Library of Congress Control Number: 2014950291

ISBN 978-0-615-91843-3

Printed in the United States of America on recycled paper.

MIX
Paper from
responsible sources
FSC® C010897
FSC
www.fsc.org

UNSPINNING THE SPIN

The Women's Media Center Guide
to Fair and Accurate Language

By
Rosalie Maggio

Preface by
Robin Morgan and Gloria Steinem

*To Pam Powers —
with gratitude!*

Gloria Steinem
&
Robin Morgan

WOMEN'S MEDIA CENTER

Our goal is to make women visible and powerful in the media. Founded in 2005 by Jane Fonda, Robin Morgan, and Gloria Steinem, the WMC works with media to ensure that women's realities are covered and women's voices are heard. We do this by: researching and monitoring media; creating and modeling original online, print, and radio content; training women and girls to participate in media; and promoting media-experienced women experts in all fields. We are directly engaged with the media at every level to work toward a diverse group of women being present in newsrooms, on air, in print and online, in film, entertainment, and theater—as sources and subjects, in bylines and credits, in the field and in the front office. This book is the first publication of the WMC Press.

Dedicated to the memory of
Mary Thom
1944–2013
for love, laughter, and language

CONTENTS

Preface

Preface

by ROBIN MORGAN and GLORIA STEINEM

For the first time ever, two forces are shrinking the world: technology is allowing us to reach across boundaries of space and culture, and English is becoming a global language. This should increase accuracy and understanding, yet different cultures receive the same word differently, the right term may not be the best known, and, in many countries, public relations now exceeds journalism as a profession.[1] With millions on the World Wide Web and no fact-checker in the sky, the danger of "spinning" or being "spun," of persuading by deception or being persuaded by it, is very high.

Unspinning the Spin was created to help everyone understand and be understood. Consumers and creators of media are the most obvious beneficiaries, but almost anyone can benefit from this up-to-date guide on the background, current uses, accuracy, alternatives, and best practices for choosing and de-coding common words and phrases. This book goes beyond the scope of a dictionary or thesaurus. It's the result of mining a wide variety of fields for accurate, inclusive, creative, and clear words and phrases. As a compendium that is easy to consult, practical, informative, and witty, it is indispensable for everyday use.

Its application is as widespread as its sources: world politics, civil society, journalism, academia, corporations, anti-racism, popular culture, social justice movements, sexual liberation, medicine, public health, disability activism, poverty and class, science, street cultures, popular music, environmentalism, slang, sports, psychology, self-help, democracy movements, film, theater, the United Nations, business, the military, philanthropy, indigenous cultures, and words and phrases in other languages that have come into popular use in English.

Some of the dilemmas this guide solves are recognizable. For example, one group's "terrorist" is another's "freedom fighter," but a thoughtful alternative is "insurgent," or describing the goal of violence factually instead of characterizing the act. Many problems have solutions that need only be popularized: for instance, "maternity leave" excludes fathers, adoptive parents, and the reality of many families, but "parental leave" or "family leave" are easy replacements. Other errors may seem small—say, using sex-marked job titles and masculine pronouns as if they were generic—yet half the world's talent rests on adding feminine pronouns and using gender-free titles. A phrase like "alternative lifestyle" assumes that a norm exists, or that sexual orientation needs a euphemism, or that people have "lifestyles" rather than lives. Expressions like "the black problem" or "the Jewish problem" turn the victim into the problem—literally—when "white racism" or "anti-Semitism" would better describe what's going on.

---

[1] In the U.S., there are more than four times more public relations professionals than journalists. The latter includes newspapers, plus TV and cable news, but the former excludes those working independently for corporations, advertising agencies, nonprofits, and the government. PR professionals earn more than journalists do, on average. Figures from the U.S. Department of Labor show that in 2014, there are 4.6 PR professionals to every one journalist.

Political realities also may be conveyed with humor: for example, a group falsely claiming "grassroots" is said to have "Astroturf." Unacknowledged realities may be conveyed by invented phrases; for example, although the U.S. has not had a military draft since Vietnam—and the wars in Iraq and Afghanistan have been fought by an "all-volunteer military"—more observant and insightful language reflects the reality of who volunteers and why: for instance, there is a "poverty draft," an "education draft," and a "Green Card draft." Other phrases are pure spin: for example, the use of "death tax" instead of "inheritance tax" makes it sound as if one were being taxed for dying, not for skewing the social order with unearned wealth; "right to life" includes fetal but not adult female life; and "right to work" denies the right of workers to organize.

In addition to such individual examples, *Unspinning the Spin* suggests common-sense democratic guidelines. Terms designating individuals, groups of people, or parts of the world should be self-chosen whenever possible. The "people first" guideline of the disability rights movement not only keeps the individual from disappearing—a "person with diabetes" is more than just "a diabetic"—but also reminds us to keep the person visible in other cases. For example, "undocumented worker" is more accurate than an "illegal," which not only characterizes someone by one act, but uses language as judge and jury. Saying "prostituted woman" makes the woman visible as more than just a "prostitute," and an "enslaved man" is more than just a "slave." Using the verb form makes the process visible. When cross-referenced to "labor trafficking" and "sex trafficking," such words and phrases also become issue briefings. Readers learn, for example, that more people are enslaved in the world today than were enslaved in the 1800s, and that 85 percent of them are women and children.

Unspinning the Spin was written by Rosalie Maggio, a distinguished authority on language for more than twenty-five years. In 1991, she published *The Dictionary of Bias-Free Usage: A Guide to Non-Discriminatory Language*, which won awards from the American Library Association and the Gustavus Myers Center for the Study of Bigotry and Human Rights. It led to her numerous authoritative and creative books on the words we use to convey the life we live.

Here, her own research has been augmented by that of the Women's Media Center, a group run for and by U.S. and international women media professionals who are working to increase accuracy and diversity in the media. Language can reveal, conceal, and even define reality. This becomes all the more evident in news reporting, entertainment, and other media, where language frames and creates imagery that becomes the basis for our actions (including elections) and shapes reality (including democracy or the lack thereof). For example, imagery that equates whiteness with positive qualities and darkness with negative qualities perpetuates a racial hierarchy that is both externally enforced and internalized. The misnaming of an issue—for instance, when adversaries of "affirmative action" put it on the ballot as "preferential treatment"—may determine whether it succeeds or fails, regardless of its content.

Indeed, one political book was entirely about language: *Don't Think of an Elephant!: Know Your Values and Frame the Debate* by George Lakoff. Even punctuation became the subject of a bestseller: *Eats, Shoots & Leaves* by Lynne Truss.

But *Unspinning the Spin* is a more comprehensive and multidisciplinary guide to words and phrases—their meanings, sources, backgrounds, suggested uses, and alternatives—than has been published so far. It's a guide for journalists and editors in this and other countries, for bloggers creating their own media and for govern-ment officials creating policy, for students and teachers at all levels, for activists, workers in communication fields, and for any reader who loves the English lan-guage. We're happy to note that the tone of *Unspinning* reflects not only Maggio's dedication to fair and accurate language, but also to her pleasure in words and their power—and her sense of humor. This is not just a useful book for scholars and laypeople; *it's fun to read*.

The guide is organized alphabetically for easy use, with cross-references to related words, phrases, and issues. Words or phrases that have been historically subject to spinning and coding are accompanied by a background briefing that explains their misuse and possible remedies.

We could not be fair and accurate about this book if we did not admit that it weathered a great blow in April 2013, when Mary Thom, its editor and the features editor of the WMC website, was suddenly killed in an accident on the motorcycle she loved and rode safely for most of her life. Mary had been involved in devel-oping *Unspinning*, and had worked with Rosalie on the voluminous manuscript, shepherding and helping shape it, with Rosalie's generously collaborative cooper-ation, and adopting suggestions from the two of us and from the Women's Media Center staff over many months. The book stands as a final monument to her skill, intelligence, and love of language and ideas. In her memory, the Women's Media Center has established an award at its Annual Media Awards: the Mary Thom Art of Editing Award. Editing—whether of film, news, books, magazines, online content, or other media—is an overlooked art, and Mary represented the best of it. Finding the right person to complete this complex task was challenging and painful. But Rosemary Ahern stepped in and brought the book home with sensitivity, expertise, and grace. Mary would be proud.

As for the two of us, we bonded decades ago, not only in terms of our feminism and other political activism but also in the shared, cheerful obsession of being writers. We procrastinate, and we both need deadlines. We both love puns, and number two pencils. We both enjoy reading Fowler's *Modern English Usage* (second edition, please) as if it were a novel, and citing E. B. White and William S. Strunk Jr.'s great *Elements of Style* with glee. Furthermore, having morphed from manual then electric typewriters to computers, each of us still prints out drafts to hand-edit—using those number two pencils—before inputting revi-sions. Neither can defend this practice, except to insist it "feels right" to *hold* the text and read it on the page. Each of us swears she sees details there that she can't spot on her computer screen. We both count ourselves incredibly fortunate to get to play lifelong with the magic of words—and call it work. We're especially grateful for this elastic, dynamic, genderless English language, in which a noun like "table" can be simply "it," and we don't have to attribute sex to chairs and pens.

Socrates, in Plato's *Phaedo*, warns, "The misuse of language induces evil in the soul." Clearly, there was "spin" in the Agora. But it was the philosopher Susanne K. Langer who wrote, "The notion of giving something a *name* is the vastest genera-tive idea that ever was conceived."

We honor this in these pages with fair and accurate naming—and with delight.

October 2014
New York City

Writing guidelines

Introduction

Language both reflects and shapes society. Culture shapes language and then language shapes culture. Little wonder that the words we use to talk to each other, and about each other, are the most important words in our language: they tell us who I am, they tell us who you are, they tell us who "they" are.

Rabbi Donna Berman says, "Language doesn't merely reflect the world, it creates it." She points out that like the eye that can't see itself, we have trouble seeing our language because it is our "eye."

The process of looking at our language, discussing it, and debating it increases our awareness of the social inequities and of the truths reflected by our word choices. There can certainly be no solution to the problem of discrimination in society on the level of language alone. Replacing *handicap* with *disability* does not mean a person with disabilities will find a job more easily. Using *nurse* inclusively does not change the fact that fewer than 10 percent of U.S. nurses are men. Replacing *black* and *white* in our vocabularies will not dislodge racism. However, research indicates that language powerfully influences attitudes, behavior, and perceptions. To ignore this factor in social change would be to hobble all other efforts.

And our biases go deep. A high school student who felt that nonsexist language was disastrous said, "But you don't understand! You're trying to change the English language, which has been around a lot longer than women have!"

The language we need to hone is the language of our differences. We have either insisted that we are all the same here in the United States ("the melting pot") or we have been judgmental about our differences.

Poet Pat Parker ("For the White Person Who Wants to Know How to Be My Friend") said it best: "The first thing you do is to forget that i'm Black. / Second, you must never forget that i'm Black." In the same way, we acknowledge our differences with respect and our samenesses with joy. "Unity, not uniformity, must be our aim. We attain unity only through variety. Differences must be integrated, not annihilated, nor absorbed" (Mary Parker Follett).

Definition of terms

Bias/bias-free

Biased language refers to people in imbalanced or inaccurate ways: (1) It leaves out certain individuals or groups. "Employees are welcome to bring their wives and children" leaves out those employees who might want to bring husbands, friends, or same-sex partners, and it implies at some level that everyone has wives and children. (2) It makes unwarranted assumptions. To write "Anyone can use this fire safety ladder" assumes that all members of the household have full function of their arms and legs. "Flesh-colored" assumes everyone is one color. Addressing a sales letter about diapers to the mother assumes that the father won't be diapering the baby. (3) It calls individuals and groups by names or labels that they did not choose for themselves (for example, *office girl*, *Eskimo*, *the elderly*, *colored man*) or that are derogatory (*illegal*, *slut*, *psycho*). (4) It is based on stereotypes that imply that all lesbians/Chinese/women/people with disabilities/men/teenagers are alike (*adolescent behavior*, *male ego*, *hot-blooded Latins*). (5) It treats groups in nonparallel ways in the same context: *Asian Americans, African Americans, and whites*; *two men and a female*. (6) It categorizes certain people when it is unnecessary to do so and when this is not done for other people: *the black defendant* when it is never *the white defendant*; *the woman lawyer* when it is never *the man lawyer*. As soon as we mention sex, ethnicity, religion, disability, or any other characteristic—without a good reason for doing so—we are on thin ice. Although there may be instances in which a person's sex, for example, is germane ("A recent study showed that female patients do not object to being cared for by male nurses"), most of the time it is not. Nor is a person's race, sexual orientation, disability, age, or belief system often relevant. "As a general rule, it is good to remember that ... you should ordinarily view people as individuals and not mention their racial, ethnic, or other status, unless it is important to your larger purpose in communicating" (*American Heritage Book of English Usage*).

Jean Gaddy Wilson (in *Working with Words*, also written by Brian S. Brooks and James L. Pinson) suggests, "Following one simple rule of writing or speaking will eliminate most biases. Ask yourself: Would you say the same thing about an affluent, white man?"

Inclusive/exclusive

Inclusive language clearly includes everyone it intends to include; exclusive language intentionally or unintentionally excludes some people. The following quotation is inclusive: "The greatest revolution of our generation is the discovery that human beings, by changing the inner attitudes of their minds, can change the outer aspects of their lives" (William James). It is clear that James is speaking of all of us.

Examples of sex-exclusive writing fill most quotation books: "Man is the measure of all things" (Protagoras). "The People, though we think of a great entity when we use the word, means nothing more than so many millions of individual men" (James Bryce). "Man is nature's sole mistake" (W. S. Gilbert).

Sexist/nonsexist

Sexist language promotes and maintains attitudes that stereotype people according to gender while assuming that the male is the norm—the significant gender. Nonsexist language treats both sexes equally and either does not refer to a person's sex when it is irrelevant or refers to men and women and to girls and boys in symmetrical ways.

"A society in which women are taught anything but the management of a family, the care of men, and the creation of the future generation is a society which is on the way out" (L. Ron Hubbard). "Behind every successful man is a woman—with nothing to wear" (L. Grant Glickman). "Nothing makes a man and wife feel closer, these days, than a joint tax return" (Gil Stern). These quotations display various characteristics of sexist writing: (1) stereotyping an entire sex by what might be appropriate for some of it; (2) assuming male superiority; (3) using unparallel terms (for example, *man and wife* should be either *husband and wife* or *man and woman*).

The following quotations clearly refer to both sexes: "It's really hard to be roommates with people if your suitcases are much better than theirs" (J. D. Salinger). "If people don't want to come out to the ballpark, nobody's going to stop them" (Yogi Berra). "People keep telling us about their love affairs, when what we really want to know is how much money they make and how they manage on it" (Mignon McLaughlin). "I studied the lives of great men and famous women, and I found that the men and women who got to the top were those who did the jobs they had in hand, with every-thing they had of energy and enthusiasm and hard work" (Harry S. Truman).

Gender-free/gender-fair/gender-specific

Gender-free terms do not indicate sex and can be used for either women/girls or men/boys (*teacher, bureaucrat, employee, hiker, operations manager, child, clerk, sales rep, hospital patient, student, grandparent, chief executive officer*).

Gender-fair language involves the symmetrical use of gender-specific words (*Ms. Cortright/Mr. Lopez, councilwoman/councilman, young man/young woman*) and promotes fairness to both sexes in the larger context. To ensure gender-fairness, ask yourself: Would I write the same thing in the same way about a person of the other sex? Would I mind if this were said of me? If you are describing the behavior of children on the playground, to be gender-fair you will refer to girls and boys an approximately equal number of times, and you will carefully observe what the chil-dren do, and not just assume that only the boys will climb to the top of the jungle gym and that only the girls will play quiet games. Researchers studying the same baby described its cries as "anger" when they were told it was a boy and as "fear" when they were told it was a girl (cited in Cheris Kramarae, ed., *The Voices and Words of Women and Men*).

Gender-specific words (*councilwoman, businessman, altar girl*) are neither good nor bad in themselves, but they sometimes identify and even emphasize a person's sex when it is not necessary (and is sometimes even objectionable) to do so. Male and female versions of a root word are also likely to be weighted quite differently (*governor/governess, master/mistress*).

One problem with gender-free terms, however, is that they sometimes obscure reality. *Battered spouse* implies that men and women are equally battered; this is far from true. *Parent* is too often taken to mean *mother* and obscures the fact that more and more fathers are involved in parenting; it is better here to use the gen-der-specific *fathers and mothers* or *mothers and fathers* than the gender-neutral *parents*. Saying *businesswomen* and *businessmen* instead of *business executives* reminds us that there are women involved, whereas *business executives* evokes a picture of men for most of us.

Amanda Smith (in *The Albuquerque Tribune*) writes, "A word like 'legislator' does not exclude women, but neither does it do anything to change the mental picture for some who already see legislators as male." She tells the story of teachers who took two groups of children to opposite ends of the playground: one group was told they were going to build "snowmen"; they made 11 snowmen and 1 snowwoman. The other group was told they were going to build "snow figures"; that group made 5 snowmen, 3 snowwomen, 2 snow dogs, 1 snow horse, and 1 snow spaceship.

Generic/pseudogeneric

A generic is an all-purpose word that includes everybody (for example, *workers, people, voters, civilians, elementary school students*). Generic pronouns include *we, you, they*.

A pseudogeneric is a word used as if it included everybody but that in reality does not. For example, "A Muslim people of the northern Caucasus, the 1.3 million Chechens are dark-haired and tawny skinned, often with lush mustaches" (*The New York Times International*). Until you get to the "lush mustaches," you assume "Chechens" is generic, including both women and men. Explaining why he felt homeless people who aren't in shelters should be locked up, Pat Buchanan (cited in *New Woman*) said, "I don't think we should have to have them wandering the streets frightening women and people."

Words like "everyone" are often used as if "everyone" can afford a new television, celebrates Christmas, can walk up stairs, is married or wants to be, can read, gets enough to eat, worries about a sunburn, and so on. Pseudogenerics are thought to include everyone because the people who use them are thinking only of themselves and their immediate world.

When someone says, "What a Christian thing to do!" (meaning kind or good-hearted), it leaves out all kind, good-hearted people who are not Christian. The speaker is undoubtedly a Christian and assumes others are too. Similarly, assuming everyone gets rosy-cheeked and goes pale in the same way ignores our diverse skin colors. When words like *mankind, forefathers, brotherhood*, and *alumni* got a foothold in the language, it was because men were visible, men were in power, and that's what their world looked like.

Certain nouns that look generic are often used as if they mean only men (*politicians, lawyers, voters, legislators, clergy, farmers, colonists, immigrants, slaves, pioneers, settlers, members of the armed forces, judges, taxpayers*). References to "settlers, their wives, and children," or "those clergy permitted to have wives" illustrate this.

See the sections below on the two most damaging pseudogenerics: "man" and "he."

Sex/gender

Sex is biological: people with male genitals are male, and people with female genitals are female. Although this is an oversimplification, in general, sex may be thought of as a physical, physiological, biological attribute.

Gender is cultural: a society's notions of "masculine" are based on how it expects men to behave, and its notions of "feminine" are based on how it expects women to behave. Words like *womanly/manly, tomboy/sissy, unfeminine/unmasculine* have nothing to do with the person's sex; they are culturally determined, subjective concepts about sex-appropriate traits and behaviors, which vary from one place to another and even from one individual to another within a culture.

It is biologically impossible for a woman to be a sperm donor or for a man to be pregnant. It may be culturally unusual for a man to be a receptionist or for a woman to be a miner, but it is not biologically impossible. To say automatically "the receptionist ... she" and "the miner ... he" assumes all receptionists are women and all miners are men, which is sexist because the basis is gender, not sex. Alleen Pace Nilsen (in Nilsen, Bosmajian, Gershuny, and Stanley, *Sexism and Language*) gives the example of "paternity suit" and "maternity suit"; they are sex-specific but they are not sexist because they involve actual sex-related differences.

Gender is a subjective cultural attitude. Sex is an objective biological fact. Gender concepts vary according to the culture. Sex is, with some exceptions, a constant.

The difference between sex and gender is important because much sexist language arises from cultural determinations of what a female or male "ought" to be. When a society believes, for example, that being a man means to hide one's emotions, bring home a paycheck, and be able to discuss football standings whereas being a woman means to be soft-spoken, to "never have anything to wear," and to love shopping, babies, and recipes, much of the population becomes a contradiction in terms—unmanly men and unwomanly women. Crying, nagging, gossiping, and shrieking are assumed to be women's lot; rough-housing, beer drinking, telling dirty jokes, and being unable to find one's socks and keys are laid at men's collective door. Lists of stereotypes appear silly because very few people fit them. The best way to ensure unbiased writing and speaking is to describe people as individuals, not as members of a set.

General guidelines

Pseudogeneric "he"

The use of *he* to mean *he and she* is ambiguous, the grammatical justification for its use is problematic, and it is not perceived as including both women and men. A number of careful studies have shown that women, men, and children alike picture only males when *he* is used to mean *everyone*. "It is clear that, in spite of the best efforts of prescriptive grammarians, *he* has not come to be either used or understood in the generic sense under most circumstances" (Philip M. Smith, *Language, the Sexes and Society*). Donald G. McKay (in Cheris Kramarae, ed., *The Voices and Words of Women and Men*) says that each of us hears the pseudogeneric *he* over a million times in our lifetime and that the consequences of this kind of repetition are "beyond the ken of present-day psychology." He describes pseudogeneric *he* as having all the characteristics of a highly effective propaganda technique: repetition, covertness/indirectness, early age of acquisition, and association with high-prestige sources; "Although the full impact of the prescriptive *he* remains to be explored, effects on attitudes related to achievement, motivation, perseverance, and level of aspiration seem likely." Linguist Suzette Haden Elgin gives this example of a pseudogeneric *he* with important consequences: "Every American child knows that he may grow up to be President."

Young children, who are unfamiliar with the grammatical rule that says *he* really means *he and she*, and who are also fairly literal-minded, hear *he* thousands of times and come to think of maleness as the general state of being and femaleness as something peripheral. In a study by Steven Gelb of Toronto's York University, young children were asked to describe pictures of sex-indeterminate bunnies, dinosaurs, and babies; 97 percent of the time boys labeled them male, and 81 percent of the time the girls also labeled them male. When parents and teachers use pseudogeneric *he* to refer to people, they inadvertently teach youngsters that maleness and humanness are equivalent.

The ubiquity of *he* is not to be underestimated. When the Minnesota legislature ordered the removal of gender-specific language from state statutes, the Office of the Revisor of Statutes deleted or replaced some 20,000 sex-specific pronouns; only 301 of them were feminine.

Defenders most often claim that *he* as a generic term is a long-standing grammatical convention and that its use is not intended to exclude anyone. But pseudogeneric *he* does, in reality, exclude over half the population, and allusions to some fundamental concept of grammar are on shaky ground. *He* was declared generic and legally inclusive of *she* by an act of the English Parliament, following a rule invented in 1746 by John Kirby, who decreed that the male gender is "more comprehensive" than the female; since then, advocates have been fond of saying "he embraces she." The 19th-century grammarians articulated the policy that between an error of number ("to each their own") and an error of gender ("to each his own"), it was preferable to make an error of gender. Thus this "convention" of grammar is based on the indefensible premise that the category "male" is more comprehensive than the category "female." In fact, it can be argued that the latter is more comprehensive linguistically: *female* contains *male*, *she* contains *he*.

The pronoun *he* (when used in any way except to refer to a specific male person) can be avoided in several ways.

Rewrite your sentence in the plural: "It's the educated barbarian who is the worst: he knows what to destroy" (Helen MacInnes). *Educated barbarians are the worst; they know what to destroy.* "When someone sings his own praises, he always gets the tune too high" (Mary H. Waldrip). *Those who sing their own praises always get the tune too high.*

Omit the pronoun entirely: "Repartee: What a person thinks of after he becomes a departee" (Dan Bennett). *Repartee: What a person thinks of after becoming a departee.* "The American arrives in Paris with a few French phrases he has culled from a conversational guide or picked up from a friend who owns a beret" (Fred Allen). *The American arrives in Paris with a few French phrases culled from a conversational guide or picked up from a friend who owns a beret.*

Substitute *we/us/our*: "From each according to his abilities, to each according to his needs" (Karl Marx). *From each of us according to our abilities, to each of us according to our needs.*

Use the second person: "No man knows his true character until he has run out of gas, purchased something on the installment plan and raised an adolescent" (Marcelene Cox). *You don't know your true character until you have run out of gas, purchased something on the installment plan and raised an adolescent.*

Replace the masculine pronoun with an article: "Can't a critic give his opinion of an omelette without being asked to lay an egg?" (Clayton Rawson). *Can't a critic give an opinion about an omelette without being asked to lay an egg?*

Replace the pronoun with words like *someone, anyone, one, the one, no one*: "He who cries, 'What do I care about universality? I only know what is in *me*,' does not know even that" (Cynthia Ozick). *The one who cries, 'What do I care about universality? I only know what is in me,' does not know even that.* "He who can take advice is sometimes superior to him who can give it" (Karl von Knebel). *One who can take advice is sometimes superior to one who can give it.*

Use genderless nouns (*the average person, workers*) or substitute job titles or other descriptions for the pronoun.

Replace the pronoun with a noun (or a synonym for a noun used earlier): "He is forced to be literate about the illiterate, witty about the witless and coherent about the incoherent" (John Crosby). *The critic is forced to be literate about the illiterate, witty about the witless and coherent about the incoherent.* "To find a friend one must close one eye—to keep him, two" (Norman Douglas). *To find a friend one must close one eye—to keep a friend, two.*

UNSPINNING THE SPIN | The Women's Media Center Guide to Fair & Accurate Language

Use *he and she* or *her and his*, but only as a last resort, and only if there are not a great many of them. *S/he* is not recommended for anything but memos or notes. "Education is helping the child realize his potentialities" (Erich Fromm). *Education is helping the child realize his or her potentialities.* There are times when it is better to use *he or she*, for example, when you want to raise consciousness about both sexes being involved in a certain activity: the new parent ... he or she; the plumber ... she or he.

Singular *they* ("to each their own") is now acceptable grammar (see dictionary entry "singular 'they'"). When nothing else works and you need to use it, remember that you can make an error of gender (use *he* when you really mean *he and she*) or you can make an error of number (using plural instead of singular). Choose your error—although it is no longer considered an error by most authorities. "Nobody is a good judge in his own cause" (St. Therese of Lisieux). *Nobody is a good judge in their own cause.* "Only a mediocre person is always at his best" (Somerset Maugham). *Only a mediocre person is always at their best.*

Recast in the passive voice: "Pessimist: One who, when he has the choice of two evils, chooses both" (Oscar Wilde). *Pessimist: One who, when given the choice of two evils, chooses both.* (Objections to the passive voice are generally valid, which is why this solution is farther down the list; at the same time, it is sometimes a good choice.)

Use masculine and feminine pronouns in alternating sentences, paragraphs, examples, or chapters, although this technique should be used sparingly and only as a last resort as it can be annoying to read.

When referring to animals and nonhuman objects, avoid arbitrarily assigning them a sex. If the sex of an animal is known (and this information is important to your material), specify it. When the sex is unknown or unimportant, use *it*. Instead of "When you see a snake, never mind where he came from," W. G. Benham could have said: *When you see a snake, never mind where it came from.* Many writers automatically use *it*: "There is nothing in nature quite so joyful as the very young and silly lamb—odd that it should develop into that dull and sober animal the sheep" (Esther Meynell). Also use *it* instead of *she* to refer to entities such as nature, nations, churches, ships, boats, and cars, and *it* instead of *he* to refer to the enemy, the devil, death, time.

Pseudogeneric "man/men/mankind"

Some people will try to tell you that *man* is defined not only as "an adult male human being" but also as "a human being," "a person," "an individual," or "the whole human race." They claim that the use of *man* does not exclude women but is merely a grammatical convention.

Two problems arise with this thinking: (1) We are never sure which meaning is intended, so *man* is ambiguous. A columnist expressed his annoyance with "the feminist campaign to eliminate the word 'man' from a lot of common, historic terms." He said women should "accept the fact" that the Founding Fathers meant to include women when they wrote "all men are created equal." He apparently forgot that it took two constitutional amendments to give women and people of color the vote, since the men created equal were exclusively and legally white, male men. Susan B. Anthony found herself in the equivocal position of not being "man" enough to vote (per the Constitution) but "man" enough (per the tax and criminal codes) to be prosecuted for trying to vote and then for refusing to pay taxes when she couldn't. (2) Even when used as if intended to be a generic, *man* has often revealed its persistent ambiguity for both writers and readers.

Researchers who studied the hypothesis that *man* is generally understood to include women found "rather convincing evidence that when you use *man* generically, people do tend to think male, and tend not to think female" (Joseph Schneider and Sally Hacker, cited in Casey Miller and Kate Swift's *Words and Women*). According to Miller and Swift, that study and others "clearly indicate that *man* in the sense of *male* so overshadows *man* in the sense of *human being* as to make the latter use inaccurate and misleading for purposes both of conceptualizing and communicating."

Few wordsmiths will tolerate an ambiguous word, especially if there is an unambiguous one available. Imagine discussing giraffes and zebras, where sometimes *zebras* is used to include both giraffes and zebras but sometimes it means simply zebras. The audience would never know when it heard *zebras* whether it meant only zebras or whether it meant zebras and giraffes.

How people hear a word is far more important than its etymology or dictionary definition. Jeanette Silveira (in Cheris Kramarae, ed., *The Voices and Words of Women and Men*) says "[T]here is ample research evidence that the masculine 'generic' does not really function as a generic. In various studies words like *he* and *man* in generic contexts were presented to people who were asked to indicate their understanding by drawing, bringing in, or pointing out a picture, by describing or writing a story about the person(s) referred to, or by answering yes or no when asked whether a sex-specific word or picture applied to the meaning." In all these studies, women/girls were perceived as being included significantly less often than men/boys. Both women and men reported that they usually pictured men when they read or heard the masculine pseudogeneric. Ask kindergarten children to draw pictures of firemen, policemen, and mailmen, and what do you think you'll get?

The justification for *man* becoming the set and *woman* the subset is linguistically, sociologically, philosophically, and psychologically indefensible. The term *human beings* clearly includes both men and women. With such a simple, commonsensical alternative available, it seems unnecessary to defend a convention that is almost surely on its last legs.

Finally, Dennis Baron (*Grammar and Gender*) says that attempts today to justify the use of the masculine generic "are but thin masks for the underlying assumption of male superiority in life as well as language; despite the attempts of the wary language commentators to include women under masculine terms, the effect is to render women both invisible and silent."

We are so used to -*man* compounds that we feel helpless without them. Worse yet, their replacements somehow don't "sound right." However, -*man* nouns are outnumbered by the common and useful -*er* and -*or* words. *Fisher* seems alien to people yet has a far stronger precedent in the language than *fisherman*. The same is true of *waiter* for *waitress*, *flagger* for *flagman*, *deliverer* for *deliveryman*, and *repairer* for *repairman*. If we had grown up hearing *shoeman*, would we balk at *shoemaker*? What about *roofman* for *roofer*, *gardenman* for *gardener*, and *teachman* for *teacher*? The following sample list may help those alternatives for -*man* words sound a little more "right" to us (and are useful alternatives for some -*man* words):

angler, barber, batter, bottler, builder, butcher, buyer, canoer, caregiver, caretaker, carpenter, catcher, commissioner, consumer, customer, dealer, doer, dressmaker, driver, employer, executioner, farmer, fitter, gambler, gamester, gardener, golfer, hairdresser, handler, healer, hunter, insurer, jogger, jokester, laborer, landscaper, leader, lexicographer, lithographer, lover, maker, manager, manufacturer, member, messenger, nurturer, officer, outfielder, owner, painter, performer, pitcher, planner, player, plumber, practitioner, producer, promoter, provider, reporter, retailer, retainer, rider, robber, roofer, runner, shoemaker, speaker, speechmaker, storekeeper, striker, subscriber, teacher, trader, treasurer, trucker, waiter, whaler, woodworker, worker, writer; actor, administrator, ambassador, ancestor, arbitrator, auditor, author, benefactor, coadjutor, conqueror, contractor, counselor, director, doctor, editor, executor, facilitator, governor, inspector, instructor, janitor, legislator, liquidator, major, mayor, mediator, navigator, negotiator, operator, professor, proprietor, protector, purveyor, sculptor, surveyor, testator, traitor, vendor, victor.

Parallel treatment

Parallel treatment of terms is essential when discussing different groups; *white* and *nonwhite* are not parallel; neither are *Jewish persons* and *Protestants*. The problems with nonparallel treatment are most easily seen in gender asymmetries.

If you refer to a woman as Margaret Schlegel, refer to a man in the same material as Gavan Huntley. If he is Huntley, she will be Schlegel; if she is Margaret, he will be Gavan; and if she is Ms. Schlegel, he will be Mr. Huntley.

Do not make of one sex a parenthetical expression: "hats off to the postal employees who manned (and womanned) the Olympic stamp cancellation booths"; "each nurse had her (or his) own explanation."

Male-female word pairs are especially troublesome. (1) Certain words are used as parallel pairs, but are in fact asymmetrical; for example, *cameragirl/cameraman, man Friday/girl Friday, mermaid/merman, makeup girl/makeup man*. The most common offender in this category is *man/wife*; the correct pairs are *man/woman* and *wife/husband*. (2) Other words are so unequivalent that few people confuse them as pairs, but it is revealing to study them, knowing that they were once equals: *governor/governess, patron/matron, courtier/courtesan, master/mistress, buddy/sissy, hubby/hussy, dog/bitch, patrimony/matrimony, call boy/call girl, showman/showgirl*. Today, a *call boy* is a page; a *call girl* is a prostitute. *Buddy* is affectionate; *sissy* is derogatory. A study of word pairs shows that words associated primarily with women ultimately become discounted and devalued. Muriel Schulz calls it "semantic derogation." (3) Acceptable words and constructions sometimes become unacceptable because of the nonparallel way they are used. For example, *a male and three women, aldermen and women*, and *two girls* [referring to women] *and a man* should read: a man and three women, aldermen and alderwomen, and two women and a man.

Gender role words

Sex-linked words like *feminine/masculine, manly/womanly, boyish/girlish, husbandly/wifely, fatherly/motherly, unfeminine/unmasculine*, and *unmanly/unwomanly* depend for their meanings on cultural stereotypes and thus may be grossly inaccurate when applied to individuals. Somewhere, sometime, men and women have said, thought, or done everything the other sex has said, thought, or done except for a very few sex-linked biological activities (for example, only women can give birth or nurse a baby and only a man can provide the sperm needed to fertilize an egg). To describe a woman as unwomanly is a contradiction in terms; if a woman is doing it, saying it, wearing it, thinking it, it must be—by definition—womanly.

Good writers have rarely used such terms—they evoke no sharp images, only fuzzy impressions that vary from culture to culture and from individual to individual. This is not a recommendation to "ban" the terms; nobody can ban words. But you might look further afield for a more precise, fresh way of conveying your meaning. Steven Pinker (*The Language Instinct*) says, "Vehicles for expressing thought are being created far more quickly than they are being lost." The aim of *Unspinning the Spin* is to inspire you to lose a few vehicles and create some new ones.

"Feminine" word endings

Suffixes like *-ess*, *-ette*, and *-trix* (1) specify a person's sex when gender is irrelevant; (2) carry a demeaning sense of littleness or triviality; (3) perpetuate the notion that the male is the norm and the female is a subset, a deviation, a secondary classification. A poet is defined as "one who writes poetry" while a poetess is defined as "a female poet"; men are thus "the real thing" and women are sort of like them. Marlis Hellinger (in Cheris Kramarae et al., *Language and Power*) says these suffixes have "a weakening, trivializing or even sexualizing effect on an occupational activity which for a man may connote power and prestige." Even the nonhuman varieties of "feminine" word endings connote a sense of being smaller than and inferior to their "mates": kitchenette, luncheonette, operetta.

The purpose of a suffix is to qualify the root word. Where is the need to qualify a standard word describing a standard human activity? A poet should be a poet—without qualification. The discounting and devaluation of the female term in a word pair is the best argument against "feminine" endings; invariably the parallelism, if it ever existed, breaks down, and the female word ends up with little of the prestige and acceptability of the male word.

Alleen Pace Nilsen (*Sexism and Language*) says, "[T]he feminine form is used as much to indicate triviality as to indicate sex." A woman conducting high-altitude tests for NASA was referred to as an aviator; a few days later, the same newspaper called a woman participating in a small-time air show an aviatrix. Harriet Tubman was a conductor, not a conductress, on the underground railway.

The recommended procedure is to use the base word (thus, *waiter* instead of *waitress*, *executor* instead of *executrix*). If the individual's sex is critical to your material, use adjectives ("At a time when male actors played female roles ...") or pronouns ("The poet interrupted her reading ... ").

The following words with "feminine" endings have all been or currently are part of 21st-century U.S. English. Not included are terms formed to ridicule (Rush Limbaugh derides those women who succeed in traditionally male-dominated professions as "professorettes" and "lawyerettes"). In general, replace the "feminine" ending as shown.

actress/actor
adulteress/adulterer
ambassadress/ambassador
ancestress/ancestor
authoress/author
aviatrix, aviatress/aviator
benefactress/benefactor
coadjutress/coadjutor
comedienne/comedian
conductress/conductor
deaconess/deacon
drum majorette/drum major
electress/elector
enchantress/enchanter
equestrienne/equestrian
executrix/executor
giantess/giant
goddess/god
governess/governor
heiress/heir
heroine/hero
hostess/host
huntress/hunter
Jewess/Jew
laundress/launderer
majorette/major
mayoress/mayor
mediatrix/mediator
millionairess/millionaire
Negress/African American, black
ogress/ogre
peeress/peer
procuress/procurer
prophetess/prophet
proprietress/proprietor
priestess/priest
sculptress/sculptor
seamstress/sewer
seductress/seducer
shepherdess/shepherd
songstress/singer
sorceress/sorcerer
starlet/star
stewardess/steward
suffragette/suffragist
temptress/tempter
tragedienne/tragedian
traitress/traitor
usherette/usher
villainess/villain
waitress/waiter
-Woman, -Man, -Person

The weak, awkward, and annoying suffix -person is not generally recommended. It was useful in making the transition to inclusive language because it was so easy to tack -person onto words, but it not only looks contrived, it is contrived. Because the -person suffix comes so readily to mind, we tend not to look any further and thus overlook more dynamic and descriptive words.

Words that end in -woman and -man are generally listed in this guidebook as a last resort, for three reasons: (1) in most cases, it is unnecessary to specify sex; (2) male-female word pairs rarely get equal treatment and thus are better avoided; and (3) the alternatives are almost always a better linguistic choice. Mail carrier and mail handler, for example, are more descriptive than mailman and mailwoman.

Sometimes the -man and -woman words are preferable in order to emphasize the presence or participation of both sexes in some activity or position: "Local businesswomen and businessmen donated their weekends to do plumbing, electrical, and carpentry work in the new downtown shelter for homeless families."

When using these suffixes, however, be aware of sex symmetry. Salesmen and women should be salesmen and saleswomen; layman and layperson should be layman and laywoman.

Word order

Because the male has been considered more important than the female, the male word has traditionally been placed first. However, this gives the impression that women are not only less important but afterthoughts as well. As any five-year-old knows, we should take turns going first. The following list of word pairs is given in their "natural" order (which you are invited to switch half the time): men and women, boys and girls, male and female, he and she, his and hers, sons and daughters, husbands and wives, brother and sister, Mr. and Mrs., kings and queens. Alleen Pace Nilsen (Sexism and Language) says we break the pattern only in words relating to the traditional women's domain of family and marriage: bride and groom, mother and father, aunt and uncle, widow and widower. We also do it in the polite but empty convention of ladies and gentlemen.

The general rule here is to vary the order.

Naming

Power belongs to those who do the naming, which is why naming is one of the most critical issues for fairness and accuracy in language. We know more about our own lives than others do; we must also assume that other people know more about their lives than we do. As Native American activist Bill Pensoneau wrote, "If we say that 'Redskins' reminds us of massacres, believe us."

Self-definition

"One of the most basic ways of showing respect for others is to refer to them by the names with which they have chosen to identify themselves and to avoid using names that they consider offensive" (American Heritage Book of English Usage). The correct names for individuals and groups are always those they have chosen for themselves. "It isn't strange that those persons who insist on defining themselves, who insist on this elemental privilege of self-naming, self-definition, and self-identity encounter vigorous resistance. Predictably, the resistance usually comes from the oppressor or would-be oppressor and is a result of the fact that he or she does not want to relinquish the power which comes from the ability to define others" (Haig Bosmajian, The Language of Oppression).

Ian Hancock, linguist and president of the International Roma Federation, uses the term *exonym* for a name applied to a group by outsiders. For example, Romani peoples object to being called by the exonym *Gypsies*; they do not call themselves Gypsies. Among the many other exonyms are: the elderly, colored people, homosexuals, pagans, adolescents, Eskimos, pygmies, savages. The test for an exonym is whether people want others to refer to them with that term—*redmen, illegal aliens, holy rollers*—or whether only outsiders describe them that way.

As a general rule, call people what they want to be called, and don't call them what they object to being called.

"People first" rule

Labels are disabling; intuitively most of us recognize this and resist being labeled. The disability movement originated the "people first" rule, which says we don't call someone a "diabetic" but rather "a person with diabetes." Saying someone is "an HIV/AIDS victim" reduces the person to a disease, a label, a statistic; use instead "a person with/who has/living with HIV/AIDS." The 1990 Americans with Disabilities Act is a good example of thoughtful wording. Name the person as a person first, and let qualifiers (age, sex, disability, race) follow, but (and this is crucial) only if they are relevant. Readers of a magazine aimed at an older audience were asked what they wanted to be called (*elderly? Senior citizens? Seniors? Golden-agers?*). They rejected all the terms; one said, "How about just *people*?" When high school students rejected labels like *kids, teens, teenagers, youth, adolescents,* and *juveniles,* and were asked in exasperation just what they would like to be called, they said, "Could we just be *people*?"

Women as separate people

One of the most sexist maneuvers in the language has been the identification of women by their connections to husband, son, or father—often even after he is dead. Women are commonly identified as someone's widow while men are rarely referred to as anyone's widower. If a connection is relevant, make it mutual. Instead of "Frieda, his wife of 17 years," write "Frieda and Eric, married for 17 years."

Marie Marvingt, a Frenchwoman who lived around the turn of the 20th century, was an inventor, adventurer, stuntwoman, super athlete, aviator, and all-around scholar. She chose to be affianced to neither man (as wife) nor God (as religious), but it was not long before an uneasy male press found her a fit partner. She is still known today by the revealing label "the Fiancée of Danger."

For some people it is difficult to watch women doing unconventional things with their names, especially when they flout the rules that connect them with men in a "readable" way. For years, the etiquette books were able to tell us precisely how to address a single woman, a married woman, a divorced woman, or a widowed woman (there was no similar etiquette for men because we have never had a code to signal their marital status). But now some women are Ms. and some are Mrs., some are married but keeping their birth names, others are hyphenating their last name with their husband's, and still others have constructed new names for themselves. Some women—including African American women who were denied this right earlier in our history—take great pride in using their husband's name. All these forms are correct. The rule of self-definition applies here: call the woman what she wants to be called.

Name-calling

It's unlikely that people come to this guidebook for help in choosing the most accurate and precise epithets when they need them. However, some are included because not everybody considers them slurs or because alternatives are often needed. See, for example, animal names for people, ethnic slurs, and food names for people, as well as individual entries (*bastard, bitch*).

Special problems

Hidden bias

Writing may be completely free of biased terms yet still carry a biased message. According to a radio news item, "More women than ever before are living with men without being married to them. And more unmarried women than ever before are having babies." An accurate, unbiased report would have said: "More men and women than ever before are living together without being married. And more single women than ever before are having babies."

Too often, language is used to make assumptions about people—that everyone is male, heterosexual, without a disability, white, married, between the ages of 26 and 54, of western European extraction. Until it becomes second nature to write without bias, reread your material as if you were: a gay man, someone who uses a wheelchair, a Japanese American woman, someone over 80 or under 16, or other "individuals" of your own creation. If you do not feel left out, discounted, and ignored, but instead can read without being stopped by some incongruence, you have probably avoided hidden bias. It is also wonderfully helpful to ask someone from a group with which you aren't familiar to read your work; they can quickly spot any irregularities.

Passive constructions

Most writing style books recommend the active over the passive voice; this is also an important concept in the language of bias. There are important differences between "she was beaten" and "he beat her," between "the first black woman who was admitted to the university" and "the first black woman who entered the university." The active voice is too often reserved for those in power while everyone else is acted upon.

Perspective

Our perceptions color our language, for example, "I am firm. You are obstinate. He is a pig-headed fool" (Katharine Whitehorn). In the same way, men are "cautious" but women are "timid"; some people are "shiftless," while others are "unemployed"; if the Indians won, it was a "massacre"; if the Cavalry won, it was a "victory." In the aftermath of Hurricane Katrina, a photograph showed a black man and a white man. The caption explained that the black man was looting; the white man was looking for groceries. "A man has to be Joe McCarthy to be called ruthless. All a woman has to do is put you on hold" (Marlo Thomas). It is helpful to mentally substitute other groups for the ones you are describing and see if your adjectives are still as precise and accurate.

Fellow, king, lord, master

Fellow, *king*, *lord*, and *master* have three things in common: (1) Either from definition, derivation, or people's perceptions of them, they are biased. All four are male-oriented: *king*, *lord*, and *master* are also hierarchical, dominator-society terms; *master* evokes the horrors of slavery. (2) They are root words: many other words, phrases, and expressions are formed from them, thus extending their reach. (3) Not everyone agrees whether all forms of them are biased. Someone who might admit that a *fellow* sitting next to them at lunch can only be a man might see nothing unacceptable in the expression *fellow student*. Those who agree that the *master* of a certain house is a man might believe that *mastering a skill* is fair language. But consider, for example, the cumulative effect on the language when such a masculine and slavery-related word as *master* is encountered in so many everyday ways: *master bedroom, master builder, master class, masterful, master hand, master key, master list, mastermind, masterpiece, master plan, master stroke, master switch, master tape, master teacher, masterwork, mastery, overmaster, past master, post-master, prizemaster, self-mastery.*

Those who prefer to use these four words only in their narrowest, male-defined meanings will find alternatives in the main text for all other uses.

Letter salutations

A state commission on the economic status of women receives a surprising number of letters addressed "Dear Sir" or "Gentlemen." In discussions of language choices, the problem of letter salutations is usually the first one mentioned. The standard "Dear ..." salutation in business letters seems to be giving way in many cases to the memo format, a subject line instead of a salutation, or beginning the letter directly after the name and address (no salutation). "Dear" is, in any case, an odd way to begin a letter to those we don't even know; you can always begin "To ... ". Below are some other suggestions for inclusive letter openings.

Dear Agent	Dear Manager
Board Member	Mr./Ms.
Citizen	Neighbor
Colleagues	Owner
Committee Member	Parent/Guardian
Councilor	Permissions Editor
Credit Manager	Personnel Officer
Customer	Publisher
Director	Reader
Editor	Recipient
Employee	Resident
Executive	Subscriber
Friend	Taxpayer
Homeowner	Teacher

Dear Friends of the Library	Dear Ellen Howard-Jeffers
Members of the ...	Acme Drycleaning
Supporters	L. Koskenmaki
Volunteers	Tiny Tots Toys
Voters	Office of the Bursar

Dear Superintendent Rajanivat
Vice-President Morris
Senior Research Specialist Jordan
Administrative Assistant Chuang

Greetings!
Hello!

To the Chief Sales Agent
To the Consumer Relations Department
To the Freestyle Credit Department
To: Chair, Commission on Language Abuse
To: Parents/guardians of Central High School students
To: J. G. Frimsted

Re: Account # 4865-1809-3333-0101
Subject: Reprints of your article on hearing loss
Please send me a copy of the most recent committee report.
I am ordering six copies of your publication.
Enclosed please find complete payment for ...

Miscellaneous

Generally, retain familiar names for nonhuman items even if they are sex-linked, for example, timothy grass, daddy longlegs, alewife, sweet william, myrtle. (These and similar items are found as entries in the main text.)

Rewriting history is not recommended. *Fathers of the Church* is a historically correct term. But we commonly refer now to the Founding Fathers as the Founders or the Framers. It may be uncomfortable or even painful to encounter the word *nigger* in a literary work, but if we erase or forget our historical and literary past, we may be doomed to repeat it. Awareness and discussion of such bias is effective and necessary; replacing biased words without comment is not.

How to make a fortune with fair and accurate language

Actually, there's not a lot of money in this business, and this section just contains some basic understandings about language, which people usually won't read. But stay; it's kind of interesting.

Who controls the language?

The correct answer is always: "You do." Language doesn't belong to grammarians, linguists, wordsmiths, writers, or editors. It belongs to the people who use it. It goes where people want it to go, and, like a balky mule, you can't make it go where it doesn't want to go.

Constructions that were once labeled incorrect are now in dictionaries because people persisted in using them. Constructions that were mandated by law (the use of *he* to mean *he and she* by an 1850 Act of Parliament, for example) were ignored by many speakers and writers of English because people wanted to say what they wanted to say. Those who understand language know there's only one reason for it to change: because a critical mass of people want it to.

An often-expressed fear of keep-it-the-way-it-is fans is that they will be forced to use language they don't want to use. And, in fact, many publishing houses, businesses, government offices, churches, mosques, synagogues, universities, and national organizations have policies on the use of respectful language. Are rights being abridged here? Freedoms taken away? Probably not. Absolute freedom doesn't exist and never did. Just as we don't spit on the floor at work, swear at customers, or send out letters full of misspellings, so too we might have to "watch our language." It is odd that the request for unbiased language in schools and workplaces is considered intolerable when other limits on our freedom to do whatever we want are not.

The rigid orthodoxy, the narrowest view of language, belongs not to those who offer 15 ways of dealing with the personal pronoun but to those who insist that the pseudogeneric *he* is right in all cases and tell us to quit "tinkering" with the language.

Tinker away. It's yours.

Does it really matter?

One objection to insisting on unbiased language is that it is really too trivial an issue when there are so many more important ones that need our attention.

First, it is to be hoped that there are enough of us working on issues large and small that the work will all get done someday. Second, the connections between the way we think, speak, and act are by now beyond argument. Language goes hand-in-hand with social change—both shaping it and reflecting it. Sexual harassment was not a term anyone used until the 1970s; today, we have laws against it. How could we have the law without the language? In fact, the judicial system is a good argument for the importance of "mere words"; the legal profession devotes great energy to the precise interpretation of words—often with far-reaching and significant consequences.

Words matter terribly. The difference between *fetal tissue* and *unborn baby* (referring to the very same thing) is arguably the most debated issue in the country. The United States changed *The War Department* to *The Department of Defense* because words matter. When President Bush used the word *hostages* for the first time in August 1990, it made headlines; up to that time, he had been using *detainees*. The change of terms signaled a change in our posture toward Iraq.

It is ironic that some of the strongest insistence that this issue is "silly" comes from political conservatives. In 1990, a pamphlet titled "Language: A Key Mechanism of Control" was sent to Republican candidates running in state elections by GOPAC, a conservative group headed by House Republican whip Newt Gingrich. One of the key points in it was that "language matters." The pamphlet offered a list of words and phrases "to use in writing literature and letters, in preparing speeches, and in producing material for the electronic media. Use the list[s] to help define your campaign and your vision of public service." Two basic lists were given, one set of words to use for one's own campaign (for example, *common sense, courage, crusade, dream, duty, peace, pioneer, precious, pride, fair, family, hard work, liberty, moral, pro-environment, prosperity, reform, rights, strength, truth, vision*) and another set to use for one's opponent's campaign (for example, *anti-child, anti-flag, betray, cheat, corruption, crisis, decay, devour, disgrace, excuses, failure, greed, hypocrisy, incompetent, liberal, lie, obsolete, pathetic, radical, red tape, self-serving, shallow, shame, sick, taxes, traitors*).

In the end, then, it appears that our choice of words is not too trivial—not for presidents, for conservatives, for any of us.

They've got to stop changing the language!

Having come of age using *handicapped, black-and-white, chairman, leper, mankind,* and the pseudogeneric *he,* some people are bewildered and upset by discussions about such terms' correctness.

And yet if there's one thing consistent about language it is that it is constantly changing. The only languages that do not change are those whose speakers are dead. Dictionary maven Ken Kister estimates that some 25,000 new words enter the language each year. So it isn't language change alone that frightens and annoys some people, but specifically language change that deals with people.

Anne H. Soukhanov, executive editor of the most excellent and useful *American Heritage Dictionary,* says in *Word Watch,* "In bringing together into one lexicon diverse linguistic elements from diverse peoples, nations, and cultures, the English language—*the* prime exponent, in fact, of multiculturalism—has been much more accepting of and tolerant to change and new ideas than some of its own speakers and writers have been."

In any case, the "changes" in language used to describe people are not so much changes as choices. For example, *firefighter* has been in the language since 1903; using it instead of *fireman* isn't so much a change in the language as a choice to use what some think is a better word. We make these kinds of choices all the time; we call it good writing. Inuits and Roms and the San never did call themselves Eskimos, Gypsies, and Bushmen; the fact that we have finally grasped the terminology is not as much a change as it is a correction or a choice to use the correct words. *Chair* (meaning the person in charge of the meeting) came into the language before *chairman*; people mistakenly think *chair* is a new and strange usage. Actually it's been there all the time.

What ridiculous word will we have next?

The most common tactic in trying to unhorse fair and accurate language—probably because it is assumed to be entertaining—is ridicule. Dozens of syndicated columnists and letter-to-the-editor writers posit some hypothetical endpoint of unbiased language, skillfully show how absurd it is, and retire from the field, victorious. In one case, the writer showed how silly the word "woperson" (for "woman") is. Quite right, too. In another case, "ottoperson" was given as the height of linguistic absurdity. No argument there. In a magazine letters column, a reader complained about the problems we were going to have with pronouns as parts of words: "'Herman was a hermit who had a hernia when climbing the Himalayas' translates to 'Itit was an itmit who had an itnia climbing the Himalayas.'" The magazine editor added: "*Italayas?*" We've also had great fun with—among dozens of others—"follicularly challenged" (bald), "cerebrally challenged" (stupid), "ethically challenged" (criminal), "personipulate," "personperson" (for mailman—William Safire's contribution), "personhole cover," and "chairperdaughter" (for chairperson).

The problem with ridicule is that nobody is asking for such silly language. Those who are serious about writing that is as graceful as it is inclusive can choose from among thousands of standard terms. There is no need to use awkward, contrived, or bizarre terms (unless you want to, of course). Anyone who says we must choose between elegant, standard language and respectful language is stuck in a binary thinking warp. In some of today's best literature you can find poetic, grammatical writing that is free of stereotypes and demeaning language.

This is not to deny that striving for fair and accurate language is occasionally awkward; cutting edges are always a little rough, and we're all still getting used to this. But then there is a great deal of bad writing in this country, and only a small fraction of it can be laid at the door of those who use unbiased language. The myth here is that either you write beautifully or you write respectfully. You *can* do both. It's work, but so is any other good writing.

But will it be better writing?

One of the rewards of breaking away from traditional, biased language—and for many people, the most unexpected benefit—is a dramatic improvement in writing style. By replacing fuzzy, over-generalized, cliché-ridden words with explicit, active words and by giving concrete examples and anecdotes instead of one-word-fits-all descriptions you can express yourself more dynamically, convincingly, and memorably.

"If those who have studied the art of writing are in accord on any one point, it is on this: the surest way to arouse and hold the attention of the reader is by being specific, definite, and concrete" (William Strunk and E.B. White, *The Elements of Style*).

Writers who talk about *brotherhood* or *spinsters* or *right-hand man* miss a chance to spark their writing with fresh descriptions; unthinking writing is also less informative. Instead of the unrevealing *adman* there are precise, descriptive, inclusive words like *advertising executive, copywriter, account executive, ad writer,* or *media buyer.*

The word *manmade,* which seems so indispensable to us, doesn't actually say very much. Does it mean artificial? Handmade? Synthetic? Fabricated? Machine-made? Custom-made? Simulated? Plastic? Imitation? Contrived?

Communication is—or ought to be—a two-way street. A speaker or writer who uses *man* to mean *human being* while the audience or reader understands it as *adult male* is an example of communication gone awry. "Meaning is not something that belongs solely to the utterance that is spoken or the piece of writing. Meaning also depends on the person who hears the utterance or reads the text" (Ronald Macaulay, *The Social Art: Language and Its Uses*).

Unbiased language is logical, accurate, and realistic. Biased language is not. How logical is it to speak of the "discovery" of America, a land already inhabited by millions of people? Where is the realism in the full-page automobile advertisement that says in bold letters, "A good driver is a product of his environment," when more women than men influence car-buying decisions? And when we use stereo-types to talk about people ("Isn't that just like a welfare mother/Indian/girl/old man?"), our speech and writing will be inaccurate and unrealistic most of the time.

Everybody is getting so sensitive!

A common complaint today is, "A person can't say *anything* anymore!" Actually, a person can. And people do. Although we have anti-disparagement laws for fruits and vegetables, we don't have them for people, which means you can say dreadful things about people, yell insults to their face, and nobody will stop you. You may get dirty looks and criticisms but, hey, you can take it.

Most stories about people failing college classes or losing jobs because "just once" they happened to refer to a woman as a *chick* are apocryphal; the courts have upheld verdicts only in the cases of the most egregious abuses and tend to favor allowing anything short of mayhem. The few stories that have some basis in fact rarely hinge solely on language, but reveal long-term patterns of harassment, dis-crimination, personality conflicts, or other factors. The fear of saying the wrong thing is the proverbial fear that springs from ignorance. Those who respect other people's realities, who read and listen carefully, and who have some common sense do not walk in fear.

There are complaints that it's hard to remember what you can say and what you can't, which words are "in" for certain groups and which words are not. And yet we started out learning that the "kitty" on the sidewalk was actually a squirrel, we learned to differentiate between fire trucks and school buses, and many people today know the difference between linguini, fettucini, and rotini. The same people who say they can't remember the "right" terms in referring to people are often whizzes at remembering which professional sports teams have moved where and are now called what.

People are tired of having to "watch what they say." But from childhood onward, we all learn to "watch what we say": we don't swear around our parents; we don't bring up certain topics around certain people; we speak differently to friend, boss, cleric, English teacher, lover, radio interviewer, child. Most of us are actually quite skilled at picking and choosing appropriate words; it seems odd that we are "tired" of being expected to be courteous, to call people what they want to be called.

Joan Steinau Lester (*The Future of White Men and Other Diversity Dilemmas*) ex-plains, "The group with the most social power usually doesn't notice its own lan-guage; it doesn't have to. So it can feel uncomfortable to suddenly become self-aware. Thus the common complaint, 'I can't say anything anymore. I have to walk on eggshells.' ... The 'free speech' we may remember wasn't actually there for everyone in the past. The excluded group long felt silenced and invisible."

Judith Martin ("Miss Manners") says, "It's no longer socially acceptable to make bigoted statements and racist remarks. Some people are having an awful time with that: 'I didn't know anybody would be offended!' Well, where have you been? I remember when people got away with it and they don't anymore."

Morris Dees (of the wonderful Southern Poverty Law Center) says, "Claims of moral ignorance ["I didn't know it was wrong"] are among the oldest tricks of bigotry."

Robin Lakoff talks about people who don't "mean" to: "It's quite possible to perpetrate, and perpetuate, sexism without meaning to, and the results are every bit as dangerous for the culture as a whole as if every word had been consciously planned to do harm."

And, as Robin Morgan once wrote, "P.C. doesn't stand for Political Correctness, it stands for Plain Courtesy."

So instead of wondering why everybody is so sensitive these days, we might wonder about those complaining: are they uninformed about the issues? Are they simply discourteous? Are they, perhaps, "insensitive?"

Additional information

In the main body of the book, in addition to entries on specific terms, there are brief guidelines on various topics:

adjectival forms as nouns
exclusive language
"feminine" word endings
inclusive language
"insider/outsider" rule
"people first" rule
pseudogeneric
salutations (letters)
sexist language
sexist quotations
sex-linked expressions
shortened forms of words
singular "they"
"the"
unconventional spellings.

Your help wanted

Language about people is constantly changing, more especially perhaps in this period than in any other in U.S. history. This book owes a great deal to all those who responded to the "Your Help Wanted" request in my earlier volumes, *The Nonsexist Word Finder* and *The Dictionary of Bias-Free Usage* (also published as *The Bias-Free Word Finder*) and *Talking About People*. If you disagree with something here, if you find biased terms not listed, or if you know of additional alternatives for biased terms, please send your comments to spin@womensmediacenter.com.

Alphabetical entries

Accuracy of language is one of the bulwarks of truth.

Anna Jameson

Words set things in motion. I've seen them doing it. Words set up atmospheres, electrical fields, charges.

Toni Cade Bambara

abandoned (dwellings) "abandoned" sometimes connotes "discarded" and carries inaccurate implications about the people who used to live there. More neutral descriptions include empty, uninhabited, vacant.

abbess/abbot appropriate sex-specific titles. "Abbess" is an exception to the avoidance of "feminine" endings; abbesses were generally equal to abbots in power, influence, and respect. In the generic sense of "abbess" or "abbot," use religious superior, administrator, director.

able-bodied this term and its buddy "temporarily able-bodied" have lost ground due to their vagueness (few people are 100 percent able-bodied, whether a toddler needs help up the stairs, a young person wears glasses, or an older one has arthritis). A one-size-fits-all term for the opposite of "people with disabilities" sets up an us/them, either/or attitude. Just describe: for example, "both those who use wheelchairs and those who don't."

ableism in use since about 1981, this term parallels sexism, racism, heterosexism, and other discriminatory social systems and describes words and actions reflecting the belief that people with disabilities are inherently inferior. See also handicappism.

abnormal see normal. See also deviant.

aboriginalism coined in 1990 by Bob Hodge and Vijay Mishra (*Dark Side of the Dream*), this term encompasses the body of "knowledge" about Aboriginals that continues to be constructed largely by non-Aboriginal people who apply terms like "legends," "myths/mythology," and "folklore" to Aboriginal creation stories. A related issue is the "settlement" of Australia, objectionable because: "This land was not 'pioneered and settled,' it was invaded and occupied" (Kevin Carmody, in *Social Alternatives*). See also aborigine/aboriginal, indigenous peoples.

aborigine/aboriginal with reference to the earliest peoples in an area, these terms are correct. However, for the earliest peoples of Australia, capitalize the terms ("Aboriginal peoples") and use the "Aboriginal/Aboriginals" instead of "Aborigine/Aborigines." (The shortened "Abo/abo" is always pejorative.) Best of all: "Koorie is the name by which those of us living in New South Wales, Victoria, and Tasmania refer to ourselves and others of our race. It does not mean a specific group. Murri is the Queensland term. Nyunga is southern Western Australia; Nyungga in Southern Australia, and so on. *Learn them all* and *use them* appropriately" (Eve Fesl, in *Social Alternatives*). "When referring to other native peoples, such as American Indians or the early Celts of Britain [use] *aboriginal* *inhabitants* or *indigenous peoples* instead of *aborigines*. While there is nothing offensive in the notion of prior habitation—indeed, it is a point of considerable pride among most native peoples—the lowercase noun *aborigine* may well evoke an unwelcome stereotype" (*American Heritage Book of English Usage*). See also aboriginalism, indigenous people, shortened forms of words, First Nations/First Nations people/First People.

abortion due to more widespread access to contraception, the number of worldwide abortions declined substantially (falling from 46 million to 42 million) between the years 1995 and 2003, before leveling off between 2003 and 2008. The Guttmacher Institute (the source for figures cited) has shown that contraceptive use reduces the probability of having an abortion by 85 percent. In countries where abortion is banned, the World Health Organization found that abortion rates are about the same as in countries where it is legal. "Access to birth control, emergency contraception (EC), sex education, and safe, legal abortion are statistically proven to reduce the number of abortions—and the pro-choice movement has worked tirelessly to ensure the availability of all these things"—from *Bitch*, in a review of Cristina Page's *How the Pro-Choice Movement Saved America*. Page says that "for all their rhetoric about saving innocent lives, the pro-life movement's policies, tactics, and agendas actually make abortions more, not less, likely to occur." When the U.S. government outlawed so-called "partial-birth abortion," it overrode a recommendation from the American Medical Association, thus confirming that the debate has been taken out of the hands of the medical establishment. The only two groups truly involved (women and their physicians) are being cut out of the decision-making. Americans have long been consistent in their support of *Roe v. Wade* and the legality of abortion. A February 2012 Quinnipiac poll which shows 64 percent of Americans agree with the high court's decision in *Roe* also shows there have not been any dramatic changes in the level of support for the decision in the preceding seven years. Abortion rights are useless if access to abortion is limited, but 87 percent of all U.S. counties have no abortion provider at all. Closing the door to another kind of access, the Hyde Amendment denies poor women, women of color, women in the military and in the Peace Corps, women in federal prisons, women who receive health care from Indian Health Services, and immigrants the ability to make their own decisions about pregnancy and childbearing; it prohibits federal funding (through Medicaid) for abortion in the majority of cases. Restrictions like this disproportionately affect American Indian women and other women of color. The 1973 Helms Amendment, which is the equivalent of the Hyde Amendment in the international arena, prohibits U.S. funding for abortion-related activities outside of the U.S., even when using their own, non-U.S. government funding. Worldwide, nearly 74,000 women die annually from unsafe abortions and thousands more suffer serious injury. For more on issues related to abortion, see the *Women's Media Center Guide to Covering Reproductive Issues*, by Sarah Erdreich, edited by Rachel Larris: http://www.womensmediacenter.com/pages/read-the-womens-media-centers-media-guide-to-covering-reproductive-issues. See also contraception.

abortion clinic women's clinic, women's reproductive health clinic. Abortion is generally only one facet of women's health clinics; most also include counseling, family planning, mammograms, referrals, and health screenings. See also abortion.

abortionist abortion provider, physician who performs abortions. "'Abortionist' ... is a highly charged word that is pejorative, derogatory, and defamatory" (Warren M. Hern, M.D., in *The New York Times*). In the past, *abortionist* described illegal providers of abortions "in a sleazy world of avaricious, incompetent criminals." Some dictionaries say the term is usually offensive, often carrying the meaning "providing abortions, especially illegally." In addition, terminating unwanted pregnancies is rarely the only work a physician does; use internist, gynecologist, obstetrician, or other specialty term. See also abortion.

abstinence (sex) a good idea for those who like and choose it, a bad idea when taught as the only line of defense against pregnancy, STDs/STIs, and HIV/AIDS. Abstinence-only sex education programs reward ignorance and don't prevent sexual activity, as research has shown—the only instance in which knowledge is valued by its absence.

acolyte depending on the denomination, this might be a woman or a man. When it means "attendant," it can also indicate either sex. See also altar boy.

acquaintance rape is often a more accurate term than "date rape" because it also includes sexual assaults that happen in contexts other than college or dating. According to a 2011 National Crime Victimization Survey, 78 percent of sexual assaults were committed by someone known to the victim. Approximately one in four college-aged women is raped or experiences an attempted date rape during her college years. The biggest issue in acquaintance rape is that prosecutors and police investigators tend to give less credit to a charge of rape from someone who knew or who may even have had previous consensual sex with the rapist. However, taking something without permission is always wrong—and rape in marriage is against the law too. Vice President Joe Biden said it's just as much a crime as if you walk down the street with a $10 bill in your hand, and someone steals it. Avoid the heterosexist assumption that date rape always involves a woman and a man. See also provoke, rape, rape victim, rapist, sexual harassment, "She asked for it," victim, violence.

activist judges see judicial activism.

act one's age it is doubtful whether there exists such an act. Use instead precise descriptions of the behavior in question.

actress actor. Women who call themselves actors point out that they are members of the U.S. Screen Actors' Guild or British Actors' Equity Association. See also "feminine" word endings.

A.D. Anno Domini (A.D.) means "in the year of Our Lord." C.E. (for Common Era) is generally used to remove the Christian basis for dating, although ironically C.E. has sometimes been taken to mean "Christian Era." See also B.C.

Adam's rib the word "adam" means "human" and "adamah" means "earth." In telling how God made the adam from the adamah, the creation story says humans are from and of the humus. This "adam" is an earthling who is not yet either male or female (Genesis 2:7). Not until the lines of poetry near the end does the story use the Hebrew words "is" and "issah," expressing male and female sex difference. Thus, biblically, common humanity precedes sexual differentiation. Dennis Baron (*Grammar and Gender*) says that the phrase "Adam's rib" (as woman-kind's point of origin) should be put in quotation marks to show its dubiousness, and its use should be reserved for discussions of the term itself. See also Eve.

adhocracy popularized by Alvin Toffler in his 1970 book (*Future Shock*), an adhocracy is the opposite of a bureaucracy, cutting "across normal bureaucratic lines to capture opportunities, solve problems, and get results" (Robert H. Waterman, Jr.). Henry Mintzberg (*Adhocracy*), who defines it as a complex and dynamic organizational form, believes adhocracy is the future, bureaucracy the past.

adjectival forms as nouns do not use adjectives as nouns when referring to something that describes only a part of a person's or a group's existence. Incorrect constructions: the blind, the poor, the learning disabled, the elderly, an amputee, a diabetic, a quadriplegic. In most cases, it doesn't help to simply put a noun after the adjective. You usually need to change the construction itself: those who have been blind from birth, poor and low-income renters, children with learning disabilities, older patients, someone with an amputation/with diabetes/with quadriplegia. See also disabilities, "people first" rule, "the."

adman advertising, creative/art director, copywriter, ad agent/writer/creator, account executive/manager/supervisor, media buyer, ad rep, advertising representative. Generic plurals: advertising executives, ad agency staff, advertising people. When possible, use specific job titles.

admitted/avowed homosexual never use these dated terms that suggest being lesbian or gay is somehow inherently shameful. If you need to mention sexual orientation and to modify it, use openly gay or openly lesbian. See also gay, homosexual, lesbian, openly lesbian/gay, queer.

adolescent this term for the period of development between youth and maturity, or from the onset of puberty to maturity, is not a specific span of years and its characteristics vary enormously from individual to individual. In addition to being vague, it has negative connotations because of its uses in terms like "adolescent behavior" and because it defines someone solely in terms of age. Either refer to a specific age ("Ali, age 16"), or use young person/people, young adult, young man/young woman. "The teen years" is preferable to "adolescence." See also ageism, children, juvenile, teen/teenager, youth.

adoption language many terms used to describe adoption and adopted children—particularly to distinguish adoptive families and children from those families and children related genetically—tend to portray adoption as a second-best, even last-resort way to build a family. Calling a biological parent a "real" parent or a "natural" parent implies that adoptive relationships are artificial and less important than are relationships by birth. The phrase "children of their own" implies that generic relationships are stronger than adoptive ones. Birth mothers and birth fathers who choose adoption for their children generally do not "abandon," "surrender," "release," "relinquish," "give up," or "put up for adoption" their children. In most cases it is accurate to say they "placed a child for adoption," or "planned for" or "chose" adoption. "International adoption" is preferred to "foreign adoption." "Hard to place" children can be called "children with special needs" or "waiting children," terms that are less damaging to their self-esteem and hopes. Avoid the qualifier "adopted" (for example, "survivors include two sons and an adopted daughter") unless there is a specific reason for mentioning the fact of the adoption. See, biological father/mother/parent, birth mother/father/parent, illegitimate/illegitimate child, "natural" father/mother/child, "real" father/mother/parent.

adulterer man or woman. This label is rarely seen today outside religious contexts—which is probably good. See also cuckold, philanderer.

advance man advance agent, publicity/press agent, agent, booker, publicist, promoter, talent coordinator, representative, rep, go-between, negotiator, producer.

advertising advertising creates and reinforces numerous sexist stereotypes: women are sex objects and men are success objects; women live to please men and men live to take care of women; men are hopeless at the simplest household tasks while women are fulfilled doing the simplest household tasks; all women really want is male sexual attention and all men really want is a fast car and a good beer. Women are shown primarily as housewife or sex partner, appear in fewer ads than men, tend to promote beauty, home, food, and clothing products, and are shown primarily at home rather than at work. "Advertising seems to encourage and magnify personal dissatisfaction in order to stimulate the demand for products. Partly because of the women's movement and partly because women are major consumers, poking outright fun at women has become financially risky. In a year-long study of over 1,000 print and television ads, Men's Rights Inc. concluded that men are portrayed as ignorant, incompetent, and at the mercy of women. Men's roles as parents and caregivers are largely ignored. In any ad in which a man and a woman appear, and one of them is a jerk, the man gets to be the jerk. Studies show that male-bashing ads are remembered far better than others. Where are the catchy, memorable ads that don't demean or stereotype either sex? Racist and ethnic stereotypes play a prominent part in advertising; today, instead of learning to portray people in diverse, respectful, and real-life ways, some advertisers are opting not to use people at all in case they "offend" someone. Advertising wrongs us in more subtle ways: Scott Russell Sanders ("Language Versus Lies," in *The Progressive*) points out the link between deceptions of advertising and those of public life: "Ubiquitous merchandising ... trains us to think of ourselves as consumers, defined by our purchases and possession, rather than as citizens, defined by our membership in communities. Worst of all, commerce appropriates and corrupts the language for everything we value, from adventure to zest, and it leads us to expect that all public uses of language will be dishonest and manipulative. Made cynical by the lies of merchants, we are more likely to shrug at the lies of politicians, generals, pundits, televangelists, and propagandists." See also anti-male bias, sex object, stereotypes, success object.

advertorial the deliberate blending of editorial content and advertising blurs the line between them and leaves readers with little idea that what they've read isn't objective reporting. Most publications will not accept advertising that closely resembles the graphics of their regular material.

aficionada/aficionado these are good sex-specific and sex-parallel terms. If you need alternatives, consider fan, enthusiast, devotee, nut, hound, buff.

affirmative action coined in 1965 as part of Lyndon Johnson's "Great Society" initiatives, this term refers to efforts to improve the employment and educational opportunities of women and members of minority groups. "To some, the term means only that an employer casts the widest possible net when searching for employees. To others, it means that minorities can be preferred over equally 'qualified' whites for the sake of 'diversity,' two other extremely controversial concepts. To some, affirmative action programs ought to be only for blacks as a historical redress for slavery. To others, women and ethnic minorities may be included or, in the case of some Asians, excluded. The questions are nearly endless," says journalist Steve Berg. In response to the current opposition (on the grounds of "unfairness," especially to white men) and dismantling of some affirmative action programs, Julian Bond says, "What they're really complaining about is that they used to have 100 percent of the slots and now they have to share, and it burns them up." Roger Wilkins, former professor of history at George Mason University, says, "White parents are telling their children that women and minorities are getting all the jobs, but that's just not true: they are teaching old-fashioned racism and sexism. What is happening is that white men are having to compete, and they're not used to that." Affirmative action has been under attack and seven states—California, Florida, Washington, Arizona, Nebraska, Oklahoma, and New Hampshire—have passed state constitutional amendments banning racial preferences in public university admissions. In *Fisher v. University of Texas* (June 2013), the Supreme Court stopped short of making race-based preferences illegal, but the Court said that colleges' use of preferences must be "narrowly tailored" and that the institutions must prove that considering race is absolutely necessary to maintaining diversity. If the outcome of *Schuette v. Coalition to Defend Affirmative Action* upholds Michigan's ban on affirmative action policies at public universities, it could prompt opponents of affirmative action to push for bans in other states. Meanwhile, concerns that affirmative action policies disadvantage white students appear to be unfounded. A 2013 study by the Georgetown Center on Education and the Workforce found that while whites make up 62 percent of the college-aged population, they represent 75 percent of the student body at the 468 most selective four-year colleges.

Afghans the people of Afghanistan are called Afghans. Their monetary unit is the afghani.

Africa whenever possible, be specific: name the African country, city, region, or people you're referring to. Africa is a huge continent. Zoë Anglesey (in *MultiCultural Review*) suggests specifying indigenous culture or heritage, for example, Ibo from Nigeria, Fon of Dahomey. If you wouldn't say "European" when you mean "German" or "Italian," don't say "African" when you mean "Kenyan" or "Eritrean."

African of or pertaining to the continent of Africa or its people or languages, this term is not a synonym for "African American" nor is it a synonym for "black" (not all Africans are black). Whenever possible, use a specific national designation (Tanzanian, Moroccan, Ethiopian). See also Africa, African American, black.

African American there has been much discussion of the appropriateness of "African American" versus "black/Black." A poll by ABC and *The Washington Post* found that 48 percent of blacks preferred the term African American (up from 22 percent in their 1989 poll), 35 percent favored black (down from 66 percent in 1989), and 17 percent liked both terms. Most people will accept either and use both themselves, but some individuals have a preference, which should be determined before writing to or about them. Most black publications still use "black" and the most commonly used strategy in all publications is to alternate the terms; there does not seem to be any resulting confusion. Another issue is whether to use African American to refer only to the descendants of slaves brought to the U.S. centuries ago, not to newcomers who have not inherited the legacy of bondage, segregation, and legal discrimination. Similarly, the number of U.S. blacks with origins in the Caribbean has grown by 60 percent in recent years; how are they African American? Work remains to be done, but in the way of language, solutions will appear. Until then, don't hyphenate the noun African American, but you can hyphenate the adjective ("African-American women"). Robin Morgan writes, "It's not good enough to say or write Native American, African American, and so on, if you don't also use European American instead of 'white,' which otherwise becomes the generic." See also African, Afro-American, black (noun), black/black-, black-and-white (adjective), Negress/Negro.

African American feminism see womanism.

Afro-American "Afro-American, first recorded in 1853, was seriously proposed in 1880, but … it was to be 80 years or more before it was to gain a measure of use" (Irving Lewis Allen, *Unkind Words*). Because African American and black are preferred in most contexts and because "Afro" seems a diminishment of "Africa," Afro-American is scarcely seen anymore. See also African American, black.

Afrocentrism an approach to the study of world history that stresses the identity and contributions of African cultures, in contradistinction to the common Eurocentric approach that too often omits them. "Despite the negative treatment in the popular press of both Afrocentric curricula and claims of African origins of civilization, *Afrocentrism* as synonymous with 'Black consciousness' remains meaningful to Black youth" (Patricia Hill Collins, *Fighting Words*).

Afro-Cuban use for a Cuban of African descent, also for music from both sources.

aged see old, senior/senior citizen.

ageism coined by Dr. Robert Butler in 1969, the term is defined as "a negative or prejudicial image of aging held by society or by individuals; ageism also exists when age is an influencing factor in situations where it is in fact inappropriate or irrelevant" (*Thesaurus of Aging Terminology*). Ageism adversely affects the young as well as the old. Although age discrimination is prohibited by law in the workplace, our cultural preoccupation with youth results in keeping older people invisible and undervalued—to society's and business's great loss. Industrial designer and gerontologist Patricia Moore (in *Modern Maturity*) says we're the only country in the world that asks age-related questions by using the word "old." In French, the question and answer are: "What age have you?" "I have 53 years." In Italian: "How many years have you?" "I have 53 years." When providing someone's age, try using "Rip Van Winkle, 78" instead of "78-year-old Rip Van Winkle." There is also a lack of respect for those who are too young; "adultism" discounts children and teenagers as too immature to know what's good for them and too inexperienced to do anything valuable. Some believe that adultism lays the foundation for accepting racism, sexism, and other oppressive re-lationships. The United States considers itself child-centered but statistics say otherwise: millions of children live in poverty, are physically and sexually abused, are involved in largely unrestricted kiddie sex and child pornography operations, and face violent death more often than in any other industrialized nation. See also adolescent, children, dirty old man, elder/elderly, frail elderly, old, old lady/old man, old maid, old-timer, old woman, oldster, senior/senior citizen, teen/teenager, youth.

aging in place the process of growing older while living in one's own residence, instead of having to move to a new home or community.

aggressive "aggressive" and its more negative synonym "pushy" are often used disparagingly of women and Jews. Deborah Tannen (*Gender and Discourse*) suggests that the "stereotype of Jews as aggressive and pushy results in part from differences in conversational style." In the lead opinion in the court case of a woman who failed to be named a partner because she was considered too aggressive, Walter Brennan wrote, "An employer who objects to aggressiveness in women but whose positions require this trait places women in an intolerable and impermissible Catch-22: out of a job if they behave aggressively and out of a job if they don't." Pollster Celinda Lake asked observers to rate women and men reading the same text at identical decibel levels. Invariably the women were described as louder, more aggressive, and shrill. Of a related term, Marlo Thomas says, "A man has to be Joe McCarthy to be called ruthless. All a woman has to do is put you on hold." See also feisty.

agnostic "an agnostic thinks it impossible to know the truth in matters such as God and the future life with which Christianity and other religions are concerned. Or, if not impossible, at least impossible at the present time" (Bertrand Russell). When asked if agnostics are atheists, Russell says, "No. An atheist, like a Christian, holds that we can know whether or not there is a God. The Christian holds that we can know there is a God; the atheist, that we can know there is not. The Agnostic suspends judgment, saying that there are not sufficient grounds either for affirmation or for denial."

aide (medical) nursing assistant, nurse assistant, N.A. Traditionally, aides and orderlies did the same work, but all aides were women and all orderlies were men. Most hospitals and nursing homes now use the inclusive terms.

aide de camp today, both military and civilian aides can be women or men, so use for both.

AIDS "an equal-opportunity pathogen," the HIV/AIDS virus crosses all cultural, economic, ethnic, sex, sex-orientation, and social lines. It is not "a gay disease"; in some parts of the world, it is found predominantly in heterosexuals. People can live with HIV (Human Immunodeficiency Virus) for decades before developing AIDS (Acquired Immune Deficiency Syndrome). A person does not die from HIV/AIDS but from complications of HIV/AIDS. When distributing information about HIV/AIDS, avoid vague, shortcut terms like "intimate sexual contact" and "bodily fluids"—tell exactly what kinds of sexual contact and exactly what kinds of bodily fluids can transmit HIV/AIDS. A person with HIV/AIDS is not "an HIV/AIDS victim" or "someone afflicted with/suffering from HIV/AIDS." Use instead person living with HIV/AIDS, someone with HIV/AIDS, person who has HIV/AIDS. See also AIDS carrier, disabilities, HIV, high-risk group, homophobia, "people first" rule.

AIDS carrier the Gay & Lesbian Alliance Against Defamation (*Media Guide to the Lesbian and Gay Community*) recommends avoiding this term as it dehumanizes people. Informing the public that someone who is HIV-infected/HIV-positive/seropositive can infect others is critically important, but it is equally important to clarify that transmission of the disease is effected only by means of high-risk activities (exchange of certain bodily fluids, sharing needles); one is not a "carrier" in the sense that a Typhoid Mary is—"a person from whom something undesirable or deadly can spread to those nearby" (*American Heritage Dictionary*). See also AIDS.

airman aviator, pilot, flier, airline/test pilot, co-pilot, navigator, flight/aeronautical engineer, aerial navigator, bombardier, air marshal, aeronaut, balloonist, aviation/aircraft worker, glider, skydiver, paratrooper, parachutist, airborne trooper, member of the U.S. Air Force. Unfortunately, the official U.S. Air Force publication is *The Airman* and the Air Force calls its members airmen, although all ranks are open to both sexes (19.6 percent of all officers and enlistees are women). Outside the Air Force, some 6 percent of commercial and private airplane pilots are women. See also birdman, wingman.

airmanship aerial navigation/flying/piloting skills, flying ability, aeronautical/flying/piloting expertise.

alderman council/city council member, city/municipal councilor, chancellor, city/ward representative, commissioner, councilor, member of the council, municipal officer, ward manager; alderman and alderwoman. In Wisconsin, they are officially called "alderpersons."

alien see illegals/illegal immigrants.

alimony other terms are sometimes more appropriate: back salary, reparations, permanent maintenance, permanent spousal maintenance, spousal support, rehabilitative/temporary alimony/maintenance. The newer terms avoid the implication that one spouse is receiving unearned financial support from the other. Either sex may receive alimony or maintenance. Today, only 15 percent of women are awarded alimony and most awards are temporary; men usually collect only when their wives earn markedly more (Jane Bryant Quinn, in *Newsweek*).

Allah the Arabic word for God. Arab Christians also use "Allah."

"all-American" aside from its use in sports, who in this diverse country could be truly "all-American"? When you picture, for example, an "all-American boy," is he black? Gay? Using a wheelchair? Probably not. Our concept of "all-American" is extremely narrow.

all boy/all girl/all man/all woman replace these vague, stereotypical expressions with specific descriptions, although no two people will agree on, for example, what "He's all man!" means: he plays baseball and spits? The common underpinnings unfortunately are usually that "all boy/all man" refers to action while "all girl/all woman" refers to physical appearance, frivolity or submissiveness.

all men are created equal all people/we are all/all of us are created equal, all women and men/men and women are created equal. "All men are created equal" is apparently one of the ten most famous quotations in the world (*Time* magazine, cited in *Random House Dictionary of Popular Proverbs and Sayings*). Unfortunately, "all men" turned out to be

not only literally true but also code for "white adult males." In 1790, after Frenchwomen realized that the liberty, equality, and fraternity won for Frenchmen in the 1789 French Revolution were just that (for French-*men*), playwright and revolutionary Olympe de Gouges published "The Declaration of the Rights of Women," modeled on the "Declaration of the Rights of Man and the Citizen." (Three years later, after opposing Robespierre and the Jacobins, she went to the guillotine.) At the first American Woman's Rights Convention (1848), the proposed "Declaration of Sentiments" began: "We hold these truths to be self-evident: that all men and women are created equal; that they are endowed by their Creator with certain inalienable rights" (Susan B. Anthony, *History of Woman Suffrage*). Not only did "all men" not include women, but it did not include black or American Indian men. It took two amendments to the U.S. Constitution to explain just who "all men" were, and into the 1970s for American Indians to be included in practice.

alma mater this gender-specific term (from the Latin for "fostering/bounteous/nourishing mother") is not perceived as particularly biased. However, if you want a sex-neutral alternative, consider the university I (he/she/we/they/you) attended, school attended, my (your/his/her/our/their) graduating institution, my (her/his/their/our/your) college or university. For the school song, use my school song/anthem, the school song, the University of Iowa school song.

altar boy server, acolyte, attendant, helper; altar girl and altar boy.

alternative the use of this term implies the existence of a single norm, and tends to marginalize the groups, activities, products, or "lifestyles" so described. Use thoughtfully. See also "alternative lifestyle," normal.

"alternative lifestyle" most often used to refer to sexual orientation, this term implies there is "a" lifestyle to which one can be alternative. People don't have lifestyles; they have lives.

alto an alto is always a woman, although you will find both men and women singing in the alto range; the countertenor is the highest male voice, and the contralto ("alto" is a contraction of contralto) is the lowest female voice.

alumna/alumnae/alumnus/alumni when used correctly to describe respectively a woman/women/a man/men, these Latin terms are gender-fair. The most common errors are the use of "alumnus" to refer to a woman and the use of "alumni" to describe both women and men. However, the trend is away from the more pedantic sex-linked Latin and toward pithier inclusive terms: graduate(s), alum(s), member(s) of the class of 1996, postgraduate(s), former student(s), ex-student(s). If you must, for some reason, use the Latin: alumna/us or alumnus/a and alumni/ae or alumnae/i.

Amazon/amazon in Greek mythology, Amazons were fabulous female warriors. The 1970 edition of *Encyclopaedia Britannica* "explains" (although a later edition deletes it): "The only plausible explanation of the story of the Amazons is that it is a variety of the familiar tale of a distant land where everything is done the wrong way about; thus the women fight, which is man's business." Not so in the African Kingdom of Dahomey (today's Republic of Benin) where a female regiment served as combat troops in the 18th and 19th centuries. Dubbed the "Dahomey Amazons" by European observers, these women warriors were renowned for their fighting skill. The word "amazon" is loaded with cultural and historical meanings; it has been used as a pejorative to describe certain women and certain kinds of women, but in other contexts it is a term of respect that women sometimes appropriate for themselves. (For example, the Amazon Bookstore, founded in 1970, is the oldest independent feminist bookstore in North America.) Use the term only if you understand its history and multiple connotations. For the casual use of "amazon," meaning a tall, strong, or belligerent woman, substitute those or other descriptive adjectives. See also warrior.

Amerasian a person of Asian and American parentage, especially the child of an Asian mother and a U.S. serviceman, "Amerasian" was coined during the Korean War but came into wider use during the Vietnam War. Because U.S. servicemen come from various backgrounds, there is no specific racial connotation to Amerasian, except that it is assumed one parent, usually the mother, is Asian. Most Amerasian children were left behind and were discriminated against by the Vietnamese people and the government, who saw them as reminders of the American presence in Vietnam (Lan Cao and Himilce Novas, *Everything You Need to Know About Asian-American History*), and also by the U.S. Government, which, unlike the French, didn't confer citizenship on the children of soldiers. In 1987, the United States passed the Amerasian Homecoming Act to facilitate the transfer to American soil of Vietnamese Amerasians born between January 1, 1962, and January 1, 1977.

America/American the United States; U.S. national/citizen/resident. The people of some forty countries (those of North America, Central America and the Caribbean, and South America) can correctly call themselves "Americans." Do not use when you only mean citizens of the United States. The terms "Asian," "African," and "European" properly refer to peoples in all the countries of their respective continents; it is puzzling to many outside the United States why "American" refers to only one of the American populations. Bernard E. Bobb, Professor of History, Emeritus, Washington State University, has one explanation: "We are the only nation in the world whose official name ["United States of America"] includes the word 'America.' Every other nation in the New World, from Canada to Argentina, has a specific name that doesn't include that word." "United Statesian" and "United Statian" have been used occasionally by enterprising writers and thinkers, as well as by former wrestler and governor of Minnesota, Jesse Ventura: "My fellow United Statians. ... I like to refer to us as United Statians. We always use the term Americans, but when you think about it there's North America, South America, Central America—I've always referred to myself as a United Statian" (interview by Misheharu Dawkins and Jonathan Miller in *The Minneapolis Observer*). No convenient shorthand term is presently available comparable to Peruvian, Angolan, Canadian, etc. "Only in Spanish is there a word for 'Americans/United Statesians': Estadounidenses" (Melanie Kaye/Kantrowitz). The American Political Science Association's style manual recommends the use of "United States, U.S., U.S. citizen, or citizen" instead of the ethnocentric "America/American" when the country is meant, reserving the use of "America/American" to refer to one or both continents. The use of "American" is ambiguous in many terms like "American history," "American heroes," and "American foreign policy," and on the grounds of clarity alone should be replaced. The exception to its use for U.S. citizens are the names used for immigrants and their descendants (Italian Americans, Japanese Americans, Native American); those terms are used only in the U.S. and are thus unlikely to be ambiguous or confused with Native Canadian, etc. See also "all-American," "hyphenated Americans."

American exceptionalism researchers and academics generally use this term for measurable differences in public opinion and political behavior between Americans and their counterparts in other developed democracies, but others use it for the theory that the United States occupies a special niche among nations in terms of its national credo, historical evolution, political and religious institutions, and unique origins. The latter argue that the idea of American exceptionalism is equivalent to ethnocentrism or jingoism and national propaganda. Tongue-in-cheek Mike Lofgren (*A Devil's Dictionary*) defines it as "a doctrine whose proponents hold that by divine dispensation America is exempt from all laws governing international norms, physics, or rationality." Know what you're talking about and whom you're addressing when using this phrase.

American Indian Ines Hernandez (in Patricia Riley, *Growing Up Native American*) says, "Native people know that the term 'Indian' is a misnomer, but we have made it our own, just as we have made 'American Indian' and … 'Native American' our own, even though in our original languages, each of our peoples had (and have) their own name for themselves and for this part of the earth that is now known as 'America.' We refer to each other by the tribe or nation that we are from—that is one of the first questions we ask each other, 'Who are your people?' and 'Where are you from?'" You may also ask, "What is your nation?" When writing and speaking about Indians: (1) It is redundant to use "Indian" following the name of a nation, for example, "Lakota," not "Lakota Indian." (2) Make no assumptions about Indians' lives, dress, beliefs, or history without careful research—many myths and stereotypes are worked into the fabric of non-Indian "understandings." In addition, there is much more diversity than stereotypes allow for. Catherine C. Robbins (*All Indians Do Not Live in Teepees [or Casinos]*) cites a study of newspaper stories on Native Americans in which some 74 percent were specifically focused on gaming and 91 percent mentioned casinos. (3) Various peoples either have changed or are in the process of changing their names from those given them by others to the names they call themselves (for example, from Nez Perce to Nimipu, from Crow to Apsaalooke, from Huron to Wyandot, from Gabrieleno to Tongva) so verify that the names are current. Paul Chaat Smith, a Comanche writer and activist, points out that names like Mao Zedong and Beethoven are not translated from Chinese or German, but Indian names were usually translated into English in an attempt to make them "easy" and incidentally primitive, thus giving us Sitting Bull instead of his Lakota name. (4) Indians are often the invisible minority; when people of color are being discussed, include Indians—and look for their presence in other issues where they should be counted. (5) Cultural appropriation is a serious issue for American Indians: they oppose their rites, ceremonies, and beliefs being taken over by non-Native do-it-yourselfers. Mary Abbe (Minneapolis' *Star Tribune*) says, "Identity theft is trouble enough in e-commerce, but imagine your whole culture snatched, abused and clichéd by outsiders. That's what some contemporary American Indian artists claim that pop culture is doing to their heritage." The late Michael Dorris (in *Teaching Toler-*

ance) said, "One thing we mustn't do is appropriate Native American symbols, which are the product of many, many years of tradition and experimentation." He says we can learn from Native American culture and experience: "We can learn that for 35,000 years this continent that we inhabit was among the most culturally diverse areas in the world, that people with many different languages, many different traditions, many different religions, existed coterminously without a great deal of violence. This is not to romanticize the past. This peacefulness did exist; no major war-making technology developed in North America as it did in Europe—reflecting a real difference in worldview." (6) "American Indian" is the most commonly used general term (but use nation, tribe, or kin names whenever you know them). "Native American" is ambiguous (it is used by the federal government for native Alaskans and Samoans and it also could mean anyone born in the U.S.), so it's not used as much today as it was. Also acceptable: First Peoples, First Nations, First Nations Peoples, Native peoples, Indian nations, Indian country. According to Clara Sue Kidwell (*Sisterhood Is Forever*), "There are more than 450 Native nations in the U.S. today, with tribal populations ranging from over 250,000 (Navajo) to less than 100. Despite their diversity, the ultimate value for Indian communities lies in our children and the metaphor of the seventh generation: all decisions being made must be judged by their effects on the seventh generation to come." See also Anasazi, brave, chief, costume, Crow, half-breed/half-caste, Indian giver, Indian summer, indigenous peoples, Injun, massacre, Nez Perce, pow-wow, renegades, roaming, Sioux, sports teams' names and mascots, squaw, tribe, warpath, white privilege.

American Indian Holocaust/Native American Holocaust (1492-1900) estimates vary, but as many as 75,000,000 to 100,000,000 indigenous Americans may have been killed in what is often referred to in history books as "Western expansion." The most conservative figure is 50,000,000 massacred. Avoid euphemisms; in some contexts, "genocide" is the correct term. Behind the mass murder was land appropriation, although the Indians never regarded the land as their property: in 1854, Chief Si'ahl (Duwamish Native American) said: "This we know; the earth does not belong to man; man belongs to the earth." See also American Indian, genocide, massacre, sports' teams names, and mascots.

American Way "The idea that the American way is better than other ways not only smacks of arrogance and selective reasoning but contributes to the divisiveness that puts false boundaries on our interest in empathizing with those who are, in so many ways, just like us" (Roy Speckhardt, *Free Mind*). After World War II, "businessmen worried among themselves that the antibusiness mentality of the 1930s might reassert itself. To counteract this possibility, corporations began to organize public-relations strategies designed to convince the public that the private-enterprise system could deliver the economic and social stability that the American people so desperately sought. The American Way reemerged as a patriotic slogan, maintaining that capitalism and democracy were two sides of the same coin and that governmental intervention was both unnecessary and dangerously 'un-American'" (Elizabeth Ewen and Stuart Ewen's *Typecasting*). The "American Way" phrase is much beloved of conservatives but grasped only in a fuzzy, feel-good way by their audiences. Before World War II, the mantra from government was "Produce! Produce!" Afterward, it was "Buy! Buy!" This, then, is the American Way. The liberal advocacy group, People For the American Way, works for a diverse democratic society, believing that there are other, better American ways. See also imperialism, patriot/patriotic/patriotism.

Amerindian/Amerind the once-popular, cobbled-together "Amerindian" (and its shortened form "Amerind") has fallen out of favor. See American Indian.

amiga/amigo these are good sex-specific parallel terms. If using Spanish would seem pretentious, substitute friend.

amputee don't refer to anyone by a surgical procedure or missing body part. Question the need to refer to a disability; if it is indeed relevant, convey the information neutrally without labeling the person by something that is only part of their life: "someone who has only one leg/foot/arm." See also handicapped.

anarchist "Anarchism is the philosophy of social affiliation unrestricted by law, government, or hierarchies of power, in which free groupings of women and men join together for the common good" (*Reader's Companion to U.S. Women's History*). Beliefs may range from extreme individualism to total collectivism, so spell out the person's essential political orientation.

Anasazi ancestral Puebloans. Because "Anasazi" is a Navajo word meaning "ancestral enemies," Hopi and other Pueblo tribes object to its use.

ancestress ancestor. See also fathers (pseudogeneric), "feminine" word endings, forefather.

anchoress retain despite the feminine ending. Julian of Norwich, for example, the first English woman of letters and the first theologian of either sex to write originally in English, is historically and respectfully known as an anchoress. For a man, use anchorite; in the broader sense, use hermit.

anchorman (newscasting) anchor, news anchor, newscaster, broadcaster, telecaster, sportscaster, announcer, reporter, TV reporter, commentator, news analyst, narrator.

ancient man early people/peoples.

androgynous/androgyny the ultimate in inclusive, these words contain the roots for both man ("aner") and woman ("gyne"). "Androgyny suggests a spirit of reconciliation between the sexes; it suggests, further, a full range of experience open to individuals who may, as women, be aggressive, as men, tender; it suggests a spectrum upon which human beings choose their places without regard to propriety or custom" (Carolyn G. Heilbrun, *Toward a Recognition of Androgyny*). According to Dr. Anne Campbell (*The Opposite Sex*), the androgynous person shows the most satisfactory psychological and social adjustment. Gloria Steinem (*Outrageous Acts and Everyday Rebellions*) says the concept of androgyny "raised the hope that the female and male cultures could be perfectly blended in the ideal person; yet because the female side of the equation has yet to be affirmed, androgyny usually tilted toward the male. As a concept, it also raised anxiety levels by conjuring up a conformist, unisex vision, the very opposite of the individuality and uniqueness that feminism actually has in mind. Radical feminist Mary

Daly (*Gyn/Ecology*) refers to the word as a "semantic abomination": "The word is misbegotten—conveying something like 'John Travolta and Farrah Fawcett-Majors scotch-taped together.'"

"(and women)" do not make afterthoughts of women by inserting them in parentheses after "men." You might also see "women (and men") or "lesbians (and bisexuals)" or some other indication that, oops, I should mention them too. The vast majority of the time the parenthetical terms are equal in weight and meaning to the preceding terms. A good writer will distinguish that rare need to put a second group in parentheses. In addition, avoid constructions like "noted funnymen and women." It's either "funny people" or "funnymen and funnywomen."

angel in many cultures and for many men, women are either angels (perfect and innocent) or devils (evil tempters). Our ideas of both angels themselves and women-as-angels are highly mythic and in some cases insulting to real women and real angels. The association of women with angels is a little puzzling; in the Jewish and Christian scriptures, there were no female angels; they were generally represented as men, although in one case they appear to be neuter. They must be somewhat intimidating; their first words are always "Do not be afraid." Not all angels are Christian (there are Jewish, Muslim, and other angels) nor are they all white.

Anglo used as a generic synonym for "white," as it is in some parts of the U.S., "Anglo" is considered inaccurate (not all whites have an Anglo-Saxon heritage) and objectionable (those who have suffered from Anglo-Saxon oppression—the Irish, for example—do not appreciate being called Anglos). "Anglo" is slang for white non-Mexican Americans in the South and Southwest and for white non-Cubans in Miami. When combining terms, no hyphen is needed when the second term is lowercase ("Anglophone") but is needed when it is capitalized ("Anglo-Saxon"). See also Anglo-American.

Anglo-American this refers to a U.S. citizen of English ancestry; it is not used generically for any white person who speaks English. The hyphen is used in both the noun and the adjective because "Anglo-" is a prefix. See also Anglo.

anima/animus in Jungian psychology, *anima* (the feminine form of the Latin for "soul") refers to the female component in a man's personality, while *animus* (the masculine form) refers to the masculine component in a woman's personality. Use as they are.

animal/he if you know the animal's gender and it is important for your audience to also know it, use it; otherwise refer to all animals of unknown or irrelevant gender as "it."

animal husbandman/animal husbandry animal scientist, animal science.

animal (man) calling men "animals" carries with it a what-can-you-expect attitude and builds tolerance for behavior that is not particularly normative for men—or for animals. See also animal names for people.

animal names for people using animal names—such as ape, bunny, chick, kitten, shark—to refer to people is generally insensitive and will not make you a lot of friends. In addition, most pejorative animal names are also sexist. "Men's extensive labeling of women as parts of body, fruit, or animals and as mindless, or like children—labels with no real parallel for men—reflects men's derision of women and helps maintain gender hierarchy and control" (Barrie Thorne, Cheris Kramarae, and Nancy M. Henley, eds., *Language, Gender and Society*). A few terms seem descriptive without being derogatory; lamb is used affectionately for both sexes. Metaphors that compare people to animals in some particular are seldom sexist and thus are acceptable, for example, merry as a cricket, happy as a lark, feeling one's oats. To distinguish between pejorative and acceptable descriptions, determine whether a person is being labeled an animal or whether the person is being likened to some animal characteristic. Saying someone is wise as an owl implies not that the person is an owl but that the person is wise as we imagine owls are wise. Strong writing depends on metaphors—even metaphors based on animals—but there is a difference between labeling people and creating vivid word associations. See also bitch, food names for people, fox/foxy/foxy lady, hen party, lone wolf, stag line, stag movie, stag party, stud, wolf.

animal rights activist/animal advocate some 68 to 80 percent of animal rights activists are women (Emily Gaarder, *Women and the Animal Rights Movement*). Vegetarians, who have always said meat doesn't belong on the feminist menu, cite, among other reasons, the link between meat consumption and exploitation of women through advertising, domestic violence, hunting and gun culture, pornography, and other forms of entertainment. Labor and environmental issues are also profoundly affected by the meat industry. According to Carol J. Adams (in *Sisterhood Is Forever*), there is ongoing debate about the appropriateness of "rights" language, and some activists have proposed that arguments on behalf of animals be placed within ethics of care theory—that is, nurturance, sympathy, and love are values that need not be directed solely toward human beings. The word "animalist" is not recommended because although sometimes it is defined as an animal rights supporter (a contraction of "animal liberationist"), it can also be used to mean the opposite in a usage parallel to ageist, sexist, racist.

animist one who generally believes that everything has a soul (Latin, *anima/animus*), that spirit and matter are all one, and that this unity has implications for everyday life. Use to describe an individual or capitalize for groups: for example, Eritrea has three major faiths; Christian, Muslim and Animist.

Anishinabe see Ojibwa/Ojibway.

anorexic someone with anorexia, person with an eating disorder. "Anorexic" may be used as an adjective ("anorexic behavior"), but not as a noun. A person is not an "anorexic." See also disabilities, "people first" rule.

anthropocentrism also referred to as human chauvinism, this is a way of looking at the world that posits human beings as the central and ultimate purpose of life. For centuries, people believed that everything in the universe literally revolved around us. Galileo was persecuted for saying otherwise and Giordano Bruno was burned at the stake in 1600 for agreeing.

anthropology the Greek word *anthropos* can be translated "human being" or "man." In practice, "anthropos" words like anthropology, anthropocentric, anthropoid, anthropomorphism, philanthropic, philanthropist, and philanthropy are defined, used, and perceived as inclusive.

anti-abortion another term for pro-life or anti-choice. See also abortion, pro-life.

anti-Arabism hatred, prejudice, and hostility toward Arabs may be expressed in slurs (raghead, camel jockey), exclusions, incorrect information about Arabs, and negative stereotypes, in particular, when Arabs are portrayed as intolerant, backward, and violent, while positive aspects of Arab culture are ignored. As with anti-Semitism, hatred of Arabs is different from political opposition to the policies of Arab states. In the U.S., many people are ignorant of the distinction between Arabs and Muslims, thus after 9/11, Arabs have been viewed as potential terrorists right along with a biased group judgment of Muslims. Anti-Arabism has also been called anti-Arab bias, anti-Arab prejudice, anti-Arab racism, Arab-phobia, Arabphobia, and Arabophobia. See also Arab, Muslim.

anti-choice another term for pro-life or anti-abortion. See also abortion, pro-life.

antifeminist man or woman who opposes equality of the sexes and measures to achieve that equality.

anti-intellectual no one actually comes out and says, "I hate smart people," but by putting "so-called" and "self-styled" in front of "intellectual" and generally deriding anything that can be construed as intellectual, the scorn is clear enough so that few intelligent people are interested in self-identifying as intellectuals. Unfortunately, the anti-intellectualism in the U.S. has become so widespread that discussions and debate about serious issues have been replaced by soundbites, news programs are now largely infotainment, and facts are considered fairly underwhelming especially if opposed to feelings or wishful thinking. Some of the disparaging words conveyed in disparaging tones to put down the intelligent include egghead, bookworm, know-it-all, highbrow, longhair, walking encyclopedia, smarty-pants, pedant, nerd, geek. Politicians like to use adjectives like out of touch, ivory tower, unrealistic, pie-in-the-sky.

anti-Islamism see Islamophobia.

anti-male bias is a rallying cry for men's rights activists (MRAs) whose grievances include economic and workplace conditions for men, the educational achievement gap that has boys lagging behind girls, violence against men, false rape reporting, father's rights in custody cases, and elevated suicide rates among men. While these issues and their causes deserve thoughtful debate, in the online world of MRAs, often called the "manosphere," what one encounters instead is violent misogyny. MRAs co-opt the language of social justice movements, but often act like hate groups.

anti-personnel bomb designed to kill people, as opposed to bombs made to destroy buildings. "These are anti-personnel weapons, like a home-made grenade, and the effect would be to tear through flesh causing terrible, lethal injuries" (the U.K.'s *Independent*). See also collateral damage.

anti-pornography movement see pornography.

anti-racist one who opposes, and works to eliminate, racism.

anti-Semitism although Semites are members of any of the peoples who speak a Semitic language, including Jews, Arabs, Assyrians, and Phoenicians, "anti-Semitism" is used and understood to mean "Jew-hating." A much nicer-sounding term than "Jew-hating," "anti-Semitism" obscures its hatefulness. Spell out what's involved: "anti-Arab hostility" or "anti-Jew publications." See also anti-Arabism, Jew.

anti-sweatshop activist anyone who works to bring needed public attention to sweatshops, to boycott products made in sweatshops, and, sometimes, to shut them down. The deaths of 200 workers in a Bangladeshi sweatshop in 2013 were particularly heinous. Workers who attempted to leave the collapsing sweatshop (extra unpermitted floors had been added to the building in order to squeeze in more workers) were driven back inside by bosses with "beating sticks." Sweatshops often have poor working conditions, unfair wages, unreasonable hours, child labor, and a lack of benefits for workers. In developing countries, an estimated 250 million children ages 5 to 14 are forced to work (www. dosomething.org). The U.S. Department of Labor defines a sweatshop as a factory that violates two or more labor laws. (But UNITE HERE, the U.S. garment workers union, defines a sweatshop as any factory that doesn't allow workers to organize an independent union.) Anti-sweatshop activists cannot take on all sweatshops. However, in the U.S., companies outsource jobs to low-paying foreign countries where there is little worker oversight (and thus lower costs). When this outsourcing goes to sweatshops, activists can apply pressure to the U.S. companies (as when the Apple company's factory in China, Foxconn, was dubbed "suicide express" because of the many work-condition-related suicides). The sweatshop issue is complex, and not all anti-sweatshop activists think alike: workers make more money than they are otherwise able to, so shutting down sweatshops is not always a solution. Arguing for a return to the U.S. of outsourced jobs also has pitfalls. The most effective anti-sweatshop activism focuses less on wages than on securing workers' rights and safety.

anti-war activist/protester this individual is not "un-American," "unpatriotic," a traitor, or a coward. Most of them support the troops. See also peace movement.

anti-Zionism Jewish anti-Zionism includes such well-known Jewish anti-Zionist movements as Satmar and Neturei Karta as well as other Jewish groups and organizations that believe any form of Zionism is heresy, directly contravening the Torah, and that the existence of the state of Israel is illegitimate. In general, non-Jewish anti-Zionists simply disagree with Israeli policies, especially with regard to the occupied territories. Dismissing critics of Israel or of Zionism as "anti-Semitic" is a means of stifling debate and masking the impact of the occupation. See also anti-Semitism, Israeli-Palestinian conflict, occupied territories, Zionism.

"ape-man" early human, prehuman, prehuman fossil, anthropoid ape.

Apostolic Fathers leave as is; historically correct.

Appalachian "*Appalachians*, because of its identity with rural poverty and its largely uncomplimentary denotation of the quasi-ethnic group of the region, holds the potential of both an ethnic and a class slur. Better, more traditional terms are available: *Southern Highlanders* and *Appalachian Southerners* could serve" (Irving Lewis Allen, *Unkind Words*). Use

"Appalachia" to refer to the area, not the people, thus "the rural populations of southern Appalachia." Some definitions of "Appalachians" specify "white residents of the mountainous regions of Appalachia." Coined by Frank X. Walker in 1992, "Affrilachian" or "Afrilachian" is sometimes used to refer to African Americans who live in Appalachia. See also hillbilly.

apron strings, tied to someone's dependent/overly dependent on, clinging, immature, timid, childish, pampered, protected, can't make a move without, no mind of one's own. Hugh Rawson (*Wicked Words*) defines the expression as being "unduly subject to one's wife or mother" and says it dates back to at least the 16th century when the legal term "apron-string hold/tenure" referred to tenure of an estate by virtue of one's wife or during her lifetime only. See also henpeck/henpecked.

Arab "Arabs are Semitic people who originated on the Arabian Peninsula. The 19 Arab countries on the west part of the Asian continent and the northern part of the Africa continent are: Lebanon, Palestine, Jordan, Syria, Kuwait, Saudi Arabia, Yemen, Oman, Bahrain, Tunisia, Algeria, Egypt, Sudan, Qatar, Mauritania, Iraq, Libya, Morocco, and the United Arab Emirates" (Joanna Kadi). The word Arab (pronouncing it as AY-rab is a slur) is not interchangeable with "Arab American," "Arab Canadian," or "Muslim." Not all Arabs are Muslims nor are all Muslims Arabs. Iranians are Persians, not Arabs. Afghans are not Arabs. Watch for stereotypes: Arab women tend to be seen as either veiled or belly dancers; men are billionaires or bombers. Usage of "al" in Arab names varies from country to country, from family to family, and even from individual to individual within a family (Al, al, al-, or attached with no space). Some Arabs use "el" instead of "al." See also anti-Arabism, Arab American, Islam, Middle East.

Arab American acceptable term for those who self-identify this way.

arbitration when discussing arbitration, double-check assumptions. Originally an informal, low-cost, and straightforward method of settling disputes between two parties, it has evolved into something disappointing to the non-corporate disputant. Jim Hightower ("The Hightower Lowdown") says the current system "is the product of years of conceptual monkeywrenching by corporate lobbyists, Congress, the Supreme Court, and hired-gun arbitration firms looking to milk the system for steady profits." Among other inequalities, third-party arbitrators are chosen by the corporation involved in the case, as is the venue where the case will be heard (making it expensive and inconvenient for the complainants). Arbitration hearings are closed to media and public; arbitrators need not give reasons for their decisions and are not legally accountable for errors; they are also not required to know the relevant law; there is virtually no right to appeal. The problem is that today most arrangements between customers and corporations include an arbitration clause—if you want the product or service, you agree, often without thinking. Most arbitration clauses prohibit any class-action cases, which means in case of a wrong done to many people, they must "arbitrate" one by one. Hightower points out that the same corporations that say arbitration is fairer, faster, and cheaper than the judicial system almost never choose arbitration for themselves in disputes with others.

Armenian genocide (1915-1923) as a result of the "ethnic cleansing" of Armenians in Anatolia (Turkey) during the Ottoman Empire, as many as a million and a half Armenians were killed. "Most scholars and experts, including a number of courageous Turks themselves, unreservedly favor the 'genocide' designation" (Sandy Berman). The Turkish government argues that these deaths resulted from the chaos of World War I and has severely sanctioned those who call it genocide (some 60 Turkish journalists were prosecuted for "insulting Turkishness" because they referred to the Armenian experience as genocide). Turkey, which refers to the genocide as "a tragedy," is a NATO ally, so in 2006 the Bush administration dismissed the U.S. ambassador to Armenia for publicly voicing the forbidden term "Armenian genocide."

army wife military/soldier's/service member's spouse. See service wife.

arthritic (adjective) don't use of individuals; joints may be arthritic but people are either people with arthritis or an individual who has arthritis.

articulate the use of "articulate" is offensive when it is used only for certain ethnic groups, the implication being that "those people" are not normally well-spoken but that this individual is surprisingly so. See also qualified.

artificial insemination see assisted reproduction.

artilleryman artillery personnel, gunner. "Artilleryman," as used in the U.S. Army, can refer to either sex. However, the average reader will still see a man, so you may have to indicate otherwise.

artist woman or man. Although 51 percent of U.S. artists are women, according to The National Museum for Women in the Arts, they are represented in public art collections at the alarmingly low rate of 3 percent. In one of the most widely used texts, *History of Art* by H. W. Janson, a woman artist was not mentioned until the book's 16th edition (1985). See also arts and crafts, Guerrilla Girls.

artiste woman or man. However, beware of a connotation of artificiality when the "e" is added.

arts and crafts "*Art* used to be definable as what men created. *Crafts* were made by women and "natives." Only recently have we discovered they are the same, thus bringing craft techniques into art, and art into everyday life" (Gloria Steinem, in *Ms*). See also artist, binary thinking.

Aryan although this term has a legitimate technical use in referring to the peoples who speak Indo-European languages, it is usually avoided because of its associations with Nazism, where it meant a white non-Jew of Nordic aspect, with the connotation that this type of human being, superior to all others, was meant to rule the world. This association has been furthered in the U.S. by such supremacist groups as Aryan Nation.

asexuality according to the online Asexual Visibility and Education Network (AVEN) group, "an asexual person is someone who is not sexually attracted to other people." *Bitch* reports that the first human studies on asexuality as a non-pathologized phenomenon found that it is not a disorder, but part of the continuum of sexuality. Dr. Nicole Prause, from the Kinsey Institute for Research in Sex, Gender, and Reproduction, says, "Our data do not support a need to pathologize asexuals." Asexual people may have romantic feelings about others (of the same-sex, opposite sex, or both sexes; asexuality has nothing to do with sexual orientation) and live full and fulfilling lives. They simply aren't interested in sex.

Asian this broad term refers to the continent, peoples, languages, and cultures of Asia. "Asian" is not interchangeable with Asian American or Amerasian, nor are "Asiatic" and "Oriental" acceptable when referring to people. Whenever known, specify nationality (Laotian/Thai/Cambodian) in the same way you would distinguish between Italian/Spaniard/German and European. See also Asian American, Asiatic, Oriental.

Asian American Shirley Geok-Lin Lim says this homogenizing label includes "hundreds of tribes, language groups, a variety of immigration histories (from first-generation Chinese Americans, arriving from Taiwan or Hong Kong or the mainland, who have different stories to tell, to the Sansei, third-generation Japanese Americans whose American roots go back to the early 19th century)." Occasionally "Asian American" may be appropriate, but in general use specific designations: Filipino/a American, Japanese American, Chinese American. Even when meant as compliments, such positive terms as quiet, serene, industrious, reserved, smiling, intelligent, studious, and philosophical tend to stereotype and render one-dimensional people from many different countries and widely varying cultures. "Asian American" is not interchangeable with "Asian" or "Amerasian." An excellent reference book is *Everything You Need to Know About Asian-American History* (Lan Cao and Himilce Novas). See also Asian, Asiatic, Issei, Kibei, Nisei, Oriental, Pacific Islander, Sansei, Yonsei.

Asian Pacific American correct form for U.S. residents with a Pacific-Island Asian heritage.

Asiatic Asian, Asian American. Or be specific: Tibetan, Chinese, Korean, Japanese American, Vietnamese American. "Asiatic" is considered offensive when used of people; it is acceptable when modifying words (Asiatic languages, Asiatic studies). See also Oriental.

assemblyman (manufacturing) assembler.

assemblyman (politics) assembly member, state assembly member, member of the assembly, legislator, representative.

assimilated groups have been reproached with both not assimilating or assimilating too much. Sometimes "assimilated" is used negatively (especially with reference to non-European minorities) to imply that an individual or a group has adopted the customs and attitudes of the prevailing culture to the detriment of their own, that they in effect assent to domination. Groups that don't learn English quickly enough are accused of rejecting assimilation. The concept goes to the heart of such issues as diversity and national unity and issues like the dominant model of society—do those who have traditionally not had power in it become assimilated and also become dominant or do they build a culture within or adjacent to the dominant culture? Use with care.

assisted reproduction according to the CDC (Centers for Disease Control and Prevention) more than 1 percent of all U.S. babies today are conceived using Assisted Reproductive Technology (ART). "Assisted reproduction" has replaced such earlier terms as artificial or alternative insemination. See also donor offspring, mother, pregnant.

assisted suicide assisted dying, aid in dying, death with dignity, assisted death. "A rational, terminally ill patient's choice to self-administer medications to shorten an agonizing dying process needs to be respected in language as well as in deed" (from the website of the nonprofit organization Compassion & Choices). As of 2014, assisted dying is legal in four states: Oregon, Washington, Montana, and Vermont. Terminally ill patients say they do not want to die and are not suicidal. Given a choice, they would choose to live, but since a disease is ending their life they seek control and the possibility of a peaceful death. The American Public Health Association, one of the nation's most esteemed health care organizations, recognizes the profound difference between what we have historically viewed as suicide and the choice of a terminally ill, mentally competent adult to take life-ending medication if suffering becomes unbearable. Noting the importance of using accurate, unbiased language, the American Academy of Hospice and Palliative Medicine has rejected what it calls the emotionally charged term "physician-assisted suicide." Oregon's landmark 1997 Death With Dignity Act models the desired language and law. Linguist Geoffrey Nunberg (*Los Angeles Times*) points out that the word suicide suggests fanaticism, desperation, or mental unbalance and that the suffix "-cide" has overtones of criminality or wrongdoing. Right-to-die supporters distinguish between taking your life when you are not otherwise dying (suicide) and the hastening, or not prolonging, of a death that is already on its way. The term "euthanasia," which is the practice of ending, in a painless way, a life that is almost ended in all but the suffering, is not often used today, perhaps because of its clinical aspect. Veterinarians use "euthanatize" rather than "euthanize" as it comes from the Greek *eu* meaning well, good, or easy, and *thanatos* meaning death.

astroturfing a term describing political or corporate campaigns that look like grassroots movements but aren't. For example, the Campaign to Fix the Debt paid college students $65 to participate in a flash mob for deficit reduction in downtown Washington, D.C., in order to make it appear that young people are passionate about the issue. This is a textbook case of astroturfing, as is the same group's placement of fake op-ed pieces, purportedly written by college students, in several regional newspapers. An editor at *The Gainesville Sun* caught the Campaign to Fix the Debt out in the fraud and wrote that "advocacy groups and others should lay off the astroturf and outright plagiarism unless they want to discredit themselves and their causes." The Campaign to Fix the Debt cites putting "America on a better fiscal and economic path" as a core principle, but it is in fact the "latest incarnation of Wall Street mogul Pete Peterson's long campaign to get Congress and the White House to cut Social Security, Medicare, and Medicaid while providing tax breaks for corporations and the wealthy" (The Editors, *The Nation*).

atheist although precise figures are difficult to pin down, some 6 percent to 10 percent of the U.S. population may be atheists. Remember these good people (by some calculations, 2.2 million atheists have fought in American wars from World War II onward, and tens of thousands have died for their country) when tempted to use terms like "divinely inspired," "God-given talent," or "Judeo-Christian ethic." The assumption that everyone believes in God, and that those who do have access to a higher morality, is pervasive—and as generally unnoticed as water is to a fish. Reporter Robert I. Sherman (*American*

Atheist News Journal) asked George H.W. Bush if he recognized the equal citizenship and patriotism of Americans who are atheists: "No, I don't know that atheists should be considered as citizens, nor should they be considered patriots. This is one nation under God." In general, atheists are the epitome of tolerance; they do not care what others believe, they ask only that others don't require them to share those beliefs, in ways abstract and concrete. Greta Christina (on www.Alter-Net.org) says, "If you don't think you're close-minded for not believing in Zeus, then please don't accuse atheists of being close-minded for not believing in your god." Two suspect terms are "militant atheist" and "fundamentalist atheist"; atheists will discuss their beliefs but are rarely evangelistic about them (they don't care what others think) and atheists have no texts or commandments or formalized dogma to be fundamentalist. Some atheists self-identify as humanists, secular humanists, freethinkers, or skeptics (although not every member of those groups may be an atheist). See also Christian cultural imperialism, deist, separation of church and state.

athlete referring to women as "female athletes" and to men as "athletes" is demeaning, illogical, and unnecessary; in sports writing, using first names for women and surnames for men is unparallel language and makes women appear childish; if male athletes are tough and sweaty, so are female athletes. Media coverage of sports and athletics differs for women and for men; work for parallel coverage. The importance of athletics to boys and men has always been a given. They are equally important to girls and women: girls and women who play sports have higher levels of self-esteem and lower levels of depression (Ms. Foundation); high school girls who play sports are 80 percent less likely to be involved in an unwanted pregnancy, 92 percent less likely to be involved with drugs, and three times more likely to graduate from high school (Institute for Athletics and Education). Today, 41 percent of athletes are women (Ms.). In 2012, for the first time, U.S. women outnumbered U.S. men at the Olympics, comprising a total of 269 women of the 530 total; in 1972, only 40 of the 400 USA athletes were women (Chris Voelz, Women's Sports Foundation). In addition, 2012 was the first year that every single participating country had men and women representing them. To see if you're writing and speaking about male and female athletes is parallel, mentally substitute one sex for the other to see if it reads sensibly. See also sportsman, Title IX.

at risk according to the *Publication Manual of the American Psychological Association*, 4th ed., "Broad clinical terms such as ... 'people *at risk*' are loaded with innuendo unless properly explained. ... Identify the risk and the people it involves (for example, "children at risk for early school dropout")." See also high-risk group.

atypical see normal.

audism "Audism is the corporate institution for dealing with deaf people, dealing with them by making statements about them, authorizing views of them, describing them, teaching about them, governing where they go to school, and, in some cases, where they live; in short, audism is the hearing way of dominating, restructuring, and exercising authority over the deaf community" (Harlan Lane, *The Mask of Benevolence*).

aunt see avuncular.

au pair girl au pair, live-in sitter/child-minder/family helper. There are few male au pairs in the U.S., although in Great Britain the term "house-boy" used to denote a similar position ("au pair" is used there now for both sexes). See also nanny.

authoress author. See also "feminine" word endings.

auto mechanic man or woman, though only 5,000 out of 845,000 auto mechanics are women.

auxiliary see ladies' auxiliary.

average man average person/citizen/human being/voter, common person/citizen/human being/voter, ordinary person/citizen/human being/voter, typical customer/consumer/reader/viewer, citizen, voter, layperson, taxpayer, resident, homeowner, landowner, passerby, non-specialist, commoner, one of the people/masses, rank and file, people in general. (In *Sister Outsider*, Audre Lorde defines the mythical U.S. norm as "white, thin, male, young, heterosexual, christian, and financially secure.")

aviatress/aviatrix aviator. See also airman, "feminine" word endings.

avuncular this is a useful term for men, but there is no equally tidy equivalent for a woman. "Auntly" and "auntlike" are possibilities, although they do not have the flavor of "avuncular." Otherwise consider adjectives with related meanings: indulgent, kindly, benevolent, genial, expansive, hearty, conspiratorial, friendly.

There are worse words than cuss words,
there are words that hurt.

Tillie Olsen

Communication provides the legs for bias,
carrying it from person to person, from
generation to generation. Eventually,
however, communication will be the
way to end discrimination.

Without Bias: A Guide for Nondiscriminatory Communication

babe/baby/baby doll (woman) picturing women as children and playthings has been highly damaging.

baby mama this term for a single mother is often sexist and racist.

babysitter this nice, inclusive word is used in one highly sexist manner. Todd Melby, Minneapolis, says that when he's out with his child, he's been "complimented" by people for babysitting. He says he is parenting, "not just giving Mom a few minutes away from the kids." While mothers are never considered to be babysitting their children, fathers often are.

bachelor a single aspect of a person's life becomes the whole of the person when "bachelor" is used. If a reference to marital status is necessary (it rarely is), use single. "Unmarried" and "unwed" perpetuate a marriage-as-norm attitude and don't include the divorced. We write and speak as if marriage and parenthood somehow grant validity to a person when in fact the married and unmarried often have more in common than not. Note the nonparallel connotations of the supposedly parallel "bachelor" and "spinster." Women go from bachelor girl to spinster to old maid but men are bachelors forever.

bachelor girl/bachelorette woman. If a reference to marital status is necessary (it rarely is), use single woman. See bachelor, single, spinster.

bachelor's degree B.A., B.S., undergraduate degree, college degree, four-year degree, baccalaureate. "Baccalaureate" means a college or university bachelor's degree and is therefore an exact synonym for "bachelor's degree" without gender-specific overtones (although its Latin roots are masculine).

backlash "backlash follows success as night follows day" (Gloria Steinem, in *Sisterhood Is Forever*). In *Backlash*, Susan Faludi says "The last decade has seen a powerful counterassault on women's rights, a backlash, an attempt to retract the handful of small and hard-won victories that the feminist movement did manage to win for women." She says the heart of the backlash movement are the messages that "women are better off 'protected' than equal" and "that women's equality is responsible for women's unhappiness." See also postfeminism.

B

backroom boys power brokers, wheeler-dealers, politicos, strategists, movers and shakers.

backward see primitive.

backwoodsman settler, wilderness settler, backsettler, pioneer, woodlander, woodcutter; hermit, recluse; backwoodsman and backwoodswoman.

bad guy bad actor/news, villain. There are few good alternatives because virtually all the "bad guy" words in our language are perceived as referring to men, even those that are not sexist per se. Although in theory the following words could be used of a woman, in practice they rarely are: bounder, brigand, bully, cad, cheat, creep, crook, deviate, double-crosser/-dealer, evildoer, four-flusher, gangster, goon, heel, hoodlum, hooligan, jerk, louse, lowlife, mobster, mountebank, mugger, outcast, outlaw, punk, racketeer, rascal, rat, ratfink, renegade, reprobate, rogue, rotter, ruffian, scalawag, scoundrel, scum/scumbag/scuzzbag/scuzzbucket, sleaze/sleazebag/sleazeball, slimebag/slimeball/slime bucket, suspect, thug, turkey, two-timer, ugly customer. In addition, the gender default for words like hoodlum, jailbird, and murderer, which are technically inclusive, is male because the majority of hoodlums, jailbirds, and murderers are men. Why this is so (classism, racism, poverty, and the cult of masculinity are big factors) and what we can do about it cannot be solved at the level of language, but recognizing male-tagged and female-tagged words can raise our consciousness of the issues—and consciousness precedes action. Negative words for women focus on sexual promiscuity (there are 10 times as many words for sexually promiscuous women in our language as there are for men); negative words for men focus on moral vileness—almost all such terms are for men, and we traditionally personalize both "enemy" and "devil" as male. See also animal names for people, bastard, devil/he, jackass, perpetrator, prisoner, Satan/he, schmuck.

bag/old bag (woman) there is no parallel for a man.

baggageman baggage checker/handler/agent, porter.

bag lady/bag man (homeless) bag woman/bag man, street person. The gender-fair use of "bag woman" and "bag man" (not the nonparallel lady/man) is sometimes appropriate although we tend to hear more about the bag woman than we do about the bag man. According to the 2010 Annual Homeless Assessment to Congress, prepared by the Department of Housing and Urban Development (HUD), 38% of individuals in homeless shelters are female, 62% are male. In the plural, use homeless people. See also homeless, the.

bagman (collector/distributor of illicit funds) bagger, go-between, shark, racketeer, peculator, receiver.

bailsman/bail bondsman bail agent, bond agent, bail bond agent/poster; provider, guarantor, bonding institution, underwriter.

ball/bang these slang terms for sex convey a number of twisted and sexist attitudes: they are violent, they are non-reciprocal, and they make objects of the partner. Avoiding these words won't change attitudes, but paying attention to language encourages awareness of the values that underpin it.

ball boy/ball girl tennis court attendant, ball/court attendant, ball tender/fetcher.

ballerina a ballerina is a principal (but not the principal) female dancer in a company, a soloist. Although the term is commonly used to refer to any female ballet dancer, this is not, strictly speaking, correct. The French word for a female solo dancer is *danseuse*; *ballerina* is the Italian equivalent and the term most commonly used in the United States. Retain "ballerina" for its narrow meaning within ballet companies, but describe anyone who dances ballet nonprofessionally as a ballet dancer. See also danseur/danseuse; premier danseur; prima ballerina.

ballet master/ballet mistress these titles are standard within professional ballet companies; in other contexts, use ballet instructor/teacher.

balls acceptable sex-specific word when it means testicles. For inclusive metaphorical use, substitute guts, moxie, courage, nerve, bravery, self-assurance, confidence, determination, stamina, spunk. Women are occasionally congratulated with "That took balls!" or encouraged with "You have the balls for it." For "ballbreaker/ballbuster," meaning a difficult or complicated task or situation, use gutbuster, tough row to hoe, killer, bad news, hell on wheels, no picnic, up a tree, hell of a note, tall/large order, tough grind/one, tough sledding, sticky business, stumper, uphill job, tight spot. For "ballbreaker," meaning a woman, see bitch, castrate/castrating, shrew. See also ballsy.

ballsy "a term that has slipped so far from its original mooring that it can be applied to females" (Hugh Rawson, *Wicked Words*). See also balls.

banana republic this derogatory term referring to a small country economically dependent on a single crop or product "trivializes the struggles that Latinas and Latinos have gone through, and still go through, to have stable sovereign governments in their own lands. The image of the so-called 'Banana Republic' continues to propagate the lie that Latinas and Latinos are hot-blooded, unstable, violent and incapable of competent self-rule, and it deflects attention away from Uncle Sam whose economic and political interests are almost always behind political upheavals and unrest in South and Central America, and the Caribbean" (Amoja Three Rivers, *Cultural Etiquette*).

Bangalore Bengaluru. Known as the Silicon Valley of India, Bengaluru has established itself as an international IT hub. Aviation and other industries are gravitating to Bengaluru and, as of 2013, the city is home to 50 percent of the top companies in India (*The Times of India*). Indians and residents of that city use these terms interchangeably, though Bangalore is more spoken and Bengaluru mostly written.

banshee this female spirit has no male counterpart, but she plays an important part in Gaelic folklore; use as is.

Bantu "applied until recently to members of Bantu-speaking tribes. … Among linguists and anthropologists it is still in carefully controlled use but is otherwise taboo in most uses because of South African whites' use of it as an offensive name for black Africans" (Kenneth G. Wilson, *The Columbia Guide to Standard American English*). "Bantu" is still acceptable when referring to the group of over 400 closely related languages in the Niger-Congo language family.

barbaric/barbarian see primitive.

barber almost half of all barbers are women, and the woman cutting your hair is not a "lady barber," "barberette," or "barberess." She is a barber.

bar boy bartender/bar helper, bar assistant/server, waiter.

bar girl with drinking age limits, the "girl" is obviously inappropriate, and the term has come to usually mean a prostitute who works out of bars. Note the different path "bar boy" has taken.

bard not itself sex-based, "bard" has acquired masculine overtones, probably from its close association with "the" bard, Shakespeare. Therefore you may sometimes want more inclusive-sounding alternatives: poet, poet-singer, epic/heroic poet, heroic versifier, minstrel, ballad singer.

bargeman barge hand, deckhand.

bargemaster barge captain.

barmaid bartender/bar helper, bar assistant/server, waiter, cocktail server.

barman bartender, bar attendant, barkeeper, barkeep. Half of U.S. bartenders are women.

bar mitzvah/bat mitzvah these terms refer both to the ceremony and to the young person initiated into adulthood in Judaism. Bar mitzvah is for boys and has been a part of classical Judaism. Bat mitzvah is for girls, was first celebrated in 1922, and has been popular since 1960. It is found only in Conservative, Reform, Reconstructionist Judaism.

baroness this title is used for a woman holding the title to a barony or for the wife or widow of a baron.

barren (referring to a woman) sterile, infertile. The alternatives are used for both sexes. "Barren," which is used only for women, carries an unwarranted stigma and many negative associations (synonyms include words like impoverished, desolate, arid, fruitless, unproductive, meager, ineffective, incompetent, useless, worthless, valueless, devoid, deficient). Describing someone as "childless" or as "having no children" is not recommended as it implies that having children is the norm. See also childfree/childless, infertile, sterile.

barrista/barista woman or man, now applied even to Starbucks personnel.

baseman (baseball) base player, baser; first/second/third baser; first-base/second-base/third-base player; first, second, third; first-base/second-base/third-base position; 1B, 2B, 3B (baseball notation); first/second/third sacker. There is good traditional support for the alternatives. According to Stuart Berg Flexner (*Listening to America*), "first base, second base, and third base" have referred to both the positions and the players since the 1840s, while "first," "second," "third," and "base player" were already being used in the 1860s. Other baseball terms use the common -er ending: outfielder, infielder, pitcher, catcher, batter. Base players may be girls/women or boys/men; Marcenia Lyle Alberga, or "Toni Stone," the first woman to play professional baseball (not softball) on all-male teams, got a hit off pitcher Satchel Paige; in 1974, nine-year-old Maria Pepe integrated Little League baseball; in 1989, Victoria Brucker competed in a Little League World Series, the first girl to do so.

basketball Mariah Burton Nelson (*The Stronger Women Get, the More Men Love Football*) notes that college basketball is still divided into "college basketball" and "women's college basketball" and that small gyms continue to be called the women's gym.

bastard when you mean someone whose parents were not married at the time of their birth (and you really, really need to mention this), use offspring/child/son/daughter of unmarried parents/of single parent/of unknown father. When you mean "bastard" in the sense of "a wretched and repellant male" (Richard A. Spears, *NTC's Dictionary of American Slang and Colloquial Expressions*), you'll have to be creative—most alternatives are unacceptable on grounds of sexism, handicappism, ageism, or unprintable language. Try ignoramus, saphead, stinker, ratfink, snake in the grass, creep, heel, jerk, bum, lowlife. "Bastard" is sexist because it is used only for men and because the insult also slyly impugns the man's mother. See also bad guy, illegitimate/illegitimate child.

batboy batkeeper, bat attendant/tender/fetcher.

batman aide.

batsman (cricket) batter.

battered wife/woman retain sex-specific terms: battered wife/woman or battered husband/man. When inclusive terms are needed, use battered spouse/partner, spouse/spousal/domestic abuse, domestic/marital/family violence. Gender-neutral terms obscure the pattern of explicit violence perpetrated on overwhelming numbers of women compared to men. Some men's organizations claim more men than women are victims of domestic abuse. While battered men definitely deserve support and social services, domestic violence activists dispute this notion, and other statistical reports, including those issued by the Department of Justice, tend to agree: four in five victims of intimate partner violence are women. The federal Centers for Disease Control reports that assaults involving intimate partners are a major public health problem in which victims are predominantly female and perpetrators are predominantly male. Battering is a system of controlling through terror, confusion, and brainwashing techniques. Many battered women are forbidden to leave their homes, use birth control, speak to their friends and relatives, and even to work. They often have no access to money, though even with such access, fear and psychological battering may prevail. Battery crosses all social classes, ethnic and racial groups. Often deprived of sleep and confused by unpredictable responses and crazy behavior, battered women may live in a state of constant terror so debilitating that they can no longer reason. According to the National Coalition Against Domestic Violence, one in every four women will experience domestic violence in her lifetime. Twenty-five to 45 percent of all women who are battered are battered during pregnancy. Thirty-four percent of all female homicide victims are killed by their intimate partners. National studies have found battering to be the greatest single cause of injury to women, exceeding rapes, muggings, or even car accidents. The cost of intimate partner violence exceeds $5.8 billion each year, $4.1 billion of which is for direct medical and mental health services. For years, the question has been: "Why doesn't she leave him?" We are now beginning to ask: "Why is he violent?" Because violence in the family and household normalizes violence, there is a move to call battering and domestic violence "original violence," but so far, the earlier terms prevail.

battle-ax (woman) tyrant, grouch, bully, petty despot, ornery/quarrelsome/domineering/strong-willed/high-handed/combative/hostile/battlesome/hot-tempered person.

"battle of/between the sexes" this adversarial approach to female-male relations legitimizes a certain hopelessness about women and men being able to coexist peaceably. So does the idea that men are from Mars and women are from Venus. In fact, we're all from the planet Earth. See also opposite sex.

bawd/bawdy house prostitute/house of prostitution. See also prostitute.

bawdy despite the connection with "bawd," this adjective can be used for both sexes.

B.C. this common abbreviation for "Before Christ" is sometimes replaced by B.C.E. (Before the Common Era) to remove the Christian element from dating—although ironically B.C.E. has sometimes been taken to mean "Before the Christian Era." See also A.D.

beau *beau* and *belle* are the masculine and feminine forms of the same French word, but the English meanings for the two words are nonparallel. For a sex-nonspecific word, use friend, lover, sweetheart. See also belle/belle of the ball, boyfriend.

beau ideal although inclusive, this term looks sexist because of the masculine *beau* (the French "ideal" is grammatically masculine in gender, thus taking a masculine adjective). If you prefer, use perfect model/type/example, standard model/type/example, paradigm.

beautician hairdresser, hairstylist, hair designer, haircutter, cosmetologist. Some people in the field still prefer "beautician," although that refers to someone who does only women's hair. See also barber.

beauty salon unless "beauty salon" is part of an establishment's name, use hair salon. The implication is that "beauty" is something definable and that it can be had for the asking (and paying).

Bechdel test created by American cartoonist, Alison Bechdel, this simple test is designed to raise moviegoers' awareness of gender disparity on screen. To pass the Bechdel test, a film must meet the following three criteria: 1) It must have at least two named female characters … 2) who talk to each other … 3) about something other than a man. The Swedish Film Institute is supporting an initiative to incorporate the Bechdel test into a rating system that would award an "A" to only those films that pass the test. See also media, movies for children.

bedfellow bedmate, ally, partner, associate, cohort, companion, mate, pair, colleague, sidekick, chum, buddy.

bedridden "bedridden," "bedfast," and "confined to bed" are more than simple descriptions; they imply "poor you!" Without euphemizing the situation, reword the sentence or use a less tragic-sounding (although perhaps less-than-ideal) alternative: on bedrest, permanent/temporary bedrest, flat on one's back, laid up; needs to stay in bed for six months; is now on total bedrest. See also disabilities.

belle/belle of the ball charming/popular/attractive person, flirt, center of attention, success, stunner, head-turner. The language never had a "beau of the ball," nor are many men described in "belle"-type terms—probably because women's successes have always been closely identified with the way they look and how they "behave" while men's successes correlate with what they have done and how they "perform."

bellboy bellhop, attendant, hotel/passenger attendant, porter.

bellman bellhop, bell captain; bellringer, crier, herald.

belly dancer in the Middle East, belly dancing is a traditional women's folk dance that was originally an exercise to strengthen muscles used in giving birth, then was reduced to an entertainment for largely male viewers. There are no public performances by male dancers. In the United States, however, professional male belly dancers perform for audiences.

Beltway I-495 circles Washington, D.C., and has come to signify the division between the federal government and bureaucracies ("Beltway insiders") and the rest of the citizenry ("outside the Beltway"). This hardens the perception that taxpayers are increasingly irrelevant to government except, of course, in the matter of paying their (nonprogressive) taxes and voting occasionally and in shockingly low percentages. It is useful but stereotypical. Use with care.

benefactress benefactor.

be one's own man/be your own man stand on one's own two feet, be one's own person, be independent/inner-directed/self-ruling/self-reliant, self-regulated/individualistic/outspoken/self-confident, be a free-thinker/free spirit, be at one's own disposal, be nobody's lackey.

Berber Imazighen. Also seen as Amazigh, Imazighen ("free people") is the original name of what we know as the Berber people. Some activists prefer the authentic name, as Berber is considered pejorative (it was derived from *barbari*, the term Romans gave to peoples they conquered).

Berdaches see Two-Spirit People.

best boy gaffer's assistant; assistant to chief electrician, chief electrician's assistant; assistant, gofer. These positions are held by both sexes, neither of which wants to be called a "boy."

best man "best man" is acceptable only if his partner is "best woman." Otherwise use attendant, attendant of honor, honor/wedding/groom's attendant, with a parallel term for the female attendant. Male and female wedding attendants did not originally have the same duties, which is perhaps why nonparallel terms developed. Centuries ago, in some cultures, men enlisted the help of their friends to kidnap a future wife or to prevent her from being kidnapped by someone else.

best man for the job best choice/candidate/applicant/person/worker for the job.

better half spouse, partner, wife/husband, mate, best friend. The perfect marriage has erroneously and destructively been touted as two half-people who are now a whole. If you must think in halves, at least use "other half" instead of "better half."

bi slang for bisexual; the plural is bi's. As with any slang or shortened form, this term should be used only if you're sure of your context and audience. See also bisexual, shortened forms of words.

bias "a learned or emotional predisposition to believe a certain way, regardless of the facts" (Marilyn vos Savant, *Parade*). If we are human, we have biases. Assumptions are two-headed critters—helpful in some cases, wrong in others. Question all assumptions about people, and assume that others know their own realities (their names, for example) better than you do.

Bible Belt use this term carefully when describing parts of the United States where fundamentalist religious beliefs generally prevail; it's a slippery generalization used to evoke feeling rather than thinking.

biblical language despite some disagreement about whether inclusive-language translations of the Bible have gone too far or not far enough, today most individuals and churches can find something to suit them. What has been important in accepting changes to what is considered the word of God is the knowledge that biased language was often a later imposition. "It is astounding how often masculine designations have entered the text in English translations and have no basis in the original language" (editors of *Lectionary for the Christian People*). Father Joseph Arackal says that going back to the original language of the scriptures eliminates 90 percent of the exclusive words in our English translations. The "newest" translations thus often turn out to be the "oldest" with their reliance on ancient Greek and Hebrew texts rather than on intermediate translations. "The Greek wording said, 'If anyone' and the translation came out 'If a man.' When Moses talked of 'God, who bore you,' the translators made it 'begot.' There was a clearly feminine reference in the original" (William Holladay, in Dorothy Uris' *Say It Again*). In addition, just as "thee"s and "thou"s are considered archaic and irrelevant and the products of translation, so are male-centered terms. (It is sometimes clearer to refer to the "Jewish Scriptures" and the "Christian Scriptures" rather than to the "Old Testament" and the "New Testament.") See also Decalogue, Old Testament, prayer language, Torah, the.

Big Brother unless referring to the Stalin-like figure watching everyone via television ("Big Brother is watching you") in George Orwell's 1949 novel *1984*, consider these alternatives: mind police, dictator, omnipresent totalitarian authority, government spy, infiltrator, stakeout, monitor, watchdog, mole, surveillant, guard, someone who keeps tab on/a sharp eye upon/a watchful eye upon.

big boss/cheese/enchilada/fish/gun/noise/shot/wheel/wig man or woman. "Big gun" and "big shot" are violent and are unnecessary with so many other choices available.

Big Government traditional conservatives see this as a pejorative and use a distorted picture of it to frighten the public. Ironically, the government has never spent so much money nor invaded our privacy so blatantly (to the point of discarding some of our civil rights) since 2000, when George W. Bush moved to Washington. Liberals understand that without infrastructure, education, health care, food and shelter, the citizenry is no longer capable of participating in a democracy—and that these foundations of a working society are government's responsibilities. "Big Government" basically means *my* kind of "big"—big military? Support for business? War? Yes, yes, and yes. Adequate safety net for people? Better infant mortality rates? Competitive schools? Safe bridges? Ah, now, there, we're talking Big Government.

bigot woman or man who "is stubbornly and unreasonably attached to an opinion or belief" (Kathlyn Gay, *Bigotry*)—said opinion usually consists of inaccurate stereotypes about other people's worth and humanity.

bikini this two-piece women's bathing suit was named after the island of Bikini, which was split in two during the first serial detonation of a hydrogen bomb on May 21, 1956; "the bomb dropped on Bikini was called Gilda [corresponding to the 1946 film *Gilda* starring Rita Hayworth] and had a picture of Rita Hayworth painted on it" (Michael Wood, *America in the Movies*). Although men conceived of and carried out the bomb project, it was symbolically linked to women; Rita Hayworth was henceforth known in France as the "Atomic Star" and women have been called "bombshells" ever since (Jane Caputi, *The Age of Sex Crime*).

billionaire woman or man. As of 2013, the U.S. has 425 billionaires, over one-third of the world's total.

bimbo from the Italian for "little boy" or "little kid," this word now has a range of meanings: sexually loose woman, giddy woman, clown-like or klutzy person of either sex. It is most often used to label supposedly brainless women. "Men in power always seem to get involved in sex scandals, but women don't even have a word for 'male bimbo.' Except maybe 'senator'" (Elayne Boosler).

binary thinking "an either/or way of thinking about concepts or realities that divides them into two mutually exclusive categories, for example, white/black, man/woman, reason/emotion, and heterosexual/homosexual" (Patricia Hill Collins, *Fighting Words*). This simplistic thinking is exemplified by the increasingly common framing of political debate as two choices: you're either a patriot or you're un-American. For a fascinating and instructive read on binary thinking, see Deborah Tannen, *The Argument Culture*.

bioguy this term is used in transgender circles to denote a biological male, whatever his gender expression might be. Use it only for those who so identify and make certain you are using it appropriately; one online "bioguy" is actually a high school biology teacher who uses his website to communicate with his students.

biological father/mother/parent everybody has biological parents, although not everyone lives with them. Biological parents are also called birth parents; they are never called "real parents." "Mother" and "father" are the terms for the people who raise and nurture a child they have adopted. Describing birth parents as "real" implies that adoptive relationships are artificial, tentative, less important, and less enduring. See also adoption language, "real" father/mother/parent.

bipartisan when describing cooperative work in Congress, note that "bipartisan" assumes just two parties; include the work and views of greens, independents, libertarians, and others.

biphobia literally meaning fear of bisexuals, this term more often translates to dislike or hatred, usually based on inaccurate associations with infidelity, promiscuity, and transmission of STDs. In addition, in a binary-thinking culture, bisexuals are a challenge to those who think that people must be attracted to one sex or the other, including some gays and lesbians who treat bisexuals as if they were too cautious or cowardly to be gays or lesbians. Although this has changed in recent years, bisexuals report being left out of discussions, groups, and texts; they have not had the visibility of other groups. Include them.

biracial "Given that 'race' is an unscientific term invented to typify pseudo criteria for racist politics and ideas—we all came from the same African origins and our differences are minor adaptations to climate—it's preferable to select a word with a different 'root' for its basic meaning. To be specific, a person's heritage from two parents or families can be characterized by saying 'of Senegalese and French descent.' When people investigate family trees of parents, it becomes apparent that both sides are usually and recently from multiple heritages or various nationalities, for example, a second-generation Puerto Rican born in New York may be of Puerto Rican, Dominican, Spanish, Irish, Arawak, and Yoruba descent" (Zoë Anglesey, "Moving From an Obsolete Lingo to a Vocabulary of Respect," *MultiCultural Review*). When necessary to specify a person's heritage (it very seldom is), use the adjective they use for themselves or name their multiple heritages. A few years ago, biracial generally meant someone with a black parent and a white parent. Today it can mean almost anything, and therefore means almost nothing. See also multiracial.

birdbrain see airhead.

birth control see contraception.

birth defect congenital disability. Or, for a person, someone born with a congenital disability, someone disabled since birth, a disability that has existed since birth. References to "abnormalities" are unacceptable except in a clinical context. See also disabilities.

birth mother/father/parent See biological father/mother/parent.

bisexual a man or a woman who has affectionate, romantic, and erotic feelings for, fantasies of, and/or experiences with both men and women is a bisexual. The person does not need to have equal experiences with women and men, or even any experience at all; bisexuality is not behaviorally defined. The bisexual community reports antagonism from both the heterosexual and homosexual worlds; our binary-thinking society tends to think people are either gay or straight. "One thing that just about everybody agrees on is that 'bisexual' is a problematic word. To the disapproving or the disinclined it connotes promiscuity, immaturity, or wishy-washiness. To some lesbians and gay men it says 'passing,' 'false consciousness,' and a desire for 'heterosexual privilege.' To psychologists it may suggest adjustment problems; to psychoanalysts an unresolved Oedipus complex; to anthropologists, the narrowness of a Western (Judeo-Christian) world view. Rock stars regard it as a dimension of the performing self. ... Bisexuality has sometimes been regarded as 'too queer' and at other times 'not queer enough'" (Marjorie Garber, *Vice Versa*). But ever since Kinsey, human sexuality has been demonstrated to be a continuum, with exclusively heterosexual or exclusively homosexual as the extremes, and many gradations in between. Bisexual has come increasingly into respect and usage. See also bi.

bishop depending on the denomination, a bishop could be a man or a woman.

bitch (noun) one of the most loaded of the sexist words, "bitch" tends to be directed at women who are "active, direct, blunt, obnoxious, competent, loud-mouthed, independent, stubborn, demanding, achieving, overwhelming, lusty, strong-minded, scary, ambitious, tough, brassy, boisterous, turbulent, sprawling, strident, striding, and large (physically and/or psychically)" (Mary Daly). Molly Hoben, co-founder of *Minnesota Women's Press*, notes that in pre-Christian Greek and Roman religions, one of the sacred titles of the goddess Artemis-Diana was "the Great Bitch," but like other words with once-positive connotations for women "bitch" has become a pejorative used by those who feel threatened. Minneapolis attorney Rebecca Palmer says, "In the workplace setting, the label of 'bitch' is often accompanied by inappropriate, demeaning behavior. … A number of courts around the country have grappled with the issue of whether, from a legal standpoint, referring to a female employee as a 'bitch' is defamatory or discriminatory." Most of its public uses constitute name-calling. In the introduction to *BITCHfest*, the editors of the outstanding pop culture magazine, *Bitch*, write: "'Cause here's the thing about 'bitch': When it's being used as an insult, the word is most often aimed at women who speak their minds, who have opinions that contradict conventional wisdom, and who don't shy away from expressing them. That said, we are aware that the word carries a difficult, complex legacy … as well as the fact that its popularity as an epithet is more sanctioned than ever. And yet we still think, ten years later, that it's the most appropriate title for a magazine that's all about talking back." Sometimes the correct alternative to "bitch" is simply woman, person, individual. Marie Shear says, "English offers a rich variety of adjectives with which to disparage people who bleepin' well deserve to be disparaged. 'Snarky,' 'malicious,' 'spiteful,' 'potty,' and 'egomaniacal' are just a few. The current ubiquity of 'bitch' and its derivatives doesn't change the fact that the word as an epithet is always anti-woman. By all means let's insult people who have it coming to them without concomitantly insulting women in general." The problem with "bitch" is that it is not a very precise word, linguistically speaking. When someone says, "She's a real bitch," you have to ask: "What did she do? What do you mean?" The word tells you nothing informative about the woman. So choose a precise, inclusive noun instead: grumbler, grouch, griper, malcontent, sourpuss, sorehead, bellyacher, crab, crank, kvetcher. Other times, you may want an adjective: hell on wheels, ruthless, aggressive, domineering, controlling, powerful, tyrannical, overwhelming, overpowering, spiteful, malicious, cruel, wicked, vicious, cold-hearted, hard-hearted, merciless (see more in bitchy). In the sense of a complaint, use instead gripe, complaint, problem, bone to pick, objection (see more in bitch (verb). In the sense of something that is difficult, unpleasant, or problematic, use tough row to hoe, tough nut to crack, heavy sledding, hornet's nest, between a rock and a hard place, bad news/one, tough grind/one, large order, predicament, no picnic, thorny/knotty problem, uphill job, backbreaker, dilemma, bind, tangle, mess, fine pickle, hell of a note. In addition to (1) name-calling, and (2) attempts to reclaim the word, there is also (3) casual use among young people. One young woman, emailing half a dozen female family members, signs off "Tootles, bitchez!" The guideline here is the "insider/outsider" rule: women can refer to themselves or friends as "bitches";

men cannot refer to women that way. Another young woman says, "It's okay for a woman to say 'I'm out with my bitches!' positively, but a man saying 'Look at those bitches' has negative connotations." In theory, it would be good if women didn't use a culturally derogatory term for themselves. The "but" here is that it is apparently not given or taken derogatorily when used that way. (John A. Hobson notes that "bitch" is the correct term for a female dog; "the corresponding male term—dog—suggests that maleness is the norm for canines.")

bitch (verb) complain, gripe, kvetch, grouse, grumble, badmouth, harp on, sound off, beef, bellyache, carp, crab, criticize, denounce, disapprove, dissent, object, protest, reproach, backbite, bawl out, call/dress down, call on the carpet/mat, cuss, make cutting remarks/dirty digs/cracks, give someone hell/the devil/a going-over, lambaste, to give someone lip, make it hot for, pick on, pitch into, put down, put someone in their place, tell someone where to get off. See also bitch (noun).

bitch session gripe session.

bitchy grouchy, cranky, crabby, spiteful, moody, rude, ill-tempered, bad-tempered, irritable, surly, complaining, cantankerous, peevish, out of sorts.

black/Black (noun) (1) These are acceptable and respected terms. (2) Do not refer to color or ethnicity when it is irrelevant to your material, as it most often is. Vivian Jenkins Nelsen (*New Voices in the Media*) says, "Persons of color are usually 'over-identified' as 'African-American writers' or 'African-American dentists,' when they would rather be identified as a dentist or a writer who is an African American. White people are 'under-identified' because most stories assume whiteness as the norm. ... write 'white' in front of every reference to a person who is not identified as a person of color, and you will see how artificial it feels." 3) Identify people the way they identify themselves (black, African American, person of color) and accept that this may vary from group to group. (4) Current style generally lowercases "black," but some writers and editors prefer it capitalized; check style guidelines before submitting material to a publication. See also African American, Afro-American, black/black-, black-and-white, denigrate, Negress, niggardly, nigger, niggling, nonwhite, people/person of color, white man's burden.

black/black- Martin Luther King, Jr. pointed out that there are some 120 synonyms for "blackness" of which at least half are offensive. Almost all the 134 synonyms for "whiteness" are positive. "The symbolism of white as positive and black as negative is pervasive in our culture" (Robert B. Moore, in Paula S. Rothenberg's *Racism and Sexism*). The good guys wear white hats and ride white horses, and everybody knows what the bad guys wear and ride. Dictionary definitions of black refer in part to evil, the devil, disaster, condemnation, dirt, sullenness, and darkness while definitions of white refer to innocence, purity, harmlessness, good fortune, and lightness. Avoiding words that reinforce the negative connotations of black will not of itself do away with racism, but we cannot unhorse racism while the language constantly tells us that black is anything but beautiful. The following terms can be replaced by those in parentheses: blackball (ostracize); black comedy/black humor (satire, sinister/morbid humor); "black day in our nation's history" ("bleak" or "sad"); black deed (evil deed); blacken (slander, defile, defame; smirch, soil, tarnish); black eye (mouse, shiner; bad name); blackguard (scoundrel, villain, ne'er-do-well); blackhearted (wicked); blackjack (bludgeon); blackletter day (evil/tragic day); blacklist (denounce, condemn, proscribe, ostracize); blackly (gloomily, hopelessly); blackmail (hush money, payola, extortion, shake-down; extort, bleed, put the arm on, shake down); black mark (mark against one, blot on one's copybook); black market (illegal market/trade/trafficking); black moment (depressed/down/dire moment); blackout (lights out; moratorium; loss of memory/consciousness); black outlook (bleak outlook); black sheep (outcast, pariah, reprobate, renegade, idler, prodigal, born/family loser, ne'er-do-well, bad apple in the barrel, family rebel). Other terms can be circumvented but with difficulty: black arts, black book, black hole, black ice, black lie (contrast with a white lie), black magic (contrast with white magic), Black Mass, Black Monday (stock market crash of October 19, 1987), Black Tuesday (October 29, 1929). The Macmillan Publishing Company advises its writers to not only avoid the negative uses of black but to apply the word's positive uses as often as possible: black pearls are the most valuable; ebony is used only on the finest guitars; oil is referred to as "black gold"; black diamonds are essential to industry; black soil is richest. They also suggest reinforcing positive attitudes toward blackness in descriptions of African Americans: too often references to "their beautiful white teeth" replace descriptions of the authentic attractions of black hair, skin, eyes. See also black-and-white (adjective), white.

black-and-white (adjective) either-or, simple, all good or all bad, either here or there, neither here nor there, binary, dualistic, dogmatic, definite, unequivocal, absolute, positive, categorical, polar opposites, diametric opposites, day and night, chalk and cheese. This highly racist expression (it refers to things being sharply divided into good and evil groups, sides, or ideas) perpetuates the positive evaluation of white and the negative evaluation of black (one of its definitions is "Expressing, recognizing, or based on two mutually exclusive sets of ideas or values" (*American Heritage Dictionary*). See also black/black-, white.

Black Carib Garifuna.

black English "contrary to the stereotypes, Black English is not substandard English; it is a separate linguistic system, although it shares much of its vocabulary, phonology, and syntax with standard English" (Francine Frank and Frank Anshen, *Language and the Sexes*). Children who use black English (also known as Ebonics, from a contraction of "ebony" and "phonics") are encouraged to understand that they are as intelligent and verbally skilled as anyone else (especially since they are familiar with two language systems) but that they will need to perfect their standard English to function effectively in a society that is based on it. "One subtle example of continued racism is 'standard' language, culture, art, and literature, which stigmatizes alternative approaches to expression" (Jane H. Hill, *The Everyday Language of White Racism*). See also English.

black feminism believing that sexism and racism are indivisible from each other, black feminists argue that the liberation of black women results in freedom for everyone, since it would end racism, sexism, and class oppression. Black feminism grew out of discontent with the Civil Rights

Movement (which often seemed sexist in practice) and the Feminist Movement (which often seemed to focus on white women). See also African American, black, womanist.

Black Muslims Muslims are Muslims; among the followers of Islam there is no color distinction. The members of the Nation of Islam, a 20th-century movement in the U.S. that has little in common with mainstream Islam, have been called Black Muslims, although they have never used the term for themselves (it was coined by the press in the 1950s). Members of the movement have always preferred simply "Muslim."

black nationalism "a political philosophy based on the belief that Black people constitute a people or nation with a common history and destiny" (Patricia Hill Collins, *Fighting Words*). In the *Encyclopedia of Rhetoric* (Thomas O. Sloane, ed.), Robert E. Terrill says that black nationalism "is an umbrella term, encompassing back-to-Africa movements, efforts to lay claim to a portion of the continental United States as a separate black nation, proposals to establish all-black political parties, and various artistic and cultural endeavors to claim African and African-American culture as sources of racial pride and solidarity. The history of black nationalism is a contentious one, marked by much disagreement about aims and strategy. In general, this rhetoric is informed by a conviction that the dominant white culture of the United States is fundamentally corrupt and that integration into such a culture would be dangerous and self-defeating, even if it were possible. ... It does not ask whites to change, but rather, assuming that white attitudes toward blacks will remain unchanged, it demands that blacks reassess their relationship to whites and to white culture." Some separatist black nationalist groups, like the Nation of Islam, are strongly anti-Semitic (*Intelligence Report*).

black sheep see black/black-.

black site Jesse Sheidlower (in *Copy Editor*) defines a black site as a "classified military site, the existence of which is officially denied." According to Dana Priest in the *Washington Post*, "The CIA has been hiding and interrogating some of its most important al Qaeda captives at a Soviet-era compound in Eastern Europe, according to U.S. and foreign officials familiar with the arrangement. The secret facility is part of a covert prison system set up by the CIA nearly four years ago that at various times has included sites in eight countries, including Thailand, Afghanistan and several democracies in Eastern Europe, as well as a small center at the Guantánamo Bay prison in Cuba, according to current and former intelligence officials and diplomats from three continents. ... The existence and locations of the facilities—referred to as "black sites" in classified White House, CIA, Justice Department and congressional documents—are known to only a handful of officials in the United States and, usually, only to the president and a few top intelligence officers in each host country." But Jane Mayer (*New Yorker*) writes that "the most common destinations for rendered suspects are Egypt, Morocco, Syria, and Jordan, all of which have been cited for human rights violations by the State Department and are known to torture suspects." See also detainee, "state secrets" defense, torture.

blacksmith use as is, or ironsmith. John A. Hobson explains that a "blacksmith makes implements from iron, as opposed to a 'whitesmith,' who makes things from silver. The term came about strictly because of the difference in the color of the metals that they work with."

black tie this refers to men's attire for social occasions; for a sex-neutral alternative, use semiformal.

bleeding heart popularized in the 1930s by right-wing newspaper columnist Westbrook Pegler, this "label implies that anyone who supports government programs for poor people must have an unduly soft heart and, very likely, a soft head, too" (Hugh Rawson, *Wicked Words*). Geoffrey Nunberg (*Talking Right*) says it's "a durable phrase that reduces all altruism to girlish sentimentality." It's time to reclaim this term by juxtaposing it with the truly heartbreaking conditions of many in the U.S. Tell just one of the Katrina stories or describe just one homeless child's days and finish up with, "Does this break my heart? You bet it does! Am I a bleeding heart? I hope so! Are we going to accept this? Hell, no."

blind this is an acceptable adjective to denote someone who is sightless or whose vision is so restricted as to be useless for ordinary purposes; "the substitution of a euphemistic expression for *blind* could itself be objectionable if perceived as implying that blindness is too piteous a condition to be stated in plain language" (*American Heritage Book of English Usage*). Do not use as a noun ("the blind"), since people are not only one characteristic. "Visual impairment" implies a range of problems that stops short of total or legal blindness ("someone with a visual impairment"). Avoid once-I-was-blind-but-now-I-see metaphors, which associate physical loss of vision with negative personal characteristics. Use naive, unaware, ignorant, obtuse, dense, unreasoning, senseless, thoughtless, uncritical, undiscerning, insensitive, unfeeling, indifferent. See also disabilities, handicappism, handicapped, "people first" rule, "the."

blogger woman or man/boy or girl.

blonde blond. Use the shorter base word as an adjective for both sexes; historically, both have been used for both sexes. The use of "blond" as a noun seems reserved for women whereas equating a man with his hair color is uncommon. Use "blond" to modify hair rather than to describe women (thus, "a woman with blond hair," not "a blond"). See also "feminine" word endings.

blood terms like "blue-blooded" and "royal blood," "full-blooded" and "mixed blood" have no validity or usefulness and the last two are highly objectionable. Tim Giago (in *Indian Country Today*), refers to a report about a "full-blooded Indian" and says, "The day this same reporter writes 'full-blooded white man' or 'full-blooded African American,' then—and only then—will I know all races are being treated equally." Use instead of mixed ancestry, or one of the terms with which people self-identify (métis, mestizo, mélange). See also half-breed/half-caste, mulatto, multiracial.

blood brother "blood sister" is also used (although not nearly as often); in the plural, use blood brothers and blood sisters/blood sisters and blood brothers.

blood diamonds see conflict diamonds.

blood libel the false accusation that Jews use the blood of Christians in their rituals. Although this canard appeared to have been discounted sometime after its anti-Semitic use in the Middle Ages, as recently as April 2013, an anti-Semitic publication had to remove an article that criticized celebrating a Passover Seder at the White House: "Does Obama in fact know the relationship between Passover and Christian blood?" (It's apparently used to make the matzo.)

blue long associated with boys, especially babies, this color was once thought to ward off the evil spirits that inhabited nurseries, perhaps because of its association with the sky and with well-disposed heavenly spirits. According to David Feldman (*Imponderables*), boys were held to be very valuable by parents, so blue clothing was used as a cheap form of insurance. No such insurance was desired or apparently needed for girl babies. See also pink.

Bluebeard the original Bluebeard, Gilles de Rais, abducted, raped, and murdered 40 to 100 peasant boys: "The most amazing part of the Gilles de Rais story is that the legend of Bluebeard's Castle that we know today has metamorphosed from a terrifying account of a sex-murderer of small boys to a glorified fantasy of a devilish rake who killed seven wives for their 'curiosity'" (Susan Brownmiller, *Against Our Will*). According to Brownmiller, it is more palatable to the sex in power to accept women in the role of victim than themselves. Do not perpetuate the recast Bluebeard story.

blue collar this imprecise term varies from somewhat to very classist and also carries a connotation of maleness; audiences will be better served by specifics (job descriptions, income ranges, education levels) or job titles: electrician, manual laborer, plumber, factory worker, skilled worker, carpenter, janitor—unless a subject wishes to be described as blue collar.

bluesman blues musician/player/singer.

blue state see red state.

bluestocking intellectual, member of the literati, wit, artistic/learned person, dilettante, dabbler, amateur, culture vulture. This derisory term for educated or literary women was originally used for both sexes, although no parallel term developed for men when this one became limited to women—even though the blue stockings worn at the small literary assemblies hosted by Elizabeth Montague, Portman Square, London, belonged to a certain Mr. Stillingfleet.

boat people first used for Vietnamese fleeing their country after the fall of Saigon, the term later denoted Haitians and Cubans emigrating to the U.S. in risky escapes that saw a great loss of life. If you need to use "boat people," limit its use and describe the individuals and situations in more precise terms.

boat/she boat/it. See also ship/she.

bobby (British) police officer. Sir Robert ("Bobby") Peel organized the London police force in the early 1800s and is responsible for the other popular British police nickname: "peeler." See also policeman.

bodily integrity growing in use as a goal or legal term, an umbrella term over all rights against assault, rape, sexual searches, involuntary testing, etc.

body image we speak and write about men's bodies and women's bodies in very different ways. Minneapolis writer Mary Morse Marti sees a direct association between a study showing that adolescent girls are almost twice as likely as boys to be depressed—primarily because of their poor body image—and, for example, media emphasis on women's bathing suit fashions that extols such virtues as "constructed bust lines" to "enhance smaller chests," "bottoms to flatter round stomachs and hips," and even suits with "built-in shape" for women and girls unfortunate enough to have none. Morse Marti wonders if she can expect to see similar articles on men's swimwear that feature "size-enhancing groin pads, rear-end boning (for that all-important pert look), and retro 'Dad' full-cut boxer trunks (for men and boys with something to hide)." There are virtually no general-interest books telling teenage boys how to dress, how to control weight, how to feel more comfortable about their bodies; countless fiction and nonfiction books address these issues for teenage girls. Twice as many women ages 30 to 64 as men think they are "overweight"; 58 percent of 17-year-old girls said they were "overweight" when only 17 percent actually were according to the charts; some 90 percent to 95 percent of those with eating disorders are female. See also fat, lookism, overweight.

boi plural: bois; use this term strictly for those who use it to self-describe. The only certainty is that it's heard in LGBTQ communities—but the boi in question may be gay, bisexual, lesbian, FTM transgender, intersex, or queer. If you're writing about a boi, verify which pronouns to use.

Bombay Mumbai. You may need to add "Bombay" in parentheses for readers who are unfamiliar with the change. In addition, you will still see such titles as the Bombay Hospital and the Bombay Stock Exchange. As with other Indian cities that have changed names, both are acceptable, with Bombay being used more in conversation and Mumbai more in writing.

bombshell/blonde bombshell (woman) these terms are militaristic, violent, and sexist (there is no parallel for a man); they portray women as destructive to men, even though superficially they appear complimentary.

bondsman (law) bonding/bond/bail/bail bond agent, surety provider, guarantor, bonding institution, lender.

bondsman/bondswoman (slave) see bondman/bondwoman.

bonhomie from the French for "good man," this is most often applied to men and groups of men, but there is nothing to say you can't use it for women and for groups of women or women and men. For a more neutral-appearing alternative, consider good-naturedness, geniality, cheerfulness, light-heartedness, optimism, happiness, joy, liveliness, friendliness, affability.

bon vivant the French is grammatically masculine and this term has become associated primarily with men over the years, but women are using it too: Catherine Deneuve—female and French—says, "I'm a bon vivant, a reveler." When you need something more neutral-looking, try connoisseur, hedonist, epicure, aesthete, sensualist, high-liver, sophisticate, enthusiast, someone with a great deal of joie de vivre.

bordello house of prostitution. See also prostitute.

borderline/borderline personality "Broad clinical terms such as *borderline* ... are loaded with innuendo unless properly explained" (*Publication Manual of the American Psychological Association*, 4th ed.). The term "borderline personality disorder ... is frequently used with the mental health professions as little more than a sophisticated insult" (Louise Armstrong, *And They Call It Help*). Some clinicians argue that the term "borderline" has become so prejudicial that it should be abandoned altogether, just as its predecessor term, "hysteria," was abandoned.

border patrolman border guard/patrol, member of the border patrol.

born-again Christian use for people who identify themselves that way. Be aware of the range of beliefs, thoughts, and political orientations to be found among born-again Christians. The term is sometimes coterminous with "fundamentalist" or "evangelical," sometimes not. See also Christian, fundamentalist.

born out of wedlock this expression is outdated and judgmental. If you absolutely need to include the information (one seldom does), use born to unmarried parents. See also bastard, illegitimate/illegitimate child, wedlock.

bossy generally reserved for women, girls, and toddlers of either sex, "bossy" has a number of colorful and sex-neutral synonyms: officious, overbearing, domineering, high and mighty, high-handed, aggressive, pushy, dictatorial, despotic, tyrannical, insolent, willful, forceful, coercive, arbitrary, imperious, authoritarian. Child psychiatrist Elizabeth Berger (author of *Raising Kids with Character*) says labeling little girls bossy is "incredibly sexist ... the same presentation in a boy would be applauded as vivid and courageous and deserving of praise." In adults, "telling other people what to do is a leadership quality," says Jennifer Allyn, a managing director at PricewaterhouseCoopers. See also aggressive.

bouncer there are exceptions, but in general bouncers are men. Bouncing is associated primarily with bars, but similar work is done in non-bar environments by women, who are then called security officers/guards/consultants, crowd controllers, patrols, bodyguards.

boy (referring to a man) man, young man. "Boy" usually refers to someone no more than sixteen and sometimes no more than twelve or thirteen, depending on the context and the individual. It is absolutely unacceptable when used of African-American men. It is used sometimes in the phrase "good old boys," but they are always white. See also good old boy/good ole boy.

boycott nonsexist; named after English land agent Captain Charles Cunningham Boycott (1832-1897), who was so harsh on the Irish tenants of his employer, Lord Erne, during a period of crop failures and famines that his neighbors shunned him and the tenant farmers refused to pay rent, stopped harvesting, and formed the Irish Land League. They drove off his servants, intercepted his mail, and tried to cut off his food supplies. See also girlcott.

boyfriend there is still no concise, appropriate, universally accepted term to describe the man we love. At least this one has the parallel of girlfriend. Those in committed relationships (whether opposite-sex or same-sex) need a word with the corresponding weight and meaning of "husband" or "spouse" or "fiancé," to denote their partners. The increasing numbers of heterosexual couples living in stable, long-term relationships have the same problem. Until the right word comes along, consider: friend; man friend (if "woman friend" is also used); male friend (if "female friend" is also used); best friend; spouse (E.J. Graff, in *Out* magazine, says "'Spouse' at least puts the pair in the same bed. Unlike 'lover,' 'spouse' knows the bedroom is just one of many rooms in the house"); partner, domestic partner, or life partner (despite its business associations, this is one of the most popular choices); companion (literally, the person with whom you share bread) or longtime companion (this is the second most popular choice); the man I'm seeing; significant other; soulmate; steady, mate, paramour, consort, lover, longtime love, live-in, live-in lover; sweetheart; sweetie, guy pal, main/major squeeze; the man in my life. See also domestic partner.

boyhood acceptable sex-specific word. If you want a generic use childhood, innocence, youth.

boyish replace this vague word with specific inclusive adjectives: ingenuous, naive, childlike, innocent, open, friendly, eager, youthful, immature, self-conscious, inept, bright-eyed, optimistic, cheerful, adolescent, childish, sophomoric, juvenile, kiddish, infantile, callow, unsophisticated.

boys and girls half the time, use "girls and boys."

boys in blue (armed forces) the armed forces now consist of both girls and boys, so use instead soldiers, members of the armed forces, armed forces personnel.

boys in the backroom see backroom boys.

boys will be boys children will be children, kids will be kids. Used archly of men when they indulge in games, adult toys, or practical jokes, this expression has also served to excuse the inexcusable: a young woman at the U.S. Naval Academy was dragged from her dormitory room and handcuffed to a urinal by male classmates while others taunted her and took pictures, but the administration determined that the incident was "a good-natured exchange that got out of hand"; the Spur Posse, "the lowlife band of high school jocks who measured their own self-worth in terms of how many meaningless sexual encounters they'd had" (Anna Quindlen) were just boys being boys; three of the jocks who sexually assaulted a young woman with mental retardation "were convicted but not before a theme emerged clearly in their defense: 'Boys will be boys,' according to one attorney." In *Boys Will Be Boys*, Myriam Miedzian says that many of the values of the "masculine mystique"—toughness, dominance, repression of empathy, extreme competitiveness, the win-at-all-costs sports world, eagerness to fight, war toys—play a major role in criminal and domestic violence and even underlie the thinking and policy decisions of many of our political leaders. From gangs to college hazings to members of the National Security Council showing how tough they are by advocating war, boys are busy being boys. "A lot of people just say it's testosterone," says Miedzian, "and throw up their hands. I take the opposite position, that because boys have potential for being this way, we have to create an environment that discourages violence." See also violence.

boy toy a man regarded as a sex object is a "boy toy."

bra burner "Legends die hard. They survive as truth rarely does" (Helen Hayes). At the 1968 Miss America Pageant in Atlantic City, "demonstrators ... flung dishcloths, steno pads, girdles, and bras into a Freedom Trash Can. (This last was translated by the male-controlled media into the totally fabricated act of 'bra-burning,' a non-event upon which they have fixated constantly ever since" (Robin Morgan, *The Word of a Woman*). The Snopes website labels the bra-burning story as false and adds, "So entrenched is this mental image that folks rarely question its validity, instead accepting it as unchallenged fact." The use of "bra burner" generally indicates hostility (you can tell by the context). The phrase has been disenfranchised by the latest *Los Angeles Times* stylebook.

brainy in 1975, Robin Lakoff said, "the word *brainy* is seldom used of men; when used of women it suggests (1) that this intelligence is unexpected in a woman; (2) that it isn't really a good trait." Although "brainy" is seen less often today, it still seems to be reserved for women; so use a substitute: intelligent, smart, etc.

brakeman braker, brake tender/holder/coupler/controller/ operator, yard coupler; conductor's assistant.

brass (high-ranking officers) men or women.

brave (Indian) a Florida radio shock jock defending Atlanta's use of "Braves" for their baseball team demanded of an Ojibway caller if it wasn't true that Indian men had been called "braves." "Yes," she replied quietly. "But not by us." See also American Indian, sports teams' names and mascots.

brazen almost always attached to women (for example, "brazen hussy"). Use fearless, dauntless, bold, daring, brash, defiant, audacious, plainspoken, outspoken, candid, frank.

breadwinner woman or man. See also provider.

brethren/brothers (pseudogeneric) brothers and sisters/sisters and brothers, people, congregation, assembly, colleagues, friends, associates, peers, community, companions, family, kin, believers, the faithful, children of God, neighbors. In direct address, use my dear people, sisters and brothers/brothers and sisters, friends, dear friends, dearly beloved. According to Jackie Graham, in the biblical epistles, the Greek *adelphoi* was usually mistranslated as brothers, although the correct translation is "siblings" or "brothers and sisters."

brewmaster brew/brewing director, head/chief brewer.

bridal if not directly modifying the bride (for example, "bridal gown" but not "bridal party"), use wedding, nuptial, marital, connubial.

bridal consultant wedding consultant.

bride and groom acceptable terms for the wedding couple, but see also bridal, bridegroom, give away the bride.

bride burning see dowry deaths, suttee.

bridegroom groom.

bride of Christ one of the important titles of the Roman Catholic Church, this metaphor is used to present the church as loved by, but subordinate to, Christ. By strong implication, this damaging bride image conveys the idea that brides are also subordinate to their god-like husbands. See also church/she, God.

bridesmaid attendant. See also best man, maid/matron of honor.

brinkmanship/brinksmanship gamesplaying, gameplaying, courting catastrophe, risk-taking bluff, bluffing, savvy, gambling, playing chicken.

bro the popular and affectionate "bro" is a nice addition to the language; the parallel term for women, "sis," has not enjoyed a parallel history.

broad (woman) no.

broken home a judgment that only a heterosexual couple makes an unbroken family; use family, single-parent home/family.

brothel house of prostitution. See also prostitute.

brother (religion) retain because of its narrow meaning and because all orders with brothers consist of men; religious orders with "brothers" and those with "sisters" both resemble and differ from each other.

brotherhood (pseudogeneric) unity, unity among humans, humanity, world unity, compassion, peace, companionship, goodwill, amity, friendship, comradeship, camaraderie, esprit de corps, conviviality; family, the human family, kinship, shared/human kinship; community, society, association, organization, social organization, common-interest group, club, corporation, federation, union, group, partnership, society; brotherhood and sisterhood. Protecting "brotherhood" from pseudogeneric use allows it to retain its strong original meaning; the word has been gaining new use as men find that other men can sometimes best understand, discuss, and reflect common joys and problems ("brotherhood" thus developing along the same lines that "sisterhood" developed as a description of a meaningful sex-specific bond). "Brotherhood" has been used since 1340 as a synonym for "guild" so we still see today, for example, the International Brotherhood of Electrical Workers. But another group calls itself the United Electrical Workers and "solidarity" is also useful in this context (for example, the Newspaper Union Solidarity Committee).

brotherhood of man human family/community/bond/solidarity, bond of humanity, humanity, humankind, global village.

brotherly this is a useful and accurate sex-specific word in most cases. Sometimes, however, it is used stereotypically when other words would be more descriptive: affectionate, loving, caring, kindly, supportive, sympathetic, protective, indulgent, friendly, humane.

brotherly love (pseudogeneric) kindheartedness, goodwill, philanthropy, charity, good-naturedness, generosity, benevolence, loving kindness, geniality, human feeling, benignity, beneficence, humanity, compassion, unselfishness, friendship, amiability, tolerance, consideration, affectionate/human love, love of others/of neighbor, other love, love of people, agape. See also City of Brotherly Love.

brothers (pseudogeneric) see brethren/brothers.

brother's keeper, I am not my use "my brother's keeper" for references to the biblical story. For alternatives to the contemporary meaning, consider I'm not anyone's keeper; don't look at me; it's none of my business; it's not my responsibility; I can't help what anyone else does; I'm not responsible for anyone but myself.

brownfields in the Small Business Liability Relief and Brownfields Revitalization Act of 2002, brownfields are defined as formerly used property "complicated by the presence or potential presence of a hazardous substance, pollutant, or contaminant." Former industrial parks, landfills, dumps, or strip mines, these 750,000 brownfield sites across the nation are to be cleaned up and turned into open spaces for public parks and recreation facilities. Apparently some golf courses have been built on brownfields. (Land that is more severely contaminated, with high concentrations of hazardous waste or pollution, such as Superfund or hazardous waste sites, does not fall under the brownfield classification.) When green spaces are being developed, residents will want to know what a brownfield is; unfortunately, long-term results of this land use won't be known for some time.

brunette although the base (male) term is "brunet," it is rarely used, most likely because referring to people's hair color is largely reserved for women. Can you imagine calling a man a brunet? Question the labeling of women by facets of their appearance and the need to talk about their hair. See also "feminine" word endings.

buccaneer see pirate.

buck (man) profoundly derogatory term when used for an African American or American Indian.

buck naked stark naked, naked, starkers, naked as a jaybird, without a stitch on, in the altogether/raw/buff, in one's birthday suit, au naturel, unclad. "Buck naked" refers either to the male animal or to the color of buckskin (which isn't everybody's skin shade); on either count, the term is better replaced.

buddy woman/girl or man/boy. This word (from the word "brother") is a positive term denoting closeness and friendship, whereas its counterpart, "sissy" (from "sister"), is never used positively. In spite of its masculine associations, "buddy" can be used of either sex. "Buddy" (for either sex) is also used to describe someone working as part of a support organization who volunteers to give companionship, practical help, and moral support to those with HIV/AIDS or related medical problems (Matthew Windibank, Steve Kluz).

bulimic can be used as an adjective ("bulimic behavior") but should not be used as a noun; use instead someone with bulimia, person with an eating disorder. See also disabilities, "people first" rule.

bull lies, exaggeration, tall tale/story, snow/snowjob, hot air, bunk, nonsense.

bull dyke (woman) this term, which is disliked by some lesbians but used by others, follows the "insider/outsider" rule: its use is unacceptable for those outside the lesbian community. See also butch, dyke, femme/fem, homophobia, homosexual.

bull session "bull" does not refer to the male animal but to fraud or deceit, from the word "boule." However, for a more neutral-appearing term (since men seem to have "bull sessions" while women have "gab-fests" and "hen parties"), you could try brainstorming/rap/buzz session, parley, talk, chat, free-for-all/informal discussion.

bully boy/man or girl/woman. "Bully" is generally defined in terms of men and it has a masculine feel to it, but it can be used of both sexes. For a more inclusive-sounding noun, use tormentor, browbeater, aggressor, terrorist, dictator, menace. For the verb, use browbeat, mistreat, tyrannize, terrorize, threaten, domineer, bulldoze, intimidate, oppress, menace. For "bully boy tactics," consider bully tactics, browbeating, intimidation, bulldozing, badgering, harassing.

bum although this theoretically inclusive term can refer to either sex, it tends to be reserved for men. You may want to use instead street person, homeless person. "Bum" and its traditional synonyms (beggar, hobo, vagabond, sponger, scrounger, vagrant, parasite) are often indefensibly pejorative given that many are homeless today because of a combination of societal values, political decisions, the economy, ill health, and bad luck. See also bad guy.

buppie/Buppie from b(lack) + (y)uppie, a buppie is a sophisticated, upperclass, well-paid professional African American. But the informal term comes with some negative spin (online example: "Terrell is such a buppie") so use it only if you know what you're doing.

Burma Myanmar. For the inhabitants, use Myanmar people or Myanmar.

burqa a loose all-enveloping garment worn by some Muslim women, the burqa (you will also see the transliterations burkha, burka, burqua) calls for respect by outsiders; only those who wear it or have worn it are authentic judges of its use, value, and meaning.

busboy busser, busperson, dining room attendant, kitchen helper, dish carrier, waiter's helper/assistant, serving/server's assistant; service worker; room service assistant/attendant; porter, runner.

Bushman San, Khwe, and other cultures are covered by this term. Better to use the specific. If used collectively anyway, use Bushpeople. Library cataloger Sanford Berman says that Africanists, anthropologists, and other educated people avoid the racist, sexist, Eurocentric, and inauthentic "Bushman/Bushmen," terms that are unacceptable to the San (*bushman* comes from *bosmanneken*, a Dutch translation of a Malay word for orangutan). He cautions against replacing them with the ethnocentric and racist "native/natives" or "tribe/tribes."

businessman executive, business executive/associate/professional, member of the business community, business leader/manager/owner, professional, merchant, shopkeeper, entrepreneur, industrialist, financier, manager, investor, speculator, buyer, trader, capitalist, retailer, wholesaler, mogul, magnate, tycoon; businesswoman and businessman (if used in parallel ways). "Businessperson" is not recommended. Or be specific: stockbroker, advertising executive, chief executive officer, public relations officer, wholesaler, banker. Plural: people in business, businesspeople.

busman's holiday working vacation. (About half of U.S. bus drivers are women.)

butch (woman) usage of "butch" follows the "insider/outsider" rule, that is, it is acceptable for lesbians who want to use the term; it is generally unacceptable for non-lesbians to use it.

butcher woman or man. (Some 30 percent of butchers are women.)

butler invariably a man.

butterfly see social butterfly.

Accuracy of language is one of the bulwarks of truth.

Anna Jameson

Political language forms a linguistic category of its own, one in which words serve not as exact descriptive symbols but as empty formulae designed to push specific emotional buttons in the guileless listener.

Brooke Allen

cabin boy cabin attendant/steward, ship's steward; in some contexts, merchant mariner, sailor.

cabinet member woman or man. Before 1933, however, when Frances Perkins was appointed, all U.S. cabinet members were men.

caddymaster caddyboss, caddy supervisor/leader/director/captain.

cad see bad guy.

Caesar's wife if you need a gender-free substitute, consider: someone whose conduct is impeccable, someone about whom there hovers the odor of sanctity, someone who is beyond reproach/above suspicion/irreproachable/unimpeachable/innocent/blameless/sinless/clean-handed.

Cajun/Cajan a Louisianian descended from French colonists originally exiled from Acadia, "Cajun" is actually a corruption of "Acadian." "Cajan" usually refers to someone of black, white, and American Indian descent living in Alabama or Mississippi. Use only for people who self-identify that way.

Calcutta/Kolkata the city name reverted to its authentic form in 2001; you may need to put Calcutta in parentheses until readers make the connection. Both are used in conversation, Kolkata mainly in writing.

calendar girl calendar model.

call a spade a spade get to the point, speak plainly/straight from the shoulder/straight out, be up front/frank/on the up and up/aboveboard. Though the expression predates the use of "spade" as a racial slur, it needs to be avoided.

call girl prostitute, prostituted woman. Call girl services and call houses are thus prostitution services and houses of prostitution. See also prostitute.

camaraderie an inclusive term, although this feeling of unity and good-will has most often been associated with men, particularly in team sports, bars, and wars. See also brotherhood, fellowship.

camel jockey see anti-Arabism.

cameragirl/cameraman camera operator/technician, cinematographer, camera crew; videographer; photographer.

campaign finance reform said to be the reform without which no other reform is possible, campaign finance reform faces nearly in-superable obstacles: the people who use vast amounts of money to buy enormous government favors in order to make even vast-er amounts of money aren't interested in stopping. And they don't have to. They have the money. "Granny D." (Doris Haddock) walked across the country at the age of 90 to protest campaign financing: "Along my three thousand miles through the heart of America, did I meet anyone who thought that their voice as an equal citizen now counts for much in the corrupt halls of Washington? No, I did not. Did I meet anyone who felt anger or pain over this? I did indeed, and I watched them shake with rage." In 2007, Bill Moyers said, "We are shouted down by the bullhorns of big money. It is money with no manners for democracy, and it must be escorted from the room. While wealth has always influenced our politics, what is new is the increasing concentration of wealth and the widening divide between the political interests of the common people and the political inter-ests of the very wealthy who are now able to buy our willing leaders wholesale. ... What villainy allows this political condition? The twin viral ideas that money is speech and that corporations are people. If money is speech, then those with more money have more speech, and that idea is antithetical to a democracy that cherishes political fairness." Moyers quoted Mark Hanna, who shook down the corpo-rations to make William McKinley President of the United States in 1896 and once said that there are two important things in politics: "One is money, and I can't remember the other one." Added Moyers: "Because our system feeds on campaign contributions, the powerful and the privileged shape it to their will. Only 12 percent of American households had incomes over $100,000 in 2000, but they made up 95 percent of the substantial donors to campaigns and have been the big winners in Washington ever since."

camp follower if you mean prostitute, use prostitute. If you mean a pol-itician who switches parties for reasons of personal gain, the term can be used for either sex.

candy-striper volunteer, junior/teen/hospital volunteer. These volunteers include girls/young women and boys/young men.

Canuck used by non-Canadians, this is usually a derisive term, especially for French Canadians. The term (origins uncertain) is not traditionally considered derogatory in Canada by either Francophones or Anglophones, so Canada has its hockey team, the Vancouver Canucks, and its national personification in Johnny Canuck.

capital punishment see death penalty.

car bra this close-fitting vinyl cover, usually black, protects the front end of an automobile from insects, gravel, and the elements and is also called front-end mask, sports-car snood, coat for nose grills. When "car bra" is used to mean a radar-absorbing carbon-filter on the front end of an automobile to resist and confuse police radar, use nose mask/cap.

career girl/career woman professional, business executive, executive trainee, longtime/full-time employee, careerist. Or be specific: sales rep, paralegal, career scientist, industry representative, social worker, professor, engineer, administrative assistant. The only use for "career man" seems to be in government service. When tempted to use "career woman," consider how "career man" would sound and handle the situation the way you would for a man. See also businessman.

caregiver man or woman, although 90 percent of all caregivers are still women (Theresa Funiciello, in Robin Morgan, ed., *Sisterhood Is Forever*). Family caregivers provide two-thirds of all U.S. home care services and more people enter nursing homes because of caregiver burnout than because of worsening health conditions (*North Star Review*).

care, withdrawing this common expression for withdrawing life support is inaccurate; care is never withdrawn even if the respirator is stopped.

car/she Referring to cars as "she" is part of the association of the feminine with men's possessions. Everything that dominator societies have traditionally run or overpowered has been imaged as female: church, nations, nature, ships, cars, etc. Use car/it.

Casanova if you need an inclusive alternative, use heartthrob, heartbreaker, lover, great romantic, dashing lover, flirt, make-out artist, smooth operator.

case the *Publication Manual of the American Psychological Association* advises, "Recognize the difference between *case*, which is an occurrence of a disorder or illness, and *patient*, which is a person affected by the disorder or illness and receiving a doctor's care." See also patient.

caste the caste system in South Asia, and particularly among Hindus, is perhaps the apotheosis of hierarchical thinking. However, in the United States, we too perceive whole classes of people as better or worse than others, more or less worthy, more or less admirable; we just don't call them castes. This topic is best approached by an insider; outsiders will rarely sound authentic. See also "Untouchables."

castrate/castrating it is not possible to "castrate" a secure, independent person; the man is not an anesthetized patient in this type of surgery. For "castrate" use disarm, disable, incapacitate, undermine, unhinge, unnerve, deprive of power/strength/courage/vigor, devitalize, attenuate, shatter, exhaust, weaken, disqualify, invalidate, paralyze, muzzle, enervate, take the wind out of one's sails, put a spoke in one's wheels. For "castrating": ruthless, aggressive, domineering, controlling, powerful, tyrannical, overwhelming, overpowering.

catfight when women disagree with each other, the proceedings are sometimes stereotyped as a catfight. Men's disagreements are not called catfights or dogfights or anything else; they are simply arguments, disagreements, debates, discussions, conflicts, or disputes.

cathouse house of prostitution. See also prostitute.

cattleman cattle owner/raiser/buyer/grower/producer, rancher, farmer.

catty malicious, spiteful, snide, sly, underhanded, disingenuous, envious. Beware of "catty," which is used exclusively of women; the alternatives can refer to either sex.

Caucasian arising from the old "racial" classifications, where it referred to peoples indigenous to Europe, western Asia, northern Africa, and much of the Indian subcontinent, "Caucasian" today is used infrequently (usually only by some police departments and hospitals) but erroneously as a synonym for "white" or "European/European American." "When it comes to the crunch, *Caucasian* doesn't mean much more than 'white people who play golf'" (Geoffrey Nunberg, *Going Nucular*). "Caucasian" is correct when used to refer to the region between the Black and Caspian seas that includes Russia, Georgia, Azerbaijan, and Armenia, but for the peoples use instead "people in or from the Caucasus." See also -oid, race, white.

cavalryman cavalry soldier/officer, horse soldier, trooper. Or specifically, Hussar, Lifeguard, Lancer, etc.

caveman/cavewoman cave dweller, early/ancient human, Neanderthal, Cro-Magnon. Plural: cave people. The use of "cavemen" as a pseudogeneric and the cartoon image of a cavewoman being dragged away by her hair have obscured women's position in prehistory: researchers now say that, contrary to common assumptions, female and male roles were often balanced more than currently, and it was women who were probably responsible for making tools and pottery and for such major technological innovations as agriculture and textiles.

celibate because this can mean someone who abstains from sexual activity (especially because of religious vows), someone who is currently refraining from sexual activity, or someone who is unmarried, it can be ambiguous; clarify your issues.

censorship the American Library Association defines censorship as "the suppression of ideas and information that certain persons—individuals, groups, or government officials—find objectionable or dangerous. It is no more complicated than someone saying, "Don't let anyone read this book, or buy that magazine, or view that film, because I object to it!" Censors try to use the power of the state to impose their view of what is truthful and appropriate, or offensive and objectionable, on everyone else." Censorship: rap music with violent lyrics is outlawed by legislative action. Not censorship: a radio station decides not to play rap music with violent lyrics. The key is whether the censorship is mandated by law, or whether it is a freely chosen expression of personal choice. Also whether the censoring act constitutes prior restraint, not just criticism or punishment after something has been published. The difference is not always so clear; when writing of censorship, note carefully the freedoms and laws involved.

CEOs although the title is so associated with the male that when an assistant wrote brokers and agents using company email, "Our CEO is very particular about where she lives," many responded with: "Great, what does he like? Where does he want to be?" Women made up 4.6 percent of CEOs in Fortune 100 companies in 2013. Interesting things to know and tell: From 1978 to 2012, CEO compensation measured with options realized increased about 875 percent, a rise more than double stock market growth and substantially greater than the painfully slow 5.4 percent growth in a typical worker's compensation over the same period. The ratio of CEO pay to average worker pay is 273 to 1, down from a high of 383 to 1 in 2000, but up from 20 to 1 in 1965. The CEO-to-average-worker pay ratio of the 250 largest companies in the Standard & Poor's 500 index ranges from 1,795 to 1 (J.C. Penney's Ron Johnson) to 173 to 1 (Agilent Technologies' William Sullivan), according to Bloomberg News. Research conducted by Equilar Inc., the executive compensation analysis firm, found that the median 2012 pay package for CEOs came in at $15.1 million—a leap of 16 percent from 2011. The *New York Times* reports that "44% of U.S. CEOs have contracts that call for them to receive severance payments even if they're fired for committing fraud or embezzlement." Inequality, says Steven Rattner, an investment manager, "isn't good as an economic matter, and it's not good as a moral or social matter." Writing in the *Boston Globe*, columnist James Carroll said the current economic system is "eroding democracy" by awarding a larger share of the economic pie to the very rich and "impoverishing more and more human beings." Roger Lowenstein, writing in the *New York Times*, says, "The United States has a pretty high tolerance for inequality. ... The extreme divergence of American incomes we see today, however, is actually rather new. For most of the 20th century, America was becoming more egalitarian. ... That CEOs have been very handsomely rewarded for failure, while many more have become exceedingly rich almost irrespective of their performance, violates every conservative piety about designing the right incentives."

chairman (noun) chair, moderator, committee/department head, presiding officer, presider, president, chairer, convener, coordinator, group coordinator, leader, discussion/group/committee leader, head, speaker, organizer, facilitator, officiator, director, supervisor, manager, overseer, administrator, monitor, clerk. Some people use "chairwoman" and "chairman," but it is better to keep this term gender-free because "chairwoman" is perceived as a less weighty word and because "chairperson" is an awkward and self-conscious term used primarily for women. There is much linguistic support for the short, simple "chair": it was, in fact, the original term (1647), with "chairman" coming into the language in 1654 and "chairwoman" in 1685. Using "chair" as both noun and verb nicely parallels the use of "head" for both noun and verb. (People who are upset about being called "a piece of furniture" apparently have no problem with the gruesome picture of a "head" directing a department, division, or group, nor is there evidence that anyone has actually confused people chairing meetings with their chairs.) See also chairman (verb), chairmanship.

chairman (verb) chair, head, lead, moderate, direct, supervise, officiate, preside, convene, coordinate, facilitate, control, oversee, organize, govern.

chairmanship chair, leadership, presidency. See also chairman.

challenged the only "challenged" term that was ever seriously used (and not for long nor by everyone) was "physically challenged." That attempt to name one of the realities of disability innocently provoked the ridiculisms that were then charged to "political correctness." Even *Fowler's Modern English Usage*, 3rd ed., which ought to be able to distinguish between genuine and deliberately farcical word usages, credits "the political correctness movement of the 1980s and 1990s" with "notorious formations" like "cerebrally challenged" (stupid) and "vertically challenged" (short). If it needs to be spelled out, the rash of simulated "challenged" words came not from the so-called PC "movement" but from the anti-PC "intelligentsia." See also disabilities, physically challenged/different, politically correct.

chamberlain historically a man. If you need a similar, inclusive term, consider treasurer, chief officer/steward, household official.

chambermaid room/personal attendant, servant, cleaner, housekeeper.

champion woman or man.

chancellor man or woman.

"change, the" this term predisposes women to expect more change than many actually experience. It's not very scientific either. See also menopause.

chanteuse this sex-specific term conveys a precise meaning; because there is no parallel for men, you might sometimes need sex-neutral alternatives: singer, nightclub singer, vocalist, balladeer. See also torch singer.

Chanukah see Hanukkah.

chaperone chaperon. See also "feminine" word endings.

chaplain woman or man.

chargé, d'affaires man or woman.

charwoman char, charworker, cleaner, janitor, maintenance worker, custodian. Plural: chars, cleaning personnel/crews, commercial cleaners, building-service employees, clean-up workers.

Chasidim see Hasidim.

chaste/chastity these terms have been used almost entirely of women (often with the implied concept of virgin/virginity); except for priests and monks, men were not held to any sexual standards. With the advent of HIV/AIDS, chastity has made a modest comeback as it is the only truly effective preventive. Use the terms for both sexes or not at all. See also celibate.

chatelaine retain in historical contexts where its companion word, "chatelain," is also used.

chauvinism although this term comes from a man's name (Nicolas Chauvin, known for his exaggerated patriotism and attachment to Napoleon), it seems male-associated not because of its etymology but because of its mid-20th-century use for men in such terms as "male chauvinist" and "male chauvinist pig" In this case, use sexist or male supremacist. Both women and men can be chauvinists in the original sense. See male chauvinist/male chauvinist pig.

checkout girl/checkout man checker, checkout/desk clerk, cashier. Note the nonparallel "girl/man."

cheerleader man/boy or woman/girl.

chef until recently, men have been chefs and women have been cooks; not too long ago, the idea of a woman chef was considered absurd. Today, however, women in the United States, France, and England wear the full title of chef. Female chefs and head cooks make up 21 percent and men 79 percent of lead kitchen positions, according to the Bureau of Labor Statistics and National Restaurant Association, and women now make up almost half the student bodies at culinary schools. Therefore, don't use "woman chef." The group without the adjective owns the noun.

chessman chess/game piece. Or be specific: pawn, rook, bishop.

Chicana/Chicano/Chican@ use these terms for people who so label themselves. Some people of Mexican descent in the U.S. (the terms are inappropriate for Mexicans living in Mexico) prefer other words (Mexican American, Latina/Latino, Hispanic). "For more than 100 years, they were Americans in name only. ... Mexican Americans were denied the rights of other citizens, and many were stripped of their land. In the 1960s, a new generation of leaders came forward and fought for change. They called themselves Chicanos—an ancient Mexican word that describes the 'poorest of the poor.' But they wore the name with pride. They walked out of fields and demanded a fair wage. They walked out of schools and demanded better education. They formed a political party and demanded full citizenship" (Judith Michaelson, in Minneapolis' *Star Tribune*). The terms Chicana/Chicano/Chican@ (always capitalized—note the recent unisex term) carry connotations of ethnic nationalism (Indian, African, and Spanish roots) and political activism, which means they are not popular with some older, more conservative Mexican Americans who want middle-class respectability and assimilation. Thus, "Mexican American" and "Chicana/Chicano/Chican@" are not synonyms, but are in fact mildly antithetical. Chicanas and Chicanos specifically reject the idea that they must deny their Mexican heritage in order to be "real" Americans. "Chicana/Chicano/Chican@" is not used for other Spanish-language groups, for example, Puerto Rican Americans or Cuban Americans, and the popularity of the term varies across the U.S. See also Hispanic, Latina/Latino/Latin@, La Raza, mestiza/mestizo, Mexican American.

chick see animal names for people.

chickenhawk a warmonger who managed not to ever go to war and has no children in the military—"do as I say, not as I do." Also an adult male who preys on children sexually.

chick flick a chick flick probably "has more dialogue than special effects, more relationships than violence, and relies for its suspense on how people live instead of how they die" (Gloria Steinem). "My boyfriend won't see anything he calls a 'chick film.' That's any film where the woman talks" (Maura Lake). Apparently first used in 1992 by Brian Shipkin in the *Chica-*

go Tribune, the term "chick flick" isn't derogatory, although one feels that it wants to be, and people occasionally use it to put down a film but, as Karen Durbin says in *O, the Oprah Magazine*, "Women's pictures used to be guilty pleasures: No more! Now they're kicking butt, getting respect, and grossing huge." Chick flicks may be companions to guy movies.

chief the use of "chief" as a generic for any American Indian man is highly offensive; when capitalized and part of a historic title of an Indian leader, it is retained. Other uses of "chief" to mean "head" are acceptable and not associated with Indians.

chief/chief justice/chief master sergeant/chief master sergeant of the Air Force/chief petty officer/chief warrant officer/chief of staff/ chief of state man or woman.

Chief Justice of the Supreme Court Chief Justice of the United States. (There is no official title "Chief Justice of the Supreme Court.")

childbirth according to Jennifer Block (in the *Los Angeles Times*), "For the first time in decades, the number of [U.S.] women dying in childbirth has increased." In addition, "pre-term births are on the rise. Nearly one-third of women have major abdominal surgery to give birth. And compared with other industrialized countries, the United States ranks second-to-last in infant survival." Black women in California are nearly four times more likely to die during childbirth than white women, with a staggering rate of 46 deaths per 100,000 births. The national picture isn't much better. Black women have three times the risk of maternal death as white women. Block attributes much of the responsibility for these statistics to overuse of the surgical birth procedure, the caesarean, or C-section: "the caesarean rate should be a major public health concern." In 1972, 5 percent of all births were by caesarean section; in 2011, they were 31 percent of total births. In a related matter, 32 states permit prisons and jails to shackle women prisoners during labor, even though the American Medical Association has condemned the practice as "unsafe" and "barbaric." Childbirth term: "drive-through delivery," referring to the very short hospital stays allowed to women after giving birth.

childcare childcare issues do not belong uniquely to women; they are family, social, political, and business issues (companies that have innovative policies on childcare and family-friendly benefits are not motivated by benevolence—their programs make good business sense). Working parents qualify for tax benefits to offset childcare costs, but the Tax Policy Center reports that in 2013, among families claiming the Child and Dependent Car Tax Credit, the largest benefit went to those with incomes between $100,000 and $200,000. Some employers offer a "childcare exclusion," which allows employees to set aside up to $5,000 of their salaries, pre-tax, to help pay for childcare. As for low-income families, the federally-funded Child Care and Development Block Grant (CCDBG) provides childcare subsidies. In 2012, the CCDBG served a monthly average of over 900,000 families with over 1.5 million children. Eighty-six percent of the families served by CCDBG were single-parent households. Parents confirm that childcare assistance, like that available through CCDBG, improves the quality and reliability of their children's care. Without assistance, parents struggle to get and keep jobs, making it extremely difficult to support themselves and their families. Research shows that access to childcare assistance increases the likeli-

C

hood that parents are employed and will remain employed for longer periods of time. The cost of childcare varies greatly based on where a family lives. The average annual cost for an infant in a day care center in 2011 ranged from $4,600 to $15,000; the annual cost for a four-year-old in day care ranged from $3,900 to $11,700. What's still needed is national recognition of and government support for universally available, high-quality childcare.

child custody damaging gender-based stereotypes about both sexes play a role in child custody. While joint custody seems consistent with equal rights and equal responsibilities, it is often not in the child's best interest; when shared responsibility, equal rights, and cooperation do not exist pre-divorce it is almost impossible to legislate them during a custody suit and ensure compliance later. In some courts, women are almost automatically given custody simply because they are women, yet men might have been the more suitable custodial parent in some of the cases. With the growth of the fathers' rights movement, men are more often being given custody—but sometimes for the wrong reasons. Reviewing *Child Custody and the Politics of Gender* (Carol Smart and Selma Sevenhuijsen), Nancy D. Polikoff concludes that the book "presents devastating evidence that mothers are losing custody of their children because of economic disadvantage, because they are judged by a 'good mother' standard vastly different from the 'good father' standard, because women's nurturing of children (as opposed to men's) is profoundly undervalued, and because, more than anything, the rhetoric of equality has outdistanced the realities of parenting." Child custody issues are highly complex and have profound, long-lasting, and sometimes devastating effects on all concerned. There are no simple solutions, but eliminating decisions based solely on gender might ensure that the child has the most suitable custodial parent. See also alimony, courts (judicial), displaced homemaker, divorce, divorced father/mother, noncustodial parent, visitation.

childfree/childless for a variety of reasons, those who self-identify as childfree have made a considered choice not to have children. According to a Center for Disease Control and Prevention survey, 6 percent of U.S. women of childbearing age were voluntarily childless in 2010, up from 4.5 percent in 1988. Jennifer Liss points out in *Bitch*, "Stats on men are harder to find, perhaps due to the built-in societal bias dictating that because only women can bear children, only women can likewise be defined as 'childfree'." Childfree individuals report experiencing social judgment against them—they are somehow offensive to those with children. Although a few childfree individuals consider themselves antibreeder, the vast majority of the childfree describe their choice as a personal decision. They have nothing against those with children. Organizations such as Childless by Choice, Child-Free Network, and No Kidding say that nonparents are trying to win acceptance for a childfree lifestyle in an age defined by "family values." Liss says, "The criticism that people without children are actively repressing a natural urge is a common one, and it's no surprise that it is so frequently directed at women, given our cultural perception of motherhood as the most sacred experience a woman can have. ... Even as the ranks of the childfree grow, the choice to parent continues to be idealized while the choice to be childfree is too often belittled and mocked. ... Parenthood should be a choice." The other side of "childfree" is having no choice at all—

being childless involuntarily. When circumstances or infertility prevent people from having the children they badly want, they describe their situations as tragic and heartbreaking (www.childlessnotbychoice.com). Again, the term is gender-weighted; Anndee Hochman (*Everyday Acts and Small Subversions*) says, "We don't refer, with quite the same sense of anomaly and pity, to 'childless' men." When faced by adults without children, how do we deal with it? We don't. We have no way of telling if they are happily childfree, despairingly childless, or somewhere in between. And it is none of our business. The childless-not-by-choice are dealing with their sorrow quietly and gracefully—we can only acknowledge them the same way.

child/he (pseudogeneric) no. When you need to use a pronoun with a child of unspecified sex: (1) Switch to the plural: "Children are remarkable for their intelligence and ardor..." (Aldous Huxley); (2) Avoid the pronoun altogether: "One of the most obvious facts about grownups to a child, is that they have forgotten what it is like to be a child" (Randall Jarrell); (3) Use "it": "Who will show a child, as it really is? Who will place it in its constellation and put the measure of distance in its hand?" (Rainer Maria Rilke). "People murder a child when they tell it to keep out of the dirt. In dirt is life" (George Washington Carver). "The finest inheritance you can give to a child is to allow it to make its own way, completely on its own feet" (Isadora Duncan).

child marriage this apparently oxymoronic phrase (defined as a formal marriage or informal union under age 18) is reality for many children around the world, although girls are disproportionately affected. Where prevalent, child marriage functions as a social norm. In affected countries, anywhere from 36 to 70 percent of women age 20 to 24 were married or in a union before age 18; worldwide, this amounts to 60 million women. Organizations working to end child marriage include UNICEF; Girls Not Brides: The Global Partnership to End Child Marriage, whose goal is to end child marriage by 2030; and The Elders, chaired by Archbishop Desmond Tutu. Gro Harlem Brundtland wants to include an end to child marriage in the U.N.'s new development goals, arguing that it would do much to empower girls, provide them with opportunities, and ensure their well-being.

children children are neither "little angels" nor "little devils"; name them in publications only when doing so will not harm them; let them speak for themselves when possible; although they are dependents of adults, they are not appendages or possessions. An "infant" is newborn up to approximately age 1; a "toddler" is usually ages 1 and 2 (when learning to crawl and walk); a "preschooler" is ages 2 to 5; "youngster" is appropriate from preschool to about 12; a "very young child" might be 3 to 6; "adolescent," "teenager," and "youth" include ages 13 to 20; "young adult" is sometimes used for older adolescents. In 2007, for the first time since it began keeping records 47 years earlier, UNICEF determined that the number of annual deaths among young children had fallen below 10 million. Among other causes for the decrease (vaccinations, anti-malarial measures) was the growing popularity of breastfeeding in place of formulas that often are mixed with polluted water. Still. Nearly 10 million deaths of children? Robin Morgan (*Saturday's Child*) cites even possibly worse numbers: "*There are approximately 250 million children in the world's labor force*, primarily in developing countries in Asia and Africa—and this is *without* counting (just as it's not counted for women) bonded labor, prostitution, pornography, domestic servitude, subsistence farming, child-rearing (of younger siblings), water hauling, fuel gathering, animal husbandry, and hidden-economy sweatshop labor. Tuberculosis, body lesions, malnutrition, and venereal disease are rife among the world's 80 million homeless street children—an estimated 30 million of whom roam in packs through the midnight streets of Brazilian cities alone." See also adolescent, ageism, teen/teenager, youth.

child-sex tourist see sex tourist, chicken hawk.

Chinaman Chinese. The offensive "Chinaman" is racist as well as sexist; use "Chinese" (or, if correct and relevant, Chinese American) for both sexes. See also Chinese, ethnic slurs.

Chinaman's chance a term both racist and sexist that arose from the years when Californians violently opposed the introduction of Chinese labor into the state; the chances of Chinese workers finding jobs were very slim as were their chances of finding justice under the law. Use instead: not a prayer, not an earthly chance, no chance, no chance at all, not a hope in hell, fat/slim chance, a snowball's chance in hell, as much chance as a snowflake in hell, doomed, unlucky, ill-omened, ill-fated, unblessed.

Chinese referring to China, its peoples, languages, and cultures, this is not interchangeable with Chinese American. "Chinese" is used in a number of expressions, some of which are benign (Chinese checkers/puzzle, various plants and vegetables), and some of which are not. Most of the negative expressions have faded from view in the post-World War II years. See also Chinaman, Chinaman's chance.

Chinese American correct term.

Chinese wall according to *Fortune* magazine, "'Chinese Wall,' which was a favored phrase of barristers and bankers looking to rationalize conflicts of interest (as in 'It doesn't matter that we also represent your arch competitor; we'll put up a Chinese Wall between their team and your team'), is now un-PC and on its way to RIP." Based on the Great Wall of China and describing a purportedly impenetrable barrier in the flow of information within a law firm or investment banking house, it's been replaced with ethics wall, information-blocking system.

Chippewa See Ojibwa/Ojibway.

chit (girl/young woman) there is no parallel referring to a boy/young man for this outdated term.

chivalrous if you want the sense without the masculine overtones, consider courteous, considerate, protective, courtly, brave, civil, generous, honorable, kindly, heroic, mannerly, gracious, well-bred, upstanding.

chivalry if you want the sense without the masculine overtones consider courtesy, honor, high-mindedness, consideration, bravery, courage, civility, valor, fidelity, mannerliness. Sexist attitudes underlie the concept of chivalry. The belief that women need protection ("for their own good"), special courtesies, and kid-glove treatment results in superficial pleasantness but deep-seated discrimination, paternalism, and oppression. "Protectiveness has often muffled the sound of doors closing against women" (Betty Friedan, *The Feminine Mystique*). Chivalry's message is that women are not the equals of men in most respects, and certainly cannot do certain heavy, dirty, dangerous (and high-paying) work. In 1915, Nellie L. McClung wrote, "Chivalry is a poor substitute for justice, if one cannot have both. Chivalry is something like the icing on the cake, sweet but not nourishing." See also lady.

choice see pro-choice.

choirboy choir member/singer, member of the choir, singer, vocalist. In the metaphorical sense, use adjectives for the traits you want to convey, or consider: cherub, angel.

choirmaster choir/music/song director/leader/conductor, director of the choir.

chorine cabaret/nightclub dancer, chorus member, member of the chorus.

chorus boy/chorus girl chorus member/dancer/performer/singer, member of the chorus, singer, vocalist, dancer, musical cast member.

Christ see Jesus/Jesus Christ.

christen term that comes from "Christian" and shouldn't be used outside of its religious context. Use instead name, dedicate, identify, label, denote, designate, entitle.

Christian "Christian" is often used as shorthand for a certain kind of goodness—for example, "that was the Christian thing to do" when what was meant was "that was the kind thing to do." During the Middle East war of 1948 the U.S. Ambassador to the United Nations urged the Arabs and Jews to resolve their disagreements "like good Christians." Use instead ethical, moral, decent, upstanding, righteous, upright, high-minded, honorable, principled, conscientious, moralistic, right, good, proper, considerate. See also Judeo-Christian.

Christian Coalition "in the late 1980s, Right-wing fundamentalists turned their attention to the political arena. Many of their leaders believed the United States had been founded as a Christian nation and should be governed by Christians sympathetic to the Right-wing political perspective. In 1989, with the formation of the Christian Coalition, the religious Right movement launched an effort to change U.S. politics fundamentally" (Cecile Richards, in *Sisterhood Is Forever*). Pat Robertson explained the goal of the Christian Coalition: "to mobilize Christians—one precinct at a time, one community at a time—until once again we are the head and not the tail, and at the top rather than the bottom of our political system." See also Christianity, Promise Keepers, religious Right, born-again Christian, fundamentalist.

Christian cultural imperialism "the overarching system of advantages bestowed on Christians. The institutionalization of a Christian norm of standard, which established and perpetuates the notion that all people are or should be Christians, thereby privileging Christians and Christianity and excluding the needs, concerns, cultural practices and life of people who do not define themselves as Christian. Often overt, but sometimes subtle, Christina hegemony is oppression by intent and design as well as by neglect, omission, erasure, and distortion" (Warren J. Blumenfeld, in *Free Inquiry*). He offers as examples of the reflexive Christian-as-default the constant, prolonged promotion of Christmas music in public spaces and on radio stations; Christmas specials on TV throughout November and December; Christmas decorations (often hung at taxpayer expense) in public areas; the president and first lady lighting the "National Christmas Tree"; and the still-common use of "A.D." (Anno Domini) and "B.C." (before Christ) to mark time. Public figures regularly confound politics with religion; as long as it is Christianity, nobody seems to mind very much; were it a Jew or a Muslim speaking similarly, everyone would mind. See also Christianity.

Christianity There appear to be at least two distinct types of Christianity in the United States today. One Christianity is based on the life of Christ and the record of his life as found in the New Testament. The highlights of this kind of Christianity are inclusiveness (even sinners and tax collectors), forgiveness, sharing, looking on everyone else as a sister and a brother, and love. The other Christianity is exclusive, judges others, and prescribes behavior by a particular interpretation of the Bible. Grace Harkness (in *Minnesota Women's Press*), says, "They call themselves the 'Christian Coalition' while they work against all the people Christ told his followers to help—the sick, the poor, the naked, the hungry, the prisoners. Listening to them, a visitor from Mars would probably think that Christianity stands for lowering the capital gains tax." In addition, some Christians want to save the souls of others by dictating their behavior and to eliminate the secular state. They are the people our European ancestors came here to escape. See also Christian Coalition, Christian cultural imperialism, fundamentalist, religious right, separation of church and state.

Christian name when you mean the name given at Christian baptism, this is correct. For its generic meaning, use instead first/given name, forename.

Christian Right, the see religious right.

Christmas with the widespread commercialization and increasingly extended celebration of this religious (for some) holiday, those who are not Christian are involuntarily exposed to "pre-Christmas sales," "Merry Christmas," Christmas cards/decorations/lights/trees, and "after-Christmas sales." In any nonreligious sense, use instead holiday, holiday season/sales/decorations/cards, Happy Holidays, Season's Greetings, year-end sales, New Year's greetings/cards. This loose usage of "Christmas" dilutes and perverts its original religious meaning and is equally abhorrent to authentic Christians and thinking non-Christians. See also Hanukkah, Kwanzaa.

church/she church/it. Everything that dominator societies have traditionally run or overpowered has been imaged as female: church, nations, nature, ships, cars. This is particularly inimical in religious matters because the image has the weight of moral "rightness" behind it. The longtime God-is-male, church-is-female metaphors have led to the "conclusion" that male must be better than female. The National Council of Catholic Bishops' document on inclusive language advises using "it" or "they" for "church." When you mention "churches," in most contexts you may also want to mention temples, mosques, and places of worship. See also bride of Christ, God, religion.

church father if you are referring to one of the apostolic or patristic Fathers of the Church, leave as is for historical accuracy. Otherwise use, for example, fourth-century religious writer, bishop, great Christian teacher, early Christian philosopher, post-Nicene writer, or other specific description.

churchman church member/worker, churchgoer, believer, member of a church; churchwoman and churchman if they are used gender-fairly. Also: religious, clergy, ecclesiastic, priest, presbyter, pastor, imam, minister, confessor, elder. See also clergyman.

Church of Jesus Christ of Latter-day Saints, The see Mormon.

circumcision for many Jews, circumcision of male infants (in a ceremony called a bris) is an important religious rite. Medically there are debated advantages and disadvantages of routine nonreligious circumcision, but some men and women oppose it, saying it is invasive, unnatural, and mutilating. It is medically necessary only 10 percent of the time. See also female genital mutilation.

cissexist someone who looks on transgender people as being fake, illegitimate, and abnormal. Cissexism is thus, like sexism, racism, heterosexism, and ageism, discrimination against a group of those seen as "other," in this case, transgender folks.

city councilman city councilor/council member. The two alternatives are so widely used today that there should be minimal need for city councilwoman and city councilman. If the sex of the council members is germane, it will be obvious from their names or the pronouns used to refer to them.

city fathers city leaders/founders/councilors/officials/administrators/bureaucrats, the powers that be. In some cases: City Hall.

City of Brotherly Love William Penn named Philadelphia after a city in Asia Minor that was the seat of one of the seven early Christian churches and known for its goodwill and generosity; "Philadelphia" comes from the Greek *phil-* ("love") and *adelphos* ("brother"). "The City of Love" and "The City of Human Love" are seen occasionally but they seem unlikely to replace the centuries-old term.

civilian contractor also called private contractors, in a new type of outsourcing that has gained currency and greater public usage due to the U.S. war in Iraq, "these civilian contractors in the non-security roles are only a degree away from what we have historically called mercenaries. They may not be carrying weapons, but they nonetheless assist, equip, sustain, and maintain the military force in Iraq" (Timothy K. Hsia, *Los Angeles Times*). Hsia says they consist of some personal security detachments (bodyguards), but most are "service support for the troops and are filled by non-Americans. ... civilian contracts have come to take a significant, vital, and cloaked role in the country's prosecution of a war in which Americans are fooled by the actual numbers required to carry out a war." Since the "launch of the 'global war on terror,' the administration has systematically funneled billions of dollars in public money to corporations like Blackwater USA, DynCorp, Triple Canopy, Erinys, and ArmorGroup. They have in turn used their lucrative government pay-outs to build up the infrastructure and reach of private armies so powerful that they rival or outgun some nation's militaries" (Jeremy Scahill, author of *Blackwater: The Rise of the World's Most Powerful Mercenary Army*). In "Mercenaries R Us" (*Los Angeles Times*), Rosa Brooks writes of "the wholesale privatization of war and U.S. foreign policy" and quotes Erik Prince, CEO of Blackwater USA (which describes itself as "the most comprehensive professional military, law enforcement, security, peacekeeping, and stability operations company in the world"): "We're trying to do for the national security apparatus what FedEx did for the Postal Service." As for the White House, Brooks asks, "Why fight another war, with all the bother of convincing Congress, if you can quietly hire a private military company to fight for you?" But these contractors operate in a sort of legal twilight zone—immune from U.S. and Iraqi law, but not held accountable under American military law either. Article 3 of the International Convention Against the Recruitment, Use, Financing and Training of Mercenaries says, "A mercenary who participates directly in hostilities or in a concerted act of violence, as the case may be, commits an offense for the purposes of the convention." "In other words," said Michael Haas (*Los Angeles Times*), "mercenaries in combat are war criminals."

civilian irregular defense soldier the Pentagon term for "mercenary," a hired professional soldier who fights for the United States, but outside regular Armed Forces channels. In the war on Iraq, these soldiers earned much more than enlisted soldiers.

civilization our notions of "civilization" and "civilized peoples" are highly ethnocentric. Heather Moorcroft, Australian reference librarian involved with Aboriginal issues, says we must challenge rigid Western ideas of what constitutes literacy, literature, art, and education when looking at other cultures. For example, oral history, told from the bottom up by many, can prove to be more accurate than written history, recorded from the top down by the few. We can contemplate thousands of gun deaths annually, people with mental disorders sleeping under bridges, the billion-dollar porn industry, the children who go to bed hungry, the size of the national debt, our bedraggled international reputation, the deaths of our sons and daughters in Iraq for no very good reason, and still manage to call ourselves civilized.

civil union committed same-sex relationships can be legally recognized. Certain legal rights accrue to those in a civil union, but not nearly the rights granted to those who legally marry. See also marriage.

claim (verb) some people are said to "state" or "say," while other people are said to "claim." The dividing line is often whether the person has favored-group or non-favored-group status. At the very least, "claim" implies dubiousness; at the most, dishonesty or guilt. Neutral alternatives: report, relate, say, state, declare, describe, disclose, tell.

clansman clan member, member of a clan.

classism as Plutarch wrote almost 2,000 years ago, "An imbalance between rich and poor is the oldest and most fatal ailment of all republics." The United States believes itself to be a classless society, yet according to the Economic Policy Institute's *State of Working America, 12ᵗʰ Edition*: "Between 1979 and 2007, the top 1 percent of households received more income growth than the bottom 90 percent. Incomes for the top 1 percent grew 241 percent, compared with 11 percent for the bottom fifth and 19 percent for the middle fifth." Between 2009 and 2012, the top 1 percent captured 95 percent of total income growth, according to University of California at Berkeley economist Emmanuel Saez. Over two decades, the income gap has steadily increased between the richest Americans, who own homes and stocks and got big tax breaks, and those at the middle and bottom of the pay scale, whose paychecks buy less. The overall tax burden has shifted from the wealthiest Americans to the middle class. The Internal Revenue Service estimates that it is able to accurately tax 99 percent of wage income but that it captures only about 70 percent of business and investment income, most of which flows to upper-income individuals, because not everybody accurately reports such figures. Class differences affect educational opportunity and achievement, material well-being, employment, health, and death rates. According to Benjamin DeMott (*The Imperial Middle*), the myth that upward mobility is available to everyone shapes our response to poverty; social programs pretend most needs are temporary (the stop-gap welfare system) or narrow (nutritional supplements for pregnant women). The editors of the pro-business magazine *The Economist*, commenting on the myth that any American can climb to the top, said that with "income inequality growing to levels not seen since the Gilded Age and social mobility falling behind, the United States risks calcifying into a European-style class-based society." Classist writing is subtle ("welfare mother," "those people," "inner city") and difficult to weed out. It helps to imagine you are speaking of a well-dressed CEO in the same situation; barring the obvious differences, would the tone still be the same? See also blue-collar, poor, welfare mother.

classman see freshman, underclassman, upperclassman.

class warfare by setting average and below-average earners at each other's throat over issues like the marriage tax, minimum wage, and Social Security, the wealthiest 1 percent of the country can tiptoe out the door with bags of taxpayer money. (Mike Lofgren, *A Devil's Dictionary*: "Class warfare: a technique by which teachers, nurses, firemen, and cashiers are believed to be oppressing derivatives traders and CEOs, which includes unreasonably complaining that their wages aren't keeping up with the cost of their health insurance.") The United States is badly in need of tax reform and tax enforcement, but we need to look higher than the little people (Leona Helmsley: "Only the little people pay taxes"). See also classism, corporate welfare, poverty, welfare.

cleaning lady/cleaning woman cleaner, domestic/office cleaner, household/domestic/maintenance worker, housecleaner, houseworker, housekeeper, household helper, janitor, custodian, charworker; men will never clean if there isn't a verbal okay.

cleft lip/cleft palate see harelip.

clergyman clergy, cleric, member of the clergy, spiritual leader. Or be specific: pastor, rabbi, minister, priest, deacon, presbyter, elder, ecclesiastic, confessor, bishop, prelate, rector, parson, dean, imam, vicar, chaplain, preacher, missionary. Some 84 Christian denominations ordain women; at least 82 still do not. Among those with female clergy are American Baptist, Christian (Disciples), Episcopal, Evangelical Lutheran, Presbyterian, United Church of Christ, United Methodist, and the Conservative, Reform, and Reconstructionist branches of Judaism. See also bishop, churchman, imam, man of God/of the cloth, minister, priest, rabbi, stained glass ceiling.

cleric/clerical may refer to either sex.

climate change is a more complete expression of the phenomenon known as "global warming" and is the term preferred by climate scientists because it encompasses effects other than warming, such as increased prevalence of droughts, heat waves, hurricanes, and other extreme weather events. The world is not just getting warmer; climate is getting more extreme. The term "climate change" predates "global warming" and was used at least as far back as 1956 in Gilbert Plass's foundational work of climate science, "The Carbon Dioxide Theory of Climate Change." According to the Union of Concerned Scientists (UCS), we are overloading our atmosphere with carbon dioxide, which traps heat and steadily drives up the planet's temperature. Today, there is a 97 percent consensus among climate scientists supporting the reality of climate change and the fact that human consumption of fossil fuels is causing it. Despite the fact that out of 2,258 peer-reviewed articles by 9,136 climate scientists published between November 2012 and December 2013, only 1 article rejected the theory that carbon emissions were responsible for climate change, climate change deniers have a strong foothold in Congress. According to the website thinkprogress.org, 56 percent (130 members) of the Republican Caucus of the 113th Congress deny the basic tenets of climate science. Sixty-five percent (30 members) of the Senate Republican Caucus also deny climate change. These are the people seeking to ease limits on industrial pollution and who oppose clean energy legislation and environmental regulation. Although it was once believed that conservative media advocated the use of "climate change" in order to suppress the term "global warming"—believed to be more frightening—the fact is that most media outlets use the terms interchangeably. NPR's climate expert, Richard Harris, reports that the public reacts equally to "climate change" and "global warming," so use of one term or the other does not constitute spin. See also global warming.

Climate Leaders according to the Environmental Protection Agency (EPA), "Climate Leaders is an EPA industry-government partnership that works with companies to develop long-term comprehensive climate change strategies. Partners set a corporate-wide greenhouse gas (GHG) reduction goal and inventory their emissions to measure progress. By reporting inventory data to EPA, Partners create a lasting record of their accomplishments. Partners also identify themselves as corporate environmental leaders and strategically position themselves as climate change policy continues to unfold." According to Paul Wasserman and Don Hausrath (*Weasel Words*), however, "only a tiny percentage of the thousands of companies that contribute to the troublesome rise of greenhouse gas emissions, which affect global warming, have signed on." Therefore look beyond the official definition.

clitoridectomy see female genital mutilation (FGM).

closet this term, which is defined in one of its meanings as "a state of secrecy or cautious privacy" (*American Heritage Dictionary*), is also used to refer to lesbians and gay men who prefer not to disclose their sexual orientation. One could say "closet chocoholic" or "closet moviegoer," but this minimizes the suffering that gave us the word. See also coming out, outing.

clotheshorse fancy/fashionable/sharp/conspicuous dresser, a person it pays to dress, clothes-conscious person. See also cross-dresser, dandy, looksism.

clothes make/don't make the man clothes make/don't make the person/individual, clothes can break/make a person, clothes aren't everything, dress for success, the right clothes make a difference, don't judge a book by its cover, appearances are deceptive, all that glitters is not gold, you can't make a silk purse out of a sow's ear, a monkey dressed in silk is still a monkey.

clubman/clubwoman club member, member of the club, enrollee, cardholder; joiner, belonger, social/gregarious person.

coach woman or man. If you use female coach to distinguish, also use male coach.

coachman coach driver, driver, chauffeur. Retain "coachman" in some historical contexts.

coalition forces the George W. Bush Administration from the beginning used this term for its war on Iraq; Arab broadcasters generally prefer the term "occupation forces." The official White House list shows 48 member states, although the accuracy of the list has been questioned: only four of the countries (the U.K., Australia, Poland, and Denmark) contributed troops (92 percent were U.S. troops) and the majority of those troops were either confined to their bases due to widespread violence or issued specific orders to avoid hostile engagement; 33 offered to send troops after the invasion was complete; at least six have no military at all.

coatcheck girl coatchecker, coatroom/cloakroom/checkroom attendant/clerk, coat attendant/checker.

co-chairman co-chair. See also chairman.

cock its slang meaning of "penis" ensures that all "cock" words carry some connotation of maleness. The barnyard cock is now a rooster; the weathercock is a weathervane. See also "cock" words below. The exception is airplane cockpit, since there cock refers to a particular instrument.

cock-and-bull story If you want a neutral-sounding alternative, use snow job, nonsense, stuff and nonsense, tall tale, yarn, preposterous/improbable story, canard, moonshine, bunkum, poppycock, hot air, hogwash, balderdash.

cock of the roost for a sex-neutral alternative, you might try arrogant, conceited, careless, overbearing, in high feather, on a high horse, sitting pretty, riding tall in the saddle.

cock of the walk for a sex-neutral alternative, consider crème de la crème, flower of the flock; tyrant, dictator, leader, ruler. ("The walk" was the chicken yard.) See also high man on the totem pole.

cockpit (airplane) flight deck. See also cock.

cocksure/cocky this is used of both sexes although it comes from the male fowl and tends to be used more often of men. If you want a sex-neutral term, use self-confident, overconfident, arrogant, self-important, in love with oneself, pushy, overbearing, swaggering, aggressive, conceited, haughty, supercilious; jaunty, brash, cheeky, flippant, saucy, nervy, impertinent, insolent, careless.

cockswain see coxswain.

cocktail there appear to be dozens of theories about the origins of this term; it is, however, functionally nonsexist. See also cock.

code words "We actually talk about race all the time, but we do it in code" (Paul Kivel, *Uprooting Racism: How White People Can Work for Racial Justice*). "Some of the code words we use are 'underclass,' 'welfare mothers,' 'inner city,' 'illegal aliens,' 'terrorist,' 'politically correct,' and 'invasion.' These color-coded words allow white people to speak about race or about people of color, whether in the United States or abroad, without having to admit to doing so. We don't have to risk being accused of racism; we don't have to worry about being accountable for what we say. We can count on a mutual (white) understanding of the implications of the words without having to specify that this comment is about race. ... Each of these three terms [underclass, welfare mothers, inner city] attempts to create a division between white people and African Americans, giving us the illusion they are different than and lower than we are. The facts are distorted to make it seem as if white people and people of color live in different worlds with different cultures and moral values. From this framework it becomes easy to blame them for their poverty and to fail to see the interconnections between their lives and ours." Patricia Hill Collins (*Fighting Words*) defines racially coded language as "language without an explicit reference to race but embedded with racial meanings nonetheless." See also inner city, racism, underclass, welfare mother.

coed (noun) student. In theory, a coed is a student at a coeducational school; in practice, it is always a young woman. Several generations ago, Joe College and Betty Coed were the popular generic couple on campus, but Joe got to be the whole college while Betty was the coed, the exception to the rule. "'Coed carries with it the connotation of perky little female students in tight sweaters, or of women who have only recently been allowed to study with their more deserving male counterparts. Only men are students; women are just co-educated'" (*Wall Street Journal*). Commented the paper: "'Tis truly sad to let go of such a headline-short word in newspapers, but let us put it on our list of sexist words to be avoided." See also feisty, perky/pert.

coffee girl/coffee man coffee maker/server. Note the nonparallel "girl/man."

cohort woman or man; also group, as in age cohort.

coiffeur/coiffeuse acceptable sex-specific terms. For a sex-neutral term, consider hairdresser. See also barber, beautician.

collateral damage replace this and other euphemisms ("unintended targets") with precise descriptions of what has taken place and who or what is dead or destroyed by whom. See also friendly fire, military language.

collective punishment the 1949 Geneva Conventions outlaw the practice of destroying civilian property for reasons of either deterrence or reprisal, and designate "collective punishment" a war crime. "International law ... prohibits an occupying power from imposing collective punishment on the occupied population" (Amnesty International).

college girl college/university student. If necessary to specify sex, use "college man" and "college woman."

colonialism "a situation in which one group of people rules another in an exploitive relationship with political, economic, social, and cultural dimensions" (Patricia Hill Collins, *Fighting Words*). Having once been a colony, the United States has avoided the appearance of colonialism and colonialization in its relations with small countries; the United States has never had colonies, only territories and possessions. Establishing aggressive markets in small countries or creating dependency through foreign aid that can only be used to buy U.S. products may be similar but is not the same historically.

colonist colonists have been both sexes and of diverse ancestry. Avoid using the word pseudogenerically (for example, "colonists, their wives and children") or implying that they were only white.

coloratura retain as is for the soprano who specializes in ornately figured vocal music.

color blindness years ago, poet Pat Parker said it best, in her poem, "For the White Person Who Wants to Know How to Be My Friend": "The first thing you do is to forget that i'm Black. / Second, you must never forget that i'm Black." The new rhetoric of "color blindness" ignores the astonishing complexity of racism and the depth to which it's become embedded in our social institutions and in the national consciousness. "Color blindness" sounds good—"We're all family here!" No, we're not. Not yet. And until we are, we need to see who's getting the biggest pieces of pie and who's not getting any pie at all. We need to be, at one and the same, aware of color—in order "to analyze what difference difference really makes" (Kimberlè Crenshaw, in Robin Morgan, ed., *Sisterhood Is Forever*)—and blind to color. Then we can also see the beauty of different skin shades and use them as a natural part of describing someone. Color blindness will no longer be defensive. See also racism.

colored as a description of African Americans, "colored" is unacceptable except in established titles (for example, National Association for the Advancement of Colored People). One possible reason for the persistence of this term: "colored people" is an older term and therefore is perceived as referring to people who "know their place" better than uppity "blacks" or "African Americans." "People of color" (which is not at all the same) is used for groups who so name themselves and is also a way of including Hispanic, Asian, American Indian, and other groups. In Cape Town, South Africa, "colored" is "Coloured" and it refers to individuals of mixed black African and other ancestry, but it is always better to specify a particular heritage—Zulu or Xhosa, for example. See also African American, black (noun), people of color/ person of color.

colorism the prejudicial or preferential treatment among persons of African descent because of skin shade (practiced by both whites and blacks). "The upper echelons of black society in particular tended to rate beauty and merit on the basis of the lightness of the skin and the straightness of the hair and features. White features were often a more reliable ticket into this society than professional status or higher education. Interestingly enough, this was more true for women than it was for men" (Michele Wallace, *Black Macho and the Myth of the Super-woman*). Colorism compounds, embeds, and diversifies racism, both economically and socially.

comedienne comedian, comic, stand-up comic, comic actor, entertainer. See also "feminine" word endings.

"comfort women" an English translation of the Japanese euphemism *ianfu*, the term "comfort women" "refers to the tens of thousands of young women and girls of various ethnic and national backgrounds who were pressed into sexual servitude during the Asia Pacific War that began with the invasion of Manchuria in 1931 and ended with Japan's defeat in 1945. Estimates of the total number of Japan's comfort women range between 50,000 and 200,000" (C. Sarah Soh, *The Comfort Women*). "The so-called 'comfort women' were, in actuality, women kidnapped and drafted into military sexual slavery by the Japanese government for the use of their troops during World War II" (Polly Mann). In fact, the sexual enslavement continued after the Japanese surrender; "Under the Recreation and Amusement Association, operating with government funds and tacit approval from U.S. occupation authorities, Japan established comfort-women brothels for *American* troops. Until the spring of 1946, when General Douglas MacArthur closed the network, tens of thousands of women were forced to service GIs—15 to 60 a day per woman" (*Ms.*). When referring to "comfort women," use quotation marks to indicate the dubiousness of the term and make clear the reality of their situation: they were sex slaves. See also trafficking (sex).

coming out the process of "coming out"—acknowledging one's sexual orientation—may be a lifelong process of forging a lesbian, gay, bisexual, or transgender identity first to oneself and then informing family, friends, and co-workers, and then perhaps the world at large, although publicly identifying oneself is often assumed to be the major or only part of "coming out of the closet" (Gay & Lesbian Alliance Against Defamation). GLAAD also says that to refer to those who have taken this step as "admitted," "avowed," or "declared" homosexuals is inappropriate because those terms imply something unsavory; "openly lesbian" and "openly gay" are preferable. See also openly lesbian/gay, outing.

commander-in-chief in the United States, this is the President, and thus gender depends on the person in office.

committeeman/committeewoman member of the committee, committee member; ward leader, precinct leader. "Committeewoman" and "committeeman" are not as equal as they seem; "committeewoman" is a much less weighty term.

committed against one's will redundant when said of an individual committed to a mental institution. Being committed means that the person is not entering voluntarily.

common-law husband/common-law wife common-law spouse, except when sex-specific terms are desirable. The woman in such a household is often disparaged where the man is not. In a few states, common-law spouses are regarded as legally married; in any case, disapproval based on lack of marriage lines is inappropriate. In the United States and some European countries, there are now more couples living together without marriage than with.

common man common citizen/person/voter, average citizen/person/ human/human being/voter, ordinary person/citizen/human/human being/voter, everyday person, layperson, taxpayer, voter, resident, householder, homeowner, landowner, passerby, one of the people, citizen, the nonspecialist, commoner, rank and file. "The common man" also translates well as "ordinary people."

community-supported agriculture (CSA) a new idea in farming that has been gaining momentum since its introduction to the U.S. from Europe in the mid-1980s, CSA is a partnership effort between consumers interested in safe food and farmers seeking stable markets for their crops. Today more than 400 CSA farms consist of a community of individuals who pledge to support farm operation, sharing the risks and benefits of food production. For detailed information, see the USDA's online Alternative Farming Systems Information Center.

companion see boyfriend or girlfriend.

companion animal see pet. See also speciesism.

company man originally someone who led a company union and represented management's hope of keeping away outside unions, a company man today is someone who always sides with the boss or the company. It's a difficult term to replace as it says so much in two words. Today, however, there are company women, too, but "company woman" may not be understood in the same way. For both sexes, use instead loyal employee/worker, staunch supporter, company spokesperson, company mouthpiece. Or use adjectives: loyal, faithful, devoted, trustworthy, true-blue. See also organization man.

comparable worth this term refers to pay schedules that offer equal pay for jobs similar in education requirements, skill levels, work conditions, and other factors. "Equal pay" means people doing the same job receive equal pay: female and male nurses of equal seniority working on the same hospital floor receive the same pay. "Comparable worth" means that a female clerk-typist might earn the same as a male warehouse employee. However, even the most carefully constructed comparable worth plans have serious difficulties weighting job dimensions. Dr. Marc S. Mentzer gives an example: women historically have been concentrated in jobs requiring communication skills (secretaries, telephone operators, teachers) while men have historically been concentrated in jobs requiring physical skills (manual laborers, construction workers). In a job evaluation plan, how should these be weighted? Are communication skills equal to, double, or half the weight of physical skills? Job evaluation is not an objective, scientific process. Underlying attitudes pose more serious issues: "In just about every [society], whatever men do or produce is valued more highly than what women do or produce, even though what a man does in one society is done by women in another society. In most societies, it is not the thing done, nor the objects produced, but the sex of the doer that confers distinctions upon acts or products" (Marilyn French, *Beyond Power*). A Temple University study found that women partners in large firms receive lower compensation on average than men despite equal productivity; women are paid less because they are women (Vanessa Kleckner, Minneapolis' *Star Tribune*). A recent Yale study revealed that identical applications for a laboratory job were judged quite differently depending on whether the hirers thought the applicant was "Jennifer" or "John." And in a Princeton study, when symphony auditions took place behind a screen, a woman's chances of advancing increased by 50 percent. A 2011 report (Joanna Barsh and Lareina Yee, *Special Report: Unlocking the Full Potential of Women in the U.S. Economy*, McKinsey & Company) noted that men are promoted based on potential, while women are promoted based on past accomplishments. National statistics compiled by the American Association of University Women show women start out behind men after college and never make up the ground regardless of whether they have children. Women who don't learn of pay disparity until months after they're hired have little legal recourse. (The outcome of the U.S. Supreme Court case, *Wal-Mart Inc. v. Dukes* et al., in which 1.5 million Wal-Mart women charged pay disparity, can be simply stated: it was good news for employers.) See also equal pay, glass ceiling, wage earner.

compassionate conservatism "sloganeering rhetoric of right-wing politics to convey their heartfelt sympathies for those less fortunate who, they profoundly believe, are best served when they help themselves through self-reliance and a strong work ethic. ... George W. Bush, for example, has clearly demonstrated his campaign promise to be a compassionate conservative by constantly displaying his compassion for conservatives" (Paul Wasserman and Don Hausrath, *Weasel Words*). The extraordinary cuts in basic human services during the second Bush's reign, the closing of V.A. hospitals while U.S. soldiers are dying in an oil war, and the distinct lack of any practical compassion for lives destroyed by Katrina (and incompetent bureaucrats) are just three examples that limit this claim to compassion.

compatriot although "compatriot" has masculine roots (from the Latin for "land of my father"), the word seems to be used in an inclusive manner today.

complain this is often used of women and members of minority groups to discount what they are saying. For example, "Women are more likely to complain of discrimination." Depending on the meaning, it should have read to "report discrimination" or "experience discrimination" or "protest discrimination." This usage may have come from legal terminology in which a complainant "complains," but using that sense in everyday language for certain people and not others is ambiguous and biased. Even at the doctor's office, notes may reveal that the man reported frequent headaches while the woman complained of them. See also claim (verb).

comptroller woman or man.

comrade man or woman.

conceive when you want the broader meaning of this term as opposed to the narrow biological meaning it conjures up, use alternatives that are not sex-linked: imagine, dream up, think, invent, fashion, create, formulate, design, devise, contrive, concoct, hatch, form, originate, initiate, bring about. See also seminal.

concentration camp restrict the use of "concentration camp" to its primary meaning ("a camp where prisoners of war, enemy aliens, and political prisoners are detained and confined, typically under harsh conditions," *American Heritage Dictionary*). Using it casually or jokingly robs it of its needed power and discounts its horrors. See also "final solution," Gestapo/gestapo, Hitler/little Hitler, holocaust, Nazi/nazi.

Concerned Women for America seriously antifeminist group.

concertmaster concert leader/director, assistant conductor, first violinist. Some concert directors, both women and men, prefer to retain "concertmaster."

concierge woman or man.

concubine this word, meaning "to lie with," refers to a woman who lives with a man outside marriage but its usage has given it the aura of being owned, imprisoned or forced. The person she is presumably lying with has no label; he is simply a man—and perhaps a slaveowner, rapist, or prison keeper. Perhaps she could simply be a woman. Use words that accurately reflect the situation. See also kept woman, loose woman, mistress, pickup.

condom it's baffling to logical people that those who so oppose abortion tend to also abominate contraceptives; but actually this position has a logic: an opposition to all sex that cannot end in conception. "Given a choice between hearing my daughter say 'I'm pregnant or 'I used a condom,' most mothers would get up in the middle of the night and buy them herself" (Joycelyn Elders, in *The New York Times*). According to a survey of more than 4,000 adolescents attending Massachusetts high schools, condom availability was not associated with greater sexual activity among adolescents but was associated with greater condom use among those who were already sexually active." We need to show responsible use of condoms in books, films, television, and films, and condoms must be "taught" in the schools.

confessor the role of confessor originated with the development of the Celtic *anamchara* or "soul friend" (5th to 10th centuries) who could be female or male, single, married, or celibate. It was not until 1215 that the Fourth Lateran Council defined "confessor" in terms of a priest. Today we return to inclusive usage: spiritual director, confidant, adviser, counselor, mentor, preceptor, therapist, mother confessor/father confessor.

confidante confidant. See also "feminine" word endings.

confined to a wheelchair wheelchair user, uses a wheelchair. Also, but less recommended, has a/in a wheelchair. Wheelchairs are often liberating, not confining. See also bedridden, disabilities, wheelchair-bound.

conflict diamonds also known as war diamonds or blood diamonds, these diamonds are obtained at great human costs and sold to finance war, insurgencies, and other military actions.

confraternity as this is based on the Latin for "brother," you may sometimes need sex-neutral alternatives: society, union, association, organization, group, club, religious society.

confrere as this comes from the French (and before that the Latin) for "brother," you may sometimes need sex-neutral alternatives: colleague, associate, co-worker, teammate, collaborator, partner, companion, comrade, confederate, counterpart, accomplice.

congressman member of Congress, representative, congressional representative, legislator, member of the United States House of Representatives, delegate, assembly member; congressman and congresswoman if they are used fairly—and if "congressman" is not used as a false generic. "Congressperson" is not recommended, although it is seen from time to time. If "member of Congress" seems cumbersome, think of how often we have heard "member of Parliament" (nobody was ever a Parliamentman). Although "congressman" or "congresswoman" is technically a correct title for senators and representatives, it is typically used to describe members of the House of Representatives; senators are always called "senator." Failing to use a false generic also reveals a real problem: worldwide rankings of women in national governing bodies places the U.S. in 79th place.

con man/confidence man con artist, swindler, hustler, confidence operator, operator, chiseler, flimflam artist, fraud, cheat, faker, grifter, charlatan, trickster, quack, shark, crook, dodger, defrauder, deceiver, sharpie, scoundrel, hoodwinker, phony, imposter, shortchange/bunko artist, scammer. Although all these terms are inclusive, many of them tend to be thought of first as male. See also bad guy.

connoisseur man or woman.

conscientious objector man or woman. So far, only one woman is an official U.S. C.O. National Guard Specialist Katherine Jashinski tells of joining the National Guard at age 19 with good intentions but, as she says, she grew to adulthood and realized she couldn't kill anyone. She was tried, dismissed with a bad conduct record, and imprisoned. She said, "I am prepared to accept the consequences of adhering to my beliefs. What characterizes a conscientious objector is their willingness to face adversity and uphold their values at any cost. We do this not because it is easy or popular, but because we are unable to do otherwise." Hundreds of men in the armed forces have also applied for conscientious objector status since 2003. The Central Committee for Conscientious Objectors (www.objector.org) has much useful information on its site. See also draft.

conservation the earth's natural resources "must be maintained if future generations are to thrive spiritually, culturally, and economically. Our mission is to conserve the Earth's living heritage, our global biodiversity, and to demonstrate that human societies are able to live harmoniously with nature" (Conservation International). The human family has not thus far been a good steward of the earth's riches. Although people don't self-identify as anti-conservationists (certainly not Big Business or the military-industrial complex), you might be able to recognize them by their actions. See also wise-use movement.

conservative see political spectrum.

construction worker women make up almost 10 percent of the construction industry. See also tradesman.

consul man or woman.

containment strategies this term appears in a number of fields—among them, politics, epidemics, and health care costs. Spell out, if you can, exactly what is meant.

contraception this issue belongs to both men and women; avoid associating it solely with women. Other acceptable terms include birth control, family planning, fertility control, reproductive freedom. When discussing contraception, do not assume that the means are accessible to everyone. See also population control.

convent in almost all cases, it is religious women who live in convents, but mendicant friars also used to live in convents. See also monastery.

conversion therapy also known as reparative therapy, sexual conversion therapy, reorientation therapy, differentiation therapy, and the ex-gay movement, this pseudo-therapeutic "treatment" purports to "cure" gay men and lesbians by making them straight—and has been condemned by the American Psychiatric Association. The American Psychological Association, the American Medical Association, the National Mental Health Association, and the American Academy of Pediatrics have also spoken out to discredit these movements. In reporting on or writing about "conversion therapy," put the term in quotation marks and spell out who's doing what to whom and why.

convict man or woman. See prisoner.

cook see chef.

copy boy/copy girl copy messenger/carrier/clerk/distributor, runner.

coquette flirt is gender-free. All other coquette-type words are specific for women (tease, vamp, belle, hussy) or for men (playboy, masher, wolf, sheik)

corporate welfare corporate welfare is shorthand for the numerous federal spending and tax measures that benefit private corporations. According to a 2013 Federal Joint Committee on Taxation estimate, there was $154 billion in special corporate tax breaks that year, contained in 135 individual provisions of the tax code. Perhaps the most shameful example of government (in actuality, taxpayer) help for huge corporations was the $700 billion authorized in 2008 (later reduced to $475 billion) to bail out Wall Street, which could not and apparently would not take responsibility for its own unsound, risky, and sometimes criminal, actions in the pursuit of ever more unfathomably large amounts of money in ever shorter periods of time. Also known as "crony capitalism," "wealthfare," and "aid to dependent corporations" (Robert Reich), corporate welfare offers benefits largely unknown to the average citizen: unlimited deduction for interest on corporate debt; money grants; intangible asset write-offs; foreign tax credits; write-offs for banks for foreign debt losses; letting large and profitable mining companies use federally owned lands at minimal cost (or buy land for a couple of dollars an acre, and pay no royalties on the minerals they extract); billions in subsidies to electric utilities designed to hold down utility rates in impoverished communities like Aspen, Colorado, and Hilton Head, South Carolina; building, at public expense, over 240,000 miles of roads for logging companies; hundreds of millions of dollars to prop up the ethanol industry; tax-free fortunes sheltered overseas; guaranteed profits for military contractors, no matter what their cost overruns and no matter how great inflation is; inflated government contracts; tax loopholes; special-interest subsidies and tax laws that actually encourage U.S. companies to ship jobs overseas while cutting them here. Then there are bailouts, export promotions, loans, loan guarantees, debt forgiveness, below-cost sales, interest-free financing, and other benefits. The largest corporate welfare program in the U.S. is the Farm Bill, with 9 billion allocated to the government subsidized crop insurance program. Most of the benefits do not go to family farmers but to huge agribusiness corporations and absentee landowners. Agribusiness turns to the government for income supports, direct payments, marketing loans, commodity loans, crop insurance premium subsidies, price supports for selected commodities, conservation program payments, and disaster assistance, among other benefits. In addition to agribusiness, some of the biggest beneficiaries of government generosity are the armaments and aerospace industries and the pharmaceutical industry. What we usually think of as "welfare" (originally meaning "the well-being of the people") or the misleadingly called "entitlement programs" (originally meaning that the federal law "entitled" you to certain benefits, not that you felt you were entitled to benefits) includes Social Security, Medicare, and Medicaid, most Veterans' Administration programs, federal employee and military retirement plans, unemployment compensation, and the Supplemental Nutrition Assistance Program (SNAP). Yet "the nation's largest corporations and richest citizens receive more welfare money than our social welfare programs," according to the Nonviolent Action Network. The Progressive Policy Institute has pointed out that corporate subsidies are deeply regressive, providing benefits to a relatively small group of upper-income Americans, largely with money taxed from those earning far less. Whenever using the term "welfare," give a thought to both types and to the relative meanings of each. See also CEOs, corporations as persons, offshoring/outsourcing, welfare.

corporations as persons corporations are, legally speaking, persons, possessing all the rights of individual citizens while being exempt from many of the controls the law places on a wrongdoer. According to Tom Stites (in *UU World*), corporate personhood is a legal fiction that undermines American democracy: "While vast corporations have helped fuel unprecedented prosperity they have also overpowered 'government of the people, by the people, and for the people.' ... Corporations' power over the government is at the root of a wide array of issues ... including campaign finance reform, the growing gap between rich and poor, environmental degradation, globalization, and whether democracy itself has been reduced to a mere charade or a sideshow in a global bazaar." In 2011, 111 out of 175 the largest economies were corporations with Royal Dutch Shell, ExxonMobil, and Wal-Mart at 26, 27, and 28 respectively (World Bank/*Fortune* magazine).

corpsman medical aide; corps member. "Corpsman," still used by the Marine Corps, may refer to either sex.

Cosa Nostra this U.S. crime syndicate is believed to be related to the Sicilian Mafia. Unless you are certain that you are referring to the Cosa Nostra itself, use organized crime, crime syndicate. See also Mafia.

costume clothing worn by indigenous peoples, native peoples, or people from other countries is often referred to as a costume when in fact it is simply clothing. Even when the clothing is more elaborate, as for rituals, ceremonies, or celebrations, it should no more be referred to as a costume than would be a wedding dress or band uniform or graduation gown.

cougar referring to a woman romantically involved with a younger man, "cougar" is either derogatory or empowering, depending on who's talking. Mostly, it's used by those who can't think of any fresher language. Andi Zeisler (*Bitch*) says that like so many of the roles assigned to women, this one takes with one hand and gives with the other: "It's celebrating the sexual agency of women and granting the idea that older women can have a sexual identity after 40, but then assigning this goofy name to it and making it into a punch line is wrong." See also animal names for people.

councilman councilor, council member, member of the council/city council, city representative, municipal officer, ward manager, commissioner; councilwoman and councilman. Beware of "councilman" as a false generic; "councilperson" is not recommended, although it is seen and heard from time to time.

countergirl/counterman counter attendant/server, waiter. Note the nonparallel "girl/man."

counterterrorism this term means you counter terrorism with terrorism of your own. And it may be exactly the word you want. However, being against and fighting terrorism is called antiterrorism, and may include strategies like capturing criminals, education, diplomacy, containment, and seeking redress in national or international courts.

country bumpkin this term tends to be used more of a man than of a woman, although it is not in itself gender-specific. It also supports a pejorative, anti-farmer, anti-rural stereotype.

countryman compatriot, citizen, inhabitant, native, resident, indigene; counterpart; country dweller, ruralist, farmer; countrywoman and countryman. See also compatriot, fellow countrymen.

country/she country/it. See also ship/she.

couple in the sense of two people with emotional, domestic, or sexual ties to each other, do not assume a couple is a woman and a man; it might be two men or two women. Instead of "married couple," try the inclusive "domestic partners." See also boyfriend, girlfriend, family, husband and wife.

courtesan historic or high-class prostituted woman. A courtesan used to be the female equivalent of a courtier; "courtier" retains most of its former meaning, but "courtesan" has been completely devalued and there is no remaining parallel. See also prostitute.

courtesy titles see social titles.

courtier attendant; flatterer. See also courtesan.

courts (judicial) gender bias in the judicial system has been the subject of a number of court-sponsored studies in various states. The conclusion in New York was that unfairness and gender bias against women as litigants, attorneys, and court employees was a pervasive problem. In Minnesota, discrimination against women was found in areas such as divorce, domestic abuse, sexual assault, employment discrimination, and access to courts. The group also found examples of judges and lawyers addressing female litigants and witnesses by first names or by such terms as "dear" or "honey" while they did not do this to men. A New York State judge was disciplined for calling an attorney "little girl." In child custody cases, there was judicial bias against men and also against working women and poor women. One study found that other factors being equal, plaintiffs tend to receive higher awards for disfigurement if they are women and for loss of future earning capacity if they are men. See also child custody, criminal/criminal class, divorce, lawyer.

couturière high fashion designer, proprietor of a haute couture establishment; couturier/couturière.

cover girl cover model, model.

cover that man (sports) cover that receiver/player, cover them.

coward/cowardly/cowardice nonsexist per se, these terms are almost entirely reserved for men/boys. From the Latin *cauda* for "tail," "coward" refers to a dog with its tail between its legs. According to Stuart Berg Flexner (*Listening to America*), "It doesn't seem to be until the 1850s that boys began to taunt each other with being timid, cowardly, or unmanly, perhaps because earlier frontier days had produced fewer such boys, or because now new diversity meant tough frontier and rural youths were meeting some milder boys." Variants on "coward" that are technically inclusive but that are generally applied to men: big baby, chicken, chicken-hearted, chicken-livered, creampuff, featherweight, fraidy cat, gutless, gutless wonder, jellyfish, lily-livered, Miss Nancy, nebbish, pantywaist, pussyfooter, quitter, rabbit, shirker, sissy, softie, spineless, traitor, twerp, weakling, weenie, wimp, worm, wuss/wussy, yellow/yellow-bellied/yellow-bellied coward. Try to describe the actual situation. The man may be called a coward because he opposes violence, killing, or war.

cowboy/cowgirl cowhand, cowpuncher, ranch hand, hand, rancher, herder, cowpoke, wrangler, range rider, drover, buckaroo, rodeo rider/roper, cowgirl and cowboy (in some contexts). Although some of the terms in the list have a masculine flavor, there is nothing to contravene their being used for girls/women. "While the cow*boy* is our favorite American hero—the quintessential man—most of us see the cow*girl* as a child who will grow up someday and be something else. The cowboy's female counterpart—who can ride and rope and wrangle, who understands land and stock and confronts the elements on a daily basis—is somehow missing from our folklore" (Teresa Jordan, *Cowgirls*).

cowboy hat Stetson, ten-gallon/western-style/rodeo hat.

cowboy shirt western-style/buckskin/fringed/rodeo shirt.

cowgirl roper, rider, rodeo entrant; cowgirl and cowboy when referring to teenage rodeo participants. See also cowboy.

coxswain "swain" refers to a servant or a boy, and most coxswains are and have been men. However, the term could be used for a woman as its sex link is related more to the lack of female coxswains than to its etymology. Or use the more neutral-sounding bosun, derived from boatswain. (A "cock" was a small boat, so coxswain and boatswain are related.) Today most coxswains are found in the Navy, on small craft, and in racing shells.

crafts see arts and crafts.

craftsman artisan, crafts worker, craftworker, skilled worker, skilled craft worker, handworker, handiworker, handicrafts worker, handicrafter, trade worker, artificer, technician, craftsperson (use as a last resort); craftsman and craftswoman. Plural: artisans, craft workers, skilled workers, handworkers, handicrafts workers, handicrafters, trade workers, handiworkers, artificers, craftspeople, craftsmen and craftswomen. Or be specific: potters, weavers, woodworkers.

craftsmanship artisanry, artisanship, craft, handiwork, skilled-craft work, expertise, handicraft, skill, artistry, quality, crafts skills, expertness. Or specify the characteristics that contribute to the piece's beauty or the skills that went into its making.

crazy see mental illness.

"credit to her/his race" when you have used this referring to a white person at least ten times, you may use it to describe a person of color. See also race.

cretin someone with congenital myxedema, not just someone with bad table manners.

crewman crew member, member of the crew, hand, employee, personnel, staff member, worker; crew/deck hand, sailor, mariner.

crime in the streets "a catch-all euphemism for the perceived threat to life and property of the white suburban dweller from the black inner-city population" (Paul Wasserman and Don Hausrath, *Weasel Words*). Specifying the crime and the streets and the situation clarifies your language and your message.

crime of passion this term usually refers to domestic violence/terrorism/murder, almost always against women. "Passion" elevates it to a somewhat defensible, almost sympathetic level. Nix the passion and name the crime.

crimes against humanity because of the rising levels of horror and number of such crimes, compassion fatigue dulls us to this phrase's unacceptable evil. Unless referring to international law's so-named criminal charge, use your writing powers to describe the specific situation.

criminal/criminal class because all those who underreport income to the IRS or who buy expensive items across state lines, falsifying place of delivery to evade sales tax, or who embezzle at the levels of upper management are never referred to as a "criminal class," it seems evident that this term has classist and racist dimensions. None of those involved in the S&L "scandal"—a much nicer word than "crime"—were called "criminals" although some were. What's left when government and corporate white-collar crime goes linguistically unemphasized is a de facto connection of "criminal" with "poor." Circular reasoning then makes the average taxpayer reluctant to back anti-poverty programs so as not to support a criminal class. This leaves the poor even poorer. See also bad guy, prisoner.

cripple person/individual with a disability/orthopedic disability/physical disability/functional limitation, someone with paraplegia/arthritis. Omit references to a disability if it is not strictly necessary to your material. "Cripple" (and "crip") follow the "insider/outsider" rule, that is, they are derogatory and absolutely unacceptable except when used by people with disabilities among themselves. "People—crippled or not—wince at the word *cripple*, as they do not at *handicapped* or *disabled*. Perhaps I want them to wince. I want them to see me as a tough customer, one to whom the fates/gods/viruses have not been kind, but who can face the brutal truth of her existence squarely. As a cripple, I swagger. But, to be fair to myself, a certain amount of honesty underlies my choice. *Cripple* seems to me a clean word, straightforward and precise. ... As a lover of words, I like the accuracy with which it describes my condition: I have lost the full use of my limbs" (Nancy Mairs). See also disabilities, handicapped, "insider/outsider" rule, wheelchair-bound.

Cro-Magnon man Cro-Magnon(s), Homo sapiens, Neanderthal, people before written history.

crone in other times, the crone was a wise, powerful elder honored by her society. Although this role is generally unacknowledged today, some women are reclaiming it for themselves. See also ageism.

cross burnings these fires still burn. Also called cross lightings, these acts of racial hatred associated with Ku Klux Klan meetings have recently been termed "important religious ceremonies" by those who continue the practice (Minneapolis' *Star Tribune*). In 2003, the United States Supreme Court ruled that burning a cross at a Klan rally is protected by the First Amendment, but also held that a statute could constitutionally proscribe cross burning when carried out with the intent to intimidate the target of the "speech." See material on cross burnings and racial terrorism at http://academic.udayton.edu/race/06hrights/WaronTerrorism/crossburn00.htm.

cross-dresser "cross-dressers use attitude, clothing, and perhaps make-up to give the appearance of belonging to the other sex or to an androgynous middle ground. Most modern women may be considered cross-dressers since they often wear clothing normally intended for men. What is a new phenomenon is the rapidly rising number of men who wear women's clothing. Because a male-dominated society frowns on its members mimicking the 'inferior' female class, male cross-dressers are usually deep in the closet" (Martine Rothblatt, *The Apartheid of Sex*). Kate Bornstein (*Gender Outlaw*) says most cross-dressers have mainstream jobs and are practicing heterosexuals. Cross-dressers who occasionally wear clothes traditionally associated with people of the other sex are usually comfortable with the sex they were assigned at birth and do not wish to change it. Cross-dressing is a form of gender expression and is a response to gender restriction, since all human qualities ought to be expressable by and acceptable in each human being. It is not necessarily tied to erotic activity. Female and male impersonators cross-dress as performing artists or stage personalities. Sometimes "female impersonator" is used as a synonym for "drag queen," but this term isn't quite accurate in that the men performing as women aren't trying to pass as women. RuPaul said, "I don't dress like a woman; I dress like a drag queen!" Use the term only for those who self-identify this way. Do not use "cross-dresser" to describe someone who has transitioned to live full-time as the other sex or who intends to do so in the future (that describes a transgender individual). And avoid "transvestite," which is considered derogatory, unless self-chosen. Humorously, "female impersonator" has also been used to describe women politicians who vote like men. See also transgender.

crotchety watch out for ageism; are young people ever said to be crotchety?

Crow Apsaalooke. The authentic, self-preferred name of this Plains people might also be seen in such alternate, but non-preferred, spellings as Absahrokee, Absaroka, Absaroke, Apsaroke; the tribe's language has become written in recent decades, so different spellings of its name have surfaced. About 10,000 "children of the long-beaked bird" live in Montana. See also American Indian.

crown prince/crown princess acceptable terms. Or, heir apparent, heir to the throne. A crown princess may also be the wife of a crown prince, whereas a crown prince cannot become one by virtue of marriage.

cruelty-free products thanks to the Internet, it is fairly quick and inexpensive to identify and buy those products that have been made without testing on animals or using animal products. See also animal rights activist/animal advocate.

crybaby used as a taunt for children of either sex or as a criticism of a whiny adult, also of either sex, this disparagement carries a special sting for boys/men, who are perhaps allowed to cry, but only for extremely important things. Since crying releases stress chemicals and is a desirable human response, avoid penalizing it. See also coward/cowardly/cowardice.

cuckold "What do they call it when a woman is cuckolded? Or doesn't that matter enough to have its own word?" (Lisa Scottoline, *Running From the Law*). Consider referring to one partner as being unfaithful while the other is betrayed. See also adulterer, philanderer.

cult originally meaning a religious practice, "cult" now more often refers to an isolated fringe sect of largely brainwashed or dominated believers. Avoid referring to authentic historical or contemporary religious groups as cults; "if the religious practices of the Yorubas constitute a cult, then so do those of the Methodists, Catholics, and Episcopalians" (Amoja Three Rivers, *Cultural Etiquette*). Geoffrey Nunberg (*How We Talk Now*) says, "There are a few certifiably deranged groups that everyone calls cults, like Heaven's Gate or the People's Temple, but beyond that it gets a little fuzzy. If you look on the web, you can find anti-cult sites that apply the word to everyone from Amway to Islam to the United Pentecostal Church." Reserve the appellation "cult" for truly extreme groups that demand a totalitarian obedience.

cultural issues usually a polite way of not really talking about racism, homophobia, classism, and other social inequalities. Define the issues.

"culturally deprived/disadvantaged" these terms imply being substandard in some vague hierarchy of cultures, whereas those so labeled are sometimes bicultural, bilingual, and rich in their own cultural traditions. Question the label; if deprivations exist, identify them and relate them to their probable causes in social or economic conditions. In the social sciences, "cultural deprivation" implies poverty; if that's what you mean, say so. Clyde W. Ford (*We Can All Get Along*) suggests using "culturally dispossessed." See also underprivileged.

culture this complex concept takes in, in one way or another, all of life. When possible, narrow the term's reach to fit your material and define it more precisely. In the U.S., there is some perception that there is one culture when in fact there are many. Beware of those who claim to know what constitutes U.S. culture (they're probably the same people who know exactly what "a real American" is, what "patriotism" is, and what you ought to be doing right now). Also beware of gender implications. As Gloria Steinem has written, "what happens to men is called *politics*, what happens to women is called *culture*." See also multiculturalism.

"culture of life" a slippery term, used primarily in anti-abortion rhetoric but not in discussions of the death penalty, poverty and lack of medical insurance that kill people, handgun deaths, and children who go to bed hungry. Behind the positive spin of "culture of life" is a single-minded effort to overturn *Roe v. Wade* and the division between church and state. Spell out exactly what the user of the term means by it.

"culture of poverty" the brainchild of the for-profit aha! Process Inc.'s CEO Ruby Payne, this term encompasses her ideas of "how poor people see and experience the world, how they relate to food, money, relationships, education, and other aspects of life. This, despite that research has shown again and again that no such culture of poverty exists. It's all too easy, for even the most well-meaning of us, to help perpetuate classism by buying into that mindset, implementing activities and strategies for 'working with parents in poverty' or 'teaching students in poverty' that, however subtly, suggest we must *fix* poor people instead of eliminating the inequities that oppress them" (*Teaching Tolerance*). As a substitute, Jonathan Kozol talks about *savage inequalities*, a more accurate term if you need one. See also poverty.

culture wars "when people first started to talk about 'culture wars' around 1980, they were referring to the controversies over PBS, the National Endowment for the Arts, the 'Great Books' requirements at universities, and the multicultural curriculum—that is, battles over 'culture' in the sense that the *Oxford English Dictionary* defines as 'the intellectual side of civilization.' But before long the phrase was being used to refer to a war *between* cultures in the anthropologists' sense, which was being fought over issues like abortion, gun control, and the teaching of 'creation science' in the schools" (Geoffrey Nunberg, *Talking Right*). Today, culture wars also center on censorship, church/state separation (school prayer, Pledge of Allegiance, faith-based government programs), same-sex marriage, equality for women and minorities, immigration, the death penalty. See also war/war on.

cunt depending on who's judging, this is (1) a deeply offensive slur for a woman; (2) a term being reclaimed and used by some women, as in buttons that said "cunt power! Worn by feminists in the 1970s (see "insider/outsider" rule); (3) a term of endearment. When the only woman to suit up for the University of Colorado Buffaloes football team alleged that a teammate called her a cunt at practice, UC President Betsy Hoffman attempted to minimize the situation by saying she had heard the word—considered one of the most derogatory terms for a woman—used as "a term of endearment." Further questioning revealed, however, that the president was referring to having seen it in Chaucer, who wrote over 600 years ago.

"curse" slang for menstruation, this term perpetuates the myth that the female body is a burden and that women do not operate on all cylinders throughout the month. It fosters incorrect and toxic attitudes in preadolescent and adolescent girls and boys.

curmudgeon because this is usually defined and used in reference to men, you may want more inclusive alternatives: grouch, grumbler, bad-tempered/peevish/cranky/petulant person, crosspatch, faultfinder, complainer, pain in the neck, nitpicker, troublemaker.

custodial parent some people find "custodial" a degrading adjective too evocative of prisons and guards, and would prefer to be simply a mother or a father or a parent. Use only when a legalism is called for. See also noncustodial parent.

custodian man or woman.

cyberbullying the misuse of technology to harm or control others. Computers, tablets, cellphones, e-mails, texts, and social media sites can all be used as tools for cyberbullying. Like traditional bullying, cyberbullying involves a repeated pattern of aggression that is based on a real or perceived imbalance of power, status, or popularity. What makes cyberbullying especially pernicious is that hurtful messages and images can be posted anonymously and instantly distributed to a wide audience. The Cyberbullying Research Center reports that one out of every four teens has experienced cyberbullying and about one in six teens has engaged in this form of bullying. Other findings: adolescent girls are just as likely as boys to experience cyberbullying (as both victim and offender). Cyberbullying is related to low self-esteem, suicidal thoughts, anger, frustration, and a variety of other emotional and psychological problems. Traditional bullying is still more common than cyberbullying, although the two are closely related: those who are bullied at school are bullied online and those who bully at school bully online. See also bully.

D

It's far easier to agree on what words should not be used than on what to replace them with.

Irving Zola

The music of difference, all alive.
The founders and this people,
who set in diversity
The base of our living.

Muriel Rukeyser

dairymaid/dairyman dairy worker/employee/milker/hand; dairy scientist. The nonparallel "maid/man" goes more than skin deep; while dairymaids were appearing in entry-level jobs in fairy tales, dairymen were becoming scientists.

dame/damsel these terms are outdated and inappropriate, and "dame" (except when capitalized and used for the official British title) is belittling. Alternatives include woman, person, adult; young woman, teenager, adolescent.

dancing girl dancer.

dandy because only men are dandies (and because not too many men like being called dandies), consider sex-neutral alternatives: fashion plate, fancy/sharp/conspicuous/fashionable dresser, clothes-conscious person.

danseur/danseuse a danseur is a principal (but not the principal) male dancer in a company, a soloist, and a danseuse is a principal (but not the principal) female soloist. Retain "danseur" and "danseuse" for their specific meaning within ballet companies, but to describe a woman or a man who dances ballet nonprofessionally, use ballet dancer. See also ballerina; premier danseur; prima ballerina.

daredevil important to use for females too so females know they *can* dare. For example, "Daredevil Marie" Marvingt (1875-1963) is virtually unknown today, but she was the most decorated woman in the world and known popularly as "the fiancée of danger." She was the third woman in the world to obtain a pilot's license, fought in World War I disguised as a man and earned a Croix de guerre for bombing a German airbase, was given the French Academy of Sports gold medal for excellence in *all* sports, dove out of a dirigible into a Venetian canal, crossed the North Sea in a balloon, invented the ambulance airplane, and is a member of the International Women's Sports Hall of Fame. Why has no one ever heard of her?

Darfur genocide use "genocide"; do not describe these massive slaughters and displacements as a "conflict" or "a war between..." The non-Arab indigenous population suffered 200,000 to 400,000 deaths, untold rapes, over 1,200 destroyed villages, deliberately poisoned wells, and 2,000,000 people forced into exile. Darfur is still in crisis today. This is not old news.

Darfuri/Darfuris person/persons from the Darfur (Realm of the Fur) region in western Sudan where the genocide of its indigenous, black, non-Arab citizens by the Sudanese government has claimed the lives of several hundred thousand Darfuri since 2003. "Darfuri" is also the adjective, as in "Darfuri survivors."

dark try to avoid using "dark" to express negatives. Use instead the word that comes closest to your actual meaning: sinister, dismal, dreary, bleak, grim, gloomy, depressed, dejected, cheerless, joyless, sad, doleful, sullen, glum, dour, moody, glowering, evil, wicked, villainous, base, vile, ominous, threatening, menacing. It's a small step, but it helps. See also black.

darkest Africa/the dark continent these phrases are Eurocentric, ethnocentric, and inaccurate (only 20 percent of the African continent is wooded savanna). See also Africa.

date inclusive term for someone of the same or opposite sex one makes arrangements to spend time with. For the person who has to pay for sex, use sex buyer. See also prostitute.

date rape see acquaintance rape.

daughter good sex-specific word for a female offspring. Inclusive alternatives: child, descendant, offspring.

daughter cell leave as is; this is a biology term with specific meanings.

daughter track this media catch phrase describes women whose careers may be threatened because of time spent caring for elderly relatives; 11 percent of caregivers with jobs (almost all of whom are women) quit or are fired from them. According to some figures, U.S. women spend an average of 18 years helping their parents. Those men and women involved in both raising children and caring for parents are referred to as the sandwich generation.

daycare "childcare" is often more accurate and inclusive when describing this need of families, since a parent may work at night. See also childcare.

deaconess deacon, except when specific denominations designate "deaconess" as the office for women; in some churches "deaconess" is the functional equal of "deacon." Although most translations of the Bible use "deaconess," the original Greek used the same word—"diakonos"—for both sexes. And these women had the game as well as the name: in the early church, both men and women functioned as deacons. Whenever possible, use the more authentic "deacon."

dead men tell no tales the dead tell no tales.

deaf/Deaf people born with a hearing loss, who can hear loud noises (like a jackhammer or an airplane) but cannot hear and/or understand speech function as and refer to themselves as "deaf." They rely on visual more than auditory cues to understand spoken messages—whether through speech reading, sign language, or some other visual method; they generally attend school with other people who are deaf; they probably use sign language; and they may be a part of Deaf culture. (This scenario differs for those who lose their hearing after living as a hearing person.) Use deaf only as an adjective ("deaf persons," not "the deaf," which characterizes a whole person by only one characteristic). According to the convention proposed by James Woodward in 1972, lowercase *deaf* refers to the audiological condition of not hearing; uppercase *Deaf* refers to a particular group of deaf people who share a culture and a language—American Sign Language (ASL), which is the native language of Deaf people in the U.S. Members of this group live in the U.S. and Canada, have inherited their sign language, use it as a primary means of communication among themselves, and share beliefs about themselves and about their connection to the larger society. Use "Deaf" for those who self-identify that way. Avoid terms like hearing-disabled/-impaired/-handicapped, auditorily handicapped, nonhearing. Because "hearing-impaired" can mean anything from hard of hearing to profoundly deaf, it is ambiguous and neither the profoundly deaf nor the hard of hearing think it means them. The International Federation of the Hard of Hearing, the World Federation of the Deaf, and other major organizations agree that "hearing-impaired" is no longer acceptable, and that "deaf" and "hard of hearing" are the terms of choice. Some Deaf individuals use "Deaf" to mean "a Deaf person" or "Deafie" as a term of affection; others dislike it. Expressions that use "deaf" metaphorically ("turned a deaf ear," "deaf to their request," "a dialogue of the deaf," "their story fell on deaf ears") associate negative personal qualities with deafness. Consider using instead: unmoved, unwilling to listen, unconcerned, indifferent, inattentive, heedless, unswerving, insensitive. See also disabilities, handicapped, "inside/outsider" rule, "people first" rule, "the."

deaf and dumb/deaf-mute/dumb these offensive terms are also usually incorrect; most deaf people have functioning vocal chords although they may choose not to use them (because of the difficulty of imitating sounds never heard) and they communicate fully and expressively by means of some form of sign language. Use deaf, someone who can't hear, someone who can't hear or speak, someone who can't speak.

dear/dearie already in 1687 playwright Aphra Behn was protesting, "Dear me no Dears, Sir." These terms are patronizing and inappropriate when used by a man or a woman to someone (most often a woman) who has not given permission to be so addressed. These terms especially do not belong in the workplace or in social interactions with strangers where the lower-power person must tolerate an unwanted and insincere intimacy. Over 20 years ago, the Ford Motor Company advised its dealers, "Never call a would-be buyer 'honey' or 'dear.'" (In service establishments where women are called "dear" or "honey," men are called "sir.")

Dear John letter, send a for a woman, use send a Dear Jane letter. If you mean in general to reject someone: jilt, brush someone off, show someone the door, swear off someone, send someone packing, break up with.

death penalty according to www.deathpenaltyinfo.org, there were 3,125 people housed in death rows around the U.S. in 2012. In general, the list of nations that retain the death penalty is dominated by repressive regimes (Iran, Pakistan, Iraq, Sudan, Afghanistan, for example); all European Union countries ban the death penalty. Studies analyzing race and the death penalty reveal that the odds of receiving a death sentence are nearly 40 percent higher if the defendant is black. The death penalty is racist, classist, ineffective, inhumane, and sometimes erroneously imposed. All that and we're birds-of-a-feathering it with repressive regimes? Donna Halvorsen (in the Minneapolis' *Star Tribune*) quotes anti-death penalty activist Sister Helen Prejean saying that executions are an unjust remedy that grows out of society's deepest wounds: racism, poverty, and a penchant for solving problems through violence. "To those who think it is a deterrent to crime, the wisecracking nun says in her Louisiana drawl: 'The people doin' the thinkin' and the people doin' the murderin' are two separate sets of people.'" And, in fact, studies have shown that the existence of the death penalty does *not* lower murder rates (John Donohue and Justin Wolfers, "The Death Penalty: No Evidence for Deterrence," *The Economists' Voice*). In addition, "there is no humane way to execute criminals... Only in the United States do we search for a humane death penalty; many other nations have ended immoral executions. So should we" (Rabbi Jerrold Goldstein, past president of California People of Faith Working Against the Death Penalty, in *Los Angeles Times*).

death tax when conservatives tried to repeal the estate tax, thus benefiting the wealthy far more than those without large estates, voters didn't care for the idea. The general feeling seemed to be, "Let those rich folks pay taxes. Fine by me!" So Fred Luntz, conservative wordsmith extraordinaire, came up with the term "death tax." Since everyone was going to die eventually, it seemed a good idea to get rid of the death tax. And they did. However, this term is not accurate. Death is not taxed, property is taxed. Death tax should only be used as an example of spinning and inaccuracy.

death with dignity see assisted suicide.

debonair because "debonair" seems limited to men (although it need not be—in *L'Allegro* Milton used it to describe a goddess), you may want alternatives: sophisticated, jaunty, lighthearted, vivacious, breezy, nonchalant, free and easy, merry, cheery, sunny, sporty; well-mannered, well-bred, polite, refined, civil, charming, suave, courteous, urbane, gracious, graceful, obliging, affable.

debutante debutant, except where "debutante" is still used for a young woman making her formal debut into society. See also "feminine" word endings.

Decalogue proper name for the Ten Commandments.

defect/defective people are not "defective" and they do not have "defects"; they have disabilities. See also birth defect, disabilities.

Defense Department it used to be the War Department. "The trouble with this country is the national passion for euphemisms" (E.S. Liddon, in her 1935 *The Riddle of the Florentine Folio*).

defenseman defense, defensive/defense player. Or use specific term: goalie, goalkeeper, goaltender, guard, linebacker. See also lineman (sports).

defense spending military spending.

deficit see tax-and-spend.

D

defoliate although originally and generally meaning to strip a tree or plant of leaves, this term grew a second life during the Vietnam War to describe using chemical (particularly napalm), incendiary, or even atomic weapons to destroy jungle growth, thus exposing supply lines and Viet Cong emplacements. William Safire (*Safire's Political Dictionary*) notes a slogan of the Air Force's flying defoliators: "Only you can prevent forests."

deformed/deformity people are not "deformed" and they do not have "deformities"; they are people with orthopedic or physical disabilities. See also disabilities.

degraded this term has a new career in the military: a number of articles and reports talk about degraded military preparedness, degraded military hardware, degraded military capabilities, degraded military readiness, degraded military medical system, degraded military sites, degraded military communication. Who knew our money could buy so little? "Degraded" has also been used in the U.S. military to describe people who have been bombed.

deist deists believe that reason and observation of the natural world indicate the existence of God, but they reject revelation, the notion of a personal relationship with this supreme power, and the idea of it involving itself in human affairs. Deism appears to have played a major role in creating the principle of religious freedom—both freedom to practice one's religion and freedom from being obliged to live according to another's religion. Framers of the Constitution who appear to have been deists include: Ethan Allen, Benjamin Franklin, Cornelius Harnett, Thomas Jefferson, James Madison, Gouverneur Morris, Thomas Paine, Hugh Williamson, and possibly Alexander Hamilton. See also atheist, secularist, separation of church and state.

delivery boy/delivery man deliverer, delivery driver/clerk, merchandise deliverer, porter, messenger, carrier, courier, runner; delivery truck/system.

dementia the *Publication Manual of the American Psychological Association*, 4th ed., says the term "dementia" is preferred to "senility"; "senile dementia of the Alzheimer's type" is an accepted term. See also senility.

demimondaine if you mean prostitute, use prostitute. If you mean someone on the fringes of society, use lowlife, riffraff, outcast, down-and-outer.

democracy Bill Moyers quoted President Woodrow Wilson explaining the rationale behind his reforms (progressive income taxation, the federal estate tax, tariff reform, the challenge to great monopolies and trusts): "The laws of this country do not prevent the strong from crushing the weak. Don't deceive yourselves for a moment as to the power of great interests which now dominate our development. There are men in this country big enough to own the government of the United States. They are going to own it if they can." Moyers added, "How we need that spirit today!" and cited a study by the American Political Science Association that found that "increasing inequalities threaten the American ideal of equal citizenship and that progress toward real democracy may have stalled in this country and even reversed." Thomas Jefferson, in his "Notes on the State of Virginia" (1781-1782), wrote, "An *elective despotism* was not the government we fought for..." (emphasis Jefferson's).

"Democrat party" Maura Reynolds (in the *Los Angeles Times*) explains that omitting the "-ic" is thought to be a partisan political slight and also code for "I'm one of you. I'm a right-wing conservative." Some say "it was adopted because it sounds annoying and echoes the word 'bureaucrat,' with its negative connotations." In the 1950s Senator Joseph McCarthy used it to deride Democrats during his HUAC hearings. "During the 1956 Republican convention, the usage was so common that it prompted the *New York Times* to report that dropping the '-ic' had become official party policy." Hendrik Hertzberg (in *The New Yorker*) says "Democrat" is a "deliberate misnaming," "a slur," and "a handy way to express contempt." It's the Democratic Party; put "Democrat" in quotes when used.

demolitions man demolitionist, demolitions expert.

demure if there are any demure men, nobody is saying so. Consider more sex-neutral alternatives: retiring, bashful, modest, diffident, reticent, taciturn.

denigrate this word means to blacken someone metaphorically (the root word is "nigr-" for black). If you don't like the sound of it, consider: disparage, defame, belittle, run down, revile, vilify, criticize, speak ill of, put down, do a hatchet job on, badmouth.

den mother should you need a sex-neutral alternative: den/group leader.

dentist man or woman. Women are not particularly new to the profession: the School of Dentistry of Paris, founded in 1884, accepted students of both sexes from the beginning and according to a guide written by Mademoiselle A. Paquet-Miller in 1891, many women practiced the profession (Eleanor S. Riemer and John C. Fout, eds., *European Women*). And while we're on the subject, a poll conducted by the Chicago Dental Society (in Minneapolis' *Star Tribune*) found that 76 percent of dentists think the phrase "about as funny as a root canal" is "inaccurate and perpetuates the myth that root canals are painful"; 55 percent think the phrase "like pulling teeth" is "inaccurate and perpetuates the concept that dentistry is painful"; and 88 percent think that children are afraid of them only because other people tip them off. Dentists in general "strongly believe" that the media are to blame for the concept that dentistry is painful.

deregulation see regulation/deregulation/voluntary regulation.

destabilize overthrow. Sometimes "destabilize" means what you think it means. However, in a political or military reference to a regime, avoid the euphemism in favor of the clearer term, "overthrow."

detainee a special category of captured enemy combatants, detainees are neither prisoners of war nor suspects in criminal cases. The Geneva Conventions protect "prisoners of war" but say nothing about "detainees," and suspects in criminal cases go to trial. By using the term "detainee," the U.S. government has been able to keep detainees from being tried and has excluded them from the protections of the Geneva Conventions. Many detainees captured after 9/11 were either transferred to the Guantánamo Bay detainment camp, where they are still held, or underwent "extraordinary rendition" (being flown to countries where torture is allowed). A Canadian engineer seized by U.S. officials when he changed planes in New York on his way home from a vacation was flown to Syria, where he was tortured for 10 months. A major obstacle to the trials of the detainees, or enemy combatants, held in Guantánamo Bay was removed when a special U.S. military court ruled in late 2007 that they were actually "unlawful" enemy combatants. The very same individuals may be enemy combatants, detainees, prisoners of war, criminals, or unlawful enemy combatants—and their fate depends on what they are called. (Until they know what they are charged with and can defend themselves in court, their guilt or innocence is unknown.) Before using the information-poor "detainee," ascertain the exact status of the individual, and use that. See also black site, enhanced interrogation, extraordinary rendition, Military Commissions Act, preventive detention, relocation, "state secrets" defense, torture.

deus ex machina this Latin phrase, "god from a machine" (because sometimes in Greek and Roman plays a god arrived onstage by means of a crane to produce a "providential" ending), is appropriate for either sex. However, since *deus* is in the masculine gender and since it is used most often in masculine contexts, you may want an alternative: last-minute rescuer, eleventh-hour deliverer; contrived solution.

developing nation/country see Third World.

developmental disability although you can use the adjective "developmentally disabled" if space requires it, it is preferable to use "person/child with a developmental disability." See also disabilities, "people first" rule.

deviant unacceptable when used to describe human beings or their behavior. Although behavior may deviate from some statistical norm for human activity, it's an oddity of our perspective that we pick and choose whom to label: we do not routinely refer to murderers or terrorists as deviants, but so label lesbians, gay men, bisexuals, and others. Once labeled deviants, individuals become stigmatized, censured, and penalized. See also dysfunctional.

devil/he devil/it. Our idea of the devil is so male that we use a prefix ("she-devil") when we want to convey anything else. Nothing but human imagination accounts for the maleness of the devil; the same is true of the maleness of God. One could say, "Win some, lose some," but both misattributions of maleness have been harmful to society, to women, and to men. Who knows, maybe men would feel more threatened—and women less so—by a devil depicted as female.

devotee woman or man. Unlike similar words borrowed from French—divorcé/divorcée, fiancé/fiancée, habitué, protegé/protegée—this one is used in the feminine form and without its accent for both sexes. Some have suggested using "-ee" for all such words, as is done with "employee."

diamonds, blood/war see conflict diamonds.

diamonds are a girl's best friend at least consider the source of this inane and demeaning expression: a 1930s DeBeers diamonds ad campaign.

dick this slang term has can mean: (1) detective (if you want alternatives use gumshoe, private eye, tail, shadow, flatfoot); (2) penis (leave as is); (3) offensive person. Dick Hannasch adds that "Dick is also a nice name."

differently abled see disabilities.

digital divide an estimated 100 million Americans have no way of accessing the Internet at home. The Internet has become an essential platform for job-hunting and education (even health care is increasingly moving online), leaving those 100 million Americans on the wrong side of the digital divide without the basic tools to secure economic advancement and stability. Forty percent of households with annual incomes below $20,000 have broadband access at home, while 93 percent of households with incomes exceeding $75,000 have high-speed Internet, according to a 2010 Federal Communications Commission (FCC) survey. The FCC is working to bring discounted broadband service, affordable computers, and training to low-income families in order to close the digital divide. See also education, unemployed.

dike see dyke.

dingbat kook, nitwit. Thanks primarily to Archie Bunker, this technically inclusive word seems reserved for women.

directress director. In 2012, only 12 percent of the 250 top-grossing films had female directors. "The Hollywood boys' club needs to start admitting women" (Women's Media Center). See also "feminine" word endings, glass ceiling.

dirty old man ageist as well as sexist. This stereotype conveys very little real information. Describe instead what the person is doing, thinking, or saying. See also lech/lecher, satyr, pederast, pedophile, womanizer, sex addict.

disabilities when writing about disabilities: (1) Mention a disability only when it bears directly on your material. (2) Do not define anyone solely in terms of a disability. Speak of the person first, then the disability (instead of "an arthritic," "an epileptic," or "a hemophiliac," use "someone with arthritis," "…epilepsy," "…hemophilia"). Instead of "is diabetic, autistic," use "with/has diabetes, autism." In the same way, people are not their missing part or their surgical procedure. Instead of "amputee" or "ostomate," use "someone who had an amputation or ostomy." (3) An illness is a disease; a disability is a condition. Cerebral palsy, epilepsy, and arthritis, for example, are not diseases; they are conditions. (4) Emphasize abilities, not limitations (instead of "uses crutches/braces," say "walks with crutches/braces"), but not to the point of euphemism, of excessive or patronizing praise, or of portraying some people with disabilities as especially courageous or superhuman as though all people with disabilities should achieve at this level. (5) Do not use adjectives as nouns, as in "the disabled," "the blind," "the deaf." (6) Delete such terms as abnormal; atypical; birth defect (replace with congenital disability, someone born with…); burden/drain; crippled; defect/defective; deficient; deformed/deformity (orthopedic/physical disability); fit (seizure); gimp; harelip (cleft palate); invalid; lame; learning disabled (someone with/who has a learning disability); maimed; normal; patient (use only for someone in a hospital or under a doctor's immediate care); physical handicap (physical disability); plight; poor; spastic/spaz (someone who has cerebral palsy); stricken with (incurred); stutterer (person with speech impediment); unfit; unfortunate; withered. (7) The adjective is "disability" not "disabled" in such terms as the disability movement, the disability rights movement, disability activists, disability advocates, disability community. (8) Disability is not a fate worse than death; avoid sensationalized words and phrases. Use emotionally neutral descriptions and avoid phrases that conjure up tragedy: suffers from, afflicted with, stricken with, bound, confined, sentenced to, prisoner, victim of, poor, unfortunate. People with disabilities are not a "drain" or a "burden" on family and friends, although they may represent "added/additional responsibilities." (9) Metaphors featuring disabilities ("deaf to our wishes," "blind to the truth") may be inappropriate or unintentionally offensive. (10) In the effort to find language to describe a reality that often had no positive descriptors, some terms have surfaced that tend to be trendy and euphemistic and are better avoided: differently abled, exceptional, handicapable, inconvenienced, mentally different, people with differing abilities, physically challenged. "Granted, some people with disabilities use the phrases.... But those of us who are active in the disability rights movement generally reject these terms as an insulting denial of our life experience, and of our hard-won community identity" (Laura Hershey, *RESIST Newsletter*). (11) When writing or speaking about people with disabilities avoid portraying them as "other": "I felt permanently exiled from 'normality.' Whether imposed by self or society, this outsider status—and not the disability itself—constitutes the most daunting barrier for most people with physical impairments, because it, even more than flights of steps or elevators without braille, prevents them from participating fully in the ordinary world, where most of life's satisfactions dwell" (Nancy Mairs, *Waist-High in the World*). See also able-bodied, accessible, adjectives used as nouns, afflicted with, amputee, bedridden, blind, cerebral palsied, challenged, confined, cripple, deaf/Deaf, deaf and dumb/deaf-mute/dumb, defect/defective, developmental disability, epileptic, exceptional, handicappism, handicapped, health appliance, idiot/idiocy, impaired, insane/insanity, learning disability, leper/leprosy, lip reading, mongolism/mongoloid, paraplegic, "people first" rule, "physically challenged," quadriplegic, retard/retarded, schizophrenic, spastic, special, suffers from, "the," victim, wheelchair-bound.

disadvantaged see "culturally deprived/disadvantaged."

"discovery" of America only by a strange twist of white ethnocentrism can one be considered to "discover" a continent inhabited by nearly 75 million people and with a settlement that once was as big as London at the time (Cahokia, near what is now St. Louis). "'Discovery' terminology demeans and trivializes Third World and indigenous peoples" (Sanford Berman). Writer Oscar Wilde said, "It is a vulgar error to suppose that America was ever discovered. It was merely detected." (Imagine that first-time travelers to France, thrilled with the snails, the Eiffel Tower, accordions, and haute couture, returned home full of their "discovery," raised money, soldiers, and settlers, and returned to plant their flag on the Ile de la Cité.) The 40-year period following Columbus's arrival in the western hemisphere saw one of the greatest losses of human life in history. The "discoverers" had little interest in or respect for nature and human beings, but a high interest in and respect for gold and wealth—attitudes still seen today. Write, speak, and teach about U.S. origins from multiple perspectives. Instead of discovery, use terms like arrival, colonization. See also savage.

discrimination discrimination exists when people's choices of and access to employment, education, housing, resources, and other public goods are limited by or dealt with differently because of their sex, ethnicity, age, religion, disability, sexual orientation, looks, or other class or category.

disinformation propaganda, usually containing incorrect statements, exaggerated claims, or lies.

displaced homemaker this sex-specific term (a woman whose principal job has been homemaking and who has lost her main source of income because of divorce, separation, widowhood, spousal disability, or loss of eligibility for public assistance) has no companion term for a man, although federal legislation dictates that financial assistance be available to men as well as to women. In 1976, lawmakers amended the Vocational Education Act to create programs to train displaced homemakers. Enrollment in these programs has fluctuated from 100,000 in 1985 to a low of less than 2,700 in 2003, but with 50,000 individuals enrolled in 2010-2011 it's clear that the issue of displaced homemakers in need of marketable skills and jobs is once again relevant. See also alimony, child custody, divorce, wage earner, working wife, working mother.

dissemination although this word (meaning "scattering seed") is related to "semen" ("seed"), it is not associated in ways that make it sexist; nor is it functionally sexist—anyone may disseminate information. Many words (for example, "family" and "familiar," "guard" and "garden") derive from a common root but still have independent lives. See also seminal, seminar.

distaff side the female line or maternal branch of a family tree is called the "distaff side" because spinning (the distaff was used in spinning) was considered women's work. The male line or paternal branch is called the "spear side" (a term that doesn't appear in most dictionaries) because fighting was considered men's work. You could also use female/male line, maternal/paternal branch/line of descent.

ditz/ditzy these terms seem used primarily of women, so you may want more inclusive-appearing alternatives: out to lunch, space ranger, flake, out of it, on another planet, with one's head in the clouds, not all there, missing some marbles, with a mind like a sieve, mindless, brainless wonder, dense, muddleheaded, not bright, half-witted, dull-witted, dim-witted, thick-headed, thick-witted, inane.

diva Beth Bernstein and Matilda St. John (in *Bitch*) say that the "very term 'diva' is used both as an acknowledgement of a woman's success ... and as disapproval of a woman's perceived overentitlement." Use with care.

diversity at its simplest, "diversity" means "variety": the makeup of the workforce, the student body, the organization would ideally reflect the diversity of the U.S. population. "When we talk about diversity now we are talking about race and gender and ethnicity. There was a time when geography was so important that the Constitution wouldn't allow a president and vice president from the same state. Diversity was a collection of white males from different places on the map. ... Critics say that the claims of diversity are splintering America, dividing and subdividing us into our warring parts. Yet Americans have become less—not more—conscious of region, religion, nationality. It can happen with race and gender as well" (Ellen Goodman, in *Boston Globe*). Business leader Lawrence Perlman says, "Diversity is so important to companies not because it is the right thing to do, although it is, but because it is critical to competitiveness."

divorce avoid phrases like "he divorced her" or "she divorced him" unless you know this was the case and it is important to say so. Use instead they filed for divorce, they divorced. Divorce in the United States is often sexist and racist. When it first appeared, no-fault divorce was hailed as a quick and equitable solution to an unsalvageable marriage. However, according to Fred Moody (in *Seattle Weekly*), "Instead of reducing inequality between the sexes, no-fault divorce has widened the gap in status between men and women, and is the leading cause of the well-documented feminization of poverty in America." Lenore Weitzman (*The Divorce Revolution*) agrees: "No fault was taken to mean no responsibility," resulting in "a systematic impoverishment of women and children." 75 percent of children with divorced parents live with their mother. 28 percent of children with a divorced parent live in a household with an income below the poverty line. See also child custody, courts (judicial), noncustodial parent.

divorcé/divorcée divorced person, divorcé. Or nothing at all (a person's marital status is seldom relevant, and descriptors like "unmarried," "unwed," and "formerly married" point to a faulty marriage-as-norm standard). It has usually been the woman who is called a divorcée (often with pejorative overtones), while a man is referred to as unmarried, a bachelor, or as someone who is divorced. Use parallel terms for both sexes. Casey Miller and Kate Swift (*The Handbook of Nonsexist Writing*) persuasively recommend the standard form of French words, that is, "divorcé" for both sexes. Note that "émigré" is used that way in English. This guideline can also be applied to such words as blond, brunet, chaperon, confidant, clairvoyant, debutant, fiancé, habitué, and protégé.

divorced father/divorced mother father/mother, single parent.

dizzy with the notable exceptions of Dizzy Gillespie and Dizzy Dean, this is used only of women (especially of women with blond hair). For inclusive alternatives, see ditz/ditzy, scatterbrained.

docent woman or man.

dogcatcher animal control officer. "Dogcatcher" is considered outdated and derogatory; it also seems to suggest a man, whereas at least as many women as men work as animal control officers.

doll/China doll/Kewpie doll/dolled up/all dolled up these terms are patronizing, belittling, inaccurate, and objectifying. The terms "dolled up/all dolled up" are generally reserved for women, but can be, and have been, used of men. As long as we have Ken, men can be dolls too, although it is not perceived as quite so patronizing to call them "dolls." See also living doll.

"do-me feminism" a derisory term originally coined by *Esquire* in 1994 in response to the supposed emergence of photogenic, unabashedly sexual feminists, sexually suggestive female musicians, and professional sex educators. Note, however, that some women self-describe as do-me feminists. See also feminisms.

domestic not sexist per se, "domestic" is sometimes used to further a sexist context—for example, the assumption that all domestic matters belong a priori to the nearest woman and are of no interest to any men.

domestic violence/domestic abuse although these terms seem firmly seated in the language, one could wish for more accurate ones. "Domestic," with its connotations of coziness and warmth, dilutes the violence and abuse; "It makes the violence sound domesticated, and it makes it sound like a special category of violence that is somehow different from other kinds—less serious" (Ann Jones, in *Ms.*). "Family violence" or "violence in the family" are variants. Both conceal the sexes of the perpetrator and the victim and the kinds of acts involved. Whenever possible, identify who is doing violence to whom, and what specifically, on the continuum of violent acts, they are doing. "It is a pattern of behavior that is used to gain or maintain power and control over an intimate partner. Domestic violence can happen to anyone of any race, age, sexual orientation, religion, or gender. Abuse includes physical, sexual, emotional, or psychological actions, or threats of action to influence another person. This includes any behavior that frightens, intimidates, manipulates, hurts, humiliates, blames, injures, or wounds someone" (Larcenia Taylor, in *The Bakersfield Californian*). Battering is the single most common cause of injury to women, exceeding rapes, muggings, and even auto accidents, and men commit 92 percent of all assaults on spouses. The National Domestic Violence Hotline receives 22,000 calls per month (which means many more go uncounted) and reports that as many as 324,000 women experience domestic violence during their pregnancy. For women in abusive relationships, abuse can often begin or escalate during pregnancy when the controlling partner feels deprived of sole attention. Some 1.3 million American women are sexually assaulted by a partner during an average 12-month period, resulting in the loss of nearly 8 million days of paid work. To clarify this issue, use the familiar "domestic violence" once or twice in your material, and elsewhere use "wife battering"—(or "husband battering," if that is the case) and specific descriptions of the violence. Avoid "spousal abuse" because it omits the sex of the abuser and victim. See also rape, "She asked for it," violence. Given the normalization of all violence by its presence in the family—and the growth of public violence from private violence—Gloria Steinem has suggested "original violence" as a future alternate term.

domestic partner this is a useful and recognized term for someone of either sex in a committed relationship with someone of the same or opposite sex. Pioneered in San Francisco in 1991, domestic partnership plans (officially recognized in 20 states) allow lesbians and gay men to register their relationships officially and extends to them some limited protections; some domestic partnerships allow city or corporate employees to be treated as married in terms of health and other benefits. When American Express announced it was offering domestic partner benefits to employees, the stated reason was to "help us attract and retain outstanding people." Chair Harvey Golub said that although committed same-sex relationships affected probably only 1 percent of the corporation, domestic partner benefits were an important symbolic and equity issue. Unfortunately, official domestic partnerships still fall far short of the rights granted to couples when they marry. See also boyfriend, girlfriend, marriage.

dominatrix dominator, dominating partner. See also "feminine" word endings.

dominionism the main idea of dominionism seems to be "that Christians alone are Biblically mandated to occupy all secular institutions until Christ returns" (Sara Diamond, *Spiritual Warfare: The Politics of the Christian Right*). Originating in God's injunction in Genesis to "Be fruitful, and multiply, and replenish the earth, and subdue it: and have dominion over the fish of the sea, and over the fowl of the air, and over every living thing that moveth upon the earth," dominionism encompasses some conservative politically active Christians' seeking to influence secular civil government through political action, with the goal of establishing either a nation governed by Christians or a nation ruled by a Christian understanding of biblical law. There is much disagreement about whether "dominion" should have been translated "control and own" or "be a good steward of" the earth. Ann Coulter (quoted in *Washington Monthly*) seems to know: "God gave us the earth. We have dominion over the plants, the animals, the trees. God said, 'Earth is yours. Take it. Rape it. It's yours.'" This has obvious implications for the environment, as does "The Rapture" and other beliefs that the end or Judgment Day is approaching anyway.

don to mean a Spanish gentleman, grandee, or Mafia leader, "don" always refers to a man. Retain "don" as it is used at a college of Oxford or Cambridge, although you can sometimes replace it with head, tutor, fellow. For its (rare) use in the U.S., its meaning is simply college/university professor.

Don Juan this term has no parallel for a woman and reinforces some stereotypes about men from Spanish-speaking countries, but has no precise ethnic-free equivalent. For a sex-neutral term, try lover, dashing lover, great romantic, paramour, heartthrob, flirt, sexually aggressive/sexually active person, seducer, bedhopper, swinger.

donor offspring persons conceived via the donation of sperm or ova, or both, either from two unrelated donors or from a couple. You may also see more clinical/technical terms: donor-conceived persons; assisted reproductive technology offspring; children of egg donors/gamete donors/sperm donors; donor egg/sperm offspring; sperm donor offspring. See also assisted reproduction.

don't ask, don't tell when President Clinton failed to get legislation through Congress to end the U.S. military's ban on gay personnel, a compromise was adopted: the "Don't Ask, Don't Tell" policy prohibited gay, lesbian, and bisexual soldiers from disclosing their sexual orientation. As long as they kept quiet, commanders were prohibited from investigating their sexuality. This was the official policy from 1993 through 2010 when Congress voted to end "Don't Ask, Don't Tell." Signing the bill repealing the ban on openly gay service personnel, President Obama said: "For we are not a nation that says, don't ask, don't tell. We are a nation that says, out of many, we are one."

doorman doorkeeper, porter, concierge, security guard, guard, caretaker, attendant, door attendant, doorkeep, gatekeeper; in some cases, bouncer.

double consciousness also called "two-ness," "double consciousness" was W.E.B. Du Bois's observation that African Americans had "a sense of always looking at one's self through the eyes of others, of measuring one's soul by the tape of a world that looks on in amused contempt and pity. One ever feels his two-ness—an American, a Negro; two souls; two thoughts, two unreconciled strivings; two warring ideals in one dark body, whose dogged strength alone keeps it from being torn asunder." Double consciousness means that blacks in our society are constantly aware of both themselves and of the way others react to them. In *Shifting: The Double Lives of Black Women in America*, Charisse Jones and Kumea Shorter-Gooden interview women who must shift between identities because of racism and sexism, a related application of Du Bois's double consciousness that sometimes becomes triple consciousness.

doublespeak language deliberately constructed to disguise or distort its actual meaning, doublespeak is most often associated with governmental, military, religious, and corporate institutions and their deliberate use of euphemism, ambiguity, distortion, misdirection, and outright untruths to disguise unpleasantness or to sell something to the citizenry that would be unacceptable in its naked form. For example, firing of employees may be "downsizing," and "outsourcing" may mean the avoidance of unions or benefits. "Vocabulary propaganda is much more subtle and effective than content propaganda.... Content propaganda misinforms about issues, but vocabulary propaganda interferes with the ability to think or talk about issues in a way that can lead to understanding" (Richard K. Moore, "Doublespeak and the New World Order," *New Dawn*). Moore says words like "market" and "competitive" have been promoted to Unquestioned Axioms of the Universe. The National Council of Teachers of English gives annual doublespeak awards. They honored George W. Bush as he "made clear the principle of democratic discussion: 'As you know, these are open forums, you're able to come and listen to what I have to say.'" See also military language, political language.

doubting Thomas there's nothing wrong with this phrase, but be aware of how many such expressions are male-based. Balance their use with female-based expressions, creative expressions of your own, or sex-neutral alternatives: skeptic, doubter, unbeliever, disbeliever, nonbeliever, cynic, questioner, pessimist, defeatist. See also sex-linked expressions.

doughboy use as is in historical context. Or World War I soldier.

Dover factor to prevent the public from seeing tragic pictures of flag-draped coffins being unloaded at Dover Air Force Base in Delaware, the Pentagon banned news coverage of the arrival of our dead. Their stated rationale is that they are protecting the dead soldiers' privacy and dignity.

dowager there is no parallel for a man. One definition of "dowager" reflects on a woman's marital status (widowed); another reflects mainly on her age. Decide if this information is relevant and then use descriptive terms that apply to both men and women.

Down Low for many ethnic and racial minorities, "gay" signifies "white." "Down low" or "downe" is a kind of oblique queer for African Americans, Asian Americans, and other groups. One can ask, "Are you downe?" and those who get it, get it, like a modern-day "friend of Dorothy" but this time with their own social networking website, DowneLink.com. The somewhat controversial term includes the phenomenon of MSMs (men who have sex with men) who publicly identify as heterosexuals and maintain sexual relationships with women. The Down Low has become synonymous with sensationalized claims that MSMs are spreading HIV into "the general population." Avoid implying that the Down Low phenomenon is exclusive to communities of color and use only for men who self-identify that way.

downsizing a euphemistic term for firing or laying off employees. When you can, put the word in quotation marks and use bald language involving the word "fired." A small rant at answers.com says, "The attempt to find even more positive-sounding ways to say 'downsize' has led business executives and people working in human resources and public relations (both euphemisms themselves) to float a number of alternatives. Companies were being 'reengineered' and even 'right-sized'; laid-off workers had to be 'separated' or 'unassigned' for being 'nonessential'; their jobs were said to be 'no longer going forward.' Most of these terms were met with scorn, being regarded as cynical attempts to sugarcoat an inherently distressing phenomenon." See also doublespeak.

Down syndrome correct form (Down's syndrome is incorrect) for the genetic, chromosomal disorder reported in 1866 by Dr. J. Langdon Down.

down under this term referring to Australia or New Zealand is a good example of perspective; it's only "down under" if you're standing in the northern hemisphere. Generally avoid it.

dowry deaths every 60 minutes in India, a woman is beaten to death, burned alive, electrocuted, poisoned, pushed out a window, or otherwise killed over dowry issues (*The Times of India*). Over 8,000 dowry deaths were reported in 2012. Experts think the true figure may be much higher because many dowry deaths (also known as bride burnings) are not reported or are disguised as accidents or suicide. Demanding dowry has been illegal in India since 1961. However, the law is rarely enforced and seldom is anyone punished for the deaths that result from a husband or his family's desire for yet another bride and more dowry. From 1995 to 2005, dowry deaths jumped 46 percent, apparently from a new acquisitiveness in a rising consumer culture. See also honor killings, suttee.

doyenne doyen. The contrived feminine form doesn't exist in French. To avoid the preciousness of a foreign word that must have seemed unbearably masculine to whoever made up "doyenne," use dean, senior/oldest member.

draft "no form of sex discrimination, against either gender, has been as devastating and deadly as the military draft" (Mel Feit, in *University of Dayton Review*). Although we no longer technically have a draft, men are still obliged to register for military service as soon as they turn 18, whereas women have no obligation to do so. In fairness, either all our children should register for military service and go to war, or none of them should. In addition to being sexist, military service is egregiously classist. Until those who make war are the same people who go to war, there will be no justice—and no peace. "All the war-propaganda, all the screaming and lies and hatred, comes invariably from people who are not fighting" (George Orwell). To find soldiers for unpopular wars, recruiters have greatly lowered enlistment requirements and offered additional inducements. They've also been thinking outside the box: the so-called backdoor draft consists of "various indirect methods of forcing people to serve in the military, especially by extending the terms of people already in service" (*Copy Editor*). With the "drug draft," young people with drug convictions, who often lose their college financial aid, are urged to see their nearest recruiter; Uncle Sam will be happy to have them. Recruiters' most frequent targets, however, are disproportionately young people with the most limited economic and educational opportunities. According to the Northeastern Anarchist, "Recruiters are relentlessly using marketing strategies to woo low-income youths with little prospects for education and good jobs into the armed forces. Painting the Army as a kind of job training and vocational school, and simultaneously as a financial aid institution, recruiters get youths in high school to sign up for the DEP (Deferred Enlistment Program)." If anyone tries to back out, recruiters often erroneously tell them it is impossible or illegal. See also conscientious objector.

draftsman drafter, artist, copyist, landscape/technical artist, designer, architect, engineer, limner, drawer, sketcher. If none of these terms works in your context and you cannot circumlocute, use draftswoman/ draftsman; avoid the cumbersome "draftsperson."

draftsmanship drafting expertise/skill.

dragoman nonsexist; comes from an Arabic word for "interpreter" and the plural is either dragomans or dragomen. If the word's sexist appearance bothers you, use interpreter, translator, travel agent, guide.

drag queen/drag king usually referring to a gay man who enjoys dressing or behaving like a woman, "drag queen" is unacceptable when used by those outside the gay community, generally acceptable when used within. Drag kings are "mostly female-bodied or female-identified performance artists who dress in masculine drag and personify male gender stereotypes as part of their performance" (Jen Aronoff, in *The University of South Carolina Daily Gamecock*). See also "insider/outsider" rule, queen.

Dream Act, the an acronym for the Development, Relief, and Education of Alien Minors Act, this legislation, if enacted, would give undocumented immigrants who entered the U.S. as children access to higher education and a pathway to citizenship. The Dream Act is not, as its opponents claim, "amnesty" for illegal immigrants. It applies only to those young people who were brought to the U.S. by their parents when they were sixteen or younger, who lived continuously in the U.S. for at least five years, who have graduated high school or obtained a G.E.D, and who have demonstrated good character. Those that meet the requirements of the Dream Act would be allowed to serve in the military, pursue higher education, and become eligible for six-year conditional status. Additional requirements would need to be met in order for individuals to achieve full legal status. According to the Immigration Policy Center, there are roughly 1.8 million DREAMers, people whose lives would be improved by passage of the Dream Act. See also illegals/ illegal immigrants, immigrant.

dressmaker tailor, custom tailor, clothier, garment designer/worker, mender, alterer, alterations expert, stitcher. See also couturière, needlewoman.

drillmaster drill sergeant/instructor.

droit de seigneur a highly sexist concept that is no longer part of our vocabulary in the same way it used to be, when it described a lord's "right" to rape a woman being wed. However, the term may be useful (in quotation marks) to describe what happens in certain cases of sexual harassment of women where there is unequal power: professors and students, bosses and staff, political candidates and campaign workers. There is no parallel term for the absolute power of a woman over a subordinate man (possibly because this has been rare, to put it mildly).

drones unmanned aircraft, known in the military as UAVs (unmanned aerial vehicles), are either controlled by pilots on the ground or pre-programmed to fly a particular mission autonomously. The military deploys drones for reconnaissance and surveillance, as well as missile and bomb attacks. The argument for use of drones is that they deliver precision strikes, eliminating the need for more intrusive military action, thus sparing troops and civilians on the ground. However, civilian deaths still occur. In Afghanistan in 2013, drone attacks accounted for 45 civilian fatalities and 14 non-fatal civilian injuries, a three-fold increase from the previous year, according to a report by the United Nations Human Rights Council. U.S. drones have been used far from the battlefield in targeted killings of suspected terrorists in Pakistan, Yemen, and Somalia. The American Civil Liberties Union has filed a lawsuit demanding that the government disclose basic information about its drone program. In response, the Central Intelligence Agency has refused to even confirm or deny that it has a drone program. Non-military use of drones includes monitoring agriculture and wildlife, tracking storms, and assisting in search and rescue missions. Although commercial use of drones is on the horizon with companies like Amazon and DHL testing drone delivery, only government agencies, some public universities, and a handful of private companies currently have Federal Aviation Administration (FAA) permits to fly private drones. But the FAA is planning to increase the number of permits and expects that 7,500 drones will be in the air by 2020, most of which will be small machines resembling model airplanes. See also terrorist, war on terror.

drug czar ironically this term covers both sides of the street, legal and illegal. Its longtime meaning is drug dealer/chief/boss/tycoon/bigwig/distributor. But it's also used by the press as an informal title for the individual charged with "the war on drugs." A czar was always male, so the term is sex-linked. However, when a woman is appointed to the ad hoc "drug czar" position, she too could be a czar, unless people get cute and call her a czarina, which they probably will. Sigh.

drum majorette drum major, baton twirler. See also "feminine" word endings.

dualistic thinking See binary thinking.

duchess retain for official title, which can refer either to the ruler of a duchy or to the wife or widow of a duke.

dude a dude can be either sex. The casual term, either as a form of address or to refer to a male friend or an especially attractive man, is usually nonpejorative. Dude is often used by men and women to address both men and women.

duenna this is always a woman. If you need a sex-neutral term, use chaperon.

dukedom duchy.

dumb see deaf and dumb/deaf-mute/dumb.

dumb blond we're pretty tired of this by now. See also blonde.

dustman cleaner, sweeper, sweep; garbage collector/hauler, trash/refuse collector, sanitation worker.

Dutch the many disparaging phrases that include the word "Dutch" grew out of the bitter trade and marine rivalry that once existed between Great Britain and Holland. Although most of the more than 70 slurs listed in A.A. Roback's 1944 *A Dictionary of International Slurs* are rarely used anymore, a few are still seen: "in Dutch" (in disgrace); "double Dutch" (nonsense; but retain as name of rope skipping game); "Dutch cheer" (liquor); "Dutching" (according to the *Oxford Dictionary of New Words*, this is jargon in the British food industry for sending substandard food intended for the U.K. market for irradiation in the Netherlands—or other European country that permits irradiation—to mask any bacterial contamination before putting it on sale in British shops.). See also Dutch courage; Dutchman; Dutch treat; Dutch uncle, talk to like a.

Dutch courage this term has probably not caused many people to think less of the Dutch. However, it is pejorative, and if you want to get around it, use sham courage, courage from a bottle.

Dutchman Hollander, Dutch citizen, Dutchwoman and Dutchman. Plural: Hollanders, Dutch people, Dutchfolk, Dutchwomen and Dutchmen (but not "Dutchmen and women").

Dutch treat this term (or "go Dutch") has probably not caused many people to think less of the Dutch or to consider them cheapskates. However, it is pejorative, and if you want to get around it, use separate checks, I insist on paying for myself.

Dutch uncle, talk to like a talk to bluntly, rebuke, upbraid, admonish, chide, reprove, reprimand, reproach, scold, chew out, lecture, lay down the law, remonstrate, call on the carpet.

dwarf although this term is still used in medical contexts for individuals whose full adult height is 4'10" or less due to a medical condition, it should be replaced with (when known) precise terminology, for example, someone who has/person with achondroplasia. (There are more than 100 different types of dwarfism.) Rarely does anyone self-identify as a "dwarf." Preferred alternatives include Little Person/little person, short-statured person, person of short stature. See also midget, short.

dyke (woman) this term, of obscure origins, is unacceptable to some lesbians, but is claimed by others; it is always unacceptable when used by outsiders. Writer Denise Ohio says that dyke is "a word being reclaimed by the people it's normally used to denigrate. It was a total insult before; now it's showing power, solidarity." When reporting the word "dyke" used in hate speech, GLAAD says it's better if reporters say, "The person used a derogatory word for a lesbian" so that such words are not given visibility in the media. See also bull dyke, butch, femme/fem, gay rights, homophobia, homosexual, "insider/outsider" rule.

Dykes on Bikes formed in 1976, Dykes on Bikes has been the leadoff contingent in the San Francisco pride parade every year since. When the group tried to trademark their name (to protect it from being traded on for profit), the U.S. Patent Office fought them for years; the government felt "dyke" was way too disparaging toward lesbians, even when used by lesbians for themselves. Our government at work. They won't let women marry each other or guarantee equal rights, but they don't mind protecting us from ourselves.

dysfunctional "the notion that being gay, lesbian, or bisexual is a psychological disorder was discredited by the American Psychological Association and the American Psychiatric Association in the 1970s. Today words such as 'dysfunctional' are often used to portray lesbians and gay men as less than human, mentally ill, or as a danger to society. If they must be used, they should be quoted directly in a way that reveals the bias of the person quoted" (Gay & Lesbian Alliance Against Defamation (GLADD).

Exclusion is always dangerous. Inclusion is the only safety if we are to have a peaceful world.

Pearl S. Buck

earth mother there is no parallel term for a man, and no inclusive term conveys quite the same idea of the wholesome, down-to-earth, back-to-nature woman. Despite the generally negative association of women with nature, this term seems positive and descriptive enough to retain. See also Mother Earth, Mother Nature, nature/she.

East Indian when referring to the people of India, this Eurocentric term is considered colonialist; they are properly called Indians. To contrast with American Indians, use "Asian Indian." In the U.S., those from India or of Asian Indian descent are known as Asian Indian Americans. (The peoples of Burma, Bangladesh, Pakistan, and Sri Lanka are not Indians.) See also Asian American, West Indian.

Ebonics see black English.

ecofeminism coined by French writer Françoise d'Eaubonne in 1974, the term represents the synthesis of feminist and ecological concerns. According to Lindsy Van Gelder (in *Ms.*), "Ecofeminists believe that the domination of women and of nature comes from the same impulse. ... In an ecofeminist society, no one would have power over anyone else, because there would be an understanding that we're all part of the interconnected web of life." Paula DiPerna (in *Sisterhood Is Forever*) says, "To the extent that the earth has been defined as 'feminine' ('Mother Nature'), it has been as subjugated as women themselves, a premise at the heart of ecofeminism." "Some call it a philosophy, others find in it a spirituality, and most believe that it calls them to political action" (Greta Gaard, *Ecofeminism*). See also Mother Earth, Mother Nature, nature/she.

economic adjustment the government likes this term, as in the Office of Economic Adjustment (OEA): "the Department of Defense's primary source for assisting communities that are adversely impacted by Defense program changes, including base closures or realignments, base expansions, and contract or program cancellations." There is also the Economic Adjustment Assistance Program (from the U.S. Department of Commerce Economic Development Administration), which provides "a wide range of technical, planning, and infrastructure assistance in regions experiencing adverse economic changes that may occur suddenly or over time." However, a clue to the real meaning of economic adjustment is found in an article about energy costs "raising new concern about the potential painful economic adjustment by households, especially low income households." "Painful" and "low-income" are key terms. When you see "economic adjustment," you might want to assume things aren't going well and shorten it to "recession."

economic deprivation use instead poverty.

economically disadvantaged the better term sometimes is economically exploited. "Many people of color have a painful history of being exploited for the benefit of European Americans. …'Economically disadvantaged' sidesteps important issues, while 'economically exploited' more accurately represents the historical plight of people of color" (Clyde W. Ford, *We Can All Get Along*). See also "culturally deprived/disadvantaged," poverty.

education education has not been and is still not an equal opportunity or parallel experience for both sexes and for various income, ability, racial, and ethnic groups in the U.S. When writing about education, include students, teachers, leaders, and experts from diverse backgrounds. According to the United Nations Population Fund website, "Despite progress in expanding primary education throughout the world, an estimated 130 million children—including 90 million girls—are not enrolled in primary school. And while enrollment in primary and secondary school totals nearly 90 million children worldwide, there are about 85 million fewer girls than boys enrolled." Women who are educated usually choose to have fewer children and to have them later. Each additional year of schooling for women has been associated with a decline in child deaths of between 5 percent and 10 percent. In the U.S., schools are more segregated today than they were in 1970 (*Time*). In the expanding field of online education, women significantly outnumber men in terms of college student enrollment in the U.S. The gender breakdown is 63 percent female, 36 percent male. Female college students (especially adult learners) appear to have a greater need than their male counterparts for the flexibility that online education affords, and this may be one reason women take more online courses and successfully complete more of them.

effeminate although this word could theoretically be used in a positive sense (and, in fact, there is a men's movement called Revolutionary Effeminism, which opposes the effects of masculinism), it's most commonly understood as pejorative and sexist, loaded with cultural stereotypes about what it means to be a man or a woman. Consider instead passive, gentle, timid, weak, agreeable, docile.

effete with reference to people, "effete" is pejorative; one of its meanings is "effeminate." Consider using less sex-linked alternatives: devitalized, exhausted; self-indulgent, decadent; overrefined. See also effeminate.

El Barrio El Barrio refers to any predominantly Hispanic community, especially a lower- or working-class neighborhood, or to the Spanish Harlem district of New York, or to parts of East Los Angeles.

elder/elderly "elder" in the sense of a respected religious, community, or other leader of either sex is acceptable; it is also used in the sense of "older" ("the elder of the two sisters"); it is not used as a noun to mean "old person." It is also used as an adjective: Elderhostel, elder care, elder legal services. "Elderly" is unacceptable as a noun ("the elderly") and isn't too popular as an adjective—rarely does anyone self-identify as an elderly person. "Frail elderly" is acceptable in sociological or medical writing to refer to those older persons who because of physical, mental, or economic problems need support from society. The preferred term for most people is "older" ("as an older man, I think ..." or "the older couple in front of us"). See also ageism, old, senior/senior citizen.

eldercare acceptable term for the care of older people, especially when referring to an organized program.

elder statesman see statesman.

Electra complex acceptable sex-specific term; the parallel is "Oedipus complex."

emancipate nonsexist; the Latin root means to free from ownership.

emasculate in the metaphorical sense, this may very occasionally be the word you mean, but too often it indicts something or someone (often a woman) for a process that depends just as importantly on a man's willingness to be emasculated, and unflatteringly implies that he is a passive victim. No parallel terms exist relating to women for "emasculate," "unman," and "castrate." For sex-neutral terms, consider disarm, disable, weaken, incapacitate, undermine, deprive of courage/strength/vigor/power. See also castrate, unman.

embryonic because of the political divisiveness over such concepts as "embryo" and "embryonic stem cells," use this term with precision or, when using it metaphorically, consider an alternative: inceptive, rudimentary, incipient, beginning, initial, immature, undeveloped, untried, fledgling, unhatched, primary, unfinished, imperfect, incomplete, elementary, half-finished, developing, sketchy, preparatory, unrefined, unpolished, becoming, unfolding, yet to come, in process. See also stem cell research.

embryonic stem cell research see stem cell research.

emerging nation see Third World.

emeritus "emeritus" is the male form; "emerita" is the female form. As fewer people are able to appreciate the Latin distinctions, "emeritus" may come to serve as a base word for both sexes, thus eliminating the reinforcement of woman as "other" by the less common term, but you're still safer using one or the other.

émigré woman or man.

éminence grise the nickname of Père Joseph, French monk, diplomat, and confidant of Cardinal Richelieu, is used today to describe a confidential agent of either sex or, in popular usage, a renowned expert. "Grise" ("gray") was not the color of his hair, as we commonly think, but of his habit.

emotional in our culture, "emotional" is not an admired trait; the word is most often used as an antonym for "rational" or "intelligent." Largely because of changing social attitudes toward women, "emotional" is not used as often as it once was to rebut a woman's arguments or generally discount her as a thinking human being. The problem today, says M. Adam (in Francis Baumli, *Men Freeing Men*), is that "women can now wax logical while men look silly waxing emotional." Until men are free to wax emotional and "emotional" is a positive word for both sexes, use it cautiously. See also irrational.

emotional disorder not a precise medical term; correct disease categories are: psychological disorders, psychiatric disorders, anxiety disorders, depressive disorders, behavioral disorders, personality disorders. According to the National Dissemination Center for Children with Disabilities, students with emotional, behavioral, or mental disorders are currently categorized as having an emotional disturbance. See the Individuals with Disabilities Education Act for more information.

empress acceptable official title. An empress may be an imperial titleholder in her own right or she may be the wife or widow of an emperor.

enchantress enchanter. See also "feminine" word endings.

endangered languages "One of the world's 7,000 distinct languages disappears every 14 days, an extinction rate exceeding that of birds, mammals, or plants" writes Thomas H. Maugh II, in the *Los Angeles Times*. The article continues "[According to] K. David Harrison, Vice President and Director of Research for the Living Tongues Institute for Endangered Languages, 'When we lose a language we lose centuries of thinking about time, seasons, sea creatures, reindeer, edible flowers, mathematics, landscapes, myths, music, the unknown, and the everyday,' he said. Half of the world's languages have disappeared in the last 500 years, and half the remainder are likely to vanish during this century."

enemy combatants see detainee.

enfant terrible although this French expression is grammatically masculine, *enfant*.

English "Speak English, this is America!" English-only adherents are generally sending racist messages that isolate immigrants from their own culture while marginalizing them from the mainstream. Beware of high-sounding, even logical-appearing words with this message. In fact, immigrants have historically wanted (especially for their children) to learn English as rapidly as possible, and bilingualism appears to be an advantage in many ways. See also black English.

enhanced interrogation a euphemism for torture. Sometimes also called "alternative interrogation," such practices flout international human rights conventions in the attempt to inhumanely extract supposedly critical intelligence. Unfortunately for all concerned, the information so acquired is often entirely pain-based and totally worthless. "Torture is not about extracting accurate information—throughout its history, its only reliable byproduct has been false confessions" (Dan Froomkin, www. HuffingtonPost.com, 2013).

enhanced interrogation techniques see torture.

enlisted man enlistee, service member, recruit, enlisted member/person/ personnel/soldier/sailor, soldier, sailor; enlisted man and enlisted woman.

enslaved worker/woman/child preferable to simply saying slave, since it keeps the person and the process of enslavement visible.

entitlement programs see corporate welfare.

entrepreneur in French, the word is grammatically masculine, but it is functionally inclusive in both English and French.

equal opportunity in 1945, Helen Gahagan Douglas said, "We cannot legislate equality but we can legislate ... equal opportunity for all." Decades later, inequalities of opportunity still exist on sexual, racial, ethnic, sexual orientation, age, and other grounds. Anecdote: a female anchor was reassured that she and the new male anchor were indeed equals, that he had been hired simply to co-anchor the show. But, as a subsequent court case showed, he was in fact the lead or primary anchor. The broadcasting company president testified that the media consultant told him a male-female anchor team should be equals. But another anchor said he was told by that same media consultant that the "male is the first among equals." The concept of equal opportunity, which has been closely tied to affirmative action programs designed to ensure equal access to jobs, housing, and schools, has been difficult for people to comprehend, whereas most people understand that equalizing the playing field in golf means that golfers of varying abilities have somewhat equal chances of competing with each other. See also affirmative action.

equal pay the Equal Pay Act of 1963 requires that women and men receive equal pay for equal work. See also comparable worth, pay equity.

Equal Rights Amendment (ERA) Women's Equality Amendment. This proposed amendment, which has so far failed by three states to obtain ratification of two-thirds of the states, consists of three brief sections. The first says, "Equality of rights under the law shall not be denied or abridged by the United States or by any state on account of sex." The second states that Congress shall have the power to enforce the article, and the third says the amendment will take effect two years after ratification. This extremely simple amendment (different by only one word—"sex"—from the amendment ensuring racial equality) has been bitterly resisted for several reasons: many people have never read the words of the amendment; equal rights for women have been confused with androgyny, sameness of function, integrated bathrooms and a supposed loss of rights for women; and perhaps, as someone once pointed out, the equality of women means the eradication of a servant class. It has been opposed for economic reasons by commercial interests benefiting from women's cheap labor or sex-based actuarial tables in insurance, and also by such religious groups as some Southern Baptists and the Church of the Latter-day Saints (Mormons) on the grounds that it is anti-family. Like much civil rights legislation, it has also been opposed as an affront to states' rights.

equestrienne equestrian. See also "feminine" word endings.

errand boy/errand girl errand runner, runner, messenger, courier, page, clerk, office helper, gofer.

escort service prostitution service. Organizations that provide drivers or companions to assist older persons with their shopping, errands, and doctor appointments are sometimes called escort services. Because of the confusion with the more common meaning, alternatives might be useful: transportation/dial-a-ride/chauffeur/elder/transportation services.

Eskimo in 1977, at the Inuit Circumpolar Conference in Alaska, the term "Inuit" ("the people") was adopted as a preferred designation for collectively referring to peoples of northern Canada, Greenland, Alaska, and eastern Siberia known as Eskimos. "Eskimo" has long been considered (incorrectly) to come from a term meaning "raw meat eaters." The native people of Alaska's North Slope call themselves Inupiat Eskimos and say that "Eskimo" comes from a word meaning "she laces a snowshoe" (Jean Craighead George, *Julie of the Wolves*). "Aleut" is the accepted designation for people of the western Alaska Peninsula, the Pribilof Islands, and the Aleutian island chain. Those native to the Cook Inlet and interior regions of Alaska refer to themselves as "Athapaskans." Inuk (or Innuk) is the singular of Inuit (or Innuit). In Alaska, "Natives" and "Alaska Natives" are accepted terms for the Inuit, Aleuts, and Indians.

Esq./Esquire it is correct to address a letter to an attorney of either sex in the U.S. using this courtesy title, for example, Marian Chernov, Esq. (In Great Britain, "Esq." signifies rank.)

-ess/-ette see "feminine" word endings.

essentialism "the belief that individuals or groups have inherent, unchanging characteristics rooted in biology or in a self-contained culture that explains their status. When linked to oppressions of race, gender, and sexuality, binary thinking constructs 'essential' group differences" (Patricia hill Collins, *Fighting Words*). As you can tell from the quotation marks around "essential," essentialism is not everyone's cup of tea. This controversial and variably understood philosophy has been used to "prove" several sides of the same issue. When discussing it, first elucidate the meanings of "essentialism" that are held. For example, some in academia have condemned as essentialist any reference to women's experience, even when the basis is cultural rather than biological.

estate tax see death tax.

ethnic/"ethnics" the adjective "ethnic" is acceptable; the noun "ethnics" is not. Use instead members of ethnic groups, ethnic-group members. Although not everyone identifies strongly or consistently with an ethnic group, by definition everybody is ethnic; "Margaret Thatcher, Susan B. Anthony and Bach are just as 'ethnic' as Miriam Makeba, Indira Gandhi, and Johnny Colon" (Amoja Three Rivers, *Cultural Etiquette*). Irving Lewis Allen (*Unkind Words*) says, "An ethnic group can be succinctly defined as any racial, religious, mother-tongue, national-origin, or regional category of culturally distinct persons, regardless of the group's size (minority or majority), social power (subordinate or dominant), or when its members immigrated to the country (immigrant, native-born, or indigenous). The *Harvard Encyclopedia of American Ethnic Groups* identifies 106 such ethnic groups who have lived in the United States. Slurs have been directed against most of these groups." "In writing about a multicultural society, authors should take care not to imply that ethnic groups are defined by their departure from some spurious norm—to imply, that is, that *ethnic* means 'not of the mainstream.' Not all minority groups are ethnic, and not all ethnic groups are minorities" (Marilyn Schwartz and the Task Force on Bias-Free Language of the Association of American University Presses, *Guidelines for Bias-Free Writing*). See also ethnicity, ethnic slurs, race.

ethnic cleansing genocide. See genocide.

ethnicity referring to a person's ethnic character, background, affiliation, or identification, this term is certainly more appropriate than "race." However, it lacks a great deal of precision in a culture in which most of us have more than one ethnic heritage. Those who self-identify with an ethnicity should be so acknowledged. In other cases, identify ethnic origin only when that information is central to your material and discuss all ethnic groups in parallel fashion. See also ethnic/"ethnics," ethnic slurs, race.

ethnic slurs epithets and slurs label people as less-than-human, which then makes them easier to discount, degrade, and destroy. In *Contreras v. Crown Zellerbach, Inc.* the Washington Supreme Court held that "racial epithets which were once part of common usage may not now be looked upon as 'mere insulting language.'" They constitute instead a tort of outrage, or "intentional infliction of emotional distress." According to Irving Lewis Allen in his excellent *Unkind Words: Ethnic Labeling from Redskin to WASP*, "Well over a thousand abusive nicknames aimed at more than one hundred different American ethnic groups have been recorded in dictionaries and other studies of our popular speech. .... If epithets were added for quasi-ethnic groups, such as the hundreds of terms for poor whites and rustics, mostly various white Protestant groups, the number of ethnic epithets in historical American slang and dialect would rise to nearly two thousand terms." Terms like the following range from moderately to deeply offensive: banana, camel jockey, chico, chink, cracker, dago, frog, gook, goy, greaser, gringo, guinea, honkie/honky, jap, kike, kraut, limey, mick, oreo, paleface, Pancho, Polack, slant, slope, spade, spic/spick, spook, white trash/poor white trash, whitey, wop. See also brave (Indian), Chinaman, Chinaman's chance, Dutch treat, half-breed/half-caste, hate speech, Indian giver, Injun, jew boy, "jew down," Jewish American Princess/JAP, nigger, Nip, ofay, Oriental, redskin, shanghai, squaw, welsh (verb), wetback, Yid.

ethnocentrism this is the belief that the ways of one's own group are (1) natural, (2) right for everybody, (3) superior to others' ways, (4) require no designating adjectives. As it is most often used, "ethnocentrism" refers to white people seeing themselves as the center and norm, with everyone else being variations on the theme.

eunuch use this word only in the literal sense of a castrated man, in which case it is a legitimate sex-specific word. For a metaphorical sex-neutral term, use substitute weakling, coward, wimp, pushover, doormat, lightweight, loser, craven. See also castrate, emasculate, sissy, unman.

Eurasian this can refer to a person of mixed Asian and European descent or to someone who lives in "Eurasia" (the land mass comprising the continents of Europe and Asia). It is ambiguous in some contexts, too broad for precision in others, and considered derogatory in still others.

European American this term is being seen more often, probably in response to the use of designations like Asian American and African American but also as a needed parallel for those designations (instead of the unparallel default "American" for whites). In your writing, alternate "European American" with white, particularly when you're alternating "African American" with black. See also "hyphenated Americans."

euthanasia see assisted suicide.

Eve Eve has traditionally symbolized the tempter, the one by whom evil came into the world; this incidentally leaves Adam looking suggestible, inept, and "belly-oriented," as one writer puts it. Misogynistic interpretations of the story of the biblical Eve have underwritten highly negative attitudes toward women throughout history. Interpreters who argue Eve's inferiority and subordination to Adam because he was created first fail to apply the argument logically: in the story, God created light, water, land, plants, stars, animals, and finally man. According to this later-is-better hierarchy of creation, woman would be God's final, most glorious effort. (Note the story in the Jewish tradition about Lilith, the woman created simultaneously with Adam; when she wanted to be treated as an equal, Adam asked God to provide him with a more submissive mate, which turned out to be Eve.) See also Adam's rib.

everyman/Everyman the typical/ordinary person, the archetypical human being, Everyman and Everywoman (always use together). See also average man, common man, man in the street.

exceptional as used in reference to people with disabilities, particularly children with mental retardation, this term is vague and euphemistic. Be specific: someone with a learning disability/an emotional disturbance/a sensory impairment, someone who is deaf/hearing impaired/blind. See also disabilities, special.

exceptionalism see American exceptionalism.

exclusive language speech and writing that excludes, intentionally or unintentionally, certain groups of people and their experiences makes them invisible to others and less valuable in their own and others' eyes. They become symbolically annihilated. For years, most of the advertising, writing, teaching, and speaking in our culture has been about, and directed toward, white, middle-class, Christian, heterosexual, able-bodied men. There is nothing wrong with this category of people; they have in fact contributed enormously to society. The problem is that there are many other members of society outside this category whose existence has been ignored by exclusive language.

executrix executor, personal representative, administrator. In some states, "executrix" is still used in official legal matters; in others, the legal term is "personal representative." See also "feminine" word endings.

exotic applied to human beings "exotic" is ethnocentric and racist. "It implies a state of other-ness, or foreign origin, apart from the norm. It is not a compliment" (Amoja Three Rivers, *Cultural Etiquette*). Why are Chinese American New Year's dancers "exotic" when those dancing the Highland fling or the Bohemian polka are not? In 2013 *Sports Illustrated* was in an "exotic" spotlight for its seven-continents swimsuit issue that juxtaposed, among others, a white, blonde model and an elderly Chinese man piloting her raft; another white bikini-clad model and a tribal-looking, half-naked Namibian man carrying a spear. By using "native" people as exotic fashion props, the photoshoot made a living mockery of human differences, contrasting the "exotic" with the beautiful and the "normal."

expatriate/ex-pat although based on the Latin for "country," *patria* (and thus on *pater*, "father"), these words are functionally inclusive and their roots not as obtrusive as some "pater"-based words ("paternal," for example). If you prefer, use American abroad, exile, displaced person, émigré.

expert when journalists, producers, or writers need an opinion from an expert, they generally end up with young or middle-aged white male experts, even when equally knowledgeable women, minorities, older people, lesbian and gay folks, and people with disabilities are available. The under-representation of women in U.S. news led to the creation of the Women's Media Center (WMC) SheSource, a brain trust of over 700 women experts. "We match up media-experienced women experts from our extensive database with journalists, bookers, and producers to ensure that women's voices are heard and the whole story is told," says WMC SheSource director, Kate McCarthy.

extraordinary rendition also known as "rendition" or "irregular rendition," this controversial kidnapping and extrajudicial transfer of a person from one country to another, which employs torture in interrogation, is often called "torture by proxy." Scott Russell Sanders defines it as "the handing over of prisoners to thuggish regimes" ("Language Versus Lies," *The Progressive*). An "obscene euphemism" (Nigel Rees, *A Man About a Dog*), extraordinary rendition also flouts the U.N. Convention Against Torture. A new term, "erroneous rendition" (or "erroneous extradition"), was required when innocent people were subjected to extraordinary rendition. Introducing the never-passed Torture Outsourcing Prevention Act, then Rep. Edward J. Markey (D-MA), said "Extraordinary rendition is the 800 lb. gorilla in our foreign and military policy-making that nobody wants to talk about. It involves our country out-sourcing interrogations to countries that are known to practice torture, something that erodes America's moral credibility." A 2009 executive order by President Obama called for more oversight, but did not end extraordinary rendition. See also black site, torture.

extremist people rarely self-identify as extremists; the label comes from others who perceive the extremist's beliefs and actions as radical, abnormal, excessive, illegitimate, unacceptable, irrational, unjustifiable, or otherwise outside the pale. Put simply, it means the person goes "too far" in the estimation of the labeler. When using "extremist," clarify in what precise ways you feel the person has exceeded your standards or society's limits.

Most of us do not use speech to express thought. We use it to express feelings.

Jennifer Stone

Language is double-edged; through words a fuller view of reality emerges, but words can also serve to fragment reality.

Vera John-Steiner

fact-finding trip before writing or talking about a fact-finding trip, determine whether it is a serious effort to obtain firsthand information that cannot be obtained any other way, or whether it's what some will call a "junket" at taxpayer expense.

faculty wives faculty spouses. Casey Miller and Kate Swift (*The Handbook of Nonsexist Writing*) say that tacking on identifiers like "faculty/ Senate/service/corporate wives" makes women appendages of both a man and an institution while detracting from their own lives and roles. The terminology also assumes that all members of the institution are men.

fag/faggot (man) these terms are extremely derogatory when used by non-gays, but may be acceptable when used positively among gay men. By reclaiming the words for themselves, gay men defuse the words' hostility and power over them. The Gay & Lesbian Alliance Against Defamation says they should not be used except in a direct quote that reveals the bias of the person quoted. So that such words are not given credibility in the media, it is preferred that reporters say, "The person used a derogatory word for a gay man." See also "insider/outsider" rule, shortened forms of words.

fair-haired boy/fair-haired girl the favorite, the apple of someone's eye, privileged person, someone with pull, front runner, person after one's own heart, in one's good graces, persona grata, teacher's pet. "Fair-haired" is problematic because (1) making "fair" the preferred coloring is racist and ethnocentric; (2) the phrases are used of adults, which makes the boy/girl designation inappropriate; (3) "fair-haired boy" is common, while "fair-haired girl" is not.

fair sex, the/fairer sex, the this phrase has lost whatever meaning it ever had.

fairy (legend) fairies are both male and female, although they most often materialize in our culture as female (for example, fairy godmother, Tinker Bell, Walt Disney's fairies, the tooth fairy).

fairy (man) this highly derogatory term has fortunately pretty much died out; a few gay men might still want to use it in a friendly and positive way among themselves, but it's off limits to others. See also "insider/ outsider" rule.

fairy godmother retain in traditional fairy tales and add fairy godfathers to modern tales. Also: good fairy/genie/genius, guardian angel, benefactor, savior, hero.

faith of our fathers faith of our ancestors/mothers and fathers.

fakir from the Arabic for "poor man," fakirs are generally men and the word is perceived as male. When you want a sex-neutral alternative, use wonder-worker, ascetic, mendicant, dervish, impostor, swindler.

Falashas Ethiopian Jews. The offensive "Falashas" means "landless aliens" in Amharic.

fallen woman if you mean prostitute, use prostitute—or better yet, prostituted woman. Otherwise use for either sex someone who is unfortunate/unlucky/sexually active/promiscuous, someone who has fallen on hard times/from grace. There are no "fallen men" just as there are no "fall women" (see fall guy/fall man); judgments about sexual activity are reserved for women, while judgments about moral evil and foolishness are reserved for men.

fall guy scapegoat, dupe, sucker, victim, fool, laughingstock, loser, sitting duck, easy/soft mark, mark, target, pushover, sap, mug, nebbish. See also bad guy, fallen woman, whipping boy.

fall of Man fall of the human race, the Fall.

family the Census Bureau's definition of a "traditional" nuclear family (married moms and dads living with their biological children and no other relative in the home) is now in the minority (Haya El Nasser, *USA Today*). When writing and speaking about family, reflect contemporary realities; the family of nostalgia ("Father Knows Best," "Leave It to Beaver," "Ozzie and Harriet"), still pictured as a "real" family, was actually only an aberration (and not even enjoyed by everyone; one-fourth of all Americans lived in poverty—without food stamps) that predominated for several decades following World War II. "The treasured belief that American families were once simpler and more innocent than they are today still exerts a powerful emotional pull on us" (Stephanie Coontz, *The Way We Never Were*). The legalistic definition of family is a group of people related by blood, marriage, or adoption, but the real-world definition is broader. A 2010 study by a team of sociologists at Indiana University found that 83 percent of the population said that an unmarried couple with children is a family and 60 percent of Americans believed that if you consider yourself to be a family, then you were one. The study identified three clusters of Americans: "exclusionists," who hold on to a more narrow and traditional definition of family; "moderates," who are willing to count same-sex couples as family if children are involved; and "inclusionists," who have a very broad definition of family. Susan Ohanian (*Ms. Class*) points out that "from George Washington on, we are a nation led by the products of single-parent families. George Washington was 11 when his father died (and Washington raised his own fatherless grandchildren); Thomas Jefferson was 14; Andrew Jackson's father died before he was born and his mother died when he was 14; Abraham Lincoln was 11 when his mother died." "Traditional" families in the U.S. are not what most people think they are, but the culture and the laws need to catch up. The Family and Medical Leave Act of 1993, for example, defines covered family as parent, spouse, child. Although some states have expanded that definition in their own FMLAs to include domestic partners, children of domestic partners, parents-in-law, step-parents, etc., the federal law needs to be more inclusive and reflective of who actual families are. Practical matters: when dealing with children, speak of their families; don't specify parents, mothers, or fathers unless you know their situation. To distinguish between the family you grew up in and the family you presently live in, consider: birth family, childhood family, family of origin, original family, first family; present family, adult family. Family policies in the workplace need to include on-site daycare, flex hours, job-sharing, parenting classes, sick-children programs, sexual harassment prevention information. See also domestic partners, "family values."

family-friendly describes such policies in the workplace as on-site childcare, flex hours, job-sharing, parenting classes, sick-children programs.

family man homebody, stay-at-home, family head, home-lover, family-oriented/family-centered/home-centered person, someone devoted to the family. Note the lack of parallel for women; all women are evidently "family women."

family of man the human family, humanity, humankind, the human family tree.

family planning this sex-neutral term is too often discussed as the exclusive province/responsibility of women. See also contraception.

"family values" this popular term is political shorthand for a rigid picture of the family (a male breadwinner and a female homemaker, a decent income, with no divorces, blended families, homosexuality, unwed or single parents). In 2010, the Pew Research Center conducted a poll measuring reactions to political words and phrases. "Family values" drew the highest percentage (89 percent) of positive response, ahead of "civil rights" (87 percent), "states' rights" (77 percent), "civil liberties" (76 percent), and "progressive" (68 percent). See also family.

farmer approximately 80 percent of all agricultural workers world-wide are women, according to UNWomen; "yet, of all the job descriptions in the English language, few jobs have a more masculine connotation than the title 'farmer.' ... In most cultures, agriculture becomes 'men's work' when it progresses to the point of being a successful commercial industry" (Lee Egerstrom, *St. Paul Pioneer Press*).

farm wife/farmer's wife most often, this woman is a farmer in all but name; give her the name. In one survey of farm women, nearly 95 percent were heavily involved in farm management, including basic farm labor and decision-making; 86 percent did the farm recordkeeping, 75 percent cared for the animals; 72 percent harvested crops. Sometimes farm wives have not only not been called farmers; they have not even been called persons. In 1988, a federal judge had to rule against the U.S. Department of Agriculture, which claimed that a farm couple was only one person. Although a father and his son or a brother and a sister farming in partnership were regarded as two people, a husband and wife were counted as only one person for USDA purposes. U.S. District Court Judge Joyce Hens Green officially rejected "the archaic notion that husbands and wives are one 'person.'"

fascism George Orwell said that the word has no meaning "except insofar as it signifies 'something not desirable.'" "Fascism" is always a slur especially when loosely used. In a meaningful discussion of fascism, define the term carefully before proceeding with your main ideas—the ideology varies with the ideologue. Even the *Oxford Companion to Politics of the World* has a tough time defining anything other than Fatherland, flag and extreme nationalism.

F

fashionista woman or man. (The "-ista" is from Spanish—for example, Sandinista, Peronista—and used like the English "-ist.") The term is rarely used disparagingly; it's more of a tongue-in-cheek, "fun" way to self-identify and find others who share your interests.

fat labeling people's appearance is often unnecessary. When description is called for, says John Paschetto, "Most politicized fat people prefer the simple word 'fat' to describe their bodies. Such words as 'heavy,' 'big,' and 'large'—while less offensive than 'overweight'—are frowned upon both because they are unclear and because they suggest that 'fat' needs euphemisms. ... The usage of 'fat,' 'overweight,' et al. is complicated by different preferences among the people being named. A lot of fat people accept the ruling group's opinion of their bodies and so are put off by the free use of 'fat.'" A principal activist organization, the National Association to Advance Fat Acceptance (NAAFA), prefers "fat." One woman asks, "When are we going to understand that fat is an adjective, not an epithet?" Eric Oliver (*Fat Politics*) says that "people who have strong anti-fat attitudes also tend to be more hostile toward minorities and the poor." A study reported in *The New England Journal of Medicine* linked being overweight to being economically disadvantaged. Other studies have found that overweight people make 10 to 20 percent less than their thinner colleagues, and one found that businessmen sacrifice $1,000 in salary for every pound they are "overweight." Fat people endure open ridicule, lectures, and insults, yet studies show that fat people actually eat less than those of average weight, and dieters exhibit more willpower than those who do not need to worry about what they eat; the non-fat partners of fat people also experience societal disapproval; unlike people with other conditions or disabilities, fat people are doubly punished by being told they could be thin if they really wanted to. The bully who yells across the cafeteria, 'Hey, Fatso!' doesn't just hurt the kid being targeted, he demoralizes other fat kids who may fear they'll be picked on next. And he makes all kids within earshot afraid of getting fat. The late Bettye Travis, clinical psychologist with a long history of activism (in the *New York Times*), fought assumptions that "fat" equals "lazy" or "ugly," and concluded that fat people were "one of the last marginal groups that are still targeted, that it's still OK to make fun of." The Yale University's Rudd Center for Food Policy & Obesity found that 72 percent of the stories they examined from the websites of CBS, ABC, MSNBC, FOX, and CNN portrayed fat people in a "negative and stigmatizing manner. These five networks all have the bad habit of pairing stories about the health impacts of obesity with stigmatizing images of people from the side or rear, dressed slovenly, eating, or acting lazy" (*Bitch*). The Rudd Center recommended using the more even-keeled terms of "weight" and "excess weight" and their media guidelines included: avoiding portrayals of overweight persons merely for the purpose of humor or ridicule; ensuring news articles about obesity are fact-based; treating fat people like people, not stereotypes—show them smiling or working, "not eating a cheeseburger on the sofa." When discussing exercise and nutrition, avoid implying that fat people are the only ones who need this information. "We're hoping to get people to realize that being fat is not a crime." said Travis. It is unacceptable for people to lose out on job opportunities, receive inferior health care, be denied access to facilities and services because of their size, and endure public disparagement.

One point of contention in the fat acceptance movement is between fat people who are attempting to lose weight and those who are not; opponents of weight loss cite high-failure rates and dangers of yo-yo dieting and weight-loss surgeries. See also fat shaming, looksism, obese/obesity, overweight, sizeism.

father (pseudogeneric noun) parent, progenitor, procreator, mother and father; source, ancestor, forebear; originator, founder, inventor, promoter. See also forefather, mother and father.

father (verb) in the sense of "to beget a child" or "to carry out the childrearing functions of a father," this is the right word. When used pseudogenerically or metaphorically to refer to actions considered analogous to begetting, it is better replaced by terms such as procreate, create, co-create, reproduce, breed, propagate, give life to, bring to life, bring into being, bring about, call into existence, cause to exist; produce, make, found, author, originate, generate, engender, establish, invent, introduce. See also mother (verb).

father (parent) when writing about men as fathers, forgo stereotypes—that they are absent, inept, distant, or cold. Some may well be, but if you're not reporting about a specific person, perpetuating these vague notions does a disservice to men who are committed, loving, and effective fathers. It also breeds social tolerance for second-rate fathering. When writing or speaking about fathers, give them a full range of behaviors, attitudes, and emotions. See also absent parent, advertising, parent.

father (clergy) leave as is in direct address ("Father Frank Friar") but when referring to someone, use the inclusive priest, minister, pastor. See also clergyman, priest.

Father (God) some Christians believe the name "Father" that Jesus Christ gives to God indicates a very specific relationship. Others, however, look back to the Gnostic and Semitic traditions from which the words "Father" and "Son" emerged, and say that these words have nothing to do with any familial roles, but that they were rather the closest worshipers could come to expressing in personal terms the concepts of Uncreated Source (God) and Reflected Image (Jesus). For these people, using metaphors for God (God as nurturing mother or loving father) is acceptable, but the idea of God having a gender is not. God is *like* a Father; the metaphor does not mean God is a father or that God is male. New metaphors for God are needed and more emphasis can be given to ones we already have (biblically, God is also light, rock, potter, mother, bread, wind, water, sun, fire, wisdom, judge, homemaker, physician, warrior, midwife, lion, leopard, she-bear, mother eagle, and shepherd, for example). Questioning God's gender poses a dilemma for some who see inclusive language (particularly the elimination of God as Father) as unconscionable tampering, and find the challenge to faith overwhelming. Scripture scholar the Reverend Joseph J. Arackal says calling God "Father" has no tradition among the Hebrews and even the word "Abba" cannot be translated into the English word "Father" since *Abba* indicates "the spiritual source of being" rather than the male parent. When using the Father metaphor, avoid masculine pronouns in order to mitigate the strongly male orientation. See also Father, Son, and Holy Spirit, God, God/he, God/his, Holy Spirit, Lord, Son of Man.

father figure this term has a specific meaning and may need to be retained. For sex-neutral alternatives, consider role model, mentor, idol, hero.

fatherland homeland, native land/country/soil, home, home/birth country, land of one's ancestors, natal place, the old country, country.

fatherless (pseudogeneric) orphaned, parentless.

fatherly replace this vague adjective with precise ones: warm, nurturing, loving, kind, kindly, protective, supportive, caring, solicitous, considerate, interested, benevolent, good-natured, fond, affectionate, devoted, tender, gentle, demonstrative, sympathetic, understanding, indulgent, obliging, forbearing, tolerant, well-meaning, sheltering, generous. These adjectives also apply to women; they are not synonyms for "fatherly" but rather what the culture seems to understand by the word.

fathers (pseudogeneric) ancestors, forebears, progenitors, precursors, predecessors, forerunners, leaders, pioneers, founders, trailblazers, innovators, fathers and mothers.

Father's Day first celebrated in Spokane in 1910, Father's Day was suggested by Sonora Louise Smart Dodd (who married John Bruce Dodd) whose father, William Smart, had raised his children after his wife died. Prompted by Mrs. Dodd and by the new popularity of Mother's Day (1908), Spokane ministers, newspapers, and stores promoted acceptance of the idea.

Fathers of the Church leave as is; historically accurate. See also church father.

Father, Son, and Holy Spirit/Ghost God, Jesus, and Holy Spirit; the God who created us, the God who redeemed us, and the God who continues to work through us to make us holy; Creator, Savior, and Healer; Source, Servant, and Guide; Creator, Liberator, and Advocate; the Holy Trinity; Three in One; One in Three; the Triune God. When choosing alternatives, be aware that some describe who God is ("God, Jesus, and Holy Spirit") while others describe what God does ("Creator, Savior, and Healer"). Some people object to the overuse of God-as-function terms.

fat shaming not always as obvious as name-calling or telling someone they'd be better off without the extra weight, fat shaming can be as subtle as a patronizing "Good for you!" to a fat person exercising or to "noticing" the choices in a fat person's grocery cart. Conveyed in myriad ways—"I see that you're fat, and that's not good"—fat shaming is anything you wouldn't say or do to a lesser-weight person or that could refer to the person's body. Note that fat shaming is outstandingly ineffective in changing other people's weight (some people use this bullying tactic under the guise of being helpful). The disdain behind fat shaming is seen in a comment on Urban Dictionary that defines it as a term used by obese people to avoid the responsibility of actually taking proper care of their body and instead victimizing themselves by pretending to be discriminated against like an ethnic group. Bottom line? Manners, people. It is incredibly rude to notice in an obvious way or to remark upon human differences. MYOB.

fatwa a religious edict, a fatwa (plural fataawa or fatwas) is an opinion issued by an Islamic scholar versed in Islamic law at the request of an individual or a judge to settle a question where Islamic jurisprudence is unclear. Marieme Helie Lucas, Algerian sociologist and psychotherapist, further clarifies (in *Conscience*): "A fatwa is an opinion by a Muslim cleric, or a well-read believer, whose knowledge of religion is recognized and appreciated by the community in which he lives or is known. In other words, it is the opinion—on religious issues, or issues that can be related to religion—of someone you know and whose knowledge you trust. ... You can decide to follow the opinion of the cleric or not. Or to seek another opinion. Your decision about how to react to the fatwa is between you and your conscience, you and your God." Collections of fatwas as well as related information can be seen at www.fatwa-online.com.

feisty during her vice-presidential campaign, Geraldine Ferraro was referred to as "spunky" and "feisty"; Michael Geis (*The Language of Politics*) says both words are normally reserved for individuals and animals that are not inherently potent or powerful; "one can call a Pekinese dog spunky or feisty, but one would not, I think, call a Great Dane spunky or feisty." And the press would certainly not have labeled George Bush, then Ferraro's opponent, as spunky or feisty. "Numerous examples of the special or sexist treatment of female leaders include ... use of the terms 'oppressive,' 'feisty,' and 'pushy' to describe behavior in women that would be called 'tough' and 'decisive' in men" (Thalia Zepatos and Elizabeth Kaufman, *Women for a Change*). See also perky/pert.

fellow (noun/adjective) "fellow" is often considered to be used inclusively; women receiving academic fellowships are called fellows, for example, and among its dictionary definitions are many inclusive concepts. However, if you say, "Today I saw a fellow throwing away $100 bills," there is no doubt in anyone's mind that the distributor of largesse was a man. The folksy "fella/feller" is also incontestably masculine. It has a history of being used for women: in 1932, for example, Gertrude Atherton (*Adventures of a Novelist*) wrote, "She may have lost her beauty and allure, but she was a good fellow, mixed cocktails for them, and was witty and amusing." If you want a substitute for the noun, consider person, partner, colleague, co-worker, companion, counterpart, associate, ally, comrade, friend, acquaintance, peer. For the adjective, use similar, alike, analogous, comparable, parallel, matching, corresponding, coinciding, like, something like, other, related, akin, equal, equivalent, associate(d), united, connected. For the academic "fellow," you can sometimes use scholar, recipient, postgraduate student.

fellow countrymen friends and neighbors, all of us, compatriots. Reword the sentence to avoid this term if the alternatives don't work. See also compatriot, countryman, fellow man/men, my fellow Americans.

fellow feeling sympathy, understanding, compassion, commiseration, empathy, rapport, link, bond, union, tie, closeness, affinity, friendship, agape, pity, walking in someone else's shoes, putting oneself in someone else's place.

fellow man/men in most cases, "fellow" is superfluous. We are so used to hearing this catch-all term in certain contexts that we don't question its necessity. Be specific: other people, you, citizens, workers, another human being, all of us here, the average person, etc. See also Man/man (pseudogeneric).

fellowship (social bond) friendship, companionship, solidarity, communion, union, unity, unity of mind and spirit, association, camaraderie, comradeship, partnership, togetherness, collaboration, participation, esprit de corps, neighborliness, sharing, amity, good will, bonding, friendliness, conviviality, sodality, human community/kinship, kinship, humanity, family, the human family; society, assembly, community, organization, club, group, federation, corporation. The substitute most often used for "fellowship" in religious materials is "communion." See also brotherhood, fellowship (scholarship).

fellowship (scholarship) when used officially, retain; otherwise consider scholarship, assistantship, internship, stipend, subsidy, honorarium.

fellow traveler traveling companion, other traveler.

fellow worker coworker, colleague, associate, teammate, partner.

female (noun) "female" is used as a noun only in technical writing (medicine, statistics, police reports, sociology). It is most often reserved for biological or nonhuman references. When using "female," use the parallel "male," not "man." "Female" is not sexist because it contains "male." Dennis Baron (*Grammar and Gender*) says, "Actually *female* derives from the Latin *femella*, a diminutive of *femina*, 'woman.' It is completely unrelated to *male*, which comes to us via Old French from Latin *masculus*, a diminutive of *ma*, 'male, masculine.'" See also female (adjective).

female (adjective) although it is preferable to use "woman" or "women" as adjectives (when it is necessary), there are times when "female" seems more appropriate. Use it, however, only when you would use "male" in a similar situation or when it is necessary for clarification; sex-specific adjectives are often gratuitous and belittling (one sees "female lawyer" but not "male doctor"). Watch especially for nonparallel usage ("two technicians and a female mechanic"). "Female" is not linguistically derived from, nor in any way related to, "male." See also female (noun).

female genital mutilation (FGM) this "procedure," undergone by more than 80 million African women, is sometimes referred to as female circumcision, but it differs radically from male circumcision: it is always a sexual mutilation; it is often performed without anesthesia by nonprofessionals (usually village healers and elderly female relatives), most often with unsterilized razor blades; it often leads to infection, life-threatening blood loss, painful intercourse, infertility, difficult childbirth, and death. This mutilation of the external female genital organs (specifically, clitoridectomy, excision, and infibulation) is a centuries-old rite of passage, intended to ensure that young women become desirable wives. It is not mandated by any particular religion, but is practiced by people of many faiths in some two dozen black African nations, in Egypt, and in the Sudan, and in immigrant communities elsewhere. Although many organizations are working to educate about FGM and laws have been passed in some affected countries, observers fear the practice is spreading rather than waning. The issue is many-layered, from the heinous and nightmarish mangling and botching of women's bodies to issues involving people's rights to self-determination. The U.S. has granted at least one woman political asylum based on the fact that if she were returned to her country she would be required to undergo female genital mutilation.

female impersonator see cross-dresser.

feminazi Rush Limbaugh began by calling feminists fascists, then shortened it to feminazi. He would probably be hurt if anyone else used it, so don't. See also Nazi/nazi.

Feminine/femininity avoid these stereotypes that convey different meanings to different people according to their perceptions of what a woman ought or ought not do, say, think, wear, feel, look like. Use instead specific descriptive adjectives for the qualities you want to express: gracious, warm, gentle, thoughtful, sensitive, loyal, receptive, supportive, compassionate, expressive, affectionate, tender, charming, nurturing, well-mannered, cooperative, neat, soft-spoken, considerate, kind. These adjectives may be used equally appropriately of a man.

feminine intuition see women's intuition.

feminine logic people who use "feminine logic" usually mean a woman is being "illogical," so they should save themselves a word and just say "illogical" if that's what they mean. Otherwise it's logic, period.

feminine/masculine (poetry, music) in poetry, rhyme with a stressed or strong final syllable is called masculine rhyme; rhyme with an unstressed or weak final syllable is feminine rhyme. In music, a masculine beginning (or ending) is a phrase that starts (or ends) on a strong beat; a feminine beginning (or ending) is a phrase that starts (or ends) on a weak beat. It would seem clearer to refer to stressed and unstressed rhymes and to strong and weak beats without bringing the sexes into it in this highly sexist manner.

feminine mystique from Betty Friedan's landmark 1963 book of the same title in which she exposed "the problem that has no name" (women's unhappiness with their role and status in society), this term refers to the then-narrow definition of women's "place" in the world.

feminine wiles wiles.

"feminine" word endings suffixes like -ess, -ette, and -trix (1) specify a person's sex when gender is irrelevant; (2) carry a demeaning sense of littleness or triviality; (3) perpetuate the notion that the male is the norm and the female is a subset, a deviation, a secondary classification. A poet is defined as "one who writes poetry" while a poetess is defined as "a female poet"; men are thus "the real thing" and women are sort of like them. The recommended procedure is to use the base word for both sexes (thus, "waiter" instead of "waitress," "executor" instead of "executrix"). For a complete discussion of "feminine" word endings and a list of examples, see the Writing Guidelines.

feminism feminism is "the belief that women are full human beings capable of participation and leadership in the full range of human activities—intellectual, political, social, sexual, spiritual and economic" (Pearl Cleage, *Deals With the Devil and Other Reasons to Riot*). Rachel Fudge (in *Bitch*) says feminism is "the theory of the political, economic, and social equality of the sexes." A feminist believes in "the full humanity of women" (Gloria Steinem). Although primarily women identify themselves as feminists, some men do too. The Reverend Jerry Falwell is not one of them: "I listen to the feminists and all those radical gals—most of them are failures. They've blown it.... These women just need a man in the house. That's all they need. Most of these feminists need a man to tell them what time of day it is and to lead them home. And they blew it and they're mad at all men. Feminists hate men. They're sexist. They hate men—that's their problem" (quoted in *Ms.*). As is evident, the definition of "feminism" varies from person to person. In general, feminism has no strictly organized agenda but is deeply concerned and activist with regard to equal rights and opportunities for both sexes, poverty, violence, education, childcare, quality of life and environmental issues, legislative-based gender equity, equal representation, comparable worth, abortion and other health care rights, sexual harassment, globalization and peace, justice and security issues. "An indigenous feminism has been present in every culture in the world and in every period of history since the suppression of women began" (Robin Morgan, *Sisterhood Is Global*). Many people now accept feminism as a historical, enduring movement that has promoted changes beneficial to society as a whole. "Today no sphere of society remains untouched by feminism" (Eleanor Smeal, in *Sisterhood Is Forever*). And Robin Morgan adds, in the same book, that "contemporary feminism is here to *stay. ... We ain't goin' backward, crazy, under, or away.*" See also feminisms, womanist, women's movement.

feminisms "Some people ... will insist on referring to 'the feminists' as if they are one big indistinguishable lump" (Rachel Fudge, in *Bitch*). A guideline for all good speaking and writing: "Don't assume that any group is monolithic" (Vivian Jenkins Nelsen, *New Voices in the Media*). Some visible feminisms: antiporn feminism, anarchafeminism, black feminism, Catholic feminism, Christian feminism, cultural feminism, ecofeminism, equity feminism, essentialist/difference feminism, girlie feminism, individualist feminism, Jewish feminism, Latina feminism, lesbian feminism, liberal feminism, libertarian feminism, Muslim feminism, neofeminism, pro-sex feminism, radical feminism, socialist/Marxist feminism, Third World feminism, womanism, and that perennial non-favorite, pseudofeminism. What all the feminisms except the last have in common is a commitment to challenge the notion that a person's gender should, in theory or in practice, be an obstacle to civil and personal liberties. See also feminism, wave (feminism).

feminization of poverty some 60 percent of the world's 1.2 billion poor are women; with their children, women make up over 80 percent of all refugee and displaced populations. In the U.S. today, 100 million Americans live on the brink of poverty; 70 percent of this number are women. Complex factors produce these numbers: much of the work that women do is unpaid; the rates of divorce, separation, and single motherhood (generally the result of relationships in which partners disappeared) have risen; many women tried part-time work so they could be home and still make money, but found they earned less and were also less likely to be promoted or to be covered by health insurance or pension plans.

fem lib feminism, women's liberation movement, women's liberation, women's movement, female liberation movement. See also shortened forms of words.

femme/fem these terms follow the "insider/outsider" rule: they are sometimes used positively among lesbians, but should not be used by non-lesbians.

femme fatale this term perpetuates the myth of woman as Eve/tempter/siren and man as helpless prey. A rule of good writing is "show, don't tell"; instead of stating that someone is a "femme fatale," show how she affects others. The parallel for a man is probably the unfortunate term "lady-killer."

fetish (religious) this term is used to refer to the religious items of peoples of color when objects in other religions often serve similar purposes but are not called fetishes. See also superstition.

fetus this is the correct term for a developing mammal after the embryonic stage and before birth; in humans, the stage properly termed "fetal" begins at week 9. Today, anti-abortion forces are both promulgating and denying the idea of granting "personhood" to fetuses: in January of 2013, the Alabama Supreme Court held that, for legal purposes, a fetus is a child ("unborn children are persons with rights that should be protected by law") while in Colorado, a Catholic hospital being sued for malpractice in the death of a woman and her twins is arguing that fetuses are not people. See also abortion, reproductive rights.

fiancé/fiancée these sex-specific terms are acceptable to most people and are still widely used. However, the trend is toward using only the base word (fiancé). According to Art Krug (in the Portland *Oregonian*, "'Fiancée' is too stuffy.... I think I'll call her my 'intendo.'" See also divorcé/divorcee, "feminine" word endings.

filial/filiation although these words come from the Latin for "son," they are defined and used inclusively in terms of children and offspring of both sexes.

Filipina/Filipino/Filipin@ a woman or man native to or living in the Philippines. In the U.S., those from the Philippines are known as Filipino Americans. Note the recent convention "Filipin@," which denotes either a woman or a man. See also Pinay/Pinoy.

"final solution" this expression should be reserved for the Nazi program of exterminating Jews during the German Third Reich. Do not use it metaphorically or analogously. See also concentration camp, Gestapo/gestapo, Hitler/little Hitler, holocaust, Jewish question, Nazi/nazi, problem.

fireman firefighter. In some instances, other terms are useful: fire chief/warden, fire/safety officer.

first baseman see baseman.

first lady the wife of a U.S. president has been given this honorary term, but it is not an official title. Thus, the "problem" of what to do with a female president's spouse is moot; he will be known simply as "Mr. Last-Name." Presidents' wives were not always referred to as "first ladies"; in 1849 President Zachary Taylor eulogized Dolley Madison: "She will never be forgotten, because she was truly our First Lady for a half-century." But the term did not become part of the vocabulary until 1911, with the hit play about Dolley Madison titled, "The First Lady in the Land." The term is seen less and less often in print. Recent presidential spouses have preferred to be known by a name, rather than by a role. (Jacqueline Kennedy said, "The one thing I do not want to be called is 'First Lady.' It sounds like a saddle horse.") Since "first lady" is not a formal title, it is never capitalized, even when used before the name of a chief of state's wife.

First Nations/First Nations people/First People see American Indian.

first-wave feminism when possible, avoid compartmentalizing feminism into "waves." A seamless garment more appropriately denotes this particular work that is never done. What is generally termed the first wave, however, is bracketed by the first Women's Rights Convention at

Seneca Falls in 1848 and women's winning the right to vote in 1920. In the intervening 72 years, feminists ushered in birth control and legal forms that granted women the right to own property, get divorced, and retain custody of their children. Elizabeth Cady Stanton, Susan B. Anthony, and Alice Paul were among the many bright, energetic, activist women changing the landscape for women during those years. For more on first-wave feminism, see *The Reader's Companion to U.S. Women's History*, edited by Wilma Mankiller, Gwendolyn Mink, Marysa Navarro, Barbara Smith, and Gloria Steinem. See also Equal Rights Amendment, feminism, feminisms, second-wave feminism, third-wave feminism, wave (feminism).

fisherman fisher, angler, fish catcher, fishing licensee (for some legal purposes); fisherman and fisherwoman if used gender-fairly. Do not be afraid of "fisher." In the following series of -er words, "fisherman" would be the odd man out: camper, hunter, canoer, skier, runner, hiker, mountain climber, birdwatcher, biker, nature lover. "Fisher" is appearing more often in print.

fishwife fishmonger, fish porter. Avoid the word to mean an abusive, scolding woman; there is no parallel for a man (fishhusband?) and we tend to attribute those qualities to women. See also shrew.

fit seizure.

flag see pledge of allegiance.

flagman signaller, flagger, traffic controller, signal giver; flag waver/carrier.

flapper use as is in historical context. Note, however, that before World War I a flapper was considered a sprightly, knowing female teenager, while afterward the term developed some negative connotations, and flappers were thought to be rather "fast."

flesh-colored this could mean anything, unless it is taken in the ethnocentric way it was used for years to mean "pinky beige." The Crayola company no longer makes a crayon in this "color." See also Indian red.

flexitarian a vegetarian who occasionally eats meat.

flower girl (vendor) flower seller/vendor, florist.

flower girl (wedding) flower bearer/carrier. Little boys are flower bearers as well as ring bearers and little girls can be ring bearers.

flyboy pilot, aviator, flier, high-flier, glamorous pilot, member of the Air Force. See also airman.

flyover country/flyover land it's difficult to reconcile the supposed disdain of the two coasts for the area of the continental U.S. that lies in between when every four years, savvy politicians head to Iowa to start the real campaigning for the presidency. See also redneck.

food names for people while some food names for people are positive ("creampuff," "peach," "stud muffin"), most are in some way belittling, trivializing, objectifying, or sexist: arm candy, babycakes, beefcake, cheesecake, cookie, cupcake, cutie pie, dish, fruit, fruitcake, fruit salad, honeycakes, lambchop, marshmallow, pudding, pumpkin, sugar, sugar and spice, sweetie pie, tart, tomato, top banana. Metaphors are more acceptable than labels: "apple of my eye" can be said of either sex and it doesn't mean the person is an apple in the same way a woman is called a tomato. Strong writing depends on metaphors—even metaphors based on food—but there is a difference between labeling people and creating vivid word associations. See also animal names for people.

food stamps an outdated term that should be replaced by SNAP (Supplemental Nutrition Assistance Program) benefits. 83 percent of all SNAP benefits go to households with children, a disabled person, or an elderly person. Considering participants as individuals, 47 percent are children, 8 percent are elderly. An individual who qualifies for SNAP benefits receives $33 per week, or $1.50 per meal. See also corporate welfare, welfare.

footman leave as is in historical contexts; a footman was always a man. Or servant. According to Alvin Silverstein (*The Left-Hander's World*), the purpose of the footman in Roman households was to ensure that guests entered the home right foot first.

forcible rape never use this redundancy except perhaps when both rape and statutory rape are involved; the latter does not necessarily involve the use of force.

forefather forebear, forerunner, ancestor, predecessor, precursor, pioneer; forefather and foremother. Also, in some senses, colonist, patriot, founder. Because genes sort randomly, "It is possible for a female to end up with all her genes from male ancestors, and for a male to end up with all his genes from female ancestors" (Sally Slocum, *Toward an Anthropology of Women*).

foreign international, world. Sometimes, of course, you mean "foreign," but when speaking of international trade, markets, travel, etc., use a more neutral term, which avoids an "us/them" implication. (Ted Turner used to fine employees $50 for using "foreign" on the air.)

Foreign Service officer woman or man. The first woman joined the Foreign Service in 1922.

forelady/foreman/forewoman supervisor, lead/floor supervisor, team/floor/work leader, line manager/supervisor, section head, manager, boss, chief, monitor, overseer, superintendent, super, inspector, director, head, leader. The British use chargehand.

foreman (jury) head juror, jury designate/supervisor/chief/chair/representative/leader. "Forewoman" and "foreperson," are seen and are acceptable enough if the pair is "forewoman and foreman" and not "foreman and foreperson," but they are not lovely constructions.

foremother while "forefather" is often used as a false generic, "foremother" may be valid to emphasize that there were indeed women before us even though they so seldom appeared in the history books, classrooms, or public halls. If you need a sex-inclusive term consider forebear, forerunner, ancestor, predecessor, precursor, pioneer; forefather and foremother. See also foresister.

foresister when a sex-specific term is useful, some people prefer this term to "foremother."

forewoman see forelady/foreman/forewoman; foreman (jury).

foster mother/father/parent acceptable terms.

Founding Fathers the Founders, Framers, writers/Framers of the Constitution; in some contexts, Founding Mothers and Founding Fathers; founders, pioneers, colonists, forebears, patriots. In the past, texts have too often assumed that these groups were male ("pioneers and their wives and children"). Although the term "founding fathers" (originally referring to the men who gathered at the constitutional convention in Philadelphia in 1787) has a venerable and ancient ring, it is of 20th-century origin when Warren G. Harding used it in 1918 and again in his 1920 presidential campaign. See also forefather, pioneer.

Fourth World this relatively new designation identifies some 6,000 nations without states, including some indigenous peoples, the Roma in Europe, the Kurds and Palestinians in the Middle East, and many Indian groups throughout the Americas. See the *Fourth World Journal* or its website for more information.

fox/foxy/foxy lady it is generally acceptable to use the adjective "foxy" but less acceptable to use the noun "fox" (the distinction lies in saying someone is like an animal or saying someone is an animal). See also animal names for people.

fragging the killing or injuring (usually by a fragmentation bomb, which leaves no fingerprints or ballistics evidence) of unpopular officers or NCOs by members of their own troops during the Vietnam War was called fragging. Supposedly there were 209 fragging incidents during that war. Alleged fragging incidents were much more rare in Iraq and Afghanistan. ("Frag" is also now a video game term—you get a frag for killing someone.)

fraternal unless speaking of a brother, you may want sex-neutral alternatives: warm, loving, friendly, kindly, teasing, protective, sympathetic, intimate. In some contexts consider sibling. Because the feminine partner for "fraternal" ("sororal") is rarely seen—an example of the discounting of female words—even women's groups have used "fraternal." The Degree of Honor Protection Association, founded more than 100 years ago, describes itself as "a fraternal insurance organization of women" and engages in "fraternal activities." "Fraternal" is used here as a synonym for "benevolent." See also sororal.

fraternal order of order of, benevolent order of. See also fraternal.

fraternal organization organization, society, association, common-interest group.

fraternal twins nonidentical/distinguishable/dizygotic twins.

fraternity organization, society, association, union, secret society, club, federation, fraternity and sorority, common-interest group; comradeship, unity, community, companionship, friendship, family, kinship. See also brotherhood, fellowship, fraternity/frat (Greek).

fraternity/frat (Greek) these terms no longer refer strictly to male organizations: there are some coed fraternities, and some sororities are officially called fraternities. For sex-neutral alternatives, use: Greek society/system, Greek-letter organization, Greek-letter society/group. Although most fraternities have social service goals and almost all have nondiscriminatory membership codes, in practice they are often exclusionary. Robin Warshaw (in *The Nation*) says, "Universities across the country are proclaiming diversity—social, sexual, ethnic, racial, economic, and cultural—as the guiding spirit behind their pursuit of academic growth and excellence. At the same time, fraternities—whose members usually select one another on the basis of conformity to homogeneous group standards—are experiencing their highest membership levels ever...it's not the blood drives, charity fund-raiser, or improved résumé potential that brings in new members; it's an attraction to a culture that often seems to say, 'Become one of us and you'll get loaded, you'll get laid, you'll become a man.'" Referring to the "inherently destructive influence of fraternities," Warshaw says, "most fraternity cultures are still centered on proving manhood In accordance with three basic beliefs: that women are sex objects to be manipulated at will; that drinking and drug-taking are endurance sports; and that all non-members, be they other male students, professors, or college administrators, are deficient weenies. Because fraternities are essentially closed shops, both morally and intellectually, members are unlikely to have those beliefs disputed in any way they will find convincing."

fraternization association, socialization, mingling, banding together, keeping company, hobnobbing, mixing, consorting, clubbing together, rubbing shoulders with. There is no parallel based on the Latin for "sister," *soror*.

fraternize associate, socialize, mingle, band together, befriend, keep company, hobnob, mix, consort, club together, rub shoulders with. There is no parallel based on the Latin for "sister," *soror*.

fratricide although most dictionaries define this as the killing of a brother or sister, the word obviously comes from the Latin for "brother" and the correct sex-specific term, "sororicide," is rarely used. "Fratricide" is also used pseudogenerically when a better choice might be internal struggle, internecine warfare, genocide.

frau there is nothing wrong with this word in German; the problem arises when it is used in English to convey a certain disdain for a narrowly defined role for women. There is no parallel English term for a man. See also hausfrau, mademoiselle.

freedman freed/former slave, ex-slave, free-issue black; freedman and freedwoman.

freegan "(free + vegan), a freegan is a person who has decided to boycott capitalist society by severely curtailing consumption of resources through reusing, recycling, and Dumpster diving" (Raina Kelley, in *Newsweek*).

freeman citizen, citizen of a free country; freeman and freewoman. "Freewoman" has had other connotations in the feminist movement; *The Freewoman*, one of the earliest feminist newspapers, was published in Great Britain as a weekly feminist review in 1911-1912.

free market in the U.S., we love the word "free" and all its permutations, from big ideas like freedom to small redundant ideas like "free gift." "Free market" sounds like something we would like, but it's deceptive. "It has major moral implications," says George Lakoff (*Thinking Points*). "Privatization and deregulation are seen as virtues that lead to 'less government.' That is a fallacy. They lead to less *responsible* government....The energy industry determines what type of energy we have access to, its impact on the environment, and how much it cost. Private testing companies determine what kids should learn and how they should learn it. These are moral decisions that ...should be made by democratically elected government, not corporate government, so they are ideally made in the interest of the public.... But when government functions are privatized and industries are deregulated, these decisions are made in boardrooms for the benefit of stockholder profits." More fundamentally, says Lakoff, "the free market is a myth." He cites the bailout of the airlines after 9/11 to the tune of $15 billion and the tens of billions spent to support the oil industry and maintaining price supports for agribusiness. "These interventions in the market promote what conservatives believe is in the vital national interest. But when government intervenes on behalf of working people, consumers, or the environment, conservatives scream foul and invoke the 'free-market' because these interventions don't mesh with their political philosophy. ... A 'free market' means business can strip the commons of its wealth, making the rest of us pay for its profits." See also corporate welfare.

Freemason a member of the Free and Accepted Masons or Ancient Free and Accepted Masons, "Freemason" always refers to a man. The Order of the Eastern Star is an affiliate, however, to which both women and men belong.

free speech freedom of speech (some prefer "freedom of expression" because it includes more than speech) is guaranteed in the United States by the First Amendment to the Constitution. Internationally, freedom of speech is assured through the Universal Declaration of Human Rights and the European Convention on Human Rights. Freedom of speech is not absolute. In the U.S., it is illegal to use your First Amendment right to, for example, defame someone (slander or libel them), to commit perjury, to infringe on someone's copyright, to sell trade secrets, to threaten someone in a way a reasonable person would consider an actual threat of violence, or to use fighting words ("insulting or 'fighting words', those that by their very utterance inflict injury or tend to incite an immediate breach of the peace"). Stanley Fish, Duke University professor who teaches First Amendment law, says, "I don't think there's a thought police or a reign of terror, partly because every time I see somebody complaining that they've been silenced, the complaint is uttered before millions on a major television or talk show program." See also hate speech.

freethinker according to the Freedom From Religion Foundation, a freethinker is someone who "forms opinions about religion on the basis of reason, independently of tradition, authority, or established belief. Freethinkers include atheists, agnostics and rationalists." Freethinkers try to base actions on their consequences to real, living human beings. Most freethinkers consider religion to be not only untrue, but harmful; it's been used to justify war, slavery, sexism, racism, homophobia, mutilations, intolerance, and oppression of minorities. Many religionists are good people, but they would be good anyway; religion does not have a monopoly on good deeds. Freethought is a philosophical, not a political, position, so freethinkers are capitalists, libertarians, socialists, communists, Republicans, Democrats, liberals, and conservatives.

free trade trading between or within countries unrestricted by legislation, taxes, or other barriers is called free trade. Bill Moyers talks about the social costs of free trade. "For over a decade, free trade has hovered over the political system like a biblical commandment, striking down anything—trade unions, the environment, indigenous rights, even the constitutional standing of our own laws passed by our elected representatives—that gets in the way of unbridled greed. The broader negative consequence of this agenda—increasingly well-documented by scholars—gets virtually no attention in the dominant media. Instead of reality, we get optimistic multicultural scenarios of coordinated global growth, and instead of substantive debate, we get a stark, formulaic choice between free trade to help the world and gloomy sounding "protectionism" that will set everyone back." When writing or speaking of free trade, spell out for your audiences what is involved so that they won't be seduced by the word "free."

free world dating from the Cold War era, the "free world" was intended to mean every nation that wasn't communist (this included many repressive regimes). You do not have to use the self-identification beloved of presidents of the U.S.: "leader of the free world." (One wants to say, "Who elected *you*?")

freshman first-year/first-semester/second-semester student, frosh, fresher, freshie, class of 2014, beginning/entering student, freshperson; beginner, novice, newcomer, greenhorn, tenderfoot. Plurals: first-year students, frosh, freshers, freshpeople, freshfolk. "Freshman" has been eliminated from the *Yale Daily News*, also from *The Yale*; Harvard refers to "first years"; Princeton says "first-year students" is now the norm; "freshfolk" is used on the Oberlin campus; Cornell uses "Class of '18"; Stanford says "frosh" is increasingly seen.

freshman congressman/freshman congresswoman first-term member of Congress, frosh. According to J.E. Lighter in "Here Come the Frosh" (*The Atlantic Monthly*), "frosh" does not appear to have come from "freshman" but rather from the 19th-century German use of *Frosch* (frog) for a student before entering the university. "That *frosh* has become the journalistic slang of choice for congressional freshmen seems inevitable in retrospect. It has a satisfying feel. It fits neatly in a headline. ... Concise, familiar, associated with the sedulous world of academe, *frosh* is now respectful enough for members of any party." See also freshman.

friendly fire both oxymoron and euphemism, "friendly fire" is the U.S. military's way of describing the killing or destruction of our own or allied forces. It is considered "collateral damage," one of the accepted costs of war. In the first Gulf War, "more American troops are thought to have been killed by 'friendly fire' than by the Iraqis, most by air-launched missiles" (the U.K.'s *Independent*). See also collateral damage, military language.

friends with benefits two friends who have a sexual relationship without the expectation of monogamy or the explicit commitment to being a couple. Friends with benefits (FWB) can alleviate the risks of more casual hookups. Sixty percent of college students participating in a 2011 Michigan State University study said they had engaged in at least one FWB arrangement at some point in their lives.

frigid (referring to a woman's sexual response) unaroused, unresponsive, uninterested, anorgasmic, nonorgasmic, preorgasmic. "Frigid" is unscientific and sexist. Beware orgasm-as-norm thinking (contrary to cultural myth, it is possible to live a full life without being frequently orgasmic or, indeed, orgasmic at all). "Frigidity" is most often traceable to an insensitive lover.

frivolous lawsuits see tort reform.

frogman military/deep-sea/scuba diver, skin-diver, underwater swimmer/explorer, diver, frog; frogman and frogwoman.

frontier this term is not much appreciated by American Indians; what for some represented the limits of the known world was for others their known and revered homeland. For "frontiersman," "European American settler/pioneer" may be appropriate.

front man/frontman (music) lead singer, vocalist, star, leader, front musician/player. Front woman is the correct term for women who front bands.

front man front, figurehead, nominal head, deputy, puppet, representative.

front office man manager, head, owner, upper-level manager, executive, policymaker; sometimes, front office, management.

fruit see food names for people.

frump/frumpy because one of the two definitions of "frump" is an unattractive girl/woman and because the terms are commonly reserved for women, you may need alternatives: slob, sloven, unkempt person, stick-in-the-mud; dowdy, slovenly, unkempt, tacky, drab, old-fashioned, unfashionable, out-of-date, staid.

FTM/FTM transsexual see MTF/MTF transsexuals, transgender.

full-blooded see blood.

fundamentalist reserve this for people and groups who self-identify as "fundamentalist." Otherwise identify the characteristic you want to convey; evangelical, militant, conservative, radical, fanatical. If you mean people who are very serious about their religion, use devout, practicing, orthodox. United Church of Christ minister Alexander Harper (in *The New York Times*) protested the increasing use of "fundamentalist" to describe those of strong religious convictions: "Within Christian fundamentalism, if the word can be used objectively anymore, there are biblical, doctrinal, and pietistic conservatives. The first typically stresses literal interpretation of the Scripture; the second, exclusive theories of salvation; the third, inner experiences of the spirit. They may or may not be political activists. One suspects that conservative Shiite Islam ... admits to at least as many distinctions as those existing among Christian fundamentalists. I call for a moratorium on the use of 'fundamentalist' ... the word only smears, casting no light but only heat, like ugly racial slurs."

funnyman comedian, comic, humorist, wit, wisecracker, punster, satirist, comedist, clown, jokesmith, jokester, jester, mime; joker, practical joker, prankster.

> We believe the concern for words that are gender-tagged is the most important shift in English usage in the last 400 years.
>
> Anne Soukhanov

> Language is also a place of struggle.
>
> bell hooks

gabby nonsexist per se, "gabby" is functionally sexist and ageist because it is used exclusively for women and older men. Consider instead talkative, loquacious, garrulous, voluble, fluent, glib, effusive, exuberant, talky, wordy, verbose, long-winded, windy, big-mouthed, talking a blue streak. See also bull session, gossip, gossipy, yenta/yenta.

Gabrieleno Tongva. See also American Indian.

gal like many male-female word pairs, "gal" and "guy" have gone separate ways. "Gal" has few acceptable uses while "guy" is very common and is used in the plural to refer to both sexes. See also guy, "you guys."

gal Friday see girl Friday.

gal pal see girlfriend.

gambler woman or man. Four to six million Americans are considered "problem gamblers," according to the National Council on Problem Gambling. Men and women apparently gamble for different reasons. Women tend to be what is termed "escape gamblers," while men are typically "action gamblers." "An escape gambler is primarily trying to avoid thoughts, feelings, pain, addiction, and trauma. In contrast, the action gambler is seeking the thrill of competition and an adrenaline rush" (Jane Burke, The Women's Addiction Foundation).

gamesman gamesplayer, strategist, tactician; gamester, gambler, someone who sails suspiciously close to the wind/skates on thin ice/cuts corners/squeaks home; risk-taker, high-flyer.

gamesmanship expertise, skill, clever tactics, strategies, sharp playing, cunning, shrewd playing, dubious tactics, sleight of hand, trickery.

gaming gambling. "Gaming" sounds more benign to entities using gambling for "revenue enhancement." Little known fact: the U.S. military has thousands of slot machines on overseas bases, generating more than $100 million annually. Although the money is used to fund recreation programs, critics say the military shouldn't be encouraging gambling or taking money out of the pockets of the troops (*The Week*).

garbageman garbage collector/hauler, trash/refuse collector, sanitation worker.

Garifuna correct for the Caribbean people living in Belize, Honduras, and Guatemala sometimes inaccurately referred to as Black Caribs.

gasman gas fitter, gas pipe repairer/installer, gas appliance repairer/installer.

"gate rape" "Since 9/11, flight crews have often had to go through screening alongside passengers, and are even pulled aside for special searches. The pilots call it 'gate rape'; many claim that screeners target them because doing so is an easy way for them to meet their quota of random searches and because screeners know crews will be punished by their airlines if they complain" (*Time*). Do not perpetuate this term—no matter how "clever" it is, it detracts from the true horror and long-lasting damage of rape.

gay (noun) do not use "gay" or "Gay" as a singular noun (*New York Times*). "Gays," a plural noun, may be used only as a last resort (in the cases of newspapers, for example, in a hard-to-fit headline). See also gay (adjective), gay community, gay "lifestyle," gay man, gay rights, homophobia, homosexual, lesbian, queer.

gay (adjective) "gay," a term whose origins seem to be in 19th-century France and turn-of-the-century England, is used for issues, events, and places of relevance to gay men and lesbians. However, although "gay rights activists" work for the rights of both lesbians and gay men and other uses of "gay" are inclusive, the preference is to make women visible: "gay and lesbian activism," "lesbian and gay readership." Throughout the 1970s and 1980s, gay publications, gay bars, and gay bookstores served men almost exclusively; to avoid confusion about who is included, use both adjectives. "Gay" is preferred to "homosexual"; the latter emphasizes sexual practice whereas "gay" refers not just to sexual orientation but also to cultural and social aspects. A person's sexual orientation is irrelevant in most situations; question the need to mention it. Some people feel they can no longer use "gay" in its meaning of merry, lively, or high-spirited. However, there is usually more anti-gay sentiment being expressed here than a legitimate linguistic grievance. Because people think of their sexuality in a much more diffuse way today, there is less binary thinking (you're either gay or you're straight) and younger people see themselves more as individuals and less defined totally by their sexuality. Check the people you're writing about and writing for; they may prefer words like "queer" or "open." So far, however, there's nothing that replaces the many uses of "gay." See also gay (noun), gay community, gay "lifestyle," gay man, Gay rights, homophobia, homosexual, lesbian, queer.

gay blade/gay dog these terms refer only to men and the use of "gay" (usually distinguishable in its different senses) could be ambiguous here. Consider using instead high-flyer, fun-lover, high-spirited person; hedonist, sensualist, flirt, bedhopper, free spirit, swinger. See also ladies' man, man about town, womanizer.

gay community this umbrella term, used like such phrases as "the Finnish American community" to describe groups with a shared trait or background, can refer to both men and women but "lesbian and gay communities" is preferred.

gay "lifestyle" Sonia Johnson says, "It's funny how heterosexuals have lives and the rest of us have 'lifestyles'" (*Going Out of Our Minds*). The fuzzy concept of a "lifestyle" has become code to convey "otherness" and "wrongness." Most lesbians and gay men have as much or more in common with heterosexuals than they do with each other; they have jobs and library cards and dental appointments, they put money in parking meters, sprain their ankles, go to ballgames, and pay income taxes.

There is no monolithic "lifestyle." The Associated Press and *New York Times* style guides have instituted rules against the use of this term.

gay man this is the preferred term for a man with a same-sex emotional and sexual orientation. See also gay (adjective), gay rights, homophobia, homosexual, queer.

gay marriage see marriage.

gay rights use in reference to the Gay Rights Movement, originally called the Gay Liberation Movement. When discussing "gay rights," use the term "equal rights for ..." or "equal protection for ..." instead. These rights are often referred to by anti-gay groups as "special-interest privileges" or "special protected status." They are portrayed as rights the average person does not have, when in fact they are simply the same rights enjoyed by other U.S. citizens—including the right to live free from discrimination in employment, housing, and education. See also gay (adjective), gay man, homophobia, homosexual, lesbian, queer.

geisha always a woman; there is no parallel for a man and no inclusive term. Use only in its narrowest definition—that is, a Japanese woman with special training in the art of providing lighthearted entertainment, especially for men.

gendarme *bien sûr*, when in France, use *gendarme* even though it is a masculine word (it means "men of arms"). There are, however, both female and male gendarmes with identical job descriptions. At one time the French experimented with the term *gendarmette* for its new female members, but the term was deemed profoundly sexist, was caricatured in a movie, and has since been retired.

gender sex is biological: people with male genitals are male, and people with female genitals are female (with apologies to intersex individuals for whom things are more complicated). Gender is cultural: our notions of "masculine" tell us how we expect men to behave and our notions of "feminine" tell us how we expect women to behave. When associating a word, activity, profession to one sex or the other, the only acceptable limitation is genetic sex: women cannot be sperm donors because it's biologically impossible; it may be culturally unusual for men to be nannies, but it is not biologically impossible. Although these are currently the ways we tend to differentiate between "sex" and "gender," it's a faulty frame. For one thing, it relies on a narrow binary system of thinking. Just as our biological sex isn't always 100 percent male or 100 percent female, "gender" has become an extremely fluid construct that exists on a broad spectrum. "Gender identity" is a person's internal sense or feeling of being female or male, which may not be the same as their biological sex. "Gender expression" is how people present their sense of gender to others through dress, mannerisms, and behavior. "Sexual identity" is independent of "gender identity" and dependent on whether they are sexually attracted to women, men, or both. Just as people determine their own gender identity, people recognize and claim their own sexual identity. Gender identity and gender expression are often closely linked with the term transgender or trans-identified. "Genderqueer" or "fluid gender" may be used by those whose gender and sexual orientation are somewhere on the continuum between or outside the binary system. Although some city and state jurisdictions forbid workplace discrimination based on gender identity or expression, a federal statute is still needed. See also genderfluid, gender roles, queer, transgender, two-spirit people.

gender bias gender bias is behavior or decision-making that is based on or reveals: stereotypical attitudes about the nature and roles of men and women; perceptions of their relative worth; myths and misconceptions about the social and economic realities encountered by both sexes (*Judicial Council Advisory Committee on Gender Bias in the Courts Report*).

gender expression this is the "external manifestation of one's gender identity, usually expressed through 'masculine,' 'feminine,' or gender-variant behavior, clothing, haircut, voice, or body characteristics. Typically, transgender people seek to make their gender expression match their gender identity, rather than their birth-assigned sex" (Gay & Lesbian Alliance Against Defamation).

gender-fair language words that treat both sexes equally constitute gender-fair language. The words may or may not reveal the person's sex. For example, "girls and boys" specifies sex but because both are included, the phrase is gender-fair.

genderfluid a term acknowledging that some people move between genders or have a fluctuating gender identity. In the broader sense, it reflects an unwillingness to categorize gender into inflexible binary distinctions. Toni Foxx (2013) says, "Discovering the term genderfluid was very freeing. ... I felt like I was owning myself." See also gender, gender roles, intersex.

gender-free language words that do not specify gender constitute gender-free language. "Students," "police officers," and "laypeople" are gender-free terms; "businessman" and "businesswoman" are not.

gender gap used in politics, economics, sociology, education, and other fields, this term gained prominence in 1982 when, for the first time in opinion-polling history, a significant sex difference in the job-approval rating surfaced during Ronald Reagan's first term; 61 percent of men thought he was doing a good job, but only 42 percent of women did. "Gender gap" has also been commonly used with respect to standardized test scores, where girls/young women used to score higher on verbal tests and boys/young men scored higher on math tests. The difference has all but disappeared in verbal scores and has greatly narrowed in math scores. "Gender gap" discussions are nearly always phrased in terms of why girls do better/worse than boys on tests/in school; the male is assumed to be the default.

gender identity everyone has a gender identity. This is one's internal, personal sense of being a man or a woman (or a boy or a girl). For transgender people, their birth-assigned sex and their own internal sense of gender identity do not match. When people tell you who they are, believe them; use the gender identity and the pronouns that a person prefers.

Gender Identity Disorder (GID) a controversial "diagnosis given to transgender and other gender-variant people. Because it labels people as 'disordered,' GID is often considered offensive. The diagnosis is frequently given to children who don't conform to expected gender norms in terms of dress, play, or behavior. Such children are often subjected to intense psychotherapy ..." (Gay & Lesbian Alliance Against Defamation). GID replaces the outdated "gender dysphoria."

gender-neutral language "there is a problem with neutral terms. A word like 'legislator' does not exclude women, but neither does it do anything to change the mental picture for some who already see legislators as male" (Amanda Smith, *The Albuquerque Tribune*). On the other hand, Smith tells about teachers who took two groups of children to opposite ends of the playground. The group told to build snowmen produced 11 snowmen and 1 snowwoman; the group building "snow figures" came up with 5 snowmen, 3 snowwomen, 2 snow dogs, 1 snow horse, and 1 snow spaceship. Sometimes the sexes need to be identified. "Spousal abuse" and "deadbeat parents" give the impression that men and women are equally involved; they are not. Use gender-neutral language to avoid stereotyping ("snow figures") but use gender-specific language to convey realities ("wife battering").

gender roles gender roles (sometimes called sex roles) involve attitudes and behaviors that society expects *because* someone is a woman or *because* someone is a man. Roles traditionally assigned to men are "provider" and "protector." Women have been assigned "caregiver" and "sex object" roles. Biologically, both women and men can provide, protect, nurture, or be a sex object, but most often "cultural influences have been misrepresented as biological imperatives" (Deborah Rhode, *Theoretical Perspectives on Sexual Differences*). Lucile Duberman (*Gender and Sex in Society*) says, "Society creates gender roles, and society can alter them." Contemporary realities offer flexibility to both sexes and freedom from rigid gender roles—if we can model this for upcoming generations of children. See also gender.

general population use only in its true sense, that is, the population to which everyone belongs. The "general population" is sometimes contrasted with lesbians and gays, with those with disabilities, with the "welfare" population, or with other groups not very much in favor with whoever is writing or speaking.

genocide the 1948 United Nations Convention on the Prevention and Punishment of the Crime of Genocide defines genocide as "any of the following acts committed with intent to destroy, in whole or in part, a national, ethnical, racial or religious group, as such: killing members of the group; causing serious bodily or mental harm to members of the group; deliberately inflicting on the group conditions of life, calculated to bring about its physical destruction in whole or in part; imposing measures intended to prevent births within the group; [and] forcibly transferring children of the group to another group." Because "ethnic cleansing" is a euphemism, always use "genocide." "Ethnic cleansing" has been used since the 1992-95 Bosnian war to mask the realities and responsibilities of genocidal acts. Kirk Allison of the Center for Holocaust & Genocide Studies states that using the term "ethnic cleansing" corrupts observation, interpretation, ethical judgment, on-the-ground decision-making and historical and legal judgment. "Ethnocide" (the mass destruction of an ethnic group, often by another ethnic group, which is in the majority) is sometimes used interchangeably with "genocide." However, there is a difference: Bartolomé Clavero (*Genocide or Ethnocide, 1993-2007*) says, "Genocide kills people while ethnocide kills social cultures through the killing of individual souls." See also American Indian Holocaust/Native American Holocaust, Armenian genocide, Darfur genocide, holocaust/Holocaust.

gentile to Jews, a non-Jew; to Mormons, a non-Mormon.

gentleman except for the still-acceptable generic public address of "ladies and gentlemen" and for an occasional, "He is a real gentleman," or perhaps its use in a legislative or political convention setting ("I call on the gentleman from New York" or "the gentlelady from Missouri"), this word ought to be retired. Its true mate, "gentlewoman," is mostly gone, and its other partner, "lady," has been retired in spite of herself. The word has lost its original meaning; Marjorie Luft, St. Paul, Minnesota, collects published reports of such "gentle" men as the "gentleman" who beat his dog to death, the arsonists whose work resulted in the death of two women (Crime Stoppers asked the public to help bring "these gentlemen to justice"), or serial killer Ted Bundy—also referred to in news articles as a gentleman. The press has also referred to "the gentleman who shot President Reagan" and "the gentleman who raped the elderly woman." See also lady.

gentleman farmer hobby/Sunday/weekend/amateur farmer, farmer.

gentleman friend see boyfriend.

gentlemanlike/gentlemanly this stereotype conveys different meanings according to one's perception of what a man ought or ought not do, say, think, wear, feel, look like. These words have nothing to do with sex and everything to do with gender. Use instead courteous, civil, refined, polite, well-mannered, polished, mannerly, brave, thoughtful, considerate, agreeable, accommodating, decent, discreet, dependable, punctilious, civilized, cultivated, dignified. These adjectives can be used equally well of women. They are not synonyms for "gentlemanlike/gentlemanly" but rather what society hears by those terms.

gentleman's agreement unwritten/informal/oral/honorable/verbal agreement, verbal/oral promise/contract, handshake, your word, mutual understanding.

gentlemen of the press representatives of the press, press corps, journalists, reporters. See also newsman/newspaperman.

gentle sex, the avoid; in its quiet way, it discriminates against both women and men.

gentlewoman see gentleman.

Gen X/Gen Y/Gen Z although demographers disagree about each generational group's exact parameters, Gen X-ers are roughly defined as anyone born between 1965 and 1980. Gen Y, more popularly known as "millennials," was born between the early 1980s and the early 2000s. Gen Z is just approaching their teen years, but trend analysts are already spotting defining traits: "Gen Z understands how scary the world can be, having grown up post-9/11, in the wake of the Great Recession, and amid countless reports of school violence. … These dark events will undoubtedly make them more cautious and security-minded, but will also inspire them to improve the world" (Emily Anatole, "Generation Z: Rebels with a Cause," *Forbes*).

gerontology this term, meaning the scientific study of old age and aging, comes from the Greek for "old man" but functions inclusively. Geriatrics, which is the branch of medicine that deals with diseases and problems specific to older people, is based on the Greek for "old age." The two words are not synonymous.

Gestapo/gestapo reserve these terms for their primary meanings (the terrorist German internal security police as organized under the Nazi regime or police organizations with very similar tactics). Using "Gestapo/gestapo" casually or "humorously" (for high-handed people) robs the words of their power and discounts horrors. See also concentration camp, "final solution," Hitler/little Hitler, holocaust/Holocaust, Nazi/nazi.

ghetto because of the negative connotations of ghetto (crime, dilapidation, persecution, poverty, "otherness"), replace it when possible: neighborhood, community, area, quarter, section of town/the city, district. By adding descriptive or geographical adjectives to these general terms, you will draw a clearer picture for your audience.

ghetto blaster boombox, portable stereo. "Ghetto blaster" is unacceptable and offensive.

giantess giant. See also "feminine" word endings.

gigolo no word describes both men and women in the way "gigolo" describes men. For women, we use "kept woman"; French slang uses *gigolette* (a woman of "easy morals"). If you need a sex-neutral term, try lover, prostitute, parasite. See also boy toy, gold digger, kept woman.

G.I. Joe GI. This nickname for U.S. armed forces personnel comes from "government issue," referring to military life, in which everything is standardized, orderly, and regimented, including the soldiers. Without the "Joe" it is perfectly inclusive. Some artists, parents, feminists, and antiwar activists apparently "surgically altered" about 300 G.I. Joes and Barbies, switching their voice boxes, so that this "mutant colony of Barbies-on-steroids" (David Firestone, in *The New York Times*) roared things like "Attack!" "Vengeance is mine!" and "Eat lead, Cobra!" The altered G.I. Joes, meanwhile, twittered, "Will we ever have enough clothes?" and "Let's plan our dream wedding!"

gird (up) one's loins perceived as sexist because it is assumed to refer to men, this term comes from Proverbs 31:17 where the loins in question actually belong to a woman. If you want an alternative, use prepare, prepare for battle, buckle on one's armor, get the steam up, get in gear, batten down the hatches, grit one's teeth.

girl (referring to a woman) woman, young woman. "Girl" is reserved for pre-teens or at the most for those 15 or under; it is objectionable and demeaning when used by men for young women or women. Among women, the term has enjoyed a resurgence of popularity, with the Guerrilla Girls in the mid-'80s and the mainstreaming of African American usages ("girlfriend" and "You go, girl!"). "Girl" is seen on T-shirts and in names like Cybergrrl and Riot Grrrls. "No longer just a badge of youth or a sign of silliness, servitude, or class difference, 'Girl!' has become a mark of pride in one's gender, a sarcastic scoff at those who for centuries patronized females with its use" (Jessica B. Baker, in *Lilith*). For others to refer to women this way is unacceptable—particularly in the workplace. Mariah Burton Nelson notes the use of "girl" as an insult in sports, as in "you play/throw/catch like a girl." See also girl Friday, girlfriend, Guerrilla Girls, "insider/outsider" rule, office boy/office girl.

girlcott coined in 1968 by Olympic track star Lacey O'Neal, more recent girlcotts have induced several companies to take products off the market or alter their advertising. See also boycott.

girl Friday assistant, office assistant/specialist, administrative/executive/ program assistant, clerk, right hand, secretary, aide, office helper, gofer. See also girl, office boy/office girl.

girlfriend there is still no concise, appropriate, universally accepted term to describe the woman we love. At least this one has the parallel of boyfriend. Those in committed relationships need a word with the corresponding weight and meaning of "wife" to denote their partners. The increasing numbers of heterosexual couples in long-term relationships have the same problem. Until the right word comes along, consider: friend, woman friend (if "man friend" is also used); female friend (if "male friend" is also used); best friend, spouse, partner, domestic partner, or life partner (despite its business associations, this is one of the most popular choices); companion (literally, the person with whom you share bread) or longtime companion (this is the second most popular choice); the woman I'm seeing; significant other; soulmate; steady, mate, housemate, paramour, consort, lover, longtime love, live-in, live-in lover; sweetheart; sweetie, gal pal, main/major squeeze; the woman in my life. See also domestic partner, girl.

girlhood acceptable sex-specific word. If you want a generic word, use childhood, innocence, youth.

girlie girls and women have recently started using the adjective to describe some interests and attitudes, but caution is advised: "girlie" is also seen as sexually titillating, as in girlie magazine/show/pictures (Nigel Rees, *A Man About A Dog*).

girlie magazine/movie/show pornographic magazine/movie/"entertainment."

"girlie man/men" lifted from a *Saturday Night Live* skit, this insult has been most famously used by Arnold Schwarzenegger of his political opponents. Joanna Grossman and Linda McClain, on the legal news and commentary website FindLaw, say that "the increasing use of the term 'girlie men' is no joke—it's an example of offensive, yet powerful sex stereotyping. ...It's damaging for America to continue to identify maleness with the qualities we hope for in political leaders—and indeed, in business leaders."

girlish for this vague and usually pejorative term, consider alternatives: ingenuous, naive, childlike, innocent, open, friendly, eager, youthful, immature, self-conscious, inept, adolescent, childish, sophomoric, juvenile, callow, unsophisticated.

girl power distinguish between the use of this term in genuine, girl-positive ways and the use of it as a rather cynical marketing device.

girls and boys use this instead of "boys and girls" about half the time.

Girl Scout the Girl Scouts of the United States of America (GSUSA) is a girls-only organization with strong gender identity that promotes self-esteem, independence, and a variety of skills and interests while also providing a supportive network for many girls. Founded in 1912 by Juliette Gordon Low, membership is currently 3.2 million. Not your mother's Girl Scouts: updated and new badges include Computer Expert, Money Manager, Product Designer, Digital Movie Maker, Website Designer, Good Credit, Locavore, the Science of Style, and others. The correct term for GSUSA adults is troop leaders. The Boy Scouts of America (BSA) and GSUSA prefer Boy Scout and Girl Scout, but there are generic terms if you need one: scout, youth scout, scouter. See also Boy Scout.

give away the bride escort the bride/accompany the bride to the altar/down the aisle. Women are not "given" by their fathers to their husbands.

glass ceiling the glass ceiling is a symbol of all the overt and covert barriers that corporate, industry, military, academic, and otherwise employed women keep banging their heads against. According to the corporate research firm Catalyst, when women did all the things they had been told would help them get ahead—using the same tactics as men—they still advanced less than their male counterparts and had slower pay growth. Even an MBA doesn't help level the playing field; on average, women with MBAs were paid $4,600 less in their first job than men. In a classic Catch-22, women with family responsibilities are seen as lacking commitment to the organization, while women who are fully committed to the organization are often seen as aggressive and unfeminine. Mary Dingee Fillmore (*Women MBAs*) asked one woman what she would need to win a top slot in her corporation. The answer: "A sex-change operation." Anne Jardim (in *The New Yorker*) says, "The ceiling isn't glass; it's a very dense layer of men." Reports of the glass ceiling's demise have been greatly exaggerated. Women hold just 4.6 percent of CEO positions at the largest U.S. companies, 16.9 percent of board seats, and 8.1 percent of top-earner positions. See also mommy track, stained-glass ceiling, wage earner.

GLBT see LGBTQIA/GLBTQIA.

globalization "the expansion of anything-goes trade among nations" (*Too Much*), globalization is supposed to be making the world more prosperous, but inequality among the world's 7.1 billion people is actually widening, and rapidly so (Robert Wade, London School of Economics, in the *Economist*). Jessica Neuwirth (in *Sisterhood Is Forever*) says, "In a corporate context, 'globalization' is a positive word because it has meant more profits and more power. ... In the international Women's Movement, 'globalization' is a negative word because it has brought great harm to many women—by facilitating the systematic exploitation of women as a source of cheap domestic and migrant labor, for example, and accelerating the international operation of organized crime, drastically increasing the trade in women and girls for various forms of commercial sexual exploitation." However, Neuwirth argues, "At the core of globalization is a communications-technology revolution that has tremendous power and potential. This revolution is neither inherently good nor bad." She sees opposing globalization as an exercise in futility and suggests that it represents an opportunity to "reorder the world in a way that serves humanity." She also says, "the real danger is that the growing influence of transnational money and power in all aspects of life will be regulated only by the corporate mandate to maximize profits."

global warming refers to the long-term trend of rising global temperatures; each of the past 37 years has been warmer than the 20th-century average. The science is unequivocal that humans are the cause of global warming. The latest climate science prepared for the World Bank by the Potsdam Institute for Climate Impact Research says that we are on a path to a 7.2 degree Fahrenheit (4 degree Celsius) warmer world by the end of the 21st century under the current rate of greenhouse gas emissions. This will have a devastating impact on agriculture, water resources, ecosystems, and human health. According to the U.S. Environmental Protection Agency, for every 2°F of warming, Americans can expect to experience the following: 1) a 5 to 15 percent reduction in crop yields; 2) a 3 to 10 percent increase of flooding risks; 3) a 200 to 400 percent increase in acreage burned by wildfires in the western U.S. See also climate change.

global war on terror see war on terror.

G-man government/federal/FBI/plainclothes/secret/un dercover agent, government investigative agent, intelligence officer, member of the FBI, spy.

God (Christian) we have not assigned God an ethnic origin or an age but have thought nothing of assigning a gender and a religion (God always belongs to the same faith we do). Too often, the default "God" is assumed to be Christian, whereas African religions, Brahminism, Chinese religions, Egyptian religions, Hinduism, Islam, Jainism, Judaism, Sikhism, and many other religions also have a God/god. In addition, theology has never ruled that God is male. In the fourth century, St. Gregory of Nazianzus summed up traditional thought writing that "Father" and "Son" as applied to the Trinity did not name their essences but rather were metaphors for their relationship to each other. John 4:24 says that God is pure Spirit (and thus is genderless) and the words for God in both Greek and Hebrew are sex-neutral. Sandra M. Schneiders (*Women and the Word*) lists some of the many metaphors we have for God (sun, rock, wind, spring, fire, lion, leopard, she-bear, mother eagle, dove, potter, builder, shepherd, hero, warrior, physician, midwife, homemaker, bread, judge, king, mother, husband, father) and says, "We create the metaphor to say something about God; but then God seems to be saying something about the vehicle of the metaphor. Thus, if God is a king, there is a tendency to see kings as divine." Theologian Mary Daly says simply, "If God is male, then male is God." God's presumed masculinity has provided a religious legitimization of the attitudes that treat women as derivative human beings. The key to inclusive God-language is to be conscious that we are using metaphors ("God is like a ..." but not "God is a...") to make a pure Spirit more accessible to us. Therefore, use a variety of metaphors and use sex-specific pronouns only for specific metaphorical uses—avoid them by (1) replacing "he" or "him" with "God" or another name for God; (2) recasting the sentence; (3) replacing the pronouns with "you/yours" or "who/whom/that." Some of the texts that the oldest books of the Bible are based on call God the Elohim, a name that signifies masculinity, femininity, singularity, and plurality. Some Orthodox Jews use "G-d" instead of "God"; in their tradition, anything with "God" written on it must be respectfully buried. See also Allah, Father (God), Father, Son, and Holy Spirit/Ghost, God/he, God/himself, God/his, God of our Fathers, Holy Spirit, Jehovah, Lord, Son of Man, Yahweh.

goddess religions in which people revered their supreme creator as female existed from approximately 7,000 B.C.E. until about 500 C.E. (Merlin Stone, *When God Was a Woman*). Retain "goddess" in references to the goddess religions and to feminist spirituality that uses the term. When "goddess" indicates a lesser god, replace it with "god"; capitalize both or neither.

godfather/godmother acceptable terms.

God/his replace phrases like "his goodness," "his love," or "by his mercy" with sex-neutral expressions ("divine goodness," "eternal love," or "out of mercy") or with the second person: "Your Goodness," "Your Mercy." The proper possessive pronoun for God is "God's," for example, "God's goodness," "God's mercy." See also God (Christian).

God of our Fathers God of our ancestors/of all generations/of our forebears/of our mothers and fathers.

go-go girl go-go dancer.

gold digger this could be used of either sex but is reserved for women. Parallel male terms in some cases might be "gigolo" or "toyboy," but try instead to describe the person you have in mind with inclusive adjectives: greedy, grasping, avaricious, self-seeking, rapacious, out for all one can get.

good old boy/good ole boy Southern sidekick, crony, pal. These terms were particularly popular in the mid-1960s when they referred to the Texas cronies of President Lyndon B. Johnson. Women don't often play a "good ole boy" role; sometimes this might be the appropriate term for a particular man. See also old-boys' network, old-girls' network.

good Samaritan woman or man

gook see slur.

gossip not sexist per se (it originally meant "godparent"), "gossip" is functionally sexist because the term is reserved for women. For the verb, use talk idly, talk over, talk up a storm, chat, converse, shoot the breeze, pass the time of day, make small talk, jaw, make chin music, wag tongues, rattle away, run off at the mouth, beat one's gums, bend someone's ear, talk someone's arm/head off; repeat everything one hears, tell secrets, spread rumors/stories, mudsling, dish the dirt. For the noun, use: rumormonger, whisperer, talebearer, blabbermouth, big mouth, mudslinger, motormouth, loose tongue, chin wag, newsmonger, windbag, idle talker; palaver, idle/small/empty talk, scuttlebutt, hearsay, chin music, talkfest, an earful. See also bull session, gabby, gossipy, yenta/yenta.

gossipy long-winded, big-mouthed, talkative, curious, loquacious, garrulous, gregarious, windy; rumormongering. See also gossip.

governess to refer to a governor of either sex, use governor. For someone who teaches young children, use tutor, private teacher, teacher, child mentor, instructor. Note what happened to the formerly parallel word pair "governor/governess" over the years. To date, 35 women (plus one in Puerto Rico) have served as governor; Nellie Tayloe Ross (D-WY) was the first woman, chosen by her party to run in 1925 after her husband died. Her two-year term began 15 days before Miriam ("Ma") Ferguson (D-TX) became the second woman governor, elected as a stand-in for her impeached husband. Janet Napolitano (D-AZ) was the first woman to succeed another woman as governor of a state. Kathleen Sebelius (D-KS) was the first whose father (John Gilligan, D-OH) was also governor of a state. The first woman-versus-woman gubernatorial race was in 1986, when Republican Kay Orr defeated Democrat Helen Boosalis to become governor of Nebraska. In 2008, Sarah Palin (R-AK) became the first woman governor to be a vice presidential nominee on a major party ticket. Arizona has had four women governors.

granddaddy/daddy of them all this is fairly harmless and it has the near relative "mother of all..." expression to balance it, but if you need something sex-neutral, try biggest/oldest/grandest/best of them all. See also "mother of all..."

grand duchess retain for official title, which can refer either to the ruler of a grand duchy or to the wife or widow of a grand duke.

grande dame a complimentary sex-linked term, except that there is no equivalent for a man.

grandfather clause leave as is in legal and historical uses. Otherwise use escape/existing-condition clause, exemption, retroactive exemption.

grandfatherly/grandmotherly these vague adjectives have no universal meanings unless it is "kindly." The terms are especially useless in describing appearance. The fact of grandparenthood is often irrelevant; when it is relevant, avoid outdated stereotypes.

Grandmaster the title "Grandmaster" for a member of the U.S. Chess Federation indicates a very specific level of ability and has no synonyms (Andy Sabl). Master, Candidate Master, National Master, and International Master are also specialized chess terms with no substitutes. Grandmaster is sometimes abbreviated GM (IGM for "International Grandmaster").

granny/grannie OK; "gramp/gramps" is for a man.

granny dress/gown use if you like; otherwise consider old-fashioned/Victorian/high-necked dress/gown.

granny dumping elderly abandonment, packed-suitcase syndrome. "Granny dumping" was one of the American Dialect Society's New Words of the Year for 1991. Anne H. Soukhanov (*Word Watch*) defines it as offensive slang for the practice in which an elderly person is left in a hospital emergency room—usually by relatives, caregivers, or apartment manager—with a suitcase of essential personal effects.

grantsmanship the fine art of obtaining grants, grant-getting, the knack of attracting grants, grant-getting/grant-writing skills/ability. There is no one-word substitute for this handy, but sexist, term. Since 1990, the share of grant dollars targeted to benefit girls and women has ranged from 5 percent to 7.4 percent.

grass widow/grass widower both terms refer to someone who is divorced, separated, or whose spouse is temporarily away. Use the terms in parallel ways, or not at all. See also widow/widower.

Great Britain "Great Britain" refers to the island comprising England, Scotland, and Wales; "England" is one of the countries of Great Britain; "United Kingdom" refers to Great Britain plus Northern Ireland; "Britain" refers to the island of Great Britain in the period before the reign of Alfred the Great (871-899).

greenwashing The U.S.-based watchdog group CorpWatch defines greenwashing as "the phenomena of socially and environmentally destructive corporations attempting to preserve and expand their markets or power by posing as friends of the environment." Governments, political candidates, trade associations, and non-government organizations have also been accused of greenwashing. Examples of greenwashing are the George W. Bush Clear Skies Initiative, which environmentalists have argued actually weakens air pollution laws, and his Healthy Forests Initiative.

groomsman best man, attendant. Avoid "groomsman"; its opposite number ("bridesmaid") is nonparallel ("maid/man"). "Best man" is used with "best woman," and "attendant" is used when the bride's witness is also called an attendant.

groupie although theoretically inclusive, "groupie" is used nearly always for young women. If you want something less sex-specific, consider admirer, fan, follower, worshiper.

grrrl in *Bitch*, Rachel Fudge says, "As the g-word became more widely adopted and popularized by girls and women who had little involvement with feminist activism of any sort, the riot grrrls' original three-*r* spelling slimmed down to two *r*s." She quotes online diarist Haley Hieronymus, "As far as I can tell, the difference between grrrls and grrls seems to be the difference between feminist politics and, uh, having none." See also girl.

guardsman guard, soldier, guardian, member of the guards, guard member/officer, National Guard member.

Guerrilla Girls defining themselves as a "bunch of anonymous females who take the names of dead women artists as pseudonyms and appear in public wearing gorilla masks...we declare ourselves the feminist counterpart to the mostly male tradition of anonymous do-gooders like Robin Hood, Batman, and the Lone Ranger." The Guerrilla Girls began papering sections of New York City with smartly designed black-and-white posters in 1985 to call out the "stale, male, and pale" art establishment, as well as a few other pale-male dominated places, like Hollywood. Using sarcasm, statistics, and bold graphics, the posters charged galleries, museums, collectors, critics, and white male artists with sexism and racism. In 2012, the Guerrilla Girls parked a "mobile billboard" in front of the Museum of Fine Arts, Boston that read: " Do women have to be naked to get into Boston Museums? Plenty of nudes in the Museum of Fine Arts are female, but only 11% of the artists are women." See also artist, girl, grrrl.

guinea see ethnic slurs.

gunman killer, armed/professional killer, assassin, robber, intruder, slayer, trigger, hired gun, gunfighter, gunner, shooter, gunslinger, gun-wielder, sharpshooter, sniper, attacker, outlaw, bandit, terrorist, gangster, racketeer, mobster, hoodlum, liquidator, executioner, enforcer, croaker.

gun moll accomplice, sidekick, confederate in crime, gangster's companion. See also girlfriend, gunman.

guns some 310 million firearms are privately held by Americans, about one gun per person, the highest ratio in the world (Minneapolis' *Star Tribune* in 2013). Guns are ostensibly purchased for hunting, protection, and collection, but these legitimate interests are outweighed by the egregious number of weapons in "other" classifications. When writing about guns, gun control, or the NRA, triple-check all facts. Dave Gilson ("Hits and Myths," *Mother Jones*) dismantles the belief that guns deter crime and protect us: states with the highest ownership rates have a gun murder rate 114 percent higher than states with low gun ownership rates; for each time a gun is used in self-defense in the home, a gun is used in the home in 7 assaults or murders, 11 suicide attempts, and 4 accidents; a Philadelphia study found the odds of being shot were 4.5 times greater if the victim carried a gun, of being killed 4.2 times greater; not one mass shooting has been stopped by armed civilians in the past 30 years; in 1 case in 5, an ER shooting involves guns taken from guards; in 2010, 6 times more women were shot by husbands, boyfriends, and ex-partners than murdered by male strangers; a woman's chance of being killed by her abuser increases more than 7 times if he has access to a gun. Countering the frequently heard threat that "they" will come for your guns, Gilson notes that "the number of guns owned by law enforcement and military is 4 million; the number owned by civilians is 310 million." He says that weak laws and loopholes backed by the gun lobby make it easier to get guns illegally: around 40 percent of legal gun sales involve private sellers and don't require background checks—40 percent of prison inmates who used guns in their crimes got them this way; in one investigation 62 percent of online gun sellers were willing to sell to buyers who said they couldn't pass a background check; 20 percent of licensed California gun dealers agreed to sell handguns to researchers posing as illegal buyers; the Bureau of Alcohol, Tobacco, Firearms, and Explosives has not had a permanent director for 6 years, due to an NRA-backed requirement that the Senate approve nominees. Erica Goode (*New York Times* in 2012) reports that some 70 percent of guns recovered at crime scenes in Virginia were purchased within one year of the crime, suggesting that in some cases guns are purchased with the intent to commit a crime or murder. For up-to-date statistics broken down in dozens of ways (police officers killed, children shot, guns used in suicides), Google "gun death statistics." It's a complicated picture and important to convey the facts: the media is often blamed for underwriting gun purchases by selling fear, fear, and more fear. In the end, fearful people with more guns tend to kill more people—with guns. See also National Rifle Association.

guru this term's original meaning (from the Hindi language) is a personal spiritual teacher, and English uses it to also mean a trusted adviser or a recognized leader in a field. Use for both sexes. If you want something perceived as less masculine, consider spiritual guide/teacher/leader/adviser, sage, oracle, adviser, counselor; leader, authority.

guy see you guys.

guys and gals this phrase is acceptable for casual use with people you know. Otherwise consider folks, people. See also gal, guy, you guys.

gyp cheat, defraud, rip off, soak, fleece, hoodwink, swindle, deceive, victimize, con, sting, put one over on, rig, fix, rook, gull, exploit, take advantage of, diddle. Avoid the pejorative "gyp," which was based on "Gypsy."

Gypsy/Gypsies see Romani/Romanies, Romani holocaust.

> The basic tool for the manipulation of reality is the manipulation of words. If you can control the meaning of words, you can control the people who must use the words.
>
> Philip K. Dick

hag although there are attempts to reclaim this word's older meaning—a mature wise-woman—it is generally perceived as pejorative.

hajji an Arabic term for those who've made the hajj pilgrimage to Mecca, "hajji" has become the slur of choice for U.S. troops, according to Chris Hedges and Laila Al-Arian (in *Los Angeles Times*) who spent several months interviewing soldiers who've fought in Iraq. The troops regularly denigrate "hajji food" and "hajji homes," and the slurs have been accompanied by abuse and undeserved killings.

half-breed/half-caste unacceptable terms when referring to people of mixed ancestry or descent. "*Half-breed* and *half-caste* are senseless. We're not half of anything. We are whole people" (Jaimie Markham, in *Colors*). Tim Giago, publisher of *Indian Country Today*, the largest U.S. Indian weekly, says, "Research has shown that these terms were created by the federal bureaucracy to place Indian people into racial pigeon holes." They are equally offensive when used of the Aboriginal peoples of Australia. See also aborigine, Indian, mélange, métis/métisse.

handicappism the attitudes, practices, and physical obstacles that lead to unequal and unfair treatment of people with disabilities constitute handicappism. A handicappist culture has a high tolerance for such bias. See also ableism, disabilities, handicapped.

handicapped someone/person with a disability, the disability/disabilities (not "disabled") community, persons with disabilities (not "the disabled"). Do not use "handicapped" as a noun or adjective referring to any of the 43 million Americans with disabilities. A disability is a condition; a handicap is an obstacle. Someone with multiple sclerosis has a disability; the two flights of stairs leading to a classroom present a handicap to that person. For a complete discussion of writing and speaking about disabilities, see disabilities.

handicapped parking this term is used in state and federal laws. Although the Americans with Disabilities Act refers to it as "accessible parking," changing existing statutes and parking-lot language will probably take some time.

handmaid/handmaiden servant, personal attendant, attendant; instrument, agent, tool, vehicle, facilitator, medium.

handyman carpenter, laborer, repairer, odd/general jobber, repairer, maintenance worker, custodian, caretaker; handywoman and handyman if used gender-fairly.

hangman executioner, public executioner, lyncher.

Hanukkah also spelled Chanukah about half as often and, less often, as Hannukah, this eight-day festival dates to 165 B.C.E. and celebrates the victory of the Jews against unbelievable odds over King Antiochus of Syria who had forbidden them to practice their religion. Because of its calendar proximity to Christmas, Hanukkah is often referred to as if it were the most important Jewish holiday while the holidays that are in fact important—Rosh Hashanah and Yom Kippur—are often overlooked by the media and non-Jews. Other major Jewish holidays include Purim, Sukkoth, Shevuoth, and Passover.

harbor master harbor chief/superintendent/officer/commander.

hardhat man or woman. (See, for example, Molly Martin, ed., *Hard-Hatted Women*). See also tradesman.

harelip cleft lip. Cleft lip and cleft palate are different conditions. "Harelip" is highly objectionable.

harem although the harem is negatively perceived in the West as a place of confinement for women, it is not always understood this way by women in some cultures. "In the Middle East, the harem is the women's quarters for living and working protected by male members of the family from outside intrusion " (Marsha J. Hamilton, in Joanna Kadi, ed., *Food for Our Grandmothers*). Use "harem" only if you understand its many culture-specific ramifications. The ethnocentric and incorrect use of "harem" to describe a man's several women friends implies an inappropriate sense of men owning women. See also purdah, sex object.

harlot/harlotry prostitute/prostitution. "Harlot" (from the Old French for "rogue") used to refer only to male vagabonds, rascals, vagrants, and entertainers. Later it was used for a person of either sex, and finally became restricted to women. See also prostitute.

harp (verb) this word is almost exclusively reserved for women; "men who are considered powerful protest, chew-out, or take action," but women harp (Susan Hoy Crawford, *Beyond Dolls & Guns*). When tempted to use "harp," decide what the same behavior in a man would be called.

harpy/harridan although "harpy" can mean a predatory person, it is usually used for "a shrewish woman"; the original Harpies were hideous, voracious monsters. A harridan is also a shrew, but vicious to boot. These terms have no male "equivalents"; even the stubborn and ill-tempered (not shrewish) curmudgeon, for example, is viewed with a certain fond tolerance. See also nag (noun), shrew, termagant, virago.

Hasidim members of the ultra-orthodox, alternative movement of popular mysticism founded in Eastern Europe in the 18th century are called Hasidim, Hassidim, or Chassidim in the plural; Hasid, Hassid, or Chassid in the singular.

hatchet man hired killer/attacker/assassin, killer, professional killer, mercenary, liquidator; someone who gives you the axe or does a hatchet job on someone. The term is harder to replace in its sense of someone who carries out a disagreeable task.

hate crime terroristic and often violent acts that target individuals or groups because of their sex, race, color, religion, sexual orientation, disability, age, or national origin are called hate crimes and include arson, bombings of homes and businesses, cross burnings, vandalism (like swastika drawings), personal assault, harassing or obscene phone calls, and threatening letters or packages. In some jurisdictions, hate crimes cannot be prosecuted independently; they need to be tried in conjunction with, for example, a crime against property.

hate groups the Southern Poverty Law Center lists 1,007 groups by name, location, and membership numbers (*Intelligence Report*). Divided into Ku Klux Klan, neo-Nazi, white nationalist, racist skinhead, Christian identity, neo-confederate, black separatist, and general hate groups, they include, among others, Supreme White Alliance, Aryan Terror Brigade, True Invisible Empire Knights of the Ku Klux Klan, Loyal White Knights of the Ku Klux Klan, Knights of the Holy Cross of the Ku Klux Klan, American Nazi Party, Aryan Nations Sinister Souls Motorcycle Club, Gallows Tree Wotansvolk Alliance, National Socialist German Workers Party, Tabernacle of the Phineas Priesthood - Aryan Nation, Confederate Patriot Voters United, Advanced White Society, Women for Aryan Unity, Blood and Honour U.S.A., Confederate Hammerskins, The Hated, Vinland Murder Squad, Volksfront, United Society of Aryan Skinheads, Church of God's Chosen, Crusaders for Yahweh, Knights of the Holy Identity, American Family Association (plus Family Research Council, Family Research Institute, Family Watch International, Illinois Family Institute—all anti-gay), Americans for Truth About Homosexuality, Mission America, You Can Run But You Cannot Hide, Aggressive Christianity, Inconvenient History (Holocaust deniers), Christ or Chaos, Slaves of the Immaculate Heart of Mary, Georgia Militia, and Holy Nation of Odin. The generalized hate is irrational: "We've got a Muslim for a president who hates cowboys, hates cowgirls, hates fishing, hates farming, loves gays, and we hate him!" (country singer Hank Williams, Jr., to an approving crowd at the Stockyards Music Festival, in *Intelligence Report*). See also hate rock, nullification, sovereign citizens.

hater someone who spreads negativity and seeks to damage others' reputations. Prevalent on the Internet and in social media, the term "hater" first surfaced in hip-hop culture, as did the equally popular comeback to hostile comments: "haters gonna hate."

hate radio see hate speech, shock jock.

hate rock typically heavy metal or aggressive punk rock music that promotes white nationalism and expresses hatred toward Jews, gays, and people of color, hate rock is seen by leaders of white-supremacist groups as the most effective way to recruit young followers and raise money. Lyrics call for a race war (the Wisconsin Sikh temple shooter was involved in the hate rock scene) and bands have names like Angry Aryans, Blue Eyed Devils, Definite Hate, End Apathy, and H8Machine. William Pierce, leader of the neo-Nazi National Alliance, sees hate rock as a way to sway the hearts and minds of young people: "Music speaks to us at a deeper level than books or political rhetoric: music speaks directly to the soul." See also hate groups, white supremacy.

hate speech the First Amendment right to free speech conflicts with the implied right of citizens to be free of hate speech, especially since the latter often leads directly to hate crimes. Brian E. Albrecht says, "Finding hate speech can be easier than defining it." But hate-monitoring groups such as Political Research Associates, the Anti-Defamation League, and the Southern Poverty Law Center know it when they see it, and they say hate speech is practiced by the National Alliance, Liberty Lobby, the Order, Aryan Nations/Brotherhood, Ku Klux Klan, the Patriot movement, John Birch, Posse Comitatus, Christian Identity, various White Aryan Nation people, neo-Nazis, skinheads, survivalists, conspiracy theorists, many private militias, and groups embracing racist, anti-Semitic, neo-Nazi, white-supremacist, antigay, and antifeminist philosophies. Chip Berlet, of Political Research Associates, says instantaneous communications technology has led to the abnormally fast creation of social movements; processes that once took decades now occur in weeks. He says, "[T]ruth emerges in vigorous if not chaotic, debate, but not when such debate is based on dehumanization, scapegoating, hate, lies, myths, and conspiracies. It's like running a sewer into your water supply and wondering why people get sick." Talk radio has been an important conduit for hate speech. Patricia J. Williams (in *Ms.*) says, "The polemics of right-wing radio are putting nothing less than hate onto the airwaves, into the marketplace, electing it to office, teaching it in schools, and exalting it as freedom." "What we need is not more law enforcement, not more FBI infiltration, not more partisan politics, says Berlet. "What we need is decent Americans standing up and saying, 'Enough.'" See also free speech, prejudice, shock jock.

hausfrau although this term means "housewife" for both the Germans and those English-speaking peoples who have borrowed it, its use is neutral-to-positive in Germany but largely pejorative in English-speaking countries. Use it only in Germany.

Hawai'i/Hawaii has two official languages; Hawai'i is the correct spelling in the Hawaiian language. Because "Hawaiian" is an English word, it has no "'okina" (glottal stop), thus Hawai'ian is incorrect. Hawaiian words are pluralized by what comes before them; therefore do not add an "s" to hula, lei, mahahlo, or other Hawaiian words. The University of Hawaii website has a helpful style guide. Ethnic Hawaiians are descendants of the original Polynesian inhabitants of the islands, and are also called Native Hawaiians. Hawaiian can also be used to refer to those of Chinese, Filipino, Japanese, Korean, Portuguese, and Puerto Rican ancestry in Hawaii. Or use Hawaii resident or islander for anyone living in the state.

he (pseudogeneric) never use "he" when you mean "he and she," or when you are referring to someone who could be a man or a woman (for example, "the consumer/he"). Make your sentence plural, circumlocute, or use one of the suggestions given in the Writing Guidelines.

headmaster/headmistress private school/school director/principal, principal, director, head administrator, head. In some instances (for example, a British boys'/girls' school) "headmaster" or "headmistress" might be correct.

head of family/head of household woman or man. See also family man, housewife, provider.

head of state man or woman. Women have served or are serving as heads of state or government in Argentina, Australia, Bangladesh, Barbados, Belize, Bolivia, Brazil, Burundi, Canada, Central African Republic, Ceylon, Chile, Costa Rica, Croatia, Denmark, Dominica, Finland, France, Georgia, Germany, Guyana, Haiti, Iceland, India, Indonesia, Ireland, Israel, Jamaica, Kosovo, Latvia, Liberia, Lithuania, Malawi, Malta, Moldova, Mongolia, Mozambique, New Zealand, Nicaragua, Norway, Pakistan, Panama, Peru, the Philippines, Poland, Portugal, Rwanda, San Marino, Senegal, Slovakia, Slovenia, South Korea, Sri Lanka, Switzerland, Thailand, Trinidad and Tobago, Turkey, Transnistria, Ukraine, the United Kingdom, and Yugoslavia.

headwaiter man or woman.

health care see universal health care coverage.

health of the mother this phrase is central to the current abortion debate as abortion opponents continue to challenge the core constitutional protections for a woman's right to terminate a pregnancy. In *Roe v. Wade*, the Supreme Court ruled that in cases where the fetus's critical organs could sustain independent life, the state "may go so far as to proscribe abortion during that period, except when it is necessary to preserve the life or health of the mother." In a companion case, *Doe v. Bolton*, the court expanded its definition of "health of the mother": "medical judgment may be exercised in light of all factors—physical, emotional, psychological, familial, and the woman's age—relevant to the well-being of the patient. All these factors may relate to health." Despite the court's clear rulings, anti-choice lawmakers continue to vote down proposed health exceptions to abortion restrictions and openly state their opposition to protecting women's health as required by law. During his 2012 campaign, Rep. Joe Walsh (R-Ill) stated that there was no such thing as a medically necessary abortion: "With modern technology, you can't find one instance [of an abortion that saved a mother's life]. … There is no exception as life of the mother, and as for health of the mother, same thing." (Walsh lost his bid for re-election.) The American College of Obstetricians and Gynecologists issued a statement in response to Walsh's comments: "Abortions are necessary in a number of circumstances to save the life of a woman or to preserve her health. Unfortunately, pregnancy is not a risk-free life event. Despite all our medical advances, more than 600 women die each year from pregnancy and childbirth-related reasons right here in the U.S. In fact, many more would die each year if they did not have access to abortion to protect their health or save their lives." Among the conditions where abortion may be necessary to save a woman's life are heart failure, preeclampsia, embolisms, severe infections, and hemorrhages. See also abortion.

hearing impaired see deaf/Deaf.

heathen defined as "one who adheres to the religion of a people or nation that does not acknowledge the God of Judaism, Christianity, or Islam" (*American Heritage Dictionary*), this term needs to be replaced by the name of the belief system under discussion. Or try areligious. "Heathen" and "nonbeliever" resemble "nonwhite" in being a catchall term for everybody who isn't "us." It also describes the supposedly unenlightened and uncivilized, an indefensible judgment. See also Pagan/Neopagan, primitive, savage.

heavyweight in the sense of an important or successful person, a heavyweight could theoretically be either sex. There is, however, a male cast to the word (because of wrestlers and boxers and because it was used for so long only of men). Consider instead VIP, big shot/wheel, bigwig, dignitary.

Hebrew this is used principally for the language of contemporary Israel and for the old Canaanite language of the Bible. See also Israeli, Jew.

heiress heir. See also "feminine" word endings.

helmsman pilot, steerer, navigator.

helpmate/helpmeet these terms are most often used for women and they imply a certain existential inferiority. While still in the White House, Louisa Adams wrote, "Man's interpretation of the word 'helpmate' as used in the Bible means this: Women made to cook his dinner, wash his clothes, gratify his sensual appetites, and thank him and love him for permission to drudge through life at the mercy of his caprices. Is this the interpretation intended by the Creator, the father of all mercy?" Probably not. Modern scholars say the meaning of the original Hebrew was actually "suitable partner," someone to walk side by side with him. See also Adam's Rib, Eve.

he-man this term perpetuates stereotypes and false expectations. Use instead precise adjectives: aggressive, hardy, rugged, husky, hearty, robust, powerful, muscular, domineering, capable, dynamic, energetic, physical.

hemiplegic someone with/who has hemiplegia (a paralysis affecting only one side of the body). See also disabilities, paraplegic, "people first" rule, quadriplegic.

henchman sidekick, hireling, underling, flunky, lackey, thug, hood, tool, puppet, accomplice, stooge, hanger-on, ward heeler, minion, myrmidon; follower, supporter, subordinate, helper, aide, right-hand, cohort; groom, attendant, page. (William Safire notes that "henchman" is used only pejoratively; "nobody ever claims to be anybody else's henchman.")

hen party all-women party, women-only party. The use of "hen party" follows the "insider/outsider" rule: women may call their gatherings hen parties; others may not. "Hen" has been a slang word for a woman since 1626. See also bull session, stag party.

henpeck/henpecked she henpecks; he is henpecked. When men have a problem, they are said to protest, object, grumble, raise a fuss, grouse, beef, criticize, censure, deplore, disapprove, chew out, remind, take action, give a piece of their mind. Use those terms for women too. Calling a man "henpecked" is also disparaging to him; consider: bossed around, bullied, browbeaten, passive, submissive, dominated, subjugated, under someone's thumb, led by the nose, at one's beck and call, ruled with an iron hand. See also castrate, nag (verb), unman.

hermaphrodite see intersexual.

hero/heroine use "hero" for both men and women. Although "hero" is the masculine form of the Greek word and "heroine" is the feminine, two of Greek mythology's best-known lovers were named Hero and Leander, and Hero was not the manly half. In English, a heroine is defined as "a female hero"—that is, a subset of hero. Although theoretically it should be possible to use "hero" and "heroine" in a gender-fair manner, they are already subtly weighted in favor of the broader, more prestigious "hero" and, given the devaluation and discounting of woman-associated words in our language, it seems best to support one neutral term. "Heroine" is still useful when referring to the female main character in a literary work. Poet Maya Angelou has suggested, and others have adopted, "sheroe." If you want alternatives to "hero" and "heroine" consider protagonist, central/main character, champion, celebrity, notable, star, paragon, good example, saint, benefactor, leader, ideal, shining example, luminary, dignitary, personage, figure, public/popular figure, social lion, big name, principal, principal character/role, feature attraction.

herstory coined by Robin Morgan in 1968, this term refers to all the parts of "her story" that have been left out of "his story." The word "history" itself is not sexist; the "his" in "history" is an English/American-language accident and has nothing to do with the male pronoun or with any male-based word. "Herstory" was never intended to replace or be a synonym for "history," but is used to "emphasize that women's lives, deeds, and participation in human affairs have been neglected or undervalued in standard histories" (Casey Miller and Kate Swift, *Words and Women*). Eleanor S. Riemer and John C. Fout (*European Women*) describe the wealth of women's writings they found in "books, women's magazines, and periodicals written, edited, and sometimes typeset and printed by women, for women. ... If historians until now have not used women's own sources to reconstruct women's past, it is only because they have not looked for them." See also history, unconventional spellings.

heteronormativity the belief that heterosexuality is the sole valid, "standard," or "normal" sexual orientation is called heteronormativity. Major social institutions, policies, public discourse and media all reinforce and privilege the heteronormative. Because heterosexuality is considered by many to be the normal or natural sexual orientation, it tends to be regarded as the only legitimate or moral way of being or acting in the world. Science is supporting what so many have known for centuries: sexual orientation is innate, thus neither abnormal nor unnatural. See also heterosexist.

heterosexist a heterosexist subscribes to the system that privileges heterosexuals and discriminates directly or indirectly against homosexuals; heterosexism often operates by a web of attitudes and systems that make opposite-sex arrangements accepted as universal, natural, and inevitable, thus appearing less offensive than overt homophobic prejudice (Jan Clausen, *Beyond Gay or Straight*). The attitude that heterosexuality is the sole valid, "standard," or "normal" sexual orientation is sometimes also called heteronormativity. Heterosexism exists when people act as if everyone is heterosexual; for example, thinking that a "couple" is always a she and a he, forgetting that Valentine's Day is for all couples, not just opposite-sex ones, assuming that only married couples celebrate anniversaries. To include everyone in general statements, remember that same-sex couples also consist of husbands and/or wives, that "couples therapy" is broader than "marriage counseling," and "parents" or "the adults" at a child's house will cover everyone. See also general population, heteronormativity, homophobia.

hick this is derogatory and classist, as are the related hick town, hicksville, hick college. See also hillbilly, redneck, yokel.

hierarchy/hierarchical thinking a system of organizing things or people, where each element (except for the top one) is subordinate to some other element, hierarchy colors most of our culture, from government, businesses, churches, educational institutions, and the military right down to some families. The pecking order in chickens has nothing on us humans. The defining factor of a hierarchy is "power over." Feminists have emphasized linking relationships instead of ranking relationships, "power with" rather than "power over." Starhawk wrote (*Truth or Dare*), "Each being is sacred—meaning that each has inherent value that cannot be ranked in a hierarchy or compared to the value of another being." And we don't have to live with the hierarchy model. Gloria Steinem points out, "What we have been raised to think of as inevitable—division and hierarchy, monotheism and nation states—actually accounts for less than 10 percent of human history."

high priestess high priest. But retain "high priestess" when discussing ancient or present-day goddess religions; it has significance and weight as a sex-specific term. See also "feminine" word endings.

high-risk group high-risk behavior. It is not the group people belong to (needle-users, gay men, heterosexuals with multiple partners) that puts them at risk for HIV/AIDS, but rather their behavior (sharing needles, unprotected sex) See also at risk.

highway patrolman highway officer/patrol officer, motorcycle officer/police.

high yellow Vivian Jenkins Nelsen (*New Voice in the Media*) says this term for lighter-colored African Americans is highly objectionable; she suggests avoiding any description of skin color or degrees of color. See also yellow.

hillbilly functionally nonsexist although it was originally based on a man's name, "hillbilly" is often classist and derogatory. It operates on the "insider/outsider" rule because some people good-humoredly self-identify as hillbillies. References to hillbilly music are acceptable. See also Appalachian.

him/himself do not use to mean "him and her/herself and himself" or when it might refer to either a man or a woman (for example, "the taxpayer/him," "the priest/himself"); replace with the plural, circumlocute, or see the Writing Guidelines on pseudogeneric "he" for suggestions.

Hindu a Hindu is a believer in the Hinduism religion; the language is Hindi. Not all Hindus speak Hindi, and many Hindi speakers are not Hindus.

hired man farm hand/worker, hired/field hand, hand, helper.

his do not use "his" to mean "his and hers," or when it might refer to either a man or a woman (for example, "the plumber/his"); replace with the plural, circumlocute, or see the Writing Guidelines on pseudogeneric "he" for suggestions.

Hispanic referring to people of Mexican, Puerto Rican, Cuban, and other Spanish-speaking countries of Caribbean, Central and South America, and Spanish descent, the term "Hispanic" dates from a Nixon-administration attempt to refine its census classifications. Concise and useful, "Hispanic" is preferred by some of those so designated but considered unacceptable by others. "No one was brought up being told, 'You are Hispanic,'" says Lorenzo Cano, associate director for the Mexican-American studies program at the University of Houston. "That's just a term bureaucracies have used for filing and government purposes. Hispanic is offensive to some; no one wants to be associated with Spain and its history of colonization and oppression in the Americas; Hispanic is too broad and offers the perfect excuse for not exploring the diversity among people who are referred to by that term." Acclaimed author Sandra Cisneros refuses to have her writings included in any anthology that uses the word "Hispanic." Critics of the term argue that it indifferently categorizes and thereby effectively camouflages the cultural, ethnic, class, religious, and historical realities of some 50.5 million Americans who share little more than varieties of the Spanish language, and sometimes not even that (the label can include Portuguese-speaking Brazilians, Europeans from Spain and Portugal who have settled in this country, French-speaking and English-speaking immigrants from Caribbean countries, and immigrant speakers of indigenous, South American Indian languages). However, Herman Badillo, then a member of Congress from New York and a founding member of the Congressional Hispanic Caucus, said that the move to "Hispanic" was cheered among the nation's various affected communities because they stood to gain more political representation and government services as a result of the designation. Chicana activist Elizabeth "Betita" Martínez (in *Teaching Tolerance*), who prefers the term "La Raza," believes "that the advertising industry had a lot to do with 'Hispanic' becoming so established because of its desire to create a market that would encompass a single population. I don't use 'Hispanic' because it is Eurocentric and denies the fact that the people being labeled are not just of Spanish origin. Nor do they all speak Spanish. 'Hispanic' denies our indigenous or Indian roots. It also denies our African roots, from the thousands of slaves that were brought to Latin America." Those who do self-identify as Hispanics tend to be politically conservative business or political leaders or professionals integrating themselves into the mainstream and corporate cultures; "Hispanic" is a term of pride for those who claim it and current usage tends to be fairly evenly divided between "Latina/Latino/Latin@" and "Hispanic." Before using "Hispanic," (1) make sure it is the term of choice of those you are describing; (2) if it is not, use the term preferred by the individual or group (Latina/Latino/Latin@, Mexican American, Chicana/Chicano/Chican@); (3) or list all the specific groups being referred to ("Mexican Americans, Cuban Americans, and Puerto Rican Americans"). See also Chicano/Chicano/Chican@, Latina/Latino/Latin@, Mexican American, La Raza, Spanish.

history from the Greek *historia* meaning "inquiry/knowing/ learning," the word "history" is not male-based. However the word "ahistoricity" has been coined to denote the ways in which the exclusion of women from history, as viewed and written by men, has been not just another exclusion, but women's most debilitating cultural deprivation (Gerda Lerner, *The Creation of Feminist Consciousness*). More than any other factor, the absence of a usable past explains why the subordination of women has persisted for so long; "Women, ignorant of their history," says Lerner, "had to reinvent the wheel over and over again." See also herstory.

Hitler/little Hitler using these terms metaphorically robs them of a horror they properly should retain; they are also painful for a Jew to hear. Either describe the person's actions or consider using fanatic, tyrant, despot, bigot. See also concentration camp, "final solution," Gestapo/gestapo, holocaust/Holocaust, Nazi/nazi.

hit man hired/professional/armed/contract killer, hired gun/assassin, assassin, killer, murderer, sniper, slayer, gunslinger, executioner, liquidator, sharpshooter, trigger, enforcer.

HIV upon the first use of "HIV," spell out the meaning and explanation, thus: "Human Immunodeficiency Virus (HIV), the virus believed to lead to AIDS..." The word virus in "HIV virus" is redundant. The test is "HIV antibody test," not "AIDS test." And people test positive or negative for antibodies to HIV, so the correct terms are HIV positive (or seropositive) and HIV negative. HIV infection is not the same as AIDS; hundreds of thousands of people who have been exposed to HIV have not developed, and may not develop, AIDS, particularly if their condition is monitored and treated with drugs that are increasingly available for that purpose.

ho no. See also whore.

hobo woman or man.

holocaust/Holocaust use "Holocaust" to refer to the Nazis' mass murder of European Jews and others. Although some regard "Holocaust" as unique to Jewish experience and limited to its World War II meaning, the word "holocaust," which has existed since the 14th century, is appropriately used in other contexts: Romanies were also part of the Holocaust—Nazis killed one-fifth to one-fourth of the total Rom population; the genocide of American Indians was a holocaust, as was the enslavement and murders of African peoples; the bombing of Hiroshima was a holocaust and "nuclear holocaust" is a part of our vocabulary. The caution is to reserve "holocaust" for the most egregious cases of humans destroying humans. See also concentration camp, "final solution," Gestapo/gestapo, Hitler/little Hitler, Nazi/nazi.

Holy Spirit (Ghost)/he eliminate masculine pronouns for the Holy Spirit, replacing them with descriptive adjectives, or, in prayer, with direct address ("you" and "your"). The Hebrew *ruah* or *ruach*, meaning "wind, breath, spirit," is grammatically feminine, and the Greek word for "spirit," *pneuma*, is neuter, which is why some writers and speakers refer to the Holy Spirit as "she" or "it." However, the most theologically and linguistically correct approach is to eliminate gender-specific pronouns.

homebody man or woman. See also family man, homemaker.

homeboy/homegirl usages of these colloquial terms seem to be sex-parallel; "homie" is also used for women and men.

home economics/home ec use this only for groups that so label their work. Preferred terms—including family and consumer sciences (FACS), domestic science, and human ecology (the term used by ecologist Ellen Swallow, who pioneered the field)—indicate the field's professional, technical, and scientific aspects, which include health care and education, aging, nutrition, dietetics, HIV/AIDS, alcohol and drug abuse; food production, processing, supplies, and technology; design and textiles; family and social sciences, safety, housing; finance and planning, farm business development; and consultation with government and industry. At least in some areas, the field is no longer so one-sexed: a 2006 survey found that at the middle school level, 49.7 percent of students enrolled in FACS education programs were male and 50.3 percent female. In high school, the percentage shifts to 37 percent male, 63 percent female. It has been proposed that home ec-type classes be required in schools to help lower obesity rates and teach basic money management skills.

homeland security following 9/11, the National Strategy for Homeland Security and the Homeland Security Act of 2002 served to "mobilize and organize to secure the homeland from terrorist attacks." The Department of Homeland Security, the DHS, has powers that have been broadened to include, for example, the establishment of the Protected Critical Infrastructure Information (PCII) Program. In typical governmentspeak, it is not so much protecting information as collecting it ("The PCII Program seeks to facilitate greater sharing of critical infrastructure information between private sector and government entities by protecting the information from public disclosure"—in other words, the people about whom the information is collected are the only ones who don't get to see it). See www.whitehouse.gov and www.dhs.gov for the full range of protections and governmentspeak that fall under "homeland security." See also Secure Flight.

homeless, the homeless people/persons. Laurel Weir (National Law Center on Homelessness and Poverty) says, "It is the Law Center's policy to say 'homeless persons' or 'homeless people' rather than 'the homeless.' We believe it's important to recognize they are people first. By using the word homeless as an adjective, rather than a noun, we recognize homelessness as a time-limited condition, rather than a permanent state of being." "People who are homeless are not social inadequates. They are people without houses" (Sheila McKechnie). Stereotypes ("shiftless") and misinformation ("they choose to live on the streets") plague homeless people. However, one in four persons reported as homeless is a child younger than 18 (Children's Defense Fund, *The State of America's Children Yearbook*). Of homeless mothers, nearly 92 percent have been physically and/or sexually abused (E.L. Bessuk, in *Scientific American*). Advocates estimate that about 40 percent of homeless youth are gay, lesbian, bisexual, or transgender, thrown to the streets by their families. In addition to children, homeless individuals include those who hold down jobs but cannot afford housing and those with a mental or physical condition or a drug addiction. Veterans account for just over 12 percent of all homeless adults. On any given night, about 58,000 veterans, mostly men, are sleeping on the streets or in homeless shelters. "Men are neither supposed nor allowed to be dependent. They are expected to take care of both others and themselves. And when they cannot do it, or 'will not' do it, the built-in assumption at the heart of the culture is that they are less than men and therefore unworthy of help. An irony asserts itself: Simply by being in need of help, men forfeit the right to it" (Peter Marin, in *The Nation*). Attempts have been made in many areas to criminalize sleeping and sitting, panhandling, and even food sharing, all aimed at homeless people. However, the United Nations International Declaration of Human Rights includes the right to "basic shelter for all" and so far homelessness is not in itself a crime in the U.S. What is a crime perhaps is that, analogous to using the ER for health care, shelters are more expensive than actually building the needed housing. "Street people" is acceptable when used respectfully—the term is sometimes a good reminder of the reality. (*Street Spirit*, published by the American Friends Service Committee, is a good way to meet homeless individuals, who write for and sell the newspaper.) In Los Angeles, Boston, and Pittsburgh, a few big-hearted, principled physicians practice street medicine. As a nation, however, we do not seem eager to address the factors—high rents and insufficient affordable housing, substandard wages (in some areas, renting a two-bedroom apartment means working three jobs), and health care—that underlie homelessness. In 2012, Rhode Island passed the first statewide Homeless Bill of Rights in the U.S. When writing or speaking about homeless people, include them: "nothing about us without us." See also bag lady/bag man, "the," veteran.

homemaker this unisex term is positive in itself. Use it to describe men as well as women, but examine the context in which you use it for hidden biases and prejudices that may tend to belittle homemakers.

hominid anthropologists use this word inclusively, and it is functionally fairly nonsexist. It is a problem only when it is defined or used as referring to "man" instead of to "human being," which is the meaning of its Latin root. For example, one dictionary defines it as "any of a family (Hominidae) of bipedal primate mammals comprising recent man, his immediate ancestors, and related forms" (*Webster's Ninth New Collegiate Dictionary*). The unambiguous choice here would have been: "recent human beings, their immediate ancestors, and related forms."

homo- words beginning with "homo-" come from the Greek word meaning "same" or "equal" and are not sexist—for example, "homosexual" does not refer to a man but to someone whose sexual orientation is toward persons of the same sex and "homoeroticism" applies to both lesbian and gay love and desire.

homo (gay man) considered a highly objectionable slur, usually employed by adolescents or anti-gay individuals. See also shortened forms of words.

homophobia defined as an irrational fear of gay and lesbian acts, persons, and sentiments, today this term includes hatred, prejudice, and discrimination, and covers a range of anti-gay behavior and attitudes. (The "homo-" refers to "same" as in "same-sex," not to "man.") Surveys indicate that almost all lesbians and gay men have suffered some form of verbal abuse, while 25 percent of all gay men and 10 percent of all lesbians have been physically assaulted because of their sexual orientation. Language is often used to express this fear and hostility (with epithets like "Miss Nancy," "pansy," and "faggot"). See also fag/faggot, heterosexist, violence.

homosexual this term (from "homo," same, not "homo," man) refers to women and men with same-sex emotional, romantic, and sexual orientations, but many people see it as outdated, sexually objectifying, limiting, and offensive. Tim Campbell, founder and publisher of the now defunct *GLC Voice*, said, "The word *homosexual* defines a person by sexual behavior whereas gayness does not necessarily include sexual behavior." Writer Gore Vidal stated categorically that "homosexual" and "heterosexual" "are adjectives that describe acts but never people." Use instead lesbian, gay man. The Association of American University Presses' *Guidelines for Bias-Free Writing* says "*homosexual* is preferable in pre-World War II contexts and in references to some traditional or non-Western cultures, where *gay* would seem anachronistic or discordant." The Associated Press, *New York Times*, and *Washington Post* restrict usage of the term "homosexual." Avoid using "homosexual" as a style variation simply to avoid repeated use of the word "gay." See also gay man, lesbian, same-sex.

honcho/head honcho a honcho can be either sex (it comes from the Japanese meaning "group leader") although it has generally been used for men. The semi-facetious "honcha" is incorrect. If you want a more neutral-sounding alternative, consider big shot/boss/wheel/cheese, leader, boss, hotshot, person in charge.

honky/honkie see ethnic slurs.

honor this term has traditionally meant different things for men and women and often has done neither sex any good. Russell Baker (*About Men*) says, "Honorable is peculiarly a man's word, as are its antonyms: dishonorable, ignoble, base, vile, swinish, caddish. Such words are rarely applied to women. Even the phrase 'a woman's honor,' referring to the high-toned sexual morality once demanded of the American female, sounds like a man's invention for burdening women with heavier moral luggage than men chose to bear." See also virtue.

honorifics see social titles.

honor killings in some cultures, some men—usually fathers or brothers—deal with the shame of rape or adultery by murdering the women involved. Often nothing at all is done to the rapist or adultery partner.

hooker prostitute. Although "hooker," whose origins are unclear, was already in use before the Civil War, it became identified with Union General "Fighting Joe" Hooker whose troops frequented prostitutes in such numbers that the women were referred to as one of Hooker's Divisions. See also prostitute.

Horatio Alger story based on over 120 enormously successful boys' books written by Unitarian cleric Horatio Alger, this phrase refers to the poor but honest newsboys and bootblacks who by hard work and virtuous living overcame obstacles and achieved success. For a more inclusive alternative, try rags-to-riches story, personal success story; make one's fortune, work/make one's way up. The Horatio Alger story has contributed greatly to the myth that anyone can be a financial success in the United States. See also classism.

horny despite its reference to the penis (horn), this term is used for both sexes.

horseman/horsewoman acceptable terms; they have not been used in sexist ways. If you want an alternative, consider: equestrian, horseback rider, horse rider/lover, rider, trainer, handler, groom, jockey, horse breeder; hunter.

horsemanship equestrianship, riding/horseriding/equestrian/horse-handling skills/technique, equitation, equestrianism.

hostess host. Also, social director, tour guide, attendant, receptionist. There are no talk show "hostesses." The docents who show visitors around the Richmond, Virginia, historic state capitol used to be called "Capitol Hostesses"; the new gender-neutral, inclusive term is now "Capitol Tour Guides." See also "feminine" word endings.

hostile environment see sexual harassment.

hot-blooded this stereotypical adjective is used for Latin peoples when Poles or Swedes or Australians behaving the same way are termed hot-headed, short-tempered, passionate, high-spirited, vehement, impetuous, ebullient, fervent, enthusiastic.

hotelier woman or man.

Hottentot Khoikhoin/Khoi-Khoin. The correct term is always the one by which a people refer to themselves.

houseboy/housegirl for "houseboy," use servant; for "housegirl" (associated with topless bars), use prostitute. Note lack of parallel. See also prostitute.

househusband this term enjoyed a flurry of popularity and while it will probably remain in the living language, it is not equivalent to "housewife" in either numbers of holders of the title or in the public's general perception of the person. Although some men care for children and home fulltime from choice, for most it is not a primary career. See also housewife, pink-collar job/worker.

housekeeper not sexist per se, "housekeeper" is too often used as an all-purpose label for a woman. Professionals who manage others' homes call themselves household technicians/workers/helpers, home managers.

housemaid servant, domestic worker, cleaner, house cleaner, household helper, housekeeper.

housemother houseparent, counselor, monitor, cottage parent, chaperon, resident assistant. There has never been a "housefather."

housewife homemaker, householder, homeowner, consumer, woman who works at home, woman, home/household manager, customer, shopper, parent, "domestic goddess" (actress Roseanne Barr). "Housewife" marries a woman to her house and identifies someone by gender and marital status (both often irrelevant in the context). See also househusband, housework, second shift, working mother/working wife/ working woman.

housewifery homemaking, housekeeping, home/household management.

housework As the woman sings in the black musical "Don't Bother Me, I Can't Cope": "Show me that special gene that says I was born to make the beds." Housework as a career is a relatively recent invention, dating from the post-industrial revolution. In 1737 in England, for example, more than 98 percent of married women worked outside the home. By 1911, more than 90 percent were employed solely as housewives. This pattern was repeated throughout the industrialized world. Today, housework "chore wars" are common features of marriage. Ellen Goodman writes, "He is doing more than his father and feeling underappreciated. She is doing more than her husband and feeling undervalued.

There is a friction between women whose lives have changed faster than the men they share them with. There is a stalemate over the household." In *The Handbook of Nonsexist Writing*, Casey Miller and Kate Swift (with credit to Marjorie Vogel for the insight), point out that "many women do not use the term *work* to describe their housekeeping or homemaking activities. Nor, in general, do members of their families. A woman 'stays home' rather than 'works at home.' She 'fixes dinner' rather than 'works in the kitchen.' In contrast, activities men traditionally undertake around the house are usually dignified by the name *work*. A man 'works on the car' or 'does his own electrical work.' He may have a 'workshop' in the basement." In summary: "Domestic work, is, after all, both tedious and repetitive, and it is not surprising that most women and all men avoid as much of it as possible" (Mary Stocks). See also housewife, man's work, second shift, working father, working mother/working wife/working woman.

hoyden (girl) this word used to refer to members of both sexes. Today it describes, with a disapproving cast, a boisterous, high-spirited girl. Try describing such a girl's actions rather than labeling them. See also tomboy.

hubby "hubby" came from "husband" just as "hussy" came from "wife" ("huswif") but with far different connotations. See also husband, husband and wife, hussy.

hula dancer woman or man.

human/humans, humanity/humankind (nouns) coming from the Latin *humanus* for "ground," "human" has been used as a noun since 1533; these terms are used and perceived today as inclusive.

humanist see secular humanist.

human rights see rights.

human trafficking also known as "labor trafficking," "sex slavery," "forced prostitution," or simply "trafficking," this term is defined by the 2000 Palermo Protocol to the U.N. Convention Against Transnational Crime as: "The recruitment, transportation, transfer, harboring or receipt of persons, by means of the threat or use of force or other forms of coercion, of abduction, of fraud, of deception, of the abuse of power or of a position of vulnerability or of the giving or receiving of payments or benefits to achieve the consent of a person having control over another person, for the purpose of exploitation." Reliable figures are impossible to come by, but between 500,000 and 2 million people are trafficked annually for prostitution, forced labor, slavery, or servitude. Women and girls account for 80 percent of detected victims. An estimated 2.5 million people are in forced labor, including sexual exploitation, at any given time as a result of trafficking. Forty-three percent of victims have been forced into prostitution, of whom 98 percent are girls and women. According to the U.N., there are currently 127 "source countries" that provide large numbers of prostitutes, and 137 "destination countries." As for labor trafficking, John Bowe (*Nobodies*) says about the coercion of recent or trafficked immigrants, "Such cases are incredibly hard to detect—and prosecute—because much of the time the perpetrators don't rely on chains, guns, or even the use of force. All they require is some method of coercion: threats of beating, deportation, death, or, perhaps most effective, harm to the victim's family." Laura Germino, a member of a workers' coalition, says, "For every case of outright slavery making splashy headlines, it is reasonable to assume that there are tens of thousands of additional workers toiling in abusive, sweatshop-like conditions." Taina Bien-Aim (Women's Media Center) estimates the number of women, children, and men bought and sold around the world for labor or sexual servitude at four to 12 million, but adds that "these numbers do not include those trafficked within the borders of their own country." Estimated global annual profits from the exploitation of all trafficked forced labor is $31.6 billion. In addition to the unfettered greed and inhumanity of traffickers, human trafficking is built on poverty, economic disparities, globalization, and unreasonable restrictions on migration. Unfortunately, without the protection of strong anti-trafficking laws, the victims of human trafficking can be treated as criminals. See also "comfort women," prostitute, sex tourist.

humilitainment "Reality porn features some of the most violent and demeaning porno scenes to hit the mainstream, what some call 'humilitainment'" (Shauna Swartz, in Lisa Jervis and Andi Zeisler, eds., *Bitchfest*).

humor humor that demeans others often masks hostility as well as a sense of inferiority. When others don't laugh at sexist, racist, or homophobic remarks, the jokester is quick to level the one accusation guaranteed to sting: "You don't have a sense of humor." In an op-ed piece on CNN.com, Julie Burton, president of the Women's Media Center (WMC), and Michelle Kinsey Burns, former online manager for the WMC, discuss the "rape-joke empathy gap:" "the presence of rape in women's lives is too real and pervasive for many to laugh at all the same jokes men can. ... When men laugh at rape jokes, they're laughing at an abstraction that's all too real for many women." Jokes about violence, rape, sexual harassment, and stereotyping may constitute free speech, but that doesn't change the fact that they are morally repugnant.

hunger in 2006, the government's annual hunger report dropped the word "hunger" and used instead "low food security" or "very low food security." The Agriculture Department, following the advice of the Committee on National Statistics of the National Academies, decided that "hungry" was not scientifically accurate: being hungry was too amorphous a way to refer to "a potential consequence of food insecurity that, because of prolonged, involuntary lack of food, results in discomfort, illness, weakness, or pain that goes beyond the usual uneasy sensation." Only a machine or a bureaucrat could write "involuntary lack of food." The *New York Times* said, "We opt for 'hunger' as a most stirring word." When addressing hunger, use the clearest terms and most recent figures available, but put a human face on it. For example, in one school district where children cannot pay for lunch, the child is brought into the kitchen where the hot lunch is taken away and exchanged for a bag lunch; in another district, the lunch tray is taken away from the child at the end of the line; in still other districts, children's hands are stamped as a deterrent to nonpayment (Minneapolis' *Star Tribune*, 2013). See also poverty.

hunk along with terms like "stud muffin," this is sex-linked and tends to make sex objects of men, but so far its use seems good-natured and men are not complaining. The biggest problem is that it tends to support lookism.

huntress/huntsman hunter. See also "feminine" word endings.

Huron Wyandot. See also American Indian.

hurricane now named after both men and women, hurricanes can be referred to as he/she or it. See also storms.

husband (noun) the "hus-band" was the Old English mate of the "hus-wif" ("hus" meaning "house") although the word "husband" fared a great deal better than either "housewife" or "wife" in terms of prestige and acceptability—possibly because "man" was used so often instead of "husband" (as in the egregious "man and wife"). Today, just as many men are redefining the husband role in positive ways, there is a subtle discounting of "husband"; advertisers portray the husband in stereotypical ways and more and more jokes and one-liners are putting down husbands. It's a pity; as British novelist Ouida wrote in 1884, "An easy-going husband is the one indispensable comfort of life." See also househusband, husband and wife, wife.

husband (verb) conserve, ration, measure, preserve, lay/put by, economize, store, reserve, accumulate, hoard, stockpile, stock, save, save for a rainy day, stow/squirrel/salt/sock/lay away.

husband and wife vary this phrase half the time to "wife and husband." Male grammarians asserted centuries ago that the male was more important than the female, and should always be placed first, thus giving us husband and wife, Mr. and Mrs., boy and girl, he and she, etc. English jurist Sir William Blackstone took that bias a step further: "Husband and wife are one, and that one is the husband." In Old English, the "hus-wif" and the "hus-band" ("hus" means "house") were parallel terms, titles of respect and honor in the community, descriptors of the couple's partnership as householders. The connotation for both terms was that of "a substantial person." Since that time, the words have taken different roads and were gradually replaced by one of the most glaringly unbalanced gender pairs in the language: "man and wife"; it's always "wife and husband" or "man and woman." Use "wife" and "husband" in parallel ways. Should you need a word to include both consider spouse, mate, partner. In 2013, the Associated Press announced that its influential stylebook now includes a single standard when referring to gay and straight spouses: "Regardless of sexual orientation, 'husband' or 'wife' is acceptable in all references to individuals in any legally recognized marriage." See also boyfriend, couple, girlfriend, housewife, husband, wife.

husbandlike/husbandly these vague words leave us little the wiser about the person so described; there are as many kinds of husbands as there are husbands. Choose instead specific adjectives: solicitous, gentle, supportive, intimate, knowing, sensitive, protective.

husbandry household thrift, thrift, thriftiness, good housekeeping, frugality, frugalness, careful management, conservation, economizing, conserving; agriculture, agronomy, agronomics, agribusiness, farming, farm management, cultivation, tillage, forestry. Or be specific: arboriculture, floriculture, horticulture, landscape gardening, viniculture.

hussy derived from "housewife," this word has taken the low road while its innocuous, affectionate mate, "hubby," has taken the high road. Try instead adjectives that convey whatever meaning it has for you: bold, brazen, seductive, shameless, immodest, immoral, indecent, bold-faced. See also femme fatale, Jezebel/jezebel, loose woman.

hustler used of either sex, although a male hustler is a man successful with women or, in some instances, a prostitute, while a female hustler is always a prostitute. In the sense of a go-getter or a con artist, a hustler is either sex.

"hyphenated Americans" this derogatory term arose from the earlier custom of joining national origin group to "American" with a hyphen. ("Hyphenates" is especially disparaging.) Today noun forms are never hyphenated (Arab American, Chinese American) and adjectival forms generally are not (Irish American Cultural Institute, *The Finnish American Reporter*, but Anglo-American). Much conservative concern about these "hyphenated Americans" suggests that they are not as fully American or loyal as the rest of us. Lynn Laitala says that the supposedly endangered species, "just plain American," was always white, male, and privileged; "Our divergent histories do not confer special privileges. They give us special perspectives." When using "Cuban American," "German American," etc., use also "European American" rather than an unqualified "American," which would imply a standard against which others are contrasted. See also multiculturalism.

hyphenated surnames hyphenated last names are not always ideal (computers sometimes don't recognize hyphens and some names are too long for most forms) but they have allowed couples to mark their relationships and children to carry their dual heritage. Even hyphenation doesn't assure gender fairness: the Nebraska Supreme Court once ruled that the father's surname has to precede the mother's in hyphenated children's names. See also maiden name, matronym/matronymic, patronym/patronymic, surnames.

hysteria/hysterical based on the Greek for "womb" (hysteria was thought to be caused by disturbances in the womb), these terms are used almost entirely and often inappropriately of women. For the medical condition, use histrionic personality disorder. For the noun use terror, fear, frenzy, emotional excess, wildness, outburst, explosion, flare-up, seizure, eruption, delirium. For the adjective, use terrified, angry, outraged, irate, incensed, enraged, furious, infuriated, livid, upset, agitated, delirious, beside oneself, carried away, raving, raging, seething, distracted, frantic, frenetic, frenzied, wild, berserk, uncontrollable; don't use it as a synonym for hilarious.

Language conveys a certain power. It is one of the instruments of domination. It is carefully guarded by the superior people because it is one of the means through which they conserve their supremacy.

Sheila Rowbotham

idea man idea machine, creative thinker, wizard, brain, genius, conceptualizer, visionary, daydreamer, ratiocinator, ideator.

idiot/idiocy because the term "idiot" is unscientific, highly demeaning, and always unacceptable, use instead someone with profound mental retardation/mental impairment/a mental disability; mental impairment/disability. Also avoid abnormal, backward, feeble-minded, freak, imbecile, moron. For the casual insult, consider using blockhead, stupid, fool. See also, disabilities, handicapped, normal, retard.

idiot savant person/someone with savant syndrome.

illegals/illegal immigrants unauthorized worker/resident/immigrants ("unauthorized immigrant" is the U.S. Census Bureau's term). In 2013, the Associated Press revised its influential stylebook, replacing "illegal immigrant" with "illegal immigration"; they "allow the use of the word 'illegal' to refer only to an action, not a person." The language issue is similar to the prostitute who is vilified by name, but whose partner is not. Why aren't companies, industries, corporations, and individuals who hire undocumented workers called illegals? In fact, most undocumented immigrants do not come to the U.S. by crossing a border illegally; six out of 10 enter legally—with student, tourist, or business visas—and remain after their visas expire. Undocumented immigrants are not eligible for public assistance except emergency medical care and nutrition programs, but most do not use these programs because they fear detection by the Immigration and Naturalization Service. In his satirical column in the *OC Weekly*, "Ask a Mexican," Gustavo Arellano responded to reader D.G.'s question, "What is it about the word illegal that Mexicans don't understand?" by saying, "Dear Gabacho, Take your pick, D.G. Mexicans don't understand the world illegal because (1) when paying their gardeners, nannies, busboys, and factory workers in cash (and forgetting to withhold payroll taxes), U.S. employers don't seem to understand the word illegal so why should Mexicans? (2) The Anglo-American trappers and traders whom you and I were taught to admire as tough, self-sufficient frontiersmen and pioneers were among the American Southwest's first illegals. Who are you calling illegal, gabacho? (3) Presidente Bush's proposal to offer amnesty and a guest-worker program to all illegal immigrants—a move designed to appease his supporters in the business community—means even Republicans don't understand the word. (4) Whether they buy a fake passport or take a citizenship oath, Mexicans will never be more than wetbacks in the eyes of many Americans, so why bother applying for residency? (5) The *Orange County Register* stylebook reportedly requires its reporters to describe as 'undocumented workers' the men and women you call illegal. (6) Little-known fact: the fragment of poetry on the Statue of Liberty ("Give me your tired, your poor, your huddled masses yearning to breathe free," etc.) does not, because of a French engraver's error, include Emma Lazarus' rarely cited footnote: 'No Mexicans, please.'" A thought from Anna Quindlen (*Newsweek*): "Latinos are opening new businesses at a rate three times faster than the national average. If undocumented immigrants were driven out of the workforce, there would be a domino effect: prices of things ranging from peaches to plastering would rise. Nursing homes would be understaffed. Hotel rooms wouldn't get cleaned. Sure, it would be great if everyone were here legally, if the immigration services weren't such a disaster that getting a green card is a life's work. It would be great if other nations had economies robust enough to support their citizens so that leaving home wasn't the only answer. But at a certain point public policy means dealing not only with how things ought to be but with how they are." (According to the *Los Angeles Times*, federal officials estimate that fully three-quarters of all farmworkers in the U.S. are here illegally.) Rinku Sen of the Drop the I-Word campaign says that "illegal immigrant" is "heavily racialized and targeted at people of color. I have yet to meet a white immigrant dealing with having that word used against them." George Lakoff (*Thinking Points*) asks what would happen if we define the issue as a problem of illegal employers: "Now the problem becomes the employers who are hiring undocumented workers so they can pay workers less or skirt paying taxes. Employers are recognized as driving down wages, hurting American workers, and exploiting immigrants, many of whom have already fled oppressive circumstances. The possible solutions that flow from such framing are much different: Fine or punish employers for hiring undocumented workers or provide a way for these workers to get the proper documents and work with due protection of the law. This is a way to unite immigrants and American workers, ensuring that all have access to decent wages, rather than dividing them—by pitting their interests against one another—and overlooking the system that drives down all of their wages." John Bowe (*Nobodies*) says, "Agribusiness has always been brutal on laborers, consistently attempting to sidestep the labor rules that have been imposed upon other industries.... Even today, farmworkers, unlike most other hourly workers, are denied the right to overtime pay, receive no medical insurance or sick leave, and are denied federal protection against retaliatory actions by employers if they seek to organize." Americans pay far less per capita for their food than citizens of every other industrialized nation. Though a raise of about $3,200 a year would be required on average for each of America's one million to two million farmworkers to receive the minimum wage, the cost to consumers would be about $50 a year per household. Language tips: acts may be illegal, but persons cannot be illegal; never use "alien"; the children of immigrants are "Americans" or, if you need to include the precision, "first-generation Americans." "What you call these women and men shapes public opinion of them, and that in turn frames the debate over how to change immigration laws" (Jean Hopfensperger, Minneapolis' *Star Tribune*). See also human trafficking, immigrant, wetback.

illegitimate/illegitimate child no human being is "illegitimate"; except for narrow legal uses, avoid these terms. Question the need to mention the circumstances of a person's birth; they are most often irrelevant. When necessary, use child of unmarried parents.

illiterate "It is good to be able to read and write. It is good to have a culture that values literacy. It is also good to have cultures that value oral tradition, which is what some people have instead of written traditions. It is a more immediate and personal form of communication and transmission of culture, and it is just as 'good' and 'smart' as a literate culture. It does not denote 'backwardness.' It is simply indicative of a world-view that differs from that of the 20th century European" (Amoja Three Rivers, *Cultural Etiquette*). "A person from an oral culture, for example, is likely to have a much more developed memory than a literate person" (*Creating Just Language*). In discussing cultures with alternative communication traditions, describe those traditions. Occasionally you might use nonliterate or aliterate, which are a little less judgmental. Internationally, two-thirds of the world's illiterate population are women; 510 million women cannot read or write. See also "culturally deprived/disadvantaged," primitive, savage.

imam this Muslim cleric is always a man.

immigrant surveys of U.S. public opinion as far back as the early 1900s show that earlier waves of immigrants were considered valuable citizens, but that the current wave is somehow "less desirable." Especially in today's climate of economic and social concerns, people are buying the inaccurate rhetoric from well-funded anti-immigrant groups that fuels the public perception that the foreign-born are flooding U.S. shores, draining welfare dollars, burdening public services, and taking jobs from citizens. Unauthorized immigrants represent less than 4 percent of the entire U.S. population. See also illegals/illegal immigrants.

imperialism the forceful extension of a nation's authority by territorial conquest, imperialism establishes economic and political domination of other nations that are not its own colonies and against their population's wishes. "...Today, ostensibly independent countries, not just colonies, can be in the thrall of Imperial powers" (Andrew Levine, *Political Keywords*). In *Naked Imperialism: The U.S. Pursuit of Global Dominance*, John Bellamy Foster says, "The global actions of the United States since September 11, 2001, are often seen as constituting a "new militarism" and a "new imperialism." Yet neither militarism nor imperialism is new to the United States, which has been an expansionist power—continental, hemispheric, and global—since its inception. What has changed is the nakedness with which this is being promoted, and the unlimited, planetary extent of U.S. ambitions." Such books as *Takeover: The Return of the Imperial Presidency and the Subversion of American Democracy* by Charlie Savage and *Imperial Hubris: Why the West Is Losing the War on Terror* by Michael Scheuer make sobering reading. The U.S. has established its control over at least 191 governments and has more than 1,000 military bases on foreign soil. The U.S. Embassy in Iraq, a massive, fortress-like, 21-building compound cost $750 million and is a major presence in a country where our footprint used to be almost nonexistent. With 4 percent of the world's population, the U.S. accounts for over 41 percent of officially acknowledged global military spending.

impersonator, male/female see cross-dresser.

impotent use "impotent" only to describe a man unable to achieve erection; someone who is sterile or infertile may be potent, but unable to father children because of, for example, a low sperm count. Currently it is more common to see, instead of "impotence," "erectile dysfunction" or "ED." Impotence in a man is not the same as "frigidity" in a woman. Erectile dysfunction and female sexual dysfunction might seem to be parallel conditions but (1) there's no Viagra for women, and (2) female sexual dysfunction is listed in the *Diagnostic and Statistical Manual of Mental Disorders* (the official catalogue of mental illnesses). See also frigid, infertile, sterile.

impregnable/impregnate there is nothing sexist about these terms, but they do have a sex-specific base. In situations in which their actual meaning might overcome the metaphorical use, consider: (adjective) unassailable, invulnerable, impenetrable, safe, unyielding; (verb) permeate, saturate, infiltrate, infuse, imbue, implant; fertilize, fecundate, generate.

impresario woman or man. For a less masculine-appearing term, consider promoter, producer, director, manager, talent coordinator, talent agent, booker, advance agent.

inamorata/inamorato meaning, respectively, a woman or a man with whom one is in love or with whom one has a relationship, these sex-specific terms are acceptable when used even-handedly. See also boyfriend, girlfriend.

inclusive language inclusive language includes everyone. Nobody feels left out or thinks, "Where am *I* in all that?" Inclusive language is advocated by the Modern Language Association, has been used to revise government job titles, and is mandated in most publishing houses, newspapers, government offices, businesses, and higher educational institutions.

incorrigible when referring to people, this may be appropriate as an adjective, but it is unacceptable as a noun.

Indian (India) this is the correct term for people living in India. When there is a possibility of confusion with American Indians, use "Asian Indian": do not use the colonialist "East Indian." In the U.S., people of Asian Indian descent are called Asian Indian Americans. (Other peoples of the former British Empire—Burmese, Bangladeshis, Pakistanis, and Sri Lankans—are not called Indians.) When referring to someone from India, identify them by state or city; all Indians are not alike, and sometimes the region is descriptive.

Indian (United States) see American Indian.

Indian giver this pejorative and highly resented term arose from a misreading of Indian customs. You may want to circumlocute as the alternatives are not wonderful: half-hearted/two-faced/sorry/repentant giver, gives with the left hand and takes back with the right.

indian red (crayon color) chestnut. In 1999, the Crayola company changed the name to "chestnut," saying, "We've received feedback that some kids incorrectly believe this color name represents the skin color of Native Americans." The name originated from a pigment commonly found near India. "This is only the third time in Crayola history that we've changed a crayon color name," the company said. "In 1958, Prussian Blue was changed to Midnight Blue because teachers said students were no longer familiar with Prussian history. In 1962, Flesh was changed to Peach in recognition that everyone's skin is not the same shade."

Indian style, sitting sitting cross-legged.

Indian summer although the origins of this term are negative ("Indian" was once used to indicate something sham or bogus, as in the "false summer" sometimes seen in the fall), today "Indian summer" is defined positively in terms of mild weather and tranquil days. How do American Indians see it? Anton Treuer, executive director of the American Indian Resource Center, says, "To me, it's kind of shades of gray, with what's appropriate and what's not. If you talk to a lot of native people about Indian summer, they'd probably say it's that period between Indian spring and Indian fall."

Indian time this term is pejorative only when it is used and meant to be so. Mary Brave Bird writes, "There is Indian time and white man's time. Indian time means never looking at the clock. ... There is not even a word for time in our language." "From the edge of Indian time overlooking infinity, there is acute perception and perspective" (Anna Lee Walters).

indigenous peoples the World Council of Indigenous Peoples uses the following definition: "Indigenous peoples are such population groups as we are who from old-age time have inhabited the lands where we live, who are aware of having a character of our own, with social traditions and means of expression that are linked to the country inherited from our ancestors, with a language of our own, and having certain essential and unique characteristics which confer upon us the strong conviction of belonging to a people, who have an identity in ourselves and should be thus regarded by others." When writing or speaking about indigenous peoples, use the names they prefer for themselves rather than the broad "indigenous," which refers to only one part of who they are (connected to the lands that they occupied before their "discovery" by others). See also aborigine/aboriginal, American Indian, Bushman.

Indochina the peninsula of southeast Asia that includes Vietnam, Laos, Kampuchea (Cambodia), Thailand, Burma, and the mainland territory of Malaysia is known as Indochina. The term also refers to the former French colonial empire, which included some, but not all, of the peninsula. To avoid confusion, you may want to use a more general term like "Southeast Asia" or name the specific countries you're discussing.

infantryman infantry/enlisted soldier, foot soldier, member of the infantry, soldier, infantry; infantryman and infantrywoman if used together.

infertile this term is used for both men and women, although most often it modifies "couple" ("an infertile couple"). "Infertile" refers to the lack of offspring in people who have been having unprotected intercourse for a certain length of time. "Sterile" usually indicates that a cause for the infertility has been found. Infertile people are not necessarily sterile. Sterile people are always infertile. Infertility is often treatable; sterility generally is not (unless, for example, a tubal ligation or vasectomy can be reversed). Do not confuse "sterile" with "impotent" or "frigid." See also barren, frigid, impotent, sterile.

infidel literally "one without faith," "infidel" is an offensive word, especially when used for a Christian or Muslim. When used by a Muslim, it means "one who denies the blessings of God" and refers to all non-Muslims. However, because the term is considered derogatory and because the Koran commands its followers to use kind words, it is a punishable offense for Muslims to use "infidel" to denote a Jew or a Christian. In Roman Catholicism, it refers to someone who doesn't believe in the divinity of Jesus or one who has not been baptized.

ingenue this well-established, narrowly defined role in the theater has no real male counterpart; "ingenu" is rarely seen. When using the term in its broader sense, consider novice, amateur, beginner, tyro, neophyte, newcomer, innocent.

in God we trust you can read the history of this motto, which first appeared on U.S. coins and bills in 1864, at the Department of the Treasury website (www.treas.gov). It's had its ups and downs (President Theodore Roosevelt, for example, took it off, expressing his "very firm conviction" that putting such a motto on coins was not a good idea). The Founders, who worked so very hard to establish the separation of church and state, would have agreed.

Injun along with "honest Injun" (which disparagingly implies the opposite), this term is derogatory and unacceptable, even when used "good-naturedly."

inner city Examine closely the use of "inner city" to describe the economic, ethnic, and business diversity found in urban areas. "Urban" is used in the same way as "inner city," a code word for ethnic minorities and their problems, while "suburban" signals white, middle-class, wholesomeness. See also underclass.

innocent women and children civilians, bystanders, innocent civilians/bystanders. In accounts of bombings, terrorism, guerrilla warfare, and other atrocities, one often finds references to "innocent women and children," the implication being that men somehow deserve what happens.

innocent victim uninvolved bystander, bystander. This phrase implies that other victims are not innocent. While this is sometimes defensible (in the casualties of gang warfare, the child who is caught in the cross-fire is surely an innocent victim), the phrase is problematic when an infant or blood-transfusion patient dying of HIV/AIDS is referred to as an innocent victim. See also victim.

insane/insanity when referring to people with a mental illness, use "has schizophrenia" or "with bipolar disorder." "Insanity" is a legal term, not a medical one. "Insane asylums" are psychiatric hospitals. See also mental illness.

inscrutable a fine word, but too often used stereotypically of Asians and Asian Americans. This usage springs from an ignorance on the part of the labeler, that is, "If I don't know anything about you, you must be inscrutable."

inside man accomplice, confederate, double/undercover agent, spy, insider; sometimes, inside job.

"insider/outsider" rule certain terms used by people within a group are derogatory and unacceptable when used by people outside that group. "Big Fag" is printed on a gay man's T-shirt; a stranger may not call him a big fag. A group of women talk about "going out with the girls"; co-workers should not refer to them as "girls." Cheris Kramarae points out that "it's important to note who uses which labels for what purposes. A term for an oppressed group might be homogenizing when used by the dominant group and unifying when used by the oppressed group" (*Women and Language*). Another rationale behind "insider" terms is the attempt to claim and rehabilitate offensive terms, using them often and positively among insiders to strip them of their power to wound. In any case, Miss Manners (Judith Martin) has decreed that "people are allowed more leeway in what they call themselves than in what they call others." See also the section on naming in the Writing Guidelines.

institutionalized racism see racism.

insurgents also known as rebels, freedom fighters, terrorists, and guerrilla fighters, insurgents are defined by a U.S. Department of Defense publication as part of "an organized movement aimed at the overthrow of a constituted government through use of subversion and armed conflict." An insurgency differs from a resistance in that an insurgency connotes an internal struggle against a standing, established government, whereas a resistance connotes a struggle against invading or occupying foreign forces and their collaborators. When used by a state or an authority under threat, "insurgency" implies an illegitimacy of cause upon those rising up, whereas those rising up will see the authority itself as being illegitimate. William Safire, in *Safire's Political Dictionary*, shows the imprecision of "insurgent": "in a positive sense, a political reformer trying to win control of a party; less positively, a rebel or revolutionary seeking to seize control of a government; pejoratively, a euphemism for a terrorist." Know your insurgent.

intelligence "Generally speaking, 80 percent of the information one needs to form judgments on key intelligence targets or issues is available in open media" (Ray McGovern, CIA analyst).

"intelligent design" creationism in new clothes, "intelligent design" (ID) is a religious belief that conservatives want taught in the schools instead of traditional science, biology, and evolution. (According to *National Geographic* news, among 34 nations polled in 2005, the U.S. ranks next to last in acceptance of evolution theory.) In a Pennsylvania court case in 2006, U.S. District Court Judge John E. Jones III found "the overwhelming evidence at the trial established that ID is a religious view, a mere re-labeling of creationism, and not a scientific theory." Although "intelligent design" was deemed in that case to be unconstitutional to teach in American schools, the issue continues to be debated in courts across the country. See also junk science, "sound science."

intentional communities (ICs) "thousands of cooperative, cohousing units, residential land trusts, ecovillages, spiritual collectives, and activist communities are thriving around the world—but almost no one outside of the intentional community network itself seems to know it" (*Bitch*). Among those listed in the Fellowship for Intentional Community (www.ic.org) international database, a few are conservative; most are progressive, interested in sustainable living and social justice.

intercourse see sexual intercourse.

interfaith multifaith/multi-faith. "Interfaith" was a useful descriptor during the growing years of ecumenism and may still be the best choice for some groups. However, Chris Seiple (*Christian Science Monitor*) says, "This term conjures up images of watered-down, lowest common denominator statements that avoid the tough issues.... 'Multi-faith' suggests that we name our deep and irreconcilable theological differences in order to work across them...."

internal nutrition force-feeding. Always replace the political euphemism with its unambiguous meaning, "force-feeding." See also political prisoners, torture.

Internet for help with Internet language and format issues, see the excellent *Elements of Internet Style* from EEI Press.

internment see relocation.

interracial referring to the presence of different races in a certain defined area or group ("interracial neighborhood," "interracial gathering"), this term has lost its validity as the concept of "race" has lost its. When it has been used it has often meant "blacks and whites," ignoring Asian Americans and other groups, or it has been code to signal the presence of African Americans. Replace the word with a precise, factual description of the makeup of the group you're describing. See also multiracial.

intersexual someone whose biological sex is ambiguous. Many genetic, hormonal, or anatomical variations can result in partially or fully developed male and female sexual organs. Parents and medical professionals have usually assigned intersex infants a sex and performed surgical operations to conform the infant's body to that assignment, but this practice has become increasingly controversial as intersex adults speak out against it. Germany officially recognizes three genders on its birth certificates: F, M, X. Intersexuality is also known as hermaphroditism; use the latter term only in scientific contexts.

intifada according to the *Oxford Dictionary of New Words*, an intifada is an Arab uprising, especially uprising and unrest by Palestinians in the Israeli-occupied area of the West Bank and Gaza Strip. The website www.intifada.com says, "Many people in the West do not know what the word 'Intifada' means. Currently, the Palestinian people are being oppressed by Israel. This manifests itself in many ways: from the use of bullets and missiles against demonstrators; to the continued building of settlements with no respect for Palestinian rights; from the removal of Palestinians from their homes; to the continuous disregard for numerous United Nations resolutions. Intifada is simply the defense of the Palestinian people against this oppression."

Inuit this is the term preferred to "Eskimo" by many Arctic and Canadian peoples. Inuk (or Innuk) is the singular of Inuit (or Innuit). Plural can also be Inuits (or Innuits). See also Eskimo.

invasion Paul Kivel (*Uprooting Racism*) notes the implications of our choice to use this term; "Why don't we say that Europeans invaded North America? Or that settlers invaded the West? Most uses of the word *invasion* are about 'us'—white Americans—being invaded by Japanese investment, illegal aliens, people of color moving to the suburbs, or Haitian refugees."

Iranian this term, along with "Persian," is acceptable to most Iranians. "Persian" is used to refer more to antiquity, to the pre-1920s era, or to ethnicity, where Iranian is used to indicate nationality.

Iraqi sects see Shiites, Sunnis, Kurds.

Irian Jaya West Papua.

Irishman Irishwoman and Irishman, native of Ireland, inhabitant of Ireland. Plurals: Irishmen and Irishwomen/Irishwomen and Irishman (but not "Irishmen and women"), the Irish, Irishfolk, natives of Ireland, inhabitants of Ireland.

Iron John a key term in the mythopoeic men's movement, "Iron John" comes from poet and essayist Robert Bly's *Iron John*, in which he reconfirms the power of ancient stories to guide and heal by using the Grimm fairy tale about Iron John to examine a masculinity that goes beyond our cultural stereotypes. He discusses male initiation, connecting with "the inner warrior," men's hunger for fathers and mentors, the missing or weak father-son bond in many men's lives, and the fashioning of a male identity that is "neither Rambo nor wimp."

iron maiden historically, this is the term used for an iron cabinet used for torture.

iron man iron woman/iron man. Originally referring to a baseball pitcher of superior endurance, this term has come to mean anyone of unusual physical staying power. Except for roundabout phrases (someone "with the strength of ten," "with stamina"), there are no good alternatives for this pithy term.

Ironman, The this triathlon championship event begun in 1978 has been open to women since 1979.

Iroquois Haudenosaunee Indians/people. "Haudenosaunee" means "people who build longhouses."

irrational this term is too often used as a rebuttal of women's arguments or applied inaccurately to women as a catch-all condemnation; use carefully in reference to women. It is not used in the same way for men. See also emotional.

Islam the name of the religion founded by Muhammad, Islam embraces all the sects now found among his followers, who are known as Muslims; a Shiite and a Sunni are both Muslims. There are about 1.6 billion Muslims, or 23 percent of the world's population, making Islam the world's second largest religion. The word "Islam" derives from the same Semitic root as the Hebrew word *Shalom*, which means peace. "Islamic" is the correct adjective when referring to the religion, but "Islamist" is usually used for political parties or governments; Islamism is the Muslim revival movement. Turkey has an Islamist Party and countries with governments controlled by religious parties are called Islamist states. See also Islamofascism; Koran; Moslem; Muhammad; Sunnis, Shiites, Kurds.

Islamofascism an oxymoron used to demonize and stereotype militant Islamists and, for some people, all Muslims. Journalist Eric Margolis states that "there is nothing in any part of the Muslim World that resembles the corporate fascist states of western history. In fact, clan and tribal-based traditional Islamic society, with its fragmented power structures, local loyalties, and consensus decision-making, is about as far as possible from western industrial state fascism. The Muslim World is replete with brutal dictatorships, feudal monarchies, and corrupt military-run states, but none of these regimes, however deplorable, fits the standard definition of fascism. Most, in fact, are America's allies." Conservative British historian Niall Ferguson says use of the term is "just a way of making us feel that we're the 'greatest generation' fighting another World War, like the war our fathers and grandfathers fought."

Islamophobia an irrational distrust, fear, or rejection of the Muslim religion and Muslims, as well as those thought to be Muslim, Islamophobia took shape early in the Reagan era, when focusing on the Muslim as enemy replaced Communism as the enemy. The indiscriminate demonizing of Muslims was greatly exacerbated by 9/11 (perpetrated by an extremist group) and the unwarranted invasion of Iraq (which angered the Muslim world and resulted in U.S. fears of that anger). Doug Saunders (*The Myth of the Muslim Tide*) says, "Muslims appear to be among the least disenchanted and most satisfied people in the West." According to Saunders, "Support for violence and terrorism among Muslims is not higher than that of the general population, and in some cases it is lower. ... The assumption among Islamophobes is that there is something intrinsically alien and incompatible about the presence of Muslims in free countries. In truth, they are not visibly different from other groups that have arrived with the mind-set of the past and found themselves transformed into tolerant, loyal and law-abiding souls who value democracy and liberty. Free societies have a way of doing that." See also Islam, Muslim.

Israeli this term originated with the creation of Israel in 1948 and should not be used to refer to people before that time. An Israeli is a citizen of Israel, but is not always a Jew. The term for the biblical peoples is Israelites. See also Hebrew, Jew, Zionism.

Israeli-Palestinian conflict this term is used by both Palestinians and Israelis, although in the wider geographical context "Arab-Israeli conflict" is often used. "Crisis" and "dispute" are also seen, but less often. See also occupied territories.

Issei literally "first generation," this acceptable term is used for a Japanese immigrant, especially to the U.S. Plural is Issei or Isseis. See also Nisei, Sansei.

it's a man's world this generalization is not true for many men—those who are unemployed, homeless, victims of street violence, soldiers fighting wars of someone else's making, divorced fathers who rarely see their children. The cliché has some use, however, as a means of expressing relative well-being: on average men still earn more, have better jobs, and sit more often in the chairs of power. See also sexism.

> Language is not neutral. It is not merely a vehicle which carries ideas. It is itself a shaper of ideas.
>
> Dale Spender

jack/jack-/-jack although the word, prefix, and suffix "jack" came from Jacob and often meant a man/boy, they have come to refer without any particular gender overtones to certain tools (for example, bootjack, hydraulic jack, jackknife), plants and animals (jack-in-the-pulpit, jack mackerel), nouns (apple jack, blackjack, jackpot), verbs (ball the jack, hijack), and adjectives (crackerjack). These can be used as they are, but one wonders: has any woman's name ever influenced dozens of words?

jackass although this word is defined as a foolish or stupid person, it means male donkey and is almost always reserved for men. It's doubtful that people shouting "jackass!" want alternatives, but more neutral-sounding terms exist: donkey, fool, nitwit.

jack of all trades, master of none this expression is nearly impossible to replace; it's familiar, pithy, and rhythmic. If the sex-specificity and the "master" are jarring, consider good at everything, expert at nothing; good at all trades, expert at none; generalist; many-talented. Where appropriate, the shortened "jill of all trades" has been used. For discussion of "master" words, see master (noun). See also handyman.

jailbait (underage female sexual partner) the use of this term implies a certain victimization and unwilling cooperation on the part of the man, and obscures the fact that the man is engaging in criminal activity (and laying the foundation for a statutory rape charge).

Jane Crow Pauli Murray said this term "refers to the entire range of assumptions, attitudes, stereotypes, customs, and arrangements which have robbed women of a positive self-concept and prevented them from participating fully in society as equals with men. Traditionally racism and sexism in the United States have shared some common origins, displayed similar manifestations, reinforced one another, and are so deeply intertwined in the country's institutions that the successful outcome of the struggle against racism will depend in large part upon the simultaneous elimination of discrimination based upon sex." Shirley Chisholm said, "Of my two 'handicaps,' being female put many more obstacles in my path than being black." See also Jim Crow.

Jane Doe acceptable legal term; use with John Doe. See also John Doe.

Jane Q. Citizen/Jane Q. Public acceptable terms; use with John Q. Citizen/John Q. Public. See also average man, common man, John Q. Citizen/John Q. Public, man in the street.

Japanese this is not interchangeable with Japanese American, and it is never shortened to the offensive "jap." See also shortened forms of words.

Japanese American acceptable term. See also Asian American, "hyphenated Americans," Issei, Kibei, Nisei, Sansei, Yonsei.

jazzman jazz musician/player, member of jazz band.

Jehovah this alteration of the Hebrew "Yahweh" is never used by Jews, is most often seen in Christian translations of the Old Testament, and is used by Jehovah's Witnesses. See also Yahweh.

jerk technically available for both sexes. Yet in a Men's Rights, Inc. study of hundreds of advertisements in which both women and men appeared, every perceived jerk was a man. Since the advent of the women's movement, it has become riskier to advertisers to make women look feeble, but since much lowbrow humor depends on putting someone down, men have become targets.

Jesus/Jesus Christ when writing about Christ, the masculine pronouns are, of course, correct. However, some people suggest eliminating unnecessary ones because "theological tradition has virtually always maintained that the maleness of Jesus is theologically, christologically, soteriologically, and sacramentally irrelevant" (Sandra M. Schneiders, *Women and the Word*). There have been few individuals in history as completely androgynous and inclusive as Christ, and it seems to do his message a disservice to over-insist on his maleness—or his usual whiteness. Theologian and biblical scholar Cain Hope Felder says the African origins of the people of the Holy Land have been ignored by European scholars. The image of Jesus as a white person was grafted onto the truth by European church leaders as a way of selling their theology to white people; "We're not saying he came from the Congo. But we are saying he was an average African-Asian man of his time." See also Christianity, God (Christian).

Jew this is always a noun, never a verb, never an adjective. The *American Heritage Book of English Usage* says the "attributive use of the noun *Jew*, in phrases such as *Jew banker* or *Jew ethics*, is both vulgar and highly offensive. In such contexts *Jewish* is the only acceptable possibility." Author and scholar Osha Gray Davidson (in *Des Moines Register*) has observed people torturing their syntax to use "Jewish person/people" when "Jew/Jews" clearly would fit the sentence structure better. He suspects that people know "Jew" is sometimes used as an epithet and so, with the best intentions, they reject that perversion. "But in the process they have cut out the word altogether, like a doctor who treats an infected finger by amputating the arm. The result: The perfectly acceptable name for a people with a 4,000-year history has, in certain circles, become the 'J-word.'" Irving Lewis Allen (*Unkind Words*) points out that the same thing has happened to "Poles" and "Swedes"; because of old derogatory uses that tainted these perfectly good proper names, they are replaced by circumlocutions. Davidson adds that "Jewish" is an adjective; "It suggests an inessential quality, a trait cobbled on and easily dismissed. Worse, the '-ish' form is the 98-pound weakling of Grammar Beach; even other adjectives kick sand in its face. It denotes tendency rather than a full-blown characteristic, a wishy-washing retreat from beingness. She is tall*ish*. It is warm*ish* out.... One doesn't need to be a Holocaust scholar to grasp that once a society considers it uncouth to *say* 'Jew,' eventually—inevitably—it will become unsafe to *be* a Jew. What are words, after all, but the womb in which tomorrow's deeds slumber?" See also anti-Semitism, jew boy, "jew down," Jewish-American Princess (JAP), Jewish mother, Jewish question, Judeo-Christian.

Jew boy completely offensive.

"jew down" this unacceptable expression is always derogatory and debasing to Judaism and to Jews. It is surprising how many people still use it unthinkingly. Alternatives include: bargain, deal, barter, haggle, dicker, negotiate, talk down, make an offer.

Jewess Jew. "I am not a Jew in the synagogue and a feminist in the world. I am a Jewish feminist and a feminist Jew in every moment of my life" (Judith Plaskow). And from Vicki Baum: "To be a Jew is a destiny." Some people feel "Jewess" is "nicer"; if you know someone who prefers being so named, do comply. But "feminine" word endings are unnecessarily sex-specific, belittling, and show again that the male is the norm and the female is a subset, a deviation, a secondary classification. The recommended guideline is to use the base word for both sexes (thus, "poet" instead of "poetess," "executor" instead of "executrix"). Online dictionaries generally classify "Jewess" as offensive. A reader recently wrote the *Economist*: "The commentator in this piece uses the extremely offensive term 'Jewess' to refer to Jews who are women. Shame on him, and shame on the *Economist* for not catching it." A similar attempt at "politeness" occurs when people circumlocute "Jew" to arrive at "Jewish person." One might as well say "of the Jewish persuasion." Ira Spiro wrote to the *Los Angeles Times*: "Unique among actual names of a people or religious group, 'Jew' makes people uncomfortable and sounds contemptuous. I'm a Jew. I'm proud to be called a Jew, not a Jewish person, but a Jew. I'm insulted that 'Jew' is insulting. ... let's call a Jew a Jew." See also "feminine" word endings.

Jewish American Princess (JAP) this term, which portrays Jewish women as self-centered, materialistic, and manipulative, appears in jokes and everyday conversation as well as in anti-Semitic graffiti. Many people use the term without realizing its powerfully damaging effects; tolerance of it has been puzzlingly strong. Some claim it is no coincidence that the term appeared when Jewish women were beginning to establish a place for themselves in Judaism, serving as rabbis and cantors, as well as in the commercial world.

Jewish mother the Macmillan Publishing Company's *Guidelines for Creating Positive Sexual and Racial Images in Educational Materials* says, "This has become a cliché used to describe the woman—Jewish or not—who tends to dominate the home, invest herself completely in her children and the preparation of food, and who views herself as a martyr. This image—a distortion of the traditionally strong role of Jewish women in the home—is degrading to Jews and women alike, and should be avoided." It seems possible, however, that the term still has some limited nonpejorative uses—when women use it in self-reference or when women reclaim the strength and courage of the Jewish mother.

Jewish question Sanford Berman (*Prejudices and Antipathies*) writes, "On the face of it, 'Jewish Question' may seem a bland, neutral term. Yet it is just the opposite, masquerading ruthlessness and inhumanity—the age-old and altogether vicious practice of scapegoating—in a deceptive, leisurely abstraction. The 'question' facing the soon-to-be-incinerated millions was not one to be calmly debated. It was fundamental: life or death." He says that Joseph Goebbels predicted in 1938, "The Jewish question will in a short time find a solution satisfying the sentiment of the German people." See also "final solution."

Jezebel/jezebel the biblical story of Jezebel depicts a murdering, controlling, rapacious person who is primarily an amoral manipulator and only secondarily a woman. Instead of focusing on Jezebel's viciousness, the common connotation of a jezebel is to her sexuality (dictionaries define her as a shameless or abandoned woman) when in fact she did not use sex to carry out her evil deeds. Consider using instead evil influence, villain, murderer, bully, plotter, scourge of the human race, devil in human form/shape.

jihadist a person who participates in a jihad, which is a "striving in the path of God," in one of four ways: the jihad of self-perfection against vice, passion, and ignorance; the jihad of the tongue; the jihad of the hand, and the jihad of the sword. Although "jihad" can mean the struggle to live a moral and virtuous life, spreading and defending Islam, or fighting injustice and oppression, "jihad" is commonly understood by the average person today as making war on behalf of Islam—thus confusing it with terrorism. "By calling the groups we are fighting 'jihadis,' we confirm their own—and the worldwide Muslim public's—perception that they are religious. They are not. They are terrorists, hirabists, who consistently violate the most fundamental teachings of the Holy Koran and mainstream Islamic scholars and imams" (Chris Seiple, *Christian Science Monitor*). See also Islam, Islamophobia, Muslim.

Jim Crow from the obsolete derogatory name for a black man, "Jim Crow" came to be a synonym for "racist," as in "Jim Crow laws." See also Jane Crow.

jock (athlete) although both sexes are referred to as jocks today, the tendency is still to think first of a man when one hears the word. The old "jock/jockum" meant "penis." Its meaning is particularly clear in "jockstrap." See also jockette.

jockette jockey. Some racing stewards have actually used the silly "jockette"—a pitiful thing to have done to a decent word like "jockey" and to the talented women who have made it into the ranks of professional jockeys. It has apparently also been used as the female "equivalent" of a jock. See also "feminine" word endings.

joe/Joe Blow/Joe Schmo/Joe six-pack "joe" and "Joe Blow" have long meant an average, typical, or ordinary man, while "schmo" comes from the Yiddish for "jerk" and "Joe six-pack" is a classist stereotype of the football-and-beer guy that we all know is out there somewhere. These are sexist insofar as there are no parallel terms for women, and two of them aren't complimentary. Less casual inclusive synonyms for both sexes are Jane Doe/John Doe, Jane Q. Citizen/John Q. Citizen, and Jane Q. Public/John Q. Public.

john sex buyer. As there is currently no term for the prostitute's sex partner equal to "prostitute" in weight, significance, and high moral judgment, the prostitute carries the economic, psychological, physical, social, and linguistic burden of a system that could not exist without the participation of "customers." There are scores of pejorative terms for prostitutes, but only three relatively innocuous terms for sex buyers: john, date, trick, score. A recent study headed by Melissa Farley, director of Prostitution Research and Education reports: "Overall, the attitudes and habits of sex buyers reveal them as men who dehumanize and commodify women, view them with anger and contempt, lack empathy for their suffering, and relish their own ability to inflict pain and degradation" (Leslie Bennetts, "The John Next Door," *Newsweek*). Since 99 percent of the research in this area has been done on prostitutes, and only 1 percent done on sex buyers, the 2011 study ("Comparing Sex Buyers With Men Who Don't Buy Sex") illuminated differences between the two groups: the sex buyers often voiced aggression toward women, and were nearly eight times as likely as nonbuyers to say they would rape a woman if they could get away with it. Asked why he bought sex, one man said he liked "to beat women up." Sex buyers in the study committed more crimes of every kind than nonbuyers, and all the crimes associated with violence against women were committed by the buyers. Prostitution has always been risky for women; the average age of death is 34, and the *American Journal of Epidemiology* reports that prostitutes suffer a "workplace homicide rate" 51 times higher than that of the next most dangerous occupation, working in a liquor store. See also prostitute.

John Doe acceptable legal term; the female form is Jane Doe. The only caution is not to use "John Doe" pseudogenerically to mean "average man." See also average man, common man, man in the street, John Q. Public.

John Hancock there is nothing wrong with using this expression, but be aware of how many like it are male-based. Balance their use with female-based expressions, creative expressions of your own, or sex-neutral alternatives: signature, name, moniker. See also sex-linked expressions.

John Q. Citizen/John Q. Public acceptable when used with Jane Q. Citizen/Jane Q. Public, these terms are sexist when used pseudogenerically to mean "the average citizen/person." See also average man, common man, man in the street.

journalism journalism, as it's been understood by journalists and news consumers, is in crisis. The cause of shrinking newspapers and falling circulations is obvious, the long-term picture less clear. "In journalism there has always been a tension between getting it first and getting it right" (Ellen Goodman). Today, the Internet and other media are always going to get it first, but will they get it right? We still need serious, talented journalists with a passion for discovery, accuracy, and words; the challenge is finding ways to pay them for work essential to democracy. It would be too easy for them to go the way of factory workers, mothers, nurses, teachers—also critical to our welfare but either unpaid or poorly paid. Web journalism can be a boon in many ways, but so far it's either a rehash of traditional news media or too often unreliable. When assessing any web journalism, fact-checking is a must, starting with factcheck.org, politifact.com, snopes.com, and others. Citizen journalism and participatory media may provide an outlet for good journalists. Privately funded to investigate issues and areas not covered by the mainstream news, people take stories into their own hands while holding themselves accountable for truth and accuracy (see, for example, the Common Language Project). Whatever journalism's future, to be the best it can be it must resolve its serious gender gap. For detailed statistics, see the Women's Media Center's latest "The Status of Women in the U.S. Media," but in general, ownership of newspapers, broadcast and cable networks, and corporate "new media" is concentrated into male hands, and men control and define journalism itself, in academia and in practice. Women are still too often relegated to writing the more "personal" stories, or writing on the "pink topics" of food, family, furniture, and fashion. Most critical is the fact that on issues of particular importance to women (abortion, birth control, women's rights), men still write (and assign) most of the articles. Although female journalism grads today are more likely to find employment than male grads, they find it in advertising and PR, not in journalism. See also media.

journeyman in the nontechnical sense, this word can be replaced by journey worker, journeyed/trained/trade/craft worker, trainee, beginner, assistant, helper, subordinate; average performer; skilled craftworker; journey level (adjective). Or, use a specific title, for example, iron worker. However, in labor law or in the trades, "journeyman" has certain specific and so far irreplaceable meanings. It may be possible in some such cases to use journeyman and journeywoman.

judas when using an expression like "judas" or one of its derivatives, be aware of how many figures of speech are male-based. Balance them sometimes with female-based expressions, creative expressions of your own, or alternatives. For "judas," use false friend, betrayer, deceiver, traitor. For "judas kiss," use kiss of betrayal. See also sex-linked expressions.

Judeo-Christian there are three problems with this term. (1) Along with "Christian," it is often used as an inappropriate synonym for morality. Use instead ethical, moral, decent, upstanding, righteous, upright, high-minded, honorable, principled, conscientious, moralistic, right, good. (2) The United States is often referred to as a "Judeo-Christian" culture. Rabbi Barry D. Cytron, of Adath Jeshurun Congregation in Minneapolis, says, "We are neither a 'Christian nation' nor a 'Judeo-Christian' one. We are not a land with one church, but of many—and of synagogues, mosques and sweat lodges, too. What makes us really unique is that we are not a nation of labels—but of people." (3) It overstates the homogeneity between the two groups. According to the *Forward*, the term "Judeo-Christian" was first used in the late 19th century by Christian scholars wishing to emphasize the Jewish roots of early Christianity, but outside that narrow context it wasn't much seen until after World War II when it was part of a reaction to the Holocaust. See also Christian.

jungle from the Sanskrit "jangala," this means uncultivated forest occupied by wild animals (Zoë Anglesey, in *MultiCultural Review*). "Jungle" is imprecise and suffers from colonialist underpinnings. Use rain forests when that is accurate; they are irreplaceable to our global welfare whereas the word "jungle" does not convey the ecological importance of these areas. In urban jargon, the word "jungle" has been used negatively of certain neighborhoods and areas; use instead neutral, descriptive terms.

junior/Jr. only boys/men are juniors; neither girls/women with feminized versions of their father's names nor girls/women named for their mothers are so tagged. The attitudes that underlie the use of "junior" have been more closely associated with boys/men (laws of primogeniture, the handing on of father-son farms, firms, businesses, etc.) but are slowly evolving to include girls/women.

junior executive executive trainee. The "junior" makes the term mildly ageist and disparaging.

junior miss ageist, sexist (there is no parallel term for boys), coy, old-fashioned, and conveying certain cultural stereotypes, this term is better replaced with young woman, high school student.

junk slang for a man's genitalia.

junk science In a startling display of linguistic legerdemain, "junk science" is actually science espoused by highly accredited scientists, while "sound science" is what conservative think tanks produce to counter "junk science," which is really sound science. According to legal scholar Wendy Wagner, industry frequently accuses governmental science agencies of producing "junk science." See also global warming, "intelligent design," "sound science."

jury foreman see foreman (jury).

juryman juror.

"just war" schoolchildren ought to discuss and analyze just war theory so that they are equipped as adults to determine when their nation must (rarely) engage in one. Kenneth Vaux (*Ethics and the Gulf War: Religion, Rhetoric and Righteousness*) outlines the conditions for a just war: it must be a last resort; must have some probability of success; the good expected from war must be greater than all the foreseen costs; can be started only by competent authorities; the central question should be "Is the justice of our cause greater than theirs?"; the war must be engaged in with an attitude of regret. "A just war is only a means to gain peace and reconciliation—not humiliation and punishment." Just causes include: vindication of justice, restoring a just international order, protecting innocent life, and restoration of human rights. (This brief summary doesn't do justice to his book or to all the just-war theory that is available.) In the context of a just war: After a 2007 visit to Iraq, George W. Bush flew to Australia where Australia's Deputy Prime Minister Mark Vaile "inquired politely of the President's stopover in Iraq." Replied the president: "We're kicking ass" (Phillip Coorey, *Sydney Morning Herald*).

juvenile because of its associations (juvenile offender, juvenile behavior), you may want to consider using young person/adult. See also adolescent, teenager, youth.

it is not that i am playing word games,
it is that the word games are there, being
played, and i am calling attention to it.

Alice Molloy

Language is neither innocent nor neutral.
Linguistic habits condition our view of the
world and hinder social change.

Carmen Martínez Ten

kaffeeklatsch/coffee klatsch in Germany, this expression is sex-neutral, referring to informal social gatherings of both sexes. In the United States, however, it has been used to belittle gatherings of women (U.S. men do not have kaffeeklatsches). The term is much less popular in recent years; people use instead get-together, tea, coffee, coffee break, social hour, visit, talk, open house, party.

Kaffir/Kaafir Xhosa. Eschew the offensive, derogatory, confrontational slur for a black person (used principally in South Africa, but on occasion in the U.S.); it comes from the Arabic for "infidel" and is roughly equivalent to "nigger" (Sanford Berman, *Prejudices and Antipathies*).

Kanakas referring to South Sea Islanders or Hawaiians of Polynesian descent, this term is derogatory and unacceptable when used by outsiders.

Kazakhstan the ninth largest country in the world, this former Soviet republic decided to drop the letter "h" from its name at one point but has since switched back. The people of Kazakhstan are Kazakhs, and the adjectival form is Kazakh.

Kelly Girl office temporary. In any case, "Kelly Girl" is a registered trademark; use only for someone who works for Kelly Services, Inc. (The firm was known as the Kelly Girl Service only from 1957 to 1966.) In 1996, the Business Women's Network recognized Kelly Services for having the second largest number of female corporate officers in the United States. See also girl.

kept woman this term is highly offensive because of the woman's supposed passivity (she is "kept") and because of the lack of a word to describe her partner. Although two people are involved, only one is labeled pejoratively—or even labeled at all. The assumption is that the man is behaving "normally" and thus is still just a man, while the woman's behavior (no different in important respects from his) is "deviant" enough to require a special term. (In the 1980s, Estée Lauder president Leonard Lauder decided against buying advertising space in *Ms.* because its readers weren't right for his product; Estée Lauder sells, he explained, "a kept-woman mentality." When Gloria Steinem pointed out that 60 percent of his customers worked, he said, yes, but they would like to be kept. It is not known whether this insight into the female mind was based on market research or something else.) See also gigolo.

Kibei a Japanese American (usually born to immigrant parents) who is educated chiefly in Japan.

kid this widely used informal word is acceptable in certain contexts, but in others it can be demeaning. For alternatives, consider child, girl/boy, young people, young women/young men, youth, youngster; student, pupil.

kike see ethnic slurs.

Kinder, Küche, Kirche the "children, kitchen, and church" slogan was used by the Nazis to reconfine women to their supposed biological roles. The phrase has since been used by various groups to describe women's "rightful place." Many women do, in fact, find deep satisfaction in children, kitchen, and spirituality. The problem arises when applying this "ideal" to every woman, just because and only because she is a woman.

king (noun) use when it is the correct formal title. For example, in 1644, Christina was proclaimed king, not queen, of Sweden. Otherwise, consider using monarch, ruler, sovereign, crowned head, majesty, regent, chief of state, leader, governor, chieftain, potentate, commander, protector; autocrat, tyrant, despot, dictator; figurehead. In religious writings, sovereign is often used for God as King. For its meaning as a superlative, use best, top, expert, superstar, boss, chief, leading light, dean, mogul, nabob, tycoon, high-muck-a-muck, big wheel, big cheese.

kingdom realm, empire, land, country, reign, rule, monarchy, domain, dominion, nation, state, world, sovereignty, principality, territory, region, protectorate, fief, commonwealth, republic, world. "Reign," "realm," and "dominion" are particularly appropriate for the kingdom of God. "Kindom" is sometimes used to express the meaning of "kingdom" without the triumphal and male overtones. "World" can be used in quasi-scientific uses, for example, the animal, mineral, and plant worlds (but retain the biology term "kingdom" in scientific writing). During the reigns of even the most powerful and influential queens (for example, Queen Elizabeth I), no one ever used the word queendom.

kingdom come the next world, the world to come, paradise, eternity, the hereafter, eternal life, life after death; the end of the world, oblivion. For the phrase "from here to kingdom come," use: from here to eternity.

kingly regal, dignified, majestic, imperial, aristocratic, autocratic, courtly, gallant, charismatic, sovereign, royal, dynastic, royalist, monarchical, imperialistic.

kingmaker except when referring to Richard Neville, First Earl of Warwick (Warwick the Kingmaker) or in the very literal sense, consider using power behind the throne/scenes, power broker, wheeler-dealer, mover and shaker, strategist, someone with political clout, string-puller, operator. Plural: the powers that be.

king of the hill/king of the mountain Or queen of the hill/mountain. Other possibilities: big wheel, bigwig, magnate, someone on the top of the heap, monarch of all they survey.

king of the jungle although this term refers to the lion (also known as "king of the beasts"), you may want sex-neutral choices when referring to someone powerful: star, superstar, mogul, nabob, boss, tycoon, high-muck-a-muck, leading light, luminary, chief, boss; "her nibs" or "his nibs"; top dog, big shot, wheel, big wheel.

K

kingpin linchpin.

kingpin (bowling) head pin.

king salmon Chinook/quinnat salmon.

King's Counsel when a queen is on the throne, it's "Queen's Counsel."

king's English standard/correct/accepted English, standard usage, correct speech. When a Queen is on the British throne, one ought to hear "the Queen's English," and one does hear it in Great Britain. In the United States, "King's English" is used, although it has not been correct since early 1952, just before Elizabeth II acceded to the throne or, better yet, since the colonists parted ways with King George.

kingship monarchy, majesty, royal position, royal office, dignity; statecraft, leadership, diplomacy.

king-size terms like this give new meaning to the roles of kings and queens as "rulers." Retain as a specific description of bed sizes and bed linen (where the use of "single," "double," "queen," and "king" is standard). Whereas "queen-size" is relative, meaning "big, but less than king-size," "king-size" has a more objective meaning: it is the largest. Because it sings that old male-is-number-one/female-is-number-two song, you might want to use alternatives: jumbo-size, jumbo, supersize, oversized, outsized, gigantic, enormous, huge, extra-large, of heroic proportions, larger than normal/life. (But who says the king is always larger than the queen?)

king's ransom not a particularly damaging little cliché. If you want something that is not sex-linked, try for a colorful new expression of your own or consider fortune, enormous/prodigious sum, priceless, beyond price, worth its weight in gold, above rubies, invaluable, matchless, peerless, inestimable, costly, of great price, precious, worth a pretty penny/a fortune.

kinsman/kinswoman use as they are or, for gender-nonspecific terms: relative, blood relative, relation, cousin, kin, kinsfolk, kith and kin, connection. Plurals: kinfolk, relatives, kin.

knave historically this was a man or boy in roughly the same pejorative sense that "boy" has been used in English for a man. For a tricky, deceitful person of either sex, use mischief-maker, rascal, trickster, troublemaker, sneak; double-crosser, four-flusher, cheater; crook, villain, evildoer, traitor, betrayer.

knavery mischief, mischievousness, monkeyshines, shenanigans, hanky-panky, trickery, roguish trick; baseness, villainy, unscrupulousness, deviltry, wrongdoing.

knight the knight of the Round Table was always a man, and there was no equivalent for a woman. Today, either a woman or a man may be knighted, although this was not always the case. Women members of British orders of knighthood are called ladies and addressed as dames; men are called knights and addressed as sirs. For inclusive modern-day alternatives to the metaphorical use of "knight," use champion, hero. Full membership in groups with "knight" in their title (for example, the Knights of Columbus) is generally reserved for men. The word "knight" is not always a clue to noble deeds and high-mindedness; the most visible (so to speak) of the infamous kind are the Knights of the Ku Klux Klan. See also knight errant, knight in shining armor.

knight errant rescuer, champion, hero errant; dreamer, idealist, romantic; philanthropist, altruist, humanitarian. See also knight in shining armor.

knighthood in the past, reserved for men; today, both women and men may be raised to knighthood. See also knight.

knight in shining armor this is still used, although there is no good parallel for a woman; perhaps the closest is "woman of my dreams." In the sense of rescuer, consider sex-neutral terms: hero, deliverer, rescuer, lifesaver, savior, champion.

knockout used colloquially to mean a wonderful thing or person, this word takes on new meaning in today's culture of violence: an ad for a woman's shelter asks, "Does your husband think you're a knockout?" Numerous men have been killed or severely injured as a result of knock-outs in the "sport" of boxing. You may want to avoid this word. See also violence, violent language.

knock someone up/knock up someone this crude slang expression for impregnating a woman is not used by anyone with any sensibilities, but illustrates a common attitude toward women that is at the same time violent and unfeeling; women are passive, throwaway objects to the speaker.

Koran Quran, Qur'an, al'Qur'an, the Holy Qur'an, Qor'an. The first term is the preferred spelling in the U.S.; in the others, the apostrophe indicates a faint glottal stop. Any of these are preferred to the anglicized "Koran" (except when used by a specific organization or in a title).

Korean American use for those who self-identify this way; do not use to describe someone based on looks or known ethnicity.

krump dancing/crump dancing a mixture of traditional African dances, street fighting, and the physical evocation of spiritual ecstasy, this form of freestyle dance originated in South Central Los Angeles and has evolved into a complex art and sometimes a network of "families" and "farms." A somewhat related activity, clowning, involves elaborate face-painting. The krumping movement is seen as a creative, vital, and nonviolent alternative to street violence.

Kurds see Shiites, Sunnis, Kurds.

Kwanzaa from the Swahili word for "first fruits," Kwanzaa (December 26 to January 1) is a celebration of African culture (not a religious holi-day) that combines traditional African practices with African American ideals and centers on the seven principles of black culture (unity, self-pride, working together, helping the community, purpose, creativity, and faith).

L

Language is the common heritage of humans; all humans must share in shaping and using it.

Francine Frank and Frank Anshen

Our language is not the special private property of the language police, or grammarians, or teachers, or even great writers. The genius of English is that it has always been the tongue of the common people, literate or not. English belongs to everybody ... to those of us who wish to be careful with it and those who don't care.

Robert MacNeil

labor trafficking see human trafficking.

lackey historically, lackeys were men. In today's sense of a servile follower, servant, gofer, or toady, a lackey can be either sex.

lad use with "lass." Or child, youth.

ladies and gentlemen when used to address an audience, this will probably not set most teeth on edge although it is old-fashioned and the correct pair for "gentlemen" is "gentlewomen." Many speakers now use terms that are more generic, contemporary, and meaningful: friends, family and friends, delegates, colleagues, members of the association, staff members. Or omit what is often a meaningless phrase and begin directly, "Welcome." See also gentlewoman, lady (noun).

ladies' auxiliary as they become less common, so will this sexist term, which indicates a secondary, helpmeet role (women's auxiliary is slightly more acceptable and some groups use "alliance" instead of "auxiliary"). Yet these organizations have contributed numerous community benefits. Use "ladies' auxiliary" for groups who so designate themselves.

ladies' room women's room. The parallel term is men's room.

ladies' man this term is problematic because there is no precise equivalent for women ("gentlemen's woman"?) and because of the use of "ladies." The lopsided and unattractive "parallels" for women would be the pejorative "femme fatale" and "man-eater." Some alternatives: popular/successful with the women/the men, heartbreaker, hottie, smooth operator, God's gift to men/women. See also femme fatale, lady, philanderer, playboy, womanizer.

ladino use this term for a Central American Spanish-speaking or acculturated Indian only if you are familiar with the culture; in some contexts, it is faintly pejorative. "Ladina" has not been seen, but it may be a possibility. Capitalized, Ladino is a Romance language with elements borrowed from Hebrew that is spoken by some Sephardic Jews.

lady (noun) woman. Many good people have trouble understanding the objections to "lady." "But isn't that a *nice* word?" they ask. "The concept of 'lady' goes far beyond a single word to a whole way of life" (Alette Olin Hill, *Mother Tongue, Father Time*). In its traditional use, "lady" defines women as ornaments or decorations rather than real people, as arbiters of both manners and morals, as members of a leisured class, as beings removed from any hint of sexuality, as needing protection from real life, as "too good" or "too special" to "dirty their hands"; as such, it is classist, condescending, trivializing, and anachronistic. However, in recent years, the term has been reclaimed and used somewhat ironically among certain groups of women. The "insider/outsider" rule applies here; others should not use it. "Lady" was once the equivalent of "knight" in the social order, and it has also been paired with "gentleman," yet neither of these terms is used today in the way "lady" is. Note too that "lady" is used sometimes to express annoyance where "woman" is not ("Hey, lady, I was here first!" or "Look, lady, we're sorry, okay?"). The use of "lady" is unobjectionable when: referring to a female member of the House of Lords; you want to convey a sense of graciousness ("She's a real lady"); when it is paired with "gentleman" ("Welcome, ladies and gentlemen"). According to the *New York Times Manual of Style and Usage*, "Except in wry contexts, *lady* is obsolete for woman, just as *gentleman* is obsolete for man." The *National Public Radio Style Guide* is more curt: "Do not use as a synonym for woman." See also chivalry, lady (adjective), ladylike.

lady (adjective) woman. A sex-identifying adjective is necessary in only rare cases; double-check phrases using one. See also lady (noun).

lady beetle/ladybird/ladybug leave as they are.

ladyfinger leave as is.

lady friend/lady love avoid; for alternatives see girlfriend. See also lady.

lady-in-waiting servant, attendant, personal attendant/servant. Use "lady-in-waiting" when it is an official title.

lady-killer this violent term has moved from metaphor to ugly reality with increasing numbers of men murdering women, most often in the context of relationships. For the usual meaning, use instead popular/successful with the women/the men.

ladylike conveying different meanings according to people's perceptions of what a woman ought or ought not do, say, think, wear, feel, look like, "ladylike" is a subjective cultural judgment. Choose instead precise adjectives: courteous, well-mannered, civil, polite, tender, cooperative, neat, soft-spoken, gentle, aristocratic, cultured, elegant, proper, correct, gracious, considerate, refined, well-bred, kind, well-spoken. These adjectives apply equally well to a man. See also lady.

lady luck luck.

lady of easy virtue/of pleasure/of the evening/of the night prostitute. These terms are sexist (there are no parallels for men), coy, and imprecise. See also prostitute.

lady of the house head of the house, householder, homeowner, registered voter, taxpayer, citizen, consumer. See also housewife, man of the house.

ladyship used of a woman with the rank of lady; the male equivalent is "lordship."

lady's maid attendant, personal attendant/servant.

lady's slipper/lady's smock/lady's thumb (plants) leave as they are.

lame some people who walk with difficulty report liking this word; it is not essentially derogatory nor is it used disparagingly of those who are lame. However, "lame" is also used metaphorically to mean "weak," as in "a lame excuse" or "That is so lame," and in a small way this usage taints the physical condition. Use "lame" of those who self-identify that way but in other uses, especially if you are writing or speaking to an audience, it is much cleverer to find a precise word to convey your meaning ("pathetic," "flimsy," "ridiculous").

landlady/landlord proprietor, owner, land owner, property owner/manager, manager, leaseholder, lessor, manager, building/apartment manager, superintendent, rent collector, householder, realtor. Note the differences in prestige conjured up by "landlord" and "landlady."

Lapps/Lapland Sàmi/Saamiland. "The term Lapp is very dated, and is considered to be pejorative, in bad taste" (*Baiki: The International Sami Journal*). "Lapp" means "outcast"; "Sàmi" mean "the People." They call their physical and cultural arctic homeland Sàpmi, which encompasses parts of Norway, Sweden, Finland, and Russia.

La Raza this term is used by some Mexican Americans to convey affinity with those blacks, whites, and Indians who share their language and culture. Thus, although it means "the race," the term is not understood the way "race" is understood in the U.S.

lass use with "lad." Or child, youth.

last name because not all cultures follow the same order of names, in some situations you may want to use instead family name, surname.

Latin American when referring to those now living in Latin America (which includes South America, Central America, Mexico, and the islands of the Caribbean), use specific designations if possible: Uruguayan, Colombian, Panamanian, Bolivian. The term is also used to refer to U.S. residents of Latin American descent, but it implies an unrealistic homogeneity and lacks precision; use it only for those so identifying themselves. See also Chicana/Chicano/Chican@, Hispanic, Latina/Latino/Latin@, Mexican American.

Latina/Latino/Latin@ these terms are preferred to "Hispanic," "Spanish-speaking," "Spanish-surnamed," or "Spanish"; for one thing, they include Brazilians. Those self-identifying as Latinas and Latinos are primarily people of Central American and Latin American descent living in the United States, although sometimes the terms may not include

Mexican Americans or Caribbeans; use the terms for—and only for—those who prefer them. The terms "Latino man" and "Latina woman" are redundant. Avoid using "Latino" or "Latinos" as generics; use instead "Latinas and Latinos," for example, or the useful new conflation, Latin@. The adjective "Latino" is a problem—is "Latino art" the work of only men? In such cases, circumlocute, use Latin@, or reword to make clear the presence of both women and men. See also Chicana/Chicano/Chican@, Hispanic, hot-blooded, Mexican American.

laundress launderer. See also "feminine" word endings, laundryman/laundrywoman.

laundryman/laundrywoman launderer, washer, clothes washer, laundry attendant/worker/hand/collector/deliverer, dry cleaner.

lawman lawmaker, lawgiver, law officer/enforcer, law enforcement officer/agent, arm/officer of the law. Or be specific: sheriff, deputy, judge, attorney, officer, FBI agent, detective, marshal, police/patrol/peace/traffic/highway officer, magistrate, justice, constable, warden, bailiff, guard.

lawyer according to the American Bar Association, 31 percent of lawyers are women; 47 percent of law school entrants are women; 25 percent of law school applicants are women and men of color; 15 percent of lawyers are men and women of color; 16.3 percent of partners in major firms are women; women earn 79 percent of their male counterparts' incomes.

"lay"/"easy lay"/"good lay" (sex partner) referring to someone this way makes them an object, an incidental scratch for the speaker's itch. See also score.

layman layperson, laic, member/one of the laity, lay Christian, congregation member, parishioner; amateur, nonprofessional, nonspecialist, nonexpert, average/ordinary person. Plurals: laypeople, laity, the laity, layfolk, members of the congregation, the lay public. Although "-person" words are generally not recommended, "layperson" has gained common acceptance and is one of the few "-person" words that does not seem to jar.

layman's terms plain/nontechnical/ordinary/uncomplicated/informal language, common/simple/nontechnical/easy-to-understand/layperson's terms.

lazy generally, only the one who says, "I am lazy" has a right to it as definitions of "success" and "ambition" as well as personal and financial resources vary greatly from person to person. It is especially objectionable when used of people of color (Vivian Jenkins Nelson) or poor people.

lazy Susan if you want a sex-neutral expression, consider revolving/relish tray.

leader female or male. The still-male flavor of "leader" is lessening as women assume leadership positions in a number of countries. In addition to such well-known past and present leaders as Benazir Bhutto, Indira Gandhi, Margaret Thatcher, Golda Meir, and Angela Merkel, there is: Jóhanna Sigurdardóttir, prime minister of Iceland; Ellen Johnson-Sirleaf, president of Liberia; Helle Thorning-Schmidt, prime minister of Denmark; Tarja Halonen, president of Finland; Pratibha Patil, president of India; Cristina Fernandez de Kirchner, president of Argentina; Sheikh Hasina, prime minister of Bangladesh; Dalia Grybauskaitė, president of Lithuania; Laura Chinchilla, president of Costa Rica; Kamla Persad-Bissessar, prime minister of Trinidad and Tobago; Julia Gillard, prime minister of Australia; Portia Simpson-Miller, prime minister of Jamaica; Dilma Vana Rousseff, president of Brazil; Atifete Jahjaga, president of Kosovo; Yingluck Shinawatra, prime minister of Thailand; Iveta Radičová, prime minister of Slovakia; Eveline Widmer-Schlumpf, president of Switzerland.

leading lady/leading man these terms, with their nonparallel "lady/man," are deeply entrenched in the language. Sometimes you may be able to use lead, principal, star, featured performer; leading woman/leading man.

leadman group leader, supervisor; star, lead singer, lead guitar player. See also foreman, frontman (music).

learning disability this term is often used unthinkingly and imprecisely. Although researchers and professionals do not agree on an exact meaning, the Learning Disabilities Association of Canada defines the term as "a heterogeneous group of disorders due to identifiable or inferred central nervous system dysfunction" that may cause difficulties in such areas as attention, reading, writing, and social competence; and may affect any individual, including those with above average intelligence. "Learning disabilities may arise from genetic variation, biochemical factors, events in the pre- to perinatal period, or any other subsequent events resulting in neurological impairment." See also disabilities.

leatherneck (Marine) woman or man. The reference is not personal; the uniform once sported a leather neckband.

lecher/lecherous/lech by definition a man, "lecher" has no precise inclusive synonyms, and "lecherous" seems most associated with men, but "lech" is used casually for women and there are several sex-neutral related terms: sex maniac/fiend, make-out artist, libertine, debaucher, swinger, bedhopper, seducer.

left/left-winger/the left/leftist/far left see political spectrum.

Legion of Honor/Legion of Merit all orders are awarded to both women and men.

legionnaire since the American Legion is open to both women and men who served in the U.S. armed forces during official conflicts as established by Congress, a legionnaire could be either sex. In historical and other contexts, a legionnaire is almost invariably male.

leper/leprosy person with Hansen's disease/Hansen's disease. A chronic, infectious, germ-caused disease, treatable with antibiotics, Hansen's is still one of the least contagious of all communicable diseases; only about 4.5 percent of the world's population is even susceptible to it. Approximately 2 million people worldwide (about 6,500 in the U.S.) have Hansen's disease. Underlying the stigma of Hansen's disease is the faulty association with biblical lepers—outcasts and undesirables. "Protestant, Catholic, and Jewish scholars are in remarkable agreement as to the biblical word *leprosy*; it was not a medical term designating Hansen's disease or any other specific disease. Rather it denoted an afflicting stigma or blemish which marked the victim as 'unclean' under Hebrew ritualistic law" (F.C. Lendrum). Do not say someone is "suffering from," "a victim of," or "afflicted with" Hansen's disease. Avoid metaphorical uses of the term ("a social leper," "leprous wallpaper"). Terminology using "leprosy"-related terms has been officially banned by the governments of Brazil, Portugal, and Suriname, and officially abandoned by the U.S. Public Health Service's regulations.

lesbian (noun/adjective) this term, which is preferred by most of the estimated 6 to 13 million lesbians in the U.S., refers to "a woman whose emotional and sexual energies are directed toward other women, and not toward men. We also extend its meaning to refer to ways of thinking and behaving that draw upon this primary identification, particularly when a Lesbian has become self-aware and consciously seeks out others like herself" (Julia Penelope and Susan J. Wolfe, *Lesbian Culture*). Examine the need to mention a person's sexual orientation; it is often gratuitous. Since "lesbian" includes the sense of "woman," the term "lesbian woman" is redundant. Respect the distinction between "gay" (men) and "lesbian" (women); when "gay" appears alone, you may generally assume it refers only to men. Occasionally "gay" is used as an adjective to include both women and men, but most often the adjective form is "lesbian and gay." See also butch, dyke, femme/fem, gay (adjective), gay rights, LGBT, LGLBTQIA/GLBTQIA, homophobia, homosexual.

lesbian separatism also known as separatist feminism, lesbian separatism "is the feminist political act of choosing to be around only lesbians or only women. In the early years of the Feminist Movement, some lesbians chose to avoid interacting with men as a way to remove themselves from male-dominated society. Their belief was that even well-meaning men were sexist and influenced by the patriarchy. They chose to be around only women in order to understand what womanhood and sisterhood is really all about. Some women moved to the country, bought land and created women-only societies. Avoiding all men was impossible, but they chose to have all of their significant relationships with women. The idea was that women could never truly understand themselves as powerful beings if they were immersed in the dominant, sexist culture. From lesbian separatism the idea of women-only space came into being at concerts, conferences, and festivals" (Kathy Belge, on www.lesbianlife.about.com). The idea that sexual disparities between women and men were irresolvable led at one time to perhaps thousands of women committing to lesbian separatism, which has been considered both a temporary strategy and a lifelong practice. See also feminisms, lesbian.

lesbie/lesbo/lezzie unacceptable terms except if used positively by lesbians among themselves. See also "insider/outsider" rule, shortened forms of words.

letterman letterholder, letter winner, letter, lettered athlete; letterwoman and letterman if used fairly.

Lewis and Clark expedition much like Columbus's "discovery" of the New World, what Lewis and Clark "found" wasn't really lost—although what was eventually lost for Native Americans were lives, lands, languages, and freedom. On their 7,400-mile trek, Lewis and Clark encountered at least 48 different tribes, says educator Judy BlueHorse of Portland, Oregon, "And yet it's always a story about these two men." Considering the earlier efforts of the Spanish, French, and British, the Lewis and Clark expedition was not one of the first, but one of the last such excursions.

LGBT acceptable shorthand for lesbian, gay, bisexual, and transgender, sometimes with a "Q" for queer or questioning. First spell out the groups involved; use the acronym only in later references. Alternate GLBT with LGBT for balance.

LGBTQIA/GLBTQIA the shorthand has changed, and it's still in flux. But let's get over ourselves; we can deal with this (and don't bother pointing out that it sounds like a sandwich; that's been done). "Youth today do not define themselves on the spectrum of LGBT," says Shane Windmeyer, a founder of Campus Pride, a national student advocacy group (Minneapolis' *Star Tribune*). The emerging rubric is LBGTQIA: L = lesbian; G = gay; B = bisexual; T = transgender, transsexual, trans-identified, two-spirit; Q = queer, questioning; I = intersexual; A = asexual, ally. (An ally is anyone, regardless of sexual orientation or gender identity, who supports the human and civil rights of LGBTQIA.) Ever-expanding categories like "genderqueer" and "androgyne" might also be included. "When you see terms like LGBTQIA, it's because people are seeing all the things that fall out of the binary and demanding that a name come into being" (Jack Halberstam, *Gaga Feminism: Sex, Gender, and the End of Normal*). A Gallup survey reported in *The Weeks* (2013) found that 3.5 percent of the population identifies as gay, lesbian, bisexual, or transgender. When discussing, first identify the groups involved and use the acronym in later references. See also gay, gender, intersexual, lesbian, queer, transgender.

lib/libber member of the women's liberation movement, liberationist, feminist. "Lib" and "libber" are derogatory and generally indicate hostility on the part of those who use them. See also shortened forms of words.

liberal see political spectrum.

lifestyle life. See also "gay lifestyle."

"like a girl" (fight like a girl/throw like a girl) an equal opportunity offender, this phrase puts down women while putting down men, or vice versa.

like father, like son this is a (usually) warm and positive phrase that can be used as is. Other variants are equally useful: like father, like daughter; like mother, like daughter; like mother, like son. To convey the concept more sex-neutrally, consider: the acorn doesn't fall far from the tree, a chip off/of the old block, like parent like child.

Lilly Ledbetter Fair Pay Act, The see wage earner.

lilywhite/lily-white this term is part of the problematic black/white dichotomy (one definition of "lilywhite" is "beyond reproach, blameless," which makes "black" ... what?).

limey see ethnic slurs.

limousine liberal see political spectrum.

limp-wristed this stereotypical adjective is inaccurate most of the time and objectionable all of the time.

line foreman line supervisor.

lineman (job title) lineworker, line installer/repairer, electrician.

line man (sports) line player, offensive/defensive tackle/guard/center; line umpire/judge/referee.

linesman line judge/referee/tender, liner.

lioness lion. By using the base word inclusively, terms like "lion's share" are also inclusive. See also "feminine" word endings.

lip reading because the person is also "reading" tongue, teeth, and related movements, the correct term is speech reading.

little boys'/little girls' room unless found in a preschool daycare center, these terms are too cute. In elementary schools, for example, use girls' room/boys' room. In most other cases, use men's room/women's room.

little lady/little man it is never correct to refer to an adult woman this way, and there is no acceptable substitute because the very notion is demeaning; "little man" is reserved for boys. It is also incorrect to refer to girls and boys this way because (1) a child is not an adult and should be allowed to be a child and (2) telling a child she is a little lady or he is a little man almost without exception is an attempt to perpetuate some cultural stereotype, for example, sitting quietly and neatly in the background (little lady) or not showing emotions (little man). The terms tell the child this is the desired, best behavior for all occasions.

Little League open to both boys and girls.

little woman, the some people who use this to mean spouse, partner, wife do so to express affection, but it is generally to be avoided.

liveryman livery worker, vehicle-rental service operator; liveried retainer; livery company member.

living apart together (LAT) couples who are committed to each other but not sharing a home are becoming more commonplace. It sounds like a new idea, but in 1923 *Cosmopolitan* published "Marriage Under Two Roofs" by Crystal Eastman: "I took a small flat for myself and the children. ... My husband took a room in a clean rooming house within easy walking distance of his office. ... It is wonderful sometimes to be alone in the night and just know that someone loves you. In other moods you must have that lover in your arms. Marriage under two roofs makes room for moods."

living doll unlike many other uses of "doll," this term refers to both sexes. Although it seems that there ought to be a general rule not to refer to people as dolls (because of all the implications of making objects of them), this particular expression has always been fairly benign, and there seems to be no difference in tone, intent, or significance between references to men and women.

living wage generally speaking, an individual ought to be able to work 40 hours a week and, with no additional income, be able to afford adequate housing, food, utilities, transport, health care, and recreation. The minimum wage is a dollar amount set by law that usually falls well below what is needed to meet basic needs. For a minimum estimate of the cost of living for low-wage families in every county in the United States, visit http://livingwage.mit.edu. Los Angeles has passed one of the nation's strongest living wage laws. See also working poor.

lobbyist Bill Moyers said, "When powerful interests shower Washington with millions in campaign contributions, they often get what they want. But it is ordinary citizens and firms that pay the price and most of them never see it coming. This is what happens if you don't contribute to their campaigns or spend generously on lobbying. You pick up a disproportionate share of America's tax bill. You pay higher prices for a broad range of products from peanuts to prescriptions. You pay taxes that others in a similar situation have been excused from paying. You're compelled to abide by laws while others are granted immunity from them. You must pay debts that you incur while others do not. You're barred from writing off on your tax returns some of the money spent on necessities while others deduct the cost of their entertainment. You must run your business by one set of rules, while the government creates another set for your competitors. In contrast, the fortunate few who contribute to the right politicians and hire the right lobbyists enjoy all the benefits of their special status. Make a bad business deal; the government bails them out. If they want to hire workers at below market wages, the government provides the means to do so. If they want more time to pay their debts, the government gives them an extension. If they want immunity from certain laws, the government gives it. If they want to ignore rules their competition must comply with, the government gives its approval. If they want to kill legislation that is intended for the public, it gets killed. I'm not quoting from Karl Marx's *Das Kapital* or Mao's *Little Red Book*. I'm quoting *Time* magazine. From the heart of America's media establishment comes the judgment that America now has 'government for the few at the expense of the many.'" To keep money out of politics, we need campaign finance reform and we need to find better jobs for all the lobbyists in Washington. See also campaign finance reform.

lobsterman lobster catcher/fisher/farmer/grower/cultivator/dealer.

locavore according to the Oxford University Press USA, that chose it as Oxford 2007 Word of the Year, the term "was coined two years ago by a group of four women in San Francisco (www.locavores.com) who proposed that local residents should try to eat only food grown or produced within a 100-mile radius. Other regional movements have emerged since then, though some groups refer to themselves as 'localvores' rather than 'locavores.'"

Log Cabin Republicans a national lesbian and gay Republican grassroots organization, Log Cabin Republicans work for the civil rights of gay and lesbians through the Republican party.

Lolita the Lolita myth ("myth" because it is not borne out very well by the book *Lolita* by Vladimir Nabokov) of a child who wants and can sustain a sexual relationship has been immeasurably harmful. Several groups argue for "sexual freedom" for children, maintaining that children actually want and need sexual experience with an adult. Kiddie sex is a flourishing business in various parts of the country, but it is not the runaway street children who want sex (although they do want the money, food, or drugs it brings them), but the unhealthy adults. There is no parallel to "Lolita" for a boy. If you need sex-neutral alternatives for the mythical Lolita, consider sexually precocious; underage and seductive. See also pornography.

lone wolf woman or man.

Long johns despite being based on the name John, this word is functionally nonsexist. If you need something more sex-neutral, consider woolies, winter underwear.

longshoreman longshore worker, stevedore, dockhand.

looksism the subtle and not-so-subtle disparagement of and discrimination against people who are not physically attractive according to unstated but entrenched cultural definitions is called looksism. While "the latitude for a woman's appearance is generally narrower than for men" (employment discrimination consultant Freada Klein, in *The Washington Post*), both men and women are spending more for plastic surgery, and, discounting for the "enhancing" effects of sexism, fat or "unattractive" men suffer discrimination nearly as often as women. Only a smattering of state and local laws have "personal appearance" protections. Although it is sometimes referred to as "appearance discrimination," the term "looksism" has much to recommend it: brevity; parallels with sexism, racism, ageism, etc.; and a fairly well-established foothold in the language. See also body image, fat.

loose woman if you mean prostitute, use it. If you mean a woman of questionable morals (which is a questionable judgment), use inclusive words: promiscuous, sexually active, indiscriminating. The language has no such expression as "loose man," yet a "loose woman" must, by definition, have a partner; avoid judging one sex by criteria not applied to the other.

lord and master (husband) the phrase will date you even if used tongue-in-cheek.

lord it over someone dominate, domineer, boss around, browbeat, bully, intimidate, tyrannize, overshadow, overpower, oppress, bend to one's will.

lordliness dignity, majesty, elegance; arrogance, haughtiness, imperiousness, insolence, overconfidence, conceit, condescension, pomposity.

lordly stately, imperial, imposing, noble, overbearing, imperious, snobbish, commanding.

lord mayor leave as is where used officially (as in Great Britain).

lord of the manor, play swagger, give oneself airs. See also lord it over someone.

Lord's Day Sunday.

lordship used of a man with the rank of lord; the equivalent for a woman is "ladyship."

Lothario for inclusive alternatives, consider heartbreaker, seducer, deceiver, libertine, lover, great/dashing lover, swinger, flame, admirer, flirt.

lounge lizard because this term is used only of men, you may sometimes need a sex-neutral term: barfly, social parasite.

love, honor, and obey (wedding ceremony) the "obey," which was meant for women, has been replaced or removed in many wedding services: love, honor, and cherish; love and honor; love, respect, and cherish; love, encourage, and accept. Many couples today make up their own pledges.

lover acceptable and useful term describing individuals of either sex and any sexual orientation. See also boyfriend, domestic partner, girlfriend, inamorata/inamorato, paramour, partner.

lowerclassman beginning student, first- or second-year student; sometimes, undergraduate. See also freshman.

low-income question the use of this term; we use it more often and with more meanings (some of them code) than we do "high-income." An employee of a utility company notes that they have two kinds of customers: customers and low-income customers.

low man on the totem pole see totem pole, low man on the.

lumberjack/lumberman lumber worker/cutter, logger, timber worker, forester, woodchopper.

lust properly (or improperly) attributed to either sex. Craig Rice (pseudonym of Georgiana Ann Randolph), wrote in 1941, "'Tis better to have loved and lust than never to have loved at all."

"When you say Man," said Oedipus, "you include women too. Everyone knows that." She said, "That's what you think."

Muriel Rukeyser

The important thing about any word is how you understand it.

Publilius Syrus

ma'am/madam used in the same way "sir" is used for men, "ma'am" (or, infrequently, "madam") is inoffensive, but neither "sir" nor "ma'am" is extremely common today. Some people dislike it: "You're more likely to hear ma'am when somebody is annoyed" (Deborah Tannen); "In theory, ma'am is a courtesy term, meant to convey respect and graciousness lightly salted with deference. Yet much evidence suggests that when it comes to fomenting a sense of good will ma'am fails even more spectacularly than 'Have a nice day'" (Natalie Angier, *New York Times*). Others like it, including Miss Manners (Judith Martin) and those familiar with languages where a polite title is tacked onto every interaction with a stranger. At one time, "madam" appeared to be losing its respectability because of its other meaning (female head of a house of prostitution). "Sir" never had an unsavory second job, but male-female word pairs (master/mistress, for example) often went in different directions. For someone connected with prostitution, use prostitute, owner/head of house of prostitution.

macho/machismo by definition, only men are macho (the word is Spanish, meaning "male") or are associated with machismo; there is no parallel for women ("macha" is incorrect). You can approximate "macho" with sex-neutral alternatives: overly aggressive, defensive, proud, swaggering, overbearing, show-off.

mademoiselle in 2012, French Prime Minister François Fillon directed that "Mademoiselle" be removed from all administrative documents. Until then, women were required to identify themselves as married ("Madame") or unmarried ("Mademoiselle") on everything from tax forms to insurance claims and voting cards. Men had only to check off "Monsieur," married or un-. Fillon wrote that the use of "Mademoiselle" made reference "without justification nor necessity" to a woman's matrimonial situation. The same groups who lobbied for the change are asking private businesses to follow suit so women do not have to self-identify as "Madame" or "Mademoiselle" for buying online music or booking an airline ticket or other business transactions. In social and marketplace interactions, where marital status is unknown, the French have tended to use *mademoiselle* for women in their teens or early to mid-twenties while *madam* was used for older women. This may continue to be seen; it is also the case with *frau* and *fräulein* (but note that *fräulein* is also no longer in official use in Germany). See also Miss, Mrs., Ms.

madman/madwoman these terms are gender-fair but they are vague and inaccurate. If a person's mental condition must be mentioned, use correct medical terminology (for example, "someone with obsessive-compulsive disorder"); avoid identifying the whole person with one aspect of their existence. See also insane/insanity, mental illness.

Madras Chennai.

maestro in some contexts, "maestro" is still considered irreplaceable and is used for both women and men. In other situations, consider conductor, orchestra leader, expert.

Mafia organized crime, the underworld. Not all Italian criminals are members of the Mafia. And in reference to non-Italian crime "Mafia" is a misrepresentation and an ethnic slur, but even to use it "in reference to Italian criminals ... implies that organized crime was begun by Italians and/or Italian Americans, when, in fact, organized crime was thriving in the United States long before our grandparents arrived here—although even the phrase 'organized crime' conjures up images of Italian-Americans for bigots" (Rose Romano).

Magi see three wise men, the.

maharaja/maharani acceptable sex-specific words.

maid/maidservant household servant/worker/cleaner/helper, houseworker, servant, housekeeper, house cleaner, custodian, janitor. See also charwoman, cleaning lady, handyman.

maid/matron of honor attendant, best woman, attendant of honor. Whichever term you choose, refer to the groom's attendant with a parallel term, for example, "best woman and best man" or "bride's attendant and groom's attendant." See also best man.

maiden (adjective) first, inaugural, initial, premier, earliest, new, untried, untested, untapped, unused, fresh, intact, inexperienced. See also single, maiden voyage.

maiden (noun) use only when quoting or in historical contexts.

maiden aunt aunt. Marital status is generally irrelevant; and "maiden" carries stereotypical implications of fussiness, lack of attractiveness, and having been rejected by men.

maidenhead hymen, virginity. See also virgin/virginity.

maidenhood youth, innocence, adolescence. There is little reason to use the outdated and problematic "maidenhood"; avoid it. See also virgin/virginity.

maiden name birth/given/birth family/family/former/original/premarital name, family of origin name, original surname. "Birth name" is the most commonly used term. Keeping one's birth name is not as widespread as it is perceived to be: only 10 percent of U.S. married women do not use their husband's last name. Since 1979, women in Quebec legally retain their surname upon marriage unless they make a special application to change it (Ruth King, *Talking Gender*). In Sicily, many women have two names—their own "public" name and their married "private" name. See also hyphenated surnames, surnames.

maiden voyage first/premier voyage, first trip/sailing; debut, initiation, premiere.

mailman mailcarrier, letter carrier, mail handler/deliverer/clerk, postal worker/clerk/officer. Both the National Association of Letter Carriers and the National Postal Mail Handlers Union use inclusive terms.

mail-order bride there has never been anything parallel for men and thus there is no sex-neutral alternative. The practice still exists.

main man (slang) this term has such a particular meaning that in most cases it is probably irreplaceable if you are writing or reporting street talk. If you need a sex-neutral alternative, try best friend, partner, hero, mentor.

mainstream a slippery notion, what is "mainstream" to one person is not to the next. It is often used as a synonym for "normal," which is also a slippery notion.

maître d'hôtel dining room/restaurant host, hotel manager/steward/proprietor.

majordomo nonsexist term (it comes from the Latin for "elder of the house"), although almost all of them have been male stewards or butlers.

makeup girl/makeup man makeup artist. Note the nonparallel "girl/man." Marie Shear on makeup (in *New Directions for Women*): "Western equivalent of the veil. A daily reminder that something is wrong with women's normal looks. A public apology."

male (noun) "male" is used as a noun only in technical writing (medicine, statistics, police reports, sociology); (adjective) use only when you would use "female" or when it is necessary for clarification; this adjective is often inserted gratuitously, for example, "male nurse," "male secretary," "male model," "male prostitute."

male bonding in *The New Republic*, Robert Wright says it's unclear "whether the intense bonds formed during war, and all the valor and sacrifice they inspire, result from 'male bonding' or simply 'person-under-fire bonding.'" The traditional meaning of male bonding (often a matter of drinking and sports) is being replaced for some men by a new sense of what it means to be with other men as friends, brothers, and companions on the journey.

male chauvinist/male chauvinist pig chauvinist. "Chauvinism" used to refer to the view that one's own country was vastly superior, right or wrong, to all other countries. Dictionaries now also define "chauvinism" as the view that one's own sex is vastly superior.

male ego ego. Make no generalizations about an entire sex.

male gaze in visual media (film, television, advertising, fine arts, comics, video), who is doing the looking and who is being looked at has enormous significance for our cultural ideas about women and men. Laura Mulvey ("Visual Pleasure and Narrative Cinema," 1975) first pointed out that women are typically the objects, rather than the possessors, of gaze. In the beginning, most cameramen and most heroes, as well as most target audiences, were men, therefore heterosexual men were the watchers and women were the watched. This male perspective underwrites the sexual objectification of women. An interesting twist in advertising is that the image being sold to men is the attractive woman ("Buy this and she will want you"), while what's being sold to women is the male gaze ("Buy this and men will pay attention to you"). The corollary is even the female adopts the male gaze, looking at herself through his eyes to see how she's doing. All power is given to the male. The implications for writers, media, and creative image makers who care about equality is to ask constantly: who is looking at whom here?

male impersonator see cross-dresser.

male privilege a few of the benefits men have traditionally enjoyed primarily because they are men include generally being paid more for comparable work, being able to ignore what women say, to be called on more frequently in the classroom, within reason to go where they like without fearing assault, rape, or sexual harassment, to do a disproportionately small share of housework and childcare, and even, in many cases and over centuries, to define reality. Along with this, however, has come the "privilege" today—simply because they are men—of registering for selective service, dying earlier than women, and living up to cultural expectations for them which include being strong, "virile," provident, and successful. Black men have the shortest average life span of any group and suffer proportionately more violence and, in the U.S., more incarceration. Public interest attorney, activist, and author Andrew Kimbrell says, "It is a lingering irony that what many call a patriarchal production system significantly degraded both fatherhood and sonship. Rejecting both the male mystique and anti-male ideology, men have begun articulating a male manifesto—a political agenda designed to re-establish ties with each other, their families, communities, and the Earth." See privilege.

mama's boy spoiled/immature/irresponsible person. "Mama's boy" is an unfortunate cultural stereotype that keeps many parents from giving their sons the nurturing they need (and that they continue to seek, often in inappropriate ways, throughout life). Daughters, on the other hand, are more often encouraged (also with sometimes unfortunate results) to be "obedient" and dependent. See also apron strings, tied to someone's.

"mammy" this term is sexist (there is no parallel term for a man), racist, and an objectionable stereotype that was probably always highly mythical.

man (adult male human being) this narrow definition is the only acceptable nonsexist usage for the noun. Dictionaries list two major definitions for "man": (1) adult male, (2) human being. However, studies have shown that people "hear" only the first meaning of the word. See Writing Guidelines for a complete discussion of pseudogeneric "man." See also bad guy, coward, gender roles, male privilege, Man/man (pseudogeneric), provider, sex differences.

Man/man (pseudogeneric) person/s, people, human/s, human being/s, the human race/family, civilization, society, individual/s, one, someone, anyone, soul/s, society, all of us, ourselves, everyone, humankind, humanity, community, the larger community, resident/s, inhabitant/s, adult/s, citizen/s, taxpayer/s, worker/s, member/s, participant/s, hand/s, party/parties, our ancestors, women and men. Or be specific: Neolithic peoples, early settlers, 15th-century Europe, civilization as we know it. Although many people, including both women and men, insist that "man" is a generic term, that usage was declared obsolete in the 1970s by both the National Council for Teachers of English and the *Oxford English Dictionary*, and a close reading of books published before the 1970s shows that "man" never was truly generic. Erich Fromm wrote that "man" needs food, shelter, and access to females. The "man/men" in our own constitution couldn't have been generic since it took two constitutional amendments to give the vote to those who were not white men. For a complete discussion of pseudogeneric "man," see Writing Guidelines. See also Fall of Man, man (adult male human being), manhood.

man- many words beginning with "man-" come from the Latin for "hand" and are not sexist: manacle, mandate, maneuver, manifest/ manifestation, manufacture, manumission, manure, manuscript. Other words that begin with "man-" have nonsexist roots: manciple (from Latin for "purchase"); mandate (from the Latin for "to command"); mandrake (from a Greek term for the plant); manege (from Italian for "horse training"); manes (from Greek for "spirit"); mangrove (from Spanish for the tree); "Manhattan" (from American Indian word for "island"); mania (from Greek for "spirit") manifold (from Old English for "many"); manor/mansion (from Latin for "dwell"); mantle (from Latin for "cloak").

-man/-men not all words that end in "-man/-men" are sex-linked. For example, a Roman or a German may be either female or male; "amen" comes from Hebrew for "truly" or "certainly"; "dolman" from "dolama," a Turkish robe; "ottoman" from French for "Turk"; "talisman" from Greek for "consecration"; "catechumen" from Greek for "someone being instructed"; "tegmen" from Latin for "covering"; "gravamen" from Latin for "burden." When in doubt, check a dictionary.

man/manned for the verb, use operate, staff, run, supply a crew/personnel for, outfit, arm, brace, fortify. For the adjective, use staffed, crewed, operated, serviced, stationed, worked, run, covered, handled. See also manned space flight.

man about town sophisticate, socially active/worldly person, swinger, mover, high-liver, high-flier. The foregoing can be used for either sex whereas there is no phrase for women parallel to "man about town." A woman who has "been around" is not being complimented. See also ladies' man, playboy, rake, womanizer.

man, act like a/be a/take it like a be brave/bold, defy, bear up, meet/ confront with courage/bravery/valor/boldness, hold up one's head, take heart, face the music, act courageously/bravely/wisely/straightforwardly/honorably, show fortitude/patience/determination/strength/vigor, stand up for oneself, be independent/resolute/unflinching/earnest. Expressions like "be a man" limit, bewilder, and oppress men while also implying that woman are not bold, courageous, straightforward, hardy. (Alternatives are for both sexes.) Russell Baker (*About Men*) says, "Before you were old enough to think for yourself, they were preparing you for a lifetime of feeling like a disgrace to your sex. …Men would rather have their eyes blackened and teeth loosened than let the whole world see that they hate being severely beaten." See also coward; manfully; man, like a; manlike/manly.

man among men one in a million, salt of the earth, one of the best.

M

man and wife never use this; it is a nonparallel construction. Use instead man and woman/woman and man, wife and husband/husband and wife, spouses, mates, partners, married couple.

man, as one unanimously, simultaneously, as one person/body, without exception, of the same mind, in concert, carried unanimously/by acclamation, everyone, all.

man-at-arms warrior, soldier, combatant; or retain in historical senses.

man, be his own stand on one's own two feet, be her own woman/his own man.

man-child use with "woman-child," not "girl-child," as is generally done. (But consider the psychology behind equating even superficial adulthood to a child.) If "girl-child" is used, then "boy-child" is the equivalent, not "man-child."

man Friday assistant, office/administrative/executive/program assistant, aide, clerk, right hand, secretary, gofer; avoid the familiar "girl/gal Friday." Note the nonparallel "man/girl."

manfully for this vague cultural stereotype, substitute precise words, which can be used for both sexes.

manhandle abuse, mistreat, maltreat, mishandle, damage, maul, batter, push/kick/knock around, paw, maul, subdue, force, handle roughly, rough up, beat up, pummel, thrash, strike, injure.

man-hater/woman-hater reserve these terms for the few cases in which they are authentic and meaningful; for too many years, lesbians, for example, were all assumed by some people to be man-haters (gay men were never, by the same token, assumed to be women-haters). See also misanthrope/misogynist.

manhole/manhole cover for the first term, use: sewer hole, utility access hole, utility hole, access hole, sewer access, service access, and (a personal favorite) sewer viewer. For the second term, use sewer cover, sewer-hole cover, cover. "Jokes" about personhole covers have been circulating since at least 1978. It's not going to get you a laugh anymore.

manhood "manhood" has four dictionary definitions. (1) Do not use it to mean "the condition of being human"; this is a pseudogeneric. A useful and popular alternative is personhood. (2) Do not use "manhood" to mean "human beings"; this is also a pseudogeneric. (3) When you are referring to manly qualities in a man, its use is correct although your sentence will almost always benefit from more specific words: pride, self-confidence, vigor, strength, courage, maturity. (4) Use "manhood" anytime to mean the condition of being an adult male human being ("womanhood" is the parallel term). See also Man/man ("generic"), man (adult male human being), mankind.

man-hours total hours, hours, worker/work/working/staff/labor/operator/employee hours, hours of work, hours worked, work/staff time, labor, time, labor time.

manhunt dragnet, chase, police search, hunt. "Manhunt" is one of the more difficult sexist words in that there currently exists no equally brief and descriptive inclusive term. When possible avoid it by circumlocution.

man in office person in authority/office, official.

man in the street average, ordinary or typical person/citizen/human/human being/voter; average woman and average man, if used together.

manipulative self-harm incidents suicide. This military term was used especially for suicides by Guantánamo prisoners (*Los Angeles Times*) while "self-injurious behavior incidents" was used for attempted suicides (William Safire, *Safire's Political Dictionary*).

mankind humanity, humankind, people, human beings, humans, human society/nature/species/creatures/populations, the human race/family, civilization, society, individuals, one, creatures, creation, all creation/generations, mortals, body, somebody, someone, anyone, souls, living souls, all living souls, society, all of us, ourselves, everyone, early peoples, we, us, mortality, flesh, folks, persons, the public, the general public, the world, community, the larger community, nation, state, realm, commonweal, commonwealth, republic, body politic, population, residents, inhabitants, adults. "Mankind" is not a generic. It's all very well and good to claim (as some people do), "When I say 'mankind,' I mean everyone." It doesn't matter what you say. It matters what people hear. And they hear "male people." With so many versatile alternatives, you will only improve your writing by avoiding the inaccurate "mankind." See also Man/man (pseudogeneric).

manlike/manly by definition, whatever a man does is manly or manlike because a man is doing it. Consider precise adjectives: courageous, strong, brave, upright, honorable, mature, noble, resolute, straightforward, vigorous, adventurous, spirited, direct, competitive, physical, mechanical, logical, rude, active, self-confident. See also man, like a.

man, like a replace this impossibly vague cultural stereotype with the characteristics you have in mind: with a high/strong hand, resolutely, courageously, competitively, self-confidently, in a straightforward manner. See also man, act like a/be a/take it like a, manlike/manly.

man-machine interface user-system/human-machine interface.

manmade artificial, synthetic, factitious, fabricated, constructed, simulated, bogus, mock, spurious, fictitious, contrived; human-constructed, of human origin, result of human activity; if you say "human-made" about fifty times, it begins to sound quite "natural" and "right."

manned space flight this phrase currently has no equally pithy and inclusive description of space flight crewed by both women and men. Circumlocution is one solution ("the Columbia space flight with six astronauts aboard"). In print, "crewed space flight" works well, but in broadcast journalism, "crude" will be heard. It is reasonable and comprehensible to speak simply of space flight. See also unmanned space flight.

mannequin although "mannequin" and "manikin" come from the Dutch word for "little man," a mannequin is often thought of as female. Should you need an alternative, consider model, dressmaker's/tailor's dummy, display figure, window display figure.

mannish replace this meaningless term with adjectives that convey your precise meaning: brusque, blunt, abrupt, direct, square-jawed, aggressive.

man of action human dynamo, ball of fire, take-charge person, active/ energetic/determined/ambitious/action-oriented person/individual, someone on their toes, woman of action and man of action.

man of affairs avoid; the ersatz parallel for women doesn't sit well in polite society. Use instead entrepreneur, mover, wheeler-dealer. See also businessman.

man of distinction important personage, person of distinction/note/ mark/consequence/importance, prominent/high-ranking individual, poohbah, nabob, man of distinction and woman of distinction.

man of few words strong, silent type; person of few words; closemouthed individual.

man of God/man of the cloth see churchman, clergyman.

man of his word/man of honor honorable person, trustworthy individual; woman of her word and man of his word.

man of letters writer, author, scholar, literary giant, one of the literati, pundit; woman of letters and man of letters.

man of means wealthy/rich/powerful/moneyed individual/person, plutocrat, capitalist, moneybags, nabob, millionaire, billionaire; woman of means and man of means.

man of the hour toast of the town, honored guest, star of the show, center of attention, star attraction, big name; woman of the hour and man of the hour.

man of the house homeowner, head of the household. "Man of the house" and "woman of the house" have been so abused that even if they are used gender-fairly they still sting. See also family man, homebody.

man of the world sophisticate, person with wide experience.

man of the year newsmaker/citizen/member/entertainer/ humanitarian of the year. From 1927, when *Time* magazine began featuring the "Man of the Year" on the cover, to the present, three women have occupied the cover alone: Wallis Simpson (1936), Queen Elizabeth II (1952), and Cory Aquino (1986). However, in 2002 three whistleblowers, all women, were featured; in 2003, it was the American soldier (two men and a woman shown); and in 2005, Melinda Gates was pictured with husband Bill Gates and Bono. (*Time* now uses "Person of the Year.")

man-of-war retain in historical context. Otherwise use warship, battleship, ship of war/of the line, war vessel. Or be specific: cruiser, destroyer, gunboat.

man on the street see man in the street.

manor nonsexist; from the Latin for "to remain."

manpower (noun) workforce, personnel, labor supply/force, staffing, human/people power/energy, staff time, payroll; muscle power, human power/energy; workload; available military personnel. "Womanpower" is seen occasionally ("the new womanpower in Japanese politics") but it is not parallel in meaning to "manpower."

manpower (adjective) staffing, occupational, employee. Narrowing your meaning will suggest precise alternatives: manpower training programs (occupational training); manpower planning (staff resources/human resources planning); manpower levels (employee/staffing levels).

manpowered muscle-/human-/people-powered.

man's best friend there is no good substitute for this phrase because it is associated like none other with the dog, whereas we all know that a woman's best friend are diamonds, and the friend of the people could be anything from Smokey the Bear to General Electric to Karl Marx. Consider using some of the time: the devoted dog, our canine friend, our faithful canine friends, a human's best friend.

manservant servant, attendant, assistant.

-manship when possible, replace words with this suffix: airmanship, brinkmanship, chairmanship, craftsmanship, gamesmanship, grantsmanship, horsemanship, marksmanship, salesmanship, sportsmanship, statesmanship, workmanship, yachtsmanship.

man's home is his castle, a my home is my castle, a person's home is a/their castle, a woman's home is her castle/a man's home is his castle, the sanctity of the home. This phrase is difficult to replace because of its familiarity, but finding alternatives is highly recommended: man's "kingship" in the home has been used to justify and tolerate behavior ranging from petty tyranny to domestic violence.

man's inhumanity to man inhumanity, our inhumanity toward each other, cruelty; Replacing this phrase with something both inclusive and elegant seems impossible, but your meaning may actually be made clearer by identifying the actions or conditions that bring this phrase to mind.

man-size(d) large-size(d), oversized, supersize(d), enormous, hefty, husky, ample, large, comfortably large, sizable, massive, weighty, impressive, considerable, capacious, towering, voracious, immense.

manslaughter this term has a specific legal meaning—use it in that sense until a nonsexist legal term is developed; in its broader sense, use murder, homicide, killing, butchery, wholesale killing/slaughter, assassination, bloodletting, slaughter, carnage, massacre, slaying.

man's man, a this term—usually defined as someone who doesn't threaten other men's egos and is accepted by them but who perhaps is not very comfortable in the presence of women—has no functional parallel for women but it doesn't seem biased against either sex.

man's work work. The only work biologically limited to men is the work they do helping propagate the species and so far it is rarely referred to as work. All other "men's work" is based on cultural stereotypes. Margaret Mead pointed out that there have been villages in which men fish and women weave, and villages in which women fish and men weave, but in either type of village, the work done by men is valued more highly than the work done by women. This may be due to (1) the association of women with nature and men with culture (see Mother Nature); (2) women's reproductive activities keeping them closer to home where their activities are domestic and largely invisible, while men's activities are public and highly visible and thus command more cultural respect; (3) boys/men defining themselves by distancing themselves from and disdaining women and women's work. If men's work has been more highly valued, it has also traditionally been very toxic; the responsibilities of the provider role, the lack of family or leisure time, and rigid and narrow expectations of what is "masculine" have denied men their full human range of expression and may be responsible for the sex difference in death rates. Today many women are also taking on toxic workloads. It would benefit both sexes to change our cultural norms for success and for what constitutes an appropriate work load.

man the barricades mount/defend the barricades.

man-to-man one-to-one, heart-to-heart, one-on-one, face-to-face, straight from the shoulder, on the level, candidly, frankly, privately, confidentially.

mantrap booby/death trap, snare, trap. If referring to a woman, don't perpetuate this tempter-Eve/helpless-Adam stereotype.

manup staff up, personnel buildup, increase in staff/personnel.

man without a country, a a person without a country/with no roots. See also expatriate/ex-pat.

marchioness or marquise/marquis (or marquess) acceptable sex-specific titles.

mare's nest there's nothing particularly pejorative in this expression, but if you want a sex-neutral alternative, consider false alarm, hoax, delusion, great disappointment, worthless, much ado about nothing; chaos, mess.

marimacha offensive Mexican slang for "lesbian" or "dyke."

marine man or woman; 6.2 percent of the U.S. Marine Corps are women.

marketing man marketer, marketing executive/associate/representative/rep, market researcher/executive; advertiser; copywriter.

marksman sharpshooter, crack/good/dead/expert shot, first-class shot/aim; markswoman and marksman. See also gunman, hitman, rifleman.

marksmanship riflery skills, sharpshooting, shooting proficiency/ability/expertise/skill.

marriage in her 1872 book, *My Opinions and Betsey Bobbet's*, Marietta Holley writes, "I took Josiah out to one side, and says I, 'Josiah Allen, if Tirzah Ann is to be brought up to think that marriage is the chief aim of her life, Thomas J. shall be brought up to think that marriage is his chief aim.' Says I, 'It looks just as flat in a woman, as it does in a man.'" In speaking and writing about marriage, keep in mind: (1) that marriage is not the norm, the be-all and end-all for everyone; (2) that couples marry each other (occasionally you see traces of the old point of usage that women cannot be the subject of the verb "to marry"; they can only be the object of it so that men marry women, not vice versa); (3) the responsibility for the marriage is not the woman's alone (Gloria Steinem: "I have yet to hear a man ask for advice on how to combine marriage and a career"); (4) by using "couples" or "relationships," you can include unmarried and same-sex couples as well as married ones. Where marriage is permitted for same-sex couples, call it "marriage," never "same-sex marriage" or "gay marriage." If you need to say so, use "marriage for gay and lesbian couples" or "the marriage of a lesbian couple" or "marriage of a same-sex couple." The construction "gay marriage" suggests that same-sex couples are seeking a separate institution that would, by definition, exclude straight couples. Gay and lesbian couples seeking the protections, rights, and responsibilities of marriage want to join the institution of marriage as it now exists, defining their relationships as "marriage," not "gay marriage." Marriage licenses provide couples access to more than 1,000 state and federal rights and protections that safeguard their families. Few of those rights can be secured through private contracts, which is why gay and lesbian couples are working for access to all the rights of the committed, long-term relationship known as marriage. See also child marriage, domestic partner, wedding.

marriage penalty some married couples pay higher taxes than they would if they earned exactly the same income but were not married to each other. However, getting angry about this inequity in the tax laws seems foolish when egregiously enormous loopholes are benefiting the very rich. By setting average and below-average earners at each other's throats over the marriage tax, the wealthiest 1 percent of the country is able to tiptoe out the door with bags full of our money. We need tax reform and tax enforcement, but we could perhaps set our sights higher than the marriage tax.

married name see hyphenated surnames, maiden name, surnames.

martinet although based on a man's name (Jean Martinet, a commander of the French infantry, instituted strict discipline based on severe punishment during the reign of Louis XIV), this term is used for both sexes.

mascots see sports teams' names and mascots.

masculine avoid this vague stereotype that conveys different meanings to different people according to their perceptions of what a man ought or ought not do, say, think, wear, feel, look like. Use instead precise adjectives: strong, upright, charming, robust, hearty, direct, straightforward, deep-voiced, protective, nurturing, attentive. These are not synonyms for "masculine" but are rather some of the qualities people seem to mean by it.

masculinity what cultural (but not biological) truth is there in this old saying? "Women have their femininity as a birthright. Men have to prove their masculinity all their lives."

masculism/masculist/masculinist Sheila Ruth says masculism is the form of sexism that mistakes the male perspective for the human perspective. Nigel Rees defines a masculist as "a person who asserts the superiority of men over women." And *The Oxford Dictionary of New Words* says a "masculinist" is someone who is antifeminist or pro-men's rights. Use only for those who claim the terms.

masher since a masher is a man who makes passes at women, there is no synonymous inclusive term. Today's masher is often found embroiled in a sexual harassment case. For inclusive alternatives, use someone who comes on strong, sex harasser.

Mason (member of fraternal organization) see Freemason.

massacre when a battle was won by Indians, it was called a massacre; when a battle was won by those moving onto Indian lands, it was called a victory. Writers and historians have conveyed the idea that Euro-americans who protected their homelands were patriots while Indians who did so were murderers and savages. Jessamyn West's *The Massacre at Fall Creek* and Elliott Arnold's *The Camp Grant Massacre* both use "massacre" to describe white killings of Indians that took place in 1824 and 1871. At least one library catalog system (Hennepin County Library, Minneapolis) has changed "Battle of Wounded Knee, 1890," to "Wounded Knee Massacre, 1890." We do not usually label the 1945 atomic bombardment of Hiroshima or the 1940 aerial bombardment of Rotterdam, for example, "massacres," yet outside our ethnocentric view, they would qualify.

masseur/masseuse these are acceptable sex-specific germs. If you need a sex-neutral term, use massage therapist.

mass evictions a repressive regime in Zimbabwe forced over 700,000 residents to burn their own homes and subsequently displaced them to rural areas with no services; another repressive regime, in Angola, evicted more than 20,000 people in order to develop the land; following Hurricane Katrina in the U.S., Trisha Miller, a public-interest lawyer working on the Gulf Coast, witnessed hundreds of people forced out of their homes for nonpayment during the months following the disaster, hundreds more illegally evicted so their landlords could raise the rent, and over 450 families in southern Mississippi that received FEMA trailers as temporary shelter received eviction letters; in Boston's Downtown Crossing area, longtime shop owners were evicted to make way for Big Business; in the Isla Vista area of Santa Barbara, California, some 55 families (mostly low-income Latino families) were evicted in what appears to be a continuing trend of annual August evictions over the last 10 years, assumed to be timed to move in wealthier students for September classes; 34 poor families in Oakland, California, faced eviction because of an Oakland housing official's act of fraud; and all over the country mobile home park conversions result in the evictions of those who must either find a new mobile home park or leave their mobile home behind. "Mass evictions"—the latest thing in human rights abuses.

master (noun) owner, manager, chief, head, leader, governor, superior, director, supervisor, employer, boss, commander, captain, controller; sovereign, ruler, monarch, autocrat, dictator, potentate; expert, authority, artist, adept, proficient, specialist, connoisseur, professional, genius; mentor, teacher, trainer, instructor, educator, tutor; victor, conqueror, winner, champion; householder, proprietor, landholder. "Master" has some inclusive meanings (owner, employer, teacher, scholar, artisan, victor, etc.) but because the principal meanings of the word are incontrovertibly masculine (for example, "male head of household"), because there is no equivalent for a woman (in the once-parallel word pair "master/mistress," the prolific male word has spawned entire pages of "master"-based words in the dictionaries while the female word has shrunk to describe only the sexual function of the woman), and because of its association with slavery, "master" and its related words are not recommended. "Master" is used as noun, verb, and adjective as well as a compound in many other words, which means its overwhelmingly masculine, hierarchical, and slave-based flavor seasons a good bit of our language. Except for its applications in trades where it has specific meaning and no currently acceptable substitutes, "master" and other forms of the word can be replaced with some of the many appropriate and easy-to-use alternatives. That said, there are times when nothing works quite as well and when the word seems to have gone beyond its associations with male dominance and slavery, for example, "master" (verb and adjective) and "mastery." Casey Miller and Kate Swift (*The Handbook of Nonsexist Writing*, 2nd ed.) say, "The presence of *master* in many combinations like *masterful, mastery, masterpiece,* and *mastermind* assures its continuance as a useful sex-neutral term."

master (adjective) expert, accomplished, proficient, skilled, excellent, competent, gifted, dexterous, adroit, deft, resourceful; controlling, main. For discussion of "master" words, see master (noun).

master (verb) excel in/at, grasp, learn, understand, comprehend, be successful at, be proficient in, acquire proficiency at, learn inside and out/ backwards and forwards, get a good grasp of, get a handle on, get the hang of, gain command of, be on top of; conquer, subdue, defeat, subject, vanquish, tame, subjugate, subordinate, suppress, get the upper hand, overcome, overpower, overwhelm, overthrow, surmount, humble, triumph over; rule, dominate, govern, control, command, dictate to, boss/order around. For discussion of "master" words, see master (noun).

Master (Christ) Teacher.

master/master mariner (sailing vessel) retain in official use; some marine occupational titles using "master" are used by the U.S. Employment and Training Administration. Otherwise use captain. For discussion of "master" words, see master (noun).

master bedroom/suite almost without exception, these are the currently used terms. When realtors tried to use "owner's suite," buyers and sellers expressed confusion. You could, however, use that sometimes or substitute main bedroom/principal/largest bedroom/suite. Or refer to bedrooms by their location, as do some designers and architects ("the northeast bedroom"). For discussion of "master" words, see master (noun).

master builder expert/award-winning/skilled/professional builder. This may refer to either sex. For discussion of "master" words, see master (noun).

master class an advanced art, music, or dance seminar led by a recognized expert (of either sex), "master class" is difficult to replace with a term that is equally concise, descriptive, and meaningful in those fields. Sometimes it is possible to use artist class (it is not limited to the visual arts), virtuoso class, expert tutorial. For discussion of "master" words, see master (noun).

master copy original copy. For discussion of "master" words, see master (noun).

masterful expert, skilled, articulate, authoritative, competent; powerful, commanding, domineering, sweeping, imperative, imperious, arbitrary, overbearing, arrogant, haughty. For discussion of "master" words, see master (noun).

master hand expert, genius, major talent, professional, authority, adept, proficient, whiz, dab hand. For discussion of "master" words, see master (noun).

master key skeleton/universal/all-purpose/pass/main/original/controlling key, passe partout. For discussion of "master" words, see master (noun).

master list overview, key, main/complete/primary/reference list. For discussion of "master" words, see master (noun).

masterly accomplished, skilled, knowledgeable, consummate, matchless, excellent, distinguished, experienced, crack, ingenious, able, felicitous, shrewd. For discussion of "master" words, see master (noun).

mastermind (noun) genius, brilliant thinker, intellectual/mental prodigy/giant, inventor, originator, creator, brains; plotter, organizer, creative organizer, instigator, planner, leader, director, head, someone who pulls the strings. For discussion of "master" words, see master (noun).

mastermind (verb) oversee, direct, head, guide, lead, coordinate, plan, contrive, engineer, launch; originate, invent, devise, develop, have the bright idea. For discussion of "master" words, see master (noun).

master of ceremonies/mistress of ceremonies host, emcee, leader/coordinator of ceremonies, speaker, main/guest speaker, facilitator, moderator, introducer, announcer, marshal, parade marshal. Although "emcee" comes from these sex-specific terms, it is used for both sexes and is perceived as neutral. For discussion of "master" words, see master (noun).

master of one's fate captain of one's soul/fate. For discussion of "master" words, see master (noun).

master of the situation in charge, in control, on top of things, reins firmly in hand, finger on the pulse. For discussion of "master" words, see master (noun).

masterpiece great/greatest/best/classic work, work of art/genius, stroke of genius, consummate art, chef d'oeuvre, magnum opus, brainchild, cream of the crop, crème de la créme, piéce de rèsistance, museum piece, flower of the flock, nonpareil, acme of perfection, perfection, brilliant achievement, ne plus ultra, tour de force, coup de maître, model, monument, standard.

master plan overall/comprehensive/ground/working plan, blueprint, project design, overview. For discussion of "master" words, see master (noun).

master print original film, original. For discussion of "master" words, see master (noun).

"master race" use this term only in its historical context and put it in quotation marks to indicate its lack of validity.

master's degree M.A., graduate/advanced degree, first advanced/first graduate degree. The spelled-out "master's degree" is still used in many cases; there is no current substitute for it.

master sergeant see serviceman.

masterstroke trump card, clever/bright idea, good/brilliant move, bold/lucky stroke, checkmate, stroke of genius, coup, complete success, stunt, exploit, victory. For discussion of "master" words, see master (noun).

master switch control/lead/main switch, circuit breaker. For discussion of "master" words, see master (noun).

master tape pattern/final/original tape, template. For discussion of "master" words, see master (noun).

master teacher leave as is where custom and usage require it. A substitute sometimes seen is artist teacher (not restricted to the visual arts). A master teacher can be either sex. For discussion of "master" words, see master (noun).

masterwork see masterpiece.

mastery proficiency, understanding, knowledge, accomplishment, acquaintance with, competency, firm grasp, command, excellence, facility, advantage, adeptness, skill, dexterity, deftness, expertise, grip; rule, sovereignty; victory, ascendancy, supremacy, authority, subjugation, conquest, control, domination, dominance, upper hand, reins in one's hands, command, order, sway. For discussion of "master" words, see master (noun).

masturbation the ultimate in safe sex, masturbation has been termed self-pleasure, self-stimulation, autoeroticism, and the witty ménage à moi. Alternatives are given since the word and concept of "masturbation" have endured centuries of, well, abuse and you might want to vary your terms. It is never called self-abuse.

matador used for both women and men. See also bullfighter.

mate used for both sexes in the sense of "partner," "spouse," or "lover" and also in navy and coast guard ranks. The Australian "mate" is also used for both sexes.

mater/materfamilias acceptable sex-specific terms, although the Latin is more often replaced with "mother/matriarch." See also pater/paterfamilias.

maternal unless you mean motherlike or mother-related ("maternal grandfather"), use parental, ancestral; kindly, kindhearted, loving, devoted, indulgent, solicitous, concerned, fond, protective, sympathetic.

maternal death rate/maternal mortality rate these rates often include women who died from abortion but who were not mothers. In compiling statistics, most countries do not differentiate among kinds of abortion-related deaths. When possible, refer to female death rates/female mortality rates.

maternal instinct nurturing/parental instinct.

maternal profiling employment discrimination against women who have, or will have, children. The term has been popularized by members of MomsRising, an advocacy group promoting the rights of mothers in the workplace.

maternity leave this term has been almost completely replaced by "family leave." In some situations, you could use parental/childcare leave. The Family and Medical Leave Act (FMLA) of 1993 is a federal law that guarantees covered employees 12 weeks of unpaid leave each year to care for a newborn or newly adopted child or a seriously ill family member, or to recover from their own serious health conditions, while ensuring they can return to an equivalent job. Although the FMLA has allowed an estimated 4 million working families per year to care for their loved ones without risking their jobs or health insurance, nearly 40 percent of the workforce is not eligible for the job-protected leave. In addition, because the FMLA guarantees only unpaid leave, some workers report they have needed but have not taken family or medical leave because they could not afford to go without salary. The United States is the only high-income country that doesn't provide paid leave for new mothers nationally.

matriarch/matriarchy because patriarchy is seen as the norm, a matriarchy tends to be viewed with alarm and disapproval; it doesn't seem "natural." In fact, the opposite of a patriarchy is not a matriarchy. Both matriarchies and patriarchies involve an imbalance of power between the sexes and are called dominator societies by Riane Eisler (*The Chalice and the Blade* and *The Power of Partnership*). The true opposite of a matriarchy or a patriarchy is a partnership society. Until we reach the point where neither sex needs to dominate the other, use "matriarchy/patriarchy" terms cautiously. The word "matricentric" puts the mother at the center of the family or system without the hierarchical overtones of "matriarchal." Sex-neutral alternatives for "matriarch" include ancestor/family elder, head of the family, family head. See also patriarchy.

matricide correct sex-specific word. Inclusive alternative: parricide.

matrilineal refers to descent through the mother's line; its word pair is "patrilineal."

matrimony marriage, union, nuptials, wedlock. "Matrimony"—from Latin, "mother"—is sex-specific and is also part of the oddly paired "matrimony/patrimony" (which may not be so odd given that men have been able to inherit money while women had to marry it). "Marriage" is also sex-linked (from Latin for "a woman's dowry") but it is less obviously so than "matrimony." For more sex-neutral alternatives for the adjective "matrimonial," consider marital, conjugal, wedded, wedding.

matron warden, attendant, police officer, deputy sheriff, bailiff, guard, prison/jail/custodial guard, superintendent, supervisor, overseer; principal, chief, director, head, manager. In its narrow legal sense, "matron" must be used until a nonsexist legal term is developed. In the sense of a middle-aged woman, replace "matron" with words that more precisely describe the person. Note the wildly different status and meaning of the word pair "matron/patron."

matronly replace this vague word with precise, inclusive terms: dignified, gracious, ponderous, heavy-set, established, grave, comfortable-looking, serene, slow-moving, well-dressed, mature, sedate. There is no such word as "patronly."

matronym/matronymic referring to a name derived from the mother or a maternal ancestor, these are correct sex-specific terms. They also have a little-recognized history: the practice of passing the father's name on to the children hasn't always been in force nor is it universally practiced in the Western world. Nelson is "Nell's son," Allison is "Alice's son," and Babson is "Barbara's son." Spanish children have their mother's names as well as their father's. In Russia, a child can take either parent's surname. Charles Panati (*Browser's Book of Beginnings*) says, "Seemingly, when surnames originated, few traces of male chauvinism historically were involved." See also hyphenated names, patronym/patronymic, surnames.

matron of honor see maid/matron of honor.

mature "an economic term for a down-sliding economy, a media term usually involving explicit sex scenes, and an advertising term suggesting their products are just what an old, retired person needs" (Paul Wasserman and Don Hausrath, *Weasel Words*).

maverick although this term comes from a man's name—a 19th-century Texas rancher named Samuel A. Maverick with a certain reputation for straying from the herd (he refused to brand his cattle)—its origins have been largely forgotten and it is perceived as sex-neutral.

may the best man win may the best person/one win.

meathead as Archie Bunker linked "dingbat" to women, so he linked "meathead" to men.

Mecca an Islamic holy city in Saudi Arabia's Makkah province, Mecca (or Makkah al-Mukarramah) is revered by Muslims for containing the holiest site of Islam, the Masjid al-Haram, and a pilgrimage to Mecca during the week of the Hajj is a sacred duty required of all able-bodied Muslims who can afford to go, at least once in their lifetime. In English, "mecca" (uncapitalized) refers to a place to which people are attracted.

media "Dictators know what they're doing when they seize control of the media even before seizing control of land or people. Image and narrative are the organizing principles on which our brains work, and the media deliver them with such power and speed that they may overwhelm our experience, actually make us feel less real than the people whose images we see" (Gloria Steinem, *Sisterhood Is Forever*). Jane Fonda says we need media that strengthens democracy, not strengthens the government; media so powerful it can speak for the powerless; media that can stop a war, not start one. We have a long way to go to achieve this. As Bill Moyers has pointed out, a "few huge corporations now dominate the media landscape in America. Almost all the networks carried by most cable systems are owned by one of the major media conglomerates. Two-thirds of today's newspaper markets are monopolies. As ownership gets more and more concentrated, fewer and fewer independent sources of information have survived in the marketplace. And those few significant alternatives that do survive, such as PBS and NPR, are under growing financial and political pressure to reduce critical news content and shift their focus in a 'mainstream' direction, which means being more attentive to the establishment than to the bleak realities of powerlessness that shape the lives of ordinary people." Further compounding the problem, "right-wing organizations have spent decades training student journalists, funding think tanks, pumping out pundits, buying up media outlets, and doing everything in their power to frame discussions about American politics on their own terms. ... The systemic underrepresentation of women's and, in particular, feminist and other progressive perspectives in American media is the result of a variety of institutional factors, including financial and political agendas of corporate media owners, news networks and entertainment studios pandering to the whims of advertisers," says Jennifer L. Pozner, executive director, Women in Media and News (WIMN). Women, who comprise 51 percent of the population, own less than 7 percent of radio and television stations. According to the 2014 Women's Media Center report, *The Status of Women in the U.S. Media*, only 28.7 percent of television news directors are women. Men have a disproportionately higher percentage (63 percent) of front-page bylines at top newspapers than women (37 percent). The picture in digital media is only slightly better, with women garnering 40 percent of byline credits. At the nation's three most prestigious newspapers and four top newspaper syndicates, male opinion page writers outnumbered female writers by 4 to 1. Across all media, women are more likely to report on health, culture, and lifestyle rather than politics, world affairs, and criminal justice. Men are far more likely to be quoted than women in newspapers, television, and public radio, even in reports covering topics of abortion, birth control, and women's rights. On the Sunday television talk shows, men account for 74 percent of roundtable guests and 86 percent of one-on-one interviews. "The average person flipping through channels on Sunday morning will be left with the quite accurate impression that politics is an arena dominated by men's voices," says Jennifer Lawless, director of the American University Women & Politics Institute. Even as women make up an increasingly large percentage of sports fans, a survey of 150 print publications and websites covering sports found that 90 percent of sports editors were male and 90 percent were white. Women accounted for just 1 percent of 183 hosts of sports talk radio shows. The lack of media inclusion of women, African Americans, Latinos, gay men and lesbians, those with disabilities and other groups means that important stories are not being told. Media influence is one of the most powerful economic and cultural forces today. By deciding who gets to talk, what shapes the debate, who writes, and what is important enough to report, media shape our understanding of who we are and what we can be. See also advertising, Title IX.

medical man doctor, physician, medical practitioner/specialist; (informal) medico. See also medicine man.

medicine man shaman, healer, magician, faith healer; medicine woman and medicine man.

mélange speaking of the mélange nation (those with "racially" diverse heritages), Jaimie Markham writes (in *Colors*), "We name ourselves *mélange* to proclaim pride in our diverse origins and to be strong in a society that makes us an embodiment of its conflicted racial relations. ... We are proud of our racial heritage, and we insist on respect for all our heritage cultures. We refuse to be forced to choose between one or the other. Our pride in both is a vitally important means for us as mélange people to deal with a racist social structure. Selecting one group over the other would require us to hate the white mother or the Filipino grandmother, the black father or the white great-grandfather." See also biracial, multiracial.

memsahib always a woman; the man is a "sahib."

men (pseudogeneric) for the military sense, use troops, soldiers, forces, armies. For the sense of game pieces, use players, pieces. For all other uses, see Man/man, man (adult male human being), mankind.

men- most words that begin with "men-" are not sex-linked, for example, menace (from Latin, "threaten"); menagerie (from French, "household"); menarche (from Latin, "month"); mendacious/mendacity (from Latin, "lie"); mendicant (from Latin, "beg"); menhir (from Breton, "stone"); menial (from Latin, "dwelling"), menorah (from Hebrew, "candlestick"); mental (from Greek, "spirit"); mention (from Latin, "call to mind"); menu (from French, "small"). See also man-, -man/-men, mensch, menopause/menopausal, menses/menstrual/menstruation, mentor.

menfolk this term is interesting in that it is probably the only "man/men" word that has never been used pseudogenerically; "menfolk" and "womenfolk" truly refer to men and women.

men of goodwill people/those of goodwill.

menopause/menopausal the "men" comes from Latin for "month." "Menopause" is a neutral term describing a physical reality that is different for different women although it does not appear to cause stress or depression in most healthy women, and may even improve mental health for some. Avoid stereotyping menopause, and do not describe a woman as menopausal unless you are writing for a medical journal.

mensch this is Yiddish for "human being" or German for "person," although in English it is often reserved for men. Use it also to mean a purposeful, upright, honorable woman who stands up for the rights of others as well as for her own.

menses/menstrual/menstruation these terms have nothing to do with men (*menses* is Latin for "months") in more ways than one. Throughout history, menstruating women have not had good press: in the Bible, they were thought to be unclean; later they were thought to be diseased, animal-like, possessing supernatural powers, and responsible for rusted-out metal tools and weapons. Still later, they were thought to be subject to mood swings that affected their judgment and mental abilities. See also "curse."

men's liberation/movement men have also found themselves oppressed—by the males-only draft (and now the males-only compulsory military registration), the provider role, rigid societal definitions of masculinity, unfair divorce and custody laws, and other biases in the culture. Men today are frustrated with their limited roles compared to the options they see available to women and uncertain about what it means to be a man or a father or a lover or a husband in this culture. Landmarks in the men's movement include: the 1970 formation of the Men's Center in Berkeley and subsequent creation of other men's centers around the country; founding of MEN International, Men's Rights Incorporated, Free Men, and other men's organizations; the appearance of voices like those of poet Robert Bly, anthropologist Michael Meade, Warren Farrell (*Why Men Are the Way They Are*), Herb Goldberg (*The Hazards of Being Male*), Jungian psychologist James Hillman, and members of activist divorce reform and fathers' rights groups. Men are examining and challenging the traditional male sex role in the belief that "men, not women, must define what it means to be a man" (Tom Williamson in Francis Baumli, *Men Freeing Men*). Men's goals, attitudes, and organizations vary widely; generalizations are risky. See also draft, Iron John, male privilege, provider.

men's studies the first men's studies courses began in the early 1970s, and there are currently hundreds of courses being taught in various disciplines. The American Men's Studies Association (AMSA) and their journal, *The Journal of Men's Studies*, are rich resources for information on men's studies. See also women's studies.

mental illness mental disorder. "Mental illness" is acceptable but "mental disorder" is often preferred to describe any of the recognized forms of mental illness or several emotional disorders that result in the inability to function independently. The most acceptable construction is "people with mental disorders" or "a person with mental illness" or, best yet, the precise disorder: "someone with anorexia." Avoid nouns like paranoiac, schizophrenic, manic-depressive, and anorexic that label the whole person by the disorder. "Mental illness" and "mental retardation" are separate conditions; one does not imply the other. "Mental institution" is almost never used and "insane/lunatic asylum" is unacceptable; the correct term is "hospital/psychiatric hospital." No one is a "mental patient" unless they are in the hospital, and then they are simply a "patient." Terms such as "mentally deranged," "mentally unbalanced," "mentally diseased," "deviant," and "demented" are not appropriate; "neurotic," "psychotic," and "psychopathic" are reserved for technical and medical writing." Insane" and "incompetent" are legal rather than diagnostic terms. Our everyday language is rife with words that reflect on mental illness: batty, certifiable, cracked, crazy, fruitcake, lunatic, loony, maniac, nuts, psycho, sicko, wacko, weirdo, off the wall, off one's rocker, around the bend, a few apples short of a picnic, the funny farm, men in white coats. Few people actually use these terms to refer to those with a mental disorder; the problem is that the derision and ridicule they convey is carried over to our attitudes toward mental illness. Kay Redfield Jamison (*An Unquiet Mind*) writes that "allowing such language to go unchecked or uncorrected leads not only to personal pain, but contributes both directly and indirectly to discrimination in jobs, insurance, and society at large. On the other hand, the assumption that rigidly rejected words and phrases that have existed for centuries will have much impact on public attitudes is rather dubious. It gives an illusion of easy answers to impossibly difficult situations." Redfield thinks aggressive public education is the answer. The California Mental Health Services Authority says: Always question your need to mention a mental disorder if it is not intrinsic to your material; if it is important, you need a reliable source for the particular mental condition; use "living with" or "has" the condition. See also disabilities, idiot/idiocy, insane/insanity, patient, "people first" rule, retard, schizophrenic.

mental retardation see retard.

mentor woman or man.

men working work zone/crew, crew/people/workers working, crew at work, workers, working.

mercenary this is still largely a male field, although you will occasionally find female mercenaries. See also civilian contractor.

mermaid/merman folklore and fantastic tradition have given us these creatures, along with nonparallel designations ("maid/man"). When possible, use instead merwoman/merman, sea creature, sea nymph, Nereid, sea god/sea goddess.

mestiza/mestizo generally understood to be a person of Indian and Spanish ancestry, these terms (female/male) have no equivalents in English. Although the terms are nonpejorative in most Spanish-language countries, not everyone in the U.S. who meets the definition self-identifies that way; "La Raza" is preferred by many (Resource Center of the Americas). Jaimie Markham (in *Colors*), says, "Of all traditional words for us, *mestizo* comes closest to satisfying me, but only because the great Brazilian writer Jorge Amado so clearly articulated the culture of *mestizaje* in his novel *Tent of Miracles*. In the Brazilian context these words speak with conscious pride of diverse racial origins, but this pride is not conveyed by the literal translations: mixed blood and miscegenation." See also Hispanic, La Raza, Mexican American.

metalhead woman or man.

meter maid (parking) meter reader/attendant/monitor/tender/officer, parking monitor/officer/enforcer, parking enforcement officer.

meter man (water/gas/electricity meter) meter reader.

métis/métisse Métis/Métisse from the French for "mixed," this refers to someone of French-Canadian and American Indian ancestry; the capitalized form is used by some people to indicate that they are a distinct ethnic group. The terms are analogous to mestizo/mestiza.

metrosexual coined in 1994 by British journalist Mark Simpson, this refers to a heterosexual man whose interest in his appearance, clothing, and personal grooming somewhat resembles that of some women and gay men.

Mexican this is not interchangeable with Mexican American. See also Chicana/Chicano/Chican@, Hispanic, Latina/Latino/Latin@, Mexican American.

Mexican American this is an acceptable term for a U.S. resident with Mexican ancestry including those whose families lived in the territories taken from Mexico in the 1846-1848 U.S.-Mexico War. Use this for those who so self-identify. See also Chicana/Chicano/Chican@, Hispanic, Latina/Latino/Latin@.

Mexican standoff three-way/four-way stalemate, standoff, impossible situation. "Mexican standoff" supposedly refers to three, four, or more people with guns trained on each other with the idea that nothing good is going to come of this—a situation that has become a movie cliché. Although "Mexican standoff" does not appear to be derogatory, one is always a bit suspicious of such constructions. Proceed with caution.

Mickey Finn there is nothing wrong with using this term, often shortened to "mickey" or "mickie," as in "slipped her a mickey," but be aware of how many such expressions are male-based. Balance their use with female-based expressions, creative expressions of your own, or sex-neutral alternatives: knockout drops. See also sex-linked expressions.

Mickey Mouse (adjective) cheap, cheaply insincere, inferior, insignificant, worthless, petty, trivial, trifling, piddling, simple, easy, childish, flimsy, paltry, trite, nonsense, time-wasting, sentimental, corny. See also sex-linked expressions.

Midas touch magic/golden touch, everything she/he touches turns to gold. See also sex-linked expressions.

Middle America a vague term that refers either to the U.S. middle class, especially its conservative- or tradition-minded members, or to the country that lies between the two coasts but with something of the same conservative, middle-class denotation. Neither speaker nor hearer can have a commonly understood, clear idea of what this means. Replace it with precise qualifiers of the demographic you're discussing. See also flyover country, "silent majority."

Middle East Joanna Kadi says "this term was given to the Arab world by Western (European) colonizers who named the region only as it related to their particular worldview. ... It is offensive to me, and not at all affirming, to use such a term to describe my identity. Using the term 'Middle Eastern' feels very much like I am adopting the oppressor's language." To a society that is generally weak in geography, it is probably in any case better to spell out exactly which countries you mean: the "Middle East" includes the 19 Arab countries on the west part of the Asian continent and the northern part of the Africa continent (Lebanon, Palestine, Jordan, Syria, Kuwait, Saudi Arabia, Yemen, Oman, Bahrain, Tunisia, Algeria, Egypt, Sudan, Qatar, Mauritania, Iraq, Libya, Morocco, and the United Arab Emirates) and the four non-Arab nations of Israel, Turkey, Armenia, and Iran. In some contexts, Somalia and Djibouti are also considered part of the Middle East.

middleman go-between, agent, contact, third party, liaison, negotiator, intermediary, broker, mediator, arbiter, arbitrator, representative, messenger, factor, intercessor, intervener, umpire, referee, peacemaker, facilitator, contact, advocate, middle party; jobber, wholesaler, distributor, dealer, contract dealer, trader, reseller.

midget Elaine Landau (*Short Stature: From Folklore to Fact*) says, "Due to the negative images connected to this term, the word 'midget' is no longer used to describe people with this body type" (a very short person whose heads and limbs are proportional for his or her body). The organization in the U.S. for short-statured people is called the Little People of America. Terms like "mental midget" and "moral midget," while not reflecting directly on little people, indirectly disparage them. See also dwarf, short.

mid-life crisis a concept that does not exist in most cultures, the so-called mid-life crisis (dramatic self-doubt and questioning of one's life and goals) is experienced in the U.S. by fewer than 10 percent of individuals in their middle years.

midshipman retain where this term is used officially; it can refer to either sex. Otherwise use cadet, naval officer in training. At the U.S. Naval Academy, women are called "female midshipmen."

midwife (noun) this term is used for both women and men practitioners and the "wife" does not refer to the person assisting but to the person giving birth ("mid" means "with"). However, the "wife" and the fact that the vast majority of midwives have always been women give it a feminine cast and you may sometimes want alternatives: birth attendant, accoucheur. The United States, Canada, and South Africa are the only industrialized nations in which midwives are not recognized and supported by the law and the medical community. Interestingly enough, in the five European countries with the lowest infant mortality rates, midwives supervise more than 70 percent of all births. See also childbirth.

midwife (verb) give birth to/beget, assist, facilitate, support, conceive of/beget (ideas), bring forth/about.

migrant used as a noun, "migrant" is vague; it is better used to modify a specific noun, for example, "migrant worker." Instead of "migrant children," use "children of migrant workers."

milady/milord sex-parallel historical terms.

militant the choice to use "militant" instead of "activist" may reveal bias; blacks are more often militants where in the same situation whites are activists.

militarism militarism might be seen as the peace movement's opposite number. Militarism, which is most evident in nation-states and empires when they engage in imperialism or expansionism, is the belief that society is best governed by military concepts, that discipline is a social priority, and that development and maintenance of the military ensures national, international, and social order. The focus is on military preparations and carrying out military operations: "Peace through strength." Full blown militarism, as seen in totalitarian or fascist nations, is essentially undemocratic and antidemocratic, therefore in the U.S., militaristic goals, concepts, and doctrines are muted but observable in certain policies and characteristics. Critics say they see characteristics of militarism in several nations and groups of nations today: the Anglo-Saxon powers (led by the United States), China, France, Israel, Russia, and Syria. See also military language, war.

"military bunker" or "civilian shelter" one of the negatives of war is that it is apparently difficult to tell the difference between these.

Military Commissions Act according to Amnesty International (AI), "On October 17, 2006, the U.S. Constitution was bound, gagged, and detained indefinitely." The Military Commission Act "makes it lawful to hold prisoners indefinitely without charge or trial, to assume guilt before innocence, to blur the definition of torture, and to use information obtained under inhumane treatment as 'evidence.'" AI asks if this makes us safer. "Experts with real prisoner-of-war experience say that people subjected to torture are as likely to lie as tell the truth." While the subsequent 2009 Military Commissions Act represents an improvement over the prior version, critics say it fails to bring military commissions tribunals in line with the Constitution and the Geneva Conventions. See also black site, detainee, torture.

military draft see draft.

military-industrial complex "Like drug dealers, American arms dealers create their own demand. First, they sell a load of weapons to one nation, and then tell its neighbor, 'Hey, did you notice that the guys next door just bought some new jets, tanks, and submarines?'" (Frida Berrigan, in *Los Angeles Times*). According to the State Department's Military Assistance Report, the Pentagon approved $44 billion in arms sales to 173 nations in 2013. Upon leaving the presidency in 1961, Dwight D. Eisenhower warned us that this "conjunction of an immense military establishment and a large arms industry is new in the American experience. The total influence—economic, political, even spiritual—is felt in every city, every State house, every office of the Federal government. We recognize the imperative need for this development. Yet we must not fail to comprehend its grave implications. Our toil, resources and livelihood are all involved; so is the very structure of our society. In the councils of government, we must guard against the acquisition of unwarranted influence, whether sought or unsought, by the military-industrial complex. The potential for the disastrous rise of misplaced power exists and will persist. We must never let the weight of this combination endanger our liberties or democratic processes. We should take nothing for granted. Only an alert and knowledgeable citizenry can compel the proper meshing of the huge industrial and military machinery of defense with our peaceful methods and goals, so that security and liberty may prosper together."

military language if you collect euphemisms, the best place to find them is in military language: "collateral damage" (dead civilians and destroyed civilian infrastructure); "traumatic amputation" (an arm or leg blown off); "neutralize" (assassinate); "ordnance" (bombs); "silos" (where we keep nuclear missiles); "farms" (where we keep our "silos"—the part of the submarine where 24 multiple warhead nuclear missiles are lined up ready for launching is called "the Christmas tree farm"); "visits" and "sorties" (bombing raids); "servicing the target" (killing); "disinformation" (lies); "operational exhaustion" (shell shocked); "soft target" (unarmored or undefended target); "administered areas" (captured lands); "extrajudicial execution" (murder); "plausible deniability" (lies that might get by); and terms that sound almost cozy—"mopping up," "skirmish," "clearing the area," and "mission." John Collins and Ross Glover (*Collateral Language*) say that "military language ... works in two directions, both making the already committed violence more palatable and softening up the public so that future military actions will seem more like video games and less like what they are—acts of violence that result in death, injury, and destruction." George Shapiro, professor of speech and communication at the University of Minnesota, says, "The language is so sanitary that it makes war bloodless. Nobody is dying, nobody is hurting, and it makes a costless, bloodless war. I think this is quite intentional." Ethicist Jeremy Iggers says, "Verbal and visual euphemisms not only hide the deaths of our enemies, they also hide their lives and their humanities. ... we have seen little of how the Iraqis live, or what they believe—very little to convey that they too are humans. Do we understand why so many of them, and their supporters, believe so passionately in the justice of their cause? Without these images and understanding, we care a lot less when they are killed. Euphemism, when it is intended to deceive, is a form of cowardice." Our own everyday language is shot through with the metaphors of war: we arm ourselves with information if we are not bombarded with it first, we take sides in the battle of the sexes, we work in the trenches or the front lines, we combat racism and sexism, poverty and injustice are the enemy. In hundreds of ways, our language reveals a war mindset; being aware of it is probably an important step in working for global peace. See also black site, civilian contractor, detainee, doublespeak, friendly fire, Peacekeeper/peacekeeper, pre-emptive strike, surgical strike, violent language.

military man soldier, member of the armed forces/the military, military officer. See also serviceman (armed forces).

military wife military/soldier's/service member's spouse.

militiaman militia member, member of the militia, soldier, citizen soldier, Revolutionary War soldier; if applicable, militiawoman and militiaman. See also hate groups, white supremacy.

milkmaid milker, dairy worker/employee/hand/worker, except for fairy tales or in historical contexts. A milkman sells or delivers milk while a milkmaid milks cows. (Note nonparallel ("maid/man"). See also milkman, dairymaid/dairyman.

milkman milk route driver, milk/dairy deliverer; sometimes, milk truck. See also dairymaid/dairyman, milkmaid.

milliner those who design, make, trim, and sell women's hats can be either sex.

milquetoast/milksop (man) timid soul, someone scared of their own shadow, someone with cold feet, timid/meek/poor-spirited/fearful/unassertive person ("The Timid Soul" was the name of H.T. Webster's newspaper cartoon featuring Casper Milquetoast.) See also coward/cowardly/cowardice, sex-linked expressions.

miner woman or man. The first woman miner in the U.S. coal industry was hired in 1973.

minister depending on the denomination, this might be a woman or a man. If you are unsure how to address a female minister, ask her; this may vary from denomination to denomination and from person to person within a denomination. According to U.S. Labor Statistics, approximately one of every eight clergy is a woman. The National Council of Churches says that women still face some discrimination but "there has been an increasing acceptance of women clergy in local church situations especially by younger people and by those of higher educational attainment." See also clergyman.

minority "at least four-fifths of the world's population consists of people of color. Therefore, it is statistically incorrect as well as ethnocentric to refer to us as minorities. The term 'minority' is used to reinforce the idea of people of color as 'other'" (Amoja Three Rivers, *Cultural Etiquette*). In addition, "minority" as used today is too often code for poor black and Hispanic people. Alicia S. Jameson says "minority" ("This extremely popular eurocentric word makes my flesh crawl") has come to be a catchword for any group being denied a full share of the American pie. However, the *American Heritage Book of English Usage* says that, despite some objections, "in the appropriate context, as when discussing a group from a social or demographic point of view, *minority* is a useful term that you need not avoid as offensive." The use of "minority" has troubled people for some time; as yet we have no good (that is, instantly graspable and clearly defined) alternatives. Being aware of its shortcomings is a beginning; restricting its use to those instances in which nothing else will do also helps; sometimes it is useful to specify what kind of minority (linguistic/ethnic/religious); in general, reserve the term for groups defined by imbalances of power rather than for groups defined by a characteristic such as sex, ethnicity, income. See also people of color/person of color, nonwhite.

minstrel although most minstrels have been men, women belonged to some medieval troupes, juggling or acting out small parts. Troubadours, who flourished during the two centuries preceding the rise of the minstrels, also numbered some women among them (Meg Bogin, *The Women Troubadours*). At the height of the popularity of 19th-century Negro minstrelsy, women were impersonated by men (for example, in the "wench performances"), so there appeared to be women on stage, but there rarely were.

minuteman retain for minutemen in the Revolutionary War or for minuteman rockets. Or soldier, citizen soldier, revolutionary soldier, Revolutionary War soldier.

misanthrope/misogynist there's a strange imbalance here: although a misogynist is a person who hates women, a misanthrope is not a person who hates men, but a person who hates all humankind. A person who hates men would be a misandrist.

miscegenation marriage, cohabitation, or sexual relations between people of different "races." According to Barbara C. Cruz and Michael J. Berson (in *Magazine of History*, published by the Organization of American Historians), "Laws prohibiting miscegenation in the United States date back as early as 1661 and were common in many states until 1967. That year, the Supreme Court ruled on the issue in *Loving v. Virginia*, concluding that Virginia's miscegenation laws were unconstitutional."

misogynist see misanthrope/misogynist.

Miss use "Miss" for those who prefer it; otherwise, especially in the workplace, use "Ms." Dale Spender (*Man Made Language*) says, "The current usage of *Miss* and *Mrs.* is relatively recent, for until the beginning of the 19th century the title *Miss* was usually reserved for young females while *Mrs.* designated mature women. Marital status played no role in the use of these terms." Today, calling women "Miss" or "Mrs." labels them in relation to men although men have never been labeled in relation to women. See also frau, honorifics, mademoiselle, Mrs., Ms.

Miss America since 1921 (the year after women obtained the right to vote), the Miss America Beauty Pageant has contributed to a competitive and unrealistic idea of beauty for women. Although making it to the pageant is a dream-come-true for many young women as well as the result of years of hard work, the pageant itself has much to answer for in its objectification of women and its unrelenting emphasis on external and physical perfection. Originally a beauty contest, the Pageant today prefers to be known as a scholarship competition.

missus/the missus this might perhaps be acceptable among an older generation to refer to one's wife, if one is very, very sure she doesn't object; it is unacceptable to refer to anyone else's wife this way, however.

mistress lover, partner. Robin Lakoff (*Language and Woman's Place*) points out the possessiveness inherent in the term: "'mistress' requires a masculine noun in the possessive to precede it. One cannot say 'Rhonda is a mistress.' One must be someone's mistress." "Mistress" used to belong to the once-parallel word pair "master/mistress." While the prolific male word has spawned entire pages of "master"-based words in the dictionaries, the female word has shrunk to describe only the sexual function of the woman. In a recent political/military scandal, a married man and a married woman were found to be having an affair; she was always referred to as "his mistress." Lisa Belkin (*The Huffington Post*) says, "Given that one can not be a mistress without a ... someone ... what does it say about our culture that we haven't given that role a name?" She suggests calling him a "mister-ess." (The online Word Spy spells it "misteress.") Belkin says, "Mostly it says that we still think of him as a bit of a stud at best, and a victim of her manipulation, at worst, while we think of her as defined in relation to him—something we can label." If you mean "mistress of the house," use householder, homemaker, head of the household. See also girlfriend, kept woman, master, schoolmistress. For "mistress of ceremonies," use host, emcee, leader/coordinator of ceremonies, speaker, main/guest speaker, facilitator, moderator, introducer, announcer, marshal, parade marshal. Although "emcee" comes from these sex-specific terms, it is used for both sexes and is perceived as neutral.

mistress of ceremonies see master of ceremonies/mistress of ceremonies.

mixed blood mixed ancestry, multiracial. Question the need to mention a person's heritage. See also blood, multiracial, half-breed/half-caste, mestiza/mestizo, mulatto.

model man or woman.

moderate a political moderate is often not so much someone who occupies the ground between left-wing and right-wing beliefs as someone who holds some mildly conservative views (on balancing the government budget, for example) and some mildly liberal views (against the death penalty, for example), which means that neither side can entirely win the moderate's heart. Psycholinguist and serious thinker George Lakoff has formulated some intriguing ideas about the importance of not deforming a political message (either from the left or from the right) in an attempt to appeal to moderates; it is better, he says, to express your deeply felt opinions in ways that will inspire moderates to pull to one side or the other. They don't seem to like being pandered to.

modern man modern people/peoples/society/civilization/world, today's people, people today, modern/contemporary civilization, the modern age. Use the term only for the Minnesota man who legally changed his name to Modern Man. See also Man/man (generic), mankind.

modiste although a person who produces, designs, or deals in women's clothes can be either sex, this term is most associated with women. Sex-neutral alternatives include clothier, clothing retailer, hatmaker, fashion/high-fashion/garment designer.

Mohammed see Muhammad.

Mohammedan as noun or adjective, this word is never correct and always highly objectionable. For someone whose faith is Islam, use Muslim. To modify a noun dealing with religious aspects of Islam, use Islamic. To modify a noun dealing with the political aspects, use Islamist. See also Islam, Muslim.

Mohawk Kaniengehagas, Kanienkehaka Native Americans. "Mohawk" means "cannibal" in Algonquian, an incorrect, derogatory exonym.

mollycoddle (noun/verb) because of "molly" (from the woman's name) but even more because the noun is defined as "a pampered, spoiled, effeminate boy or man," this word is thoroughly sexist. For the noun, use spoiled/immature/irresponsible person, timid/gentle/sensitive person. For the verb, use indulge, spoil, pamper, dote on, overprotect. See also mama's boy, sissy.

mommy track writing in the *Harvard Business Review*, Felice N. Schwartz said, "The cost of employing women in business is greater than the cost of employing men" (citing more career interruptions, plateauing, and turnovers for women) and asked employers to distinguish between "career-primary" and "career-and-family" women managers and to devise policies so that the latter could "trade some career growth and compensation for freedom from the constant pressures to work long hours." Although Schwartz added, "The costs of employing women pale beside the payoffs," her approach was labeled the "mommy track" (Schwartz herself never used the term) and criticized on a number of grounds: except for two unpublished studies by anonymous corporations, Schwartz offered no data to support her claim about the costs of employing women; she divided women into two groups while the diversity of men was ignored; the paper reinforced the assumptions that you can have either a family or a career but not both if you're a woman and that it is always the woman's responsibility to care for children; it tried to fit women into the existing culture instead of questioning the values of the culture; her theory supported the contemporary situation in which women at upper levels of management mostly do not have children while their male colleagues do. See also executive, glass ceiling, wage earner, working father, working man, working mother/working wife/working woman.

mommy wars this catch-phrase makes for great headlines, but there's no "there" there. The supposed antagonists are mothers at home and mothers in the workplace. Entire books have been written about the benefits and disadvantages of each situation. In the end, however, the only conflict is between the kind of women with intelligence and compassion who understand that every other woman is doing the best she can and making the wisest of the possible choices available to her ... and the other kind of women, if there are any. In our absurdly binary culture, if we identify one group, we seem to need an equal and opposite group, ignoring the fact that sometimes we're all in it together.

monastery most monasteries house or housed monks, but some abbeys and convents are also considered monasteries and Benedictine, Cistercian, Carmeline, Brigittine, and Visitandine nuns all live in monasteries.

moneyman financier, backer, sponsor, bankroller, benefactor, donor, angel.

Mongolian acceptable term when referring to the central Asian region of Mongolia or its people.

mongolism/mongoloid Down syndrome/someone with Down syndrome. "Down's syndrome" is not pejorative, but it is less correct (Down is the physician who first reported it); "mongoloid" is objectionable but fortunately obsolete.

monk correct sex-specific term; the approximate equivalent for women is nun. There is no precise synonym for "monk" that is sex-neutral, but in some contexts you could use religious, recluse, hermit, solitary.

monogamist woman or man. See also polyandrist/polygynist, polygamist.

monsignor always a man; it means "my lord" or "my sir."

Montezuma's revenge there is nothing wrong with this expression (it doesn't appear to be used in any derogatory or ethnocentric way, but is rather a recognition of the harm done Aztec peoples by the Spanish conquest); alternatives: dysentery, intestinal flu, travelers' tummy/scourge.

moonbats and wingnuts respectively left-wing and right-wing bloggers or ranters. If one must name-call and label everything, these picturesque terms are at least nicely balanced. Coined and defined by London blogger Adriana Cronin-Lukas of Samizdata.net ("someone who sacrifices sanity for the sake of consistency"), "barking moonbat," or simply "moonbat," is "most often applied derisively to extreme partisans on the left, but we use it as originally intended, to apply to all far-out cases whose beliefs make them oblivious to facts, regardless of party or ideology" (Brooks Jackson and Kathleen Hall Jamieson, *UnSpun: Finding Facts in a World of Disinformation*). According to the Urban Dictionary, "it was always intended as a much more ecumenical epithet and has been correctly used to describe certain paleo-conservative and paleo-libertarian views (also see idiotarian)." Although "wingnut" is generally leveled at the right, indicating extreme and irrational political views, often with religious overtones, it is also sometimes used for anyone whose views seem outlandish.

Moonie Unificationist, Unification Church member. "Moonie" is derogatory.

moonlighter man or women. Moonlighting is an equal employment opportunity: government studies show that 5.6 percent of working women and 4.8 percent of men work two or more jobs.

moral injury defined as "a betrayal of one's sense of right and wrong by someone who holds legitimate authority in a high-stakes situation" (Dr. Jonathan Shay, Department of Veteran Affairs psychiatrist), this largely unaddressed issue faces combat veterans. According to American Public Media, about a third of veterans returning from Iraq and Afghanistan who visit VA medical centers have experienced some kind of mental health issue. This has presented, in some instances, a massive guilt and shame about their rewired consciences. Shay says that when a person's moral horizon shrinks, so do a person's ideals and attachments and ambitions. Use the term without quotation marks; it is a valid concern for many veterans. See also war.

more bang for the buck although this probably refers more to a fireworks-type "bang" than to a sex-type "bang," it is an expression that makes many people wince. An alternative might be get the most for your money/your money's worth.

Mormon member of the Church of Jesus Christ of Latter-day Saints. "'Mormon' is just a nickname (taken from *The Book of Mormon: Another Testament of Jesus Christ*). It is customary in our church to address someone of our faith as 'L.D.S.' (short for 'Latter-day Saint'), and so instead of 'Mormon Bishop,' it is more respectful and proper to write 'L.D.S. Bishop' (or 'LDS Bishop,' without the periods)" (Colleen D. Taylor). In the correct form of the Church name, there is no "the" before "Latter-day," which is hyphenated; "-day" is lowercased.

Moslem see Muslim.

mother (noun) "mother" is a good word. However, when appropriate use "mother and father" to avoid associating all the responsibility for parenting with the mother (a breakfast cereal box has "kid-tested, mother-approved"). Using "parent" tends to be understood as "mother"; specifically mention fathers when they are involved. A woman expecting a child is a pregnant woman, not a mother, unless she has other children. Medical science divides mothers into three categories: the genetic, the gestational, and the social mother; these mothers may be represented by as many as three different individuals—the one whose eggs are donated, the one who carries the fetus, and the one who mothers the child for life. Mothers may also be adoptive, biological, birth, lesbian, ovarian, step-, surrogate, and uterine—although the most popular word is still the unadorned "mother." See also pregnancy.

mother (verb): "To 'father' a child suggests above all to beget, to provide the sperm which fertilizes the ovum. To 'mother' a child implies a continuing presence, lasting at least nine months, more often for years" (Adrienne Rich, *Of Woman Born*). When you need inclusive sex-neutral alternatives for the verb "mother," consider parent, nurture, support, protect, take care of, look after, care for, be responsible for, rear children, caretake, supervise. See also father (verb).

mother and father use "father and mother" half the time. Although there are inclusive alternatives (the best is "parents"), in this situation it seems important to make both sexes clearly visible; children need both fathers and mothers whenever possible. See also father (noun), mother (noun), parent (noun).

motherboard this is the most commonly used term. "System board" is also seen, and for some computers and in some contexts you may be able to use analog/logic/CPU/primary circuit board. See also daughterboard.

mother cell this biology term has a long-standing and specific meaning; leave as is. When mother cells split, they form daughter cells.

mother country see motherland.

Mother Earth Earth. For the rationale on not feminizing nature, see Mother Nature.

mother hen overprotective/indulgent/hovering person/parent.

motherhood every woman experiences motherhood in a unique way; avoid generalizations, including canonizing or vilifying mothers. "There is only one image in this culture of the 'good mother.' ... She is quietly strong, selflessly giving, undemanding, unambitious; she is receptive and intelligent in only a moderate, concrete way; she is of even temperament, almost always in control of her emotions. She loves her children completely and unambivalently. Most of us are not like her" (Jane Lazarre, *The Mother Knot*).

motherhouse correct sex-specific term for religious order headquarters, although there is no parallel "fatherhouse."

mother-in-law there are no father-in-law jokes and virtually no father-in-law put-downs.

motherland homeland, native land/country/soil, home, home/birth country, land of one's ancestors, country of origin, natal place, birthplace, the old country.

mother lode main/principal lode.

motherly replace this vague adjective with precise ones: warm, nurturing, loving, kind, kindly, protective, supportive, caring, solicitous, considerate, interested, benevolent, good-natured, fond, affectionate, devoted, tender, gentle, demonstrative, sympathetic, understanding, indulgent, obliging, forbearing, tolerant, well-meaning, sheltering, generous. These words also apply to men; they are not synonyms for "motherly" but rather what people seem to mean by it.

Mother Nature Nature. The earth is made easy to rape, exploit, and subjugate by being considered female; "in our culture, words matter: The masculine dominates the feminine. To consider the Earth in terms wholly female implies that it is to be acted upon at our will. Plowing fields, cutting timber, mining ore, burning rain forests, and dumping our garbage into landfills and oceans are actions that characterize this view of the Earth as an entity we dominate" (Mary Morse, in *Utne Reader*). Elizabeth Dodson Gray (in *Creation*) says giving nature a traditional feminine image is reassuring to us for "surely a mother will always be loving toward us, continue to feed us, clothe us, and carry away our wastes, and never kill us no matter how much toxic waste we put into the soil or CFC's into the ozone." In the same way Nature has been hurt by the association with the feminine, women have been discounted because of their association with Nature. Sherry B. Ortner (in M.Z. Rosaldo and L. Lamphere, eds., *Woman, Culture, and Society*) attributes the secondary status of woman in society ("one of the true universals, a pan-cultural fact") to the way every culture distinguishes between "nature" and "culture" and then associates women with nature and men with culture. Woman is perceived as being closer to nature because of (1) her body and its functions—which place her in (2) social roles that are considered to be at a lower order of the cultural process than man's and which lead to a (3) psychic structure which is seen as being closer to nature; "proportionately more of a woman's body space, for a greater percentage of her lifetime, and at some—sometimes great—cost to her personal health, strength, and general stability, is taken up with the natural processes surrounding the reproduction of the species." In contrast, man, lacking natural creative functions, asserts his creativity externally, "artificially," through technology and symbols. "In so doing, he creates relatively lasting, eternal, transcendent objects, while the woman creates only perishables—human beings." The association of women with second-class nature is reinforced by her association with incontinent, unsocialized children (who are, being "uncivilized," closer to nature) and by her traditional confinement to the domestic sphere (originally because of bearing and nursing children), which is always considered "less" than the public sphere since society is logically at a higher level than the domestic units of which it is composed. "Since it is always culture's project to subsume and transcend nature, if women were considered part of nature, then culture would find it 'natural' to subordinate, not to say oppress, them." See also ecofeminism.

mother of all ... according to the American Dialect Society's journal, *American Speech*, neologists have recorded more than 70 variations of the phrase, including *mother of all victory parades, mother of all bagels,* and *mother of all mothers.* "All of the *mother of all* forms are joke uses, or at least playful allusions to Saddam Hussein's boastful "mother of all battles," says the journal. If you want alternatives consider the ultimate ..., the last word in ..., the ... to end all. ... See also granddaddy/daddy of them all.

mother of pearl (mollusks) this term is acceptable but you can also use nacre.

mother of vinegar leave as is.

Mother's Day proposed by Anna Jarvis, Mother's Day was first observed on May 10, 1908, in Philadelphia. No florists, greeting card companies, or candy makers were involved at the time.

mother's helper babysitter, childcare worker, family/parents' helper, live-in babysitter, child minder/monitor/attendant, housekeeper. See also nanny.

mother ship supply ship.

mother superior retain when it is someone's title.

mother tongue if you want a sex-neutral alternative, consider native language/tongue, birth/first/original language.

mother wit native wit, natural wit/intelligence.

motorman driver, streetcar/railway/subway driver, streetcar/motor operator, motor-power connector, motoreer (a clever older word that was put together from motor + engineer), railway/railroad conductor.

mountain man/mountain woman acceptable if "mountain man" is not used as a pseudogeneric. Plural: mountain people/folk.

Mountie both men and women belong to the Royal Canadian Mounted Police Force.

movies for children commissioned by the See Jane program, researchers from the Annenberg School for Communication at the University of Southern California studied the 129 top-grossing G-rated films released from 2006 through 2011, analyzing a total of 5,839 speaking characters, and found the films were dominated by white male characters and male stories (72 percent of speaking characters are male). Gender imbalance is also reflected in the percentage of female speaking roles within each film; only 11 percent of family films feature girls and women in roughly half of all speaking parts. The See Jane program seeks to engage film industry professionals and parents to dramatically increase the percentage of female characters—and to reduce gender stereotyping—in media made for children under 11. See Jane founder Geena Davis says, "By making it common for our youngest children to see everywhere a balance of active and complex male and female characters, girls and boys will grow up to empathize with and care more about each other's stories." When writing or discussing movies for children, let parents and teachers know how balanced they are in terms of women/girls. See Bechdel test, media.

Mr. and Mrs. without hoping to actually see "Mrs. and Mr." very often, this entry is here to highlight the language usage that always puts the male first (except—and you are welcome to make of this what you will—"bride and groom"). Even phone books, in their vast impassivity, line us up as Willie and Mattie, Gene and Becky, Chuck and Sondra, Duc and Thu Huong. We have male and female, boy and girl, husband and wife, man and woman. Half the time, mix 'em up.

Mrs. some women prefer this title; respect their wishes. When their wishes or marital status are unknown, use "Ms." Dale Spender (*Man Made Language*) says, "Contrary to the belief of many people, the current usage of *Miss* and *Mrs.* is relatively recent, for until the beginning of the 19th century the title *Miss* was usually reserved for young females while *Mrs.* designated mature women. Marital status played no role in the use of these terms." (In French and German, *mademoiselle* and *madame*, *frau* and *fräulein* are still understood this way.) "Mrs." and "Miss" reflect a tradition of labeling women in relation to men although the converse has never been true. About 10 percent of married women use their birth names rather than their husbands' names. African American woman generally prefer taking their husbands' names because their "history denied them the legal right to that designation. What signifies bondage to one woman may mark freedom to another" (Francine Wattman Frank and Paula A. Treichler, *Language, Gender, and Professional Writing*). In the workplace, this social title gives way to the more common "Ms." See also frau, mademoiselle, Miss, Ms.

Ms. pronounced "miz" and originating in secretarial manuals of the 1940s, this title is used for women where "Mr." is used for men. If you use "Mr. Seifert," use "Ms. Ayallah"; if you call Seifert by his last name, do the same for Ayallah. "Ms." is generally acceptable when you don't know what social title (Ms., Mrs., Dr., Miss) the person uses; you may also omit the social title for both sexes ("Dear Irene Nash"; "Dear David Koskenmaki"). Where a woman indicates she prefers Miss or Mrs., use that instead. The greatest objection to "Ms." has been that you can't tell if she's married or not. The only sensible reply is that we have managed for centuries to get along without knowing whether a "Mr." is married or not. According to the *American Heritage Book of English Usage*, "the term stands as a highly successful language reform—probably because people value its usefulness." The plural is Mses., Mss. Fun things to know and tell: in 1972 Bella Abzug passed her "Ms. Bill," which forbade the federal government from using prefixes indicating marital status. See also mademoiselle, Miss, Mrs., salutations (letters).

M

MTF/MTF transsexual Julia Serano, author of *Whipping Girl: A Transsexual Woman on Sexism and the Scapegoating of Feminism*, says the feminist and queer communities tend to dismiss MTF (male-to-female) transsexuals while celebrating their counterparts on the FTM (female-to-male) spectrum. Balance coverage of these two groups. See also transgender.

muezzin always a man.

Muhammad this is the correct spelling of the name of the Muslim prophet of Allah. See also Islam, Moslem.

Muhammadan as noun or adjective, this word is never correct and always highly objectionable. See also Moslem.

mulatto "*Mulatto* is a slaveholder's word derived from the notion that, like mules, we were unable to have children. Racist pseudo-science said that since inter-species breeding produces infertile offspring, the children of whites (humans) and Africans (sub-humans) would be sterile. Hopefully, sensible people have abandoned the notion that human genetic pools—races—are different species and will therefore abandon this offensive word" (Jaimie Markham, in *Colors*). Use instead (if a reference is needed at all) biracial, multiracial, mélange, métis/métisse.

mullah this Muslim scholar is always a man.

multicultural this adjective modifies programs, curricula, and publications. It does not modify human beings (despite being seen describing a group of women from diverse backgrounds as "multicultural women"). See also multiculturalism.

multiculturalism a cluster of ideas and attitudes that have come to the fore in developed capitalist countries in recent decades, "multiculturalism" is "a term of wholly uncertain meaning" (Timothy Garton Ash, *The New York Review of Books*). Ash says, "Painful though this will be to those who have expended their academic careers on multiculturalism, the term should be consigned to the dustbin of history. ... To be clear: it is the 'ism' that should be a 'wasm.' Although the adjective 'multicultural' questionably gathers in one tag what are in reality multiple kinds of human differences—religion, ethnicity, language, nationality, color, etc.— it has become a generally understood shorthand for the mainly postmigrant diversity of these societies." Some of the ideas from the years of enthusiasm for multiculturalism were positive: "Multicultural education is, simply put, teaching and learning that effectively include the histories, contributions and perspectives of all groups and individuals who make up our national identity.... Genuine educational excellence recognizes multiple histories, cultural values, and learning styles.... Partial or exclusive knowledge results in partial and exclusive truth" (Carol Miller, chair, Department of American Indian Studies, University of Minnesota). Near-synonyms, which have their own shortcomings, include: cultural diversity, diversity, pluralism, cross-culturalism, ethnic inclusiveness. See also multicultural.

multiracial "For the first time in U.S. history, birth data indicate that the number of children born to parents of different races is growing faster than the number born to single-race couples" (Seth Schiesel and Robert L. Turner, *Boston Globe Sunday Magazine*). It seems illogical to retain terms like "biracial" and "multiracial" when the concept of "race" itself is incorrect, but do use them for those who self-identify that way. (It often isn't necessary to mention one's heritage at all.)

mumbo jumbo Mumbo Jumbo is an object of worship in parts of West Africa. For its borrowed, disrespectful, and ethnocentric use in English, you may want alternatives: nonsense, gibberish, twaddle, jargon, drivel.

mum's the word this has nothing to do with "mum" ("mother") but with an old command to be quiet.

murderess murderer. See also bad guy, "feminine" word endings.

muscleman hired muscle, muscler, goon, thug, bully, menace, bruiser, ugly/rough customer, enforcer, big tuna, hard case; powerhouse, weightlifter. See also bad guy.

Muslim never use "Moslem," which is an unacceptable westernized corruption. "Muslim" is both adjective and noun, referring to a follower of Islam or modifying anything of or pertaining to Islam. Never use "Mohammadan" or "Mohammedanism" since they imply worship of the prophet Muhammad, considered by Muslims to be a blasphemy against the absolute oneness of God. See also Black Muslims, Islam, Islamofascism, Islamophobia, Mohammedan, Muhammad.

Muslima/Muslimah referring to a Muslim woman, "Muslima" or "Muslimah" is not accepted by most Muslims, but some groups and individuals use it. Retain it for those who self-identify this way.

mute this is acceptable in its sense of refraining from speaking ("when questioned, he remained unwaveringly mute"); it is less acceptable when referring to those who are incapable of speech or to those who are capable of producing vocal sounds but do not speak (usually because of deafness and the difficulty in reproducing sounds never heard). "Deaf-mute" is always unacceptable. The *American Heritage Book of English Usage* suggests "aphonic" as an adjective for someone who has lost the ability to speak, as for those who physiologically could speak but don't, "many deaf people today are brought up in a sign-oriented community that rejects the notion that speaking is necessary or, to some, even desirable; they are best referred to simply as *deaf*, or, if appropriate, *Deaf*." See also deaf/Deaf.

My fellow Americans former presidential speechwriter Peggy Noonan writes just before the 2007 state of the union speech (in the *Wall Street Journal*): "Someone at just about this moment is suggesting changing the opening—'My fellow Americans'—to 'Fellow citizens.' And someone else is penciling in 'My brothers and sisters.' Down the hall someone is writing, 'Why don't we make it new, edgy—how about "Hey Dawg?"' Somewhere a speechwriter is screaming." Although "my fellow Americans" seems hallowed by familiarity and time, there are phrases that don't use the masculine "fellow": Friends, Neighbors, Citizens; Good People of America; Brothers and Sisters; My Partners in Democracy; Women and Men of America; Compatriots. See also America/American.

Language is the perfect instrument
of empire.

Antonio de Nebrija

Language is the road map of a culture.
It tells you where its people come from
and where they are going.

Rita Mae Brown

nabob historically the governor or deputy of a Mongol or Indian district or town was always a man, and there was no parallel term for a woman; in the broad sense of a wealthy, high-ranking, or prominent person, it can be used of both sexes.

nag (noun) because this is used to refer only for women (with no parallel word for men) consider using grouch, grump, grumbler, fussbudget, crosspatch, faultfinder, complainer, nitpicker, sorehead, crank, griper.

nag (verb) although "nag" is not sexist per se, it has been used almost exclusively for women, while in the same situation men are said to bully, chew out, complain, or just plain talk. Consider using one of the many available alternatives: complain, gripe, criticize, scold, kvetch, badger, pick on, find fault, pester, harass, grumble, grouse, irritate, harp at/on, bicker, drive up the wall, fuss, raise a fuss, have a bone to pick with; persist, lobby, push, press, ask again, tell, say, remind, repeat, reiterate. See also bitch, henpeck/henpecked, whine.

name-calling the late Peter Opie, authority on children's rhymes, said that the well-known doggerel on name-calling should be rephrased: "Sticks and stones just break my bones. / It's words that really hurt me." Name-calling tends to be associated with children, and it is indeed childish, but many political debates degenerate into a more sophisticated, pseudo-intellectual kind of name-calling. Miss Manners (Judith Martin) says, "The whole country wants civility. Why don't we have it? It doesn't cost anything. No federal funding, no legislation is involved. One answer is the unwillingness to restrain oneself. Everybody wants other people to be polite to them, but they want the freedom of not having to be polite to others." Long ago, Daniel Webster pointed out that "anger is not an argument." Neither is name-calling.

naming naming is power, and the right to name ourselves is one of the most basic rights. It seems a simple enough thing—to call other people what they want to be called and *not* to call them what they don't want to be called—but some people have a hard time with this. When Peg turned 40 she asked her friends to call her "Margaret." She'd been nicknamed Peg, never liked it, and wanted to spend her remaining years with her "real" name. A friend thought the whole thing was silly: "I'll call her Peg if I want to." And that's where we are today. Some people call other people what *they* feel like calling them.

nanny historically this described a woman servant who had charge of young children. In Great Britain today it refers to a woman who has two or more years of formal training, has passed a national examination, and sometimes has served an internship. No certification boards or examinations are offered for nannies in the United States, but a few programs offer nanny training. A U.S. nanny is usually someone who cares for children full-time in the home. Otherwise use inclusive terms: babysitter, live-in babysitter, family/parents' helper, childcare worker/specialist, child minder/monitor/attendant, nursery worker, tutor.

natalism the idea that reproduction is the most important facet of existence.

nation/she nation/it.

National Guardsman apparently a woman cannot correctly be referred to as a National Guardswoman; she is either a soldier or a Guard member (Norm Goldstein, in *Copy Editor*).

national health insurance see universal health care coverage.

National Organization for Women (NOW) established in 1966 by Betty Friedan, among others, to "take action to bring women into full participation in the mainstream of American society now," this liberal feminist organization's mission is to make "legal, political, social, and economic change in our society in order to achieve our goal, which is to eliminate sexism and end all oppression." (Sometimes the "for" in the title is incorrectly replaced by "of.") See also feminism.

National Rifle Association (NRA) the largest gun-rights lobbying organization in the U.S., the NRA is also possibly the single most powerful nonprofit association. (Handgun Control, Inc. is the largest gun-control lobbying organization.) With nearly three million members and deep pockets, the NRA has thus far gotten everything it wants from Congress. Although the NRA offers information and gun-safety classes, which are useful, it is unwilling to give up any gun, no matter how inappropriate for personal use, or close any of the many loopholes allowing illegal gun sales. They fear that any tightening of gun laws will lead inevitably and immediately to a ban on all guns. Most people believe the NRA represents U.S. gun owners, but it appears that only about 5 percent of gun owners belong to the NRA (John Side, Poly-Sci Perspective, *Washington Post* online). Whoever could be funding them? See also guns.

nation building originally, nation building referred to newly independent countries shaping and creating themselves, their institutions, and their national identities. Today it is used more often in the case of a super power (well, okay, the United States) going in to shape a country the way it ought to be. This is not as easy as it sounds, as the neoconservatives are finding out. One school of thought believes we could use some of that nation-building energy right here at home.

native (noun) this term carries certain stereotypical connotations (in particular the notion of "uncivilized") that make it offensive in many situations. The first choice is to call people by the name they use for themselves. The second is to use "native" as an adjective (see below) or use, depending on context: indigenous/original/aboriginal population/ peoples. See also Aborigine/aboriginal, native (adjective).

native (adjective) the selective use of "native" as an adjective is generally acceptable. For example, Native American, native American, Native Alaskan/Hawaiian/Australian, native Indian (a Canadian term referring to indigenous peoples of Canada, excluding the Inuit), native peoples, peoples native to.

native American someone who was born in the United States. See also Native American.

Native American when both words are capitalized, this universally acceptable term refers to an American Indian. However, partly because of its imprecision (it could also mean a native American), the term has been replaced in many cases by "American Indian." The best approach is to use the particular Indian people's own name (Dine, for example) and ask whether they would prefer the use of "Native American" or "American Indian" in other references. See also American Indian, Indian, native American, sports teams' names and mascots.

Native People see American Indian.

nativism this political position seeks favored status for established inhabitants of a nation, and typically opposes immigration or, at least, seeks to speed assimilation of newcomers and immigrants (particularly with respect to language). Max J. Castro (in Han B. Entzinger et al., *Migration Between States and Markets*) says nativist movements combine elements of ethnic prejudice and nationalism. Nativism descends from earlier incarnations: in the 1920s xenophobic upsurges in the U.S. led to restrictionist legislation and four decades of scant immigration; Nazi Germany in the 1930s and 1940s typifies it; in the 1990s another "invasion of the other" (largely from Latin America) provoked a nativist reaction without, however, affecting immigration levels. Castro calls the current version neonativism, marked by its anti-immigration lobbies and its intellectual and vigilante activity. For information on nativists, see their flagship organization, Federation for American Immigration Reform, or English Only (originally allied with the FAIR), or the Center for Immigration Studies (an anti-immigration organization). Good news: According to the Southern Poverty Law Center (*Intelligence Report*, 2013), the number of nativist extremist groups (those that go beyond pushing for legislative change or stricter border controls to personally confronting suspected undocumented workers and border crossers) has fallen dramatically in the last several years, apparently due to criminal scandals, sniping among the various groups, and the co-optation of the movement's goals by state legislatures. Note: Steven Pinker (*The Stuff of Thought*) says that "in cognitive science, the term 'nativism' refers to an emphasis on innate mental organization; it has nothing to do with the political term for anti-immigrant bigotry."

nativist someone who opposes immigration and distinguishes between those people born in the United States and those who immigrated to it, with sometimes strong feelings against the latter.

"natural" father/mother/child biological mother/father/child. See also adoption language.

natural because it is difficult to know (scientifically, psychologically, philosophically) whether something is indeed "natural" and, secondarily, whether being natural is good, it is better not to use these terms with respect to sex roles, age, race, sexual orientation, disabilities, or other human variables. These terms are often a substitute for informed thought, an opinion on what seems "right." "For centuries people have appealed to the 'natural' to back up their moral and social recommendations. ... it is often taken for granted that if one persuades us that '"X" is natural,' he has also persuaded us that '"X" is good" (Christine Pierce, in Vivian Gornick and Barbara K. Moran, eds., *Woman in Sexist Society*). Consider using automatic, instinctive, essential, idiosyncratic, usual, often-seen, common, habitual, accustomed, customary, established, time-honored, regulation, traditional, general, prevailing, frequent, popular, predictable, expected.

nature/she nature/it. For the rationale on not feminizing nature, see Mother Nature.

Navaho Dine.

Nazi/nazi using this term for anything but a member of the National Socialist German Workers' Party robs it of an evil it properly should retain; it is also painful for a Jew to hear the word. There has been a recent outbreak of "humorous" -nazi forms, which desensitize us to a cruel piece of history. For alternatives, either describe the person's actions or consider using fascist, neo-Nazi, fanatic, extremist, bigot, racist, supremacist, white supremacist. See also concentration camp, feminazi, "final solution," Gestapo/gestapo, Hitler/little Hitler, holocaust/Holocaust.

Neanderthal man Neanderthal, the Neanderthal, Neanderthals, early human, Pleistocene/Ice Age peoples, archaic human, Homo erectus. The colloquial insult "Neanderthal" is sexist because it is reserved for men and ethnocentric because it represents early peoples unfairly. See also prehistoric man, primitive man, troglodyte.

necessity is the mother of invention if you need a sex neutral expression, try necessity gives rise to/fosters/breeds/spawns/provokes/generates invention.

née because men don't change their names when they marry, the parallel French word meaning "born" for men (*né*) is not used in English; he always is what he was *né*. *Née* has outlived its usefulness, appearing only now and then in an obituary, society column, or crossword puzzle. Use either "born Ella Gwendolen Rees Williams," "the former Virginia Stephen," or both the woman's names: Anna Eleanor Roosevelt Roosevelt, Hillary Rodham Clinton.

needlewoman needleworker, tailor, mender, alterer, stitcher, alterations expert, custom tailor, garment worker/designer.

negative economic growth sometimes called "a technical recession," you should probably just call it a recession or at least spell out the bad news and what it means in plain English.

negative employment growth unemployment.

Negress/Negro except in established titles (for example, United Negro College Fund), the terms "Negro/Negress" are considered unacceptable, offensive, slavery-based, and contemptuous. Use instead African American, black. See also African American, Afro-American, black (noun).

neoconservative see political spectrum.

Neopagan see Pagan/Neopagan.

nerd male or female.

nervous Nellie this can be used to describe either a man or a woman, but for a sex-nonspecific term, consider fussbudget, worrywart, hand-wringer, terminal worrier.

New Age do your homework. Because "New Age" refers to such a broad range of late 20th-century and contemporary beliefs and practices, it is difficult to know which tenets are held by any given individuals or which aspects of New Age spirituality are included in any reference to it. Characterized by an eclectic and personal approach to spiritual exploration, the New Age movement has no holy text, central organization, membership, formal clergy, geographic center, dogma, or hard-and-fast creed. Instead, it draws on all the major world religions for inspiration with particular emphasis on Buddhism, Hinduism, Shamanism, Sufism, Taoism, New Thought, Neo-Paganism, and Spiritualism. Many New Agers graft additional beliefs onto traditional religious affiliations.

newsboy newspaper carrier/vendor. See also paperboy.

newsman/newspaperman reporter, newspaper reporter, journalist, news representative/writer, correspondent, representative/member of the press/media/Fourth Estate, newscaster; newsmonger. Or be specific: war/special/foreign correspondent, columnist, commentator, wire/roving/investigative reporter, feature writer, sportswriter, stringer, editor, publisher, radio correspondent, television commentator, anchor, news anchor/director, announcer, reviewer, gossip columnist, photojournalist. See also anchorman, media.

New World this highly Eurocentric term disregards the fact that the world in question wasn't new at all to the people who had lived there for centuries. See also "discovery" of America.

Nez Perce Nimipu. This American Indian tribe was named by French trappers ("Pierced Nose"). Although Nez Perce is used (see www.nez-perce.org) and they were once also called Chuta-pa-le, the preferred name is Nimipu ("The People"). Variations include: Ni-Mii-Puu, Nimiipu, Nimiipuu, Nimapu, Namipu, Numipu, Neemepoo, Noomeepoo, Chopunnish, Taoopnitpalu, Tautpeli. When possible, verify the name. When not possible, use Nimipu.

niggardly although by definition and derivation "niggardly" and "nigger" are not remotely similar, the use of "niggardly" elicits uncomfortable reactions in many people. It's just too close. There are many descriptive alternatives available: stingy, miserly, parsimonious, skinflinty, reluctant, ungenerous, grudging, begrudging, cheap, moneygrubbing, grasping; scanty, skimpy, piddling, measly, puny.

nigger/nigga in 1933 Fannie Hurst (*Imitation of Life*) wrote, "Nigger is a tame-cat word when we uses it ourselves ag'in' ourselves, and a wild-cat word when it comes jumpin' in at us from the outside." Always deeply offensive and off-limits when used by others, the word is under considerable debate among African Americans. Some believe that their open use of it among themselves will strip it of its racist meaning; others say that no matter who uses it, such a hideous pejorative needs to be stricken from the national vocabulary. Geneva Smitherman (*Talkin and Testifyin*) suggests the division may be classist—"the bourgeoisie, the upper-class ... may not want white folks to get the wrong impression. But among black folks in the plants and places like that, it's fine." Carla Hall (*Los Angeles Times*) writes, "As epithets go, it's a knife. It doesn't just cut, it slashes." Eugene Grigsby, director of UCLA's center for African American studies, says, "It's the ultimate way to remind someone you were once property, once chattel. To slip back into that terminology is to hurl an insult." "The word is inextricably linked with violence and brutality on black psyches and derogatory aspersions cast on black bodies. No degree of appropriating can rid it of that blood-soaked history" (Neal A. Lester, in *Teaching Tolerance*). Years after he made his 1974 comedy album, "That Nigger's Crazy," Richard Pryor returned from a visit to Africa and told audiences he would never use the word again as a performer because he never once saw a "nigger" in Africa. Public Enemy, one of rap's most respected and popular groups, has a song on its third album, "I Don't Wanna Be Called Yo' Nigga." The most common argument against use of it by blacks is that whites who hear it may think they too can use it. Rapper Q-Tip says, "The more and more hip-hop culture is being accepted into the white community, the more chances are greater for a white person to start saying it, and I'm really trying not to hear that." In 2007, a mock funeral for "the n-word" was held in Detroit by delegates of the NAACP to do away with the racial slur, its spirit, and all its associations. Also in 2007, the New York City Council approved a symbolic resolution banning it. (See www.AbolishtheNWord.com and www.BantheNWord.org.) Errol Louis (*New York Daily News*) says, "The 'N-word' is on the way out." Some critics feel bans are a pointless public relations tactic that doesn't address gentrification, joblessness, racial profiling, police brutality, and urban killings. For writers and speakers, it's simpler: never use "nigger." For the completely unacceptable phrase "nigger in the woodpile," substitute catch, hitch, snag, drawback. "Timber nigger," a highly offensive term describing American Indians involved in the fishing and hunting rights debate, has no good alternative except "American Indians involved in the fishing and hunting rights debate." See also African American, black (noun), "insider/outsider" rule, racism.

niggling of possible Scandinavian origin, this term is unrelated to "nigger" and less questionable to the ear and eye than "niggardly." Although most people will find it unobjectionable, those who want to replace it can choose from among a number of alternatives: petty, trivial, puny; piddling, trifling, fiddling; silly, inane, foolish, pointless.

night watchman night guard/watch, security guard/officer, guard, building guard, watch, guardian, caretaker, gatekeeper, custodian, sentinel, sentry, lookout, patrol, patroller; the night watch.

Nip a derogatory clipping of the word Nipponese (meaning Japanese, from "Nippon," another name for Japan), "Nip" is never acceptable.

Nisei literally, "second generation," this acceptable term is used for a U.S.-born Japanese American whose parents immigrated to the United States. It is sometimes used to refer to all Japanese Americans. Plural is Nisei or Niseis. See also Issei, Kibei, Sansei, Yonsei.

no better than she should be this phrase reeks of judgment, sexism (there is no parallel for a man), and a conception of virtue based solely on sexuality.

nobleman noble, member of the nobility, aristocrat, peer; noblewoman and nobleman. Or be specific: countess, duke, princess, earl, marquis, baroness.

No Child Left Behind the federal government's funding program for public schools, No Child Left Behind (NCLB) aims to insure that all students are 100 percent proficient in reading and math. As outcome-based education, success of NCLB depends on good test scores so teachers are motivated "to teach to the test." Peg Tyre (*Newsweek*) writes that NCLB "puts pressure on schools to have their kids pass...scores on statewide exams have become the single yardstick by which school success is measured. Struggling schools are being penalized—and some are even slated to be taken over if tests scores fail to rise. Teachers are under pressure to show that kids are learning more, and if they do that, even by fudging the results, they can help their borderline school survive." Under NCLB, states have an incentive to lower standards and emphasis is placed on punishing failure rather than rewarding success. Schools that don't meet "Adequate Yearly Progress" (AYP) benchmarks are subject to interventions such as replacing teachers, transferring students to higher-performing schools, and even closing schools. As of the 2011-2012 school year, 54 percent of schools were failing to meet their AYP goals. Concern is growing that the culture of test taking and teaching to the test that NCLB has produced has left even the brightest students ill-prepared for the critical thinking, high-level reading and writing, and demands of working independently required by college and the workplace.

no man is a prophet in his own country no one is a prophet in their own country (see singular "they"); we are slow to see the prophet in our midst; prophets are not without honor, save in their own country and among their own kin and in their own house; prophets are seldom recognized in their own land; prophets go unhonored in their own country; people rarely recognize the prophet in their midst. (The original phrase reflected earlier biblical translations; many current translations no longer use that version.)

no-man's-land limbo, wasteland, Death Valley, nowhere land, uninhabited/uninhabitable/uncharted/unclaimed/lawless/noncombatant/unclaimed land/zone/territory, demilitarized/buffer/dead zone, hostile country, nowheresville, gray area, vacuum, dead space/zone, arid zone, the desert, the wild. This is a difficult phrase to replace at times, not so much because there are no alternatives, but because we are seduced by its familiarity and by the ease with which it springs to mind.

nomenclature nonsexist; the "men" comes from *nomen*, Latin for "name."

non-alien and you thought you were a citizen ... ! The federal government used this extremely circuitous synonym for citizens during World War II because it sounded so much better to be interning non-aliens than to be interning U.S. citizens. The latter had constitutional rights, but who knew what rights "non-aliens" had?

noncustodial parent don't assume that this is always the father, nor that a noncustodial mother is somehow lacking; our ideas of mothering and fathering are sometimes so narrow that we have difficulty imagining a mother who would give up custody of her children or a father who is devastated when he fails to get custody of his. The force of these sexist attitudes is enough to pressure some women into taking custody of children who might be better off with their fathers. Women may choose to avoid custody battles because they want to spare their children the conflict or are unable to support them financially. Threats of physical violence and harassment can also be a factor in a woman surrendering custodial rights. See also custodial parent.

nondisabled you could do worse than use this term, but you could do better too. Be specific about the group you are referring to. Not everyone accepts or uses "nondisabled," but given limited space and the need for something nonpejorative and succinct, this can work.

nonracist someone who is not racist or someone who is unprejudiced about race.

nonsexist language language that carries no bias (good or bad) toward one sex or the other is nonsexist. It may be gender-fair ("businesswomen and businessmen") or gender-free ("parents").

nontraditional career/employment female-intensive occupation/career, male-intensive occupation/career. Using "nontraditional" implies work that is unacceptable or abnormal for one sex. Statistics indicate that women's increasing interest in male-intensive occupations has not been matched by a comparable increase in men's interest in female-intensive occupations. See also pink-collar job/worker.

nonwhite this ethnocentric, imprecise term assumes white is the standard and lumps everyone else together without any individual identity. As Joan Steinau Lester said, "I wouldn't want to be a 'non-male.'" Replace the term with specifics.

normal referring to some people as "normal" makes everyone else "abnormal" or at least "not normal." Although there are some appropriates uses (for example, when referring to statistical human normalities), in general it is better replaced or circumvented: instead of "normal child," use "normally developing child" or "child with normal eyesight"; instead of "normal classroom," use "mainstream classroom"; the opposite of "persons with disabilities" is not "normal people" but "people without disabilities"; the opposite of gay men and lesbians is not "normal people" but "heterosexuals" (one man wrote, "As a gay man, I have waited a long time for the media to finally ... limit the term *normal* to stories detailing automatic dryer cycle options"). "Abnormal" and "atypical" are equally suspect; which of us counts ourselves absolutely normal or typical? See also deviant, special.

Norseman ancient/early Scandinavian, Scandinavian, peoples of old Scandinavia, Viking, Norseman/Norsewoman, Northwoman/Northman, Norsefolk. Inhabitants of Scandinavia since the 10th century are properly called Scandinavians. Before that they are Northmen and Northwomen. Scandinavian sea-warriors who plundered the coasts of Europe from the 8th to the 10th centuries are Vikings.

nosy this is too often used to describe women when men in the same situation are simply said to be curious. Consider using instead curious, overcurious, supercurious, interested, interfering, intrusive, officious, snoopy, prying, spying, eavesdropping, tending/minding other people's business.

nosy parker man or woman. From the word "parker" (park keeper), a "nosy parker" was someone who hung about London's Hyde Park around the turn of the century for the vicarious thrill of spying on lovemaking couples.

nubile there is no parallel for a man. The main objection to this word is that it defines a woman primarily in terms of her readiness for a relationship with a man.

nuclear event not widely known outside the nuclear community (did you know there was "nuclear community"?), the International Nuclear Event Scale (INES) is the mechanism used to classify and report nuclear "events." To most people, an event is a birthday party or perhaps a wedding or a trip to the beach. To the International Atomic Energy Agency (IAEA), an event can range from an "anomaly" (a level 1 "event") to an "incident" (level 2) to a "serious incident" (level 3) and so on up to level 7, a "major accident."

nuclear option this "mock-alarming name for a tactic to prevent filibusters on judicial nominations" (William Safire, *Safire's Political Dictionary*) should be called the "constitutional option." In November 2013, the Senate pushed the button on the nuclear option to end the unprecedented number of filibusters blocking President Obama's political and judicial nominees. See also military language.

nude beach putting aside the issue of whether a beach can be nude, this expression is acceptable if you mean nothing but. If you want to convey the idea that all are welcome, use clothing-optional beach.

nudist camp/colony nudists or naturists (the preferred term in parts of the world) never use "colony" and rarely "camp." Members of a naturist community call their gathering place a sun club, a naturist club, or by its specific name.

nukespeak see military language, nuclear event.

nullification "a fringe legal theory which claims that states have the right to ignore federal laws they consider unconstitutional" (Leah Nelson, *Intelligence Report*, 2013). See also hate groups.

number-one man/number-two man number one, boss, chief, head; number two, second in command, key/chief aide. See also front man; right-hand man; totem pole, highman on.

nun acceptable sex-specific term. Religious orders restricted to one sex were in fact advantageous for women because (1) women themselves often chose to live this way; (2) inasmuch as the hierarchical church allowed any group autonomy, these women governed themselves; (3) religious orders offered women the first alternative to "belonging" to earthly father or husband; (4) nuns were some of the first women to work professionally outside the home (as teachers and nurses). Many nuns today consider themselves feminists and were among pioneers in the women's movement. Today not all nuns live in a convent or a motherhouse; increasing numbers live in apartments, shared houses, and other non-convent homes.

nuncio so far, always a man.

nuptial/nuptials functionally nonsexist, these terms nevertheless come from the Latin meaning "to take a husband." Should you want something truly sex-nonspecific, use wedding, marriage.

nurse man or woman, although only around 6 percent are male. Unless necessary for clarity, "male nurse" is not used.

nursemaid/nurserymaid childcare worker, child minder/monitor/attendant, family/parents' helper, live-in babysitter, babysitter, nursery worker.

nurseryman nursery owner/manager/operator/worker, tree farmer/grower, landscaper, gardener, horticulturist, florist, forester.

nurture (verb) both men and woman can nurture. They can also mentor, encourage, train, reassure, motivate, support. You may want to zero in on the particular aspect of "nurture" you are detailing.

Nuyorican emerging during the early 1970s to identify Puerto Ricans born or raised in the continental U.S., Nuyorican is used primarily to refer to the generations of artists and writers born or raised in the U.S.—regardless of whether they live in New York—who write in English or bilingually (Edna Acosta-Belén, in Wilma Mankiller et al., *The Reader's Companion to U.S. Women's History*).

nymph because this is a "beautiful maiden" and there is no parallel for a man, you may sometimes need a sex-neutral alternative: nature god, sprite.

nymphet the *American Heritage Dictionary* defines a nymphet as "a pubescent girl regarded as sexually desirable." How does it happen that the person who is doing nothing but breathing gets a label while the (usually older) man who is breathing heavily, metaphorically speaking at least, goes unlabeled, unremarked?

nymphomaniac defined as a woman with excessive sexual desire, "nymphomaniac" is, in theory, paired with "satyr," a man with abnormal or excessive sexual craving. In practice, we hear "nymphomaniac"—or "nympho"—much more often (and used much less precisely and with far less justification) than "satyr." Mignon McLaughlin (*The Neurotic's Notebook*) defined "nymphomaniac" as "a woman as obsessed with sex as an average man." Unless you use both terms gender-fairly, choose inclusive terms: indiscriminate lover, oversexed/promiscuous/sexually active/insatiable/sensuous/sensual person, "sex maniac/fiend," someone who sleeps around, bed hopper, bedswerver.

O

Omissions are not accidents.

Marianne Moore

Language, as symbol, determines much of the nature and quality of our experience.

Sonia Johnson

oarsman rower, competitive rower; boater, boathandler; paddler, canoer, canoeist, oar puller; punter, sculler.

Oaxaquita / Indito innocent-appearing, these terms ("little Oaxacan" and "little Indian") are used as bullying epithets, and have been banned by at least one school district.

ObamaCare/Obamacare The Patient Protection and Affordable Care Act, signed into law in 2010 and upheld by a Supreme Court ruling in 2012, consists of over 1,000 pages of provisions that give Americans more rights and protections, and expand access to affordable quality health care to tens of millions of uninsured. When discussing it, be specific about who likes or dislikes exactly which elements, and avoid broad, inaccurate labels of the Act, particularly "socialist," a flabby word that today only means "They're gonna give my money to poor people, aren't they?" and does not describe the Act and its workings. See also universal health care coverage.

obese/obesity these terms along with "morbid obesity" have medical definitions (although they vary somewhat) and, as such, they are not discriminatory. Generally reserve "obese/obesity" for clinical writing. Outside the medical profession, the terms are often used to make prejudiced statements seem more scientific. Virtually no one self-identifies as obese, unless joking. Nigel Rees (*A Man About A Dog*) lists "obese" as a synonym for "fat": "Originally obese was more precisely used to describe the very fat and fleshy and the excessively corpulent." If describing someone you think is obese, try instead using adjectives as interesting as his. See also fat.

occupied territories this term is commonly used to describe the area occupied by Israeli troops after the Six-Day War and includes the Gaza Strip, the West Bank, and the Golan Heights. The United Nations uses the term "occupied Palestinian territory" to refer to Gaza and the West Bank. The Golan Heights is claimed by Syria and not by the Palestinians. A small area of Golan called Shebaa Farms is claimed by Lebanon. Many Israelis argue that the West Bank and the Gaza Strip do not belong to any other sovereign state, are part of the former Mandate for Palestine, and therefore fall legitimately within Israel's jurisdiction. Because they were "occupied territories" before 1967 (the occupying powers being Egypt and Jordon), many Israelis prefer the term "disputed territories." The demographics are informative: the Gaza Strip has a population of 1.76 million, essentially 100 percent Muslim. For the West Bank, Muslims make up 75 percent of a total population of 2.68 million. See also Israeli-Palestinian conflict.

Occupy movement an international, nonviolent protest movement against social and economic inequality, the Occupy movement focuses on the way large corporations and the global financial system control the world in basically unstable ways that disproportionately benefit a minority and undermine democracy. The movement's slogan, "We are the 99%," highlights the concentration of wealth among the top 1 percent of income earners compared to the other 99 percent. One of the most visible movements in recent years, it began in Spain in 2011 and has been particularly effective in disseminating information on the growing income gaps worldwide. See also classism, corporate welfare, globalization, poor, poverty.

odd-job(s)-man odd-jobber, odd-job laborer, general jobber, do-it-yourselfer, do-all, factotum, fixer, fixer-upper, repairer, maintenance worker, janitor, custodian, caretaker. See also handyman.

odd man out odd one out, loner, left out, third wheel, extra.

Oedipus complex acceptable sex-specific term; the parallel is "Electra complex."

ofay this disparaging term for a white person evidently comes from the pig Latin for "foe" (Stuart Berg Flexner, *I Hear America Talking*).

office boy/office girl office worker/assistant/helper/staff member, staffer, assistant, right hand, aide, bureau assistant, co-worker, gofer. Or be specific: secretary, clerk, bookkeeper, typist, receptionist, switchboard operator, messenger, courier, runner, deliverer, page. See also girl Friday.

office spouse "a co-worker with whom one has an emotionally close but usually nonsexual relationship" (Jesse Sheidlower, *Copy Editor*). They can also be office husband, office wife.

offshoring/outsourcing moving a company, factory, subsidiary, or other enterprise to another country to take advantage of cheaper labor, lower costs of doing business, lower taxes, and also to avoid paying U.S. taxes. "New York police tickets are processed in Ghana, New Jersey food-stamp questions are answered from India, airline reservations may be processed by prisoners in Tennessee" (Ellen Bravo, in *Sisterhood Is Forever*). U.S. companies are increasingly moving jobs (over 2.6 million of them in 2013) overseas because they can get the work done at much lower wages without the annoyance of dealing with safety regulations, labor unions, and other restrictions on their ability to make really big bucks. At least one company sees another way of doing things: "In a twist on offshoring that Northrop [Northrop Grumman Corp.] has dubbed onshoring, the global defense and technology corporation has been shipping computer work to small-town America, shunning India's Bangalore and Mumbai" (*Los Angeles Times*). They've set up locations for employees in seven small towns (Corsicana, Texas, and Lebanon, Virginia, for example) and find that it costs them about 40 percent less to have the work done there than in Los Angeles—"savings similar to what would be achieved by sending jobs overseas." See also anti-sweatshop activist.

-oid as "racial" categories, Australoid, Caucasoid, Mongoloid, and Negroid have no scientific validity; they are also pejorative and offensive.

oil "Today's wars are about oil. But alternate energies exist now—solar, wind—for every important energy-using activity in our lives. The only human work that cannot be done without oil is war" (Grace Paley, in *Sisterhood Is Forever*).

oilman oil company executive/sales representative, oil field worker, petroleum engineer, driller, wildcatter, wholesaler, retailer, refinery operator.

Ojibwa/Ojibway some members of this American Indian people are known as "Chippewa"; others prefer "Anishinabe." All three are acceptable terms; to determine which is correct in the particular instance, use people's self-identification or ask for clarification. Although referred to that way, they have never been a Plains nation. See also American Indian.

old "as long as it's shameful to be called old, it will be shameful to be old" (Barbara Macdonald, in *Sisterhood Is Forever*). Question the use of "old" in describing people; it is often irrelevant. Although "old" can be positive, connoting experience (an old pro/hand), its use as a pejorative intensifier (old bag, old bat, old biddy, old buzzard, old codger, old coot, old duffer, old fogy, old fuddy-duddy, old geezer, old goat, old hat, old witch) makes it less than neutral. Sometimes, those terms are trying to convey non-age-related ideas like eccentric, character, card, odd duck, original, crackpot, oddball, fanatic; stick-in-the-mud, crank. If you need to mention advanced age, however, "old" is preferred to euphemisms. Consider using "older," which suggests a younger person than "old" (an old woman versus an older woman), for those beyond middle-age but not yet elderly. According to the *American Heritage Book of English Usage*, "Where *old* expresses an absolute, an arrival at old age, *older* takes a more relative view of aging as a continuum—older, but not yet old. As such, *older* is not just a euphemism for the blunter *old* but rather a more precise term for someone between middle and advanced age." There is official support for "older" in the Older Americans Acts (the Older Americans Act Title IV provides for, among other things, research; Older Americans Act Title V supports senior communities). See also ageism, old lady/ old man, old maid, oldster, old-timer, old woman.

old as Methuselah there is nothing wrong with this phrase, but be aware of how many such expressions are male-based. Balance them with female-based expressions, creative expressions of your own, or sex-neutral alternatives: old as the hills/as history/as time, an old chestnut. See also sex-linked expressions.

old-boys' network to keep up with changing realities in the workplace, use network, professional/career network, connections, business connections, contacts. See also old-girls' network.

old-girls' network what began as a tongue-in-cheek takeoff on the powerful and long-established old-boys' networks today functions as a valuable means of sharing information for some women. However, to keep up with changing realities in the workplace, it is often appropriate to use network, professional/career network, connections, business connections, contacts.

old lady/old man these terms have been used for generations (usually with "my") to refer disrespectfully to one's spouse, live-in partner, or parent. "Old man" has also been used to refer quasi-admiringly to one's boss or to a high-ranking male officer; "old lady" never was used this way. Note the nonparallel "lady/man." See also old woman.

old maid woman. This term invariably appears in a negative context. Unless a person's marital status is relevant, avoid even such apparently benign expressions as "unmarried woman" and "single woman"; they perpetuate the marriage-as-norm stereotype. Why have unmarried women gone from bachelor girl to spinster to old maid while unmarried men of all ages have simply been bachelors? See also bachelor, spinster.

old-maidish replace this vague term with a more precise adjective depending on your meaning: particular, fussy, finicky, fastidious, pernickety, set in one's ways, solitary, precise, old-fashioned, repressed, nervous, fearful. These adjectives can be used for both men and women and are associated with unmarried older women only insofar as they convey the inaccurate, stereotypical meaning of "old maidish."

Old Man Winter there is a long poetic tradition of making a metaphorical man of winter: "Barren winter, with his wrathful nipping cold" (Shakespeare); "Lastly came Winter ... [c]hattering his teeth" (Edmund Spenser); "winter [hath] his delights" (Thomas Campion); "Winter... [w]ears on his smiling face" (Samuel Taylor Coleridge); "O Winter, king of intimate delights" (William Cowper); "Winter ... with all his rising train" (James Thomson). There is nothing untoward in this convention, but it is useful to be aware of it. What are the implications of personifying winter, time, and death as men?

old masters since the old masters were all men, and they were masters in the Western European system of master-apprentice relationships, this term is historically correct. When not referring to painters and works known as old masters, use: distinguished/great/classic painters/paintings, the classics, 13th-/14th-/15th-/16th-/17th-century artists/works. Or use specific names and painting styles. The concept of "old masters" assumes a consensus on what constitutes great artists and artworks. "Master" and "mistress" illustrate what commonly happens to male-female word pairs: the male word takes on new and broader meanings while the female word shrinks to refer only to a woman's sexual function. Lord Beaverbrook underlined the absurdity of this word pair: "Buy Old Masters. They fetch a much better price than old mistresses." For discussion of "master" words, see master (noun).

oldster does anyone self-identify as an "oldster"? See also youngster.

Old Testament reserve this for the first of the two main divisions of the Christian bible; for the corresponding writings in Judaism, use Hebrew Scriptures/Bible. See also biblical language.

old-timer this is more of an affectionate term of respect than a negative reflection on age and people sometimes self-identify this way. Although it has a masculine cast (forever associated with the grizzled prospector of yore), it can be used of women too.

old wives' tale folk wisdom, superstitious belief/story/folklore, popular belief/folklore, common knowledge, ancestral wisdom, superstition, myth, silly myth, legend, folktale, tale, misconception.

old woman this put-down does triple duty: it insults the man being so described, makes an epithet of "woman," and is also ageist. Use instead for both sexes fussbudget, fuddy-duddy, weakling, worrywart, handwringer, worrier. See also old lady/old man.

oligarchy a government in which a few people have all the power.

ombudsman ombuds, ombud, ombudscommittee, ombudsteams, watchdog, investigator, referee, representative, surveillant, intermediary, go-between, censor, monitor, guardian of the public good, regulatory agent, protective services, complaints investigator, troubleshooter. The Swedish word is inclusive—the "man" means "one"—but its English use is not. University campuses now have Student Ombuds Services and at least one large metropolitan area has an ombudscop program under which police officers respond to neighborhood concerns.

one man, one vote one person/citizen/member/legislator/voter, one vote, one vote per voter/person/citizen/member/legislator.

one-man/two-man/three-man, etc. (adjective) one-person, or substitutes such as two-seater boat, two-way mayoral race, three-person tent, three-way contest, four-passenger plane. Or use a noun: two-seater, tent for two. For "one-man" try: individual, lone, solo, singlehanded, solitary. For two-man/three-man block use double/triple block. Terms like twelve-man jury can use twelve-member jury. Alternatives for "one-man show" include: one-person/solo/individual/single-artist show/exhibition/exhibit/performance. As there is no parallel nonsexist phrase for "one-man band," use one-woman band or one-man band.

one of the boys one of the gang, a regular person.

one small step for man, one giant leap for mankind unless quoting Neil Armstrong, use one small step for a human being, one giant leap for the world/human race.

oneupmanship one-upping, oneupness, the art of one-upping, one-uppance, going one better, keeping a jump ahead, getting the jump on, trying to get the best of, competitiveness, competition, competitive skill, rivalry, outdoing someone, quest for superiority, keeping up with the Joneses, vying for top honors. Stephen Potter, who popularized "oneupmanship" with his book *One-Upmanship,* used "one-upping" and "oneupness" in the same book. With use, the shorter and punchier "one-upping" quickly begins to sound "right": "Keeping score of old scores and scars, getting even and one-upping, always makes you less than you are" (Malcolm Forbes).

openly lesbian/gay "openly" is acceptable in referring to someone who self-identifies as lesbian or gay in public and/or professional life. See also admitted/avowed homosexual, coming out, outing.

Operation Iraqi Freedom the official name of the war on Iraq, it was initially called Operation Iraqi Liberation until someone realized that the acronym would be OIL. See also oil, war, war of liberation.

opportunity scholarship check carefully as all manner of scholarships fly under this bird's wings, including educational vouchers to allow white flight.

opposite sex this phrase is sometimes used coyly in sexist contexts. It also perpetuates an unnecessarily adversarial attitude between women and men. Dorothy L. Sayers wonders why it has to be the "opposite" sex; why not the "neighboring" sex? See also battle of the sexes.

opting out in "The Opt-Out Revolution" (*New York Times Magazine*), Lisa Belkin wondered why more career women don't get to the top. Her answer? "They choose not to." Belkin's essay about herself and eight other Princeton grads who no longer work full-time concluded that well-educated women are fleeing their careers and choosing instead to stay home with their babies. But E.J. Graff ("The Opt-Out Myth," *Columbia Journalism Review*) says although the moms-go-home story is based on some kernels of truth (women *do* feel forced to choose between work and family), there is no opt-out revolution. "The U.S. has seen steady upticks in the numbers and percentages of women, including mothers, who work for wages. Economists agree that the increase in what they dryly call 'women's participation in the waged workforce' has been critical to American prosperity, demonstrably pushing up our GDP. The vast majority of contemporary families cannot get by without women's income—especially now, when upwards of 70 percent of American families with children have all adults in the work force, when 51 percent of American women live without a husband, and when many women can expect to live into their eighties and beyond. ... Census numbers show no increase in mothers exiting the work force."

orderly nursing/nurse assistant, N.A. Aides and orderlies traditionally did the same work, but all aides were women and all orderlies were men. Most hospitals and nursing homes now use the inclusive terms.

organization man "One of the interesting changes that has taken place in today's business climate is that many organization 'men' are now women" (Don Ethan Miller, *The Book of Jargon*). Until a more compact, inclusive term appears, use organization woman/women and organization man/men. Although they don't carry quite the same meaning, you could also consider team player, loyal employee. See also company man.

Oriental Asian, Asian American. Or be specific: Japanese, Vietnamese, Korean, Chinese. The word "Oriental" (created from our perspective) has been used for generations in the U.S. with increasingly negative connotations and is unacceptable when used for individuals. (Rugs, art, and objets d'art may be described as Oriental.) The Chinese Exclusion Act (1882) and the internment of Japanese-Americans during World War II left scars for Asian Americans; the language shouldn't perpetuate the "otherness" implied in "Oriental."

outcall service prostitution business. See also prostitute.

outdoorsman nature-lover, outdoors enthusiast/person, fresh-air lover/type, fan of the great outdoors; outdoorswoman and outdoorsman. Or be specific: hunter, camper, fisher, hiker, birdwatcher, canoer, mountain climber. See also fisherman.

outing compared to coming out, which is the choice to acknowledge one's sexuality to oneself and to others, outing is an aggressive act, informing the public that a person is lesbian or gay despite that person's desire to keep the information private. Although there have been some impassioned defenses of outing, most lesbian and gay political groups oppose outing and support the right to privacy. Sexual orientation is nobody else's business, they say, and individuals have the right to "come out" (if they do) in their own idiosyncratic time, place, and manner. Outing, on the other hand, is a controlling, violent, and dominating act. Dragging unwilling victims to the sacrificial table went out of style a long time ago. People are also outed in another way; as novelist Bruce Benderson writes, "You could hide in the closet from your family, you could hide in the closet from your bosses, but you could not hide in the closet from the virus. AIDS is outing." See also coming out.

outsourcing see offshoring/outsourcing.

overdevelopment when natural resources are affected by construction, building, and development, the area is said to be overdeveloped, although there is little agreement between developers and environmentalists about the distinction between "developed" and "overdeveloped" and the extent to which the environment has to be affected before it is considered a problem.

overlord supervisor, overseer, boss. See also master.

overmaster overpower, overcome, overset, outwit, outflank, out-maneuver, defeat, conquer, vanquish, discomfit, confound. For discussion of "master" words, see master.

overmastering overpowering, overwhelming, all-powerful, irresistible, invincible, unconquerable, indomitable, unquenchable, incontestable. For discussion of "master" words, see master.

overmature trees the definition of overmature trees depends on whether you are an environmentalist, in which case you think these long-standing, healthy trees should stay right where they are, or whether you work for a lumber company or for the U.S. Forest Service, in which case you think these trees definitely need to be logged out.

overseas sometimes the correct term is foreign; "overseas" is not synonymous with "every country but us"; for example Mexico and Canada aren't "overseas markets" whereas Hawaii actually is but isn't likely to be so categorized.

oversensitive sensitive, considerate, thoughtful; thin-skinned, touchy, easily hurt. Nick Levinson points out that "oversensitive" is used to characterize uppity minority folk. It has also been used as an epithet for people working on diversity, anti-discrimination, justice, and multicultural issues. It is not clear what the opposite of "oversensitive" would be. Since even being "sensitive" is suspect, it must be "insensitive."

overweight this term implies that there is an objective, standard, "normal" weight for each person. It is also unhelpfully vague (a person could be from two to 200 pounds "overweight"). Most members of the National Association for the Advancement of Fat Acceptance dispute the term; they prefer "fat." Question the relevance of including "overweight" or rephrase your material in more meaningful terms ("He weighs more than he wants to"). See also body image, fat, looksism.

owner when referring to those who "owned" slaves use terms that do not carry the legitimacy of "ownership": slaveholder, slaveholding master, slave master. The "ownership" of human beings saw its most evil and incomparable expression in slavery. In a much different, but also harmful way, men have often felt they "owned" women, children, and, sometimes, workers. *Esquire* magazine once offered its readers a tear-out section, "Your Wife: An Owner's Manual." A number of works have documented women's treatment as property, along with the consequences, which range from petty humiliation to murder. One study of women's deaths at the hands of lovers and husbands showed that the critical moment often occurred when the woman tried to leave. Chuck Niessen-Derry, who works with batterers through an intervention project, says it's "the ultimate expression of sexism, of ownership: 'If I can't have you, nobody can.'" There is only one person entitled to an owner's manual on a woman (see The Diagram Group's *Woman's Body: An Owner's Manual*).

"ownership society" as popularized by President George W. Bush, an ownership society would restore control of their lives to the people. In addition to owning their own home, citizens would "own" their own health care, their children's education, and their retirement funds. That's right, no government oversight, regulation, or assistance. (In 2008 President Barack Obama described the ownership society as a "you're on your own" society.) When Bush said, "We're creating ... an ownership society in this country, where more Americans than ever will be able to open up their door where they live and say, welcome to my house, welcome to my piece of property," two of the unforeseen consequences of his policies toward establishing an ownership society were the housing bubble and the near collapse of the global financial system. When you see this phrase, read the fine print.

Prejudice squints when it looks,
and lies when it talks.

Laure Junot, Duchesse de Abrantés

Real, live creatures are spinning the web
of language all the time, making it as they
use it, without the slightest regard to the
formulas of professors or the precepts
of pedants.

Gamaliel Bradford

Pacific Islander this is an acceptable term to refer to a person from any of the hundreds of Pacific Islands, which lie in the middle of the Pacific Ocean in a region traditionally known as Oceania. It is always preferable, however, to be as specific as possible (New Caledonian, Fijian). Micronesia includes the Marshall Islands, the U.S. territory of Guam, and Saipan in the Mariana Islands (peoples from Guam and Saipan are collectively referred to as Chamorros); Polynesia includes the Hawaiian Islands, Cook Islands, French Polynesia, American Samoa, Western Samoa, and Tonga; Melanesia includes many countries, among them New Caledonia, Papua New Guinea, Fiji, the Solomon Islands, and New Hebrides. In the U.S., someone with Pacific Island ancestry is called Asian Pacific American. See also Asian, Asian American.

paddy wagon a derogatory shortening of "Patrick," "Paddy" is considered offensive by the Irish.

Pagan/Neopagan a "pagan" (from the Latin for a rural dweller) is usually identified by negatives; the first three definitions in the *American Heritage Dictionary* are: one who is not a Christian, Muslim, or Jew; one who has no religion; a non-Christian. The term also implies someone hedonistic, heathenish, and irreligious. Instead of the poorly understood "pagan," identify the person by the precise belief system: polytheist, animist, Buddhist, etc. Many non-Muslim, non-Jewish, and non-Christian religions are deeply spiritual. Use only when someone self-identifies as a pagan. Neopaganism is an umbrella term for religious or spiritual movements that reconstruct pagan belief systems for contemporary believers. It ranges widely from monotheism to polytheism, and some of its adherents practice a spirituality that is entirely modern in origin, while others attempt to reconstruct or revive culturally historic Pagan and indigenous belief systems. For example, the Druidic religion is based on the faith and practices of the ancient Celtic professional class; followers of Asatru adhere to the ancient, pre-Christian Norse religion; Wiccans also trace their roots back to the pre-Celtic era in Europe. Other Neo-pagans follow Hellenismos (ancient Greek religion), Religio Romana (ancient Roman religion), Kemetism (ancient Egyptian religion), and other traditions. Some Neopagans practice Neopaganism along with adherence to another faith, such as Christianity or Judaism. Some believe in a Supreme Being. Many believe in God and Goddess—a duality. Many believe there are countless spirit beings, gods and goddesses, in the cosmos and within all of nature—God is all and within all; all are one God. The Great Mother Earth, or Mother Nature, is highly worshiped. No human incarnations are worshiped in particular, as all of nature and the universe are considered embodiments of God and Goddess, worthy of respect and reverence. Paganism and Neopaganism have nothing to do with Satanism. As more Neopagans have gone public with their faith, more non-Pagans have realized the benign nature of Neopagan religious traditions; opposition by religious conservatives has lessened. Many Wiccans and other Neopagans refer to themselves simply as "Pagans." Because the word has many different meanings—some quite negative—the term "Neopagan" is less ambiguous. But call people what they want to be called.

pal from the Romany for "brother" or "friend," "pal" is more often used of boys/men, but is also correctly used of girls/women.

paladin historically a man; for an outstanding champion of a cause, a paladin could be either sex.

palimony this court-ordered allowance may be made to either member of a former relationship.

pallbearer woman or man.

Pandora's box the majority of our sex-linked metaphors, expressions, and figures are male-based; female-based ones, like this one, are often negative. However, the familiar and evocative "Pandora's box" is probably the best choice for this meaning. If you need sex-neutral alternatives, consider opening a can of worms, the curiosity that killed the cat, unforeseen consequences, the unknown, mischief, the ills that flesh is heir to, machinations of the devil, all hell breaking loose.

pansy see homophobia.

Papago Tribe Tohono O'odham Nation. The Tohono O'odham people reside primarily in the Sonoran Desert of the southwest U.S. and northwest Mexico. "Tohono O'odham" means "People of the Desert" whereas the rejected name was given to them by conquistadores who heard their enemies calling them "Papago" ("tepary-bean eater").

paperboy newspaper/paper carrier/deliverer, news carrier, newspaper vendor; paperboy and papergirl (if sex-specificity is necessary and if the carriers are under the age of thirteen or fourteen).

Papist derogatory term for Roman Catholics.

papoose this is unacceptable when used by non-Indians.

paramour woman or man.

paraplegic someone with/who has paraplegia. If necessary to mention a disability (and it often isn't), information can be conveyed neutrally without labeling the whole person by something that is only part of their life. Paraplegia is a complete paralysis of the lower half of the body. See "people first" rule. See also disabilities, hemiplegic, quadriplegic.

parent (noun) three recommendations: (1) use "fathers and mothers" or "mothers and fathers" rather than the inclusive "parents," in order to make both sexes visible. (2) Do not assume "parent" translates to "mother"; mail on infant care is addressed "Dear Mother" and an ad for an adhesive tape makes "diapering so easy, even Dad can do it." While the reality is that more women than men are active parents, it is also a reality that many more men than before are becoming involved in parenting and should be given the name as well as the game. A step in the right direction: some stores now have diaper-changing counters in both the men's and the women's restrooms. (3) When working with children, do not assume that the child lives with both parents; many children live with only one parent, with a parent and stepparent, with a guardian, with grandparents, in a foster home, or with two parents of the same sex. Teacher David Salmela asks his elementary-school pupils to take notes home to "the adults" at their house. See also babysitter, mother and father.

parent (verb) "to mother" a child is very different from "to father" a child, which is why "to parent" is so useful.

parlormaid servant. See also cleaning lady/cleaning woman, maid/maidservant.

parson depending on the denomination, this may be either sex.

"partial-birth abortion" emergency abortion, late-term removal of a non-viable fetus, intact dilation and extraction (term used by the American College of Obstetrics and Gynecology), dilation and evacuation. "Partial-birth abortion" is not a medical term, but a highly biasing phrase coined by abortion opponents. No medical procedure known as "partial-birth abortion" exists. If it is necessary to use "partial birth" as part of the title of legislation, it should be preceded by "so-called." See also abortion.

partner this word is used by many lesbian, gay, and unmarried heterosexual couples to denote the person with whom they are living or to whom they are romantically attached. "Partner" may suggest a business association, but until a better word is found, it is one of the more useful possibilities available today. Other terms in use are companion, long-time companion, and lover. See also boyfriend, girlfriend.

pasha retain as a male term in the context of Turkish or North African political life. However, there is nothing to say you can't use "pasha" metaphorically to describe a powerful or high-ranking official of either sex.

pastor depending on the particular denomination, a pastor may be either sex.

pater/paterfamilias acceptable sex-specific terms, although the Latin is more often replaced with "father/patriarch." The original paterfamilias, head of the clan, tribe, or family, had unlimited power over his wives, concubines, children, slaves, servants, animals, and property. At times, his power extended even to deciding who would live and who would die (girl children, for example, or disobedient wives and slaves). Be sensitive to the history and legacy of this concept when using these terms. See also mater/materfamilias.

paternal unless you mean fatherlike or father-related ("paternal grand-mother"), use parental, ancestral; kindly, kindhearted, loving, nurturing, devoted, indulgent, solicitous, concerned, fond, protective, sympathetic. "Paternal" has been overused, and often the paternal verges on the patronizing.

paternalism (pseudogeneric) parentalism, authoritarian parentalism, authoritarianism, protectionism, political intrusion/intervention, benevolent despotism. "Paternalism" is entrenched in certain academic, philosophic, and political circles, and is difficult (but not impossible) to replace with a commonly recognized one-word term. The concept of paternalism resonates negatively with many women and minorities; paternalistic societies, laws, churches, and husbands have been a fact of life throughout history. Former U.S. Supreme Court Justice William Brennan said, "Our nation has had a long and unfortunate history of sex discrimination ... rationalized by an attitude of 'romantic paternalism' which, in practical effect, put women not on a pedestal, but in a cage." See also chivalry.

patient use "patient" only if the person is under a doctor's care or has a disease that requires such care. "For the 43 million people now designated as having a physical, mental, or biological disability, only a tiny proportion are continually resident in and under medical supervision and are thus truly patients" (Irving Kenneth Zola, in Mark Nagler, *Perspectives on Disability*). The *Publication Manual of the American Psychological Association*, 4th ed., says to reconsider such terms as patient management and patient placement; "In most cases, it is treatment, not patients, that is managed; some alternatives are 'coordination of care,' 'supportive services,' 'assistance.'" See also case, disabilities.

patient as Job there is nothing wrong with using this phrase, but be aware of how many such expressions are male-based. Balance their use with female-based expressions, creative expressions of your own, or sex-neutral alternatives: long-suffering, stoic, forbearing, uncomplaining, longanimous, abiding, patient, extraordinarily patient, patient as the grave, through fire and water, keeping the faith. See also sex-linked expressions.

patient bias called one of medicine's open secrets, the refusal of some patients to be treated by medical personnel of another race is being highlighted by several recent lawsuits. In one case, a white man with a swastika tattoo insisted that black nurses not touch his newborn. Although the ethics code of the American Medical Association prohibits doctors from refusing to treat people based on race, gender, and other factors, there are no policies on race-based requests from patients. (Some patients severely traumatized by rape or combat might reasonably need caregivers who did not aggravate their condition.)

patient dumping the inappropriate or premature discharge or transfer of patients, mostly poor people and seniors, to other facilities, homeless shelters, or the streets for economic reasons. In one instance, a Nevada state psychiatric hospital unsafely discharged a homeless man who was given a Greyhound bus ticket to Sacramento where he knew no one and where he had never been before. A 63-year-old homeless woman, found wandering near Los Angeles' Skid Row dressed only in a hospital gown and diaper, had been put in a taxi by the hospital and dropped off there. The 1986 Emergency Medical Treatment and Active

Labor Act (EMTALA, a part of COBRA) governs when and how patients may be refused treatment or transferred from one hospital to another when in an unstable medical condition. Unfortunately, the practice continues to put uninsured Americans at risk, according to a national team of researchers led by a professor at the George Washington School of Public Health and Health Services (*Health Affairs*, 2012).

patriarchy "the basic principle of all major relationship systems in the western world" (Sandra M. Schneiders, *Women and the Word*), patriarchy refers to a hierarchical system (that is, exercising power over subordinates) where some men, and virtually no women, have controlled social, political, religious, military, and other prominent institutions. Schneiders, theologian Rosemary Ruether, former president of the World Council of Churches Willem Visser't Hooft, and others say that the patriarchy principle supports racism, colonialism, ageism, classism, and clericalism as well as sexism. While it is true that "dominator models of society" (Riane Eisler, *The Chalice and the Blade*) have been established and maintained almost entirely by men, it was not their maleness that was destructive and oppressive as much as their hierarchicalness and their abuse of power. In addition, not all men were involved in the dominator system; many of them, especially those who did not conform, suffered under it. It is entirely possible to be a father (patriarch) without being oppressive. The opposite of a patriarchy is not a matriarchy as both matriarchies and patriarchies involve an imbalance of power between the sexes; the true opposite of a matriarchy or a patriarchy is a partnership society. True or false: "A patriarchal state is one rehabilitating from war, presently at war, or preparing for war" (Berit Ås, in Robin Morgan, *The Word of a Woman*). To clarify contemporary systems of oppression, replace "patriarchy" with: dominator system/society, dominator model of society, hierarchy, hierarchical/authoritarian society (the first two terms from Eisler). Until neither sex needs to dominate the other, use "matriarchy/patriarchy" terms cautiously. Sex-neutral alternatives for "patriarch" include ancestor/family elder, head of the family, family head. The word "patricentric" puts the father at the center of the family or system without the hierarchical overtones of "patriarchal." See also chivalry, hierarchy/hierarchical thinking, matriarch/matriarchy, paternalism, sexism.

patrician this word shares the same Latin root (*pater*) as other "father" words and there is no parallel "matrician." It is not functionally sexist, but it tends to be classist and you may sometimes want alternatives for the adjective: elegant, well-bred, formal, stately, graceful, courtly, debonair, delicate, decorous, majestic, exquisite, polite, seemly, refined, genteel, cultivated, urbane, sophisticated, worldly, stylish, cosmopolitan, classy. The best alternative for the noun is aristocrat, although we tend not to use "patrician" in that sense, perhaps because of our democratic underpinnings.

patricide accurate sex-specific word. Inclusive alternative: parricide.

patrilineal refers to descent through the father's line; its word pair is "matrilineal."

patrimony inheritance, estate, family estate, birthright, legacy, bequest, succession, inherited property, heirship, heritage, endowment, portion, share, lot. Note the nonparallel "patrimony/matrimony."

patriot/patriotic/patriotism from Latin for "land of my father," these terms function today as inclusive words, although their connection to "father" words (patriarchy, paternalism, patrimony, patronizing) tends to emphasize the male-dominated, hierarchical, war-prone elements of our country. George Lakoff (*Thinking Points*) describes two ways of viewing patriotism. Conservatives believe that patriots "do not question the president or his war policies. To do so undermines our nation and its troops. Revealing secret, even illegal, government programs is treasonous. The Constitution should be amended to criminalize political dissent in the form of flag desecration." Liberals believe that the "greatest testament to one's love of country is when one works to improve it. This includes principled dissent against policies one disagrees with and against leaders who promote those policies. Times of war are no exception. Our first loyalty is to the principles of our democracy that are embedded in our Constitution, not to any political leader." In general, conservatives tend to be loyal to their leaders (president, other conservatives), where liberals tend to be loyal to the Constitution and the Bill of Rights. Loyalty, not love, motivates the patriot. "Because the term carries a generally positive connotation, it is susceptible to misappropriation for propagandistic purposes. Political elites and the manufacturers of consent for their rule are wont to use the idea to characterize thoughts, deeds, and even persons that they favor; and to describe what they want to disparage as unpatriotic" (Andrew Levine, *Political Keywords*). If you need an alternative for "patriotic" without sex-linked roots, consider civic-minded, public spirited, nationalistic, loyal.

Patriot Act the Uniting and Strengthening America by Providing Appropriate Tools Required to Intercept and Obstruct Terrorism Act of 2001, also known as the USA PATRIOT Act (the first initials of the long title give you this acronym) or simply the Patriot Act, actually threatens fundamental freedoms, according to the American Civil Liberties Union (ACLU). The Act gives the government the power to access our email and telephone communications, medical records, tax records, information about the books we buy or borrow without probable cause, and the power to break into our homes and conduct secret searches without telling us for weeks, months, or indefinitely. The Act also expanded the definition of terrorism to include "domestic terrorism," thus enlarging the number of activities to which the Patriot Act's expanded law enforcement powers can be applied. Some people think we need this Act, but the government already has the authority to prosecute anyone whom it has probable cause to believe has committed or is planning to commit a crime and already has the authority to engage in surveillance of anyone whom it has probable cause to believe is a foreign power or spy—whether or not the person is suspected of any crime. Other people feel that the government uses these powers in our best interests and would never abuse them, but the secrecy clauses of the Act mean that we can't really know how the Act is being used. The ACLU says flatly, "The little information that we do have suggests that the FBI is abusing its powers." In addition, federal courts have ruled that a number of the Act's provisions are unconstitutional. For example, in violation of the Fourth Amendment, the FBI need not show probable cause, nor even reasonable grounds to believe, that the person whose records it seeks is engaged in criminal activity; the FBI need not have any suspicion that the subject of the investigation is a foreign power or agent of a foreign power. Those who are the subjects of an FBI surveillance are never notified that their privacy has been compromised. In short, the Patriot Act is unnecessary and unconstitutional. Its main goal is to increase governmental powers at the expensive of the citizenry, something the Framers worked very hard to avoid.

Patriot Movement composed of present and former members of law enforcement and the military, the anti-government Patriot Movement has grown from 149 Patriot organizations in 2008 to 1,360 groups in 2012 (Southern Poverty Law Center's *Intelligence Report*, 2013). Of these, 321 are militias. Before the first wave of the Patriot movement died down at the end of the 1990s, law enforcement officials had broken up scores of terrorist plots aimed at the government and others. The current resurgence is fueled by hatred of gun control, the election of "the liberal traitor" President Obama, and the economy. A report from the Combating Terrorism Center at West Point, "Challengers from the Sidelines: Understanding America's Violent Far-Right" shows that violence by far-right groups and individuals is increasing every year. At the same time, the Department of Homeland Security gutted its non-Islamic domestic terrorist unit after unjustified criticism from the political right; it needs to rebuild its intelligence capabilities to monitor these growing and increasingly active groups.

patrolman patrol/highway/law enforcement/peace/police/traffic officer, patroller, state trooper, trooper, officer, police.

patron both women and men are patrons today, and the word functions fairly inclusively, but it comes from the Latin for "father," it has been used more of men than of women, it is part of the exceedingly non-parallel word pair "matron/patron," and it has some fairly sexist relatives ("patronage," "patronize," "patronymic"). For those reasons, you may want alternatives: benefactor, sponsor, backer, donor, supporter, promoter, philanthropist, booster, champion, partisan, angel, guardian angel, bankroll, advocate, mentor, helper, protector; library user, customer, shopper, buyer, purchaser, subscriber, client. See also matron.

patronage from the Latin for "father," this term has no female partner ("matronage"), is closely related to "patronize," and reflects centuries of "father"-inspired domination. These associations may inspire you to consider alternatives: sponsorship, support, auspices, advocacy, defense, championship, assistance, encouragement, promotion, protection, influence; business, trade, custom, customers, clientele, commerce, shopping, trading. See also patron.

patroness patron. "Patron" may not always be the word of choice, but it is far better than "patroness." See also "feminine" word endings, patron.

patronize "patronize" has highly sexist roots and associations (for example, what some men did to some women for so long, but rarely vice versa) and can be easily replaced: support, favor, uphold, promote, defend, sponsor, show favor to, defer to, tolerate; condescend to, treat condescendingly, underestimate, disparage, discount, look down on, talk down to, deign, stoop, be overbearing/arrogant; trade with, buy/purchase from, do business with, give business to, shop at, frequent. See also patron.

patronizing condescending, scornful, supercilious, overbearing, snobbish, superior-acting, offensive, humiliating, haughty, presumptuous, insulting, insolent. See also patronize.

patron saint namesake/guardian saint, special saint (for example, "Saint Appollonia, special saint of dentists"). See also patron.

patronym/patronymic referring to a name derived from the father or a paternal ancestor, these are correct sex-specific terms. If you mean the term in the generic sense, use surname, last name, birth name. Author Una Stannard believes that giving children their fathers' surnames sprang from ignorance about the facts of life. Before the female ovum was discovered in 1827, people assumed that men contributed the seed of life while women's wombs simply provided the soil in which it grew. "Since the female role in generation was thought to be negligible, it seemed only logical that children would receive their names from their fathers, seen as their sole progenitors." See also hyphenated names, matronym/matronymic, surname.

patsy the origins of this word do not appear sex-linked and it is not perceived as particularly gender-specific. For a more neutral-appearing term, use scapegoat, goat, loser, born loser, dupe, nebbish, victim, mark, target, laughingstock, sad sack, doormat, sap, hard-luck story, pigeon, pushover, fool. See also fall guy, whipping boy.

pay equity see comparable worth, equal pay.

paymaster payroll agent/supervisor/manager, financial officer, treasurer, bursar, purser, receiver, accountant, cashier, teller, bookkeeper, controller, comptroller, steward.

Peacekeeper/peacekeeper the Peacekeeper is a four-stage intercontinental ballistic missile (ICBM) that can target, with supposedly greater accuracy than any other ballistic missile, up to 10 cities with atomic bombs. "Its design combines advanced technology in fuels, guidance, nozzle design, and motor construction with protection against the hostile nuclear environment associated with land-based systems. The Peacekeeper is much larger than the Minuteman, over 70 feet long and weighing 198,000 pounds" (Federation of American Scientists). A "peacekeeper" is also a member of an occupying force of soldiers, different from traditional soldiers in that they use minimal force, distribute humanitarian aid, and on rare occasions take offensive action; they are generally viewed as an impartial third-party force with no stake in the conflict, except in maintaining peace. The U.N. peacekeepers familiarly known as "blue helmets," comprise soldiers, military officers, police, and civilian personnel from many countries who monitor and observe peace processes in post-conflict situations and assist conflicting parties to implement their peace agreement. Women represent 3% of the military personnel, 9% of police officers, and 30% of civilian staff. The original intent of the U.S. peacekeeping organization is laudable, and they have done much good around the world. However, the U.N. is presently dealing with multiple and egregious incidents of sexual exploitation and abuse by "blue helmets" in Sudan, Somalia, Morocco, Congo, Darfur, Liberia, Bangladesh, Burundi, and Haiti. According to Colum Lynch (*Washington Post*), "Some U.N. officials and outside observers say there have been cases of abuse in almost every U.N. mission, including operations in Ivory Coast, Sierra Leone, and Kosovo."

peace movement the peace movement is oriented toward ending a particular war as well as working toward eliminating all wars through education, conflict resolution, diplomacy, boycotts, moral purchasing, and supporting anti-war candidates. Using nonviolent resistance, the principles of pacifism, demonstrations, and political lobbying groups to create legislation, the movement shares the common goals of peace and sustainability, but loosely encompasses scores of groups with motivations as diverse as humanism, nationalism, environmentalism, anti-racism, anti-sexism, decentralization, ideology, and theology. One of the most difficult issues for peacemakers is conveying an image of "peace." Say "war," and everyone can visualize it. Say "peace" and what happens? Usually nothing. Peace is more than "not war," and until peace is visualized as a concrete good it will probably not be a priority for most of us. See also anti-war activist/protester, military language.

peace on earth, good will to men peace on earth, good will to all/all God's creations/all God's children.

peach see food names for people.

peacock/peafowl/peahen use the generic "peafowl" instead of the male "peacock" when referring to both males and females.

Peck's bad boy enfant terrible, in the avant garde, innovative/unorthodox/unconventional/nonconforming director/artist/musician, etc., heretic (in nonreligious sense), questioner; embarrassment; mischievous child. See also enfant terrible.

pederast child molester/abuser, habitual child molester. The Greek root word means either "child" or "boy," but "pederast" is defined today as a man (usually someone over age 18) who uses boys (usually under age 16) as sex objects, and thus is sex-linked; there is no parallel for women/girls. Pederasts are not gay, as such; they are unlikely to form relationships with men of their own age (Matthew Windibank). Alternatives are given not to provide inclusive terms but to make clear exactly what a pederast does. See also pedophile.

pedestal human beings were never meant to be put on pedestals—question all pedestals. "As a general rule, when something gets elevated to apple-pie status in the hierarchy of American values, you have to suspect that its actual *monetary* value is skidding toward zero. Take motherhood: nobody ever thought of putting it on a moral pedestal until some brash feminists pointed out, about a century ago, that the pay is lousy and the career ladder nonexistent. Same thing with work: would we be so reverent about the 'work ethic' if it wasn't for the fact that the average working stiff's hourly pay is shrinking, year by year" (Barbara Ehrenreich, *The Worst Years of Our Lives*). "Writers are hoisted up onto a pedestal only to scrutinize them more closely and conclude that it was a mistake to put them up there in the first place" (Simone de Beauvoir, *Force of Circumstance*). See also chivalry.

pedophile child molester/abuser, habitual child molester. "Pedophile" is not sexist per se, but it is often associated with men since they are the principal abusers. Use alternatives because they appear more inclusive, but, more important, they do not dress up an ugly practice with a fancy name. Child molesters are generally men attracted to prepubescent boys and girls; most abusers identify as heterosexuals (Matthew Windibank). See also pederast.

peeping Tom this term is based on the legendary tailor who tried to get a look at Lady Godiva as she rode naked through the streets of Coventry. The contemporary male peeper is not, however, the harmless voyeur he has been thought to be: statistics indicate that such individuals are usually involved or will be involved in more harmful deviant behavior including rape and other sex crimes. Avoid treating this offender lightly or humorously.

peeress peer. See also "feminine" word endings.

Peking man early human, Peking fossil, Homo erectus.

penman writer, author, scribe, calligrapher.

penwoman writer, author, scribe, calligrapher. But note the National League of American Penwomen, an organization of professional women writers and editors.

penmanship handwriting, writing, longhand, hand, script, calligraphy, manuscript.

"people first" rule Haim Ginott taught us that labels are disabling; intuitively most of us recognize this and resist being labeled. The disability rights movement originated the "people-first" rule, which says we don't call someone a "diabetic" but rather "a person with diabetes." Saying someone is "an HIV/AIDS victim" reduces the person to a disease, a label, a statistic; use instead "a person with/who has/who is living with HIV/AIDS." Instead of "crack babies," use "babies addicted to crack." The 1990 Americans with Disabilities Act is a good example of correct wording. The "people first" rule is useful not only in speaking and writing of those with disabilities. Readers of a magazine aimed at an older audience were asked what they wanted to be called (elderly? Senior citizens? Seniors? Golden agers?). They rejected all the labels; one said, "How about just *people*?" When high school students objected to labels like kids, teens, teenagers, youth, adolescents, or juveniles, and were asked what they *would* like to be called, they said, "Could we just be people?" Name the person as a person first, and let qualifiers (age, sex, disability, ethnicity) follow, but (and this is crucial) only if they are relevant. See also disabilities, handicappism, victim.

people of faith this phrase "became popular about 25 years ago as an ostensibly inclusive way of referring to believers of all creeds and religions, about a decade after 'people of color' was revived as an inclusive term for nonwhites. The phrase was actually introduced out of a New-Agey aversion to identifying with organized religions, but it soon caught on among conservative Christians who saw the advantages of comparing themselves to other oppressed groups," says Geoffrey Nunberg (*Talking Right*). "And *of faith*, like *of color*, was soon spun off as a suffix, so that you see references to 'journalists of faith,' 'physicians of faith,' and 'Texans of faith,' usually with the implication that those people are conservative Christians."

people of color/person of color these terms are acceptable when groups or individuals self-identify this way; when used to label others from without, it is problematic, masking people's individuality and diverse origins, and functioning like the ethnocentric "nonwhite." Elizam Escobar (in *Prison Legal News*) wonders if everybody doesn't have some color; "'people of color' has this fastidious 'picturesque' element so familiar to the vocabulary of tourism. It sounds like a color Polaroid photograph of 'nice' and 'cute' people; innocent, inoffensive, and domesticated people, where everyone is homogenized with this attribute of color. And who is this photographer who has so carefully taken this picture? A 'white' tourist with 'good intentions?' Or, in fact, is no one to be blamed but ideology itself?" On the other hand, the *American Heritage Book of English Usage* points out that "*person of color* stands *nonwhite* on its head, substituting a positive for a negative."

perky/pert "No more stories describing women athletes or other women as 'perky,' please. It is demeaning" (Nancy Greiner). A similar caution might be applied to "pert." When have you heard a boy or a man described as perky or pert? See also coed, feisty.

perpetrator "The words 'perpetrator' and 'male' are used interchangeably" (William Betcher and William Pollack, *In a Time of Fallen Heroes*). Alternatives, like "criminal" or "rapist" or "assailant," are also heard as male. While certainly not all perpetrators are men, there is statistical support for the idea that perpetrators are mainly men, making it difficult to deal with this on the level of language. See also bad guy.

person/person-/-person not sexist; the Latin *persona* means "human being." In the plural, "people" is preferred to "persons." Women-Are-Persons-Too Department: in 1988, a federal judge ruled against the U.S. Department of Agriculture, which claimed that a farm couple was only one person. Although a father and his son or a brother and a sister farming in partnership were regarded as two people, a husband and wife were counted as only one person for USDA purposes. U.S. District Court Judge Joyce Hens Green officially rejected "the archaic notion that husbands and wives are one 'person.'" For years, African Americans were designated "nonpersons" in order to maintain the institution of slavery. Although using "person" as a suffix has been helpful in making the transition to inclusive language, it should be avoided whenever possible; it is awkward, contrived, unnecessary, and not always neutral. Except for "personhood," "person-" has been used as a prefix only by those who were making up words ("personhole cover") to make fun of nonsexist language. According to a story contributed by M. Larson in *Reader's Digest*, when a male college friend said he was a freshperson, a puzzled bystander interrupted: "A freshperson? But I thought only women were 'persons.'" See also Writing Guidelines for a discussion of -man, -person, and -woman.

persona grata/persona non grata man or woman.

personal accounts for a time called "private accounts" (until the second Bush administration realized "personal" sold better to the citizenry than "private"), these accounts were suggested as a "reform" to Social Security. People would essentially save and manage their own retirement funds (probably investing them in the stock market), thus freeing the government from repaying or fixing Social Security. But, as the *Washington Post* pointed out, they "would transfer investment uncertainty to individuals, the poorest of whom may arguably be ill-placed to shoulder it. It would transfer resources out of the traditional Social Security program, which is attractively progressive." *Business Week* said, "President Bush and other free-market advocates are suggesting the most sweeping change to this core social program since its inception, based on a simple premise: Let the stock market help fix it."

personal injury lawyer trial lawyer. "Wordsmiths who supply Republicans with terms designed to prejudice the listener suggested using 'personal injury lawyer' rather than the less emotion-charged 'trial lawyer' when referring to the 2004 Democratic vice-presidential candidate John Edwards" (Paul Wasserman and Don Hausrath, *Weasel Words*). Frank Luntz, conservative wordsmith, goes further and advises Republicans to add "predatory" to the term. See also tort reform.

personal is political, the this phrase "pointed out how politics permeated everyday life. It also prescribed how actions in everyday life were important in challenging structural power relations" (Patricia Hill Collins, *Fighting Words*). Robin Morgan (*Saturday's Child*) said the feminists first using the phrase meant that "politics is about power. That insight has genuinely altered our national consciousness ... understanding that the personal is political has helped change the way we see things, and helped change the rules. By the way, the political is also personal."

"person first" rule see "people first" rule.

person of color see people of color.

persons people, individuals. Although "persons" is an acceptable plural, it's avoided in general prose: "Its use should be restricted to certain fixed phrases (such as 'persons unknown' and 'missing persons') and to specific numbers in restricted contexts ('capacity: 120 persons'). 'Persons' can also be used in official references to small numbers ('The death toll stands at nine persons') or precise numbers ('The number of persons who held more than one job...') but even these uses are often considered overly formal outside official documents" (*Copy Editor*).

pervert defined as one who practices a sexual act considered abnormal or deviant, "pervert" has most often been used to derogate lesbian, gay, bisexual, and transgender individuals. According to the Gay & Lesbian Alliance Against Defamation, "the notion that being gay, lesbian, or bisexual is a psychological disorder was discredited by the American Psychological Association and the American Psychiatric Association in the 1970s." GLAAD suggests that if the word "pervert" must be used, the speaker should be quoted directly in a way that reveals their bias.

pet although the word "pet" is seen and heard more frequently, many people prefer "companion animal" (the term of choice for years for groups such as the Humane Society of the United States and the American Society for the Prevention of Cruelty to Animals) or "animal companion." Instead of owner/master, recommended terms are caretaker, guardian, steward. When writing about animals, you might want to alternate terms between the familiar and the preferred. See also speciesism.

Peter principle/Paula principle in his 1968 book, *The Peter Principle*, Laurence Peter formulated the notion that in a hierarchy every employee tends to rise to their level of incompetence. In 1986, Elizabeth Filkin (in *The Observer*) offered the Paula principle, that is, that women stay below their level of competence because they aren't adequately promoted.

petite this is used only of women, and its masculine companion, "petit," has a rather important and meaningful life in the legal world—an example of yet another female-male word pair that bit the dust. If size is relevant, use inclusive terms: small, tiny, miniature, pint-sized, teeny, short, trim, slight, slender, thin, lean.

pharaoh pharaohs were all men (the word means "king"); women married to a pharaoh or who served as regents were called queens. Christiane Desroches Noblecourt (*La femme au temps des pharaons*) notes that Egyptian women of the pharaonic periods had as many rights as men, being able to rule, teach, make their own decisions, and own property.

pharmaceutical industry conservative wordsmith Frank Luntz suggests to Republicans that they use "pharmaceutical profession" instead. It sounds better when you're paying high prices for drugs, but "pharmaceutical industry" is more accurate.

philanderer this means "lover of men" but is defined as a man who flirts with women (it may have originally referred to gay lovers). In practice, it's used for men who seem to buzz from woman to woman. Like womanizer and ladies' man, it doesn't have the negative connotations you might think it would; the "equivalents" for women are on the order of "slut." Use philanderer in balanced ways for both men and women, or replace: heartbreaker, flirt, indiscriminate lover, seducer.

philanthropic/philanthropist/philanthropy see anthropology.

Philippines this is the correct name for the country in eastern Asia. See also Filipina/Filipino/Filipin@, Pinay/Pinoy.

physically challenged/different see challenged, disabilities.

pickup (woman) this term says the woman is passive (she is "picked up") and also implies that she is the guilty party (by giving her, but not her partner, a special derogatory label). We pay lip service to the two-to-tango notion, but our language says that a man's actions are literally unremarkable while the woman's actions deserve a judgment. Eliminating words like "pickup" from the language will not eliminate the double standard, but it is a necessary part of the process.

pied piper in the fairy tale, the pied piper was a man, but the term itself is gender-free and can be used for either sex.

pig see animal names for people.

Pilgrim Fathers Pilgrims.

pillar of society/of the community "Even when women occupy professional and community positions of great solidity and centrality, they are not called pillars of society: pillars, it seems, are male. Yet no society could contrive to function for even a day without the support of women, as the Greeks seemed to recognize when they used fully draped female figures as columns or pilasters supporting the entablatures of their buildings" (Marilyn French, *Beyond Power and Morals*).

pimp by definition, a man. See also prostitute.

pink unlike blue, which can be worn by female infants, girls, and women with impunity, pink has remained largely associated with the feminine. According to European legend, girl babies were found inside pink roses (boys in blue cabbages), thus giving rise to the traditional pink-for-girls and blue-for-boys rule. And it's not over yet. The opening screen on Barbie's website pulses pink. On the other hand, pink is also used in a defiant-to-revolutionary way by the activist, peace, and social justice group CODEPINK. See also blue, sexism.

pink-collar job/worker a "pink-collar job" is a job into which a majority of salaried women are clustered—usually relatively low-paying, low-status, female-intensive occupations. About half of all employed women are found in occupations that are at least 70 percent female. For example, 90 percent of dental assistants/hygienists, 95 percent of childcare workers, 92 percent of registered nurses, 89 percent of nursing aides, 83 percent of librarians, 84 percent of teachers, 97 percent of secretaries and administrative assistants, and 75 percent of all cashiers are women. However, in the wake of the recession, there's been a shift in workplace gender patterns. More and more men are entering fields traditionally dominated by women. "These men can expect success. Men earn more than women even in female-dominated jobs. And white men in particular who enter those fields easily move up to supervisory positions, a phenomenon known as the glass escalator—as opposed to the glass ceiling that women encounter in male-dominated fields" (Shaila Dewan and Robert Gebeloff, "More Men Enter Fields Dominated by Women," *The New York Times*). See also nontraditional career/employment, secretary.

pinko coined in 1926 by *Time* magazine (from the term "parlor pink" denoting social justice activists), this term is given to those who hold moderately leftist views (to contrast with radical leftist views of the "red" variety—no doubt Communists and revolutionaries).

pin money an outdated term for an outdated concept whereby husbands gave their wives spending money (to buy pins). Use instead: pocket/mad/household/spending money, petty cash; loose change.

Pinay/Pinoy these terms for a woman or a man from the Philippines are used by Filipinos only; they are offensive when used by others. See also Filipina/Filipino/Filipin@.

pinup girl model, photographic/calendar model.

pioneer we too often incorrectly assume that all pioneers were not only male, but white.

Piraha Indians Hiaitiihi. Replace the alien ethonym for this people from the Brazilian Amazon (Pirah) with the self-preferred, authentic name.

pirate noted pirates (or buccaneers or freebooters) included Anne Bonny, Mary Read, and Grace "Gráinne" O'Malley.

pitchman sidewalk vendor/seller, barker; hawker, promoter, high-pressure seller, celebrity endorser.

pitman (industry) pit/underground miner/worker, miner.

pivotman (basketball) post/pivot player, pivot, center.

placeman political appointee, government official, bureaucrat, functionary, agent.

plainclothesman plainclothes/undercover officer/detective, detective, investigator, police officer.

Plain Language Around the world, governments and communicators are promoting, teaching, and using easy-to-understand language. "Plain English is clear, straightforward expression, using only as many words as are necessary. It is language that avoids obscurity, inflated vocabulary, and convoluted sentence construction. It is not baby talk, nor is it a simplified version of the English language. Writers of plain English let their audience concentrate on the message instead of being distracted by complicated language. They make sure that their audience understands the message easily" (Professor Robert Eagleson, Australia). New software prompts users to get rid of jargon and to substitute active verbs for passive ones, urges them to strive for specificity, eschew modifiers, and be direct. Government offices that use Plain Language relate its use to fewer telephone calls from bewildered or anxious citizens. For more information, see www.plainlanguage.gov.

plainsman plains dweller/inhabitant; plainswoman and plainsman.

Plan B (contraceptive) available over-the-counter at most pharmacies for those 17 and older (those under the age of 17 need a prescription), Plan B is billed as an emergency contraceptive for instances of contraceptive failure, unprotected sex, or rape—not as a regular means of contraception. Women are advised to call their pharmacy first because some refuse to carry Plan B. The chances of pregnancy are reduced by up to 88 percent but Plan B must be taken within five days of intercourse—and the sooner, the better.

playboy swinger, bed hopper, philanderer, mover, hustler, free spirit, flirt, libertine, seducer, high-roller, high-liver, high-flier, hedonist, fun-seeker, pleasure-lover, good-timer, sport, gadabout, party animal, dissolute/promiscuous/sexually active person, someone who sleeps around, make-out artist, lover. See also ladies' man, man about town, rake, womanizer.

playgirl/playmate centerfold, model, nude model. If you mean "playgirl" in the same way "playboy" is used, see playboy for alternatives.

"playing the race card" don't use this pejorative, assumption-heavy phrase before considering the way other cards are played, notably legacy college admissions and "connections," usually of the old boys' club variety. Anna Quindlen (in *Newsweek*) says, "The fallacy at the heart of most discussions of affirmative action is twofold: that it replaced true meritocracy, and that it means promoting the second-rate. The meritocracy theory requires us to believe that for decades no women and no people of color were as qualified as white men, who essentially had every field locked up. Belief in the ascendancy of the second-rate requires us to demean the qualifications of countless writers, jurists, doctors, academics and other professionals who gained entry and then formed superlatively. Part of the tacit deal for most of them was not that they be as good as their lackluster white male counterparts, but as good as the best of them." Supreme Court Justice Sonia Sotomayor (*My Beloved World*) has said, "I was given a chance to get to the start of the race, and it made all the difference."

pleased as Punch in the standard "Punch and Judy" show, Punch carries a stick with which he "belabors" Judy—and then bursts into screams of laughter. 'Nuff said.

pledge of allegiance when the owners of the popular children's magazine, *Youth's Companion*, were selling flags to schools, they asked Christian Socialist author and Baptist minister Francis Bellamy to write something for their advertising campaign. The result was the pledge of allegiance, which was first used in public schools in 1892. It did not have the phrase "under God" in it. On Flag Day in 1943, the Supreme Court ruled it was unconstitutional (violating the First Amendment) to oblige schoolchildren to recite the pledge and salute the flag. In 1951, the Knights of Columbus began a campaign to get Congress add the words "under God" to the pledge. Their attempts failed until one of them personally convinced President Eisenhower of the need for it; the change was passed by Congress in 1954. The Founders thought they had covered all the bases in their efforts to maintain separation of church and state; judging by their own words, not one of them would think adding "under God" was a good idea. See also separation of church and state.

plowboy/plowman plow driver/operator, farm worker, farmer, cultivator, sower.

plutocracy *The American Heritage Dictionary* defines a plutocracy as "government by the wealthy" or "a government or state in which the wealthy rule." Does this ring any bells?

PMS see premenstrual syndrome.

poetess poet. Adrienne Rich said that whenever she was introduced as a poetess, she became a terroristress. See also "feminine" word endings.

poilu this World War I French soldier was always a man, with at least one exception: Marie Marvingt, the Frenchwoman known as the Fiancée of Danger, disguised herself as a poilu and fought in the front lines for three weeks until she was discovered.

point man high-scoring player/ballplayer, high-scorer, scorer. "Point-person" is occasionally seen, but it looks awkward and self-conscious.

policeman officer, police, police/peace/law/highway/patrol/law enforcement/beat/traffic officer, officer/agent/arm of the law; policewoman and policeman. Or be specific: sergeant, detective, sheriff, chief, deputy, lieutenant, etc. In 1910, Alice Stebbins Wells was appointed to the Los Angeles Police Department. Invariably accused of using her husband's badge for the free streetcar rides offered police officers, she was issued "Policewoman's Badge No. 1."

policeman of the world watchdog/police officer of the world. "Policeman of the world" has a specific and instantly recognizable sense in some disciplines. However, with a little effort one could get used to a new expression. If one were really, really fortunate, the concept itself would fade away and one wouldn't need to worry about the phrase.

political language words are the most important tool in the service of a democratic government and its political system and they are often manipulated to make us feel, act, or vote a certain way; words are a means of controlling the public's perception of government or political initiatives. For example, the Tax Simplification Act of 1993 ran hundreds of pages with section titles like "Diminimis Exception to Passive Loss Rules." The Job Creation and Wage Enhancement Act of 1995 was actually a cost-benefit analysis to limit new regulations. A group called Northwesterners for More Fish were not intending, "as its name suggests, to protect the area's dwindling salmon populations, but to uphold the complex of hydroelectric dams on the Columbia River blamed for decimating salmon numbers" (*High Country News*). Efforts to limit welfare have been titled the Work Opportunity Act, the Personal Responsibility and Work Opportunity Act, and the Family Self-Sufficiency Act. Public Citizen called the Common Sense Product Liability Reform bill the "Death to Americans Act" because "The legislation is based on a complete set of myths and phony anecdotes about lawsuits." Being a good citizen means analyzing every word that comes from politicians, elected officials, and government representatives for the truth. It is helpful to consider: who is saying it, what do they have to gain by persuading you this way or that way, where did they obtain their information, what is being left out of the picture, and what might "the other side" say? Be aware of how political language makes you feel. Feeling optimistic, pessimistic, triumphant, hopeless, or patriotic is not a good way to judge the truth of what you hear ("That must be right because it makes me want to stand tall as an American!"). Evaluating political language needs not feeling, but thinking.

"politically correct" "There are few things more wearisome in a fairly fatiguing life than the monotonous repetition of a phrase which catches and holds the public fancy by virtue of its total lack of significance." Agnes Repplier wrote this in 1897, but surely she had some precognition of the term "political correctness" because she also wrote, in 1916, "People who pin their faith to a catchword never feel the necessity of understanding anything." The term "politically correct" is a loose term from much flabby living; its meanings run along the lines of "I hate what you're doing," "Stop it! Stop it right now!" and "For heaven's sake, why would we change anything?" Many people can no longer even identify what specifically they are decrying. Your writing and arguments will be much clearer if you drop "political correctness" altogether and state your objections: it is "bias-free language" or "multiculturalism" or "hate speech codes" or "affirmative action" or "diversity"—not "all that PC stuff." The final word perhaps belongs to Robin Morgan: "P.C. doesn't stand for Political Correctness, it stands for Plain Courtesy."

political prisoners according to U.N. investigations, as of 2010 there were more than 27,000 prisoners held by the U.S. in more than 100 secret prisons around the world and on 17 ships that serve as floating prisons. They are almost entirely Muslim prisoners. According to the Center for Constitutional Rights, 92 percent of the prisoners held just at Guantánamo are not "Al-Qaeda fighters" by the U.S. government's own definitions and records; 22 were under 18 years of age when captured. Of the 155 men who remain at Guantánamo as of January 2014, approximately half were cleared for release years ago. The vast majority will never by charged with any crime. Guantánamo remains; the only recent action was to close the office of, and eliminate the post of, special envoy to Guantánamo Daniel Fried in 2013. "Political prisoner" is correct as far as it goes, but when possible indicate when a prisoner is unlawfully or secretly held, not given due process, or has not been charged with a crime. See also detainee, extraordinary rendition, unlawful enemy combatants/unlawful combatants.

political spectrum political labels provide shorthand identifications for people, policies, and organizations, but they are grossly inadequate as to specifics, nuances, and useful information. Pair the use of a label with details of the issue under discussion. Reading from left to right is among the most commonly used descriptors: progressive, green, liberal, left, right, conservative, libertarian, reactionary, neoconservative. In general, concerns for peace, poor people, social inequities, and justice belong on the left; concerns for business, low taxes, gun ownership, and military spending belong on the right. When you see "far left" or "far right," the "far" just means "very." "Radical" is also used as an intensifier meaning "very, very, very" (radical right, radical reactionary, radical left—there is even a book about the radical middle) as well as being a noun in its own right: someone who's really "out there." "Radical" is often used to discredit otherwise modest expressions of concerns for, for example, women's most basic civil rights. It can, in fact, be used to dismiss almost anything you don't like. *CONSERVATIVE*: the word, which comes from Latin *conservare*, to keep, guard, and preserve, appeared in the late 18th century as a description of Edmund Burke's opposition to the French Revolution. "The development of society and culture depends upon a changing balance, maintained between those who innovate and those who conserve the status quo. Relentless, unchecked, and untested innovation would be a nightmare.... If repetition and rigidity are the dark side of the conservative coin, loyalty and stability are its bright side" (Judith Groch). But Brooke Allen (*Los Angeles Times*) says, "Too many people of a generally conservative temperament, people who value traditions, customs, and institutions, have been fooled by the current cynical use of the word 'conservative' into identifying their own interests with those of the political right, which today, far from being genuinely conservative, actually espouses a program of radical change." *PROGRESSIVE/LIBERAL*: since the late 1990s, "liberal" has been replaced by "progressive," possibly because the "L" word had been used so often as a pejorative (basically, "horrible people who are giving away all our tax money to deadbeats"), but they stand for approximately the same wish list of social goods. "Liberal" comes from Latin *liberalis* meaning noble, generous, and pertaining to or befitting a free individual (from Latin for "free," *liber*). To be liberal, traditionally, was to be generous and open-minded, concerned with the liberties of others, to be tolerant and free from prejudice. (In *Going Nucular*, Geoffrey Nunberg mentions right-wing talk radio shows that "start sentences with 'Liberals are ...' and go on to describe liberalism as something between a personality disorder and a market segment.") "Progressive" means favoring progress toward better conditions; progressive business leadership is, for example, a very good thing. Progressivism historically advocates the advancement of workers' rights and social justice; progressives were early proponents of anti-trust laws and the regulation of large corporations and monopolies, as well as government-funded environmentalism and the creation of National Parks and Wildlife Refuges. Liberals, as liberals, have historically worked to end slavery, institute child labor laws, fight anti-Semitism, support better working conditions, enact civil rights, establish open housing as well as openness in government, reduce military spending, allocate more money for education and good quality childcare, and protect the environment. Derivatives of the pejorative liberal include "bleeding heart liberal," "limousine liberal," "silk stocking liberal" (the last two are almost humorous if you compare net worths of conservatives to liberals), and "liberal elites" and "liberal media bias." Given that a handful of very conservative corporations own the media in the U.S., it's a marvel that they don't throw the liberal bums out. *TEA PARTY MOVEMENT*: although lacking structure, hierarchy, and a defined agenda (one main goal is to lower the national debt and federal budget deficit by reducing government spending and taxes), the Tea Party movement has made its influence felt mostly by obstructing legislation or stalling forward movement. The movement has been described as partly conservative, partly libertarian, and partly populist, so being specific when writing about it is even more important for clarity. *NEOCONSERVATIVES*: a group as small as it is scary, the neoconservatives have a blueprint for the United States that involves: empire building or world domination, whichever you prefer; gathering to themselves unlimited masses of power and money; aggressive unilateral U.S. foreign policy so that the U.S. global footprint allows us to place profitable markets wherever we choose; an unshakeable belief in their own vision and morality for the world (which needs to be democratic—their version—and Christian); a paternalistic modus operandi that undergirds their belief that elites protect democracy from mob rule; a decided belief that bombing is better than diplomacy; an unlimited and arrogant disdain for the citizenry (everyone but those in the top 1 percent of income); and an unswerving dedication to dismantling all government that does not directly serve Big Business. Naomi Klein (*The Shock Doctrine*) says they are characterized by "privatization, deregulation, and cuts to social spending—in which governments dismantle trade barriers, abandon public ownership, reduce taxes, eliminate the minimum wage, cut health and welfare spending, and privatize education." She calls this program "disaster capitalism." Conservatives may think that neoconservatives are just the "new, improved Tide of politics," but they are a whole new breed of cat. Everything that conservatives hold dear (small government, fiscal stinginess, and keeping ourselves to ourselves) has been turned on its head. After the years of Neoconservative rule, the U.S. is dangerously deep in debt, the government is reading our e-mails, wiretapping our phones, tracking our travel, decrying what's going on in our bedrooms, and invoking the "state secrets" defense to keep from telling us what else it's doing, and we've highhandedly decided to fix Iraq and are fixing to fix Iran next. Dimitri Simes of the Nixon Center, a Washington think tank, says of the neocons, "Their foreign-policy manifesto seems to be 'We're right, we're powerful, and just make my day.'" According to Michael Hirsh (*Newsweek*), the common theses for Neocons are: willingness to use military power, a tendency to group all radical Islamist groups together as a common enemy, strong support for Israel, and an aggressive posture toward Iran." They "favor the assertive use of American power abroad to spread American values." See also military language, political language.

politician the United States ranks 86th in the world in the number of women elected to public office. Not only have centuries of discrimination, invisibility, and inaccessibility hindered women from being adequately represented among legislators and public officials, but contemporary obstacles pose a continuing problem. One of them is easily remedied: media needs to change the way it presents female candidates. Name It Change It, a nonpartisan project of the Women's Media Center and She Should Run, released two new studies in 2013 showing that neutral, positive, and negative descriptions of the woman candidate's appearance all had detrimental impacts on her candidacy; her male opponent paid no price for this type of coverage. When a female candidate or a third-party responding directly by saying this coverage had no place in the media and that her appearance was not news, she regained the lost ground. Julie Burton, president of the Women's Media Center, said, "The press is part of the problem—it may be more fun to focus on a woman's shoes than her views, but this coverage has a real impact on women candidates." The test of reversibility applies here: if it wouldn't be said of a man, it shouldn't be said of a woman. (In New Hampshire in 2013, the governor and the entire congressional delegation were women; no other state has done that and many have yet to send even one woman to the Senate.)

politics makes strange bedfellows unless quoting Charles Dudley Warner, use politics makes strange bedmates.

pollution rights yes, it's true. You—well, not you, but some people—have the right to pollute. The government allows companies to pollute, but wisely limits how much they may pollute. If they are lucky enough not to use up all their pollution allowance, they may sell what's left over of their rights to a company that needs to pollute a little more than usual. "The Bush II White House continued to enlarge such rights in this pay-to-sin program invented way back in the Reagan years" (Paul Wasserman and Don Hausrath, *Weasel Words*). See also global warming.

Pollyanna if you need a sex-neutral term, consider irrepressible/eternal/persistent/unflagging/perennial/cockeyed/incurable optimist, daydreamer, romantic, visionary, castlebuilder, utopian, idealist, victim of terminal cheerfulness, one who lives in a fool's paradise, wearer of rose-colored glasses.

polyamorist someone who desires, practices, or accepts having more than one loving, intimate relationship at a time with the full knowledge and consent of everyone involved is a polyamorist. According to the Polyamory Society (www.polyamorysociety.org), polyamory emphasizes consciously choosing how many partners one is involved with rather than accepting the social norms that dictate loving only one person at a time. This bond usually, though not necessarily always, involves sex. An umbrella term, polyamory embraces sexual equality and all sexual orientations. The term is sometimes abbreviated to poly, especially as a form of self-description, and is sometimes described as consensual, responsible, ethical, or intentional non-monogamy. Polyamory is usually taken as a description of a lifestyle or relational choice and philosophy, rather than of someone's actual relationship status at a given moment.

polyandrist/polygynist correct sex-specific terms meaning, respectively, someone with more than one husband, someone with more than one wife. See also polygamist.

polyfidelity a term that originated within the Kerista Village commune in San Francisco, which practiced polyfidelity from 1971 to 1991, polyfidelity is a form of polyamorous group marriage wherein all members consider each other to be primary partners and agree to be sexual only with other members of their group. Eve Furchgott describes polyfidelity as "a new multi-adult family structure in which clusters of best friends come together around shared values, interests, life goals, and mutual attraction. Inside such a Best Friend Identity Cluster (B-FIC), family members are non-monogamous, relating to all their partners without a hierarchy of preference. Thus in a heterosexual polyfidelitous B-FIC, each of the women has a sexual relationship with each of the men, and no group member relates sexually to anyone outside the family group. While different groups might work out different methods for determining who will sleep with whom every night, the method used successfully by actual polyfides in the United States is the 'balanced rotational sleeping schedule.' This arrangement has each person sleeping with a different partner each night, sequentially (using the chronological order of when people joined the group as the sequence), until at the end of the list, at which time she/he comes back around to the first person again."

polygamist this term refers to a woman or a man who has more than one mate at the same time. We tend to use it as if it means "several wives" instead of "several mates"; the correct term for "someone who has several wives" is "polygynist." Bring a different perspective to "polygyny" and instead of one man having many wives, it could also be defined as a group of women sharing one husband (Joan Steinau Lester).

polysexual see polyamorist, polyfidelity.

pontiff so far, always a man.

pontificate although this term comes from the Latin sex-neutral word for "bridge-building," its associations with the male papacy suggest the need for alternatives in some cases: orate, declaim, hold forth, harangue, expound, wax pompous, declaim; preach, lecture, sermonize, dogmatize.

pooh-bah although the original character from the opera *The Mikado* (1885) was a man, this term can be used to describe a self-important person or pompous functionary of either sex who occupies a high position, holds several positions at once, or wields great influence.

poor when possible, be specific about the ways you mean "poor" (low income, substandard housing, illiteracy, without medical insurance). Do not use as a noun ("the poor") and make sure it's not code for "black" or other minority groups. Avoid classist assumptions about poor families' values, lives, choices, and behavior. See also criminal, poverty, "the," welfare.

popular culture sometimes abbreviated to pop culture, popular or mass culture encompasses all that entertains and brushes up against the vast majority of us every day: film, television, sports, music, books, newspapers, magazines, comic books, the Internet, consumer goods, fashion, art, dance, celebrities, advertising, toys, foods, and the next public obsession coming over the horizon. The serious study of popular culture is fairly recent, although sociologists have long found the materials with which Americans amuse themselves fascinating for what they reflect about the people and the world around them. One way for thinking individuals and progressives to keep up with the meaning of pop culture is a regular reading of the astute *Bitch: Feminist Response to Pop Culture*.

population control reproductive freedom. Also: reproductive rights/responsibility/information, birth control, contraception, family planning, fertility control. The term "population control" reveals a paternalistic, patronizing attitude toward people in general, toward peoples in non-aligned countries, and most particularly toward women. "Population control" also had racial connotations since it was perceived as being—and often was—more directed at groups and countries that were not white. The phrase "reproductive freedom" has allowed people to come together across racial lines, whether they were working for legal abortion or against coerced sterilization. The alternatives shift the emphasis to individual control. In countries in which women have reproductive rights and control their own reproductive choices, population figures decrease. See also contraception.

populist someone who professes to represent the interests of the common people against an unprincipled or self-serving elite is a populist. But every politician would like to be thought a populist long enough to get elected, so judge a populist by deeds; in our contemporary Orwellian seas, words are paper boats. A real populist—now that would be worth talking about.

pork barrel the term "pork barrel" dates to the early 1800s when meat was packed in barrels, and hungry farm hands reached in for slabs of salt pork. In 1879, it was adopted as political slang to mean goodies for the local district, paid for by the taxpayers at large. The Collins & Aikman site helpfully categorizes recent pork-barrel spending into (1) absurd projects, (2) federal spending for private concerns, and (3) presents for Congress itself. See also earmarks.

pornography "Pornography is the attempt to insult sex, to do dirt on it" (D.H. Lawrence); "It is heartless and it is mindless and it is a lie" (John McGahern); "Pornography is the undiluted essence of anti-female propaganda" (Susan Brownmiller); Susan Sontag says it drives "a wedge between one's existence as a full human being and one's existence as a sexual being—while in ordinary life one hopes to prevent such a wedge from being driven." Perhaps the most comprehensive and precise definition is a 1983 suggested civil rights ordinance written by Andrea Dworkin and Catherine MacKinnon: "Pornography is a systematic practice of exploitation and subordination based on sex that differently harms and disadvantages women. The harm of pornography includes dehumanization, psychic assault, sexual exploitation, forced sex, forced prostitution, physical injury, and social and sexual terrorism and inferiority presented as entertainment." Pornography is often associated with the rising tide of sexual and violent crime against both children and adults, the desensitization of individuals toward the horror of violence and rape, and the inability of many men to relate to women with any mutuality or respect because of their pornography-inspired but unrealistic expectations of women and of sex. Susan Griffin (*Pornography and Silence*) says pornography teaches men that sex has nothing to do with emotions. Child porn flourishes, and is even defended by a few well-organized political pressure groups (for example, the North American Man-Boy Love Association and the René Guyon Society, whose motto is "Sex by Age 8 or Else It's Too Late"). As many as one million children have been used to create the child porn in some 275 monthly magazines (Carol Gorman, *Pornography*). Addiction is also a factor. Men may buy pornography but women pay for it—in terms of exploitation, rape, violence, and a society that sees them as disposable sexual objects. Pornography associates women with pain, inferiority, and humiliation; the assumption for the user is that this is real and normal and, besides, the women seem to like it. Good sex is also a victim; a graduate of the School of Pornography is a sex-illiterate. Erotica differs from pornography in celebrating rather than degrading human sexuality; it preserves the mutuality of sexual activity, is not exploitive, controlling, objectifying, addictive, a "using" activity, or effected for prurient interests; it also does not embarrass you if you are found reading it by a friend. The differences between pornography and erotica can be seen in their Greek roots: *pornē* means female slaves or female slavery, thus pornography is the depiction of female slavery (or men in the position of female slaves); erotica derives from *erōs* and has a connotation of love, mutual pleasure, and free choice. Ann Simonton (in *Z Magazine*) says there "is a determined movement of millions of women and men nationally and internationally who are working on every level possible to help the public understand the consequences of our culture's addiction to pornographic images and to expose the fact that real people are being hurt through the making and distribution of pornography. Pornography, for many of us, is a form of hate propaganda designed to keep women subordinate to men; it is also a system of sexual exploitation for profit that targets women for rape, battery, and harassment." "In early 1991, a furor was created by the U.S. government's initial denial and later admission that bomber pilots on aircraft carriers in the Gulf were deliberately shown films of violent pornography before taking off on missions over civilian areas in Iraq" during the Persian Gulf War (Robin Morgan, *The Word of a Woman*). Gail Dines (in *Sisterhood Is Forever*) says that "it was the success of *Playboy*, followed by *Penthouse* and *Hustler*, that laid the groundwork for the current almost $60-billion-dollar-a-year industry. Today's porn videos, DVDs, and computer websites are the outcome of the legal, economic, and cultural spaces that the pornography magazines of the 1950s, '60s, and '70s created through marketing techniques they developed." As for any censorship of Internet pornography, Mike Royko wrote, "That, of course, is the traditional defense of pornographers and other creeps: If they are censored, it's just a matter of time until the rest of us will be censored. Maybe, but I've never believed it. As far as I can tell, anytime the rights of pornographers are threatened, it just makes it more difficult for pornographers to ply their grubby trade." Pornography has "been credited with helping to drive the evolution of the camera, the home-video business, cable TV, and DVDs. As the operator of a bondage website boasts, 'Technology is driven by adult entertainment ... because sex then sells the technology.' Businesses that fail to follow this strategy pay a price; entertainment analysts maintain that Sony, by refusing to license its Betamax technology to pornographers, allowed VHS to monopolize the market by the early 1980s." Interesting things to know and tell: "About 70 percent of the visits to Internet porn sites come during regular office hours" (*The Weekly Standard*). See also rape; revenge porn; sex object; trafficking, sex; violence.

poseur this grammatically masculine French word is used (in French and English) for either sex. If you need a less masculine-appearing term, try pretentious person, mannerist, lump of affectation, charlatan, quack, humbug, pedant, pedagogue, pseudo-intellectual.

postfeminism feminists—who ought to know—are not calling this a postfeminist world. Whoever could be saying these things? Writer and *Bitch* editor Rachel Fudge notes that, for one, the *New York Times* has been a contributor ever since 1982 when it "was already signaling the death knell of feminism and using the term 'postfeminist.' Postfeminism is the notion that the feminist movement has outlived its usefulness, because, after all, we have a few female senators, it's illegal to discriminate against women in job hiring, there's a women's pro basketball league, and record numbers of women are attending college. Put down your torches, gals, 'cause the struggle is over! While such sentiments do point to feminism's far-reaching success, they also tend to re-personalize the political by assigning any continuing gender-related struggles to individual circumstances. ... It pretends that everything is peachy and suggests that if, for you, it isn't, then the problem lies with you and your personal choices, not with any large systems of, oh, let's say patriarchy or capitalism or racism or classism." Lisa Jervis and Andi Zeisler (in *BITCHfest*) say, "Postfeminism is, perhaps not surprisingly, very similar to old-fashioned antifeminism. ... The term was (and still is) an insult to the legacy of feminism, an eye-rolling suggestion that we need to get over it and move on, already. But postfeminism can only exist in a postsexist world, and we're not there by a long shot." "It's a continual source of wonder: the consistency with which feminism has been wishfully declared dead at least once a month since 1968" (Robin Morgan, in *Sisterhood Is Forever*). Gloria Steinem wonders, "Would we say post-democracy?"

postman see mailman.

postmaster/postmistress retain for titles in current use; otherwise use postal chief/manager, post office supervisor/manager.

postmaster general retain for current titles; otherwise use federal postal director/chief/supervisor.

postmodern churches also known as emerging churches, these congregations defy simple definition. Wander about the Internet to read descriptions of many types of postmodern Christian churches as well as lengthy disagreements about what constitutes a postmodern church. For those congregants involved in the nontraditional creation and support of their churches, the reality is that this is a meaningful church to them.

postmodernism "A conceptual framework applied to the social world based on decentering power relations, deconstructing universal truths about the world, and recognizing multiplicity or differences of experiences and perspectives on the world" (Patricia Hill Collins, *Fighting Words*).

postracial a term that suggests we have achieved a colorblind society and that discussions of race and racism are no longer relevant. Some have deemed America "postracial" since the election of Barack Obama—the nation's first African American President—in 2008. But as race and racism continue to play a role in maintaining social and economic disparity between blacks and whites, "postracial" remains a theoretical concept. See also interracial, multiracial, nonracist, race, racism.

potentate in certain contexts today, this could be either sex; historically it was always a man.

"pound of flesh" see shylock.

poverty according to the United States Census Bureau (2013), the average poverty threshold is an annual income of $12,119 for an individual; $24,028 for a family of four. One in 6 Americans (15 percent) live in poverty. The percentages are even higher for women (17.8 percent) and children (22 percent). Research at Syracuse University and Columbia University confirms that the U.S. has the highest child poverty rate of any major Western industrialized nation. There is a sharp racial divide in the incidence of poverty; the U.S. Census Bureau reports poverty rates among African Americans, Native Americans, and Latinos at or near 27 percent for each group. "Inequality in America is greater than it's been in 50 years. In 1960, the gap in terms of wealth between the top 20 percent and the bottom 20 percent was 30-fold. Today it's more than 75-fold" (Bill Moyers). The top 1 percent earned one-fifth of the nation's household income, and the top 10 percent captured a record 48.2 percent of total earnings. Poverty is strongly linked to poor health; research has shown that low-income people typically have relatively poor outcomes for health and mortality compared to those with higher incomes. The risk of dying before the age of 65 is three times greater for those living in poverty. The 2010 Affordable Care Act (ACA) was partly designed to mitigate the consequences of poverty and inequality for health. Prior to passage of the ACA, over 50 million people were uninsured; 70 percent of this number were individuals living at or near the poverty threshold. Access to health care is a key issue for those living in poverty, and the ACA contains financial incentives for health care providers who choose to locate in areas designated as underserved. The ACA also calls for the expansion of Community Health Centers (CHCs). Currently, 8,000 CHCs serve 23 million people each year; the ACA provides funding for CHCs to serve 40 million people a year. Why haven't we won the war on poverty? Racial and gender inequality continue to hinder lives and result in higher poverty among minorities and families headed by single mothers. Also, "We've been drowning in a flood of low-wage jobs for the last 40 years. Most of the income of people in poverty comes from work. … Half the jobs in the nation pay less than $34,000 a year, according to the Economic Policy Institute. A quarter pay less than $23,000 annually. Families that can send another adult to work have done better, but single mothers (and fathers) don't have that option. Poverty among families with children headed by a single mother exceeds 40 percent" (Peter Edelman, author of *So Rich, So Poor: Why It's Hard to End Poverty in America*"). See also classism, corporate welfare, feminization of poverty, poor, war on poverty, welfare, welfare mother.

powder room restroom, washroom, lavatory, bathroom, lounge. This word is sexist in an unexpected way: the "powder" in the phrase comes from the powder men used on their wigs in colonial times, yet today the powder room, coy and exclusive, is reserved for women. See also john.

pow-wow "All too often the word 'pow-wow' is used out of context by writers. For those of us who are American Indian, a pow-wow is a dance and social gathering celebrating our traditions and cultures. It is a beautiful and powerful experience. I am offended by the coopting of the word to describe a nonspiritual dialogue between two people" (Pauline Brunette). For alternatives, consider talk, discussion, negotiation, dialogue, conversation, chat, confab, conference, parley, meeting.

prattle "prattle" and most alternatives ("babble," "jabber," etc.) are used of women and children, and rarely of men. Examine your material to see if by choosing "prattle" you are making a subtle statement about women. For more inclusive-sounding alternatives, use rattle, rattle away, ramble, blabber, blather, spout, spout off, run off at the mouth, talk nonsense, talk through one's hat, talk idly, shoot the breeze, make chin music, bend someone's ear.

prayer language prayer and liturgical language is being rendered inclusive in many temples, churches, and mosques in the U.S.; the nation's largest Jewish movement, Reform Judaism, has adopted its first new prayer book in 32 years, with four versions of each prayer so as to offer something for everyone—traditionalists, progressives, and even those who don't believe in God. Works like Marcia Falk's *The Book of Blessings* offer prayers in English and Hebrew that avoid anthropomorphisms and the language of male domination. Most Christian denominations in the U.S. have addressed sexist and racist language in their prayers, readings, and hymns. In Canada, the United Church of Canada and the Anglican Church of Canada have produced nonsexist guidelines, and the pastoral team of the Canadian Conference of Catholic Bishops has advocated a move from exclusive to inclusive language in official texts and also in the everyday language of the church.

preacher depending on the denomination, may be a woman or a man.

precision bombing see surgical strike.

pre-emptive strike "the right of self-defense has always been understood to include the possibility of preemptive self-defense. Hugo Grotius, the 17th century Dutch philosopher who laid the foundations for international law, wrote that 'it be lawful to kill him who is preparing to kill,' although he also acknowledged that this principle could be dangerous" (Joshua Muravchik, in *Los Angeles Times*). When George W. Bush said: "We will not allow the world's most dangerous regimes to threaten us with the world's most dangerous weapons," critics argued that he was advocating not pre-emption but 'preventive war.' See also military language.

"preferential treatment" the Civil Rights Act of 1964 forbid states to "discriminate against, or grant preferential treatment to, any individual or group on the basis of race, sex, color, ethnicity, or national origin" in public employment, university admissions, or contracting. The phrase "preferential treatment" has been lifted from the Act, turned around, and used against Affirmative Action programs, which, in the spirit of the Civil Rights Act, have attempted to redress centuries of discrimination. A California Affirmative Action referendum was effectively killed because the public debate was framed in terms of "preferential treatment for unqualified candidates." In their paper, "Ending Affirmative Action: Public Opinion and Media Depiction of the California Civil Rights Initiative," Marnie Rodriguez and Elaine Hall reported that "people were more supportive of affirmative action than framing of the issue would suggest." Supporters have evidently not adequately conveyed to voters that Affirmative Action is not about preferences but about promoting basic equality and fairness through such efforts as diversity-recruitment by state universities, gender-specific healthcare, training, and posting official notices in languages other than English. Companies, schools, and other organizations have not, in the past, included people in anything approaching their representations in the population; something besides self-regulation is required to ensure that there is equal access to education and work opportunities. See also affirmative action.

pregnancy nonsexist term, but sometimes found in sexist contexts. Is pregnancy treated as an illness, disability, misfortune, or inferior state of being? Is the pregnant woman assumed to be moodier and less capable than other people? Are pregnant women penalized in the workplace? Sex-neutral terms for "pregnant" in its metaphorical sense include expectant, suspenseful, waiting, teeming, meaningful, profound, momentous, ominous. Note the difference between a gestational pregnancy and a surrogacy pregnancy: in the former, the gestational carrier is not related to the fetus but carries it for a couple when the woman is unable to carry a pregnancy to term; "surrogacy pregnancy" is used less often, because it implies traditional surrogacy in which a woman is inseminated with the sperm of a man who is not her partner to conceive and carry a child for him and his partner. In this form of surrogacy, the woman gives her own genetic child to the other couple; the biologic father and partner adopt the child after birth. See also assisted reproduction, pre-pregnant.

prehistoric man prehistoric/early peoples/humans, prehumans, fossil humans. "Prehistoric" is imprecise; indicate a specific geologic period. Because history is defined as "a record of events," "prehistory" is correct because it refers not to a time before history as we commonly think of it, but to a time before recorded history.

prehominid see hominid.

prejudice in *The Nature of Prejudice*, Gordon W. Allport describes the ladder of prejudice: the first rung is speech, the second, avoidance, the third, discrimination, the fourth, physical attack, and the fifth, extermination. "Beware how you contradict prejudices, even knowing them to be such, for the generality of people are much more tenacious of their prejudices than of anything belonging to them" (Susan Ferrier, *The Inheritance*, vol. 1). "Prejudices such as sexism and the deeply related homophobia, racism, and classism are not just personal problems, sets of peculiar and troubling beliefs. Exclusions and devaluations of whole groups of people on the scale and of the range, tenacity, and depth of racism and sexism and classism are systemic and shape the world within which we all struggle to live and find meaning" Elizabeth Kamarck Minnich, *Transforming Knowledge*. See also ageism, anti-Arabism, anti-Semitism, classism, disabilities, hate speech, homophobia, Islamophobia, racism, sexism, sizeism/sizism.

pre-industrial referring this way to certain "countries or societies assumes that other societies, economies, or nations should or will progress toward mirroring industrial models like the United States and Western Europe and dismisses the inherent value in any other systems" (*Creating Just Language*). See also Third World.

prelate so far, always a man.

pre-literate society this term "sometimes assumes that written communication is superior to other forms, that people who can't read or cultures and religious communities that rely more heavily on oral communication are inferior. A person from an oral culture, for example, is likely to have a much more developed memory than a literate person" (*Creating Just Language*, a publication of the 8th Day Center for Justice). Use instead nonliterate or aliterate. Better yet, instead of the quick label, describe how the group communicates and preserves their history.

premenstrual syndrome/PMS this term, which describes a recognized medical condition, is troublesome when it is either over-identified (using it as an explanation for anything a woman does that one doesn't like) or under-identified (discounted as a reality in the lives of some—but far from all—women). See also "curse."

premier danseur a "premier danseur" is the principal male dancer in a company; his opposite number is the "prima ballerina." Retain "premier danseur" for its narrow meaning in ballet companies. See also ballerina; danseur/danseuse; prima ballerina.

prenuptial agreement "nuptial" has probably moved far enough from its roots ("to take a husband") to be functionally inclusive. Should you want alternatives, consider pre-marriage/pre-wedding agreement/arrangement/contract.

preparedness any discussion of preparedness needs to acknowledge two vastly different views, represented by George Washington ("To be prepared for war is one of the most effectual means of preserving peace") and James Monroe ("Preparation for war is a constant stimulus to suspicion and illwill").

pre-pregnant a 2006 report from the Centers for Disease Control (CDC) recommends classifying all women as pre-pregnant, detailing measures to be taken to intervene in the life, health care, and behavior of all women, "from menarche to menopause ... even if they do not intend to conceive." Sunsara Taylor (truthdig.com) says that as far as the CDC is concerned, "if you are one of the 62 million U.S. women of childbearing age, you are pre-pregnant—a vessel. You are a future fetal incubator." She says the report "calls for a radical shift in medical care so that at every point of interaction, women's doctors are to stage 'interventions' to make sure they are healthy and prepared to give birth. Want to take your newborn in for a checkup or your 8-year-old in for a high fever? Expect an 'intervention' into your eating habits, weight, and behavioral risk factors. Got diabetes or epilepsy and looking for the care that is best for you? Wrong approach, says the CDC: 'Separating childbearing from the management of chronic health problems and infectious diseases places women, their future pregnancies, and their future children at unnecessary risk.'" See the complete article and Taylor's outlining of the implications of such a measure at www.truthdig.com.

presidentress apparently Edith Bolling Wilson was known as the "Presidentress of the United States" when she was first lady. It never caught on.

pressman press operator/tender/feeder/worker, printer, presser, compositor, typesetter, typographer. See also newsman/newspaperman.

preventive detention following 9/11, the Bush administration, for the third time in U.S. history, cited "preventive detention" to jail thousands of people suspected of being terrorists. "Preventive detention" was used in 1919 after terrorist bombings; thousands of foreign nationals were arrested, hundreds were deported, although no links were found to the bombings. During World War II, 110,000 persons were interned because of their Japanese ancestry; no links between the incarcerated and espionage were found. See also detainee.

prick (man) the Title-Says-It-All Department: "'Pricks' and 'Chicks': A Plea for 'Persons,'" (Robert Baker, in Robert Baker and Frederick Elliston, eds., *Philosophy and Sex*).

priest in some denominations, a priest may be a man or a woman; in others, they are always men. Knowing how to address a woman priest is not difficult; the most common practice is the use of first names for both female and male clergy. Some women clergy are comfortable being called "Mother," while others say they are not disturbed when they are called "Father"; they accept it pro tem in the spirit in which it is meant. It is never in poor taste to ask a priest what she or he likes to be called. This is a time of transition and few people, including the clergy themselves, have hard and fast guidelines. (Neither male nor female priests are properly addressed orally as "Reverend," however.) There does not appear to be a biblical or first-generation Christianity basis for the ban on women priests; the four verses often quoted to defend the ban (1 Cor. 11, Eph. 5:22, I Tim. 2, and I Cor. 14) do not address the issue directly and cannot be defended by an indirect approach. The requirement that priests resemble Christ has been taken to mean only his maleness; it is not equally required that they be short, bearded Jews. See also clergyman, minister, priestess, rabbi.

priestess retain "priestess" in historical or present-day contexts where the term reflects a reality that is very positive for women, for example, in the goddess religions. In many instances, the term is not second-best but one that offers a model of power and inspiration for women. When "priestess" is just a subset of "priest," use priest.

prima ballerina gender-specific terms are still used in professional ballet companies to distinguish between the female first dancer ("prima ballerina") and the male first dancer ("premier danseur"). Retain the narrow usage when referring to members of professional ballet companies, but use inclusive language for others: ballet dancer, first dancer, star dancer, principal dancer. See also ballerina, danseur/danseuse, premier danseur.

prima donna lead, lead opera singer, opera star, leading role, opera/lead/principal singer/performer. There is no parallel for men. When describing an overly self-absorbed and temperamental person, it is used (in spite of its plainly feminine cast) for both sexes.

primitive referring to early peoples, indigenous peoples, or other cultures as "primitive" is unacceptable; anthropologists see the term as unhelpful and "loaded." Such a use of "primitive" depends on subjective judgments about such debatable concepts as civilization, intelligence, and social development. "Within the cultures of many people, more value is placed on relationships, and on the maintenance of tradition and spirituality than on the development and acquisition of machines. It is ethnocentric and racist to apply words like backward, primitive, uncivilized, savage, barbaric, or undeveloped to people whose technology does not include plumbing, microwaves and micro-chips. Are people somehow more human or more humane if they have more technological toys?" (Amoja Three Rivers, *Cultural Etiquette*). "Every society is primitive in some ways and complex in others. If we put aside our fascination with technology and material wealth, we may find that for many people in U.S. and European societies today, life is primitive and stunted in terms of family values, spiritual life, commitment to the community, and opportunities for rewarding work and creative self-expression" (Sanford Berman). Berman says the term "is heavily overlaid with notions of inferiority, childishness, barbarity, and 'state of nature' simplicity, whereas the societies, arts, economic modes, music, and religions it purportedly covers may be extremely complex, ingenious, creative, human, and—depending on taste and *Weltanschauung*—admirable." Replace "primitive" with precise descriptors of what you mean to convey. You might also be able to use some of the following alone or in combination: folk, traditional, kin-organized, nonmechanized, early, indigenous society. See also "culturally deprived/disadvantaged," heathen, illiterate, savage, Third World.

primitive man early people/peoples/societies/human being, cavedweller, Cro-Magnon, Neanderthals. See also caveman, prehistoric, primitive.

primogenitor because the "genitor" comes from the word for begetting, "primogenitor" refers to male ancestors. For a sex-neutral alternative, use ancestor, forebear.

primogeniture in its narrowest sense (the inheritance rights of the firstborn son), "primogeniture" is the correct term to use, although the concept itself is very sexist. In the larger sense of being the firstborn of all the children of the same parents, use firstborn, firstborn child, eldership, seniority, rights of the firstborn.

prince correct sex-specific term for royalty. In the generic sense, its supposed feminine parallel ("princess") has quite different connotations and there are no female equivalents for such expressions as "he's a prince," "a real prince," "a prince of a fellow," "a prince among men." For inclusive alternatives, use a real paragon, an ace, the acme of perfection, a trump, a marvel, a real lifesaver, a one-off, one in a million, salt of the earth, one of the best, outstanding human being, hero, champion, shining example.

princely replace with precise, inclusive adjectives: generous, liberal, bounteous, magnanimous, lavish, profuse, sumptuous, rich, abundant; luxurious, glorious, brilliant; noble, stately, grand, august, awesome, majestic, dignified.

princess use only for royalty. See also prince.

princess dress this term is probably harmless enough in itself, although all the "princess" language has not been good for women. For alternatives, describe the dress precisely or consider flared/close-fitting/waistless dress.

prioress this term denotes a woman with power and stature usually equal to that of a prior's. For the generic sense of "prioress" or "prior," you might use religious, superior, administrator, director. See also "feminine" word endings.

prisoner according to the latest statistics from the U.S. Department of Justice, more than 2.2 million men and women are now behind bars; the U.S. incarcerates a higher percentage of its people than any other country in the world (the New York-based Human Rights Watch). Some

93 percent of inmates in state prisons are men. However, the number of women admitted to state prison for violent offenses increased by 83 percent between 1991 and 2011. Contrary to popular perception, violent crime is not responsible for the quadrupling of the incarcerated population in the United States since 1980. Nearly three-quarters of new admissions to state prison were convicted of nonviolent crimes; only 49 percent of sentenced state inmates are held for violent offenses. About 14 percent of the total prison population is in federal prison. The most serious charge against 51 percent of federal prison inmates is a drug offense. Only 4 percent of federal inmates are incarcerated for robbery; only 1 percent for homicide. The most serious charge against 20 percent of state prison inmates is a drug offense, a larger percentage than any other single category of offense. The national "war on drugs" is the single greatest force behind the growth of the prison population. More troubling than the absolute number of persons in jail or prison is the extent to which those men and women are African American; although blacks account for only 13 percent of the U.S. population, 44 percent of all prisoners in the United States are black. Several states are questioning whether statutes, rules, or practices in the court systems cause unfairness; other groups are looking at social causes. One recent study showed that two-thirds of Americans prefer sentences of mandatory drug treatment and community service over prison time. Putting things in perspective: in the state of California alone, in 2007 the state spent $3.3 billion on its state university system and $9.9 billion on its prison system (*Los Angeles Times*). See also bad guy, war on drugs.

privilege meaning "private law," privilege comprises the covert and overt benefits or immunities that society grants certain individuals based solely on their social standing. An obvious example is the judicial outcome of a wealthy white embezzler with a well-paid lawyer compared to the outcome for a poor black thief with a court-appointed lawyer (studies show court-appointed lawyers are generally less effective, and there is currently talk of a shortage of them because of budget cuts). People who can afford to put up bail are in a more advantageous position as are those who can afford to fly in expert witnesses. Although we are all in some sense born equal, some people are more privileged than others. At the top of a list of privileges would be wealth (which depends on other, prior privileges such as family, whiteness, inheritance, education, social status, powerful networks, etc.). Greta Christina (*AlterNet*) says, "I am privileged as a white person, a college-educated person, a middle-to-upper-middle class person, a more or less able bodied person, an American. I am marginalized as a woman, a queer, a bisexual, a fat person, an atheist." Check your writing and speaking for unconscious privilege bias, assuming, for example, that an activity or a profession or a reference is familiar to or even possible for your audience. Along with the unearned benefits of privilege goes the stigma that the privileged are somehow better. Examine your words for subtle hierarching when speaking of people. See also male privilege, white privilege.

PR man PR agent.

problem expressions like "the Indian problem," "the black problem," and "the Jewish problem" have disgracefully associated victims with their abuse. Where there is a problem, there must be a solution; Hitler's "final solution" to "the Jewish problem" illustrates how inappropriate "problem" terminology is. There was no "black problem" until four million people were brought to the U.S. as slaves (and without racism and discrimination it is possible there would be no "black problem" today); there was no "Indian problem" until virtually an entire people was killed, dispossessed, impoverished, and isolated; there was no "Jewish problem" until Nazi Germany needed a scapegoat. Identify instead the real issues: oppression, discrimination, racism, poverty, race relations, restitution for stolen lands, violence. See also "final solution," Jewish question.

processing (of animals) killing, slaughtering.

pro-choice this term has long been used by women and men who believe that women (not government or clergy) should make the decision about abortion; the term "pro-abortion" is inaccurate and highly offensive. Current thinking is that "choice" may not be the best descriptor of this issue. Linguist and cognitive scientist George Lakoff wants to move away from "the linguistically inaccurate word 'choice.'" He argues that "choice" is less serious and derives from a consumer, rather than a moral, vocabulary. He would prefer the emphasis to be on personal freedom. Summer Wood (in *Bitch*) says "substituting 'choice' for 'rights' as both a legal framework and a common language proved successful in attracting some libertarians and conservatives to vote for the 'pro-choice' position in numerous contests during the '80s. Because 'choice' is, in essence, an empty word, people with vastly divergent political viewpoints can be united under its banner. In retrospect, this is both the word's greatest strength and its ultimate weakness. As various constituencies brought their own political prerogatives and definitions of 'choice' to the negotiating table, parents, physicians, husbands, boyfriends, and religious leaders all came to be included as rightful participants in making the abortion choice, significantly weakening the idea that women have a right to make this decision on their own. The result has been a rapid depoliticizing of the term and an often misguided application of feminist ideology to consumer imperatives, invoked not only for the right to decide whether to terminate a pregnancy but also for the right to buy all manner of products marketed to women, from cigarettes to antidepressants to frozen diet pizzas." Katha Pollitt (in *The Nation*, 2013) agrees: "Today we are so bombarded with choices the word sounds 'frivolous'—like choosing your cellphone plan." She adds, however, that no matter what the issue is called, it will get devalued. Other objections to the term "pro-choice" include the fact that many women have no choice: according to the Guttmacher Institute, one out of every four women enrolled in Medicaid who would otherwise choose abortion has to carry an unwanted pregnancy to term because she can't get Medicaid to pay and can't cover out-of-pocket costs herself; the editors of *The Nation* recently noted that "87 percent of U.S. counties lack an abortion provider, and several states have only a clinic or two staffed by a doctor who flies in from another state." Marlene Fried of SisterSong lists other inadequacies of the choice framework: choice is not a sufficiently powerful moral argument, especially when you have to challenge the "pro-life" framework of those opposed to women's rights; choice is not a compelling vision, the vision needed to mobilize the kind of movement capable of winning clear and consistent victories for women's rights. Whenever feasible, use "reproductive rights" in place of pro-choice. For more on issues associated with reproductive rights, see the *Women's Media Center Guide to Covering Reproductive Issues*, by Sarah Erdreich, edited by Rachel Larris: http://www.womensmediacenter.com/pages/read-the-womens-media-centers-media-guide-to-covering-reproductive-issues. See also abortion, abortionist, anti-choice, fetus, pro-life, reproductive rights.

proconsul Roman proconsuls were all men, as are almost all modern administrators of colonies, dependencies, and occupied areas.

procreate procreation is shared equally by men and woman. When speaking of it, sometimes use "beget" and sometimes use "give birth to."

procuress procurer. See also "feminine" word endings.

prodigal son prodigal, returned prodigal, the prodigal one, the prodigal, one who returns to the fold, lost lamb; profligate, wastrel, squanderer, waster, spendthrift, high liver.

professional/pro these terms have always been complimentary when referring to men, but have often been synonymous with "prostitute" when referring to women. This usage is no longer so prevalent, but occasionally the terms might be ambiguous (and their dichotomous usage reveals much about our sexism). Although the differences between "the professions" and "the trades" and between "white-collar" workers and "blue-collar" workers might occasionally be useful, many times the distinctions are gratuitous and classist. See also businessman, glass ceiling.

Professional Secretaries Day/Week Administrative Professionals Day/Week.

progressive see political spectrum.

progressive taxes if everyone pays 20 percent of their income for taxes, the person making $25,000 will have $20,000 left over after taxes, but the person making $25 million will have $20 million left over. Progressive taxation says that those with lots of money left over should pay a little more for taxes because, as George Lakoff explains (*Thinking Points*), "Great wealth can be accumulated only by using other people's money—through infrastructure paid for by taxpayers and through transfers of wealth directly from taxpayers to you, through government subsidies, writing off business expenses, tax breaks, no-bid contracts, and so on. ... If you make great wealth, you have a responsibility to pay back an appropriate amount to maintain the common wealth infrastructure so that others can use it, too." Under the George W. Bush Administration, taxes became seriously less progressive, with the richest taxpayers enjoying most of the "tax relief."

project subsidized housing, public housing development. "Project" is code for poverty, crime, and dilapidation, all usually attributed to minority groups. See also ghetto.

pro-life this term is preferred by men and women who oppose abortion; pro-life stances range from rejecting abortion for any reason whatsoever and also opposing birth control to favoring birth control and accepting abortion as a possibility in a few narrowly delimited instances. Most pro-life individuals are one-issue-oriented (abortion only) while some define "pro-life" by a spectrum of concerns (death penalty, poverty and justice, global peace). Newspapers prefer "anti-abortion" because "pro-life" implies others are anti-life; it also focuses on the group's principal objective:

although some people in the movement may be dedicated to other issues, all pro-life individuals oppose abortion. "Pro-lifer" is derogatory. One of the problems not yet defused by the pro-life movement is that "those most obsessed with saving it also oppose doing anything for this 'person' once it becomes a real person in need of food, clothing, shelter, education and health care. In nine months it goes from being a 'miracle of life' to a 'welfare cheat'" (Marie Alena Castle, "Fertility Worship: Alive and Well and Turning Primitive Beliefs Into Law," *The Moral Atheist*, 2011). The terms "pro-life" and "pro-choice" have been problematic. They are best replaced by "anti-abortion" and "reproductive rights." See also abortion, abortionist, anti-choice, fetus, reproductive rights.

promiscuous this term tends to be judgmental and imprecise, referring to the lack of discrimination in the choice of (multiple) sexual partners. But it is difficult to know when to start labeling someone "promiscuous"—after three partners? Ten? Twenty? If they choose partners who are unemployed, less educated than they, with bad reputations? Women are labeled promiscuous much more often than men; Julia Penelope Stanley found 220 terms in English that describe a sexually promiscuous woman, but only 22 for a sexually promiscuous man. She notes that there is no linguistic reason why the first set is large and the second set small. In its sense of indiscriminate and irresponsible, it may have some uses, but generally look at it twice before using.

Promise Keepers the religious movement of men started in the 1990s, Promise Keepers set out to re-establish men's "rightful place" as leaders at home and in society. Founder Bill McCartney said, "There's coming a day when the strongest voice in America will be that of a Christian male."

pro-natalist see natalist.

pronouns for information on pseudogeneric "he," see the Writing Guidelines. See also animal/he, automobile/she, church/she, devil/he, enemy/he, nature/she, singular "they."

propertyman/prop man property/prop coordinator/attendant/handler/supervisor.

prophet in his own country, no man is a unless you need to quote a specific translation of the Bible, use the inclusive version given in some translations: Prophets are not without honor except in their own countries and in their own houses. Variations include: we are slow to see the prophet in our midst; prophets are not without honor, save in their own country and among their own kind; prophets are seldom recognized in their own lands.

prophetess prophet. See also "feminine" word endings.

proprietress proprietor. See also "feminine" word endings.

prostitute a prostitute may be either sex. Use "prostitute" or "prostituted woman" instead of the hundreds of slurs and euphemisms: baggage, bawd, B-girl, call girl, chippie/chippy, doxy, drab, fallen woman, fancy girl/woman, floozie/floozy, hussy, lady of the night, magdalen, painted woman, pavement princess, piece, pro/pross/prossie/prostie/prosty, round heels, scarlet woman, sidewalk hostess, streetwalker, strumpet, tail, trollop, trull, woman of easy virtue/ill fame/ill repute, working woman. The male-dominated language has been slow to demean male prostitutes, which is why all the foregoing words apply to women. Prostitution involving adults is a takes-two-to-tango operation and could not survive without the active and continued participation of both parties. Yet our language in no way treats prostitute and prostitute buyer equally. The prostitute is often disadvantaged, compelled by poverty, homelessness, a pimp, or drugs to maintain the system. The prostitute user does not suffer from similar life-and-death compulsions. Yet by naming prostitutes pejoratively, society apportions to them all the blame, all the "badness." When it comes to the men who do with prostitutes that which supposedly makes the prostitutes bad women, we have only four words for them: john, trick, score, date. "John" is a nice word. Many people name their sons John. "Trick" and "score" are not too shabby either; they are both used (although not in that sense) in polite society. And "date" is even more innocuous. Virtually none of the prostitute words have this double life; they live only on the streets. Vednita Carter (in *Sisterhood Is Forever*) says, "Prostitution is based on acute economic inequality: being driven to "choose" prostitution because of poverty is force, is coercion." She reports that the average age of entry into prostitution in the U.S. is 14, and says, "This 'victimless crime' leaves a devastating impact on its victims. ... There is a sexual war against women and children in this world. It has been going on for a long time. This war has managed to disguise itself as 'the oldest profession' when, in reality, it is the oldest oppression." Prostitution has always been risky for women; prostitutes have a death rate that is 40 times higher than women who are not involved in prostitution. Avoid all terms for prostitutes except "prostitute" or "prostituted woman/man" or "woman/man working as a prostitute." Call the prostitute's partner a "prostitute user" (linguistically connecting the two) or "sex buyer." Eliminate cover-ups like outcall service, escort service, red light district, call girl service, brothel, bordello, call house; they are houses of prostitution or prostitution services. See also camp follower, courtesan, demimondaine, harlot/harlotry, ho, hooker, Jezebel/jezebel, kept woman, lady of easy virtue/of pleasure/of the evening/of the night, loose woman, madam, sex industry, sex worker, slattern, slut, tart, tramp (woman), wench, whore.

Protect America Act, The passed in 2007, the Protect America Act is a dramatic, across-the-board expansion of government authority to collect information without judicial oversight; it authorizes open-ended surveillance of Americans' overseas phone calls and e-mails. "The law's most important effect is arguably not its expansion of raw surveillance power but the sloughing away of judicial or Congressional oversight. In the words of former CIA officer Philip Giraldi, the law provides 'unlimited access to currently protected personal information that is already accessible through an oversight procedure'" (Aziz Huq, *www.thenation. com*). In addition, according to Huq, the vague wording of the law is troubling: "It remains deeply unclear how much domestic surveillance this allows." The government "has to meet an extraordinarily low standard, in a one-sided judicial procedure in which the court has no access to details of the program's actual operation." Jay Leno perhaps says it best: "President Bush said that Congress needs to give him more power to spy on Americans by making changes to the Protect America Act. Did you ever notice they always give these pieces of legislation names you can't disagree with? The Protect America Act. ... Give it a fair name. At least call it the Ignore the Constitution Act."

protectress protector. See also "feminine" word endings.

protégé/protégée protégé for both sexes. "Protégée" is defined in most dictionaries as "a female protégé" thus removing women one step from the real thing. See also "feminine" word endings.

provider just as the caregiver role—as the primary option—has limited, dehumanized, and oppressed some women, the provider role—as the primary option—has limited, dehumanized, and oppressed some men. Men bring home more bacon than women, but many of them consider the economic benefits associated with their gender to be a mixed blessing. The notion that "it's a man's world" has obscured the fact that along with benefits have come severe lifestyle restrictions, stress, economic pressures and responsibilities, unrealistic social expectations, and being judged by criteria not applied to women. As more women providers join men in taking on toxic workloads, personal and societal goals may need to be re-evaluated to help fashion a more life-giving balance between work life and non-work life. The following words are theoretically inclusive, but we use them largely to penalize men for not being providers or "good enough" providers: also-ran, born loser, deadbeat, derelict, do-nothing, down-and-outer, dud, failure, freeloader, goldbricker, good-for-nothing, hard-luck case, idler, layabout, lazybones, lightweight, loafer, mooch, ne'er-do-well, nonstarter, parasite, piker, prodigal, schlemiel, schmo, shirker, skinflint, slacker, sponge, washout, wastrel. Traditionally, a male "loser" is a financial failure—someone who can't "provide"; a woman who is a "loser" fails to be sexually attractive. See also breadwinner, bum, male privilege, success object.

provocative when describing ideas or intellectual properties, "provocative" is useful and meaningful. In a social or sexual situation, however, the word's connotations make it difficult to use fairly and factually. Too often it is women who are "provocative"—eternal Eves luring endless numbers of passive Adams. See also provoke.

provoke this word is used as a "reason" for beating, raping, and even killing women. A man in a family violence program explains, "I know I shouldn't hit her, but I can't seem to stop. The bitch really asks for it, you know? She really provokes me." When Carol S. Irons, the first female judge in Kent County, Michigan, was shot to death in her chambers by her estranged husband, the jury convicted him of a lesser crime (voluntary manslaughter instead of the first-degree murder charge) because, as one juror put it, "Everybody felt he was provoked by his wife to do this." A judge ruled that a five-year-old girl was a "temptress" in "provoking" a sexual encounter with a 20-year-old man (Nijole V. Benokraitis and Joe R. Feagin, *Modern Sexism*). After Linda Simmons's husband, a hospital pathologist, killed her as she was walking out the door with their two young children, he told police, "She just wouldn't quit bugging me"—presumably about his long-standing alcoholism. A man who strangled his woman friend after they had argued about Christmas toys said, "I did it, I did it. ... I can't believe I killed her, I did it, I can't believe she made me that mad." See also "She asked for it."

prudent man (legal) prudent person/individual. See also reasonable and prudent man.

pseudogeneric words that purport to include everyone, but that do not are called pseudogenerics. "A Muslim people of the northern Caucasus, the 1.3 million Chechens are dark-haired and tawny skinned, often with lush mustaches" (*The New York Times International*). "People" here is a pseudogeneric; it was intended to mean all Chechens, but "lush mustaches" betrays the writer's sense that real people are men. (FYI: Pseudogeneric "man" was declared obsolete by the *Oxford English Dictionary* in 1971.) See also he (pseudogeneric), Man/man (pseudogeneric), mankind.

pseudoscience see junk science, "sound science."

puberty in general, puberty refers to bodily changes of sexual maturation when moving physically from child to adult, whereas adolescence refers to the social and psychological achievements between childhood and adulthood. Puberty and adolescence overlap, but not precisely, and body changes are more easily charted than psychological changes.

public diplomacy according to the U.S. Department of State, Dictionary of International Relations Terms, "public diplomacy refers to government-sponsored programs intended to inform or influence public opinion in other countries; its chief instruments are publications, motion pictures, cultural exchanges, radio, and television." Discussion has often focused on whether "public diplomacy" and "propaganda" are similar.

public relations man publicist, public relations/P.R. agent/practitioner/director/executive/representative/specialist, promoter, publicity/press agent, booster, promoter, advance agent, propagandist, public information manager/officer, publicity writer. See also adman, spokesman.

puerile the Latin *puer* means either boy or child. If you want a more strictly neutral alternative, consider juvenile, childish.

Puerto Rican since Puerto Rico is an independent commonwealth of the United States, Puerto Ricans are U.S. citizens. José Cuello says many Puerto Ricans who live on the island as well as Nuyoricans on the mainland reject the image and heritage of being colonized by Europeans and use the term Boricua, derived from Borinquen, the indigenous name of the island, instead of Puerto Rico (Wayne State University, for example, has a Center for Chicano-Boricua Studies). See also Nuyorican.

Pullman car/Pullman porter named after its inventor George M. Pullman. You can avoid the masculine look of "pullman porter" with porter, train attendant, red cap.

pundit see expert.

purdah literally, "curtain," purdah is the pattern of veiled and secluded domesticity that characterizes the lives of certain Muslim, South Asian, and Hindu women. Emily C. Smith, member of Muslim Women of Minnesota, says, "Muslim women do not aspire to feminism on the Western model. Instead, they pursue the rights guaranteed to them in their own religious law, which 1,400 years ago granted them independent legal status and rights of voting, inheritance, and divorce. The adoption of Islamic dress is often a political statement by which the wearer rejects the sexual exploitation of women while reaffirming that she does not need to mimic customs and manners foreign to her own culture. To assume that the Muslim woman is universally oppressed is an insult which disregards the achievements of millions of our Muslim sisters worldwide." Leila Ahmed (in *Feminist Studies*) says, "Although universally perceived in the West as an oppressive custom, the veil is not experienced as such by women who habitually wear it. More than anything perhaps, it is a symbol of women being separated from the world of men, and this is conventionally perceived in the West as oppression." Women Living Under Muslim Laws, formed in 1984, is an international solidarity network that provides information, support and a collective space for women whose lives are shaped, conditioned or governed by laws and customs said to derive from Islam. "Our name challenges the myth of one, homogeneous 'Muslim world.' This deliberately created myth fails to reflect that (1) laws said to be Muslim vary from one context to another and (2) the laws that determine our lives are from diverse sources: religious, customary, colonial, and secular. We are governed simultaneously by many different laws: laws recognized by the state (codified and uncodified) and informal laws such as customary practices which vary according to the cultural, social, and political context." In speaking and writing, then, respect the customs and beliefs of others and know that if change is needed, it will come from inside out, not vice versa.

purple state a U.S. state where the Democratic and Republican Parties have similar levels of voter support. The term alludes to the fact that the color purple is a blend of red (Republican) and blue (Democratic). In presidential elections, purple states are also known as "swing states."

purse strings despite the "purse," this isn't particularly sex-linked; historically both sexes carried purses and today the term is functionally nonsexist. Should you want alternatives, consider financial support/resources, control over financial support/resources; hold all the cards, lay down the law, run the place/show, call the shots/plays, be in the saddle/driver's seat, have under control, wear the crown, boss.

pushy see aggressive, bossy.

pussy this vulgar slang for the vulva is used as a euphemism for "cunt" and is also a derogatory term for a woman. It has come to be synonymous with "wimp," "loser," and other derogatory terms.

pussy-whipped this is like "henpecked," except vulgar. For alternatives, consider bossed around, bullied, browbeaten, passive, submissive, dominated, subjugated, under someone's thumb, led by the nose, at one's beck and call, ruled with an iron hand. See also henpeck/henpecked, pussy.

PWA/PLWA/PLA acceptable acronyms for a person with HIV/AIDS or a person living with HIV/AIDS. See also AIDS, innocent victim, victim.

pygmy there are no peoples who call themselves "pygmies"; replace this ethnocentric, Eurocentric term with specific, authentic peoples' names (Mbuti, Twa).

Q

To speak of "mere words" is much
like speaking of "mere dynamite."
C.J. Ducasse

in a ward on fire, we must
find words
or burn.
Olga Broumas

quadriplegic someone with/who has quadriplegia. If necessary to mention a disability, information can be conveyed neutrally without labeling the whole person by something that is only part of them. Quadriplegia is a paralysis of the body from the neck down. See "people first" rule. See also disabilities, hemiplegic, paraplegic.

Quakeress Quaker. Although the word "Quaker" was at one time used derogatorily, it was adopted early on by the members of the Religious Society of Friends. Today the word Quaker has a long and honorable history; it is used interchangeably with Friend. See also "feminine" word endings.

qualified this is a good word sometimes found in the wrong places, that is, "qualifying" people whose qualifications would be taken for granted if they were, for example, white, male, young, and able-bodied. "Why is the word "qualified" applied only to those who have to be more so?" (Gloria Steinem, *Moving Beyond Words*). Use with care.

quarryman quarrier, quarry worker.

quartermaster in the Army, this term refers to a field of specialization, not to an individual; members of this branch include supply sergeants, supply officers, and supply NCOs. In the Navy and Coast Guard, "quartermaster" is a job title or rank used for both women and men involved in navigation. Civilian equivalents might include: petty officer, quarterdeck; commissary, provisioner, storekeeper, victualer; navigator, small craft/large ship operator. The Air Force and the Marine Corps do not use the term "quartermaster"; they call their supply branches Individual Equipment (Air Force) or Supply (Marines).

queen (noun) acceptable sex-specific word for royalty. If you need a gender-free term, try ruler, monarch, sovereign, crowned head, leader. In the world of slurs, "queen" can be used to demean a man considered to be "effeminate." "King" has not been similarly misused and downgraded. If you are reporting hate speech, set the term in quotation marks to show the bias of the speaker. Better yet, to avoid giving the word an airing, report that the person "used a derogatory word for a lesbian, gay, bisexual, or transgender person." Gay men might use "queen" among themselves, but its use is unacceptable by non-gays. See "insider/outsider" rule.

queen (verb) women "queen it over" others, while men "lord it over." While somewhat asymmetric, the terms are functionally benign. Should you need inclusive alternatives, consider: have the upper hand, hold something over someone's head, wear the crown, hold court, have/get it all one's own way, have the game in one's own hand/corner/court.

queen bee correct when referring to the inhabitant of a hive. If you want a less sex-specific expression for its metaphorical use, consider big wheel. For additional terms, see prima donna; totem pole, high man on the.

queen consort in referring to the wife of a reigning king, it is acceptable to drop the word "consort" except in some narrow circumstances (legal or historical references and official titles).

queenlike/queenly there is nothing particularly biased about these sex-specific words, but, like most stereotypes, they are vague. If you want more precise adjectives, consider: regal, imperial, noble, dignified, imposing, impressive, stately, majestic, commanding, haughty.

queen-size terms like this give new meaning to the roles of kings and queens as "rulers." The term is irreplaceable because of its specific descriptions of beds and bed linen (where the use of "single," "double," "queen," and "king" is standard) and its euphemistic use for such items as queen-size pantyhose. However, it undergirds the female-as-lesser/smaller perspective and if you simply mean "very large," you might consider one of the many synonyms of huge. See also king-size.

queer although this term was used pejoratively for many decades, "many gay people have reclaimed 'queer,' using it to describe the many and sometimes outrageous facets of our gay selves and communities. 'Queer' is sometimes used as shorthand for 'LGBT,' and some people even use the word 'queer' to describe those straight people who have a cutting-edge attitude toward their own sexuality" (Lynn Witt et al., eds., *Out in All Directions*). The Gay and Lesbian Alliance Against Defamation (GLAAD) says the term has been appropriated by some gay men and lesbians to describe themselves: "Some value the term for its defiance and because it is inclusive—not only of lesbians and gay men but of bisexuals and transgender people as well. Nevertheless, it is not universally accepted within our communities, and used out of context it is still derogatory." Internet postings show that some people love "queer," some only tolerate it, and some feel the word is despicable, alienating, inaccurate, and profoundly pejorative. Use "queer" with gay abandon when you self-identify this way or when you believe your audience will appreciate it. Otherwise, avoid it and all related terms. See also gay "lifestyle," homosexual, transphobia.

questioning a relatively recent term used to emphasize the fluidity of the sexual/gender continuum. Those who self-identify as questioning are often in the process of distinguishing and accepting their individual sexuality. You'll see LGBTQ or GLBTQ, meaning lesbian, gay, bisexual, transgender, and either queer or questioning. "Questioning" is an identity that is claimed, not bestowed.

quotas see affirmative action.

quotation marks quotation marks are used to question the legitimacy of a word or phrase, for example, "Indian giver," "all American," "Yellow Peril." Sometimes they impute dubiousness where there is none. Journalist Susan Berkson writes, "George Will came up with another boffo idea: To silence any radical feminist criticism, put basic facts—'sexual violence,' 'survivors,' 'silencing'—in quotation marks, calling into question their very existence." In a review of the work of a respected archaeologist, the writer's opinion of "feminist archaeology" was underlined by putting the term in quotation marks. Use quotation marks to imply that something is "so-called" or "alleged" or to express your disagreement with a concept; be wary of using them to disparage other people's realities.

Qur'an this is the preferred term for the sacred text of Islam. See also Koran.

They say that there is no reality before it has been given shape by words rules regulations. They say that in what concerns them everything has to be remade starting from basic principles. They say that in the first place the vocabulary of every language is to be examined, modified, turned upside down, that every word must be screened.

Monique Wittig

Nowadays a word is a deed whose consequences cannot be measured.

Heinrich Heine

rabbi women are rabbis in the Conservative, Reform, and Reconstructionist branches of Judaism, and they are addressed "rabbi." There are no women rabbis in the Orthodox branch.

race the use of this word "to refer to a group of persons who share common physical characteristics and form a discrete and separable population unit has no scientific validity, since evolutionary theory and physical anthropology have long since demonstrated that there are no fixed or discrete groups in human populations.... However as a folk concept in Western and non-Western societies the concept of race is a powerful and important one, which is employed in order to classify and systematically exclude members of given groups from fully participating in the social system controlled by the dominant group" (*Macmillan Dictionary of Anthropology*). "There are no pure races in any meaningful sense, only large geographical groupings whose genetic histories can never be fully known. ... The terminology of race has shifted in recent years from anthropological classifications toward a more flexible language of geography, culture, and color" (*American Heritage Book of English Usage*). Amoja Three Rivers (*Cultural Etiquette*) says, "If there ever was any such thing as race (which there isn't), there has been so much constant cross-crossing of genes for the last 500,000 years, that it would have lost all meaning." Clyde W. Ford (*We Can All Get Along*) suggests discarding "this outmoded term" and replacing it "with another term like ethnic group, ethnicity, cultural background, nationality, or human variation when speaking about differences among human beings. The term race is loaded with a history of fiction, conflict, violence, and racism." In *The Concept of Race*, Ashley Montagu says, "The idea of 'race' as a widespread secular belief is, in fact, no older than the 19th century. ... In part because of that phrase, 'All men are created equal,' and, of course, because of all those other conditions that bound them to support the institution, the defenders of slavery felt it necessary to show that the Negro was biologically unequal to the white man, both in his physical traits and in his mental capacities. ... it was in this way that the doctrine of racism was born." As long ago as 1936, biologist Julian Huxley and anthropologist Alfred Cort Haddon found the biological concept of race wanting: "It is very desirable that the term *race* as applied to human groups should be dropped from the vocabulary of science" (*We Europeans: A Survey of "Racial" Problems*). Although the term "racism" is necessary to a discussion of these issues and to denote the entrenched bias that the false concept of "race" has underwritten, the word "race" itself is best avoided as being devoid of meaning in itself. See also interracial, multiracial, racism.

racialization "the assignment of a racial meaning to a previously racially neutral event" (Patricia Hill Collins, *Fighting Words*).

racial preference race-based remedies, affirmative action program, policies designed to benefit women and racial minorities. The National Association of Black Journalists advises against using "racial preference," and recommends using the alternatives given, which are more accurate and neutral. See also affirmative action.

racism any attitude, action, social policy, or institutional structure that discriminates against a person or a group because of their color constitutes racism. More specifically, racism is the subordination of people of color by white people. "While an individual person of color may discriminate against white people or even hate them, his or her behavior or attitude cannot be called 'racist.' He or she may be considered *prejudiced* against whites and we may all agree that the person acts unfairly and unjustly, but *racism* requires something more than anger, hatred, or prejudice; at the very least, it requires *prejudice plus power*. The history of the world provides us with a long record of white people holding power and using it to maintain that power and privilege over people of color, not the reverse" (Paula S. Rothenberg, *Racism and Sexism*). "Racism is not just the sum total of all the individual acts in which white people discriminate, harass, stereotype or otherwise mistreat people of color. The accumulated effects of centuries of white racism have given it an institutional nature which is more entrenched than racial prejudice. In fact, it is barely touched by changes in individual white consciousness. We often find it difficult to see or to know how to challenge institutional racism because we are so used to focusing on individual actions and attitudes" (Paul Kivel, *Uprooting Racism*). Patricia Hill Collins (*Fighting Words*) defines institutionalized racism as the "combination of practices whereby Blacks and other people of color as a group or class receive differential treatment within schools, housing, employment, healthcare, and other social institutions. Unlike bias and prejudice, which are characteristics of individuals, institutionalized racism operates through the everyday rules and customs of social institutions." Zora Neale Hurston (*Dust Tracks on a Road*) wrote, "Light came to me when I realized that I did not have to consider any racial group as a whole. God made them duck by duck and that was the only way I could see them." Seeing people duck by duck may be a start to dismantling stereotypes. See also African American, black, code words, color blindness, prejudice, race.

racketeer functionally sexist; although women may be involved in racketeering, there are not many of them and they are rarely called racketeers. See also bad guy.

raconteur this French word is grammatically masculine (and its partner, "raconteuse," evidently stayed in France) but is used in English for both sexes. If you want a more inclusive-sounding alternative, consider storyteller, anecdotist, teller of tales, taleteller, talespinner, spinner of yarns, romancer, monologist, narrator.

radical see political spectrum.

radioman radio technician/operator/repairer/engineer.

raghead this slur is used against Arabs, Indian Sikhs, and other peoples, denigrating them for wearing traditional headdress such as turbans or keffiyehs.

ragman ragpicker, rag collector, junk dealer/collector.

raiders see renegades.

raise Cain there is nothing wrong with this phrase, but be aware of how many such expressions are male-based. Balance their use with female-based expressions, creative expressions of your own, or sex-neutral alternatives: make mischief/a fuss, carry on, lose one's temper, fly off the handle, flare up, run amok, raise a rumpus/a storm/a hue and cry/the devil/hell, castigate, lecture, rail, fulminate, find fault; be boisterous/loud/rowdy/disorderly, disturb the peace. See also sex-linked expressions.

rajah always a man; his wife is a "rani."

rake because this term is used only for men and there is no true parallel for women, consider libertine, swinger, bedhopper, free spirit, high-roller, dissolute person. See also ladies' man, man about town, womanizer.

Ramadan "Happy Ramadan" or "Happy New Year and Happy Ramadan" are appropriate greetings during the month of Ramadan (considered the most blessed and venerated month of the Islamic year when prayer, fasting, and charity are accompanied by reflections on self-accountability).

randy this adjective has no connection with a male name (it most likely comes from "to rant").

rape every two minutes in the United States, someone is sexually assault-ed (calculation by the Rape, Abuse & Incest National Network based on the U.S. Justice Department's *National Crime Victimization Survey, 2006-2010*). One in six American women are victims of sexual assault, and one in 33 men. There is an average annual 207,750 victims (age 12 or older) of rape, attempted rape, or sexual assault each year. About 44 percent of rape victims are under age 18, and 80 percent are under age 30. Since 1993, rape/sexual assault has fallen by over 69 percent. Males are the least likely to report a sexual assault, though it is estimated they make up 10 percent of all victims. Young females are four times more likely than any other group to be a victim of sexual assault. Rape of either sex remains the most underreported violent crime. As of 1993, all 50 states have laws against marital rape. Cultural support for rape: one of eight Hollywood films has rape scenes. Fewer than 3 percent of charged rapists go to prison; one man who admitted raping a woman was given no prison time (despite guidelines and a plea agreement for at least four years in prison) because the judge knew the woman from a divorce case he handled several years earlier and thought she was "pitiful" (the judge advised the man to be more careful in choosing women); police departments are either ill-equipped or ill-motivated to pursue rapists—a few years ago, the Oakland, California, police department had to reopen 203 rape cases that had been dropped without even minimal investigation. Myths about rape: (1) No one can be sexually assaulted against their will; in fact, 87 percent of all adult rape victims are faced with weapons, death threats, or threats of bodily harm, and nearly one-fifth of all rapes involve two or more assailants. In almost 90 percent of the cases, victims attempt self-protective measures such as physical force, threats, or calling for help. Rape victims range from infants to people over 80; about one-fifth of all rape victims are aged 12 to 15. (2) Women "ask for it" by dressing or behaving seductively or by being in the wrong place at the wrong time. Studies indicate that 60 percent-70 percent of rapes are planned in advance; victims' actions have little effect on the outcome. Since rape does not involve sexual desire, but rather violence and power, "seductiveness" is not a factor. We react differently to property crimes than to crimes against persons. A prosperous-looking man who is robbed is rarely accused of "asking for it" by the way he was dressed (rape victims' attire and manner are often a big issue in court). Women's sex lives are often cited against them in rape cases on the theory that this wasn't anything they hadn't done before. And women who report date rape or husband rape are told that since they have previously been willing to have sex, they have no recourse when sex is forced on them. (3) Finally, the racist twist to rape is not the one of myth: "The rape of black women by white males has been far more commonplace than the white fantasy about black men raping white women suggests" and it is "still a serious problem for black women in some parts of the United States" (Nijole V. Benokraitis and Joe R. Feagin, *Modern Sexism*). Some cautions in using the term "rape": (1) Say "men raping women" rather than "women are being raped"; Sonia Johnson (*Going Out of Our Minds*) says that when we say, "'Women are raped,' the syntax helps convey the impression that *women* do the acting, that *women* are responsible. But when I say instead, 'Today, men in this country raped over 2,000 women,' I lay the responsibility exactly where it belongs. Rape is *not* passive. Women are not raped. *Men rape women.*" (2) Avoid using "rape" in the figurative sense ("rape of the taxpayers")—it devalues the original meaning. See also acquaintance rape, provoke, rape victim, rapist, sexual harassment, "She asked for it," victim, violence.

rape culture a form of social conditioning that causes us to dismiss, excuse, tolerate, or expect sexual violence. It is culture that is supportive of sexualized violence occurring. It puts the focus on the behavior or status of the victims instead of the perpetrators. Rape culture includes TV, movies, music, advertising, pornography, jokes, laws, words, and imagery that essentially sanction rape and make it seem normal. "Rape culture exists because we don't believe it does," says Jessica Valenti (co-editor of *Yes Means Yes: Visions of Female Sexual Power in a World Without Rape*). "Violent masculinity and victim blaming are the cornerstones of rape culture and they go hand in hand. When an instance of sexual assault makes the news and the first questions the media asks are about the victim's sobriety or clothes or sexuality, we should all be prepared to pivot to ask, instead, what messages the perpetrators received over their lifetime about rape and 'being a man.' Here's a tip: the right question is not what was she doing/wearing/saying when she was raped? The right question is 'What made him think this was acceptable?'" Examples of rape culture are when a woman is told not to dress provocatively, to take a self-defense class, not to drink with men, with friends, or at all and otherwise make herself responsible for preventing her own rape; when a movie seems to frame rape as a compliment to a female character's beauty and desirability or to imply that a character "deserved" what is coming to her by her actions; when college athletes accused of rape become the focus of sympathy and support over the threat to their bright futures; when a comedian tells a joke where the punchline is rape because some people deserved to be raped or rape is funny when it happens to some people or because being raped is no big deal. See also acquaintance rape, rape, rapist, sexual harassment, "She asked for it," victim, violence.

rape victim avoid using "victim" in speaking and writing about rape; "survivor" is sometimes used. Tami Spry (*Women and Language*) says that "the agency of a woman as meaning maker of her own experience is denied in having to choose between the categories of victim or survivor. The pain and confusion following the assault is further complicated by having to structure and make sense of her experience within the assailant's language. ... How can one tell a story of sexual violence from a woman's bodily narrative point of view? ... The language of victor or survivor defines the meaning of the assault in relation to his action rather than her experience; she survived it or was a victim of it. ... the narrative focus, the primary experiential focus is on the male perpetrator, what he did and why he did it." The most important caution in writing or speaking of those who have been raped is to avoid indirectly blaming them. "We all want injustice to be the victim's fault" (Hortense Calisher). We like to think that most sexual assaults are provoked by, or preventable by, the victim, when in fact 60 percent to 70 percent of all rapes are planned in advance; nothing the victim does or doesn't do can avert it. Publicly identifying those who have been raped is debatable. Use someone's name only with permission as there are good reasons not to further expose the person at such a vulnerable time. Then again, not using a name seems to imply that there is something shameful about having been raped, when in fact there was something criminal about it. Suzette Haden Elgin (*The Lonesome Node*) says the ugly truth about not publicizing the name of those who have been raped "is because most of our society looks upon them as damaged goods." Although nearly all reported rape victims are women, men are raped, particularly in prisons where rape is a common way of maintaining an inmate power structure; do not exclude men from discussions of rape or assume that victim and violator are of different sexes. See also date rape, rape, rapist, "She asked for it," victim, violence.

rapist "Why isn't it called a raper?" asks Naomi Lifejoy (St. Paul's *Pioneer Press*). "It seems that some words that describe what people do have an 'ist' at the end, and they command a certain degree of respectability, such as scientist, archeologist, biologist, balloonist. Rapist sounds like too soft a word to me. We say robber, not robbist; killer, not killist; abuser, not abusist. Why then do we not say raper, rather than rapist?" A comparison of prestigious "-ist" words (dentist, scientist, therapist, geneticist, ophthalmologist, gynecologist, metallurgist) with criminal "-er" words (murderer, slayer, poisoner, strangler, sniper, knifer, slaughterer, destroyer, bloodshedder, shoplifter, mugger, stalker) supports Lifejoy's point. See also man-hater/woman-hater, rape, rape victim, violence.

Rastafarian not all Jamaicans are Rastafarians; not all Rastafarians are Jamaicans; not all people with dreadlocks are Rastafarians. Use only for those who self-identify this way.

reactionary see political spectrum.

"real" father/mother/parent biological mother/father/parent, birth father/mother/parent. Describing birth or biological parents as "real" implies that adoptive relationships are artificial, tentative, less important, and less enduring. See also adoption language, biological father/mother/parent, birth mother/father/parent.

real McCoy, the this is used of men, women, and objects, even though the original was a man. According to *Why Do We Say It?*, a prize fighter by the name of McCoy was being annoyed by a drunk whose friends tried to tell him that this was the great McCoy. McCoy eventually fought the man who, when he came to, said, "You're right. He's the real McCoy."

reasonable and prudent man (law) reasonable and prudent person/individual; reasonable, prudent person; reasonable person; the ordinary, reasonable, prudent person (ORP person); the average person; objective standard of reasonableness. See also reasonable woman (law).

reasonable woman (law) "In determining whether conduct or statements are sufficiently severe to rise to the level of unlawful sexual harassment, some state courts have relied upon a 'reasonable woman' standard. Under federal law, however, an objective standard, the 'reasonable person' standard, as well as the victim's subjective perception are applied to determine whether a hostile or abusive work environment exists" (N. Elizabeth Fried, *Sex, Laws & Stereotypes*). The "reasonable man" does not always agree with the "reasonable woman" about what constitutes sexual harassment. See also reasonable and prudent man.

rebel "rebel" by itself isn't very revealing. Some rebels are fighting oppression and unjust systems. Some rebels are murderers and terrorists. Give readers a context and a clear description of the rebels' methods and goals.

recruit woman or man. See also draft.

rector depending on the denomination, this may be either a woman or a man.

redhead this is much more likely to be used of a woman than of a man. It's not offensive in itself and has its uses but, in general, question the labeling of women by facets of their appearance and the need to talk about their hair.

red light district prostitution district. (One explanation for the term is that train crews left their red lanterns outside the house of prostitution so they could be located in case of an emergency. When owners of brothels realized this was an excellent way to advertise, the custom spread.)

red man American Indian, Native American, first American. Or use specific name (Chippewa, Dine). See also American Indian, Native American, redskin, sports teams' names and mascots.

redneck this classist, judgmental, and inflammatory term is used mostly of men. If you mean "bigot" or "racist" or "conservative," use those terms instead of the vague "redneck"; all it conveys is that you think the person is beneath you. Geoffrey Nunberg (*Talking Right*) offers a surprising perspective on the use of the term: "The word *redneck* is about 20 times more likely to appear in the pages of conservative publications like *National Review* than in the *Nation* or the *American Prospect*, chiefly because conservatives are fond of setting the word in the mouths of imaginary left-wing elitists in the course of reminding the good people of the heartland how much contempt liberals have for them. The same ratio applies to the dismissive 'flyover country,' which is ten times as likely to appear in *National Review* as in the *Nation* or the *American Prospect*."

redskin this reference to American Indians is always absolutely unacceptable; "Redskin, whose earliest known written instance is 1699, was one of the first slur-names given by white settlers to the Native Americans they encountered" (Irving Lewis Allen, *Unkind Words*).

red state a state that votes primarily Republican. Blue states vote primarily Democratic Party, and purple states are split.

referee in 1997, Dee Kantner and Violet Palmer became the first women to officiate in men's professional sports (*USA Weekend*). See also umpire/ump.

reform when used in politics, this word should elicit scrutiny of the most ferocious sort. Behind "reform" lies doing away with government programs, turning them on their heads, passing laws for the greater honor and glory and bottom line of big business and their political friends, and other unseemly activities. When George W. Bush talked about "reforming" Social Security, he had in mind doing away with it. However, highly successful Republican wordmaker Fred Luntz (*Words That Work*) says they should use "strengthen Social Security" instead. In that case, "reform," "strengthen," and "gut" would all refer to the same solution to the Social Security problem. See also personal accounts, tort reform.

reformed alcoholic recovering alcoholic. In writing or speaking about alcoholism, treat it as a disease, not as a moral offense, although the consequences of alcoholism (deaths caused by drunk drivers, for example) are certainly matters for discussion.

refugee by definition, a refugee is fleeing war, political oppression, or religious persecution; "refugee" is not interchangeable with "immigrant" (someone who leaves voluntarily) and it is not used for people who have been in a country long enough to be settled. However, "refugee" has been used in the sense of "fleeing from" in the case of Hurricane Katrina and the 2004 Asian tsunami. (George W. Bush said in the case of Katrina that the flood victims "are not refugees, they are Americans.") See also illegals/illegal immigrants.

regal/regalia/regent these words are based on the Latin *rex* for king, but they no longer have any strong male associations, except perhaps for those who know Latin. Either a woman or a man may be regal or a regent.

regime "the media tend to use regime much more often when they're talking about governments that are unfriendly to the United States than when they're talking about U.S. allies, independent of how unstable or undemocratic the governments are" (Geoffrey Nunberg, *Talking Right*). Governments rarely self-identify as regimes; for a neutral term, use government, administration, political system, ruling party. In general, use "regime" only when quoting a government official. See also regime change.

regime change a euphemism for the forcible overthrow and replacement of a government by another nation, regime change is considered by many to be a violation of international law.

regulation/deregulation/voluntary regulation the term "regulation" is met with instinctive and deep-seated resistance by the average citizen. "Deregulation," on the other hand, sounds to most people a lot like "freedom!" No one wants to be regulated; the independent-minded national character likes to make its own decisions. This is truly unfortunate as "regulation protects the public from harmful products and fraud by unscrupulous or irresponsible businesses" (George Lakoff, *Thinking Points*). Without regulation, food products and pharmaceuticals are likely to be harmful, working conditions dangerous, interest rates usurious, pollution uncontrolled, baby cribs unsafe, clothes flammable, and cars, toys, and equipment defective. When a product is recalled, we can thank federal and state regulations. Deregulation has brought us higher prices, virtual monopolies in many industries, and a lack of oversight along with the inability to fix things gone wrong. As for voluntary regulation or self-regulation for corporations, it simply doesn't work. When faced with self-regulating or making a larger profit, there is no contest for most businesses. It's critical when writing or speaking about regulation and deregulation to define each with examples from real life. People have heard these terms so often they no longer attach significant meaning to them, but hear in them their own personal dislike of being "regulated" while failing to understand that their interests and the interests of profit-making corporations are often at odds.

religious right terms like "the Christian right" and "the religious right" are sometimes—but not always correctly—used interchangeably. The terms are also considered by many to be pejorative as they are used mostly by opponents. However, the Christian Coalition, which describes much of what is understood by these terms, is a self-chosen name and thus acceptable. Because this coalition is a many-tentacled thing, verify who and what it includes before writing about any of its aspects. For example, Citizens for Excellence in Education, a division of the National Association of Christian Educators, was formed to take over school boards across the U.S. (Cecile Richards, in *Sisterhood Is Forever*). Other well-funded and highly activist organizations with a heavily Christian orientation and huge memberships include the American Family Association (designated a hate group by the Southern Poverty Law Center), Focus on the Family, and Concerned Women for America. See also Christian Coalition, Christianity, Promise Keepers, stereotypes.

relocation "Years ago the term used to describe the internment was 'relocation.' That it is still used in textbooks to describe the internment is discouraging" (Mark Sweeting, in *Rethinking Schools*). "Relocation center" was the term used by the federal government to describe the 10 camps where more than 120,000 people of Japanese ancestry were held without charges for three years during World War II. West-coast Japanese Americans (two-thirds of whom were U.S. citizens) were forced into hastily built prisons in western desert regions. Among violated Constitutional rights were freedom of speech, freedom from unreasonable searches and seizures, the right to be informed by charges, the right to a speedy and public trial, the right to legal counsel, the right to a trial by jury, and the right to equal protection under the law. Instead of "relocation," use the factually accurate term, which might be: internment, incarceration, imprisonment, genocide. "Relocation" (with "some untoward incidents") is also the term used by the Turkish Historical Society for the slaughter of more than a million Armenians between 1914 and 1918 (Elif Şafak, *The Bastard of Istanbul*). See also Armenian genocide, resettlement.

Renaissance man the *American Heritage Dictionary* gives identical definitions for "Renaissance woman" and "Renaissance man."

renegades along with "raiders," this term is often used with bias, depending upon which side you're taking. For American Indians, for example, their story is one of resistance and survival, fighting to maintain land, culture, and community. Adjectives often used of Indians ("warlike," "bloodthirsty," or "treacherous") do not ask whether a group resorted to war in self-defense or whether their opponents might not also have been warlike, bloodthirsty, and treacherous, in addition perhaps to greedy and racist. See also American Indian, sports teams' names and mascots.

reorientation therapy see conversion therapy.

repairman repairer, service rep/technician, servicer, adjuster, technician, mechanic, fixer, troubleshooter, custodian. Or be specific: plumber, electrician, carpenter, roofer, etc. In England a "repairman" is a "fitter," a tidy, useful word.

reparative therapy see conversion therapy.

repo man repossessor, the repo.

representative see congressman.

reproductive justice Laura Jiménez of SisterSong Women of Color Reproductive Health Collective, says reproductive justice includes working "for the physical, mental, spiritual, political, economic, and social conditions for women and all people to be able to make healthy decisions about their sexuality and reproduction." SisterSong believes these choices must be informed by accurate, accessible, and culturally relevant sexuality education; healthy dialogues between young people and their families, peers, and communities; and the creation of a positive-sex culture. The group also believes that reproductive justice includes the human right to a healthy and satisfying sexuality, the right to have a child, the right not to have a child, and the right to parent the children we already have.

reproductive rights the rights of human beings (in practice, it is women who are most often denied all or some of these rights) to sex education, contraception, safe childbirth, abortion, health care, and childcare. Access to some reproductive rights for many women is limited or nonexistent because of financial, legal, religious, or other restraints. For example: 22 states enacted 70 abortion restrictions in 2013; the Hyde Amendment bans federal Medicaid coverage of abortion, and since only 17 states pay for abortion care with their own revenue, low-income women in most of the country must pay for an abortion out of pocket, making the right to abortion an empty promise for millions of women; provisions in state and federal law known as "refusal clauses" or "conscience clauses" allow healthcare providers (including pharmacists) to deny women contraceptives at will. Language is currently changing to subsume the pro-choice defense of the right to abortion into the reproductive rights continuum. Replacing the weaker "choice" with a "right" is more accurate, more compelling, and more defensible. Use "reproductive rights" unless you are quoting someone or writing about a group who uses "pro-choice" or self-identifies that way. For more on reproductive rights, see the *Women's Media Center Guide to Covering Reproductive Issues*, by Sarah Erdreich, edited by Rachel Larris: http://www.womensmediacenter.com/pages/read-the-womens-media-centers-media-guide-to-covering-reproductive-issues. See also abortion, fetus, pro-choice, pro-life, reproductive justice.

resettlement this term most often describes a benign endeavor to move populations because of economic, political, or weather disasters. However, it has also served occasionally as a euphemism for malignant endeavors like mass murder or deportation to detention camps. Verify its meaning for your particular use. See also relocation.

restaurateur woman or man.

retard person with mental disability/impairment/retardation, someone with developmental/cognitive delays. "Mental illness" and "mental retardation" are separate conditions; one does not imply the other. Labels such as feebleminded, idiot, imbecile, mental defective, mentally deficient, moron, cretin, and retard are highly offensive, stigmatizing, and inaccurate when used of anyone with a disability. They are also offensive, damaging, and inexcusable when used as slurs for other people because they associate extreme negativity with disabilities. In the past few years, a number of states have removed "mentally retarded" from state laws. See also disabilities, handicapped, idiot/idiocy, "people first" rule.

revenge porn websites that post revealing photos, mostly of women, without their consent and with their full names and identifying information (phone numbers, Facebook snapshots) are popularly known as revenge porn. The owner of the first such site is currently out of business, having lost a defamation lawsuit for $250,000. But a copycat website directs victims who want to be removed from the site to a "takedown service" that costs $250. According to a CBS report, that website's proprietor is straightforward about his desire to turn the controversial business of involuntary porn into a big moneymaker, claiming his site should be considered entertainment and not extortion. "I would say our business goal is to become big and profitable." "Only two states, California and New Jersey, make it illegal to post a sexual photo online without the subject's consent" (ABA Journal.com).

revenue enhancement regard this term with deep suspicion. It only means "bringing in more money," which has the same number of syllables but is much clearer, and it often involves some end-justifies-the-means thinking that nobody but the government or top executives is going to like.

reverend (adjective) depending on the denomination, this title may be used for a woman or a man. Use "The Reverend Dinah Morris" when writing, but in general do not use "reverend" as a noun, as in "How are you today, Reverend?" Use instead the person's first name, "Father" or "Mother," or the title the person prefers. Clergy today welcome a question like, "What shall I call you?" See also clergyman, minister, priest.

reverse discrimination although this term has its own dictionary definition now, its linguistic and real-life legitimacy is still much debated. On the level of language, the word "reverse" is illogical: discrimination is discrimination; how is discrimination somehow different, needing a special label, if it is leveled against traditionally dominant groups? Mary Daly (*Wickedary*) says it helps see the issue if you replace "discrimination" with "oppression." "The ludicrousness of *reverse oppression* is more obvious.... We can see that oppression is something done by the institutionally powerful to the powerless. That is, the agent is exposed. We can then see that 'reverse oppression' would imply oppression of the institutionally powerful, an obvious and absurd contradiction." On the level of everyday experiences by individuals, affirmative action may not be administered as effectively as it should be, but remember that the line after "I never promised you a rose garden" was "I never promised you perfect justice" (Hannah Green). And "studies using equally qualified black and white testers to apply for the same job have consistently found that whites are disproportionately favored in hiring; this speaks to the myth that white guys can't get jobs because women and minorities are taking them all" (Demetrius P. Junior, Minneapolis' *Star Tribune*). In *Fighting Words*, Patricia Hill Collins relates the astonishing story of the secretly taped Texaco executives' meeting to discuss Bari-Ellen Roberts's bias suit. First they referred to her as a "smart-mouthed little colored girl" and then said, "This diversity thing. You know how black jelly beans agree." And then one said, "That's funny. All the black jelly beans seem to be glued to the bottom of the bag." See also affirmative action.

rewrite man rewriter. See also newsman/newspaperman.

rhyme, feminine/masculine see feminine/masculine (poetry, music).

rich as Croesus there is nothing wrong with this phrase, but be aware of how many such expressions are male-based. Balance their use with female-based expressions, creative expressions of your own, or sex-neutral alternatives: well-to-do, made of money, worth a bundle/a pretty penny, rolling in money, on Easy Street, has a goldmine, has money to burn, flush, someone whose ship has come in. See also sex-linked expressions.

ridiculisms those who object to accurate, inclusive language rely principally on making up silly words and then showing us how silly they are. Of course they're silly! But nobody is using them except the people who made them up—talk about a straw argument! Professor Claire Caskey, for example, is still "manning the barricades" against "assaults" on the language; to kill with humor is his way and his after-dinner speeches are very popular. He gets laughs with every ridiculism he introduces: personkind, persondate, person your battle stations, person the lifeboats, foreperson, workpersons, personhole cover, person those pumps. Among scores of expressions created for the sole purpose of ridiculing them are: parasitically engaged (pregnant), follicularly challenged, ottoperson, vertically challenged. Using a particular to condemn a universal is a fault in logic. But then ridicule, it is said, is the first and last argument of fools.

rifleman sharpshooter, carabineer, crack shot, sniper, sharpshooter, shooter, gunner, soldier. See also gunman, hit man, marksman.

right/right-winger/the right/far right see political spectrum.

right-hand man right hand, deputy, lieutenant, assistant, right-hand/chief/invaluable assistant, aide, key aide, helper, attendant, co-worker, sidekick, subordinate.

rights "Food, shelter, education, and health care are all basic rights for all people" (George Lakoff, *Thinking Points*). Mary McCarthy pointed out in 1961, "Once the state is looked upon as the source of rights, rather than their bound protector, freedom becomes conditional on the pleasure of the state." These two basic principles are not obvious to many in the United States. Conservatives believe in individual responsibility; they consider social welfare programs morally weakening. Because the people at or near the top have "made it," they believe everyone should be able to do likewise. Unfortunately, poverty, disabilities, lack of education, dangerous neighborhoods, innutritious food, and other factors negatively affect one's ability to "make it." In most developed countries, the assumption is that people have rights to the basics so as to sustain life, work, and the pursuit of happiness. When addressing rights, be alert to rights to something (the right to a fair trial, to free speech, to practice your religion without interference) as well as the right to be free from something (from being assaulted, from having someone's religious beliefs imposed on you). The differences between freedom to and freedom from need to be recognized in such areas as guns, hunger, education, and economic activity. See also compassionate conservatism, liberal, poverty, safety net/social safety net, welfare.

right to die see assisted suicide.

right to life acceptable adjective for pro-life groups. "Right-to-lifer" is not taken as positive. See also pro-life.

right-to-work laws it's a pity we don't have a right to work in the Bill of Rights. The right-to-work laws are actually anti-union (Gloria Steinem in *Sisterhood Is Forever*), restricting union activities, often making it more difficult for workers to be adequately compensated and protected in the workplace. See also unemployed, union man.

ringmaster this term is entrenched in the language and has high meaning for most people; it almost invariably refers to a man, thus justifying its male character; and the "master" is overlooked by many people. If you want an alternative, consider ringleader, ring supervisor, circus announcer/leader/producer, announcer, host, leader. See also master of ceremonies/mistress of ceremonies.

riot grrrls see grrrl.

risk see at risk, high-risk group.

riverman river logger/jobber.

road sister this colorful term was used for girls/women when they first became hoboes in the 1930s. If you need a sex-neutral term, use hobo.

roaming indigenous or native peoples are often described as "roaming" or "wandering," which is defined as moving without purpose or direction, whereas in fact their movements had both; describe instead what they were actually doing: moving between winter and summer homes, going on religious pilgrimages, following food supplies.

riot think twice before using "riot" in connection with communities of color; it's a clichéd choice that may not always be accurate. "The white community riots, too—by moving to the suburbs or cutting back on social services" (Robin Morgan, *Saturday's Child*).

Robin Hood tax the French financial transaction tax (FTT) passed in 2012 is expected to be levied by nine other European countries as well. The FTT affects all transactions involving French companies valued at over $1.5 billion. Looking to raise half a billion euros the first year, the tax will be used partly to fight climate change, global poverty, and HIV/AIDS.

rob the cradle in the case of a partner below the age of consent, there are legal terms with associated criminal penalties that are more accurate. In the case of adult couples with an age difference, both women and men marry or date younger people, so the phrase isn't sexist, but it is ageist, judgmental, and unwelcome.

rock art petroglyphs, pictographs. Cave drawings were actually communication tools and maps left along migratory routes for other clans to follow.

roger although based on a man's name (from the old communications code for the letter "r"), this term meaning, "OK," "that's right," or "over and out" is not functionally sexist.

rogue nation/rogue state according to an opinion piece in *The Nation*, "After the cold war, we labeled our potential adversaries 'rogue nations'—violent, lawless, willing to trample the weak and ignore international law and morality to enforce their will. Now ... there is a growing consensus that the world's most destructive rogue nation is the most powerful country of them all." On the lighter side, a rogue nation has been defined as a "country that buys its military hardware from France, China, or Russia and not from the United States" (Justin Rezzonico, in Katrina vanden Heuvel, *Dictionary of Republicanisms*).

Roman Catholic "The female sex is in some respects inferior to the male sex, both as regards body and soul" (*Roman Catholic Encyclopedia* of 1912). And that was when they were (1) trying to be nice, and (2) relatively enlightened. Its unyielding stance on abortion (which was enunciated only in the 19th century) and on contraceptives (which is theologically, logically, and morally indefensible) plus the astonishingly high numbers of abusive priests and higher-ups who protected them and its current opposition to liberation theology have all left the Roman Catholic Church hierarchy in a weakened position with regard to many of its members.

Romani/Romanies the singular noun and the adjective is Romani or Romany; plural is Romanies. The word Roma is seen as a less precise adjective for those populations that speak, or at some time in the past spoke, the Romani language (for example, Roma National Congress). In the U.S., they are Romani Americans. In the Romani language there is no word for "Gypsy," and no Romanies accept it as a name for themselves. The pejorative "Gypsy" is an issue for parents who want to give their adopted Romani children a positive sense of culture identity, especially when Gypsies are so often portrayed as fairy-tale characters or thieves (remember the Gypsy who stole Pinocchio?). Ian Hancock, the leading authority on Romani culture, history, and terminology, says the Romanies and the Jews are the only two people to have occupied Europe for so many centuries without countries of their own. "We always lived in other peoples' countries as outsiders." Some 12 to 14 million Romanies are dispersed today in pockets across all seven continents, from India, considered their ancestral home, to America, where about one million live. Romani culture is so diverse it may be more accurate to speak of "cultures." And there are more than sixty dialects of Romany in Europe, at least 18 in Bulgaria alone. In the *Los Angeles Times*, Colum McCann writes that if Europe, where 10 million Romanies live, "recognizes itself, and ultimately critiques itself, on how it treats its most downtrodden, then surely the acid test for the EU is its ongoing treatment of the Roma. They can be found living in the housing projects of Paris, the toxic dumps in Kosovo, the ruined outskirts of villages in eastern Slovakia, the warren of backstreets in old Polish towns and the gray flatlands of Dublin. Each place has its own—sometimes tiny—community. But when taken together, these groups form a giant cultural mosaic, one that leans overwhelmingly toward poverty. There are, of course, Romani doctors, psychologists, poets, and scholars who ... point to Romani contributions to the world of arts, politics, and music by figures of Gypsy descent as diverse as Pablo Picasso, Django Reinhardt, Bob Hoskins, Charlie Chaplin, flamenco legend Carmen Amaya, and even President Clinton. But the old clichés of lying, cheating, stealing and breaking curfew with violin endure." If you think your audience will not recognize "Romani," you may have to relate it to "Gypsy" (capitalized and in quotation marks). Whenever possible, refer to specific Romani groups (Romanichal, Kalderash, Bashaldo). See also gyp, Romani Holocaust.

Romani Holocaust from 1933 to 1945, an estimated 1 to 1.5 million Romanies were exterminated by Hitler's policies of racial supremacy (victims of the Nazis numbered nearly 12 million). Romanies lost a higher proportion of their total number in Nazi Germany than any other targeted population, although they have received no war crimes reparations as a people. Ian Hancock (*Pariah Syndrome: An Account of Gypsy Slavery and Persecution*) says, "During the first few months of Nazi rule, an SS study group proposed that all Gypsies then in Germany should be killed by drowning them in ships taken out into mid-ocean and sunk... The authorities began a lengthy process of codifying persons of Romani origin. ...

Some Gypsies were sterilized as early as 1933 ... beginning in the same year, camps were being established by the Nazis to contain Gypsies in Vennhausen, Dieselstrasse, Mahrzan, and Dachau. In 1936 the anti-Gypsy campaign became globalized through the establishment of the International Center for the Fight Against the Gypsy Menace by Interpol in Vienna. ... In 1939 Johannes Behrendt, speaking for the Party, declared that 'elimination without hesitation of the entire Gypsy population had to be instigated immediately.' Only Jews and Gypsies were singled out for annihilation on racial grounds. Gypsies faced deportations, mass murders, slave labor camps, and extermination in concentration camps; an estimated 500,000 Gypsies died. Their dark skin and curly hair was a threat to the purity of German blood." Catherine Kjos (in Minneapolis' *Star Tribune*) says "Tens of thousands were recorded killed at Auschwitz, while others perished at other camps. Many more were massacred in fields and forests and shooting pits dug on the edge of towns—where no lists were ever drawn up." See also gyp, Romani/Romanies.

Romeo this evocative name conveys a whole story and complex understandings to those familiar with its origins. Should you need a less specific but inclusive term, consider lover, doomed/young/dashing lover.

rookie man or woman.

roommate inclusive term describing someone you share quarters with; so far, it is not generally used as a euphemism for lover.

roughhouse/roughneck although culturally reserved for men, particularly because one meaning of "roughhouse" is "an oilfield worker" (a traditionally all-male field), this term may also be used for women when appropriate.

roundsman deliverer; inspector, police officer, watch, patrol; relief cook.

roustabout a roustabout has invariably been a man, but inclusive alternatives are available: deckhand, wharfhand; circus worker/laborer; oilfield worker/laborer.

rowdy can be said of women/girls or boys/men, although girls have often been reproached for being rowdy, while in boys it was considered "natural."

royal/royalty although these terms are based on "roy" ("king"), they no longer have perceived male associations.

rubbing noses Eskimos don't rub noses and they object to the characterization; also, most of them aren't called Eskimos. See Eskimo.

rube based on a man's name and used more of a man than of a woman, this term is also a derogatory anti-rural stereotype. More sex-neutral and less pejorative terms include: country cousin, rustic, provincial.

rugged individualism this phrase, most often associated with policies of the Republican party, refers to the belief that if people can't succeed on their own they just aren't trying hard enough—and that therefore government support for individuals is unnecessary. Failure to prosper is seen as a personal defect, with no credence given to systemic or individual inequities that may limit people's attainments (economic policies that favor the wealthy, low wages, racism, classism, mental illness, poor health, personal catastrophes, inadequate schools, unemployment levels, etc.). The working poor can testify that even if you work as hard as the average CEO, some people still can't make it in the U.S. today. Republican President Herbert Hoover liked to talk about "rugged individualism," but of course he oversaw the Stock Market Crash of 1929 and the beginning of the Great Depression.

rule of thumb there has been much debate about this term and its association with the right of a man to chastise his wife with a switch no thicker than his thumb. The original "rule of thumb" had nothing to do with wife-beating (among the provenances: the last joint of the thumb is about an inch and so was commonly used as a measure; artists used a thumb to gauge perspective; the thumb was used to test the degree of fermentation of malt in making beer in 19th-century England; the thumb was used as a tiny writing pad to calculate the exchange of Spanish dollars for French francs by French contractors in the early 1800s in southern France). In "*Rule of Thumb* and the Folklaw of the Husband's Stick," *Journal of Legal Education*, Henry Ansgar Kelly writes, "Printed references to 'rule of thumb' as a guideline antedate references to it in the context of wife-beating by almost several hundred years. An 1868 case, *State v. Rhodes* appears to be the only case on record in which a husband was let off because 'His Honor was of opinion that the defendant had a right to whip his wife with a switch no larger than his thumb.'" Kelly points out that the verdict was overturned by *State v. Oliver* (1874): "We may assume that the old doctrine, that a husband had a right to whip his wife, provided he used a switch no larger than his thumb, is not law in North Carolina. Indeed, the Courts have advanced from that barbarism until they have reached the position, that the husband has no right to chastise his wife, under any circumstances." The overturning of the case apparently got less press than the original suit. In 1881, Harriet H. Robinson (*Massachusetts In the Woman Suffrage Movement*) wrote, "Thirty years ago, when the Woman's Rights Movement began, the status of a married woman was little better than that of a domestic servant. By the English common law, her husband was her lord and master. He had the sole custody of her person, and of her minor children. He could 'punish her with a stick no bigger than his thumb,' and she could not complain against him." In Margaret Deland's 1924 *New Friends in Old Chester*, a woman said to the man who had "jokingly" threatened to beat her, "Let's see ... you can use a stick no bigger than your thumb, can't you?" "Rule of thumb" may not have originated in wife-beating, but it has acquired that association for many people. Use instead general rule, rough guideline, commonsense/ballpark/approximate measure.

rule the roost this phrase is sexist because, although the roost is invariably "manned" by a rooster, the expression refers to a woman who dominates her family. The expression developed from the nonsexist British variant "rule the roast" where "roast" refers either to a governing body or to the roasted beef served for Sunday dinner (and it is moot who ruled it: the woman who roasted it or the man who carved it). If you want an alternative, consider call the shots/the tune/the plays, have it all one's way, lay down the law, be in the saddle/driver's seat, hold all the cards.

Rwanda/Rwandan genocide the 1994 mass killing of between 500,000 and 1,000,000 ethnic Tutsis and moderate Hutu sympathizers in Rwanda was not a conflict, not a war, not trouble between groups, but genocide.

> Words can destroy. What we call each other ultimately becomes what we think of each other, and it matters.
>
> Jeane J. Kirkpatrick

saboteur this grammatically masculine French word is used for both sexes in French and in English.

sacristan depending on the denomination, a sacristan may be either sex.

safe-haven laws nearly all states have enacted safe-haven legislation for the noncriminal relinquishment of unwanted newborns. In the *Columbia Law Review*, Carol Sanger addresses these laws' relatively small impact on infant abandonment in terms of their more long-term goal: overturning *Roe v. Wade*. Sanger says that by connecting infant life to unborn life, and abandonment to infanticide, proponents of these quickly passed laws have blurred distinctions between pregnancy and motherhood, fetus and child, and abortion and infanticide.

safe sex this ought to be "safer sex," since 100 percent safe sex is only no sex at all. When using "safe sex," define terms and spell out relative margins of "safety."

safety net/social safety net the net is not only full of holes, but it's been mended so often by careless (care-less) officials that it barely keeps some people from drowning and rarely actually helps anyone out of the water. Most conservatives believe in the bootstrap method of climbing into the boat and seem unable to grasp the effects of the economy, unemployment, lack of health insurance, being born into poverty, classism, and racism on certain individuals. As a result, insult is added to injury when the safety net shrinks and we blame the people in the water for their situation. See also compassionate conservatism, liberal, poverty, rights, welfare.

sahib always a man; the woman is a "memsahib."

salesgirl/saleslady/salesman/saleswoman salesclerk, clerk, sales associate/rep/agent/representative/broker/manager, floor assistant, agent, seller, door-to-door seller, canvasser, commercial traveler, vendor, dealer, marketer, merchant, retailer, wholesaler, trader, solicitor, shop assistant, peddler. These terms are not interchangeable: "salesclerk" is appropriate for a retail store employee, while "sales representative" describes someone employed by a large manufacturing company who is a combination business manager, product specialist, and sales trainer. For "salesmen," use plurals of the alternatives given as well as sales force/staff/personnel, salespeople.

salesmanship sales ability/expertise/technique/skill, high sales potential, selling ability; vendorship, sales record; hucksterism.

salutations (letters) when you know the person's name but not their sex or social title, write Dear Lane Busby; when you don't have a name, either address yourself to the company (Dear Gates-Porter) or to a job title (Dear Credit Manager) or to a role (Dear Neighbor). The trend in non-personal letters is toward replacing the salutation with a subject line (Re: enclosed contract). For more information and lists of salutation possibilities, see the Writing Guidelines.

salvage man salvage worker/inspector/repairer, salvager, parts salvager.

Samaritan, good man or woman.

Sambo possibly from a Hausan personal name meaning "second son," Sambo was popularized by Helen Bannerman's 1899 book, "The Story of Little Black Sambo," in which a clever boy outwits some determined tigers. Republished in 2003 with new illustrations to replace the condescending originals, the book re-evoked a debate over its ethnic stereotypes. On one level, it is a charming story (and was even chosen as one of the top 40 children's books on the Kirkus Reviews' 2003 Editor's Choice List), but it's been called racist for its stereotypical characters and derogatory names (Sambo's parents are Mumbo and Jumbo). Some say no amount of revision can sanitize the pejorative "Sambo," which dates to the mid-19th century (Irving Lewis Allen, *Unkind Words*). "Sambo" shouldn't be used to refer to anyone, but recommending or mentioning the book is up to you and your perception of your audience.

same-sex this adjective is used (1) to refer to situations that include only one sex (same-sex school, same-sex friends), and (2) as an inclusive adjective meaning lesbian or gay (same-sex couples, same-sex dating).

same-sex marriage see marriage.

samurai this member of the historical Japanese warrior class was always a man.

sanctions in *Newsweek*, Fareed Zakaria says, "Sanctions are the Energizer Bunny of foreign policy. Despite a dismal record, they just keep on ticking." He says with some countries, sanctions have become a substitute for an actual policy. "By design, sanctions shrink a country's economy. But the parts of the economy they shrink most are those that aren't under total state control." The end result is that "the government gets stronger." Workers are forced out of jobs (with many of the women ending up in the sex trade), legitimate businesses are replaced by black markets and drug trafficking, while "the military, which controls border crossings, ports and checkpoints, always prospers. ... One of the lessons of Iraq surely is that a prolonged sanctions regime will destroy civil society and empower the worst elements of the country, those who thrive in such a gangland atmosphere. If the purpose of sanctions is to bring about a better system for that country, devastating its society is a strange path to the new order."

Sandman, the derived from an old European tale, the Sandman is harmless enough in himself; the problem is that so many of his ilk are male (Santa Claus, Jack Frost) and small children are especially susceptible to the subliminal messages about maleness and femaleness in a world overrun with "he"s. If you're interested in establishing your own terms, consider Sandy Eyes, the sleep/sand fairy, sand sprinkler, the sleep genie.

sand nigger see anti-Arabism.

sanitation man sanitation worker/engineer.

sanitized censored, approved for public release.

Sansei literally, "third generation," this acceptable term is used for the U.S.-born grandchild of Japanese immigrants to the U.S. Plural is Sansei or Sanseis. See also Issei, Kibei, Nisei, Yonsei.

Santa Claus Father Christmas, Pére Noel, Saint Nicholas, Kris Kringle, and Santa Claus are better left as they are, even with the acknowledgment that these male figures reinforce the cultural male-as-norm system. Mrs. Claus goes largely unrecognized; she doesn't even have a first name. There is nothing inherently wrong with a male Santa Claus; the problem is that nearly every cultural icon of this magnitude is male. (The Santa Claus World Union is currently debating opening its membership to female Santas—Mrs. Claus or Mother Christmas.) Those interested in promoting female as well as male heroes could introduce Befana, or La Befana, the Italian version of Santa Claus, who carries a cane and a bell and traditionally drops down the chimney on the twelfth night of Christmas.

sapphic acceptable term meaning of or relating to lesbianism.

sassy/saucy because these are used only of girls and women, you may want to consider instead impudent, insolent, mouthy, bold, nervy, forward.

Satan/he Satan/it.

satyr by definition, a satyr is male. If you want sex-neutral alternatives, consider libertine, bedhopper, swinger, lover, seducer. See also nymphomaniac.

savage this highly ethnocentric term has been used to justify invading, dispossessing, and subjugating entire populations. In the case of American Indians, their manner of defending themselves was called "savage" and Indian victories were called "massacres" while unprovoked attacks and indiscriminate killings of Indians were simply called "victories"; "any attempt to evaluate war as 'civilized' or 'savage' usually depends on which side one is on" (Thomas R. Frazier, ed., *The Underside of American History*). Slavery was made possible by labeling kidnapped Africans "savages." See also "discovery" of America, heathen, illiterate, massacre, Pagan/Neopagan, primitive.

savant the French word is grammatically masculine but is used in French and English for both sexes. See also idiot savant.

scalper (tickets) the first meaning of "scalper" is "one (especially an American Indian) who removes scalps" (*The Oxford English Dictionary*, 2nd ed.). The second meaning refers to selling tickets (or stocks) for higher (or lower) prices than usual. The term is objectionable, even though users don't associate it consciously with Indians; if you're an American Indian, however, it bites. There is currently no easily recognized equivalent. Write when you find one. Until then, experiment with combinations like ticket shark/sharp/hustler/runner, stock rustler (related by marriage to cattle rustlers).

scarlet woman there is no parallel term—nor any expressed condemnation—for the men who are the "partners in crime" of scarlet women.

scatterbrained see ditz/ditzy.

schizophrenic person who has/with schizophrenia; never use "schizophrenic" as an adjective for a person. In addition, "Schizophrenia is not characterized by dual personality and to perpetuate this myth is a great disservice to those persons already suffering from a brain disorder" (Helen L. Klanderud, in *Conscience*). The National Alliance for Research on Schizophrenia and Depression says, "Schizophrenia does not mean 'split personality...' It ... is an illness with a biological cause, like cancer or heart disease.... [It] is one of the most common mental illnesses—about 1 percent of the world population will develop it. In the United States, more than two million people suffer from this disease in a given year. Schizophrenia causes more hospitalization than almost any other illness." Schizophrenia involves incoherent, hallucinatory, delusional thinking; be careful of using it to denote a split, dual, binary, or otherwise divided personality. See also disabilities, handicapped, mental illness.

schlemiel woman or man.

schmoozer man or woman.

schmuck this term and its lesser-known euphemism, "schmo," are reserved for men; they are from the Yiddish for "penis," which is why Yiddish-speaking individuals don't use it in polite company. To non-Yiddish-speakers, the term means something like "stupid jerk." It might be better to use that.

scold (noun) a common scold was legally defined as a troublesome, angry woman who broke the public peace (and the law) with her brawling and wrangling and was punished by public ducking (Abby Adams, *An Uncommon Scold*); a woman was booked (but not convicted) on a common scold charge as recently as 1971 in the United States.

scold (verb) instead of this, use for a woman the term you would use for a man in the same situation: chide, reprimand, lecture, admonish, criticize, remonstrate, upbraid, chew out, rebuke, chastise, give a piece of one's mind, lay down the law.

schoolboy/schoolfellow/schoolgirl schoolchild, schoolmate, classmate, peer, youngster, elementary school child, child.

schoolmarm/schoolmaster/schoolmistress schoolteacher, teacher, educator, instructor, tutor, principal.

score the concept of scoring (a man "getting" or "having" a woman sexually) underlies much that is skewed with female-male relations. Thinking of a woman in this way makes her a notch on the bedpost; she is certainly not a partner in any meaningful sense. Lack of mutuality underlies a "score" ("Man is the hunter; woman is his game," wrote Alfred Lord Tennyson in *The Princess*). "Score" is also an inclusive term for the client of either sex of a male or female prostitute. See also "lay"/"easy lay"/"good lay," sex object, sexual conquest.

Scotch a contraction of "Scottish," this term is not in high favor although it is accepted in certain fixed expressions (for example, "Scotch whisky"). It is always avoided in reference to people. See also Scotsman, Scottish.

Scotsman Scot, Scotlander, inhabitant of Scotland, Scotsman/Scotswoman. Plural: Scots, Scotlanders, inhabitants of Scotland, Scotswomen and Scotsmen. This form is preferred to "Scotchman/Scotchwoman." See also Scotch, Scottish.

Scottish this adjective is acceptable for referring to Scotland or its people, language, or culture. "Scots" is the Scottish shortened form, "Scotch" the English (and thus less acceptable) form. Whether to use "Scots" (informal) or "Scottish" (formal) depends on your style.

scout girl or boy. See also Boy Scout, Girl Scout.

scoutmaster scoutleader.

scrapman scrap worker/separator/collector.

script girl/script man script supervisor; continuity, continuity supervisor. Note the nonparallel "girl/man."

Scrooge there is nothing wrong with using this colorful and highly evocative name, but be aware of how many such expressions in the English language are male-based. Balance their use with female-based expressions, creative expressions of your own, or sex-neutral alternatives: tightwad, money-grubber, penny pincher, pinchpenny, miser, skinflint, cheapskate, piker, cheeseparer. See also sex-linked expressions.

sculptress sculptor. See also "feminine" word ending.

seamstress seamster, sewer, tailor, mender, alterer, stitcher, alterations expert, custom tailor, clothier, dressmaker, fashion sewer, garment worker/maker/designer, needleworker.

seaman seafarer, sailor, enlisted sailor, naval recruit, mariner, merchant mariner, marine, navigator, pilot, tar, salt, gob, captain, skipper, mate, first mate, crew member, deck hand, boater, yachter. "Seaman" and "seaman recruit" are official U.S. Navy terms, but refer to either sex.

seaman apprentice apprentice sailor/crew member, marine apprentice. "Seaman apprentice" is an official Navy term used for both sexes.

seamanlike/seamanly shipshape, sailor-like. Or be specific: tidy, orderly, skilled.

seamanship navigation/ship-handling skills, marine strategy, navigational/ship-handling/sailing expertise/techniques.

second shift, the from Arlie Hochschild's *The Second Shift*, this term refers to the unpaid job a woman comes home to after a day of paid work. The idea that women work two—or three—shifts is not new. In 1918, Alexandra Kollontai wrote, "The wife, the mother, who is a worker, sweats blood to fill three tasks at the same time: to give the necessary working hours as her husband does, in some industry or commercial establishment, then to devote herself as well as she can to her household and then also to take care of her children" (in Eleanor S. Riemer and John C. Fout, *European Women*). See also housewife, housework, working father, working mother/working wife/working woman.

second-story man cat burglar, burglar, housebreaker, professional thief.

second-wave feminism when possible, avoid compartmentalizing feminism into "waves." A seamless garment more appropriately denotes this particular work that is never done. What is generally termed the second wave, however, is the period from the early 1960s to the mid-1980s. During this time, the birth control pill became available, Betty Friedan published *The Feminine Mystique*, the Civil Rights Act passed, women established the National Organization for Women (NOW), Title IX was enacted, lesbian and gay rights were sought, *Sisterhood Is Powerful* (Robin Morgan, ed.) struck a nerve, and the *Roe v. Wade* decision legalized abortion. During this period, black women, Latinas, and lesbian women expanded the feminist movement through their activism and contributions to feminist theory. Gloria Steinem, Jane Fonda, Robin Morgan, Angela Davis, Bella Abzug, Adrienne Rich, Alice Walker, and Dolores Huerta are just a few of the prominent second-wave feminists whose contributions continue to inspire women everywhere. For complete, accurate, and fun-to-know-and-tell information on the history of feminism, see *The Reader's Companion to U.S. Women's History*, edited by Wilma Mankiller, Gwendolyn Mink, Marysa Navarro, Barbara Smith, and Gloria Steinem. See also feminism, feminisms, first-wave feminism, third-wave feminism, waves (feminism).

secretary office administrator. Legal secretaries have discussed changing to "legal support professionals"; some judges' secretaries are now called "judicial assistants" or "administrative assistants"; other titles include administrative professional/assistant/coordinator, executive secretary, executive assistant, and office administrator/professional/manager. "But whatever they're called—and although the office could not run without them—they remain at the bottom of the heap in status, treatment, and pay" (Ellen Bravo, in *Sisterhood Is Forever*). Although the number of men in this pink-collar occupation has increased, more than 97 percent of all secretaries are still women—which is a switch. Until the 1870s, when the typewriter was introduced, the secretarial profession was considered strictly men's work. From the Middle Ages onward, a "secretarius" (from the Latin for "secret") was a confidential male officer who could be trusted with state secrets. When the YWCA hired eight women to be "typewriters" in 1873, physicians were brought in to certify that the women's physical and mental abilities could withstand the pressure; many people predicted the women's minds would snap. In 1880, the all-male First Congress of Shorthand Writers issued a statement saying, "Some day women will be smart enough to write shorthand." See also Administrative Professionals Secretaries Day/Week, girl Friday, pink-collar job/worker.

Secret Service man Secret Service agent, member of the Secret Service, bodyguard, intelligence agent/officer, plainclothes officer. The Secret Service employs women and men.

secular humanist see secularist.

secularist "Secularism is the belief that ecclesiastical institutions and their concerns should not impinge upon governance and, more generally, on institutional arrangements and modes of thought" (Andrew Levine, *Political Keywords*). "Secularist is beginning to rival liberal as an epithet—in media discussions of domestic politics, it's five times as common as it was a decade ago," says Geoffrey Nunberg (*Talking Right*). "Secular" simply means "not religious" or "without religious significance": children playing on swings are indulging in a secular activity, one that has nothing to do with religion; if they stop to say a prayer, they've moved from a secular to a religious activity. Those described as secularists or secular humanists simply want religion to have its own sphere and government to have its own sphere; in separating church and state, the Constitution set us up as a secular, not a religious, nation. A secular humanist is someone with a philosophy of humanistic values or practice of good behavior independent of religion. Sometimes equated with ethical atheists, humanists include not only atheists but also agnostics and others belonging to organized religious. Note that to the Muslim ear, "secular" tends to equate with "godless" (Chris Seiple,

Christian Science Monitor); "pluralist" is a much better word in some contexts, encouraging those with and without a God-based worldview to have an equal place in the public square.

Secure Flight in the *Los Angeles Times*, Patt Morrison discusses the Department of Homeland Security and its Transportation Security Administration's Secure Flight program. She says if you haven't heard of it, "That's the way they like it in D.C. But some of the people who do know about it are not pleased." She says Canadians are peeved: some airline flights that merely fly over the United States, without so much as touching a wheel to U.S. soil, would have to fork over more information about passengers, and do it as much as three days before the flights take off. The AFL-CIO is also peeved: then-Homeland Security chief Michael Chertoff notified the European Union that they were required to provide the following information about EU passengers: "racial or ethnic origin, political opinions, religious or philosophical beliefs, trade union membership and data concerning the health or sex life of the individual." Morrison asks, "Since when is union membership—not to mention the sex lives of French, Dutch, British, or Italian tourists—a terrorist risk factor?" Privacy advocates are peeved: Could EU data collection apply to Americans too? Even some senators are peeved: why isn't the agency inspecting a jet's cargo as rigorously as it inspects passengers and their toiletries and why are there no security checks for foreigners repairing U.S. jets in places such as Egypt and Singapore? See also Protect America Act, the; rights.

seductive both men and women can be seductive; don't limit the word to women.

seductress seducer. See also "feminine" word endings.

see a man about a dog/horse see somebody about a dog/horse. Or replace the phrase with whatever you really mean. This Victorian circumlocution was designed to avoid mentioning anything inconvenient or embarrassing: visiting the restroom, going to a bar or tavern for a drink, seeing a prostitute. (Dorothy Parker once said, "Excuse me, everybody, I have to go to the bathroom. I really have to telephone, but I'm too embarrassed to say so.")

seigneur/seigneury retain in historical context. Alternatives: member of the landed gentry, feudal property owner, elder, local authority; landed estate, manor house.

selectman representative, city representative, commissioner, council member, member of the council, councilor, municipal/board officer, board member, chancellor, ward manager; selectwoman and selectman.

self-determination "the power to decide one's own destiny" (Patricia Hill Collins, *Fighting Words*), self-determination is considered by many to be a moral and legal right for nations and individuals as long as they aren't interfering with the rights of others.

self-made man self-made individual/person, entrepreneur, go-getter, hard-worker, rags to riches story; self-made woman and self-made man.

self-mastery self-control, self-discipline. For discussion of "master" words, see master (noun).

self-regulation see regulation/deregulation/voluntary regulation.

seminal because "seminal" is the adjectival form of "semen," than which nothing could be more male, the word is clearly sex-linked. In addition, as Marie Shear (in *New Directions for Women*) points out: "If we believe what newspapers and magazines tell us, intellectual and literary prowess flows from Man's Most Cherished Protuberance." She suggests using such synonyms as: creative, pioneer, pioneering, groundbreaking, pathfinding, trailblazing, unprecedented, precedent-setting, influential, original, landmark, milestone, inspiring, inventive, innovative, originative, departure from, germinal, germinative, primary, primal, primordial, prototypal, prototypical, exemplary, fresh, novel, pivotal, first of its kind, historic, initial, earliest, source, unorthodox, nonconforming, unconventional, rudimentary, inceptive, catalytic, influential, far-reaching, productive. She adds, "The apologist for biased usage will, of course dismiss such matters as trivial. But I think they make a vas deferens."

seminar although "seminar" is related to "semen" by the back door (it comes from the word for "seed plot"), it is a nonsexist term, etymologically and functionally.

seminary both sexes have attended seminaries in the past, but their experiences have not been parallel: seminaries for women enrolled high school-aged girls while seminaries for men trained clergy. The former is now a rarity, while the latter includes women, depending on the denomination. See also clergyman.

senator see congressman.

senility dementia. The *Publication Manual of the American Psychological Association*, 4th ed., says the term "dementia" is preferred to "senility"; "senile dementia of the Alzheimer's type" is an accepted term. Avoid the casual use of "senile/senility" as a synonym for "forgetful/forgetfulness" or "old/old age" and do not use it as though it is something inevitable for everyone, which is not true.

senior airman this official U.S. Air Force term is used for both sexes.

senior/senior citizen although not universally liked, these terms might be around for a while. The best alternatives: older adult/person. Or use the person's age or age group ("those over 65," "patients aged 75-90"). References to age are often irrelevant or used in nonparallel ways (we see "elderly man catches burglar" but not "middle-aged man wins cooking contest" and "robs elderly woman" but not "robs young woman"). Avoid euphemisms like "Golden Agers" or the term "retirees" when not all the group are retired, and probably not idle either. The "citizen" in senior citizen at least acknowledges that age is not the only relevant characteristic of people over 65, although the National Gray Panthers, the American Association of Retired Persons, and the National Retired Teachers Association all prefer "older person/people/American" to "senior citizen." See also ageism, old, old man/old woman, oldster, old-timer.

separate the men from the boys separate the sheep from the goats/wheat from the chaff/professionals from the amateurs/strong from the weak/good from the bad/able from the incompetent/mature from the immature.

separation of church and state reviewing Garry Wills' book, *Head and Heart: American Christianities*, Tim Rutten writes (in *Los Angeles Times*) that the separation of church and state was the U.S. Constitution's single wholly original contribution to the political tradition. "It is precisely this innovative separation, Wills contends, that has allowed religion to flourish in America as it does nowhere else in the developed world. Wills points out that at the time of the founding, historians estimate that only about 17 percent of Americans professed formal religious adherence, a historic low point. The framers were deists, who believed in a divine providence knowable only through reason and experience and not prone to intervene in the affairs of men." Deism was "the religion of the educated class by the middle of the 18th century. Legal scholar William Lee Miller writes that the chief founders of the nation were all Deists—he lists Washington, Franklin, John Adams, Jefferson, Madison, Hamilton, and Paine, though many more leaders of the founding era could be added." The Constitution of the U.S. does not mention God at all. Wills says that today "The right wing in America likes to think that the United States government was, at its inception, highly religious, specifically highly Christian, and—more to the point—highly biblical." This was not true of that or any later government. The separation of church and state "has been upheld by every Supreme Court since 1879—until 2002, when the court approved school vouchers" (Robin Morgan, *Fighting Words*). Wills mentions Karl Rove's part in bringing this about. "He shaped the hard core of the Republican Party around resentments religious people felt over abortion, homosexuality, Darwinism, women's liberation, pornography and school prayer. ... Rove made the executive branch of the United States more openly and avowedly religious than it had ever been, though he had no discernible religious belief himself." Thomas Jefferson specified that "civil powers alone have been given to the President of the United States, and no authority to direct the religious exercises of his constituents." When George W. Bush established an Office for Faith-Based Initiatives inside the White House, he was in clear violation of a 1971 U.S. Supreme Court Decision that said, "Any statute [or public policy] must have a secular legislative purpose." The Bush administration provided funds for faith-based social-service programs to practice religious discrimination and to hire only people belonging to their church. That administration also instituted a "religious test" for judges, promising to appoint only "commonsense judges who understand that our rights were derived from God." Robin Morgan (*Fighting Words*) quotes George W. Bush, "But the key thing is, is that we do have the capacity to allow faith programs to access enormous sums of social service money" and the Texas Republican Party Platform of 2002, "Our Party pledges to do everything within its power to dispel the myth of separation of church and state." She also cites Ulysses S. Grant: "Leave the matter of religion to the family altar, the church, and the private schools supported entirely by private contributions. Keep the church and state forever separate"; James A. Garfield: "The divorce between Church and State ought to be absolute"; and Supreme Court Justice Robert H. Jackson: "The day that this country ceases to be free for irreligion, it will cease to be free for religion."

serf man or woman.

seropositive see HIV.

serve two masters serve God and mammon, have divided loyalties, be torn in two. For discussion of "master" words, see master (noun).

serviceman (armed forces) service member, member of the service/ armed forces, enlistee, recruit, officer, sailor, soldier, Marine, flyer; service personnel, servicewoman and serviceman. Or use specific service titles—all of which may now refer to either a woman or a man. Some of the following sample titles still appear "masculine" as we are unused to women in these ranks—and women may not to date have filled all of them—but they may potentially be held by either sex: adjutant, admiral, brigadier general, captain, colonel, commandant, commander, command sergeant major, commodore, corporal, ensign, field marshall, first lieutenant/sergeant, fleet admiral, general, gunnery sergeant, lance corporal, lieutenant/lieutenant colonel/lieutenant commander/ lieutenant general/lieutenant junior grade, major, major general, master sergeant, military police, NCO (noncommissioned officer), paratrooper, petty officer, private/private first class, rear admiral, second lieutenant, senior naval officer, sergeant/sergeant at arms/sergeant first class/sergeant major, squadron commander/squadron leader, staff officer/staff sergeant/staff sergeant major, subaltern, technical/top sergeant, vice admiral, warrant officer, wing commander. See also airman, draft, midshipman, wingman.

serviceman (repair) servicer, service contractor, repairer, technician, maintenance/repair worker, troubleshooter, fixer, mender, adjuster; gas station/service station attendant, mechanic.

service wife military/soldier's/service member's spouse. Casey Miller and Kate Swift (*The Handbook of Nonsexist Writing*) say that tacking on identifiers like "service wives" makes women appendages of both a man and an institution while detracting from their own lives and roles. The terminology also assumes that all members of the institution are men, whereas today a number of service spouses are men.

session man (music recording session) session player/musician, studio musician/player; session man and session woman; freelance musician.

set-asides a certain percentage of government contracting and buying is set aside for small businesses, minority-owned, and women-owned businesses.

settler those who moved onto Indian homelands have generally been referred to by historians as "settlers" whereas to Indians they were trespassers or invaders. Be conscious of the perspective from which this term is viewed.

sex understanding the difference between sex and gender is crucial to the appropriate use of language referring to women and men. Sex is biological: people with male genitals are male, and people with female genitals are female. Gender is cultural: our notions of "masculine" tell us how we expect men to behave and our notions of "feminine" tell us how we expect women to behave—but these may have nothing to do with biology. When deciding whether a word is restricted to one sex or the other, the only acceptable limitation is genetic sex. A woman cannot be a sperm donor because it's biologically impossible. It may be culturally unusual for a man to be a nanny, but it is not biologically impossible; to assume all nannies are women is sexist because the issue is gender, not sex. Gender signifies a subjective cultural attitude while sex is an objective biological fact.

sex change operation see sex reassignment surgery.

sex differences in 1947, Dorothy Sayers wrote, "The first thing that strikes the careless observer is that women are unlike men. ... But the fundamental thing is that women are more like men than anything else in the world." In 1955, Ivy Compton-Burnett observed, "There is more difference within the sexes than between them." Thirty-five years later, a *Newsweek* article concurs: "Social scientists agree that the sexes are much more alike than they are different, and that variations within each sex are far greater than variations between the sexes." According to *The Opposite Sex* (Anne Campbell, ed.), "As soon as we finish with sexual anatomy and move on to questions about behavior, abilities and social roles, 'obvious' differences [between the sexes] turn out to be not nearly as obvious as we may have thought at first." The differences between the sexes can be examined along three axes: (1) anatomy, or how we are physically different from each other; (2) biology, or how we behave innately differently from each other because we are male or because we are female; (3) culture, or how we live out certain social roles as women/girls and men/boys. A sperm donor is always a man, not because of the culture, but because of anatomy and biology. A CEO today is far more likely to be a man than a woman, not because of anatomy or biology, but because of culture. It is easy to see when anatomy determines behavior (only women give birth, only men can impregnate women). It is not quite so easy to see when culture determines behavior and when biology determines it. Are girls innately better at verbal tasks and boys innately better at spatial tasks? Or is it the culture that determines the small statistical test-score variations between the sexes? (Sex differences in abilities are only averages, which means that men/boys can do as well on verbal abilities as the best women/girls, and girls/women can do as well as the best boys/men on spatial abilities.) Is it biology or culture that determines who is "the weaker sex"? Research shows that when adults are told a baby is a girl, they view the child as delicate, fragile, or small in size. But when told the *same* child is a boy, they think of him as strong, alert, and large. Increasingly, social scientists emphasize that society as much as nature turns girls into women and boys into men. James M. Dubik (in *Newsweek*) explains how he came to see, via his two daughters and his experiences teaching male and female cadets at West Point, that "many of the characteristics I thought were 'male' are, in fact, 'human.'" Infant psychiatrist Dr. Taghi Modarressi says, "When we talk about inborn, intrinsic maleness and femaleness, we really don't know what we're talking about." Our western, hierarchical thinking says that if two things are different, one must necessarily be better or worse, higher or lower, than the other. Applied to the differences between the sexes, this attitude has been particularly malignant. (Which is "better," an apple or an orange, a lake or a river, geology or astronomy, the way women think or the way men think?) Deborah Rhode (*Theoretical Perspectives on Sexual Differences*) says we can deny sex differences, we can celebrate them, or we can "dislodge difference as the exclusive focus of gender-related questions." Anatomically, there are great differences between the sexes; biologically, there are some interesting differences (among the possibilities are that men generally appear to have greater muscle mass, cardiovascular capacity, more lefthandedness, and a higher concentration of red blood cells while women generally have more good cholesterol, handle stress better, sing and smell better, and live longer—in addition, neurobiologists report structural differences in at least two regions of the human brain); culturally, there remain great differences in attitudes, behaviors, opportunities, and expected roles for women and men. Anatomy and biology may be immutable; culture is not. See also gender roles.

sex discrimination see sexism.

sex industry the multi-billion-dollar sex industry is blatantly sexist: those who profit from it financially are almost all male; the majority of victims are female, although boys/young men are also victims. One of the most vicious and appalling aspects of this "industry" is the large number of children involved. According to an insider, "The word on the street is johns prefer chickens—kids." The most common scenario involves a middle-class suburban male who pays for sex with underagers. Abuse, degradation, drugs, disease, poverty, and death are facts of life for the young victims of this man's idea of "consensual sex." See also human trafficking, prostitute, sex worker.

sex industry worker see sex worker.

sexism both boys/men and girls/women are objects of discrimination based on their sex; "sexism" is an inclusive term when viewed primarily as discrimination. However, sexism is often defined specifically as the subordination of women by men; "While some women may dislike men intensely and treat them unfairly and while some women may be equally guilty of prejudice toward other women, the balance of power throughout most, if not all, of recorded history has allowed men to subordinate women in order to maintain their own privilege" (Paula S. Rothenberg, *Racism and Sexism*). Unequal, discriminatory treatment of the sexes touches almost every aspect of society, from large issues like the males-only compulsory registration, the feminization of poverty, the disparity in income between women and men, and the glass ceiling for many working women, to everyday issues like lifestyle ("work wives" are more socially acceptable and admired than "house husbands"), clothing (women wear just about anything men wear, including for a while, boxer shorts, while men aren't culturally approved for skirts, dresses, or most women's wear), crossover colors (women can wear blue, but men don't dare to wear pink unless it is called "salmon"), activity (girls can be "tomboys" but boys better not be "sissies"). Nijole V. Benokraitis and Joe R. Feagin (*Modern Sexism*) say, "Although both men and women can be targets and victims of sex discrimination, a vast literature indicates that being a woman is frequently a better predictor of inequality than such variables as age, race, religion, intelligence, achievements, or socioeconomic status." In all but two respects, that is true: today people with same-sex orientations are likely to be more discriminated against than any other group; the fact that only men were sent to war provided a stunning inequality for men for centuries while today's males-only compulsory registration remains discriminatory. See also blue, glass ceiling, draft, pink, wage earner.

sexist (adjective) this is used to describe attitudes, practices, behavior, language, codes, laws, and cultures but generally not people. Instead of "Dale is so sexist," say, "She uses sexist language" or "He encourages sexist practices in the office," or "Your attitude seems very sexist to me."

sexist language sexist language promotes and maintains attitudes that stereotype people according to gender; it favors one sex, demeans or excludes one sex, or portrays members of one sex as all alike. Writing for members of the Foreign Service Institute, Mortimer D. Goldstein sums up the status of sexist language in his chapter title, "Sexist Language Is Yesterday's Style: Besides, It's Against the Policy" (*Disciplined Writing and Career Development*). See Writing Guidelines for specific information on identifying and dealing with sexist language.

sexist quotations it is standard practice not to rewrite quotations, even ones with sexist language. However, for reasons of space or meaning, we often paraphrase or use only parts of quotations—even those without sexist language. Especially when using quotations in educational settings, it may be important to call attention to the sexism so that it is not absorbed unthinkingly; Ann Daly Goodwin used to write quotations on the chalkboard, but place—without comment—an "X" under any sexist terms. It did not take her students long to figure it out. When you need to work around sexist language (for example, Wendell Phillips, "The best use of laws is to teach men to trample bad laws under their feet"), there are several possibilities. (1) Omit the quotation marks and paraphrase the remark (still attributing it to the author): Wendell Phillips suggested that the best use of laws is to teach people to trample bad ones underfoot. (2) Replace the sexist words or phrases with ellipses and/or bracketed substitutes: "The best use for laws is to teach [people] to trample bad laws under their feet" (Wendell Phillips). (3) Use "[sic]" to show that the sexist words come from the original quotation and to call attention to the fact that they are not inclusive: "The best use of laws it to teach men [sic] to trample bad ones under their feet" (Wendell Phillips). (4) Quote only part of it: Wendell Phillips said the best use for laws was to teach people "to trample bad laws under their feet." (5) Replace the quotation with one that isn't sexist.

sex-linked expressions our rich and colorful language contains hundreds of striking, evocative, and useful metaphors, expressions, and figures of speech. As is true of the rest of the language, the sex-linked among these phrases are dominated by male images. There is nothing wrong with any of them per se, but this sourcebook lists several dozen expressions with comments and possible alternatives, *not so that they will be removed from the language*, but so that you will be aware of how many such expressions there are. It is the story of Lilliput again: one Lilliputian is harmless enough, but an army of them can overtake a Gulliver (Marie Shear). Each individual male-based expression is acceptable; to use only or principally male metaphors is not. Aware of their weight, you can then use only the most dynamic and appropriate of the male-based expressions, otherwise creating original ones of your own, using neutral or female-based expressions, or choosing from among listed alternatives for the less important terms. In the end, this attention to literary expressions improves our writing; many of the old phrases have become clichés; readers and audiences are sparked by fresh, new uses of language. And when we do use the time-tested expressions, we will have first given them a good sharp look to make sure they are exactly what we need.

sex object for centuries, women have been treated as sex objects ("piece of ass"), things ("skirt," "doll"), possessions ("my woman"), and commodities ("birds," "chicks"). Heavily reinforced by advertising, which uses women's sexuality to sell everything from razor blades to cars, this concept has had invidious results: prostitution, rape, laws and societies that "protect" women and relegate them to the status of children, words and attitudes that label women solely by their sexuality, even murder when the mythic cultural promise that women exist for the sexual pleasure of men goes unfulfilled. Men absorb the message that they must compete for women—as if women were passive things for the having. Watch for subtle ways in women are treated as sex objects—and delete them. See also gender roles, owner, score, success object.

sexploitation a category of independent, low-budget films from the 1960s, which featured softcore pornography, "sexploitation" also encompassed slick magazines connected with such films from about 1963 to 1973.

sexpot used only for women, "sexpot" supports the stereotype of woman as tempter and narrows her entire personhood to her sexuality.

sex reassignment surgery (SRS) according to the Gay & Lesbian Alliance Against Defamation (GLAAD), SRS refers to surgical alteration, but this is only one part of the transition for individuals who work to have their internal sexual identity match their external sexual identity. Altering one's birth sex is not a one-step procedure; it is a complex process that occurs over a long period of time. Transition includes some or all of the following cultural, legal, and medical adjustments: telling one's family, friends and/or coworkers; changing one's name and/or sex on legal documents; hormone therapy; possibly (though not always) some form of surgical alteration. Don't refer to "sex change" or "re-operative" and "post-operative." They inaccurately suggest that one must have surgery in order to truly change one's sex. Not all transgender people choose to or can afford to have SRS. GLAAD advises journalists to avoid overemphasizing the importance of SRS to the transition process. While estimates vary greatly concerning the number of male-to-female (MTF) transsexuals compared to the number of female-to-male (FTM) transsexuals, all indicate the number of MTF transsexuals exceeds the number of FTM transsexuals by a ratio of 3 or 4 to 1.

sex roles see gender roles.

sex slavery see human trafficking.

sexting the sending of sexually explicit messages or images by cellphone. As new technologies and software emerge, they are often co-opted by users to privately send each other sexually explicit material. Sexting is typically viewed by the senders of "sexts" as a means of privately sharing material not meant to be seen by anyone but the receiver. Some software providers such as SnapChat offer users the ability to control or limit such exposure of sexually explicit material, but, as with much that is digital, there are many ways images may be shared beyond the original receiver. Because it is illegal for anyone to send or receive sexually explicit photographs of a person younger than 18 via a cellphone, teenagers who have sexting photos of themselves, their friends, or their partners have been charged with distribution of child pornography, even when the image is of their own body. Intercepted sexts or, rather, sexts shared beyond the original receiver, sometimes play a role in cyberbullying. Education of both parents and kids is having an impact, and sexting among young people is less of a scourge than media hype portrays. See also cyberbullying.

sexton woman or man.

sex tourist most sex tourists are interested in sex with children despite a 2003 law under which U.S. citizens can be prosecuted for having sex abroad with children under 18. Men from the U.S. account for 80 percent of the child-sex tourists in Latin America. Worldwide, U.S. citizens account for one-quarter of sex tourists. An estimated 2 million child prostitutes are involved in the global sex trade. If there are people more repulsive than these sex tourists, it is difficult to imagine them. Taina Bien-Aime, (Women's Media Center) relates how Equality Now, a New York-based international human rights organization, discovered Norman Barabash's sex tour operation, Big Apple Oriental Tours, in Bellerose, Queens. For $2,195, the tour would fly American men to the Philippines or Thailand for 12 nights of "real sex with real girls—all for real cheap." Although the business violated state laws against promoting prostitution, the Queens district attorney's office showed no interest. Equality Now enlisted Gloria Steinem and Congresswoman Carolyn Maloney in an intensive campaign to engage the media and pressure the legal establishment, but Barabash continued to profit with impunity. Finally, Steinem wrote to Eliot Spitzer, who had just been re-elected state attorney general, urging him to look into the case. In July 2003, after a year-long investigation, Spitzer issued a temporary restraining order, the first of its kind in the country, to severely restrict Big Apple Oriental Tours from organizing or advertising sex tours and followed up with a criminal indictment. Other organizations help young sex slaves: Captive Daughters (www.captivedaughters.org), the Child Sex Tourism Prevention Project (www.worldvision.org), and ECPAT-USA (www.ecpatusa.org). See also human trafficking.

sexual assault any attempted or actual physical touching or sexual activity of any kind directed against another person that is initiated for the sexual pleasure of the perpetrator and that is unwanted by the victim is sexual assault. The broad term therefore includes, but is not limited to, rape. See also rape.

sexual conquest whether by one sex or the other, is "conquest" an appropriate term? See also "battle of/between the sexes," score, sex object.

sexual freedom for most people, this is understood to mean a toleration for, and the absence of social or legal restrictions on, all areas of mutually acceptable adult sexual behavior, one's sexual orientation and relationships, and control over one's own reproduction. Implicit in the conviction that every human being has moral jurisdiction over their own body is that no harm will be done to others.

sexual harassment sexual harassment consists of unwelcome, unsolicited, nonreciprocated sexual advances, requests for sexual favors, sexually motivated physical contact, or communication of a sexual nature, usually by someone who has power over another; it includes comments, jokes, looks, innuendoes, and physical contact, and emphasizes a person's sex role over their function as a worker. The three most common forms of "friendly" harassment are inappropriate flattery, hostile humor, and psychological intimidation. When these incidents happen more than once, or when they are objectionable enough, a hostile work environment is created—and the courts take hostile environments seriously. A government report puts the annual cost of sexual harassment just among federal workers at $95 million—not including legal fees or settlements. Women who report sexual harassment or who are driven to the courts because management will not act on their reports are sometimes accused of "acting like a victim." Going to court is seen as being weak and needing protection. However, when a man sues his neighbor over a fence dispute, he is not viewed as weak and needing protection; he's seen as standing up for himself. A number of studies have reported that the majority of girls and women from elementary school through doctoral programs and in every type of workforce, and particularly in the armed forces, have encountered sexual harassment. With increasing education and courts responding to reports, sexual harassment is declining. See also battered wife/woman, date rape, provoke, rape, rape victim, "She asked for it," victim, violence.

sexual intercourse sex, sexual activity. "Intercourse" is heterosexist.

sexual orientation this is the accurate term for an individual's deep-seated and enduring physical, romantic, emotional and/or spiritual attraction to members of the same and/or opposite sex, including lesbian, gay, bisexual, and heterosexual orientations. "Sexual preference" is never used; it suggests that one's sexual orientation can be chosen rather than be a given, inextricable aspect of one's identity. It also wrongly implies that you can be "cured." A person's sexual orientation is very often irrelevant; mention it only if it is central to your material and if its relevance is made clear to your reader. Gender identity (who you are) and sexual orientation (whom you're attracted to) are not the same. Transgender people (a gender identity) may be heterosexual, lesbian, gay, or bisexual (sexual orientations). It helps to look at sexual orientation on a continuum, and not as a set of absolute categories. See also conversion therapy, gender, transgender.

sexpert woman or man.

sexsomnia see sleepsex/sexsomnia.

sexual conversion therapy see conversion therapy.

sexual preference see sexual orientation.

sexual reorientation see conversion therapy.

sexual revolution "In the 1960s, any sex outside marriage was called the Sexual Revolution, a nonfeminist phrase that simply meant women's increased availability on men's terms. By the end of the seventies, feminism had brought more understanding that real liberation meant the power to make a choice; that sexuality, for women or men, should be neither forbidden nor forced" (Gloria Steinem, *Outrageous Acts and Everyday Rebellions*).

sex worker this term for a woman or a man who works in the sex industry was apparently coined by sex worker-activist Carol Leigh in 1978 (Margo St. James, in *Bitch*, 2013). "A sex worker might work on a pay-telephone fantasy line, dance topless, strip, perform in simulated or real sex shows, sell sexual services to individuals, be a sexual surrogate, or work as an explicit sex demonstrator" (Sallie Tisdale, *Talk Dirty to Me*) or in "massage, exotic dance, out-call, Lesbian videos, hard-core magazines" (Sue Grafton, *"K" Is for Killer*). Gloria Steinem (in *The Humanist* 2012) says, "If someone wants to be called a sex worker, I call them a sex worker. But there is a problem with that term, because while it was adopted in goodwill, traffickers have taken it and essentially said, 'Okay, if it's work like any other, somebody has to do it.' In Nevada, there was a time when you couldn't get unemployment unless you tried sex work first. The same was true in Germany. So the state became a procurer because of the argument that sex is work like any other. This is not a good thing. We have to be clear that you have the right to sell your own body but nobody has the right to sell anybody else's body. No one has that right." Since its first appearance, "sex worker" has been debated: does it confer dignity on people who do in fact work hard to make a living or is it a euphemism disguising the egregious nature and effects of such work? In *Stripped: Inside the Lives of Exotic Dancers*, Bernadette Barton uses the metaphor of the Möbius strip—a length of paper twisted and then fastened at the ends so the inside is continuous with the outside—to describe the relationship between empowerment and exploitation in sex work. See also prostitute, sex industry, human trafficking.

Shaker this term for a member of the United Society of Believers in Christ's Second Appearing has come to be respected and respectable even though it was originally a pejorative. The term "Shaker" referring to styles and furniture is a prestigious one.

shaman woman or man.

shamus although this could refer to either sex, it tends to be heard as masculine, and so do its equally "neutral" alternatives: cop, copper, flatfoot, gumshoe, private eye, shadow, sleuth, tail. With the advent of good fictional female gumshoes, these words are beginning to seem more inclusive.

shanghai it's not easy to replace this compact, instantly comprehensible term, but its negative—and unmerited—reflection on the Chinese city should at least be acknowledged: English sailors were kidnapped (often after being drugged) to work the ships sailing to Shanghai. Possible alternatives might include impress, conscript, kidnap, abduct, commandeer, force, trick.

"She asked for it" this corrupt and specious "explanation" has been used to excuse everything from unwanted sexual attentions to rape. No woman ever asks to be harassed, abused, or violated. See also battered wife/woman, date rape, domestic violence/domestic abuse, provoke, rape, rape victim, victim, violence.

sheikh/sheik always a man.

shelters see homeless, the.

sheroe see unconventional spellings.

shiftless when used of African Americans, this word is incredibly objectionable because it has been reserved almost solely for that use. If you need to convey this idea, instead of using a label, describe the specific behavior.

Shiites, Sunnis, Kurds the two major religious branches of Islam are Shi'a and Sunni; their followers are Shiites and Sunnis (98 percent of Iraqis are Muslims). The two principal ethnic groups in Iraq are the Arabs and Kurds (the two minor groups are Assyrian and Turkoman). The Kurds are an ethnic group of between 27 and 36 million people inhabiting the northern provinces of Iraq and adjacent areas in Turkey, Iran, and Syria. The largest ethnic group in the world without a state, they speak Kurdish, a language related to Persian. The majority of Kurds are Sunni Muslims. Their overriding, longterm desire is for more autonomy leading to statehood. Under the new Iraqi constitution, the Kurds are entitled to return to lands from which they were driven under Saddam's regime. Sunnis and Shiites differ in doctrine, ritual, law, theology, and religious organization. After decades of repression, the Shiites want power now, no matter the price. They say they accept the Sunnis, but think that some "Sunnis will either kill us or make us slaves" (Sheik Sayak Kumait al-Asadi, in *The Nation*). Even though the Sunnis return the animosity, "Sunnis and Shiites are much more intertwined by bonds of tribal affiliation and family than is commonly understood in the United States" (Dahr Jamail, in *The Nation*). Acknowledging their divisions, one of Jamail's interviewees says, "Our enemies are waiting for us to start fighting each other, [but] that will never happen." The media use of "sectarian violence" to describe violence in Iraq is often a catch-all term to label any violence that is not directed against the U.S. and Iraqi troops and where specific knowledge of the event is unavailable. Dr. Wamid Omar Nadhmi, a senior political scientist at Baghdad University and a Sunni, says, "It will take Iraqis something like a quarter of a century to rebuild their country, to heal their wounds, to reform their society, to bring about some sort of national reconciliation, democracy and tolerance of each other." See also Islamofascism.

shiksa this Yiddish word for a non-Jewish woman has roots in the Hebrew *shakaytz*, meaning to abominate or loathe an unclean thing. Because of this, "the term has never been neutral, and along the way has picked up associations—most of them sexual—like lint. At her most basic, the shiksa is a non-Jewish, sexually available female on the make for a Jewish prince or what a Jewish man is supposed to practice on before he marries a Jewish woman" (Christine Benvenuto, author of *Shiksa*, writing in *Bitch*). No real parallel exists for a man—*goyische* means simply foreign, but even "goy" has picked up unflattering connotations of inferiority. Know what you're doing if you use "shiksa" as it is considered offensive by some people.

ship/she ship/it in the early days of sailing, a new ship was customarily dedicated to a goddess, under whose protection it sailed. Referring to ships and boats as "she" today is outdated, unnecessary, and unacceptable because of the association of the feminine with men's possessions. Everything that dominator societies have traditionally run or overpowered has been imaged as female: church, nations, nature, ships, cars. *Lloyd's List*, the international shipping industry newspaper, no longer uses the feminine pronoun for ships. Editor Julian Bray says, "I decided that it was time to catch up with the rest of the world, and most other news organizations refer to ships as neuter."

shock and awe also known as "rapid dominance," shock and awe is an intent to display such overpowering military might that the enemy loses its will to resist. Historical examples of shock and awe include the blitz-kriegs carried out by the Nazis and the bombing of Hiroshima. "The notion is that the United States needs to intimidate countries with its power and assertiveness, always threatening, always denouncing, never showing weakness" (*Newsweek*). See also military language.

shock jock man or woman. Of about 40 current, well-known radio talk-show hosts who think nothing of ignorantly airing their bigotry, at least two are women. See also free speech, hate speech.

shoeshine boy shoeshiner.

shogun always a man; no parallel for women.

shoot the bull this phrase doesn't refer to the male animal, but probably comes from the Old French *boul* meaning "fraud/deceit." To avoid its masculine orientation (it is almost always used of men rather than women), use shoot the breeze. See also gossip.

shop girl shop clerk/assistant/employee/manager/owner, salesclerk, clerk.

shoreman shorehand, dockworker, dockhand, stevedore, shoreworker, longshore worker, wharfworker, wharfhand.

short Elaine Landau (*Short Stature: From Folklore to Fact*) says, "We live in a society in which 'bigger' is often believed to be better. Consider the popularity of such fast-food favorites as the Big Mac or the Whopper. On the other hand, phrases such as 'falls short of' or 'comes up short' are often used to describe something that is less than desirable." She uses "short-statured people" and says that "negative feelings about short-statured people have often made it difficult for them to find employment." Most often, it's unnecessary to mention anyone's height. See also dwarf, midget.

shortened forms of words while personal names are shortened as an expression of affection (Liz, Pat, Jack), shortening of names of groups usually indicates hostility: abo (for "Aborigine"), lib, libber, women's lib, fag (even more hostile than "faggot"), Yid, jap, nip, bi, homo, lezzie, spic (from "Hispanic"). Marc Wolinsky and Kenneth Sherrill (*Gays and the Military*) note the further derogation of shortened words like "homo" that end in "-o": chico, dago, fatso, gringo, lesbo, oreo, psycho, sicko, wacko, weirdo, wino.

showgirl dancer, performer, performing artist. See also showman.

showman performer, entertainer, limelighter, razzle-dazzle/stage artist, theatrical person, exhibitionist, someone with a flair for the dramatic, ham, show-off, actor, theatrician, show manager/producer/stager. Note the nonparallel "man/girl" and the differences in prestige and type of work between a showgirl and a showman. See also impresario.

showmanship showcraft, stagecraft, razzle-dazzle, performing/staging skills, production genius, virtuosity, dramatics, theatercraft, theatrics, showiness, flair for the dramatic, dramatic flair. None of these terms may be as satisfactory as "showmanship." Try showing what you mean (by examples and description) rather than just telling.

shrew in theory nonsexist, in practice "shrew" is reserved for women. Consider using instead grouch, grumbler, crosspatch, faultfinder, complainer, pain in the neck, nitpicker, troublemaker, bad-tempered/peevish/cranky/petulant person. Ethel Strainchamps has pointed out that the root of "shrew" is the same as that of "shrewd," which is more commonly used of men.

shrill see strident.

shylock this term, from Shakespeare's usurer of the same name in *The Merchant of Venice*, is both sexist and anti-Semitic. Use instead loan shark, usurer, extortionist, moneylender, parasite. Shylock demanded the original "pound of flesh" (meaning today spiteful penalty, harsh demand).

shyster although the roots of this word are not very nice, they are not related in any way to "shylock." There may be lawyers who are shysters, but for every shyster there are a thousand honest, effective lawyers who are our neighbors, serving on community and charitable organizations, donating their time, talents, and money to local fine arts groups, school boards, food shelves, zoos, educational activities, and in general contributing to the larger good as well as practicing good law (Patrick J. Maggio). Shun the loose use of "shyster."

Siamese twins conjoined twins.

Siberia Nick Levinson points out that "Siberia" (which is often used to indicate banishment—as when someone is sent to the branch office) is home to the Siberians; the forced labor camps were not all of Siberia.

sibyl retain in historical contexts and in those present-day contexts where the term finds validation among women. If you need an inclusive alternative, use prophet, fortuneteller.

sideman musician, instrumentalist, member of the band, band member. Or be specific: bassist, drummer, clarinetist.

signalman signaler, signal operator.

significant other used for a woman or a man in a same-sex or opposite-sex relationship, this is still occasionally seen, but it is a little too arch and cumbersome for most people. See also boyfriend, girlfriend.

"silent majority" "a term used by President Richard Nixon to indicate his belief that the great body of Americans supported his policies and that those who demonstrated against the involvement of the United States in the Vietnam War amounted to only a noisy minority" (*The New Dictionary of Cultural Literacy*, 3rd ed.). Paul Wasserman and Don Hausrath (*Weasel Words*) say, "The idea persists that there is a group of citizens who constitute the majority of the voting population, who seldom express their views in public forums but demonstrate their feelings only in the voting booths. The problem for politicians is identifying who they are, where they are, and then, how to influence them since their actual values are anyone's guess."

silk stocking district posh neighborhood, wealthy/aristocratic area, deluxe section/fashionable part of town, the Gold Coast.

silk stocking liberal see liberal.

Simon Legree "Simon Legree" and its common synonym "slave driver" have negative associations and no equivalent for women. They are not easily replaced with terms as familiar and evocative, but sometimes you can reword or use an alternative: hard/brutal taskmaster, ogre, tough/strict boss, martinet, stickler, severe disciplinarian.

simon-pure there is nothing wrong with using this term (from the character Simon Pure in Susanna Centlivre's 1718 play, "A Bold Stroke for a Wife"), but be aware of how many such expressions are male-based. Balance them with female-based expressions, creative expressions of your own, or sex-neutral alternatives: pure, genuine, untainted, sterling, honest, truthful, pure-hearted, flawless, upright, highminded, reliable, real, veritable, authentic, exact, precise, credible, worthy; clean as a whistle. See also sex-linked expressions.

single "singles sometimes find themselves outside the cultural loop in a society that considers marriage the natural state for healthy adults. People are expected to grow up, get married and stay married—or risk the wrath of politicians who brandish spouses and children like banners of morality" (Barbara Yost in *The Arizona Republic*). In *Going Solo*, Eric Klinenberg says that today more than 50 percent of American adults are single, and 31 million (roughly 1 out of 7 adults) live alone (excluding the 8 million Americans in voluntary and nonvoluntary group quarters, such as assisted living facilities, nursing homes, and prisons). People who live alone make up 28 percent of all U.S. households, which means that they are now tied with childfree couples as the most prominent residential type—more common than the nuclear family, the multigenerational family, and the roommate or group home. He notes that living alone is one of the most stable household arrangements: over a five-year period, people who live alone are more likely to stay that way than everyone except married couples with children. Our language nevertheless often reflects a Noah's Ark view of society, where singles are overlooked, ignored, or excluded. At company events, employees' "guests," not "spouses and families" can be welcomed.

single mother/single father there are times when it may be necessary to specify "single"; most of the time it is not. It is better to use "single father" or "single mother" as "single parent" is too often thought to refer to a woman. The inclusive term may also obscure the gender breakdown: in 2012, 24 percent of children under eighteen lived with a single mother; 4 percent lived with a single father. In Great Britain, "lone parent" or "solo parent" is used, to avoid the connotation of "unmarried" in single. However, in the U.S. "single" has long been used without pejoration for unmarried, divorced, separated, or widowed parents.

single-payer health insurance/single-payer system see universal health care coverage.

single-sex colleges as of 2014, there are 47 women's colleges (down from 224 in 1969) and four males-only private educational institutions. Private institutions justify single-sex status by their specific alternative missions, lack of federal support, and, in the case of women's colleges, an affirmative action rationale. Single-sex colleges appear to be highly advantageous for women: compared to students enrolled in coeducational institutions, women in single-sex colleges participate more fully in and out of class, develop measurably higher levels of self-esteem, score higher on standardized achievement tests, choose more male-intensive majors, and are more are likely to graduate. Afterward they are more successful in their careers (for example, hold higher positions, are happier, earn more money), are twice as likely to receive a doctoral degree, six times more likely to be on the boards of Fortune 500 companies, and even appear to have lower divorce rates. While graduates of women's colleges constitute only 2 percent of all college-educated women, they make up 20 percent of female members of Congress. See also education.

singular "they" since medieval times "they," "their," and "them" have been used as singular pronouns (for example, Jill Ruckelshaus's "No one should have to dance backward all their lives"). "'They' has been in continuous use as a singular pronoun in English for over 600 years. Two centuries of vigorous opposition, including concerted efforts by the education and publishing industries and an 1850 Act of Parliament declaring the masculine pronoun to be the proper third singular generic pronoun, have not eradicated it" (Miriam Meyers). Singular "they" is now accepted or endorsed by many authorities: *Oxford English Dictionary* ("The pronoun referring to *everyone* is often plural"); *Chicago Manual of Style*; *American Heritage Dictionary of the English Language* ("may be the only sensible choice in informal style"); *American Heritage Book of English Usage* ("The alternative to the masculine generic with the longest and most distinguished history in English is the third-person plural pronoun"); the National Council of Teachers of English ("In all but strictly formal usage, plural pronouns have become acceptable substitutes for the masculine singular"; *Random House Dictionary II*; *Webster's Third New International Dictionary* (their definition of *everyone* reads in part, "Usually referred to by the third person singular ... but sometimes by a plural personal pronoun" and they give the example of "Everyone had made up their minds"). Singular "they" was proscribed in 1746 on the theory that the masculine gender was "more comprehensive" (whatever that means) than the feminine. But it wasn't until the 19th century that prescriptive grammarians tried to enforce it; many writers continued to use singular "they." Casey Miller and Kate Swift (*The Handbook of Nonsexist Writing*) say that "the continued and increased use of singular *they* in writing as well as speech—and the restitution of the status it enjoyed before grammarians arbitrarily proscribed it—now seems inevitable." Among the many writers who have used singular "they" are Jane Austen, Samuel Johnson, Anaïs Nin, Shakespeare, Elizabeth Gaskell, Agatha Christie, George Eliot, Charles Dickens, Anthony Trollope, George Bernard Shaw, William Congreve, Thomas Malory, William Thackeray, L.E. Landon, Anne Morrow Lindbergh, W.H. Auden, F. Scott Fitzgerald, Jonathan Swift, Lawrence Durrell, and Doris Lessing. You can find it today in the *Christian Science Monitor*, *Washington Post*, *New York Times*, and *Wall Street Journal*. ("You" is also used as both singular and plural, and no major campaign has been mounted to change it—people seem able to understand when it is singular and when it is plural.)

sins of the fathers are visited on the children, the unless quoting Euripides (in which case it is "The gods visit the sins of the fathers upon the children"), use the sins of the parents are visited on the children (if you can stand this expression in the first place).

Sioux "most of the people once called 'Sioux' by the white man now call themselves by their traditional name, Lakota, Dakota or Nakota, which means 'allies' rather than 'little snake'" (Tim Giago, in *Indian Country Today*).

sir "sir" and "dame" are parallel sex-specific titles for those raised to knighthood. "Sir" and "madam" are parallel and useful sex-specific terms for everyday social exchanges.

siren the definition of a siren sounds flattering (a woman seen as beautiful and seductive), but the stereotype of a woman luring a man to his destruction belittles both sexes.

sissy from "sister," this pejorative word denotes excessive timidity. "Buddy," from "brother," is a positive term describing a good friend. "Tomboy" is often paired with "sissy," but since it has the masculine connotation, society is more tolerant of so-called tomboy behavior than it is of so-called sissy behavior. Dr. Eugene R. August points out that our language lacks "a favorable or even neutral term to describe the boy who is quiet, gentle, and emotional." Instead of "sissy," consider using nothing at all with this connotation. If you must, try timid, gentle, sensitive; weakling, pushover, wimp, doormat, easy mark, weak stick. See also coward/cowardly/cowardice, mama's boy.

sister (adjective) the use of "sister" in such constructions as "sister cities/plants/companies" is not pejorative to women or to men ("brother" doesn't operate similarly). However, it introduces sex where it is superfluous. If you prefer something else try related, twin, cousin, co-, companion, neighboring, paired, partnered, affiliated, allied, associated. None of these feels as comfortable as "sister," but you can also circumlocute ("both magazines are published by...").

sisterhood unlike "brotherhood," which has been overused as a pseudogeneric, "sisterhood" has meaning for women as a description of a sex-specific, unique bond and should be retained in most instances. When you want an inclusive alternative, consider unity, unity among humans, humanity, compassion, peace, companionship, goodwill, amity, friendship, comradeship, camaraderie, conviviality; family, the human family, kinship, shared/human kinship; community, society, association, organization, social organization, common-interest group, club, corporation, federation, union, group, partnership, society; sisterhood and brotherhood. See also brotherhood.

sisterly this is a useful and accurate sex-specific word in most cases. If you need a sex-neutral substitute, consider affectionate, loving, caring, kindly, supportive, sympathetic, protective, indulgent, friendly.

sizeism/sizism this term refers to discrimination and prejudice based on body size (especially fatness or shortness). Tenaciously entrenched in U.S. culture, sizeism knows no limits: in 2011, ABC News reported that nearly half of all three- to six-year-old girls worry about being fat. An early Barbie doll used to come with her own scale, set at 110 and her own diet guide: "How to Lose Weight: Don't Eat" (Louise Bernikow, *The American Women's Almanac*). "Sizeist" is the adjective for materials or viewpoints. See also fat, looksism, midget, obese/obesity, short.

skank see name-calling.

skinhead skinheads may be completely apolitical, progressive, or neo-Nazi white supremacist/racist. Use for those who self-identify as "skinheads," but do not assume a homogeneity in attitudes, politics, or style.

skirt/a bit of skirt (woman) these terms make of a woman an object, by inference a sex object, and there is no parallel for men. See also suit.

slattern for prostitute, use prostitute. If you need a sex-neutral alternative for the meaning of an unkempt, slovenly woman, consider sloven, slob, unkempt person. See also frump/frumpy, prostitute.

slave/slavery "Next time you read the word slaves substitute Africans forcefully removed from their families and homes, or African people held in captivity" (Clyde W. Ford, *We Can All Get Along*). We tend to have lost the impact and tragedy of what these words denote, partly from familiarity, partly from not wanting to look too closely at this part of our history, and partly by the casual use of terms like slave driver, slavish imitator, work like a slave, work for slave wages, slave of fashion, slaving away. Consider finding other ways to express "slave" concepts. When writing or speaking of slavery include the black point of view instead of discussing slavery merely as a boon, and later a problem, for whites (Macmillan Publishing Company, *Guidelines for Creating Positive Sexual and Racial Images in Educational Materials*).

slave girl in addition to its association with slavery, this sexist, racist, demeaning term perpetuates the false notion that most women secretly enjoy being enslaved.

slaveholders historically these were both men and women.

sleepsex/sexsomnia apparently both men and women can be afflicted with an advanced form of sleepwalking that includes the full gamut of sexual activity without the patients having any conscious awareness of what they're doing and, when awakened, having no recollection of it (*Newsweek*).

slum substandard/inadequate housing. Aim for accurate, non-euphemistic language without painting people's homes with shaming language. Precise, neutral description of the area will convey the truth without reflecting so negatively on those who live there. On the other hand, for a sex-neutral term for "slumlord," go ahead and use slum boss, slumholder, slum owner/manager, absentee slum owner, absentee fat cat slum owner. It seems almost impossible to shame some of these individuals.

slur in *Unkind Words*, Irving Lewis Allen says, "The overt purpose of an ethnic epithet is to insult and to injure. The use of ethnic slurs is also an effort, whether quite consciously realized or not, to control the behavior of the disparaged group. A primitive belief lingers in all societies that if one can name or attach a label to an object, in this case an ethnic individual or group, then one can wield power over it simply by calling its name. ... Ethnic slurs are used to produce and maintain social class and privilege." We know a slur when we hear it and there are extensive lists online for those who are interested in their stories, but it's worth mentioning that on the ladder of prejudice, it all starts with speech.

slut one survey of teenagers (*USA Weekend*) indicated that "when people find out that a boy and a girl have had sex, he is a 'stud,' but she is a 'slut.'" Only 22 percent of boys and 15 percent of girls say sex hurts a boy's reputation, while 70 percent of boys and 87 percent of girls say a girl's reputation is damaged. Both sexes conclude it's not fair, but that's the way it is. However, "slut," says Stephanie Rosenbloom (*New York Times*), "which originated in the Middle Ages, has emerged from a schoolyard barb to become commonplace in popular culture, marketing, and casual conversation." She points to novelty shops and websites that sell Slut lip balm, bubble bath, soap and lotion, to a cocktail known as the Red-Headed Slut, to casually described voraciousness ("coffee slut," "TV slut"). But Leora Tanenbaum (*Slut! Growing Up Female With a Bad Reputation*) says being labeled a slut is still painful and humiliating despite pop culture's semi-embrace of the term. After interviewing more than 100 women between 14 and 66 who had been pigeonholed as sluts, Tanenbaum found that the label can be a self-fulfilling prophecy, leading to greater promiscuity, or it can act as a brake, leading a woman to shut down sexually. As for the liberal use of the word today, "It's still too hurtful."

smart aleck this expression comes from the man's name Alexander, but it is used for both sexes. Should you need a more sex-neutral alternative, consider know-it-all, blowhard, egomaniac, braggart, big/swelled head, arrogant/conceited/mouthy person/individual.

snowman snow figure/sculpture/creature/statue, snowwoman or snowman. Yes, it seems bad-tempered to question the venerable "snowman," but as it is children who are primarily exposed to it, it's an important term in painting their world more male than it actually is and establishing the primacy of the male; on another level, it limits their creativity: if they hear "snowman," that is what they are most likely to make—instead of dragons and snow castles and huge birthday cakes.

sob sister sob story writer/journalist, yellow journalist; bleeding heart, pushover.

soccer mom at the height of the soccer mom's popularity, Harrison Hickman, a Democratic pollster, said, "The soccer mom is this year's hula hoop." Jacob Weisberg (www.slate.com) wrote that there is "something intrinsically misleading about the category, and indeed about all such categories. ... The notion that there is a single demographic group that determines each election, then recedes back into the anonymity of the general populace, is useful for political consultants and reporters. But as the impermanence of such categories suggests, they are usually clichés that obscure as much as they reveal."

social butterfly this phrase generally refers to a woman, but there are no good inclusive alternatives for it. "Social butterfly" conveys a sense of light-mindedness along with the sociable, gregarious character of the person. Either use "social butterfly" for men too or consider sex-neutral adjectives and nouns: gregarious, outgoing, social, sociable, socially active, convivial, extroverted; a joiner. See also socialite.

socialite replace this empty, sexist, demeaning term with a precise description: frequently entertains, community-minded, member of several boards, civic figure, on charitable foundations. See also social butterfly.

socialized medicine see universal health care coverage.

social justice they asked Thucydides, "When will justice come to Athens?" And he answered, "Justice will not come to Athens until those who are not injured are as indignant as those who are." Social justice and social action is about the uninjured working alongside their injured sisters and brothers to root out the causes of those injuries.

social safety net see safety net.

social titles use the titles people use for themselves. If you don't know, ask. Omitting honorifics before a name is acceptable and has the advantage of clarity and brevity. Even in letterwriting, you can use "TO: Myriam Durand" or "Dear Shawn Clayton." In work situations, "Ms." is generally acceptable for women. See also Esq./Esquire, Miss, Mrs., Ms., salutations.

social welfare conservatives are calling a new plan to privatize helping the needy "social welfare." Government welfare will be phased out and replaced by private services. Details so far are vague.

sodomite from the inhabitants of the biblical city of Sodom, this term is often taken to be synonymous with "homosexual," when in fact it refers to anyone of either sex and any sexual orientation who performs, according to the wording of most laws, an "unnatural act" (oral or anal sex or bestiality). The Gay & Lesbian Alliance Against Defamation says this term constitutes hate speech and shouldn't be used except in a direct quote that reveals the bias of the person quoted.

sodomy laws "historically used to selectively persecute gay men, lesbians and bisexuals, the state laws often referred to as 'sodomy laws' were ruled unconstitutional by the U.S. Supreme Court in 2003. 'Sodomy' should never be used to describe gay, lesbian, or bisexual relationships, sex, or sexuality" (Gay & Lesbian Alliance Against Discrimination).

"soft on crime" put-down of some progressives by conservatives. The issue of criminal justice is much more complicated than this extremely vague phrase indicates, but to counter the charge one needs to discuss complex issues, and most voters will take simple over complex any day.

soft targets unarmed civilians. Avoid the euphemism except when quoting someone, in which case, define the term after the quote.

soldier see armed forces, combat, draft dodger, males-only registration, serviceman, sexism, warrior.

soldier of fortune generally a man. See also civilian contractor.

soldier-statesman soldier-politician/-diplomat/-lawmaker.

solicitor (British) man or woman.

solitary confinement most people do not grasp the true dimensions of "solitary confinement"; it sounds like the "time out" given a misbehaving child. The reality constitutes what many, including human rights activists and some international law, define as torture. Its short-term and long-term effects meet all rational definitions of "cruel and unusual punishment." If you need to use this term, give your audience enough detail to understand what the punishment entails. A new wrinkle: "Solitary confinement in immigration detention centers across the nation is often overused and arbitrarily applied. According to data obtained by the National Immigrant Justice Center, as many as 300 immigrants, or about 1 percent of all detainees in the 50 largest facilities in the country, are confined to small cells on any given day, even though many pose no security risk. In many cases, they're held there for 23 hours each day without a break, often for weeks. The use of solitary confinement is troubling enough in regular state and federal prisons, where inmates held in such conditions for prolonged periods are at risk for severe mental illness and suicide, according to medical experts. But its use in immigration facilities is even more alarming because those detainees aren't serving criminal sentences but are awaiting civil deportation hearings. Moreover, prolonged solitary confinement not only puts detainees' health in jeopardy but undermines their ability to fight their cases. Access to telephones and contact with attorneys are often severely restricted because detainees are allowed to spend just one hour each day outside their cells" (*Los Angeles Times*, 2013). Some 34,000 legal and undocumented immigrants are held in a sprawling nationwide network of 250 jails and privately run facilities. The op-ed piece concludes, "If the federal government is to continue to hold so many people before trial, it has an obligation to ensure that they are treated humanely."

solon although this derives from Solon, the Athenian lawgiver (560 B.C.E.), it can be used for wise legislators of both sexes.

"some of my best friends are..." there is nothing wrong with this phrase if you don't mind betraying your bias against the group you are about to mention. Ironically, it's often used to defend oneself: "I'm not prejudiced! Why, some of my best friends...."

sommelier traditionally, sommeliers have been men, but today a handful of the world's top sommeliers (known as "master sommeliers") are women. You can also use wine steward/waiter for both women and men.

songbird singer. See also songstress.

songstress songster, singer, vocalist, balladeer. See also bluesman, crooner, chorus girl/chorus boy, prima donna, torch singer.

sonny avoid this patronizing and sexist (there is no parallel expression for girls/women) term.

son of a bitch avoid. This insult, aimed at a man, ricochets off a woman—his mother. There is generally no dearth of good swear words; replacing this expression is a matter of choice. When you want to refer to a person this way, use so-and-so, ignoramus, saphead, stinker, ratfink, snake in the grass, creep, heel, jerk, bum, lowlife. When using the term to describe a difficult job or situation, use instead a tough one, uphill job.

son of a gun most often a meaningless interjection or a cheery back-slapping greeting between two men (preceded by "you old"), this relative of "son of a bitch" is genial and unobjectionable most of the time. Finding an alternative that women could use is difficult, mainly because women have their own ways of greeting each other in similar circumstances, few of which resemble the male scenario. *Vive la difference.* See also son of a bitch.

Son of God (Christ) Beloved of God, Only Begotten, God's Own, Eternally Begotten, Chosen One.

Son of Man (Christ) the original phrase, translated simply "member of the human race," emphasized the humanity as well as the divinity of Jesus Christ. Christ describes himself often with this phrase, underscoring its profound significance, and those rendering "Son of Man" inclusive will want to express "member of the human race" in a way that is theologically correct, scripturally sound, and acceptable to both congregations and hierarchies. This is a difficult phrase to retranslate, but there are several possibilities: the Incarnate One, the One who became human/flesh, the One made human/flesh, Son/Child of Humanity/Humankind/the People, one like you, one of you. You can also reword, for example: Christ, who was flesh and blood even as you and I are flesh and blood.

sons (pseudogeneric) children, heirs, offspring, progeny, daughters and sons/sons and daughters.

sons of God daughters and sons/sons and daughters of God, children of God, believers, the faithful. Because of its brevity and familiarity "children of God" is a good choice, although it doesn't work in all contexts because of the difference between "children" and "adult children."

sons of man children/daughters and sons of humanity/humankind, daughters and sons/children of the earth, our children/sons and daughters.

sorceress sorcerer. See also "feminine" word endings.

sororal from the Latin for "sister," this is the little-known sibling to "fraternal." Forms of it are seen principally only in "sorority" and Soroptimist International of the Americas (SIA), a service organization of professional women. "Sororal" could be used to describe all-women groups, activities, and friendships. Like other female-male word pairs, "sororal" and "fraternal" have developed along very different lines, with "fraternal" taking on many meanings, associations, and uses—some of them pseudogeneric. See also fraternal, fraternal order of, fraternal organization, fraternal twins, fraternization, fraternize.

sorority unlike "fraternity," which in the case of the Greek society is sometimes coed or which as a pseudogeneric refers to groups including both women and men, "sorority" refers strictly to women. If you want an inclusive alternative for the Greek society, use Greek society/system, Greek-letter organization, Greek-letter society/group. Otherwise use organization, society, association, union, secret society, club, federation, fraternity and sorority, common-interest group. See also fraternity, fraternity/frat (Greek), sororal.

soubrette retain for the well-defined stage and opera role; there is no precise synonym and no parallel for a man.

sound-effects man sound-effects coordinator/specialist/technician/crew; sometimes circumlocute with simply sound effects.

sound man sound controller/technician/specialist/coordinator; sound mixer.

soul brother/soul sister acceptable, parallel sex-specific terms.

"**sound science**" when you see this phrase, it's very possible that what follows is neither sound nor science as it is practiced by actual reputable scientists. President George W. Bush said, "We've got some regulatory policy in place that makes sense, but it says we're going to make decisions based upon sound science, not some environmental fad or what may sound good—that we're going to rely on the best of evidence before we decide." He may have been referring to the Data Quality Act (DQA), also called the Information Quality Act by the Government Accountability Office. The Data Quality Act is "a below-the-radar legislative device that defenders of industry have increasingly relied upon to attack all range of scientific studies whose results or implications they disagree with, from government global warming reports to cancer research using animal subjects" (Chris Mooney, *The Boston Globe*). The DQA directs the Office of Management and Budget (OMB) to ensure everything it issues is high-quality information. "Sound science" means that whatever scientists you can find in the OMB will be vetting any scientific or statistical information to be sure it's, well, sound and, in particular, that it agrees with Administration policies. The DQA has been criticized by the scientific community and journalists as a ploy of corporations and their supporters to suppress the release of government reports contrary to their economic interests. See also global warming, "intelligent design," junk science.

Southeast Asian American this refers to ethnically, culturally, and geographically diverse peoples: the Vietnamese; the ethnic Lao, Mien, and Hmong of Laos; the Khmer of Cambodia, the Thai, and the various ethnic groups of Indonesia, Myanmar, Brunei, Singapore, and Malaysia. The majority of Southeast Asians in the U.S. are Vietnamese, Laotian, and Cambodian. Use the more information-rich terms.

sousveillance/souveillance a new word, first cousin to surveillance except that it means watching below from below, instead of above; it refers to monitoring the authorities. An early example is the footage of the police officers beating Rodney King. *New York Times Magazine* points out that today, "with the spread of cheap, lightweight cameras and the rise of Web video sites like YouTube, sousveillance has proliferated." They mention civilian footage of police abuse in Malaysia, gay-bashing in Latvia, and union-busting in Zimbabwe. A global phenomenon, the website www.ihollaback.org "encourages women to post a photo of any man who tries to harass them."

sovereign citizens these zealots, who refuse to recognize government authority in virtually any form, have killed at least six police officers since 2000 (David Zucchino, *Los Angeles Times*, 2013). Some 15,000 police officers and 5,000 public officials have received special training in dealing with what the FBI calls a "domestic terrorist movement" numbering between 100,000 and 300,000. They do not believe in paying taxes, they write their own deeds to homes they do not own, and they pay with coupons or photos of silver money. RuSA (Republic for the united States of America) is the largest group of antigovernment sovereign citizens, although at the moment its president has been arrested for trying to pay his taxes with a fictitious $300 million bond, and then helping others do the same with similar bogus securities; as one member put it, "We as a Republic look very, very, very bad with our president sitting in jail." See also hate groups, nullification.

Soviet someone from or something pertaining to the former U.S.S.R. Not interchangeable with Russian.

sow wild oats both young men and young women do this while their parents pray for crop failure.

spaceman astronaut, cosmonaut, astronavigator, celestial navigator, member of the space program/space exploration team, space explorer/traveler/aviator/pilot/ranger/walker, rocketeer, spacewoman and spaceman; extra-terrestrial, person from outer space.

Spanish of or relating to Spain or its people or culture, this term is not interchangeable with Mexican, Latina/Latino, Hispanic, Cuban American, Puerto Rican, Latin American, or any other peoples not specifically from Spain.

spastic someone with spasticity/spastic muscles/uncontrolled muscle spasms. "Spaz" is naturally unacceptable. See also disabilities.

special in referring to disabilities, use "special" only when it is part of a title (Special Olympics, Department of Special Education). "Special" sets apart those with disabilities, implying that they are not just different, as we are all different from each other, but of a different species; it is considered by the disability-rights community to have definite negative connotations. It's unpleasant to hear the word "special" with all its ordinarily wonderful connotations used to label you, exclude you from full participation, and keep you on the sidelines of life. Instead of "special buses," for example, use "separate buses" or "specially equipped buses" or "accessible buses," depending on what you mean. See also disabilities, exceptional.

special-effects man special-effects coordinator/technician/crew.

special interests "in political theory, interest groups are collections of individuals joined together by common interests" (Andrew Levine, *Political Keywords*). In real-life politics, the other side always favors special interests that are undesirable, leaving it to voters to decide which special interests they support. In general, liberals prefer issues and legislation favoring the poor, minorities, environmentalists, women, small businesses, workers, students, older individuals, and the unemployed. In general, conservatives prefer issues and legislation favoring financial institutions, trade associations, large corporations (especially aerospace, pharmaceutical, agribusiness, and insurance), and military spending. Back to theories, Levine says, "In political theories that construe political processes as efforts by competing interest groups to gain advantages, capitalists and other beneficiaries of the system in place also constitute interest groups. But in mainstream political discourse, this is not usually acknowledged. Instead, their interests are effectively identified with the interests of the whole community, which is then depicted as being besieged by 'special interests.'" Unless quoting someone, avoid the rubbery "special interests" or spell out what those interests are.

"special rights" see gay rights.

"special treatment" see "preferential treatment."

S

speciesism the assumption of superiority of humans over other animal species, especially to justify their exploitation, the term "speciesism" was coined either by philosopher Peter Singer or psychologist Richard D. Ryder "to denote a prejudice toward the members of one's own species as against the interest of members of other species. ... speciesism is analogous to racism and sexism and is as morally unacceptable" (Timothy J. Madigan, in *Free Inquiry*). Tad Clements says, however, "If by 'speciesism' is meant favoring one's own species above others, then speciesism is universal in nature. Natural selection through evolutionary mechanism leads to decline or extinction of any species if its population fails to promote the long-range success of that species. Whatever the mechanism employed—parasitism, predation, symbiosis, or whatever—the bottom line for every species is success as a species. So speciesism—preferring, whether consciously or not, one's own species—is the natural state of affairs throughout the biotic world." Defined more broadly as a lack of respect for other species, "speciesism" is still a useful term.

spend money like a drunken sailor this phrase perpetuates an outdated stereotype and is sexist in that the "drunken sailor" is never visualized as a woman. Consider instead spend money like water, throw money around, squander one's money, spend foolishly/ extravagantly/ outrageously/lavishly/imprudently/immoderately.

spin/spin control "spin" is a polite word for deception in the attempt to minimize public knowledge of or reaction to mistakes, unpopular decisions, unfulfilled promises, slips of the tongue, accidents, and other events that make one (usually political) party look ineffective to the other (usually political) party and to the public. Tennis and badminton players know how important spin is in (1) controlling the ball and (2) keeping your opponent from "getting" it. "Spin paints a false picture of reality by bending facts, mischaracterizing the words of others, ignoring or denying crucial evidence, or just 'spinning a yarn'—by making things up" (Brooks Jackson and Kathleen Hall Jamieson, *UnSpun: Finding Facts in a World of Disinformation*). Used by both government and corporations to "manage" communication between them and the public, spin ranges from shading the truth to outright lying.

spinning jenny this generally refers to a specific machine; sometimes you can use the generic spinning machine.

spinmeister "spin-doctor" is the more common term for a political aide or public relations agent who gives a positive spin to facts that are negative or awkward (for their side). The less-prevalent "spinmeister" has a masculine flavor but could be used for either sex. See also spin/spin control.

spinster using "spinster" turns something that is only one part of a person's life (being single) into the entirety of the person; references to marital status are usually unnecessary. When they are necessary, use an adjective instead of a noun: single. Avoid "unmarried" and "unwed" because they perpetuate the marriage-as-norm stereotype (that marriage somehow confers validity). Historically, single women enjoyed more civil powers than married women who were dependent upon and secondary to their husbands. Note the nonparallel connotations of the supposedly parallel terms "spinster" and "bachelor" (and was there ever an "eligible spinster" as there are "eligible bachelors"?). Women go from bachelor girl to spinster to old maid but men are bachelors forever. See also bachelor, celibate, maiden aunt, old maid, single, spinsterhood.

spinsterhood singleness.

spirits liquor, alcohol. "Spirits" sell better, but unless you're selling, use the clearer terms.

spirituality differentiate between spirituality and religiosity, between someone who is "spiritual" and someone who is "religious." The latter holds a belief system connected to an organized religion, while the former enjoys a more amorphous, independent belief system usually taken from a number of philosophies and theologies.

spokesman official, representative, speaker, source, company/union/White House official, publicist, prolocutor, company/White House/union representative, advocate, proponent, voice, agent, press/publicity agent, PR coordinator, proxy, stand-in, intermediary, mediator, medium, go-between, negotiator, arbitrator, speechmaker, keynoter, promoter, aide, deputy, diplomat, mouthpiece, spokester, public information manager/officer, public relations director, news bureau manager. "Spokesman" (first used in 1540) and "spokeswoman" (first used in 1654) are acceptable if used gender-fairly. "Spokesperson" (1972) is not only awkward and contrived, but is generally reserved for women; it is not recommended. There are some excellent (and more descriptive) terms in the list of alternatives; "prolocutor," for example, is an exact synonym meaning "speaker for." Be creative: Actress Elizabeth Hurley was referred to as a "spokesmodel" for Estée Lauder. You can also use speaking for the group/on behalf of, representing or "the company/firm/department said."

spoonerism switching the initial sounds of two or more words ("It is kisstomary to cuss the bride," "one swell foop," or "the queer old dean," in a reference to Queen Victoria) results in a spoonerism, named after Oxford educator William A. Spooner. Retain the term; some linguistic sex balance is provided by Mrs. Malaprop and the term malapropism that describes her own brand of confusion.

sport of kings there is no good alternative to this expression, which has been associated for centuries with horseracing.

sportsman sports lover, sport, sportster, sports/outdoor enthusiast, athlete, gamester, hobbyist, competitor; gambler; honorable competitor, good sport, honest/fair player; sportswoman and sportsman. Or be specific: angler, hunter, fisher, tennis player, canoer, ballplayer, golfer.

sportsmanlike/sportsmanly sporting, fair, fair-minded.

sportsmanship sporting behavior, fair play, fairness, fair-mindedness, playing fair, sense of fair play, being a good sport/good loser, sportslike behavior, honor, honorable competition, competing honorably. See also sportsman, sportsmanlike/sportsmanly, unsportsmanlike.

sport teams' names and mascots announcing that *The Oregonian* would no longer print racist team and mascot names, editor William Hilliard said, "These names tend to perpetuate stereotypes that damage the dignity and self-respect of many people in our society ... this harm far transcends any innocent entertainment or promotional values these names may have." The use of Indian names for team names and mascots is considered by national and regional Indian and non-Indian groups to be derogatory, demeaning, disparaging, defamatory, racist, offensive, and insensitive. The National Congress of American Indians says, "Our sacred songs, dances, ceremonies, languages, and religions are precious to us as a people." Bill Pensoneau (St. Paul's *Pioneer Press*) writes, "The bottom line is that only Indians can say what is offensive, regardless of the intent. If we say 'Redskins' reminds us of massacres, believe us." Jack Shakely (*Los Angeles Times*) says, "The irony that the football team in our nation's capital is called the Redskins is not lost on a single Native American." In addition to the Washington Redskins (with its invidious tomahawk chop) are the Atlanta Braves, Cleveland Indians, Kansas City Chiefs, Cincinnati Reds, Chicago Blackhawks, Florida Seminoles. After a four-year legal battle, the University of North Dakota retired the "Fighting Sioux" nickname for good. Perhaps the most damaging mascot is Chief Wahoo (his "idiotic grin, shifty eyes, and fire-engine red face are a devilish declaration of insensitivity and callousness"). Jon Lurie (*The Circle*) reports good news: "Some 3,000 elementary, middle, and high schools in the U.S. have dropped racist team names over the past 30 years, according to research conducted by News Watch Project at San Francisco State University." In a related issue, Daniel A. Buford (in *Conscience*) writes, "The macabre practice of naming weapons of death after native American people [H-13 Sioux, CH-21 Shawnee, UH-1A Iroquois, H-19B Chickasaw, OH-58A Kiowa, T-41 Mescalero, CH-47A Chinook, Chief combat command vehicle, AH-64A Apache, OV-1 Mohawk, Tomahawk cruise missile, U-8F Seminole] is ... linguistic racism and cultural imperialism. The use of coopted names is more than word play. Names, cultures, and lands have been expropriated and consumed in areas where indigenous people once predominated. The practice of coopting the names of defeated enemies is analogous to ancient rites of battle wherein the heart or the liver of a defeated opponent was eaten in order to symbolically internalize the vanquished power of the opponent. ... The appropriation of Native American names by the U.S. military is a practice even more offensive, if less culturally pervasive, than racist athletic team symbols." Newspapers that no longer print racist sports teams' names use instead "the Washington football team" or simply "Washington." See also American Indian.

spouse "spouse" has had a straightforward, nonpejorative history referring to a marriage partner of either sex. It is also used sometimes in same-sex or nonmarried heterosexual relationships. "Spousal equivalent"—which may sound either officious or tongue-in-cheek—has been sighted.

spry this hackneyed, ageist term is almost always used of older people to indicate that they are livelier than you would expect. As Mary Pettibone Poole said, "There are no old people nowadays; they are either 'wonderful for their age' or dead."

spunky see feisty.

squaw this racist, sexist, demeaning term may have originally meant simply "woman" but it was used by white settlers as a slur for Native American woman and as slang for "vagina." Most American Indians consider it insulting. In the U.S., the names of some 1,000 lakes, creeks, springs, ponds, bays, narrows, islands, mountains, gulches, bluffs, valleys, gaps, cities, reservation communities, and other places included the word "squaw." The U.S. Board on Geographic Names has a Derogatory Name Policy, which was invoked, for example, in 1963 to change all instances of the word *Nigger* to *Negro*, and in 1971 all instances of *Jap* to *Japanese*. Beginning with Minnesota in 1995, a number of states have replaced the offensive "squaw" with other names. (In Maine, one frustrated county changed all "squaw" names to "moose" in one fell swoop to avoid thinking up new ones.) See also sports teams' names and mascots.

squire (noun) always a man; there is no parallel for a woman.

squire (verb) accompany, escort (used of either sex).

stableboy/stableman stable hand/worker/attendant, groom, handler.

stag line a group of dateless, danceless men at a dance, the stag line is rarely seen today. It was, however, a terrifically sexist concept, burdening men with the social duty of requesting dances of women and restricting women to passive-object status. Compare "wallflower," applied to groups of dateless, danceless women, to "stag line."

stag movie pornographic movie.

stag party for men only, a stag party can mean simply a gathering of men unaccompanied by women (perhaps a parallel for "hen party") or it can mean a raunchy party where prostitutes perform, pornographic movies are shown, or other socially questionable behavior occurs. If you mean the party for a man about to be married (which can be either of the above), you could also use pre-wedding/bachelor party. "Going stag" (that is, attending a party or event without a partner) used to be applied only to men; women also use it now.

stained-glass ceiling headline from *The Catholic Voice, Diocese of Oakland*: "Catholic women debate whether to abandon struggle against 'stained glass ceiling.'" See also clergyman.

stand pat nonsexist; the "pat" is not a person.

starlet aspiring/promising young actor, neophyte/novice/beginning/young/inexperienced/rookie actor, rookie/young performer, newcomer to the stage/screen, young/future/minor star. Or use whatever term you would use for a male actor at the same level of professional experience.

star wars officially called the Strategic Defense Initiative, this was a Reagan administration's weapons program, which was as unrealistic as it was expensive, or vice versa.

state rape refers to state-mandated vaginal or transvaginal probes for women seeking an abortion in the first trimester. This procedure has no medical rationale: its proposed intention is to oblige women to see what is in their womb and then, it is hoped, have them change their minds about an abortion. There are no published studies in peer-reviewed literature demonstrating that viewing ultrasound images persuades women seeking abortion to continue the pregnancy. As of 2013, eight states (Alabama, Arizona, Florida, Kansas, Louisiana, Mississippi, Virginia, and Texas) mandate that abortion providers perform ultrasounds on women seeking to terminate pregnancies. See also abortion.

"state secrets" defense a recent example of the "state secrets" defense (David G. Savage, in *Los Angeles Times*): a German car salesman was stopped by the CIA at a border crossing, blindfolded, taken to an airport and stripped of clothes by a team of masked men, drugged, chained inside the plane, flown to Afghanistan, beaten repeatedly and tortured in a CIA-run prison for five months, and, when it was discovered he was the wrong man, received no apology; "Instead, he was dropped from a truck on a hillside in Albania." German officials said the U.S. "admitted this man had been taken erroneously." When he attempted to sue for the torture and wrongful imprisonment, his case was denied "to protect classified intelligence sources." In their appeal, ACLU lawyers said it made little sense to use secrecy as a reason to throw out a case whose facts had been broadcast and discussed throughout the world." Savage says "the state secrets rule dates to 1953 with a case involving the crash of a B-29 bomber. When the widows of three crewmen sued and sought the official accident report, the Air Force refused, saying the plane was on a mission to test secret electronics equipment. The court ruled, in *U.S. v. Reynolds*, that the need to protect the nation's security outweighed the widows' claim. Recent disclosures show that the justices apparently had been misled. When the accident reports were declassified, they revealed the plane had been poorly maintained but did not contain military secrets." Another recent use of the "state secrets" defense: "administration lawyers have said judges cannot hear challenges to the warrantless wiretapping of Americans because doing so would expose secret details about the National Security Agency's program." See also black site, detainee, torture.

statesman diplomat, world/government/political leader, politician, legislator, lawmaker, public figure, political/government strategist, public servant/official; stateswoman and statesman. Avoid "statesperson"—it's not only awkward, but so far it's been used only for women. Replace "elder statesman" with more descriptive phrases: presidential adviser, well-respected world political figure, renowned political elder, longtime political resource.

statesmanlike/statesmanly diplomatic, politically savvy.

statesmanship statecraft, diplomacy, government/world leadership, leadership, political savvy.

stationmaster station manager/head/chief.

stem cell research many researchers see virtually unlimited potential in stem cells to treat and cure such human diseases and disorders as Parkinson's disease, Alzheimer's, diabetes, heart disease, cancer, multiple sclerosis, burns, and spinal cord injuries. Stem cells come in two general types: (1) adult stem cells, which researchers have been investigating for two decades but which have limited flexibility; not all of the 220 types of cells found in the human body (for example blood cells, heart cells, brain cells, nerve cells) can be coaxed from them. (2) embryonic stem cells are more primitive but do permit developing into most or all of the 220 types of human cells. A news release from the National Institutes of Health (NIH) says it believes the potential medical benefits of human stem cell technology "are compelling and worthy of pursuit in accordance with appropriate ethical standards." This is all good news so far. The problem is that anti-abortion groups feel that embryos are little people and should not be used for research. But stem cells used for research are typically obtained from surplus frozen embryos left over from in-vitro fertilization (IVF) procedures at fertility clinics. A couple undergoing IVF has four choices for their 16 or so surplus embryos: discard them, donate them to another infertile couple, donate them for research, or preserve them at very low temperatures for possible future use. Very few parents are willing to give their embryos to another couple for a variety of emotional reasons (and very few couples are willing to receive them for emotional reasons and because thawed embryos have a lowered chance of starting a pregnancy). Preservation can be expensive. So most couples ask that the remaining embryos be discarded. There are currently hundreds of thousands of surplus embryos in clinics. It's difficult to see the difference between discarding embryos and using them for research with so much promise. George Lakoff (*Thinking Points*) says, "Conservative language experts have for years been insisting that it be called 'embryonic' stem cell research to reinforce" the idea of stem cells as embryos, pre-born babies, children who need resculng. Stem cells are "actually blastocysts, hollow spheres with only stem cells—no brain cells, arm cells, heart cells, nerve cells, or any other kind of cell." It can never become a child as it is.

stepfather/stepmother these are acceptable terms, although some people prefer "mother/father by marriage." See also stepmother, wicked.

stepmother, wicked leave this phrase in the old fairy tales but do not write any new ones using it. It is sexist because there is no equally developed wicked stepfather persona; its mythic influence has unnecessarily complicated many blended family situations.

stereotype a stereotype (the word comes from the process of duplicating printing plates made from set type) is "the continual portrayal of a group of people with the same narrow set of characteristics. ... It shows a cultural bias toward the characteristics of one's own culture, painting characters outside that culture in limiting and sometimes dehumanizing ways" (Linda Seger, *Creating Unforgettable Characters*). Stereotypes are quick and convenient because they require no thought. For the same reason, they are often inaccurate—and racist, sexist, homophobic, ageist, handicappist, or ethnocentric. "The holder of a stereotype will accept any information, no matter how improbable, which reinforces the image. Conversely, the holder will discard as irrelevant any data which does not confirm the stereotype" (Marsha J. Hamilton, in Joanna Kadi, *Food for Our Grandmothers*). In his classic 1922 study of the forces that shape popular consciousness, Walter Lippmann said that when the "charm of the familiar" was imperiled, people will go to extremes to preserve and defend their version of things as they are. "No wonder," he wrote, "that any disturbance of the stereotypes seems like an attack on the foundations of the universe. It is an attack upon the foundations of our universe, and, where big things are at stake, we do not readily admit that there is any difference between our universe and the universe." Lippman said that stereotypes "mark out certain objects as familiar or strange, emphasizing the difference, so that the slightly familiar is seen as very familiar, and the somewhat strange is sharply alien." According to Elizabeth Ewen and Stuart Ewen (*Typecasting: On the Arts & Sciences of Human Inequality*), "The Christian Right has played an important role in the resurrection of typecasting as a strategy of power. ... Ministers routinely tell their congregations that God is angry with those who question stipulated stereotypes of family, community, religion, and patriotism. Challenges to sexual codes of belief are particularly diabolical and rampant across the land. It is the responsibility of good Christians, congregations are instructed, to uphold timeless definitions of good and evil, to save America from the devils of secularization. At the vortex of this imperative, homosexuality and the autonomy of women are typecast as the most ominous threats to morality and to life."

sterile this term is used for both women and men. "Infertile" refers to the lack of offspring in people who have been having unprotected intercourse for a certain length of time. "Sterile" usually indicates that a cause for the infertility has been found. Infertile people are not necessarily sterile. Sterile people are always infertile. Infertility is often treatable; sterility generally is not (unless, for example, a tubal ligation or vasectomy can be reversed). See also barren, frigid, impotent, infertile.

stevedore nonsexist; from the Spanish for "to pack."

steward (manager) the word itself is nonsexist and can be used for both sexes, but stewards have traditionally been men so it seems to have a male cast to it.

steward/stewardess (flight crew member) flight/cabin attendant, attendant, crew member. Plural: flight crew.

stock boy/stock girl/stock man stockkeeper, stock/stockroom clerk/assistant, stock gatherer.

stockman rancher, cattle owner/raiser/breeder, sheep farmer/owner/raiser/breeder.

Stone Age this is the correct term for the earliest known period of human culture. It is derogatory when used to refer to non-Stone Age cultures and people, implying that they are somehow inferior, backward, or unchanging.

storms in 1979, the National Weather Service stopped naming storms exclusively after women; half are now named for men. See also hurricane.

straight (adjective) "straight" and "gay" are adjective mates referring to people who have respectively other-sex and same-sex attractional orientations. Despite its dictionary definitions ("exhibiting no deviation from what is established or accepted as usual, normal, or proper," *Webster's Ninth New Collegiate Dictionary*; "right; correct ... not deviating from what is considered socially normal, usual, or acceptable," *American Heritage Dictionary*), the term "straight" is acceptable to lesbians and gay men.

straw man straw argument/figure, nonexistent problem, diversionary tactic, hoax, imaginary/weak opposition, carefully set up just to be knocked down, front, cover; red herring; nonentity, hot air, ineffectual person, weakling; sitting duck. Bankers use the term "straw borrower" for a nonoccupying co-borrower.

street people see homeless, the.

stress positions see torture.

strict constructionists in contrast to judicial activists, who attempt to apply the Constitution to contemporary issues—issues the Founders could not have imagined—strict constructionists read the Constitution very narrowly and literally. Like literal readings of the Bible (the earth is 6,000 years old and Noah really had two of each animal on the Ark), literal readings of the Constitution are sometimes a poor fit for our technological and increasingly complex society.

strident used primarily to describe women (especially feminists) indiscriminately and discriminatingly, "strident" (as well as "shrill") has become a stereotype that means little more than "She makes me sick!" Alternatives include: harsh, jarring, raucous, dissonant, discordant, unharmonious, clashing, sharp.

strongarm man strongarm guard, bodyguard, the muscle; enforcer, goon, ugly/rough customer, bully, hard case, big tuna.

strongman dictator, tyrant, military dictator, weightlifter, iron pumper, powerhouse.

stud (man) used colloquially to mean someone who is successful with women, this term seems to have found a niche for itself in the language. There is no equivalent for "a woman successful with men" that doesn't emphasize her promiscuity or have a negative spin. He is a stud; she is a slut. See also ladies' man, man about town, playboy, rake, slut, womanizer.

stuffed shirt this term is appropriate for both sexes, but if you need a more neutral-sounding alternative, consider prig, someone who is stuffy/stuck-up/conceited/smug/self-important/parochial/provincial/supercilious/snobbish/puffed-up/complacent/self-satisfied/pleased with oneself.

strumpet see prostitute.

stuntman "stuntwoman" is an equally acceptable sex-specific word. If you need inclusive alternatives, consider stunt performer/driver/actor, professional acrobat, daredevil, breakneck, acrobat, aerialist, contortionist, gymnast.

suave technically inclusive, this term is curiously reserved for men. There is nothing to say it can't be used of women. You could also consider sex-neutral alternatives: sophisticated, smooth, worldly, polite, diplomatic, civil.

subjects terms like "subjects" and "sample" are acceptable when discussing statistics, but the *Publication Manual of the American Psychological Association*, 4th ed., suggests replacing the impersonal term *subjects* with a more descriptive term: participants, individuals, college students, children, respondents. "Scientists who refer to people as *subjects*, businessmen who refer to people as *personnel*, teachers who refer to people as *culturally disadvantaged* are not merely describing; they are committing themselves to a point of view" (Neil Postman, *Crazy Talk, Stupid Talk*).

subkingdom retain this biology term as it is.

submissive promoting submissiveness as a "natural" attitude for women has often been based on the biblical injunction for wives to be submissive to their husbands. That this use of "submissive" may have arisen from factors in the mid-Eastern culture of the first centuries C.E. or from subsequent translations is not taken into account. In addition, it doesn't seem at all natural to most women.

subsidy the same people who bring you the free market ("Just leave everything alone—things will come 'round right in the end") also bring you subsidies. When a little company gets in trouble, the government says, "Go fish." When a big company gets in trouble because of "market weakness" or "price instabilities" (little companies refer to these as lousy sales and rising supply costs), the government can't get its checkbook out fast enough—usually because it knows that what goes around comes around. A corporation has to convince the givers-of-subsidies that what they do is important to the country. Fortunately, this isn't too difficult. For example, Wal-Mart, the world's largest corporation, made $9 billion in profits in 2003. The following year a report was published showing that Wal-Mart had been the recipient of at least $1 billion in federal and state subsidies ("Shopping for Subsidies: How Wal-Mart Uses Taxpayer Money to Finance Its Never-ending Growth" by Philip Mattera and Anna Purinton at goodjobsfirst.org). Whoever posted this to Wikipedia was possessed of a fine sense of irony: "In economics, a subsidy is a type of financial government assistance, such as a grant, tax break, or trade barrier, in order to encourage the production or purchase of a good. The term subsidy may also refer to assistance granted by others, such as individuals or non-government institutions, although this is more commonly described as charity." See also corporate welfare.

substandard English when this is code for black English, use nonstandard English.

substandard housing see slum.

success object (man) if women have traditionally been viewed as sex objects, men have traditionally been viewed as success objects; both roles are artificial, highly limiting, and destructive. For men, economic success is still the crucial criterion of self-worth—witness the bumper sticker "He who dies with the most toys wins." Avoid writing and speaking of men solely in terms of their achievements, finances, possessions, and social rank. This is not to belittle accomplishment, hard work, or success, but to say that men are more than machines that endlessly crank out "product" for the boss, the family, the neighborhood, and the IRS. See also provider.

suffers from (a condition) someone who has (a condition), someone with (a condition). In referring to people with disabilities, avoid all forms of the afflicted with/suffers from/victim of construction. Use instead, for example, has diabetes, has multiple sclerosis. See also disabilities, handicapped.

suffragette suffragist. Although women in Great Britain chose to call themselves "suffragettes," U.S. women did not want the demeaning "-ette" ending ("majorette," "usherette," "farmerette") and were called "suffragettes" only by those periodicals and speakers hostile to the women's goals. See also suffragist.

suffragist this term describes anyone of either sex who works for the voting rights of others, especially women's, but it most often refers to a woman. In 1912 Mark Twain wrote of suffragists: "For forty years they have swept an imposingly large number of unfair laws from the statute books of America. In this brief time these serfs have set themselves free—essentially. Men could not have done as much for themselves in that time without bloodshed, at least they never have, and that is an argument that they didn't know how." See also suffragette.

sugar daddy there is no parallel term for a woman who supports a younger man, but if you need to convey this concept, a possible inclusive alternative might be meal ticket. ("Sugar" has meant money since 1859.)

suicide evidence has suggested that certain types of media reporting are tied to an increase in suicides (suicide contagion). Some factors appear to raise the risk of suicide for imitators: placement (story on the front page or using "suicide" in headlines); details (specific methods and locations given); photos and videos (grieving friends and family, memorial services, locations, methods); language (instead of "committed," "succeeded," "failed," use the neutral "died by suicide" or "took their life"; simplification (naming a single cause like "recent financial worries" or "divorce"). On the other hand, with the growth of social media, it is more important than ever that factual information be given to dispel fast-mushrooming rumors. Mental health disorders and/or substance abuse are associated with 90 percent of suicides. See also assisted suicide, manipulative self-harm incidents.

suicide bomber man or woman.

suit this jargon for "manager" or "boss" can be used of either sex (women wear suits too) although at present it tends to be more male-associated. It can be used or understood derogatorily.

suitor in affairs of the heart, this term has traditionally been reserved for men. Today, it is not so much the case that women may also be suitors as that the term is no longer necessary because forming a relationship tends to be a mutual activity. No longer is one person the supplicant, the pursuer, while the other is the "sued."

sultan/sultana acceptable sex-specific terms.

Sunni see Shiites, Sunnis, Kurds.

superhero/superheroine these denizens of popular comic book/strip genres might seem to be equals, but as long as "heroine" is defined as "a female hero," she is a subset and thus the lesser of the two. In most comics, the female superhero was a sidekick to the superhero or had "Girl" in her name (Trina Robbins, in Wilma Mankiller et al., *The Reader's Companion to U.S. Women's History*). Call all such characters "superheroes." See also hero/heroine.

superman/superwoman these are fairly equivalent gender-specific terms and they can be used as they are. The inclusive alternative is superhero.

superpatriot this term describes flag-waving extremists and is also an attack phrase on those who protest too much their love of country (William Safire, *Safire's Political Dictionary*). He quotes President Eisenhower in 1962: "I don't think the United States needs super-patriots. We need patriotism, honestly practiced by all of us, and we don't need these people that are more patriotic than you or anybody else."

superstition "To this day, unverifiable Christian beliefs are respected as tenets of faith, while unverifiable non-Christian beliefs are negatively referred to as superstition (Eleanor Moore, *Creating a New Community*). Nick Levinson points out that every religion requires faith for at least some of its beliefs, but "superstition" is applied only to other people's beliefs. The creeds and rituals of numerous religions fit dictionary definitions of "superstition."

"support our troops" two kinds of individuals in the U.S. support the troops: those who have bumper stickers that say so and those who don't. The false equation of anti-war sentiment with anti-troop sentiment has created a synthetic dichotomy maintained by people who know a good thing when they see it. Refined during the George W. Bush's administration, which "systematically shortchanged the wounded and maimed who made it back from harm's way" (Brett Cunningham, in *Columbia Journalism Review*), the pro-troop propagandists charged that critical discussion of the wars in Iraq and Afghanistan was unpatriotic and an insult to the brave men and women fighting and dying for our freedoms. All reasonable Americans appreciate our armed forces and their profound sacrifices. Supporting our troops should mean outfitting and paying them adequately (we paid "contract soldiers" or mercenaries in Iraq many times what soldiers earned) and offering resources when they leave the military; an estimated 18 to 22 veterans commit suicide every day (Veterans for Peace, Inc.). The issue is bigger than bumper stickers.

surgical strike also called "precision bombing," a "surgical strike" is intended to kill or damage only its chosen legitimate targets, the "surgical strike" is not dependably precise. In the war on Iraq, civilians have been killed, hospitals bombed, and infrastructure destroyed by surgical strikes. However, the phrase makes the business of war more palatable to the U.S. public. When Washington talks about "surgical strikes," it is often camouflage for horrors the public doesn't want to know about. See also military language.

surnames use parallel treatment for men's and women's surnames: if you use his surname alone (Tascher), don't add a social title to hers (Ms. Demeter); if you call her Magnolia, don't call him Mr. Bartleby. With reference to married couples, too often he is the main Primrose while she is Mrs. Primrose, Deborah, or Deborah Primrose; they should be referred to as Charles Primrose and Deborah Primrose, Mr. Primrose and Ms. Primrose, or Deborah and Charles. Some 90 percent of married women in the United States take their husband's last name, according to a poll conducted for *American Demographics* magazine; those breaking with tradition are more likely to be young, affluent achievers. Only nine states recognize a statutory right for men to take their wives' last name. A man who wants to take his wife's name must petition the court, advertise in a newspaper, and pay hundreds of dollars in fees; a woman needs only to fill out a marriage license application (*Ms.*). See also hyphenated surnames, maiden name, matronym/matronymic, patronym/patronymic.

surrogate mother surrogate. "Coined in 1981, 'surrogacy' describes the arrangement in which a woman gestates a fetus for others after artificial insemination. Current terms include contract pregnancy, intrauterine adoption, or preconception arrangement. ... Most feminist writers strongly oppose surrogacy's valorization of women's biological role and its potential for exploitation of low-income women who become surrogates because they need money. Others argue for surrogacy as a low-tech, woman-controllable method for alleviating infertility that enables alternative family structures and they oppose limiting women's freedom to choose how to use their bodies" (Helen Bequaert Holmes and Laura M. Purdy, in Wilma Mankiller et al., *The Reader's Companion to U.S. Women's History*).

survivor see rape victim, victim.

suttee "It was once a common practice in many parts of the world to kill the wives, concubines, and female (and sometimes male) servants of deceased patriarchs, perhaps in the hope that they would continue to serve their masters in the next world. Widow-sacrifice has existed not only in India, but in Scandinavia, Slavia, Greece, Thrace, Scythia, Ancient Egypt, among the Tongans, Balinese, Fijians and Maoris, in some African and Native American tribes, and in China. India is unusual only in that there the practice has continued into modern times" (Mary Anne Warren, *Gendercide*). Although burning widows alive on their husbands' funeral pyres was outlawed in India in 1829, immolations continued. Human rights groups have suggested sanctions against countries that practice gender apartheid and tolerate violence against women. See also dowry deaths.

swain admirer. "Swain" comes from the Middle English *swein* meaning "boy" or "servant." See also boyfriend, suitor.

swami from the Hindi for "owner, lord," this word is perceived as male. Unless you are using it in its narrowest sense, you may substitute teacher, religious teacher, ascetic, pundit, seer, mentor, leader, guide, spiritual guide, guru.

swamp wetlands.

swarthy although references to complexions are not in themselves unacceptable, "swarthy" always seems to convey a little something negative; "dark-complexioned" says the same thing without also implying that this person is possibly someone to keep an eye on.

swashbuckler this term seems ineradicably associated with men, although there have been women who have behaved like swashbucklers, among them pirates Anne Bonny, Mary Read, and Grace "Gráinne" O'Malley and the French daredevil Marie Marvingt. More neutral-appearing words include daredevil, adventurer, sensation-seeker, thrill-seeker, show-off, exhibitionist.

swear like a trooper troopers and soldiers include both sexes now, but if you want something else, try turn the air blue, cuss a blue streak, curse up hill and down dale/up one side and down the other, badmouth.

sweater girl if it is truly necessary to describe a woman in terms of her voluptuousness, use adjectives ("curvaceous," "well-built," "voluptuous") instead of a noun so that a piece of clothing (emphasizing one part of her) does not become the whole woman. "Sweater girl" implies a great deal more than what the woman looks like: it also hints at her lifestyle and her intelligence. See also body image.

sweet sixteen (and never been kissed) as this always refers to a young woman, it is sexist. No sixteen-year-old wants to hear it anyway.

sweet william leave as is.

swingman (basketball) swingplayer.

switchman switcher, switch/switchyard operator, technical equipment operator/technician, switching equipment technician/operator.

swordsman fencer, dueler, duelist, blade, swashbuckler, sword fighter; swordswoman and swordsman.

T

If you are a thinker, you will change the language. You will not use words the way others do.

Gertrude Stein

Words are name tags which save us the trouble of thinking about the objects or ideas which they represent. Here exactly lies their capacity for mischief.

Judith Groch

tailor woman or man.

take off one's hat to this formerly male custom has all but disappeared; the term is used inclusively today.

Taliban plural for "talib," meaning student, uppercase Taliban ("Students of Islamic Knowledge Movement") is the Sunni Muslim Pashtun organization that gained the outside world's notice in 1994 and in 1996 captured Kabul, Afghanistan's capital, with the intention of creating the world's most pure Islam state. Their close ties with Osama bin Laden and their radically fundamentalist Islamism set them in conflict with most of the international community. You will see the spelling "Taleban" in British materials.

talisman nonsexist; the "man" is not sex-linked but comes from a Greek word for "consecration ceremony." The plural is talismans.

tar baby a doll made of tar and turpentine, Tar Baby was used to entrap Br'er Rabbit in one of the Uncle Remus stories. The more Br'er Rabbit fought the Tar Baby, the more entangled he became. Since then, a tar baby has referred to a sticky situation that only gets worse the harder you try to fix it. Although "tar baby" originated in African folklore and the Uncle Remus stories were told in a manner acceptable (that is, not racist) to many people of the time, by the mid-20th century, the dialect and the "old Uncle" stereotype of the narrator, long considered demeaning by many blacks, as well as Harris's racist and patronizing attitudes toward blacks (he was white) and his defense of slavery in his foreword, rendered the book indefensible to many. When the stories were recently reissued with more acceptable illustrations, one critic wrote, "Isn't it just like liberals to diminish genuine racial and cultural diversity in the name of respecting it?" Actually, it's not liberals as much as some African Americans who find the stories demeaning. It's only fair to say that other African Americans are pleased that the folktales were collected and saved—and they are, considered out of context, rather delightful. The bottom line? Avoid "tar baby" until further notice.

tart if you mean prostitute, use prostitute. If you mean a woman considered to be sexually promiscuous, consider describing her behavior factually rather than labeling her judgmentally. (Originally "tart" was used as an endearment, much as "honey" or "sugar" is used.) See also prostitute.

taskmaster/taskmistress supervisor, boss, job boss, task sergeant, disciplinarian, inspector, instructor, overseer, monitor, martinet, surveyor, superintendent, director, manager, employer. For discussion of "master" words, see master (noun).

tax-and-spend a pejorative epithet applied to politicians or policies that increase the size of government, this phrase appears, like the emperor, without its clothes—to wit, ignoring that all politicians tax and all of them spend. It really means that we don't like the way *you* are taxing and spending. It is most often used by Republicans who claim Democrats are driving the U.S. economy into the ditch by taxing the rich and spending on the poor. But historically, the U.S. economy has fared better under Democratic presidents than under Republican presidents. In a recent study (2013), Princeton economists Alan Blinder and Mark Watson note that "the performance gap [between Republican and Democratic presidents] is startlingly large—so large, in fact, that it strains credulity, given how little influence over the economy most economists (or the Constitution, for that matter) assign to the President of the United States." For the phrase "tax-and-spend," substitute who is objecting to what, and why. See also taxes, tax loopholes.

taxes "Even though the first purpose of the tax system is to raise revenue for government functions, historically it has also been used to shape the behavior of taxpayers" (Martha Burk, *Ms.*), for example, the mortgage interest deductions encouraged home ownership and marriage taxes reduce the incentive for married women to be employed outside the home. In addition to getting out of the business of social engineering, the tax code needs serious reform: revoke the pay-no-taxes status of nonprofits who discriminate against certain segments of the popular or who use their tax free funds to influence politics (Catholic and Protestant churches were among the biggest contributors to anti-abortion referenda in the 2006 election); close barn-sized loopholes and collect all owed taxes (according to a Senate subcommittee investigation, "Americans hiding money in offshore tax havens such as Switzerland, Liechtenstein, and the Cayman Islands, cheat the U.S. out of $100 billion a year"); ensure that members of Congress live, earn, and spend by the same rules U.S. taxpayers do—no exceptions; remove the caps on Social Security taxes; institute a Social Security credit for caregiving; vet the tax code for inequities; and restore the levels of taxation that led to one of the healthiest U.S. economies in history. "Taxes were far higher on top incomes in the three decades after World War II than they've been since. And the distribution of income was far more equal. Yet the American economy grew faster in those years than it's grown since tax rates were slashed in 1981" (Robert Reich, marketplace.org, 2012). He says, "Fairness isn't incompatible with growth. It's necessary for it." What if taxpayers were allowed to indicate where 50 percent of the taxes they're paying should go: education? Military? Infrastructure? Social services? Perhaps the citizenry could do some social engineering, while feeling much less helpless about their taxes going for programs that do not approve of. The point of this entry? When discussing taxes, know your audience, know your material, and be specific; "taxes" means something different to everyone.

taximan taxi driver.

tax loopholes "We've got over $1 trillion worth of loopholes in the corporate tax code. This isn't the invisible hand of the market at work. It's the successful work of special interests" (Barack Obama). Corporations avoid paying billions of dollars in federal and state income taxes by shifting their U.S. earnings to offshore tax havens. Ironically, tax avoidance is actually bad for corporations in the long run, but this is the land of opportunity: what matters is money in the corporate pocket today for executives who may be leaving tomorrow. In 2014, EU Competition commissioner Joaquin Almunia announced that regulators will be examining corporate tax loopholes across Europe—loopholes and weaknesses in the laws that allow companies like Starbucks, Apple, Amazon, and others to cut their tax bills by shifting their profits into tax havens. This is one way, albeit an indirect one, of closing tax loopholes. Closer to home, in 2003, Montana deleted the so-called "water's edge" tax loophole that companies used to evade state tax liability on profits stashed in offshore bank accounts. In the last 10 years, that move brought in $40 million—substantial for a small state that typically spends about $1.8 billion a year. In 2013, Oregon followed Montana's lead and expects to bring in $17 million in tax revenue from offshore corporate holdings. If 21 other states and the District of Columbia had also closed their "water's edge" loopholes, they would have brought in $1.015 billion in additional tax revenue in 2012 (according to the U.S. Public Interest Research Group). Most taxpayers know that these loopholes must be closed; now they know a few ways to do it. See also taxes.

taxman tax collector/inspector/agent/preparer/consultant.

tax relief by repeatedly dinning "tax relief" into U.S.-owned brains, the conservative right has indoctrinated us to think of taxes as onerous—right up there with headaches and hemorrhoids, only worse. We seem to have forgotten, as George Lakoff (*Thinking Points*) reminds us, "Taxation brings together the common wealth to build a common infrastructure that we all need to fulfill our individual needs and dreams." Taxes mean more than some faceless government taking our hard-earned money. Taxes buy us roads and schools and police protection and firefighting capabilities and emergency services and the Internet and dams and bridges and defense systems. When taxes are fair (which they are not at present since the wealthiest pay the smallest percentage), we get a lot for our money. The only reason conservatives work so hard at selling "tax relief" is that voters are likely to go along with "tax reforms," failing to read the fine print that says almost all of the "relief" will go to those who need it least. See also tax loopholes.

teacher some 98 percent of preschool and kindergarten teachers and 86 percent of elementary school teachers are women, while 86 percent of public school superintendents are men and 95 percent are white. Statistics like these wouldn't seem to lead to the best educational outcomes.

Tea Party movement see political spectrum.

tease (woman) the dangerous myth that women are "teasing" when they say no to a man's advances has been responsible for much grief, criminal behavior, and even murder. The notion of woman-as-tease is often in the eye (and elsewhere) of the beholder.

teen/teenager acceptable age-specific terms, although less acceptable in generalizations; young people (the preferred term) reject a one-size-fits-all label and particularly dislike being called kids, girls and boys/boys and girls, youths, adolescents, juveniles, or teenyboppers (which is also sexist, as it's reserved for girls). Older teens can be called young adults, and secondary students can be called high schoolers. One career teacher addresses his high school students as scholars. See also adolescent, ageism, juvenile, youth.

teen moms 305,420 babies were born to girls ages 15-19 in 2012. Teenage girls with older partners are more likely to become pregnant than those with partners closer in age, according to a study by Planned Parenthood. Teens who date older partners were less consistent about contraceptive use; for each year of age difference between a teenage girl and her partner, the likelihood of contraceptive use decreases by 11 percent. Much societal disapproval and anger (expressed concretely by "reforms" in welfare programs) is directed against "teen moms" (there is no corresponding label for the men) but very little is said or done about their partners. According to Bill Albert, deputy director of the National Campaign to Prevent Teen and Unplanned Pregnancy (in *Conscience*), teen pregnancy rates in the U.S. have declined 36 percent since 1990, and the teen birth rate has plummeted by one-third since 1991. Even more encouraging, adolescent pregnancy and childbearing have declined in all 50 states and among all racial and ethnic groups. The results are thought to be due to better sex education and the availability of contraceptives.

Tejana/Tejano U.S.-born person of Mexican descent living in Texas; use for those who self-identify this way.

telephone man telephone installer/repairer/worker

telephone operator man or woman.

television largely sexist, racist, homophobic, ageist, and violent, television is not an equal opportunity medium—not perhaps surprising considering that over two-thirds of television writers are white men. Men are featured much more often, in more lead roles, and for a wider range of roles. While men are shown often at work, women are usually presented in family roles and given explicit marital status (most female characters are married, about to be married, or in a serious relationship with a man, while most male characters are single). Men are more likely to dominate women than vice versa, and even when they have equal status, men are more likely to assume control, both physically and emotionally. Men are the movers and shakers who earn the money; women are responsible for the wellbeing and cleanliness of the family. Despite exceptions, women are often shown as half-clad and half-witted, needing to be rescued by quick-thinking, fully clothed men. On the other side of the camera, women make up approximately 34 percent of writers, 38 percent of producers, and 12 percent of directors. See also advertising.

tell it to the marines nonsexist since marines are now both women and men. Or use: pull the other one.

temp short for temporary worker/employee, this informal term applies to both men and women, although since women make up the majority of temporary office workers, it is likely to be perceived as female.

temptress tempter. See also "feminine" word endings.

termagant since this term is reserved for women and there is no parallel for men, you may want sex-neutral alternatives: faultfinder, grouch, grumbler, crosspatch, loud/overbearing/bad-tempered person. See also shrew.

terminate/terminate with extreme prejudice kill, assassinate, execute. This euphemism, derived from the employment contract language of "termination with prejudice" was used by the CIA during the Vietnam War when "sacking" its locally hired operatives (Douglas Valentine, *The Phoenix Program*). The phrase appeared in Bernard Conners' 1972 *Don't Embarrass the Bureau*, and continues to appear in books and movies; whether it is currently used by military or intelligence operations is doubtful.

terrorist with the exception of blatantly terroristic acts, like the bombing of a civilian airliner, the use of "terrorist" varies according to the writer's perspective. A terrorist in one situation might be a freedom fighter, guerrilla, resistant, or commando in another. "This has become a code word for Arabs. When using it we can mask anti-Arab statements and politics while ignoring the terrorist acts of white people and European and U.S. governments, such as the bombings of civilian areas in Panama and Iraq" (Paul Kivel, *Uprooting Racism*). From *Creating Just Language*: to create or reinforce prejudices, a useful tool of governments is to demonize their enemies as terrorists. "The English would have called the rebellious colonists 'terrorists,' while the colonists would have called themselves 'freedom fighters.' The term is always applied to the less powerful adversaries and promulgated by the more powerful to cultivate disdain for the enemy. Unfortunately, once the term 'terrorist' is applied to a group of individuals with similar ethnic origins, the negative reverberations spill over to all persons of that particular ethnic background. There is seldom, if any, analysis of which of the adversaries are the real terrorists." Don Irish (in *North Country Peace Builder*) says, "Killing those labeled terrorists will not end terrorism, unless the despair which recruits them is addressed. Terrorists do not arise in a vacuum! There are reasons for their existence. They have personal hopes, dreams, and talents which are unfulfilled. They do not become suicide bombers willy-nilly, not caring for life. They have families whom they love and are loved by. If they don't have tanks, helicopters, bombers, and so on for physical opposition, they use what they have—rocks, or homemade bombs, or their bodies. Ultimately, the dominant group must deal with the real problems rather than the terrorism, which is a symptom." Reserve "terrorist" for those who create terror in the lives of others, killing bystanders and destroying infrastructure, but use it for all sides of a conflict when it is deserved.

terror, war on see war on terror.

testimony nonsexist; terms like "testimony," "protest," "New Testament," and "testicles" all come from the Latin *testari* meaning to testify or to witness (the word "testes" developed as a supposed "witness" to virility). The connection between testes and testimony was reinforced by the old Roman custom whereby men swore oaths by laying a hand on their genitals while women swore by their breast. (Freud was puzzled as to how women, not fearing castration, developed a conscience.)

testosterone testosterone circulates in both sexes but is much more abundant in males; post-pubertal men have testosterone levels about ten times higher those in women. Some studies have indicated that testosterone is a likely source of aggression and that men who dominate in social situations have higher testosterone levels than their peers While the presence of high levels of testosterone may have some behavioral consequences, scientists warn against generalizations and are skeptical that testosterone is a strong, direct cause of specific human activity when so many other social factors determine if and how testosterone translates into such behavior as aggression, dominance, or competitiveness. It appears, for example, that women can be as competitive as men, even with much lower testosterone levels. To imply that the violence men commit is inherent and unavoidable is not only unscientific but dangerous insofar as it gives a kind of permission to male acting out. With so little factual evidence, it is indefensible to accuse men ("jokingly" or not) of "testosterone poisoning." Just as menstrual cycles and menopause have been blamed for unrelated behavior in women, men are beginning to hear more unscientific remarks about their testosterone levels. Refrain yourself.

testy this comes from Latin for "head" and has nothing to do with testicles or testosterone.

that's so gay a young woman who used this currently popular expression with classmates explained that it means only, "That's so stupid, that's so silly, that's so dumb." But Morgan Kroll (in *The Advocate*) says, "Many don't think 'That's so gay' is so innocuous," and Kevin Jennings, executive director of the Gay, Lesbian, and Straight Education Network, agrees: "It's not about this one student—it's about a pervasive and serious problem that far too few schools are addressing."

"the" (before people) when used before adjectives to make a noun phrase (the elderly, the poor, the blind, the homeless, the aged, the disabled), "the" is disparaging and objectifying, and it reduces people to an anthropological category; it also betrays the writer or speaker as an outsider. Couple the adjective with an accurate and specific noun (elderly residents, poor taxpayers, blind students). "'The,' followed by an adjectival noun stereotypes and renders a diverse group of people as generic. It was a powerful tool then ("the Jews"), and is today. People disappear behind the label "the." ... Reducing people to labels is the first step toward prejudicial behavior. Person-first language, as in 'Americans with Disabilities' and 'person with cerebral palsy' help everyone see the person first" (Harold A. Maio, in *American Libraries*). See also adjectives as nouns.

"the" (before countries) most writers no longer use "the" before countries like Ukraine, Congo, and Sudan. Michelle Dzulynsky (in *Copy Editor*), says, "Ukrainians do get irate when the article *the* is added in front of Ukraine because of the many years our people and our nation were forced to be a part of the Soviet Union. It may seem petty, but to a nation that struggled for many years to have its voice heard or even its identity recognized" the small difference is important. Patricia M. Godfrey had written earlier, "The Ukrainians contend that using *the* before the name of their country implies that it is less than a sovereign, independent member of the nations of the world. If so, then neither are *the* United States, *the* United Kingdom, and *the* French Republic." However, a further look at the lack of strict parallels among country names has inspired most people to use whatever English form the country itself uses. The next time you see "Ukraine" in print, note that there is no "the" there.

thealogy see unconventional spellings.

their/them/they see singular "they."

the n-word see nigger/nigga.

theocracy a nation literally ruled by God, by means of a class of ruling priests, is called a theocracy. This is different from a nation that has a national religion or one that favors a religious orientation. There are no strict theocracies today. Although some think Iran qualifies, Iran self-identifies as a religious democracy.

theodicy "the body of doctrine that attempts to reconcile cruelty, horror, and injustice with the idea of a benevolent God" (Frederick Crew, *Follies of the Wise*).

therapy although dictionaries define "therapy" using "treatment," and vice versa, the two terms differ slightly. Therapy is often long-term with no clear-cut ending. Treatment is shorter, more directed to a particular outcome, and is usually curative. For example, contrast talk therapy with medication treatment for depression, or occupational therapy with antibiotics following an injury.

thinking man thinker, thinking/reflective/intelligent/learned person, thinking/intelligent being, intellectual, philosopher, sage, scholar, brain, highbrow.

think tank centers for research and analysis of public issues, social policy, political strategy, science or technology issues, industrial or business policies, or military advice, think tanks vary from authentic hatching grounds for improving the common lot to public relations fronts and manufacturers of ideology product. Go to www.sourcewatch.org to be astonished at the long list of U.S. think tanks. "We've got think tanks the way other towns have firehouses," *Washington Post* columnist Joel Achenbach says. "This is a thoughtful town. A friend of mine worked at a think tank temporarily and the director told him when he entered, 'We are white men between the ages of 50 and 55, and we have no place else to go.'" Almost all think tanks have a decided political leaning. There are twice as many conservative think tanks as liberal ones, and the conservative ones generally have more money. Claire van Breemen Downes (in St. Paul's *Pioneer Press*) responded to an op-ed piece by Mitchell Pearlstein by saying, "Pearlstein is listed as president of the Center of the American Experiment, apparently another of those unthinking think tanks which hijack fine-sounding names and phrases. Their role in life seems to be facing 20th-century problems with 16th-century minds, coming up with simplistic nonsolutions designed to comfort the comfortable by blaming the afflicted." She was speaking, of course, of a rather conservative organization. When you write or speak about think tanks, treat them duck by duck because their political bias, funding sources, and members differ dramatically from each other.

third-wave feminism when possible, avoid compartmentalizing feminism into "waves." A seamless garment more appropriately exemplifies this particular work that is never done. Writer and political activist Naomi Wolf is credited with helping launch the third-wave movement with her 1991 book, *The Beauty Myth*; in a 1992 *Ms.* article, "Becoming the Third Wave," Rebecca Walker wrote about and further popularized this new phase of feminism. Walker, Catherine Gund, Dawn Luncy Martin, and Amy Richards established the Third Wave Foundation, and published landmark books: *Manifesta: Young Women, Feminism, and the Future* (Jennifer Baumgardner and Richards) and *To Be Real: Telling the Truth and Changing the Face of Feminism* (Walker). According to Jennifer Baumgardner, "The Third Wave rejected the idea of a shared political priority list or even a set of issues that one must espouse to be feminist. ... Third Wave feminism was portable—you didn't have to go to a meeting to be a feminist; you could bring feminism into any room you entered. ... Reclaiming words like "slut" and "girl" replaced protests. For an in-depth look at this era, see *The Women's Movement Today: An Encyclopedia of Third-Wave Feminism*, ed. by Leslie L. Heywood. Feminist organizer Shelby Knox has identified a fourth wave and Jennifer Baumgardner describes the new movement: "By the time Obama and Hillary were facing off in the Democratic primaries, a critical mass of younger feminists began expressing themselves. They were tech-savvy and gender-sophisticated ... creating blogs, Twitter campaigns, and online media with names like Racialicious and Feministing. ... Because of media advances and globalization, waves of mass change are coming faster and faster. The waves are all part of the same body politic known as feminism, and combine to become a powerful and distinct force." See also feminism, feminisms, first-wave feminism, second-wave feminism, waves (feminism).

Third World this term refers to countries that are marginalized economically and politically in the international system (also infrequently used to describe minority groups as a whole within a larger culture). The First World supposedly included industrialized democracies, the Second World was the communist bloc, and the Third World was everyone else. However, with the disappearance of the communist bloc as such, this already simplistic geopolitical system no longer works. Critics of the term "Third World" call it imprecise (definitions vary), simplistic (the countries differ widely from each other), antagonistic (like "nonwhite," it's a catch-all way of marking "us" and "them"), and demeaning (no matter how you look at it, being third is not as good as being first or second). "The Third World is gone. ... The countries once assigned to the Third World are still there, but the concept of the Third World is no longer connected to any reality" (Robert J. Samuelson, *Newsweek*). "Nonaligned" and "unaligned" are political rather than economic concepts. Left are such labels as: emerging/emergent nations, developing nations, overexploited (or economically exploited) nations, newly industrializing/industrialized country (NIC), nonindustrialized nations, impoverished populations, post-colonial regions. The World Bank uses LICUS (Low-Income Countries Under Stress) and the British government refers to those at the bottom as "fragile." The *New York Times* style guide recommends "economically underdeveloped or emerging nations." As in all good writing and speaking, precise description is better: name the relevant nations and identify what they have in common. Bonus thought: "Study after study has taught us that there is no tool for development more effective than the empowerment of women" (former U.N. Secretary-General Kofi Annan). See also "culturally deprived/disadvantaged," illiterate, primitive, savage.

"those people" see "you people."

three-man (adjective) see one-man/two-man/three-man.

three sisters the main crops of some American Indian nations: corn, beans, squash. There seems to be no parallel for brothers.

three wise men, the Magi. A committee of the Church of England said the term "Magi" was a transliteration of the name used by officials at the Persian court, and that they could well have been women. In the authorized 17th century King James Bible used by up to 70 million worshipers in Anglican churches around the world, the gift-bearing visitors are referred to as "The Three Wise Men." Henceforth, they are "Magi" and no longer gender-specific in the Anglican prayer book.

thug the original thugs were members of a professional gang of thieves and murderers in India who strangled victims, and the term still seems male although there is nothing to prohibit it being used for women too. See also bad guy.

tigress tiger. By using the base word inclusively, terms like "tiger's eye," "tiger lily," and "have a tiger by the tail" are not sex-specific either. In its meaning as a daring or fierce woman, "tigress" is a judgment call. See also "feminine" word endings.

tillerman tiller, tiller operator.

timberman timber cutter/worker, logger, tree cutter, forester, woodcutter, log roller.

time-study man time-study engineer.

time waits for no man time waits for no one.

tin lizzie Model T. The innocent-sounding "tin lizzie" comes from the name Elizabeth (also Liza or Lizzie), which was such a common name for black women (H.L. Mencken posited that its popularity came arose from Eliza in *Uncle Tom's Cabin*) that it was used from the 1880s until the late 1920s as a generic name for any black woman, but especially a servant, maid, or cook (Stuart Berg Flexner, *I Hear America Talking*). Flexner says the name was given the car because it, like the maid, "worked hard all week and prettied up on Sundays." (Henry Ford said the car was available in "any color you choose as long as it's black.")

tinman tinsmith, tin manufacturer.

Title IX under the Educational Amendments of 1972 was a short section on gender equity known as Title IX, mandating equality in sports access for girls in high schools and universities. It is arguably the most important legislation for women in the 20th century after the right to vote, and 82 percent of Americans approve of it. The dramatic increase in female participation in sport since Title IX was passed—560 percent at the college level and 990 percent in high schools—indicates that it was lack of opportunity, not lack of interest, which kept girls and women out of high school and college athletics for so many years. According to the Women's Sports Foundation, if a girl doesn't participate in sports by the time she is 10, there is only a 10 percent chance she'll participate when she's 25. The Ms. Foundation says that girls and women who play sports have higher levels of self-esteem and lower levels of depression. The Institute for Athletics and Education found that high school girls who play sports are 80 percent less likely to be involved in an unwanted pregnancy, 92 percent less likely to be involved with drugs, and three times more likely to graduate from high school. There are still inequities for girls in sports programs, and women and girls are underrepresented, often due to myths about Title IX. It does not require quotas; force schools to cut sports for boys and men; cause a decline in male sports; require schools to spend equally on male and female sports; or oblige football and basketball to subsidize female sports. One of the problems with the perception of sports for women is shown by a report on sports journalism from the Institute of Diversity and Ethics in Sports: 90 percent of sports editors are male and 90 percent are white. See also athlete, sportsman.

T-man Treasury agent.

to a man without exception, unanimously, of one mind/accord, with one voice, at one with each other, willingly, agreed on all hands, in every mouth, carried by acclamation/unanimously, to a one; like-minded; every last one of them, everyone.

toastmaster/toastmistress these are difficult to replace as they have specific meanings particularly because of the many toastmasters clubs around the country. When possible, replace with emcee, host, speaker, announcer, introducer, lecturer, talker, guest lecturer, orator, declaimer, speechmaker, rhetorician, elocutionist, preacher, interlocuter.

to boldly go where no man has gone before in the first "Star Trek" TV series in the 1960s, this phrase was used; in the late 1980s, "Star Trek: The Next Generation" used to boldly go where no one has gone before (Ruth King, *Talking Gender*).

to each his own to each their own, there's no accounting for tastes, it takes all kinds, *chacun son goût*, to each her own/his own. See also singular "they."

toff refers to men only; there is no parallel for women.

token defined as someone hired to deflect accusations of discrimination against the employer, this often implies the person was unqualified for the job; use cautiously.

tomato see food names for people.

tomboy active/agile/athletic/boisterous/adventurous/physically courageous/competitive child, live wire, one of the gang, strong/vigorous/direct/spirited/self-confident child, rude/blunt/messy/rough/tough child, logical/mechanically minded child. "Tomboy" used to refer only to boys, then to both girls and boys, and now only to girls. In *Women of the World*, Julia Edwards says of foreign correspondent Dickey Chapelle: "Although she called herself a tomboy, she was better described as a tomgirl, for she didn't want to be a boy. She just wanted to do the things boys get to do." Sociologists and behavior experts suggest that the concept of tomboy (along with the term) is obsolete; behavior that another generation found tomboyish is considered normal today.

Sociologist Barrie Thorne spent 11 months observing boys and girls on a playground; only twice did she hear them use the word "tomboy" although adults did so fairly commonly. Many children were clearly unfamiliar with the term and several said they'd never heard of it. She predicts the word will disappear within the next decade. See also sissy.

tomcat Hugh Rawson (*Wicked Words*) says this originated from the hero's name in a 1760 bestseller, *The Life and Adventures of a Cat*. In reference to a cat, use only for male cats. To mean a man who is sexually active with more than one partner, it may be clearer to describe rather than label the behavior.

tomfool/tomfoolery/tommyrot if the connection with the man's name is a problem in your context, consider for the adjective: foolish, imprudent, irresponsible, unwise, hasty, shortsighted, foolhardy, reckless, pointless, nonsensical, ridiculous, silly, crazy, daft, simpleminded, stupid, mindless, thick-witted; for the nouns: foolishness, nonsense, rubbish, shenanigans, monkeyshines, monkey business, mischief, hanky-panky, trick, buffoonery, silliness, malarkey, baloney, poppycock, balderdash, moonshine, gobbledygook, garbage, stuff and nonsense, hogwash, bunkum, craziness, goofiness.

Tommy retain in historical contexts. Or British soldier.

tommy gun nonsexist; named after the gun's inventor, John T. Thompson.

Tom Thumb this is the hero of English folklore; if you should ever need a sex-neutral expression like it, he was known in some accounts as hop-o'-my-thumb.

tom-tom nonsexist; from the Hindi word "tamtam."

tonto this unacceptable term is borrowed from the Lone Ranger's loyal Indian companion.

too big for one's britches said of both sexes.

top banana/top brass/top dog use for both sexes.

Torah, the consisting of the five books of Moses (Genesis, Exodus, Leviticus, Numbers, and Deuteronomy), the Torah is only part of—not synonymous with—the Hebrew Bible or Scriptures. (The other two parts are the Prophets and the Writings). See also biblical language.

torch singer this has always been a female singer with a husky, passionate voice who has generally lost her man. The term may include in the future male singers in gay bars. An inclusive alternative (although it is not an exact synonym) is blues singer. See also bluesman, songstress.

tort reform conservatives are working very hard to do away with "frivolous lawsuits" by reforming the tort laws. If this were all there were to it, they wouldn't have to work so hard. But "tort lawsuits are the last possibility—the baseline of protection—for dissuading irresponsible companies from harming the public" (George Lakoff, *Thinking Points*). Lakoff points out that tort reform "has been made to sound like it is just about capping large damage awards and lawyers' fees. It is really a destruction of the civil justice system's capacity to deter corporations from acts that harm the public, since it is the lawyers' fees that permit the system to function." Nobody wants frivolous lawsuits, but that's a matter for the courts, not for law, which couldn't possibly draw all the fine lines in advance of hearing each individual case. The problem with tort lawsuits for conservatives is that they imperil corporate and investor profits. At www.corpreform.com, Justinian Lane explains that tort reform isn't about fixing a "broken" justice system; it's about protecting the public image and bottom lines of the biggest and most powerful companies in the world. Tort reform isn't about protecting doctors from high insurance rates; it's about protecting their insurers from having to pay large judgments. Tort reform isn't about keeping "greedy lawyers" from filing frivolous lawsuits; it's about keeping those who are severely injured out of the court system and away from the public eye. The truth about tort reform is that "it punishes people to protect profits. That's it."

torture despite statements that "this government does not torture people," the U.S. does in fact use torture. The *New York Times* reported that the Justice Department was secretly endorsing "harsh interrogation techniques" at the same time that then-President Bush was denying it. The *Washington Post* said you can call these techniques anything, but according to common sense, to say nothing of international law, they are torture. Andrew Sullivan (*New York Post*) said if the Nazis developed a technique we shouldn't use it—and many of the methods approved by the Justice Department were, in fact, treated as war crimes after World War II. He says that even officialdom's preferred euphemism, "enhanced interrogation," is "the exact term innovated by the Gestapo." Philip Zelikow, executive director of the 9/11 Commission, said that key European allies were balking at working with the U.S. on terrorist operations because of fears that their agents could be prosecuted for human-rights violations. The *New York Times* said that "by late 2005, European officials were angry over disclosures that CIA officials had been interrogating prisoners at secret 'black sites' in Eastern Europe. Meanwhile, U.S. officials began receiving reports that European military commanders were releasing captured terrorists in Afghanistan rather than subject them to U.S. interrogators." Waterboarding (simulated drowning), light and noise bombardment, isolation, sleep deprivation, slapping, and stress positions are only those tactics that have been admitted. The Taxonomy of Torture at www.slate.com uses official military and government documents to describe what is meant by various interrogation techniques. "Euphemisms like 'stress position' cover a wide range of practices, from the merely uncomfortable to the wickedly cruel and painful" (Phillip Carter). "The torture at Abu Ghraib and Guantánamo and Bagram and Qaim and Bucca and Gardez and Mercury and Cropper and the salt pit and all the other islands in our war-on-terror prison archipelago was not the acts of a few bad apples or rogue soldiers. It was U.S. policy" (Dr. Steven Miles, in *Women Against Military Madness*). What makes the use of torture not only inhuman and illegal, but insane is that, as former CIA field officer Robert Baer says (*Time*.com), "Torture doesn't work. When prisoners are in great pain or in great terror, they'll say everything and anything, and you can't tell what is true and what is not." Information obtained by torture at Guantánamo, for example, is thought to be inadmissible in a U.S. court of law—and might not be allowed in their military commissions, some former officials and legal experts said. Even if the information from the CIA interrogations is allowed, they said, it would probably risk focusing the trials on the actions of the agency and not the accused (*Los Angeles Times*)." "Torture is not about extracting accurate information—throughout its history, its only reliable byproducts has been false confessions. Torture is about power, revenge, rage and cruelty. It's about stripping people of their humanity. That's why torture is almost universally condemned as a human rights violation and the mark of totalitarian regimes that want to control people, not get information" (Dan Froomkin, *Huffington Post*, 2013). A 2013 report from the Constitution Project, a nonpartisan Washington think tank, said there was "indisputable" use of torture during George W. Bush's presidency. It concluded that "there is no firm or persuasive evidence that the widespread use of harsh interrogation techniques by U.S. forces produced significant information of value. There is substantial evidence that much of the information adduced ... was not useful or reliable." See also black site, detainee, enhanced interrogation, extraordinary rendition, solitary confinement, "state secrets" defense.

totem pole, high man on the number one, second to none, front-runner, star, the favorite, person on top, high-ranking individual, someone with seniority, winner, top scorer, cream of the crop, influential person, big shot/boss/wheel/cheese, hotshot, bigwig, someone at the top of the ladder/heap/tree. The phrase is ethnocentric as well as sexist. See also lord it over someone.

totem pole, low man on the lowest ranking individual, new kid on the street, someone with no seniority/clout, the last one in, washout, loser, three-time loser, hard-luck case, defeatee, the low scorer, also-ran, plebian, neophyte, proletarian, rookie, beginner, tyro, gofer. The phrase is ethnocentric as well as sexist.

tough cookie/tough guy although of nonparallel construction ("cookie/guy"), these terms for a woman and a man mean approximately the same thing. Sex-neutral alternatives include toughy/toughie, tough, bully, someone who is hard as nails, hard-nosed, callous, unsympathetic, hard-boiled, unfeeling.

tough titty tough luck, tough, too bad, that's the breaks. Its origins are unclear, but its association with the slang for a breast makes this a term to avoid.

towerman tower tender/operator/attendant.

townsman town-dweller, local, native, resident, citizen, neighbor, member of the community; townie, city slicker; urbane person. Plural: townspeople, townsfolk.

toyboy defined as a young man, more handsome than intelligent, who dates older female celebrities, this term is ageist, highly judgmental, and as sexist as "kept woman." Our national obsession with other people's lives and our willingness to judge those we don't even know encourages the popularity of stereotypes fashioned to sound-bite dimensions.

tradesman shopkeeper, storekeeper, small business owner, merchant, retailer, dealer, store owner/manager/worker/employee, tradeswoman and tradesman; trades worker, skilled/construction worker. Or be specific: electrician, mason, machinist, sub-contractor. Plural: tradespeople, people in the trades. See also hardhat.

"traditional" family see family.

trafficking, labor see human trafficking.

trafficking, sex see human trafficking.

tragedienne tragedian. See also "feminine" word endings.

trailer manufactured home.

trailer park manufactured home community, mobile home community, mobile home park. These terms are preferred to the sometimes-derogatory "trailer park."

trailing spouse see two-person single career.

tramp (hobo) woman or man. See also bum, hobo, road sister.

tramp (woman) for prostitute, use prostitute. For someone with questionable morals (a questionable judgment), consider inclusive terms: promiscuous/sexually active/indiscriminating person/individual. Women are often judged by criteria not applied to men; "tramp" is used for men only in the original meaning of a vagrant or hobo. See also prostitute.

transgender "to those who consider themselves transgender, there's a disconnect between the sex they were assigned at birth and the way they see or express themselves. Though their numbers are relatively few—the most generous estimate from the National Center for Transgender Equality is between 750,000 and 3 million Americans (fewer than 1 percent)" (*Newsweek*). Transgenderism is "an umbrella term that refers to all identities or practices that cross over, cut across, move between, or otherwise queer socially constructed sex/gender boundaries. The term includes, but is not limited to, transsexuality, heterosexual transvestism, gay drag, butch, lesbianism, and such non-European identities as the Native American berdache or the Indian Hijira" (Susan Stryker, in Paisley Currah et al., *Transgender Rights*). Anne Enke (in *Our Lives*) reports "a transgender social movement that has made it possible for an increasing number of people to insist on their right to gender self-determination, to come out as trans, and to do so at an ever younger age. It is perhaps also due to the fact that even people who conform to conventional gender norms may see that in our everyday world, gender is far more varied than those norms would suggest." The Transgender Law Center in San Francisco (in *Collective Voices*) says, "Transgender people (very broadly conceived) are those of us whose gender identity and/or expression do not or aren't perceived to match stereotypical gender norms associated with our assigned gender at birth." Transgender people face extreme levels of discrimination and violence. According to "Injustice at Every Turn," a report by the National Center for Transgender Equality and Taskforce, 53 percent of anti-LGBT homicide victims in 2012 were transgender women. Transgender people experience unemployment at twice the rate of the general population and are four times more likely to live in poverty. Forty-one percent of those interviewed for the report had attempted suicide, compared to 1.6 percent of the general population. Ninety percent of transgender people report experiencing harassment or discrimination on the job. Sixteen states plus Washington, D.C., have enacted antidiscrimination laws that protect transgender people—and the U.S. House of Representatives has passed a hate-crimes prevention bill that included gender identity. And 125 Fortune 500 companies now protect transgender employees from job discrimination (up from 3 in 2000). Transgender individuals may identify as MTF (male-to-female) or FTM (female-to-male). Because this is a community with an evolving language, those who speak and write about transgenderism need to respect people's gender choice and the terms and pronouns with which they self-identify. The word transgender never needs an extraneous "-ed" at the end. And "transgender" is used only as an adjective, never as a noun; use "transgender people" or "a transgender person." It is never appropriate to put quotation marks around either a transgender person's chosen name or the pronoun that reflects that person's gender identity. "Trans" is sometimes used as an adjective: trans-related medical care, trans clients, a trans take on things. In addition, gender identity is about who one is; sexual orientation is about who one is attracted to. Therefore, some transgender people are straight, some are gay, some are bi, some are queer. The use of "transgender" is greatly preferred to "transsexual" (or "transexual"); use "transsexual" only if an individual self-identifies that way. "Tranny" and "she-male" are offensive terms. Most often, it is unnecessary to refer to a person's gender identity. "Transgender activists have long called for this diagnosis [gender identity disorder] to be revised or removed altogether from the DSM, arguing that being transgender is not a disease but a human variation—more like being left-handed than schizophrenic" (Beth Schwartzapfel, "Transgender People Want Shrinks to Stop Calling Them Crazy," *Mother Jones*, 2012). Guinevere Turner wonders in *The Advocate*, "Are those people who choose to live in between traditional male and female identities being gender-revolutionary or simply trandy?" See also cross-dresser, gender, sex reassignment surgery (SRS), transphobia.

transphobia "irrational fear of people whose actual or perceived gender identity/expression departs from stereotypical gender roles and expectations" (Alvin M. Schrader and Kristopher Wells, *Challenging Silence Challenging Censorship*). Transphobia is expressed by stereotyping, discrimination, harassment, and violence. See also transgender.

transsexual see transgender.

transvestite see cross-dresser.

trash see white trash/poor white trash.

trashman trash collector.

travel FYI: "The U.S. government is collecting electronic records on the travel habits of millions of Americans who fly, drive, or take cruises abroad, retaining data on the persons with whom they travel or plan to stay, the personal items they carry during their journeys, and even the books that travelers have carried, according to documents obtained by a group of civil liberties advocates and statements by government officials" (Ellen Nakashima, in the *Washington Post*). These personal travel records are meant to be stored for as long as 15 years.

traveling salesman traveling sales agent/rep, commercial traveler. See also salesgirl/saleslady/salesman/saleswoman.

treatment see therapy.

tribal warfare "Conflicts among diverse peoples within African nations are often referred to as 'tribal warfare,' while conflicts among the diverse peoples within European countries are never described in such terms. If the rivalries between the Ibo and the Hausa and Yoruba in Nigeria are described as 'tribal,' why not the rivalries between Serbs and Slavs in Yugoslavia, or Scots and English in Great Britain, Protestants and Catholics in Ireland, or the Basques and the Southern Spaniards in Spain?" (Robert B. Moore, in Paula S. Rothenberg, *Racism and Sexism*). In the same way, "We hear about 'black on black' violence in Africa, but Eastern European warfare is called an 'ethnic clash'; we never hear about 'white on white' violence. It's just people from 'ethnic' groups clashing. How much more understandable than those enigmatic 'tribal bloodbaths'" (Joan Steinau Lester, *The Future of White Men and Other Diversity Dilemmas*).

tribe nation, people, peoples. Or use specific designation (Cheyenne, Ibo, San). Ward Churchill (in *Global Justice*) says, "Words such as 'nation' and 'tribe' are not, all protestations of government officials and 'responsible tribal leaders' notwithstanding, 'interchangeable' in either political or legal contexts. To the contrary, phrases such as 'tribal sovereignty' add up to near-perfect politicojudicial oxymorons.... No native language in North America ... contains a word which translates accurately as 'tribe.' The literal translation of most American Indian people's names for themselves was, traditionally, exactly that: 'people.'" Originally, Indian peoples were treated as nations, complete with ambassadors and treaties. In the 1860s and 1870s, "tribe" began completely displacing "nation" in the legal discourse leading to congressional termination of treaty-making with Indians and full and absolute power over Indians' property and affairs. The use of "tribe" for African peoples is also rejected. "How an ethnic group with two or ten million people in East or West Africa, with a parliamentary government, can be described as a tribe and not the Irish, the Scot, the Welsh, the French or the English, still baffles the non-European" (Sanford Berman, *Prejudices and Antipathies*). "It's easy to say the Yoruba of Nigeria, the Hausa people, the Makah of the Olympic Peninsula in Washington State, or the Iroquois nation. When using specific name and locale, we are conveying information and knowledge (Zoë Anglesey, in *MultiCultural Review*). See also American Indian, tribal warfare, tribesman.

tribesman tribe/tribal member, member of a tribe. However, the use of "tribe" is generally considered ethnocentric or racist; it is particularly inaccurate and inadmissible with respect to African ethnology (use "people"). For American Indians, use "nation," "people," or a specific group name. See also savage, tribal warfare, tribe.

trick prostitute's customer. See also john, prostitute.

triggerman professional/armed killer, killer, gangster, gun, hired gun, gunner, gunfighter, gunslinger, assassin, slayer, gun-wielder/-toter, sharpshooter, sniper, attacker, outlaw, bank robber, bandit, terrorist, racketeer, mobster, hoodlum, liquidator. See also gunman, marksman, rifleman.

Trinity, the see Father, Son, and Holy Spirit.

troglodyte this term for the very early or mythical peoples who lived in caves or dens is now used inclusively but derogatorily to denote someone who is thought to be reactionary, out of date, reclusive, boorish, or backward.

trooper/trouper all meanings of these words are inclusive.

troops soldiers, service members. Allan Reeder (in *Copy Editor*) says, "The word *troop* means 'a group of people or animals' so the plural *troops* should be used to denote several such groups." He thinks the first use of "troops" to mean "individual soldiers" might have been an AP headline: "Pentagon to Keep 135,000 Troops in Iraq." Newspapers across the country followed suit. Norm Goldstein of the AP stylebook said they found the "rule" on *troops* universally misused, and changed their style to accept the inevitable; the updated style guide explains that when *troops* appears with a large number, "it is understood to mean individuals." However, since then, "troops" is used for as few as three "troops" (but never for "one troop was killed" because the construction was never meant to be used this way). Using "troops" distances and depersonalizes the dead, dying, injured, and fighting soldiers from those who sent them to war. If you have any control over what gets published, use "soldiers" instead of "troops."

troop sergeant historically, it was undoubtedly a man; if used today, it could refer to either sex.

trophy wife introduced in *Fortune* magazine's 1989 article, "The CEO's Second Wife," this term describes a pattern among chief executives to discard longtime spouses for women typically younger, "sometimes several inches taller, beautiful and very often accomplished."

troubadour woman or man. For information on the little-known women troubadours, see Meg Bogin's *The Women Troubadours*.

truck driver man or woman. Some 5 percent of truck drivers are women.

truthiness Stephen Colbert gave the old word "truthiness" new life when he defined it as knowing in one's heart what the truth is, the facts be damned. He explained, "Truthiness is 'What I say is right, and [nothing] anyone else says could possibly be true.' It's not only that I *feel* it to be true, but that *I* feel it to be true. There's not only an emotional quality, but there's a selfish quality." In a nation where politicians appear to be making decisions by what "feels" right instead of by what the facts, logic, evidence, and information indicate is right, Colbert's word struck a chord with many people. Frank Rich (*New York Times*) concurred: "We live in the age of truthiness."

Tuareg Kel Tamasheq, Kel Tamajaq, Kel Tagelmust, Imuhagh, Imazaghan, Imashaghen. These North African peoples were called "Tuareg" by early explorers and historians. They prefer the names listed. When writing or speaking about these groups, verify beforehand the name by which they want to be identified.

turfman racetrack regular, horseracing/track fan, devotee of horseracing.

tweens a Madison Avenue term for 8- to 12-year-olds who more often than not have a TV, computer, iPad, and a video-game player in their rooms. What we used to call kids are now a targeted market worth over $15 billion a year in sales, and better yet, are still on the bottom rung of that golden ladder of consumerism (Paul Wasserman and Don Hausrath, *Weasel Words*).

twinkie although this could refer to both sexes, it's generally reserved for teenage girls/young women. If you want a more neutral-sounding alternative, consider space ranger, flake, brainless wonder.

twit man/boy or woman/girl.

two-man (adjective) see one-man/two-man/three-man.

two-person single career introduced by Hanna Papanek in 1972, this term describes women's vicarious achievement through their husbands' jobs. Formal and informal institutional demands made of both members of a married couple (of whom only the man is employed by the institution) were prevalent for many years in middle-class occupations in the United States, and still exist in some ways today. These wives' contributions to their husbands' work include status maintenance, intellectual contributions, and public performance. Their rewards consist of raises in salary and perquisites granted to the husband; open acknowledgment of collaboration was infrequent. Although this phenomenon was problematic when it was unquestionably assumed that all women would be willing to be supporter, comforter, backstage manager, home maintainer, and main rearer of children, today it is a valid, satisfying, and practical choice for the couples who freely choose it. Anne Soukhanov (*Word Watch*) also notes the phrase "trailing spouse": the partner in a two-career marriage who relinquishes employment in order to follow to a new locale where the other has obtained employment.

two-spirit people Indian people who identify as gay, lesbian, bisexual, transgender, or intersex are called two-spirit people, a term that, since the early 1990s, has replaced the anachronistic "Berdaches," which has been explicitly rejected by the relevant Native American community. Clara Sue Kidwell (in *Sisterhood Is Powerful*) explains, "Individuals who crossed gender lines were recognized in many tribes. Their behavior was generally associated with visions that conveyed special spiritual powers. The Lakota winkte has this meaning. Some Aboriginal people also self identify as two-spirited. Historically, in many Aboriginal cultures, two-spirited individuals were respected leaders and medicine people, often accorded special status based upon their unique abilities to understand both male and female perspectives.

tycoon woman or man.

typical when referring to individuals or groups and their behavior or beliefs, be leery of identifying anything as "typical." When possible, use statistics and studies to illustrate trends or patterns.

typist man or woman.

tzarina see czarina.

It is well that we should become aware of what we are doing when we speak, of the ancient, fragile, and (well used) immensely potent instruments that words are.

C.S. Lewis

umpire/ump in 1988, Pam Postema became the first woman to umpire in professional baseball; in 2007, Ria Cortesio became the second. Umpires of both sexes work at other levels of baseball and in other sports.

un-American from flabby usage as a pejorative (generally meaning "If I had you in a jar, I wouldn't give you air"), the literal meaning of "un-American" as being contrary to our founding principles has been lost. Use instead unconstitutional or illegal, if that's what you mean, or specify what you object to.

unborn child/unborn children do not use these oxymorons. "The phrase 'unborn children' is a misuse of two words with clearly accepted meanings. Because of the meanings of the two constituent words, 'unborn children' is a logical impossibility, just like the phrase 'round squares.' 'Children' are young human beings from the ages of perhaps two to eighteen. A human fetus that has the potential to continue to develop to the point of birth and, subsequently, to the age at which we would use the word *child* (rather than *newborn* or *baby* or *infant* or *toddler*) is not a child. It cannot—*logically* cannot—be any kind of a child, including an unborn child" (Andrew S. Ryan, Jr., in *Free Inquiry*, June/July 2013).

uncivilized see primitive.

uncle, I'll be a monkey's this term could be reduced to "Well, I'll be!" although anyone who wants to be a monkey's uncle is probably not a threat to the language. (Correspondent par excellence Bob Considine wrote of female war foreign correspondents: "In Korea, they landed with both feet, and if they aren't in war to stay, I'm a monkey's aunt.")

Uncle Sam while some countries are personified by men, others are personified by women (for example, France's Marianne and Great Britain's Britannia). If you need a sex-neutral replacement for "Uncle Sam," use: the United States, the United States of America, the U.S., the U.S.A., the U.S. government; the armed forces, the military.

uncle, say surrender, give up, throw in the towel/sponge, knuckle under, raise the white flag, call it quits, throw oneself at the mercy of, pack it in, throw up one's hands, capitulate, eat one's words.

Uncle Tom it's difficult to imagine being knowledgeable enough of another person's behavior and motives to use this term. As well as being sexist (there is no equivalent for a woman), it can be highly racist. Possible alternatives include: collaborator, traitor to one's race, toady, sycophant, stooge, backscratcher, bootlicker, puppet, rubber stamp, dupe, doormat, flunky, subservient/obsequious person. Today we might speak of someone who has been co-opted.

unconventional spellings to highlight social and linguistic inequities, certain words (for example, herstory, sheroe, thealogy, wimmin, womyn) are spelled unconventionally. None of these terms has replaced the standard term; their use is optional. In the case of "wimmin" and "womyn," follow the alternate spelling for individuals and groups who use it. See also herstory.

underclass this term is often used as code for African Americans living in poverty. "It suggests that they are a separate group from other poor people, a class by themselves which is 'below' the rest of us. It connotes hopelessness, desperation and violence, and implies that this group lives by values which are different from ours and is therefore immune to efforts to change their economic circumstances" (Paul Kivel, *Uprooting Racism*). He points out that African Americans have no monopoly on poverty; there are over twice as many poor whites as poor blacks in the U.S. "Nor is there a special 'culture of poverty' (another racially coded phrase). There are certainly negative effects of poverty, but well-paying jobs, access to decent housing and schooling would mitigate most of these." See also classism, code words, "culture of poverty," poverty, racism.

underclassman undergraduate. Or be specific: first-year student, second-year student; class of 2012. See also freshman.

undercover man undercover agent/officer, private eye, eye, plainclothes detective, sleuthhound; sometimes, spy. See also plainclothesman.

underdeveloped/undeveloped countries see Third World.

undermanned understaffed.

underprivileged as words go, this one is a corker. It seems to imply that the people so denoted are privileged—just not quite as privileged as other people. Instead of using this vague, five-syllable code word for poor, specify the conditions under which people live or the obstacles that prevent them from being more privileged. See also "culturally deprived/disadvantaged."

underutilized inadequately exploited. "Underutilized" is most often seen when public resources aren't made available to profitmaking companies.

undocumented immigrant/worker see illegals/illegal immigrants.

undomestic domesticity is a talent found in both women and men; either may also be "undomestic." The term is vague; spell out what you mean.

uneconomical unprofitable.

uneducated compared to what? Some people who graduated from Yale still sound uneducated—and some individuals with a fourth-grade education can hold their own in a complex political discussion. Specify: self-educated, with a high school or GED degree, college educated. Or describe the traits that you mean by "uneducated."

unemployed this term covers people who are temporarily unemployed, on disability, formerly employed but recently "downsized," working part-time, or working in the home. Put "unemployed" in context for your audience. "Of all the aspects of social misery nothing is so heartbreaking as unemployment" Jane Addams, *Twenty Years at Hull-House*).

Nikki Giovanni (in Gloria Wade-Gayles, ed., *My Soul Is a Witness*) says, "The ability to take pride in your own work is one of the hallmarks of sanity. Take away the ability to both work and be proud of it and you can drive anyone insane." Or the great Maria Montessori: "There can be no substitute for work, neither affection nor physical well-being can replace it." And Dorothy Sayers (*Unpopular Opinions*): "A human being *must* have occupation, if he or she is not to become a nuisance to the world." Sigmund Freud, for all his faults, wisely pointed out that we absolutely need two things in this world: Love. Work. We tend to forget how critically important work is, not only for the income it produces, but for our greater human welfare; the lack of employment is a dangerous societal ill. See also right-to-work laws, union man.

unfeminine avoid this vague, self-contradictory cultural stereotype. A woman's clothes, behavior, words, feelings, and thoughts are, by definition, "feminine" because a woman is wearing them, saying them, feeling them. Words like "womanly/unwomanly," "manly/unmanly," "feminine/unfeminine," "masculine/unmasculine," "ladylike/unladylike," and "gentlemanly/ungentlemanly" are based on cultural, not biological, expectations. Language should not underwrite this illogic. The only truly unfeminine things are those things biologically reserved to men. Replace the unhelpful and inexact word "unfeminine" with descriptive adjectives: cold, hard, selfish, abrupt, analytical, direct, competent, logical, etc. These adjectives can apply equally well to a man and are not synonyms for "unfeminine" but rather reflect the cultural spin on this word.

ungentlemanly see "unmasculine" for an explanation of the subjective cultural meanings attached to this word. Define what you mean by "ungentlemanly" in precise terms: impolite, crude, rude, insensitive, thoughtless, discourteous, poorly behaved, ill-mannered, uncivil, disagreeable, inconsiderate. These adjectives (which can apply equally well to women) are not synonyms for "ungentlemanly" but rather reflect the way this word is most often used.

Union Jack the correct term for the normal-size flag of the United Kingdom (flown on land, or at sea from the starboard yardarm) is Union Flag (or Union Flag of 1801). The Union Jack is a flag smaller than usual flown from a jackstaff at the stern of a British ship. By definition, a "jack" is a small flag, usually indicating nationality, located at the bow of a ship.

union man union member, labor/trade unionist, unionist, union backer, member of a union, organized worker. Currently, women account for 45 percent of 14.3 million American union workers and will be the majority of the unionized workforce by 2020. Unionization raises a female worker's wage by two dollars per hour (or 11.2 percent) and makes it 19 percent more likely that she will have employer-paid health coverage and 24.7 percent more likely that she'll have a pension. Public-sector workers have a union membership rate of 35.3 percent, more than five times higher than that of private-sector workers (6.7 percent). Unionization is at its lowest level since 1916. Labor specialists attribute the steep decline in union membership to new laws that have weakened unions in Wisconsin, Indiana, and other states; the continued expansion of manufacturers like Boeing and Volkswagen in non-union states; and the growth of sectors like retail and restaurants, where unions have little presence.

United Kingdom the official title is the United Kingdom of Great Britain and Northern Ireland; it is commonly called Britain or Great Britain and it is abbreviated U.K. or UK; it includes England, Scotland, Wales, and Northern Ireland. See also Great Britain, Irishman, Scotsman, Welshman.

"United we stand" in *Collateral Language* (John Collins and Ross Glover, eds.), Eve Walsh Stoddard and Grant H. Cornwell say, "Within the United States unity has become a moral imperative, with the U.S. flag as its icon and 'United we stand' its motto." Too often, this unity has been translated to mean, "We must all think the same." We need more national discussion on what unity means to us and how we will know when we are united.

universal health care coverage the United States remains the only significant industrialized country without universal health care (or a system of single-payer health care, under which government pays health care costs). Because the concept of universal health care coverage is poorly understood, it has been simple for opponents to inaccurately relabel it "socialized medicine," "nationalized medicine," "state medicine," or "nationalized medical insurance." (Ed Gillespie, former Republican National Committee chair, says in *Winning Right*, "We finally defeated Hillary-care by defining it as 'government-run health care.'") As a nation, we cannot make an informed decision about universal health care or a single-payer system unless citizens know what the terms mean. When using "universal health care coverage," first define it for your audience (the World Health Organization says its goal is "to ensure that all people obtain the health services they need without suffering financial hardship when paying for them"). When appropriate, compare it to similar, known programs for illustration (for example, Medicare successfully serves over 49 million people and the Department of Veterans Affairs provides "socialized medicine" to 22 million veterans and their families). See also Obamacare.

Unknown Soldier, the this World War I soldier is a man.

unladylike see "unfeminine" for an explanation of the subjective cultural meanings attached to this word. For the vague and often inappropriate "unladylike," substitute insensitive, indelicate, awkward, uncharming, unkind, rude, undignified, ill-mannered, ungracious, impolite, abrupt, etc. These adjectives apply equally well to a man and are not synonyms for "unladylike" but rather reflections of what society tends to understand by the word.

unlawful enemy combatants/unlawful combatants "Suspects targeted by the U.S. for assassination, without criminal charges or trial, became 'unlawful combatants,' a ruse designed to exclude them from protection under the Geneva Conventions" (Scott Russell Sanders, "Language Versus Lies," in *The Progressive*). But the term is also sometimes defined as "prisoners of war." Except when used in a direct quote, replace this fuzzy term with a precise description and military standing of the individuals. See also detainee.

unman unnerve, disarm, weaken, devitalize, incapacitate, disable, unhinge, undermine, frighten, paralyze, petrify, terrorize, appall, horrify, deprive of courage/strength/vigor/power, render hors de combat, attenuate, shatter, exhaust, disqualify, invalidate, muzzle, enervate, take the wind out of one's sails, put a spoke in one's wheel, undo. In the

U

narrower sense of emasculate or castrate, use "unman" sparingly as it implies, unflatteringly, that the man is a passive victim. There are no parallel terms referring to women for "unman," "emasculate," and "castrate." See also castrate/castrating, emasculate.

unmanliness/unmanly see "unmasculine" for an explanation of the subjective cultural meanings involved here. Replace these limp terms with descriptive adjectives: dishonesty/dishonest, cowardice/cowardly, deviousness/crooked, weakness/weak, fearfulness/fearful, timidity/timid. These words can be applied equally well to a woman and are not synonyms for "unmanliness/unmanly" but simply the stereotypical and unreflected notions of a sexist society on what it means to be a man.

unmanned unstaffed, having no staff aboard, unpeopled, unpopulated, uninhabited, lacking crew, crewless, remote control, on automatic pilot; frightened, undone. See also unman.

unmanned space flight remote-controlled/mission-controlled/control-operated/unpiloted/crewless/automatic space flight.

unmarried woman/unmarried man use single woman/single man to avoid implying that marriage is the default, the norm. "Unmarried households (single people or partners who share an address and a 'close personal relationship') have outnumbered married households in the U.S. since 2005" (*Ms.*).

unmarried mother see unwed mother.

unmasculine avoid this vague, self-contradictory cultural stereotype. A man's clothes, behavior, words, feelings, and thoughts are, by definition, masculine because a man is wearing them, saying them, feeling them, etc. Words like "womanly/unwomanly," "manly/unmanly," "feminine/unfeminine," "masculine/unmasculine," "ladylike/unladylike," and "gentlemanly/ungentlemanly" are based on cultural, not biological, expectations. Language should not underwrite this illogic. The only truly unmasculine things are those things biologically reserved to women. Replace the unhelpful and inexact word "unmasculine" with descriptive adjectives: timid, craven, weak, indirect, fearful, soft, faint-hearted, gentle, overemotional, comfort-loving. These adjectives can apply equally well to a woman and are not synonyms for "unmasculine," but stereotypical cultural notions of what it is to be a man.

unsalaried see unwaged.

unsportsmanlike unsporting, unfair, unfair play/playing, unsporting behavior, dishonorable, underhanded, unprincipled, behavior of a poor loser.

unstatesmanlike undiplomatic, impolitic, imprudent, lacking stature/grace and diplomacy, showing poor political strategy/ineffective government leadership. No good substitute for "unstatesmanlike" exists, but then neither do we have very many real "statesmen" anymore.

"Untouchables" Dalits (literally, "the oppressed") is preferred to "Untouchables," which is approximately the equivalent of "niggers."

unwaged/unsalaried not a synonym for "unemployed," this term recognizes the contributions and economic issues of groups whose work is unpaid (for example, full-time mothers, community volunteers, activists). See also working mother/working wife/working woman.

"unwanted child" in some instances, the more precise term is unwanted pregnancy; with those wishing to adopt children outnumbering adoptable babies, the child may be wanted, but by someone else.

unwed mother mother, woman, head of household, single parent. Or use, if necessary and appropriate, unmarried parents. The term "unwed mother" disregards the also unwed (at least to this woman) father. In addition to not getting the label, the father also avoids getting the child, the poverty, and the social disapproval. According to a radio news item, "More women than ever before are living with men without being married to them. And more unmarried women than ever before are having babies." Why not: "More men and women than ever before are living together without being married. And more unmarried couples than ever before are having babies." If it's not possible to speak of "parents" (perhaps because the father is no longer in the picture), at least do not linguistically stigmatize the woman who has accepted the consequences of her actions. An "unwed father" shows no external signs of his fatherhood—and thus does not make a good target for censure. "Unwed mothers" and their children, on the other hand, are all too visible. See also teen moms.

unwomanly see "unfeminine" for an explanation of the subjective cultural meanings attached to this word. Use instead cold, hostile, sharp, unloving, ungentle, uncharming, ungiving, unsupportive, ill-mannered, unmannerly, ungracious, undignified, indecorous, unattractive, unappealing. These adjectives apply equally well to a man and are not synonyms for "unwomanly," but rather reflections of what society tends to understand by the word.

unworkmanlike unprofessional, unskillful, slipshod, unskilled, inexpert, inexperienced, untrained, inefficient, unsystematic, unbusinesslike, incompetent, sloppy, careless, unsuitable, irresponsible, unhandy, imprecise, unproficient.

upperclassman upperclass student. Or be precise: third-year student, fourth-year student; junior, senior; class of 2014.

urban often a code word for black or inner-city. See inner-city.

urban unrest riots.

uxoricide although this term, meaning the killing of a wife by her husband, is not commonly seen, its parallel ("mariticide," the killing of a husband by a wife) does not appear in any dictionary although "mariticidal" (*wanting* to kill one's husband) appears in a few.

A very great part of the mischiefs that
vex this world arises from words.
Edmund Burke

Words are seductive and dangerous
material, to be used with caution.
Barbara W. Tuchman

vagina Eve Ensler (in *Sisterhood Is Forever*), creator of "The Vagina Monologues," says, "When I first began to perform these monologues, I realized that just saying the word '*vagina*' caused enormous controversy, because *vagina* is in fact the most isolated, reviled word in the English language. The words *anthrax* or *plutonium* never caused anywhere near such a stir. The taboo on this word is no accident—for as long as we cannot *say* vagina, vaginas do not exist. They remain isolated and unprotected."

Valentino this evocative name is usually just what you want. For inclusive alternatives, use heartthrob, great/dashing lover.

valet/valet de chambre personal/room attendant.

valet parking parking service. Those who park the cars are "attendants."

valley girl the valley girl seems to be history now, and as such the term is correct; there never was a "valley boy."

vamp (woman) short for "vampire," this word posits hypnotic power for women and helplessness for men, which disserves both. "Vamp" was popularized by Theda ("Kiss me, my fool!") Bara in the 1915 *A Fool There Was*. She and Pola Negri played many vamps, strongly identifying the role with women.

vampire if there are vampires, they are both women and men; in the metaphorical sense, the word is also used of both.

varlet historically varlets were always young men. If an alternative is needed, consider: attendant, menial, page.

vassal although taken to mean a man, this word is defined as "a servant, slave, dependent, or subordinate," and historically it included all members of the household of the feudal tenant, male and female.

vegetarian most vegetarians do not eat meat "because of its many overlapping exploitative practices—including the oppression of workers who must kill, process, and package the slaughter animals" and because "raising and then killing animals also involves the extensive exploitation of the natural world—water, fossil fuels, land use, deforestation for pastureland, etc.—as well as requiring the deaths of close to 10 billion land animals per year in the United States alone" (Carol J. Adams, in *Sisterhood Is Forever*).

verger man or woman.

vestryman vestry member, member of the vestry, parish council member.

veteran man or woman, referring both to someone who has served in the armed services and to an experienced person. The "Support Our Troops" sentiment often does not extend to veterans who have been frustrated by the closings of VA hospitals, cheated out of service-connected disability benefits, and denied essential rehabilitation and mental health services. In one of the most unjust situations in society today, nearly 200,000 veterans are homeless on any given night, and nearly 400,000 experience homelessness over the course of a year (U.S. Veterans Administration estimates). The V.A. says most are men; 4 percent are women. The vast majority are single, most come from poor, disadvantaged communities, 45 percent suffer from mental illness, and half have substance abuse problems. These homeless veterans have served their country in World War II, the Korean War, the Cold War, the Vietnam War, Grenada, Panama, Lebanon, Operation Enduring Freedom (Afghanistan), Operation Iraqi Freedom, or the military's anti-drug cultivation efforts in South America. Some 47 percent of homeless veterans served during the Vietnam Era. More than 67 percent served for at least three years and 33 percent were stationed in a war zone. According to the National Survey of Homeless Assistance Providers and Clients (U.S. Interagency Council on Homelessness and the Urban Institute), veterans account for 23 percent of all homeless people in America. How can we tolerate this? For more information, see the website for the National Coalition for Homeless Veterans. See also compassionate conservatism.

vicar depending on the denomination, a vicar may be either sex.

vice-chairman vice-chair, second in command, deputy, deputy director, vice-president.

vicereine/viceroy these sex-specific titles (literally, "vicequeen" and "viceking") denote the governor of a country, province, or colony, ruling as the representative of a sovereign; "vicereine" can mean either a ruler in her own right or the wife of a viceroy. For unofficial uses, consider deputy, ruler, sovereign, governor, regional governor, vice-consul.

victim in reference to those with disabilities, never use this word. Instead of "polio victim" or "victim of multiple sclerosis," say "someone who has polio" or "someone with multiple sclerosis." According to *The Disability Rag* (now *Ragged Edge*), "'Victim' sensationalizes a person's disability. Instead, avoid emotional language by using 'has': 'has HIV/AIDS,' 'had polio.'" In the case of the crime of rape or other violent attacks, often the individuals do not want the "victim" label; they may prefer to be known as survivors. Verify your choice of words with the people you're writing about. In addition, be careful that your material doesn't blame those injured. "We all want injustice to be the victim's fault" (Hortense Calisher). This is seen in reflections like "What was she doing at a bar at one o'clock in the morning?" or "Why did he leave his car unlocked?" See also acquaintance rape, disabilities, handicapped, provoke, rape, rape victim, "She asked for it," "victimization, culture of," violence.

"victimization, culture of" in commenting on the "recent spate of letters, books, and columns blaming feminism for creating a 'culture of victimization' in which women are supposedly wallowing every time they stand up for their right not to be raped, beaten, sexually harassed, or denied employment or a promotion on the basis of their gender," Brian Ashley says, "It would seem rather obvious that when a person fights back when *others* attempt to make her a victim that she is not 'wallowing in victimhood'; she is, in fact, fighting against it. [The very people] who are having such fun castigating women are the ones who've consistently promoted attitudes, lifestyles, and even laws that not only victimize women but establish barriers preventing women from being able to speak against their oppressors. This 'culture of victimization' baloney is nothing more than another such barrier created by these people in their attempt to recreate a 'natural order' in society. A 'natural order' in which white men are on top and everyone else, especially women, is on the bottom." Those complaining about the "culture of victimization" say that when women resort to the law for redress in sexual harassment or other such suits it only shows they are weak and need to be protected. But Jodie L. Ahern says we never think that when men go to law. Is the man who sues his neighbor for a tree overhanging his property weak and in need of protection? Why doesn't he just go *tell* the guy to cut down his tree?

victory for mankind victory for the world, victory for humankind/all peoples/everyone, our common victory. See also one small step for man, one giant leap for mankind.

Vietnam War among Vietnamese, this is often called the American War to distinguish it from other wars, against the Chinese and the French, for example.

vigilante woman or man.

villainess villain. See also "feminine" word endings.

violence violence has sexist and racist implications: men are more likely than women to be perpetrators of a wide range of violent activities; of all those arrested for violence in any year, the great majority (for the United States the figure is around 90 percent) are men. They are also more liable than women to be victims of violence, while black men are victims more often than white men. Although most violence is not sex-biased in that the sex of the offender or victim is not a contributing factor in the violence, there are two exceptions: (1) Men have died in wars solely because of their sex. While civilians of both sexes also die in wars, and while women have died in combat, particularly in recent years, their deaths were not institutionalized and their sex was not a factor in their deaths. Young men still face prison and fines for failing to register for the draft; young women do not. (2) Women suffer disproportionately from violence by men, primarily because they are women. According to the Justice Department, the majority of women can expect to be victims of at least one violent attack in their lifetime. A nationwide Louis Harris Poll found that 25 percent of the men in the sample approved of a husband slapping his spouse. "Men are raised with a sense of entitlement, privilege and expectation that women can and should do what we want them to do," says Edward Gondolf, a researcher on male violence. "And if they don't we resolve the problem with aggression and force." The violence continuum includes sexist language, anti-woman jokes, abusive rap lyrics, film and TV violence against women, sexual harassment, pornography, wife beating, rape, and murder. Chuck Niessen-Derry of BrotherPeace says men need to "start making the connection between the rape joke on Tuesday and the rape on Thursday." And Myriam Miedzian (*Boys Will Be Boys*) says, "At least 235 studies of the effects of showing violence in films and on television have overwhelmingly shown that watching violence increases violent behavior." Men are also abused by their wives and murdered by them, although in far smaller numbers. Many of the more serious assaults by wives have been reported as self-defense in response to abuse. This is not to discount the reality of abused men, but to give it perspective: men do not fear for their physical safety when passing a group of women on the street. (However, gay men as well as women may experience fear when approaching a group of men standing on a corner.) One of the indications of the violence in our culture is the violent death rate of our children; the U.S. has the highest homicide rate for children of any industrialized nation in the world. The most recent U.S. Bureau of Justice Statistics show that men, blacks, and those 24 or younger continue to be victimized at higher rates than females, whites, and those 25 or older. Women were most often violently victimized by someone they knew (64 percent) while men were more likely to be victimized by a stranger (54 percent). Rape and sexual assault rates were down 69 percent compared with 1993 rates. Andrea Dworkin (in *Sisterhood Is Forever*) says, "Through political activism, the culture has changed enough to stigmatize rape and battery against women. Over the past three decades, rape crisis centers, sexual abuse and battery shelters, sexual assault laws, marital rape laws, third-person battery intervention laws, laws forbidding convicted batterers (including police officers) to carry guns, date and acquaintance rape prosecutions, police precinct and emergency room special training for dealing with survivors, and passage of the 1994 Violence Against Women Act—all these changes and more have been won by feminist activism." See also battered wife/woman, date rape, knockout, lady-killer, provoke, rape, sexual harassment, "She asked for it," victim, violent language.

violent language our language reflects our violent ways; it also helps perpetuate them. Consider avoiding these common expressions: kill two birds with one stone, big gun/shot, going great guns, gun-shy, under the gun, shoot full of holes, shoot from the hip, shoot down, shoot one's mouth off, shoot oneself in the foot, shot in the dark, take a shot at, call the shots, straight shooter, big shot, quick on the draw, half-cocked, deploy, half the battle, win the battle but lose the war, pick your battles, battle scars, arsenal, smash hit, hit below the belt, on target, kick an idea around, crack the whip, hit on someone, how does that strike/hit you, knock someone dead/for a loop/out, knock heads together, take a beating, sock it to 'em, give a black eye to, haul someone over the coals, hit someone up for something, slap on the wrist, skin someone alive, search and destroy, beat the tar/stuffing/living daylights out of someone, call in/out the troops, hair-trigger, blow one's top, blow somebody away, skin someone alive, bite/snap/take someone's head off, blast them out of the water, explode onto the scene, blow up, blow them away/out of the water, twist someone's arm, loose cannon, nuke your coffee, meltdown, fallout, mobilize, strategic, dead meat, dead soldiers, closing ranks, bite the bullet, magic bullet, hit them where it hurts, take a stab at it, hit or miss, pack a wallop, wipe somebody out, beat one's brains out, knock one's head against a wall, knock oneself out, kill oneself with work, this'll kill you, this'll knock 'em flat, fight the good fight, hold the fort, in the trenches, make a killing, get someone in the crosshairs, attack an argument, tell war stories, deep-six something, a real coup, heads roll, spearhead the discussion, terminate people at work. After seeing this list, consider the cumulative effect on people who use and hear this language. See also knockout, military language, political language, violence.

violently examine the use of "violently" (as in "objected violently") when what you really mean is intensely, severely, excessively, virulently, stringently, urgently.

virago the first dictionary definition of "virago" is "a loud, overbearing woman: termagant." The second is "a woman of great stature, strength, and courage" (*Webster's Ninth New Collegiate Dictionary*). As such, it is being reclaimed by some members of the women's movement.

virgin/virginity/virginal if these terms are intrinsic to your material, apply them to both sexes with equal weight and meaning; in general, there are few good reasons for talking about anyone's sexual status. The double standard associates virginity or virginal behavior with women while it rewards men in subtle and unsubtle ways for being experienced. The concept of virginity is heterosexist, euphemistic, difficult to define physiologically with any precision, and alive today. Jessica Valenti (*The Purity Myth: How America's Obsession With Virginity Is Hurting Young Women*) describes hundreds of purity balls, "where young girls pledge their virginity to their fathers at a promlike event." (The balls were apparently federally funded.) Valenti reports a number of purity groups on Facebook, "schools holding abstinence rallies and assemblies featuring hip-hop dancers and comedians alongside religious leaders. ... So what are young women left with? Abstinence-only education during the day and Girls Gone Wild commercials at night." And she sums up the moral of it all: "A woman's worth lies in her ability—or her refusal—to be sexual." Replace "virginal" with one of the dozens of neutral, more telling terms, for example: untouched, innocent, unused, uncorrupted, unsullied, wholesome, fresh, pristine, spotless, unblemished, untainted, unadulterated.

virgin forest/virgin soil use only when necessary because of specific legal designations. Otherwise consider unspoiled, untouched, pristine, unused, untainted, uncharted, undeveloped, unprocessed, pure. "Virgin paper" is "nonrecycled paper." John A. Hobson points out that for computer people, "virgin" means "unused, pristine; in a known initial state" ("Let's try writing it on a virgin diskette and see if it gets corrupted"). In reference to things of nature, "virgin" alludes to their being unused by man (sex-specific word intended). See also Mother Nature.

virile this is a properly sex-specific word when it refers to a man's ability to function sexually. In its broader sense, you may want inclusive alternatives: energetic, vigorous, forceful, strong, powerful, dynamic, spirited, daring, fearless, venturesome, courageous, intrepid, tough, audacious, dashing, potent, hardy, hearty, rugged, bold.

virtue/virtuous these terms, which come from the Latin *vir* for "man," have two general connotations: the first involves high-minded traits of morality, honor, integrity, and uprightness and is applied generally to men; the second deals with sexual purity (closest synonyms for this sense are chastity, virginity, and purity) and is almost always used for women. Today we rarely refer to a man as virtuous, and if we hear of "a virtuous woman," we know two things: she is chaste and her eyes are probably modestly cast down.

visitation (child custody) for some people, this is a common, unambiguous word (it is also the legal term); others find it too closely associated with visits to prisoners, and prefer access, parenting time. (The term "access" was used instead of "visitation" in the 1988 Family Support Act.)

visual-effects man visual-effects coordinator/supervisor/specialist/technician.

visual impairment see blind, impairment.

vital interests the current bottom-line needs of the most generous financial supporters of our administration and politicians are generally said to be in our vital interests. If you look carefully at our so-called vital interests, they are usually what are actually special interests. A related issue is what, exactly, is in the public interest. Unfortunately, public interests usually end up competing with "vital" (i.e., corporate) interests, and losing.

vivacious as Francine Frank and Frank Anshen point out (*Language and the Sexes*), both girls and boys may have lively personalities, but when did you ever meet a "vivacious" boy? Two-thirds of the *American Heritage Book of English Usage*'s panel on usage felt that "vivacious" could be used only of a female subject. You could either begin describing appropriate men as vivacious or use more inclusive substitutes: spirited, high-spirited, full of pep, breezy, animated.

vizier has always been a man.

voluntary regulation see regulation/deregulation/voluntary regulation.

volunteer a volunteer can be either a woman or a man, of course, but volunteer work has traditionally been apportioned along sexist lines: "For men it usually means serving in prestigious policymaking or advisory capacities, with the encouragement of the employer to take time off from work to serve as the company's 'goodwill ambassador' to the community. For women, volunteerism means providing direct services at their own expense (transportation, lunch). Second, because women volunteers work almost exclusively at the lowest levels of the volunteer hierarchy, they obtain little valuable work experience or training. Popular mythologies to the contrary, displaced homemakers have been continuously frustrated to find that their résumés, which have meticulously translated fifteen to twenty-five years of volunteer activities into marketable skills, elicit ... negative responses from prospective employers" (Nijole V. Benokraitis and Joe R. Feagin, *Modern Sexism*).

voodoo as used in expressions like "voodoo economics," the word disparages someone else's religion.

voyageur history records only male voyageurs.

voyeur although the term is inclusive, factually voyeurs are much more likely to be male, and recent studies indicate that far from being the relatively harmless deviants they were once thought to be, many voyeurs graduate to rape and other sex crimes. Use of "voyeur" should reflect the gravity of the behavior.

W

Few would suggest that sexual or racial inequality exists because of language use. Nor would many argue that banishing sexist and racist labeling would in itself result in a just society. At the same time, it is clear that language not only reflects social structures but, more important, sometimes serves to perpetuate existing differences in power; thus a serious concern with linguistic usage is fully warranted.

Francine Wattman Frank and Paula A. Treichler

A broken bone can heal, but the wound a word opens can fester forever.

Jessamyn West

wage earner the term itself is inclusive, but what it means in dollars and cents reveals deep societal sexism and racism: female college graduates generally make less than male high school graduates, with the average black female college graduate often earning the same as the average white male who did not finish high school; more than two-thirds of minimum-wage workers are women; disproportionate numbers of women and members of minority groups lack employment-related benefits such as health and pension coverage. Pay discrimination—where less-favored groups receive less pay for the same work done by, say, white men—has been a fact of life for generations. One big obstacle to pay fairness has been removed by the Lilly Ledbetter Fair Pay Act of 2009, which says that the 180-day statute of limitations for filing an equal-pay lawsuit for pay discrimination resets with each new paycheck affected by that discriminatory action. The Supreme Court had earlier decided that an employee had only 180 days from the first paycheck to sue for pay discrimination. As employees rarely know from the start that they are being discriminated against, it became virtually impossible to sue an employer for pay discrimination. The next step in the struggle for fair pay is the Paycheck Fairness Act, intended to expand the scope of the Equal Pay Act of 1963 and the 1938 Fair Labor Standards Act (which broadly prohibited pay discrimination based on sex, race, etc.). The new Act would address female-male income disparity, but it has been so far twice rejected by our lawmakers. See also living wage, working poor.

waiter woman or man. This is the preferred term for both sexes. See also waitress.

waitress waiter, server, attendant, table/restaurant server; serving staff. Also being used in some areas: wait, waitron, waitperson. Plural: waiters, servers, waitstaff.

wallflower although it theoretically could refer to either sex, it's reserved for women/girls and it reflects outdated customs and attitudes.

Walter Mitty there is nothing wrong with evoking Mr. Mitty to convey a ready-made picture of someone like James Thurber's character, but be aware of how many such expressions are male-based. Balance their use with female-based expressions, creative expressions of your own, or sex-neutral alternatives: daydreamer, escapist, secret adventurer. See also sex-linked expressions.

wandering see roaming.

wanton this is used only for women, holding them to a higher arbitrary moral standard than men are held to. If you must use it, do so gender-fairly to describe behavior but not people ("They behaved wantonly," not "They were wanton").

war the United States has been at war for 216 of its 237 years (*Real Time With Bill Maher*, 2013). Maher says, "We need to start defining peace as strength." Referring to the long list of wars (he excepts World War II), he suggests it's time the U.S. begins to realize "Maybe it's me." See also moral injury.

"war"/"war on" Richard E. Norred (*Los Angeles Times*) wonders "if we as a nation can couch any issue except in terms of war." We've seen the war on poverty, the war on drugs, the war on terrorism, the cultural wars, and the mommy wars. Ross Glover (*Collateral Language*) says, "'The War on—' plays on our competitive heartstrings like a football cheer. 'Yes,' we seem to respond, 'fight the good fight, O fearless President, fight the war for us, fight the war for the good of humanity, but most importantly just fight.' It matters little that most fights end up only wasting time, money, and lives, or that every time we begin fighting, conditions get worse rather than better." "Obviously, it makes no sense to wage war on a tactic or on an abstract noun. ... That this usage could be accepted so widely attests to the fact that our political vocabulary, along with our general political culture, has become extraordinarily debased" (Andrew Levine, *Political Keywords*). How debased? It's likely that the national familiarity with "war on" language kept us from realizing after 9/11 the critical importance of "the decision to describe the attacks in the language of 'war' rather than as a criminal act" (Brent Cunningham, "The Rhetoric Beat," *Columbia Journalism Review*) "so that by Sept. 13 the assumption that America was 'at war' with all of that idea's sobering implications, was irrevocably established in the national consciousness. Polls released on September 12 indicated that more than 90 percent of respondents considered the attacks as an 'act of war.'" Had 9/11 been described instead as "mass murder," the response would have fallen under the domain of police investigation, criminal justice, and the safeguards of law (as correctly happened in the 2013 Boston marathon killings). Cunningham proceeds to lay out the logic that followed: once talk of war is established, a national enemy must be identified. The invasion of Iraq was the solution. Heretofore, the U.S. and other countries have treated terrorist attacks as a breach of civil and criminal law—the idea is to deny the perpetrators legitimacy and thereby defuse the political power of their actions. Investigations, trials, convictions were the primary response to Pan Am Lockerbie, Scotland, in 1988, and embassies bombed in east Africa in 1998. Careless use of "war" or "war on" has consequences. Rephrase such phrases to accurately describe the issues. And why is going to "war" so attractive? Arthur Silber says that "a huge swath of our economy is now devoted to preparing for war, making war, and cleaning up after war. To one degree or another, most members of Congress are beholden to the economic powers that drive the obsessive concern with war, and its cornucopia of economic opportunity. Both parties are enmeshed in the War State, and the current corporatist warmaking apparatus devours almost all those who go into public service. Until this intricate and complex system is altered, nothing else will change, except in comparatively superficial ways." See also culture wars, military language, mommy wars, oil, war on drugs, war on poverty, war on terror.

war bride were there ever any war grooms? Retain in historical contexts.

war diamonds see blood diamonds.

"war of liberation" among other rationales for the invasion of Iraq was the U.S. goal of liberating the Iraqi people from Saddam Hussein. Other peoples have seemed to need liberating more urgently than did the Iraqis (Rwanda? Darfur?) but they had no oil (Operation Iraqi Freedom was originally named Operation Iraqi Liberation—until the first time the acronym was used). Invading a country to help them, without being asked, reminds one of Becky: "The little entourage of friends and relatives whom she completely dominated was fond of saying, 'Becky would give you the shirt off her back.' And it was true. The only trouble was that she neglected to take it off first, and what you found on your back was not only Becky's shirt but Becky too" (Margaret Halsey, *No Laughing Matter*). See also oil, "war"/"war on."

war on drugs "after many years this pseudo-war rages on with few visible signs that victory is anywhere in sight" Paul Wasserman and Don Hausrath (*Weasel Words*). Ross Glover (*Collateral Language*) says, "While using the vague and often unspecified term 'drugs' after the phrase 'the War on,' U.S. foreign policy makers potentially justify any global military activity. However, the frightening reality is that the war on drugs has had much more to do with promoting U.S. business interests than with any drugs. In the name of democracy, the Reagan-Bush Administration actively used drug trafficking to fund a rebel army in Nicaragua. These so-called Contras, groups often trained by the CIA, and also called 'Freedom Fighters' by President Reagan, murdered supporters of socialist democratic ideals. These ideals sought an end to poverty and a beginning to national education and healthcare for all citizens, not to mention a stable economy. Reagan, while producing the most fervent fear and the most viciously articulated war on drugs, was simultaneously supporting and funding the narcotics trade in Central America; these drugs, primarily cocaine, were destined for the U.S. market. Not simply carrying out blind-eye policies, the CIA, Oliver North, Vice President Bush, and numerous others actively supported, paid for, and traded with those trafficking in narcotics, ostensibly to pay for the overthrow of governments concerned with their citizen's poverty and to support some of the harshest dictatorial regimes in the Americas. These activities took place under the rubric of a 'war on drugs.'"

war on poverty in 1964, President Lyndon B. Johnson declared a war on poverty. Through programs such as Medicaid, Head Start, Job Corps, and Legal Services for the poor, among others, poverty was reduced by 43 percent over the next decade. Fifty years later, we've lost a lot of ground. Economic inequality and social immobility are much greater and affect far more women and children than men. Rather than pointing the finger at low wages, lack of jobs, and educational opportunity, pundits and politicians routinely advance the contemptible idea that poverty is caused by the bad attitudes and shiftless habits of the poor. "Sadly, this has become the means by which the wealthiest country in the world manages to remain complacent in the face of alarmingly high levels of poverty: by continuing to blame poverty not on the economy or inadequate social supports, but on the poor themselves. It's time to revive the notion of a collective national responsibility to the poorest among us, who are disproportionately women and especially women of color" (Barbara Ehrenreich in *The Shriver Report: A Woman's Nation Pushes Back from the Brink*).

war on terror replace this imprecise term with a description of who is doing what to whom. "Terrorism is not an enemy but a technique" (Zbigniew Brzezinski, *Washington Post*). Peter Beinart (also in the *Washington Post*) agrees that "war on terror" has always been a flawed term, since terror is a tactic, not an enemy. But the alternatives, Beinart acknowledges, are also problematic. The George W. Bush administration once spoke of the "global struggle against violent extremism," but there are plenty of violent extremists whom the U.S. chooses to ignore. The "war on jihadism" insults Muslims. The "war on al-Qaida" once may have made sense, Beinart said, but al-Qaida now appears to be more of an inspiration than a cohesive organization, and "war against al-Qaidism" is a mouthful. "How strange. We're engaged in a violent struggle that could last years, and we don't even know what to call it." Historian and writer Howard Zinn said that "the category of 'terrorism' continues to be applied selectively, and in a way that serves the goals of U.S. policies, despite the fact that these very policies often cause or support more human suffering than is caused by the so-called 'terrorists' the United States opposes. Ultimately this leads to operative official definitions of 'terrorism' that are so vague and redundant as to defy logic...." Ross Glover (*Collateral Language*) points out at that the word "terrorism is so vague, the BBC World Service has stopped using the term altogether." See also black site, detainee, "state secrets" defense, torture, "war"/"war on."

wardrobe mistress wardrobe supervisor/manager/clerk/handler/department/coordinator.

warehouseman warehouse laborer, warehouser.

war hawk/warmaker/warmonger although studies show that the tendency toward warfare is characteristic of men across many cultures (the only nonbiological characteristic that can be attributed consistently to one sex), distrust generalizations: many men have devoted their lives to peace issues and some women are hawks.

warlock "witch" (female) and "warlock" (male) are strong, evenly balanced words when used together. If you want sex-neutral alternatives, consider conjurer, sorcerer, magician.

warlord because of the sex-linked "lord," consider using military commander/leader, supreme military leader, militarist, warmonger, jingoist. Another caution is using the term fairly; Joan Steinau Lester (*The Future of White Men and Other Diversity Dilemmas*), says "Warlords? This is a term reserved exclusively for Asians and Africans abroad, and African-American or Latino gang leaders at home. Europeans in a similar feudal spot were 'lords of the manor'—or, if they were especially warlike, 'knights.'"

"war of/between the sexes" see "battle of/war between the sexes."

warpaint (woman's makeup) no.

warpath this is considered offensive and disparaging. In any case, it's an overworked cliché that wants to be retired. See also American Indian, pow-wow, renegades, sports teams' names and mascots.

warrior both women and men have been and are warriors—whether this means fighting in battles or living out the warrior archetype. In *The Warrior Queens*, Antonia Fraser describes female warrior-rulers who have often been the focus for what a country afterwards perceives to have been its golden age, for example, Queen Elizabeth I of England, 12th-century Queen Tamara of Georgia, or 15th-century Queen Isabella of Spain. In more recent times, women have taken part in every American military crisis since the Revolutionary War. Harriet Tubman planned and led a military campaign for the Union Army in South Carolina in 1863. At least some men—the traditional warriors—are becoming "new warriors" today. Acknowledging and coming to terms with the warrior within, the new warrior is ideally without guilt, shame, or apology about being a man; both fierce and compassionate, he holds himself accountable for his actions. Feeling truly powerful, he does not need to dominate anyone. He directs his considerable energy in constructive, non-threatening ways and is able to renew connections with self, others, and the world. See also Amazon/amazon, warrior (Indian).

warrior (Indian) Indians were always called warriors, where in other circumstances, in other lands, they would have been called soldiers. Consider the implications of the words "soldier" and "warrior" as they are used for various conflicts. See also renegades.

washerman/washerwoman/washwoman launderer, laundry worker, cleaner, drycleaner.

WASP this acronym for White Anglo-Saxon Protestant has become a simplistic synonym for oppression, discrimination, and spurious superiority. Hugh Rawson devotes chapter 10 of *Unkind Words* to WASP, "one of the most ingenious codewords, with several layers of covert meaning." Bypass the vague cliché and describe the person or event with specific adjectives.

watchman security guard, watch, night guard/watch, guard, building guard, security officer/consultant, gatekeeper, guardian, sentry, sentinel, lookout, caretaker, custodian, patrol, patroller; guardian; crossing tender/guard.

waterboarding see torture.

water boy water carrier.

watermanship swimming/boating/rowing/sailing/water sports skills, canoeing expertise, etc. Or reword to describe the person with these skills: competent swimmer, professional boater, skilled canoeist, veteran rower, proficient/expert/talented/ knowledgeable/skillful swimmer/boater.

water witch water dowser.

wave (feminism) in *Sisterhood Is Forever*, Robin Morgan says that "'wave' terminology got started with a well-meant, off-hand remark in the late 1960s by Kate Millett; it was picked up by the media and thereafter institutionalized." But waves, she says, "are accurate only if we define feminism narrowly: polite organizing done in the U.S. by primarily white, middle-class women, for a limited number of equal rights (however important) attainable under the social, economic, and political status quo. And 'wave' terminology makes *no* sense internationally. There were twelfth-century harem revolts in what is now Turkey; Christine de Pisan penned her furious feminist tracts in 13th-century France; all-female armies fought for women's rights in China during the 1780s White Lotus Rebellion, the 1851 Taiping Rebellion, and the 1899 Boxer Rebellion; Gandhi acknowledged that he copied his nonviolent resistance tactics from the Indian women's rights movement; Argentina's Feminist Party was founded as early as 1918—you get the point. 'Wave' oversimplification makes no sense domestically, either. Beverly Guy-Sheftall's essay [in *Sisterhood Is Forever*] on black feminism is a superb example of the buried history of activism by U.S. women of color, from colonial times through slavery, westward expansion, and immigration, to the present. ... Actually, today's Women's Movement is more like 'the ten thousandth wave.'"

way to a man's heart is through his stomach, the the way to a person's heart is through their stomach (see singular "they"); the quickest way to the heart is through the stomach, the way to the heart is through the stomach.

weaker sex, the this is, for good reason, rarely heard anymore.

weapons of mass destruction (WMD) any weapons—nuclear, chemical, bacteriological, radiological, thermonuclear, explosive—that could kill great numbers of people as well as destroy infrastructure, other life forms, and habitats. Technically, the term is imprecise; replace it with the specific weapons and outcomes under discussion. Politically, WMD is used to create fear and to underwrite policies that need to avoid scrutiny.

weathergirl/weatherman weathercaster, meteorologist, weather reporter/forecaster/prophet, forecaster, climatologist. Note the nonparallel "girl/man."

webmaster director of website.

wedding same-sex couples have weddings, commitment ceremonies, and civil unions; there are lesbian and gay wedding registries, a national magazine focusing on LGBT ceremonies, and companies that supply everything you need from gay- and lesbian-friendly vendors. See also marriage.

wedlock the "lock" in this word is from the Anglo-Saxon for "gift" while "wed" means "promise." Marriage, or wedlock, is thus the promised gift of happiness.

weekend warrior an inaccurate and derogatory way to refer to military reservists, especially in light of their importance in Iraq where many have served several tours of duty, lost jobs and families, and returned home with mental and physical injuries. Others have not returned at all. Activated during times of war and at other times engaged in humanitarian services, reservists work hard, live with disrupted lives, and contribute immeasurably to the good of the commonwealth. They are soldiers.

welder man or woman. Approximately 8 percent are women.

welfare "'Welfare,' as a word, has fallen far from its heights as one of the basic national purposes described in the Constitution: 'to promote the general welfare'" (William Safire, *Safire's Political Dictionary*). Most people think of "welfare" as government money (our taxes) that goes to individuals in need. They rarely think of government money (our taxes) that goes to large corporations. See the entry on "corporate welfare" for the other half of the story. As for individuals, the myth is that typical welfare recipients are unemployed, inner-city members of minority groups whose families have received public assistance for generations. However, the percentage of African American (33 percent), Hispanic (29 percent), and white (31 percent) families receiving aid under the Temporary Assistance for Needy Families (TANF) program is roughly equal. Another welfare myth is that those who are poor will remain for years on public assistance, but 40 percent of TANF families receive assistance for 12 months or less. Over the last 15 years, TANF's role as a safety net has declined sharply. In 1996, for every 100 families with children living in poverty, TANF provided cash aid to 68 families. By 2010, only 27 in 100 families in poverty received cash aid. Evidence suggests that poverty among young children not only impacts learning and performance in school, but it also decreases their earnings as adults. Poverty researchers Greg J. Duncan of the University of California, Irvine, and Katherine Magnuson of University of Wisconsin found that among families with incomes below $25,000, children under age six whose families received an additional $3,000 annual income boost through public assistance earned 17 percent more as adults than did otherwise similar children whose families did not receive the income boost. As for the cost of welfare, extra tax breaks for the wealthiest 2 percent of Americans costs more than the combined total expenses for the TANF program, Supplemental Nutrition Assistance for Women, Infants, and Children (WIC), the Low-Income Home Energy Assistance program, and the Housing Choice Voucher Program (also known as Section 8 Tenant-Based Rental Assistance). See also corporate welfare, poor, poverty, welfare mother, working poor.

welfare mother welfare/public assistance client/recipient. Myths, stereotypes, misinformation, and unjustified hostility surround "the welfare mother." For example, although the prevailing public notion is that welfare families are larger than most, those who use public assistance have the same average family size as those who don't. Likewise, although the average person believes that most welfare mothers are black, white women make up an equal percentage of "welfare mothers." "Being a mother is a noble status, right? Right. So why does it change when you put 'unwed' or 'welfare' in front of it?" (Florynce Kennedy, in *Ms.*). The most egregious "welfare queen" (if there is such a thing) in the country can't possibly compete with white-collar criminals who make millions in fraud, embezzlement, income-tax evasion, offshore banking, and clever accounting. It's astonishing that "she" is regularly demonized, while "they" don't even have a label, much less receive heartfelt public scorn. See also corporate welfare, poverty, welfare.

welsh (verb) renege, default, backpedal, back/pull out, weasel/worm out of, cheat, swindle. Although this term may or may not have anything to do with the people of Wales, it is considered a slur by them; the Welsh American Legal Defense and Development Foundation has persuaded several news organizations to avoid the terms "welshing" and "welsher."

Welshman inhabitant/native of Wales, someone from Wales, Welshman and Welshwoman. Plural: the Welsh, people of Wales, Welshfolk, Welshwomen and Welshmen (but never "Welshmen and women").

wench retain in the earlier, historical sense ("young woman" or "female servant"). Today, "wench" is fluid—it can mean a promiscuous woman (and "wenching" is what men do with wenches), but it's sometimes used affectionately and even claimed as a positive word (International Wenches Guild).

werewolf although this term comes from the word *wer* for "man" and is most often perceived as male, the *American Heritage Dictionary* defines it as "a person transformed into a wolf or capable of assuming the form of a wolf"; use it of either sex (there is no parallel for a woman).

West, the this term, "the East," "the Far East," and "the Middle East" are holdovers from the days when Europe thought itself the center of the world. These phrases probably aren't going to go away anytime soon, but you can be aware of their flawed origins.

Western civilization beware if a subtext in your material that implies that everything good and effective originates in the West (or in the U.S.) and that Western civilization is that by which the measure of everything else is taken.

West Indian Caribbean. "West Indian" is a term given by Columbus, whereas "Caribbean" is derived from an ancient indigenous word naming the pre-Columbian inhabitants, sea, and islands (Zoë Anglesey, in *MultiCultural Review*).

wetback undocumented resident/worker. This term for someone from Mexico in the U.S. without a visa is derogatory and unacceptable. See also ethnic slurs, illegal alien, immigrant.

wet nurse legitimate gender-specific word.

whaleman/whalerman whaler. A whaler can also refer to the ship.

wharfman wharfworker, wharfhand, dockhand, dockworker, stevedore, shoreworker, shorehand, longshore worker.

wharfmaster wharfinger, harbor manager. The nonsexist "wharfinger" is actually the older term (1552); "wharfmaster" came into the language in 1618. For discussion of "master" words, see master (noun).

what evil lurks in the hearts of men? what evil lurks in our/people's/human hearts? What evil lurks in the hearts of humans?

whatsoever a man sows, that shall he also reap whatsoever you sow, that too shall you reap; whatever we sow we will also reap.

wheelchair-bound wheelchair user, someone who uses/navigates in a wheelchair. Never use: wheelchair-bound, confined/bound/restricted to a wheelchair. A wheelchair is a tool, not a prison, something that frees rather than restricts. See also confined to a wheelchair, cripple, disabilities, handicapped.

wheelsman pilot, steerer, navigator.

whine this word is functionally sexist since it is used primarily of women and children, while in similar circumstances men are said to ask, tell, repeat, complain, criticize, or just plain talk. Use instead complain, grumble, grouse, gripe, criticize, harp on, fume, find fault, be dissatisfied, pester, harass, fuss, raise a fuss. See also bitch (verb), complain, nag (verb).

whipping boy whipping post, scapegoat, goat, victim, dupe, tool. The most precise synonym, "whipping post," is violent and might be rejected for that reason. In the historical sense of whipping a substitute for the prince, it was always a boy. See also violent language.

whirling dervish although a dervish is the Muslim equivalent of a monk or a friar (some of whom whirled), the metaphorical sense is used of both women and men.

white (noun, referring to people) this is the generally accepted term for those who are not people of color, sometimes including, sometimes in addition to, those of Latin ancestry. The tendency is to underuse, not overuse, "white"; if skin color or ethnicity is pertinent to your material, check for parallel usage across named groups and include references to "white" if you have included, for example, references to "black." If you alternate the use of "black" and "African American" in your material, similarly use "white" and "European American" (if applicable). Too often, "white" is assumed to be the default. Do not so assume. "White" is usually spelled lowercase, although the style for some publications and writers is uppercase. It is not a synonym for Caucasian or Caucasoid ("white" refers to light-skinned peoples of Europe and parts of Asia; "Caucasian" and "Caucasoid" refer to a now-discounted racial categorization that included Europeans, North Africans, Middle Easterners, and some people of the Indian subcontinent). "The word 'white,' which has been used to describe European Americans, does not reflect anyone's skin color so much as a concept of racial purity which has never existed" (Paul Kivel, *Uprooting Racism*). See also black/black-, Caucasian, privilege, white (adjective), white privilege.

white (adjective) avoid the metaphorical use of "white" to symbolize purity, goodness, rightness (the opposite of all this being, of course, black). Replace phrases like "that's white of you" ("that's good of you") and "white lie" ("social/innocent lie"), and circumvent others like "white knight," "white hope," and "whitewash." See also black/black-, Caucasian, white (noun, referring to people), white privilege.

white-collar worker people who work sitting down (desk jobs) are referred to as white-collar workers while those who work standing up (manual labor) are blue-collar workers. These tidy labels aren't very informative, however, and tend to set up an adversarial relationship between the two groups. Instead, name the specific professions or positions or jobs.

white knight although the original white knight was saving Alice (in Wonderland) from a wicked red knight, in our culture the antonym for a white knight (the friendly party in a takeover bid for a company) is a black knight (the unfriendly party). Try to avoid the black/white terms by describing the parties' actions or by creating fresh terms that might make the story clearer for readers.

white man's burden one of the most egregious expressions in the language (from Rudyard Kipling's 1899 poem of the same name), this refers to the alleged duty of white peoples to manage the affairs of "less developed" nonwhite peoples. It was the inescapable duty of white conquerors, he wrote, to rule over their "new-caught, sullen peoples, Half devil and half child." This concept served to justify immeasurable horror and injustice, and lingering colonial/domineering/protectionistic/patriarchal attitudes stemming from this phrase still color much Western thought.

whiteness studies a growing and controversial field of scholarly research, critical whiteness studies approaches racism by trying to understand a previously unexamined part of the equation. "The assumption has been that for many white Americans, race is something other people have," said Doug Hartmann, a sociology professor at the University of Minnesota and co-author of 2007 study showing that 74 percent of white Americans interviewed said their racial identity was important—a number that surprised researchers, who believed that whites simply took their race for granted. "Likewise, the white Americans said they understood that they benefited from their race." While more than 80 percent said access to schools and social connections were important in explaining "white advantage" over racial minorities, 62 percent said prejudice and discrimination against nonwhites also explained those advantages.

white privilege a range of obvious and less obvious benefits and immunities that people with "white" skin appear to enjoy beyond what people of color experience in the same situation. "I have come to see white privilege as an invisible package of unearned assets which I can count on cashing in each day, but about which I was 'meant' to remain oblivious. White privilege is like an invisible weightless knapsack of special provisions, assurances, tools, maps, guides, codebooks, passports, visas, clothes, compass, emergency gear, and blank checks" (Dr. Peggy McIntosh, in Harriet Lerner, *Life Preservers*). Sharon Martinas (*Challenging White Supremacy*) calls the web of institutional and cultural preferential treatment "300 years of affirmative action for white people." The ubiquity and ingrained nature of current racial advantages and disadvantages make the status quo seem normal to those unaffected by it. As James Baldwin said, "To be white in America means not having to think about it." In the same way that "money makes money," privilege makes privilege, and after centuries of accumulated and interrelated advantages, white privilege shows up in differences in life expectancy, health, wealth, education, and other statuses, partly due to different accesses to resources and opportunities. These disparities are maintained both by denying that they exist and by refusing to address them at the policy level. Note that non-ruling-class white people retain white privilege but they may be significantly unprivileged on the basis of age, ethnicity, sexuality, culture, religion, physical abilities, or other factors. Try to view life in these United States through the lens of "privilege" so that your writing does not reinforce it, ignore it, or assume it.

white slavery female sexual slavery.

white supremacy the belief that white or light-skinned people are innately superior to, and should control, all others; overt and covert anger as well as violence and ignorance are usually hallmarks of white supremacist groups. In the U.S., groups vary from the nonviolent pseudo-intellectual to those labeled by the FBI as domestic terrorists. Obama's re-election in 2012 triggered fear and fury: "Welcome to a truly white minority world," wrote one commenter on Stormfront, the world's largest white supremacist website. Another wrote, "You will never see another white man occupy the White House again." See also hate groups, hate rock, nullification, sovereign citizens, white privilege.

white trash/poor white trash see ethnic slurs.

whore prostitute. "Whore" used to be a nonjudgmental term describing a lover of either sex; now it is a highly offensive term describing a woman. "Ho" is the "friendly" version. See also prostitute.

whorehouse house of prostitution. See also prostitute.

whoremonger this ambiguous term can mean either a pimp or a prostitute user; it is rarely seen anymore, which is just as well since it is based on the highly pejorative "whore."

Wicca this pagan nature religion with roots in pre-Christian western Europe is undergoing a contemporary revival. In 2008, some 342,000 people identified themselves as Wiccans. Wiccans stress that their beliefs have nothing to do with black witchcraft or Satanism (they don't even believe in Satan). One Wiccan describes her faith as a mixture of Native American and Celtic influences and rituals. Others say it keeps alive teachings on reincarnation and karma while focusing on harmony with nature and an enhanced spirituality. While Wicca may involve the practice of magic and witchcraft, it cannot be solely defined by those elements. In 2007, Wiccans persuaded the Department of Veterans Affairs to add their symbol (the Wiccan pentacle representing earth, air, fire, water, and spirit) to veterans' government-issued grave markers (57 symbols are permitted). Wiccans might best be summed up by their saying, "Do what thou wilt, an it harm none" (Robin Morgan, *The Word of a Woman*).

wicked stepmother See stepmother, wicked.

widow/widower these are acceptable sex-specific words. If you need an inclusive term, use surviving spouse. "Widow" and "widower" are also used by lesbian and gay couples when one dies. "Widower" is one of the only male words that is the marked term—that is, the female "widow" is the unmarked or default word and the male word is based on it. Notice how often a woman is referred to as someone's widow—and how very seldom a man is referred to as someone's widower.

widow burning see suttee.

widowhood the word "widowerhood" exists, but you have probably never seen it.

widow lady widow, surviving spouse. See also lady, widow/widower.

widow's mite one's last cent/dime, giving of one's all, giving out of one's need, giving till it hurts. Retain the term sometimes to balance the many male expressions in the language.

widow's peak there appears to be no good inclusive alternative to this recognizable and concise term. Either a man or a woman may have a widow's peak, although the term arose from the superstition that it heralded early widowhood.

widow's walk leave as is. Or, railed observatory platform.

wife an acceptable word in itself (from a Germanic term meaning "female human being"), "wife" is sometimes used gratuitously or in highly sexist ways. An effective test is to see if you would use "husband" in a similar way. Casey Miller and Kate Swift (*The Handbook of Nonsexist Writing*) point out that in the traditional marriage service provided in the Book of Common Prayer, the couple was initially referred to as "the Man and the Woman"; it was not until the words of marriage were pronounced that they were referred to henceforth as "Man and Wife"; "Symbolically, two have been made one, but also symbolically the man's status as a person remains intact whereas the woman's is changed from person to role." This language is history now in many churches, but we have inherited much of its spirit in the use of "wife" today. When *Esquire* offered its readers a special tear-out section entitled "Your Wife: An Owner's Manual," editor-in-chief Lee Eisenberg introduced it: "We are gathered together in the sight of our readers to come to grips with the subject of a man's wife, his partner, the little woman, the missus...." The issue included a list of "synonyms" for "wife," some of which were positive or neutral and some, acknowledged as offensive, that illustrated what some men and some husbands think of wives: bitch, hussy, old lady, the gadget, Darth Vader, the hag, the nag, the rag, the bag, the spandex monster, my little piranha fish, the war department, twitface, the mouse queen, Evita, the terminator, the queen, the princess, Her Majesty, the boss, the worse half, exec-u-wife, the fishwife, the shrew, the mouth, the ballbuster, the creature, squaw, the powers that be, the ball and chain. See also farm wife/farmer's wife, husband (noun), husband and wife, owner, working mother/working wife/working woman.

wife-beater tank top this offensive term for a sleeveless T-shirt that trivializes intimate violence is one of the most jarring in the language. At least one newspaper (*The Boston Globe*) has banned it. Go thou and do likewise.

wifehood/wifelike/wifeliness/wifely our ideas of "wifelike," "wifely," "wifeliness," and "wifehood" depend entirely on subjective cultural stereotypes. Replace these terms with words that are gender-fair, precise, and descriptive. For example, for "wifely" use companionable, helpful, supportive, sympathetic, sensitive, affectionate, intimate, loving, approving, admonishing. These words would do equally well for "husbandly." See also wife, woman, womanlike/womanliness/womanly.

wife-swapping spouse-swapping, swinging. Why don't we speak of "husband-swapping"?

wildcrafter one who gathers edible plants and herbs from the wild in an environmentally sensitive manner is a wildcrafter.

wilderness European Americans generally referred to the lands they settled as "wilderness." American Indians called these same lands their "homelands" or "sacred geography" (Arlene B. Hirschfelder, in *Library Trends*).

wild Indians used to explain to children how not to behave, this term is not appreciated by American Indians.

willy-nilly this term is male-based, but not because of a man's name; the original expression was "will he or nill he." Even so, it functions inclusively and it would be a rare individual who perceived it as sexist.

wimmin/wimyn/womon/womyn some women favor spellings for "woman/women" that leave out "man/men." These terms should be used for groups and individuals that so name themselves. See also unconventional spellings, woman.

wingman wingmate, flying partner. "Wingman" is used in the Air Force for either a woman or a man. See also airman.

wingnuts see moonbats and wingnuts.

Winnebago Ho-Chunk Indians. The Wisconsin peoples once referred to as "Winnebago" have replaced that ethnonym with their ancestral, authentic name, Ho-Chunk. "Winnebago Indians" refers only to the Winnebago Tribe of Nebraska. Other spellings you might see include Ho Chunk, Hocak, Hocank, Hochank, Hochunk, Nipegon, Puant.

wireman wirer, electrician; wiretapper.

wise as Balaam's ass/Solomon there is nothing wrong with using these phrases, but be aware of how many such expressions are male-based (or at least in this case, we know Balaam and Solomon were men; the sex of the ass is unknown). Balance their use with female-based expressions, creative expressions of your own, or sex-neutral alternatives: wise as an owl/a serpent/a judge. See also sex-linked expressions.

wise man wise person/one, elder, leader, sage, philosopher, oracle, mentor, luminary, learned person, pundit, scholar, savant, authority, expert, guru, thinker. "Wise man" or "wise woman," which are currently used gender-fairly, will sometimes be the terms of choice. See also three wise men, the.

wise-use movement this loose-knit coalition of groups was formed in opposition to the environmental movement, which it believes is (1) too radical, (2) wrong about its science, and (3) trying to control the land. A good part of wise-use movement funding appears to come from land development and resource extraction industries.

witch woman or man. Although "witch" has undeservedly negative connotations for many people, it is being reclaimed with pride by the estimated 150,000 witches in the U.S. who tend to be gentle people who believe in responsibility toward self, others, and the world. Write or speak about today's witches only if you are knowledgeable about their beliefs and activities. Genuine benevolent witchcraft does not in any way include, let alone worship, Satan.

wizard in the sense of a sorcerer, magician, conjurer, or witch, we tend to picture a wizard as a man. However, a computer wizard or a wizard (expert) in some field could be either sex.

wolf (man) there is no alternative for this term. Should you want a sex-neutral approximation, consider flirt, seducer, predator, someone who comes on strong. See also lone wolf, womanizer.

woman (noun) the Old English word from which "woman" is taken ("wif-man") came from "wif" ("female") plus "man" (Old English for "human being"). Women continued to be "female human beings," which is fairly decent, but the word for "male human beings" ("wer-man") was gradually lost (it survives only in "werewolf") and men got to be human beings, period, full stop, no qualifications for sex. Although suggestions are made from time to time to replace the word "woman," it appears to be solidly positioned in the language. The problem with "woman" is really "man" (when used to mean "everyone" when everyone knows it doesn't). When "human being" is used for everyone, "man" for adult males, and "woman" for adult females, the word "woman" is respected, acceptable, and in every way equal to the word "man." A neat if facile summary of female-male issues might be Theodor Reik's maxim: "In our civilization, men are afraid that they will not be men enough and women are afraid that they might be considered only women." See also farm wife/farmer's wife, female (noun), girlfriend, lady (adjective), lady (noun), prostitute, wage earner, wife, wimmin/wimyn/womon/womyn, woman (adjective).

woman (adjective) female (adjective) Occasionally, very occasionally, it is necessary to modify a noun to indicate whether it's a man or a woman: male nurse, female archbishop. You never read about a man gynecologist or a man babysitter; it's always a male gynecologist or a male babysitter. In the interests of parallel treatment, which always seems a sound principle, use "female" for women: female driver, female prime minister. The best check is to substitute the opposite sex in place of your adjective and see how silly it looks: "oddly enough, the man candidate never once called on a woman in the audience." The 2013 *AP Style Guide* very plainly says to always use "female" as an adjective, never "woman." See also female (adjective), woman.

woman-hater see man-hater/woman-hater.

womanhood both definitions of this word are acceptable—"the state of being a woman" and "women or womenkind." If you want a broader, sex-neutral term, use personhood, selfhood, adulthood, majority, maturity.

womanish replace this vague and pejorative stereotype with descriptive words: fussy, particular, overparticular, choosy, fastidious, anxious, overanxious, worried, nervous, timid, weak, indecisive, unathletic, vapid. "Womanish" used of a man manages to disparage both sexes with a single word.

womanist in her 1983 book, *In Search of Our Mothers' Gardens*, Alice Walker coined this word to denote a black feminist. Black feminists and other women of color wanted to broaden the scope of feminism beyond a white middle-class perspective and to explore the intersections of ethnicity, race, class, and gender. (Walker said, "Womanist is to feminist as purple is to lavender.") See also feminisms, feminist.

womanize/womanizer philander, bedhop, sleep around, seduce, be promiscuous/sexually active/sexually aggressive/indiscriminate, have many love affairs; swinger, philanderer, seducer, bedhopper, sensualist, free-lover, flirt, freethinker, free spirit, voluptuary, sybarite, hedonist, lover, operator. It's difficult to find appropriate inclusive substitutes for "womanize" and "womanizer" because we so rarely need that exact word for anything except a man who pursues or courts women habitually or illicitly. Women who philander are either "man crazy" or "promiscuous." Gay men who have many affairs are also "promiscuous" or they have "one-night stands." Ellen Goodman says "manize" hasn't made it into the language because women have always associated sex with danger (rape, pregnancy, the double standard), because getting men on their backs isn't a power trip for most women, and because so far the power of successful older women does not seem to act as an aphrodisiac on younger, good-looking men. There have been too few highly public and powerful women to know if "manizing" is something women would do (Golda Meir? Indira Gandhi? Maggie Thatcher?). See also ladies' man, man about town, playboy, rake.

womankind there is a legitimate use for "womankind," whereas "mankind" is problematic since it has been misused for so long as a pseudogeneric.

womanlike/womanliness/womanly these vague and subjective cultural stereotypes convey different meanings to different people according to their perceptions of what a woman ought or ought not do, say, think, feel, and look like. Choose words instead that express precise characteristics: gracious/graciousness, warm/warmth, gentle/gentleness, receptive/receptivity, supportive/supportiveness, tender/tenderness, charming/charm, sympathetic/sympathy, nurturing/nurturance, well-mannered/good breeding, considerate/consideration, kind/kindness, intuitive/intuition, strong/gentle strength. These words may be used equally appropriately of a man. They are not synonymous with the sexist terms, but are rather what people generally seem to mean by them. See also gender.

woman's place is in the home, a when a man's "place" is also in the home and when the woman truly wants to be there, this is a powerful sentiment. It also rings true if we substitute "heart" for "place" and apply it to both sexes. Unfortunately, this dictum has been used with all the finesse of a sledgehammer and promulgated as a "natural" law as well as a test of patriotism, "femininity," conjugal love, and right-thinking. Working in the home is an excellent choice for many women and one that society ought to value and support with positive attitudes and practical assistance. This expression becomes a problem when it is used as a mandate for all women and ignores men's involvement with the home.

woman suffrage movement this term is the one used most often by historians.

woman's work except for what goes on during childbirth, there is no work biologically specific only to women. "[I]t is a retrogressive idea to call any particular sphere of work 'Women's'. We do not know what women's work will be, we only know what it has been" (Caroline Boord, *The Freewoman*, 1911). See also man's work.

women and children/women and children first pairing women with children is illogical, belittling to women, and a paternalistic attempt to perpetuate the subordination and powerlessness of women. The Napoleonic Code (1804) did much to legitimize the second-class status of European women. Among other things, the code grouped women and children with "persons of unsound mind," judging them all equally incapable of entering into contracts. When you see women and children grouped together, delete or replace the phrase (in the case of "women and children first" it should be "those who need extra assistance first"). This expression probably arose not so much from some medieval idea of chivalry as from a more ancient fact of life: an early society's main chance for survival rested on its being able to reproduce itself. Men can father children every day but women need nine months to produce a child and a child represents a considerable investment in the future. Thus in times of crisis, women and children were protected so as to ensure the future of the society. Today the future of our society depends on both sexes. See also innocent victim.

"women and other minorities" women and minorities. Women are not a minority in the U.S. or in the world.

womenfolk acceptable when also using "menfolk." Otherwise use folk, folks, people.

women-only spaces because some women have been so abused by men, the only way they feel safe and relaxed is in a women-only space. The most important example of this might be the Michigan Womyn's Musical Festival, which has a "womyn-born-womyn-only" admission policy. Because this excludes MTF transgender people, the policy is still being debated.

women's intuition intuition, sixth sense, hunch, perspicacity, insight. As concepts, "women's intuition" and "feminine intuition" don't do much for either sex: they impute insensitivity to men and erratic reasoning to women.

women's issues by using this vague label, politicians and others are able to discount and stereotype issues such as abortion rights, ageism, childcare, comparable worth, divorce, domestic violence, the Equal Rights Amendment, flextime, parental leave, poverty, rape, and sexual harassment, when they are in fact family, political, social, ethical, economic, and human issues.

women's lib/women's libber women's movement, feminism, feminist movement, women's liberation movement; feminist, supporter/member of the women's movement. "Women's lib" and "women's libber" are considered derogatory, patronizing, trivializing, and hostile. Gloria Steinem says that because of the putdown implicit in the cavalier shortening, "and because of the vast enlargement of the numbers of women involved, women now tend to say 'Women's Movement' rather than "Women's Liberation' ... comparable to 'Civil Rights Movement' as a phrase." See also shortened forms of words.

women's movement/women's liberation movement/women's rights movement in 1838, Adelaide Anne Procter wrote to her friend Anna Jameson: "The men are much alarmed by certain speculations about women; and well they may be, for when the horse and ass begin to think and argue, adieu to riding and driving." In the same year, Sarah M. Grimké wrote, "I ask no favors for my sex. All I ask of our brethren is, that they will take their feet from off our necks." In 1739 it was Sophia, identified only as "A Person of Quality": "What a wretched circle this poor way of reasoning among the Men draws them insensibly into. Why is learning useless to us? Because we have no share in public offices. And why have we no share in public offices? Because we have no learning." Or Mary Astell in 1694: "Women are from their very infancy debarred those advantages with the want of which they are afterwards reproached.... So partial are men as to expect bricks when they afford no straw." Choose almost any year and you will find women writing, agitating, outlining arguments we are still using today. There has always been a women's movement. However, the "women's rights movement" as a formal movement commonly dates from 1848 when women met in Seneca Falls, New York, to draw up the first public protest in the U.S. against the political, social, and economic repression of women. The "women's liberation movement," which grew out of leftist politics in the 1960s, was never one monolithic organized group, but its proponents generally espoused more radical issues than those of the women's movement; they were also the first to promote consciousness raising. See also feminism, feminisms.

women's studies in 1972, two U.S. colleges had women's-studies programs. As of 2007, there were at least 754 women's-studies programs in U.S. colleges, and increasing numbers of courses in high schools (*Ms.*).

womyn see wimmin/wimyn/womon/womyn.

Wonder Woman Wonder Woman is not a female parallel for Superman, Batman, or Tarzan. Cheris Kramarae (*Women and Men Speaking*) points out that, without belittling her strength, magic, courage, and independence, it must be said that Wonder Woman is an aberration rather than a super specimen of her gender: "She lives in a community that is dominated by women; however, there are no men living on her island. Even on the island, the queen is given insight, wisdom, and knowledge by two men from another world. All the women except Wonder Woman are spectators to the action of the story."

woodsman in the sense of someone who lives and works in the woods or who enjoys the outdoors, "woodsman" has few good sex-neutral alternatives. Fortunately, "woodswoman" is a functional, independent term, thanks to Woodswomen, an organization for outdoorswomen who like outdoor sports and adventure travel (trekking to Nepal, llama packing in the West, biking in Brittany and Cozumel, climbing in Alaska and Ecuador, rafting in the Northwest and Costa Rica). Rebecca A. Hinton writes in *Women's Outdoor Journal*, "Women have been enjoying the outdoors since the beginning of time, but if we'd all been wearing camouflage we couldn't be more invisible." In some contexts, you can use: woodlander, forest dweller, backsettler; woodworker, carver, woodcrafter, carpenter; forester, logger, woodchopper, woodcutter, woods worker.

work ethic the belief that hard work, done well, develops a virtuous character, that it is a good and a goal in itself. The work ethic is much admired, but usually by those who don't need to work hard themselves (the wealthy), those who pay minimum wage or employ the working poor, and those who like to fiddle (in a negative way) with programs aimed at getting people on their feet financially. Large numbers of those with a good work ethic, who actually create profit by their work, are employed at 50 highly successful U.S. national retail and fast food chains for minimum wages. These same companies routinely pay their top execs an average of $10 million a year, not counting perks and stock options, and have since 2006 provided some $175 billion in dividends to shareholders. Their workers routinely apply for food stamps and Medicaid, which equates to additional corporate subsidies financed by taxpayers. Roughly 60 percent of jobs created since the 2008 Wall Street collapse fall within the minimum wage category (Joe Bahlke, in *The Progressive*, 2013). See also comparable worth, working poor.

workfare shorthand for the requirement that individuals seeking cash assistance for food, housing, or medical needs must seek and obtain employment in order to receive benefits. The TANF (Temporary Assistance to needy Families) program is a block grant to states to fund cash assistance, work supports, and other services for low-income children and families. In 2012, over 1.75 million families and 3.1 million children received TANF benefits. More than 8 in 10 adults served by TANF are women. The National Partnership for Women and Families says that "TANF beneficiaries are more likely to work in low wage jobs that offer little or no flexibility or benefits, such as sick leave. Lack of work flexibility means that being available to take a child to the doctor or a parent to chemotherapy, to attend a parent-teacher conference, to supervise children before or after school, can place job security in jeopardy." In an effort to overhaul the workfare program, the Health and Human Services department now allows states to apply for a waiver for the work requirements of the TANF program if they are able to demonstrate credible progress toward increasing employment by 20 percent compared with the state's past performance.

working father according to the Bureau of National Affairs, fathers still define themselves primarily as providers and continue to face traditional pressure to be good workers, but they are increasingly torn between work and family, wanting to connect with their children in stronger ways than their own fathers did. In one study, 50 percent of fathers and 56 percent of mothers reported difficulty in balancing work and family. Men often keep quiet about their family interests because of workplace attitudes, but fear of reproducing their fathers' absence and detachment sets up conflicts for them as they move through their careers. See also childcare, parent (noun), provider.

working girl worker, employee, jobholder, wage earner, laborer. O be specific: typist, programmer, mechanic, librarian, pipefitter, teacher, physician, electrician. "Working girl" is sexist (we have no "working boys"), inaccurate (if she's old enough to work, she's not a girl), and has unpleasant overtones; in the late 1940s, it was synonymous with prostitute. See also businessman, career girl/career woman, working mother, working wife, working woman.

working man worker, employee, jobholder, wage earner, laborer, day laborer, average/typical worker, blue-collar/industrial worker, professional. Or be specific: programmer, mechanic, librarian, pipefitter, teacher, physician, electrician. See also wage earner, working father, working mother, working wife, workman.

working poor this term should be an oxymoron. If you work full-time, if you work hard, you should not be poor. Yet one in four American workers have jobs that pay $10 an hour or less and 10.4 million Americans qualify as the "working poor." Roger Weisberg, who produced and directed the documentary "Waging a Living," said he wanted viewers to understand "what it's like to work hard, play by the rules, and still not be able to support a family." Despite all their hard work and determination, people find themselves, as one subject in the documentary observes, "hustling backwards." Since 1994, more than 100 cities have passed local living wage laws that require employers who do business with the government—who get taxpayer subsidies, in other words—to pay workers enough to lift their families out of poverty.

working mother/working wife/working woman "While women represent half the global population and one-third of the labor force, they receive only one-tenth of the world income and own less than 1 percent of world property. They also are responsible for two-thirds of all working hours" (former Secretary General Kurt Waldheim, "Report to the U.N. Commission on the Status of Women"). All women work. Most often, you do not need labels to distinguish among them, nor is their sex usually relevant (sometimes it is) or the fact that they are mothers. (At work, too often men with children are men, and women with children are mothers.) Should you need to convey something specific, use a job title (programmer, lawyer, librarian, teacher, physician, electrician, farmer) or one of the following: worker, employee, employed at ..., employed outside the home/in the paid workforce, laborer, member of the labor force, wage-earner, salaried worker, job-holder. If you must specify the status of a woman who is not in a paying job, consider: woman who works as a homemaker, woman who is her own childcare giver (these first two are used by the U.S. Department of Labor), homemaker, nonsalaried/unsalaried worker/woman/mother, woman/mother who is working/employed inside the home/at home, at-home parent, home-working mother. (Lady L. McLaren pointed out in 1908, "The great majority of wives are devoting their time to unpaid work, and when the importance of the work is considered, it appears extraordinary that the services of wives have no money value placed on them.... A wife who works diligently and devotedly to the family service should be entitled to such wages of a servant or housekeeper as are usual in that station of life in which she lives and this in addition to her board.") When there are two adults and they both work, use: a two-income/two-paycheck family, two-earner/dual-career/dual-income couple/household. Avoid terms that imply a woman who cares for her children at home doesn't work; even phrases like "stays home" imply passivity. The issue of women employed outside the home seems to be such a contemporary one, yet women have always worked—and in great numbers. The 1861 census in Great Britain, for example, indicates that of the total adult female population, some 60 percent were salaried (Eleanor S. Riemer and John C. Fout, eds., *European Women*); in the late 19th century, guidebooks were written for women on how to choose an occupation or profession. Although working mothers have been criticized for destroying the traditional family, they have, on the contrary, kept millions of children from sinking below the poverty line; two-thirds of the women in the workforce today are either the sole support of their children or have husbands who earn less than a living wage. Senator Christopher J. Dodd once wrote to Ann Landers, "Ann, please keep telling your vast readership that American women haven't turned their backs on their children by entering the workforce. They have gone to work to keep their families together." See also career girl/career woman, family, housewife, housework, maternity leave, opting out, second shift, "traditional family," woman's work, working poor, workman.

workman worker, artisan, crafter, employee, laborer, operator, hand, staff. Or be specific: repairer, landscaper, electrician. See also handyman, odd-job(s)-man, repairman, working man.

workmanlike/workmanly skillful, skilled, expert, professional, businesslike, competent, efficient, careful, precise, proficient, first-rate, top-flight.

workmanship artisanship, work, construction, handiwork, handicraft, artisanry, skilled-craft work, skill, technique, style, expertness, expertise, competence, proficiency, finish, quality, polish, execution, technique, performance. "Workmanship" may need to be retained in the legal sense as case law often uses it.

workmen's compensation workers' compensation.

workplace in *Taking on the Big Boys: Or Why Feminism Is Good for Families, Business, and the Nation*, Ellen Bravo identifies bosses' tactics in keeping employees in their places: minimize, trivialize, patronize, demonize, catastrophize, and compartmentalize.

writing guidelines for guidelines on using fair and accurate people language, see the Writing Guidelines where you will find definition of terms, issues on naming, information on pseudogeneric "he" and "man/men/mankind," and special problems. See also such entries in the main part of this sourcebook as adjectival forms as nouns, feminine word endings, "insider/outsider" rule, salutations (letters), "people first" rule, sexist language, sexist quotations, sex-linked expressions, shortened forms of words, singular "they."

wuss/wussy see coward.

Our native language is like a second skin, so much a part of us we resist the idea that it is constantly changing, constantly being renewed.

Casey Miller and Kate Swift

xenophobia contempt or fear of foreigners, usually taken to mean those from other countries. It can also, more broadly, include a hatred of "the other." (Willa Cather was perhaps describing a mild xenophobe: "He had the uneasy manner of a man who is not among his own kind, and who has not seen enough of the world to feel that all people are in some sense his own kind.")

Xmas this term is "etymologically innocent of the charge that it omits Christ from Christmas" (the *American Heritage Dictionary of the English Language*) because the "X" represent the Greek *chi*, or the first letter of Christ's name. It's been used as shorthand for Christ in religious writings for centuries. However, it is currently in disfavor with many Christians. Know your audience if you use it.

The dictionary is … only a rough draft.

Monique Wittig and Sande Zeig

yachtsman yacht owner/captain/racer/sailor, yachter; yacht club member; yachtswoman and yachtsman. See also seaman.

yachtsmanship yachting skills/techniques/proficiency, yacht sailing techniques.

Yahweh (YHWH) because this personal name for God is not gender-specific, it has been used by groups seeking inclusive terms. However, observant Jews neither use nor speak this sacred word, and out of respect for this belief system, many non-Jews have chosen to forego its use also. Jews use instead "Ha-Shem" ("The Name"). Jews also refer to God as "Adonai," "Lord," and "Eloheino"—but never "Jehovah." See also Father (God), God (Christian), Jehovah.

yammer nobody yammers very much, but apparently men absolutely never do. For alternatives to this functionally sexist word, see gossip, prattle.

Yankee/Yank/Yanqui a positive term today when used to refer to New Englanders, "Yankee" was originally derogatory and is still occasionally used that way in other countries to refer to the United States ("Yankees, go home"). During the Civil War, it referred to any Northerner; traces of this antagonism can sometimes be heard in it today. During World War II, however, "Yankee" and "Yanks" were a positive term. Like all shortened forms, "Yank" is otherwise disparaging; "Yanqui" is the Spanish-language term sometimes used as an epithet. "Yankee" also has some negative overtones of cleverness verging on sharp practices.

yardman yard worker/laborer, caretaker, odd-job laborer; gardener, landscaper; yard supervisor/chief; stockyard handler/laborer; railroad worker.

yellow according to the *American Heritage Book of English Usage*, "Of the color terms used as racial labels, *yellow*, referring to Asians, is perhaps the least used and the most clearly offensive." Yellow has also been used to single out Jews: in some countries during the Holocaust, they were forced to wear a yellow badge; the Nazis required yellow stars. The color has also been associated with cowardice. See also high yellow, yellow/yellow-bellied, etc., "Yellow Peril."

yellow/yellow-bellied/yellow-bellied coward/yellow belly/yellow streak down one's back wholly reserved for boys/men, these insults indirectly discount girls/women (who have not been expected—or indeed often allowed—to accept challenges that call for courage, bravery, or risk-taking) and hold men/boys to impossibly high, dubious, and constantly shifting standards of courage. Boys/men are acculturated to be sensitive to taunts of "coward." Most people would not use these terms; they are included here to show the cultural bias that expects too much of men and too little of women. See also coward/cowardly/cowardice.

"Yellow Peril" this term, expressing turn-of-the-century fear of being overrun by peoples from the East, is rarely seen today. In discussing it historically, use quotation marks to show the dubiousness of the concept.

yente/yenta this Yiddish word for a constantly talking, meddling, or scolding woman is defined fairly negatively (synonyms include "gossip" and "blabbermouth"), but few people hear it that way today—partly because it's not commonly used as an epithet, perhaps partly because of the Barbra Streisand movie *Yentl*, and partly because the yenta has a good heart. For inclusive alternatives, see gossip.

yeoman/Yeoman of the Guard/yeomanry/yeoman's service some of these terms have historical (yeoman, yeomanry, yeoman's service) or official (Yeoman of the Guard, yeoman) meanings that defy substitution, but others can be variously replaced: retainer, attendant; military corps personnel attached to the British royal household; smallholding/freeholding farmer, smallholder, freeholder; petty officer, clerical officer; clerk, paralegal, typist, copyist, transcriber; helper; beefeater, warden, bodyguard. See also yeomanly, yeoman's job.

yeomanly there isn't a great call for this adjective so it is not overwhelming us with its manly presence. If you need a sex-neutral term, consider loyal, faithful, courageous, stalwart, staunch, steadfast, true, true-hearted; unwavering, unswerving, firm, stable, solid.

yeoman's job this is difficult to replace; consider making up your own metaphor or using impressive/remarkable/extraordinary/outstanding/valiant/heroic/superexcellent/first-class/bang-up/a-number-one job, massive/enormous effort.

yes man yea-sayer, toady, rubber stamp, sycophant, flunky, puppet, stooge, dupe, brown-noser, apple polisher, bootlicker, backscratcher, flatterer, hanger-on, follower, doormat, tool, minion, myrmidon; an obsequious underling.

Yid offensive slang, from "Yiddish," but one that is sometimes used by Jews themselves. See also shortened forms of words.

yogi woman or man. Indians call the woman a "yogini."

yokel this disparaging, anti-rural, usually classist term is also functionally sexist, as it is almost always used for a man.

Yonsei this is an acceptable term for fourth-generation Japanese Americans. See also Issei, Kibei, Nisei, Sansei.

Yorkshireman inhabitant/native of Yorkshire, someone from Yorkshire, Yorkshirewoman/Yorkshireman. Plural: Yorkshirewomen and Yorkshiremen (but never "Yorkshiremen and women").

you guys when you say, "See that guy over there?" everyone, but everyone, looks for someone of the masculine persuasion. Singular "guy" is an all right word, limping a little only in that its natural mate, "gal," doesn't have nearly the use, standing, or linguistic influence that "guy" does. The problem arises when "you guys" refers to mixed-gender groups or groups consisting entirely of women. Fast becoming part of standard language in all but the most formal speech, the ubiquitous "you guys" neither demeans nor excludes anyone. Nor is the plural "guys" heard by most people as referencing males. It also resolves our linguistic lack of an all-purpose, generic, emphatic "you." One study found "you guys" the default expression of choice in all U.S. regions but one (Harvard Survey of North American Dialects). But, Audrey Bilger writes (in *Bitch*), "Can the same culture that says 'it's a guy thing' to refer to anything that women just don't get about male behavior view a woman as one of the guys?" She points out that "terms signifying maleness have been more readily perceived as universal than those signifying femaleness," and adds, "If you call a group of men 'you gals,' they're not going to think you're just celebrating our common humanity....Calling women 'guys' makes femaleness invisible. It says that man—as in a male person—is still the measure of all things." Alice Walker is absolutely opposed to its pseudogeneric use: "Isn't it at least ironic that after so many years of struggle for women's liberation, women should end up calling themselves this?" Advice? Avoid it in writing. In speech, know your friends—who is okay with it, who is not. Alternatives, besides the simple "you": y'all, you all, folks, people.

young lady young woman. See lady.

youngster female or male. When used of a child, it is respectful and correct if somewhat less common today than it used to be. When used jocularly to refer to or address older people, it is rarely received jocularly.

"you people" this phrase is not so much objectionable—although it is that too—as it is a galloping indication of the speaker's feelings (hostile, disparaging, shaming) about "those people" (a companion term). Vivian Gornick once wrote ("On the Progress of Feminism"), "If I hear 'you people' just once more...!"

youth male or female. The term "youth" for young people aged thirteen to nineteen sounds slightly clinical and in the singular usually means a young man (the plural "youth" is understood to be inclusive). You may want to use young person, young adult. See also adolescent, ageism, juvenile, teenager. The gender-, classist-, and ethnic-neutral term "youth" has been used in all the school shootings to describe the middle-class or upper-middle-class white males who did the killing, thus concealing the real connotations. Yet when there's a shooting by African Americans they are always identified as black. In Virginia the killer was an "Asian shooter." In the same way, in some killings of "youth," the victims have all been girls. It's important to know who's doing what to whom; don't let the use of "youth" obscure critical information.

"You've come a long way, baby!" although this phrase looks gender-free, it has been so profoundly associated with a cigarette advertisement aimed at helping women catch up to men's lung cancer and cardiac death rates that "baby" is assumed to be female. In addition, it is generally women who have been called "endearments" that make of them babies, babes, girls, and other young, helpless dependents. If you want to defeminize it, men's groups have been known to use: "You've come a long way, Bubba!" It's also being used simply without the "baby."

yuppie/Yuppie from Young Urban Professional, "yuppie" has the usual defects of a facile label: imprecision, thoughtless and unsupported usage, and a distancing from the reality and humanity of those being tagged. Although the term sounds flattering, it implies a materialistic, egocentric approach to life and fails the self-naming test: rarely has anyone announced with genuine pride, "I am a yuppie." Use it with care, naming the characteristics you're singling out. See also buppie/Buppie.

No dictionary of a living tongue ever can be perfect, since while it is hastening to publication, some words are budding and some falling away.

Samuel Johnson

zamba/zambo referring to people with significant amounts of both African and Amerindian ancestry, this term should be used only for those who self-identify this way. It has, in the past and in some cases, been used derogatorily.

zines not your parents' fanzine, zines have a heterogeneity that defies precision, so beware of attributing anything to them as a monolithic group.

Zionism coined in 1890 by Nathan Birnbaum, Zionism was the striving to establish a Jewish state in its ancient homeland and is now the maintaining, support, and protection of the nation of Israel. Not all Jews are Zionists, nor are all Zionists Jews. (Christian Zionists believe that the return of the Jews to the Holy Land, and the establishment of the State of Israel in 1948, is in accordance with Biblical prophecy. However, Christian Zionists also commonly believe that to fulfill prophecy, a significant number of Jews will accept Jesus as their Messiah, and that in the last days, such Messianic Jews will practice a Hebraic form of Christianity. Many Christian Zionists believe that the people of Israel remain part of the chosen people of God, which effectively turns Christian Zionists into supporters of Jewish Zionism.) See also anti-Semitism, anti-Zionism, Israeli-Palestinian conflict, occupied territories. See also Israeli.

zoo in an effort to signal the more humane organization of zoos, the World Conservation Society (formerly the New York Zoological Society) decided to rename its zoos "wildlife conservation parks." However, the Humane Society of the United States strongly believes that under most circumstances wild animals should be permitted to exist undisturbed in their natural environments. People for the Ethical Treatment of Animals (PETA) say that despite their professed concern for animals, "zoos can more accurately be described as 'collections' of interesting 'specimens' than as actual havens or homes. Even under the best of circumstances at the best of zoos, captivity cannot begin to replicate wild animals' habitats. Animals are often prevented from doing most of the things that are natural and important to them, like running, roaming, flying, climbing, foraging, choosing a partner, and being with others of their own kind. Zoos teach people that it is acceptable to interfere with animals and keep them locked up in captivity, where they are bored, cramped, lonely, deprived of all control over their lives, and far from their natural homes." PETA points out that while zoos claim to provide educational opportunities, "most visitors spend only a few minutes at each display, seeking entertainment rather than enlightenment. Over the course of five summers, a curator at the National Zoo followed more than 700 zoo visitors and found that 'it didn't matter what was on display—people [were] treating the exhibits like wallpaper.' He determined that 'officials should stop kidding themselves about the tremendous educational value of showing an animal behind a glass wall.'" Using "zoo" metaphorically is often negative. See also jungle.

Z

Zulu 17 to 22 million Zulu, who form South Africa's largest single ethnic group, live mainly in the province of KwaZulu-Natal, while small numbers also live in Zimbabwe, Zambia, and Mozambique. Under apartheid, Zulu people were categorized as third-class citizens and suffered from state-sanctioned discrimination; today they have equal rights along with all other citizens. The caveat with Zulu is to use it only for the South African people, never for a non-Zulu black person in the U.S.—that use is considered derogatory and pejorative.

List of entries

abandoned
abbess/abbot
able-bodied
ableism
abnormal
aboriginalism
aborigine/aboriginal
abortion
abortion clinic
abortionist
abstinence
acolyte
acquaintance rape
activist judges
act one's age
actress
A.D.
Adam's rib
adhocracy
adjectival forms as nouns
adman
admitted/avowed homosexual
adolescent
adoption language
adulterer
advance man
advertising
advertorial
aficionada/aficionado
affirmative action
Afghans
Africa
African
African American
African American Feminism
Afro-American
Afrocentrism
Afro-Cuban
aged
ageism
aging in place
aggressive
agnostic
aide (medical)
aide de camp
AIDS
AIDS carrier
airman
airmanship
alderman
alien
alimony
Allah
"all-American"
all boy/all girl/all man/all woman
all men are created equal

alma mater
altar boy
alternative
"alternative lifestyle"
alto
alumna/alumnae/alumnus/alumni
Amazon/amazon
Amerasian
America/American
American exceptionalism
American Indian
American Indian Holocaust/Native American Holocaust
American Way
Amerindian/Amerind
amiga/amigo
amputee
anarchist
Anasazi
ancestress
anchoress
anchorman (newscasting)
ancient man
androgynous/androgyny
"(and women)"
angel
Anglo
Anglo-American
anima/animus
animal/he
animal husbandman/animal husbandry
animal (man)
animal names for people
animal rights activist/animal advocate
animist
Anishinabe
anorexic
anthropocentrism
anthropology
anti-abortion
anti-Arabism
anti-choice
antifeminist
anti-intellectual
anti-Islamism
anti-male bias
anti-personnel bomb
anti-pornography movement
anti-racist
anti-Semitism
anti-sweatshop activist
anti-war activist/protester
anti-Zionism
"ape-man"
Apostolic Fathers
Appalachian
apron strings, tied to someone's
Arab
Arab American
arbitration

Armenian genocide
army wife
arthritic
articulate
artificial insemination
artilleryman
artist
artiste
arts and crafts
Aryan
asexuality
Asian
Asian American
Asian Pacific American
Asiatic
assemblyman (manufacturing)
assemblyman (politics)
assimilated
assisted reproduction
assisted suicide
astroturfing
atheist
athlete
at risk
atypical
audism
aunt
au pair girl
authoress
auto mechanic
auxiliary
average man
aviatress/aviatrix
avuncular

b

babe/baby/baby doll
baby mama
babysitter
bachelor
bachelor girl/bachelorette
bachelor's degree
backlash
backroom boys
backward
backwoodsman
bad guy
bag/old bag
baggageman
bag lady/bag man
bagman
bailsman/bailbondsman
ball/bang
ball boy/ball girl
ballerina
ballet master/ballet mistress
balls
ballsy

banana republic
Bangalore
banshee
Bantu
barbaric/barbarian
barber
bar boy
bar girl
bard
bargeman
bargemaster
barmaid
barman
bar mitzvah/bat mitzvah
baroness
barren
barrista/barista
baseman
basketball
bastard
batboy
batman
batsman (cricket)
battered wife/woman
battle-ax
"battle of/between the sexes"
bawd/bawdy house
bawdy
B.C.
beau
beau ideal
beautician
beauty salon
Bechdel test
bedfellow
bedridden
belle/belle of the ball
bellboy
bellman
belly dancer
Beltway
benefactress
be one's own man/be your own man
Berber
Berdaches
best boy
best man
best man for the job
better half
bi
bias
Bible Belt
biblical language
Big Brother
big boss/cheese/enchilada/fish/gun/noise/
  shot/wheel/wig
Big Government
bigot
bikini

billionaire
bimbo
binary thinking
bioguy
biological father/mother/parent
bipartisan
biphobia
biracial
birdbrain
birth control
birth defect
birth mother/father/parent
bisexual
bishop
bitch (noun)
bitch (verb)
bitch session
bitchy
black/Black (noun)
black/black-
black-and-white (adjective)
Black Carib
black English
black feminism
Black Muslims
black nationalism
black sheep
black site
blacksmith
black tie
bleeding heart
blind
blogger
blonde
blood
blood brother
blood diamonds
blood libel
blue
Bluebeard
blue collar
bluesman
blue state
bluestocking
boat people
boat/she
bobby (British)
bodily integrity
body image
boi
Bombay
bombshell/blonde bombshell
bondsman (law)
bondsman/bondswoman (slave)
bonhomie
bon vivant
bordello
borderline/borderline personality

border patrolman
born-again Christian
born out of wedlock
bossy
bouncer
boy (referring to a man)
boycott
boyfriend
boyhood
boyish
boys and girls
boys in blue (armed forces)
boys in the backroom
boys will be boys
boy toy
bra burner
brainy
brakeman
brass (high-ranking officers)
brave (Indian)
brazen
breadwinner
brethren/brothers
brewmaster
bridal
bridal consultant
bride and groom
bride burning
bridegroom
bride of Christ
bridesmaid
brinkmanship/brinksmanship
bro
broad (woman)
broken home
brothel
brother (religion)
brotherhood
brotherhood of man
brotherly
brotherly love
brothers
brother's keeper, I am not my
brownfields
brunette
buccaneer
buck (man)
buck naked
buddy
bulimic
bull
bull dyke (woman)
bull session
bully
bum
buppie/Buppie
Burma
Burqa

busboy
Bushman
businessman
busman's holiday
butch (woman)
butcher
butler
butterfly

C

cabin boy
cabinet member
caddymaster
cad
Caesar's wife
Cajun/Cajan
Calcutta/Kolkata
calendar girl
call a spade a spade
call girl
camaraderie
camel jockey
cameragirl/cameraman
campaign finance reform
camp follower
candy-striper
Canuck
capital punishment
car bra
career girl/career woman
caregiver
care, withdrawing
car/she
Casanova
case
caste
castrate/castrating
catfight
cathouse
cattleman
catty
Caucasian
cavalryman
caveman/cavewoman
celibate
censorship
CEOs
chairman (noun)
chairman (verb)
chairmanship
challenged
chamberlain
chambermaid
champion
chancellor
"change, the"
chanteuse

Chanukah
chaperone
chaplain
chargé, d'affaires
charwoman
Chasidim
chaste/chastity
chatelaine
chauvinism
checkout girl/checkout man
cheerleader
chef
chessman
Chicana/Chicano/Chican@
chick
chickenhawk
chick flick
chief
chief/chief justice/chief master sergeant/chief master
  sergeant of the Air Force/chief petty officer/chief
  warrant officer/chief of staff/chief of state
Chief Justice of the Supreme Court
childbirth
childcare
child custody
childfree/childless
child/he
child marriage
children
child-sex tourist
Chinaman
Chinaman's chance
Chinese
Chinese American
Chinese wall
Chippewa
chit
chivalrous
chivalry
choice
choirboy
choirmaster
chorine
chorus boy/chorus girl
Christ
christen
Christian
Christian Coalition
Christian cultural imperialism
Christianity
Christian name
Christian Right, the
Christmas
church/she
church father
churchman
Church of Jesus Christ of Latter-day Saints, The
circumcision

cissexist

city councilman

city fathers

City of Brotherly Love

civilian contractor

civilian irregular defense soldier

civilization

civil union

claim (verb)

clansman

classism

classman

class warfare

cleaning lady/cleaning woman

cleft lip/cleft palate

clergyman

cleric/clerical

climate change

Climate Leaders

clitoridectomy

closet

clotheshorse

clothes make/don't make the man

clubman/clubwoman

coach

coachman

coalition forces

coatcheck girl

co-chairman

cock

cock-and-bull story

cock of the roost

cock of the walk

cockpit

cocksure/cocky

cockswain

cocktail

code words

coed (noun)

coffee girl/coffee man

cohort

coiffeur/coiffeuse

collateral damage

collective punishment

college girl

colonialism

colonist

coloratura

color blindness

colored

colorism

comedienne

"comfort women"

coming out

commander-in-chief

committeeman/committeewoman

committed against one's will

common-law husband/common-law wife

common man

community-supported agriculture (CSA)

companion

companion animal

company man

comparable worth

compassionate conservatism

compatriot

complain

comptroller

comrade

conceive

concentration camp

Concerned Women for America

concertmaster

concierge

concubine

condom

confessor

confidante

confined to a wheelchair

conflict diamonds

confraternity

confrere

congressman

con man/confidence man

connoisseur

conscientious objector

conservation

conservative

construction worker

consul

containment strategies

contraception

convent

conversion therapy

convict

cook

copy boy/copy girl

coquette

corporate welfare

corporations as persons

corpsman

Cosa Nostra

costume

cougar

councilman

countergirl/counterman

counterterrorism

country bumpkin

countryman

country/she

couple

courtesan

courtesy titles

courtier

courts (judicial)

couturière

cover girl
cover than man (sports)
coward/cowardly/cowardice
cowboy/cowgirl
cowboy hat
cowboy shirt
cowgirl
coxswain
crafts
craftsman
craftsmanship
crazy
"credit to her/his race"
cretin
crewman
crime in the streets
crime of passion
crimes against humanity
criminal/criminal class
cripple
Cro-Magnon man
crone
cross burnings
cross-dresser
crotchety
Crow
crown prince/crown princess
cruelty-free products
crybaby
cuckold
cult
cultural Issues
"culturally deprived/disadvantaged"
culture
"culture of life"
"culture of poverty"
culture wars
cunt
"curse"
curmudgeon
custodial parent
custodian
cyberbullying

d

dairymaid/dairyman
dame/damsel
dancing girl
dandy
danseur/danseuse
daredevil
Darfur genocide
Darfuri/Darfuris
dark
darkest Africa/the dark continent
date

date rape
daughter
daughter cell
daughter track
daycare
deaconess
dead men tell no tales
deaf/Deaf
deaf and dumb/deaf-mute/dumb
dear/dearie
Dear John letter, send a
death penalty
death tax
death with dignity
debonair
debutante
Decalogue
defect/defective
Defense Department
defensemen
defense spending
deficit
defoliate
deformed/deformity
degraded
deist
delivery boy/delivery man
dementia
demimondaine
democracy
"Democrat party"
demolitions man
demure
denigrate
den mother
dentist
deregulation
destabilize
detainee
deus ex machina
developing nation/country
developmental disability
deviant
devil/he
devotee
diamonds, blood/war
diamonds are a girl's best friend
dick
differently abled
digital divide
dike
dingbat
directress
dirty old man
disabilities
disadvantaged
"discovery" of America
discrimination

disinformation
displaced homemaker
dissemination
distaff side
ditz/ditzy
diva
diversity
divorce
divorcé/divorcée
divorced father/divorced mother
dizzy
docent
dogcatcher
doll/China doll/Kewpie doll/dolled up/
  all dolled up
"do-me" feminism
domestic
domestic violence/domestic abuse
domestic partner
dominatrix
dominionism
don
Don Juan
donor offspring
don't ask, don't tell
doorman
double consciousness
doublespeak
doubting Thomas
doughboy
Dover factor
dowager
Down Low
downsizing
Down syndrome
down under
dowry deaths
doyenne
draft
draftsman
draftsmanship
dragoman
drag queen/drag king
Dream Act, the
dressmaker
drill master
droit de seigneur
drones
drug czar
drum majorette
dualistic thinking
duchess
dude
duenna
dukedom
dumb
dumb blond

dustman
Dutch
Dutch courage
Dutchman
Dutch treat
Dutch uncle, talk to like a
dwarf
dyke
Dykes on Bikes
dysfunctional

 e

earth mother
East Indian
Ebonics
ecofeminism
economic adjustment
economic deprivation
economically disadvantaged
education
effeminate
effete
El Barrio
elder/elderly
eldercare
elder statesman
Electra complex
emancipate
emasculate
embryonic
embryonic stem cell research
emerging nation
emeritus
émigré
éminence grise
emotional
emotional disorder
empress
enchantress
endangered languages
enemy combatants
enfant terrible
English
enhanced interrogation
enhanced interrogation techniques
enlisted man
enslaved worker/woman/child
entitlement programs
entrepreneur
equal opportunity
equal pay
Equal Rights Amendment (ERA)
equestrienne
errand boy/errand girl
escort service
Eskimo

Esq./Esquire
-ess/-ette
essentialism
estate tax
ethnic/"ethnics"
ethnic cleansing
ethnicity
ethnic slurs
ethnocentrism
eunuch
Eurasian
European American
euthanasia
Eve
everyman/Everyman
exceptional
exceptionalism
exclusive language
executrix
exotic
expatriate/ex-pat
expert
extraordinary rendition
extremist

f

fact-finding trip
faculty wives
fag/faggot
fair-haired boy/fair-haired girl
fair sex, the/fairer sex, the
fairy (legend)
fairy (man)
fairy godmother
faith of our father
fakir
Falashas
fallen woman
fall guy
fall of Man
family
family-friendly
family man
family of man
family planning
"family values"
farmer
farm wife/farmer's wife
fascism
fashionista
fat
father (pseudogeneric noun)
father (verb)
father (parent)
father (clergy)
Father (God)

father figure
fatherland
fatherless
fatherly
fathers (pseudogeneric)
Father's Day
Fathers of the Church
Father, Son, and Holy Spirit/Ghost
fat shaming
fatwa
feisty
fellow
fellow countrymen
fellow feeling
fellow man/men
fellowship (social bond)
fellowship (scholarship)
fellow traveler
fellow worker
female (noun)
female (adjective)
female genital mutilation (FGM)
female impersonator
feminazi
Feminine/femininity
feminine intuition
feminine logic
feminine/masculine (poetry, music)
feminine mystique
feminine wiles
"feminine" word endings
feminism
feminisms
feminization of poverty
fem lib
femme/fem
femme fatale
fetish (religious)
fetus
fiancé/fiancée
filial/filiation
Filipina/Filipino/Filipin@
"final solution"
fireman
first baseman
first lady
First Nations/First Nations people/First People
first-wave feminism
fisherman
fishwife
fit
flag
flagman
flapper
flesh-colored
flexitarian
flower girl (vendor)

flower girl (wedding)
flyboy
flyover country/flyover land
food names for people
food stamps
footman
forcible rape
forefather
foreign
Foreign Service Officer
forelady/foreman/forewoman
foreman (jury)
foremother
foresister
forewoman
foster mother/father/parent
Founding Fathers
Fourth World
fox/foxy/foxy lady
fragging
fraternal
fraternal order of
fraternal organization
fraternal twins
fraternity
fraternity/frat (Greek)
fraternization
fraternize
fratricide
frau
freedman
freegan
freeman
free market
Freemason
free speech
freethinker
free trade
free world
freshman
freshman congressman/
  freshman congresswoman
friendly fire
friends with benefits
frigid
frivolous lawsuits
frogman
frontier
front man/frontman (music)
front man
front office man
fruit
frump/frumpy
FTM/FTM transsexual
full-blooded
fundamentalist
funnyman

gabby
Gabrieleno
gal
gal Friday
gal pal
gambler
gamesman
gamesmanship
gaming
garbage man
Garifuna
gasman
"gate rape"
gay (noun)
gay (adjective)
gay blade/gay dog
gay community
gay "lifestyle"
gay man
gay marriage
gay rights
geisha
gendarme
gender
gender bias
gender expression
gender-fair language
genderfluid
gender-free language
gender gap
gender identity
Gender Identity Disorder (GID)
gender-neutral language
gender roles
general population
genocide
gentile
gentleman
gentleman farmer
gentleman friend
gentlemanlike/gentlemanly
gentleman's agreement
gentleman of the press
gentle sex, the
gentlewoman
Gen X/Gen Y/Gen Z
gerontology
Gestapo/gestapo
ghetto
ghetto blaster
giantess
gigolo
G.I. Joe
gird (up) one's loins
girl

girlcott
girl Friday
girlfriend
girlhood
girlie
girlie magazine/movie/show
"girlie man/men"
girlish
girl power
girls and boys
Girl Scout
give away the bride
glass ceiling
GLBT
globalization
global warming
global war on terror
G-man
God (Christian)
goddess
godfather/godmother
God/his
God of our Fathers
go-go girl
gold digger
good old boy/good ole boy
good Samaritan
gook
gossip
gossipy
governess
granddaddy/daddy of them all
grand duchess
grande dame
grandfather clause
grandfatherly/grandmotherly
Grandmaster
granny/grannie
granny dress/gown
granny dumping
grantsmanship
grass widow/grass widower
Great Britain
greenwashing
groomsman
groupie
grrrl
guardsman
Guerrilla Girls
guinea
gunman
gun moll
guns
guru
guy
guys and gals
gyp
Gypsy/Gypsies

h

hag
hajji
half-breed/half-caste
handicappism
handicapped
handicapped parking
handmaid/handmaiden
handyman
hangman
Hanukkah
harbor master
hardhat
harelip
harem
harlot/harlotry
harp
harpy/harridan
Hasidim
hatchet man
hate crime
hate groups
hater
hate radio
hate rock
hate speech
hausfrau
Hawai'i/Hawaii
he (pseudogeneric)
headmaster/headmistress
head of family/head of household
head of state
headwaiter
health care
health of the mother
hearing impaired
heathen
heavyweight
Hebrew
heiress
helmsman
helpmate/helpmeet
he-man
hemiplegic
henchman
hen party
henpeck/henpecked
hermaphrodite
hero/heroine
herstory
heteronormativity
heterosexist
hick
hierarchy/hierarchical thinking
high priestess
high-risk group

highway patrolman
high yellow
hillbilly
him/himself
Hindu
hired man
his
Hispanic
history
Hitler/little Hitler
hitman
HIV
ho
hobo
holocaust/Holocaust
Holy Spirit (Ghost)/he
homebody
homeboy/homegirl
home economics/home ec
homeland security
homeless, the
homemaker
hominid
homo-
homo (gay man)
homophobia
homosexual
honcho/head honcho
honky/honkie
honor
honorifics
honor killings
hooker
Horatio Alger story
horny
horseman/horsewoman
horsemanship
hostess
hostile environment
hot-blooded
hotelier
Hottentot
houseboy/housegirl
househusband
housekeeper
housemaid
housemother
housewife
housewifery
housework
hoyden
hubby
hula dancer
human/humans, humanity/humankind
humanist
human rights
human trafficking
humilitainment
humor

hunger
hunk
huntress/huntsman
Huron
hurricane
husband (noun)
husband (verb)
husband and wife
husbandlike/husbandly
husbandry
hussy
hustler
"hyphenated Americans"
hyphenated surnames
hysteria/hysterical

i

idea man
idiot/idiocy
idiot savant
illegals/illegal immigrants
illegitimate/illegitimate child
illiterate
imam
immigrant
imperialism
impersonator, male/female
impotent
impregnable/impregnate
impresario
inamorata/inamorato
inclusive language
incorrigible
Indian (India)
Indian (United States)
Indian giver
Indian red (crayon color)
Indian style, sitting
Indian summer
Indian time
indigenous peoples
Indochina
infantryman
infertile
infidel
ingenue
in God we trust
Injun
inner city
innocent women and children
innocent victim
insane/insanity
inscrutable
inside man
"insider/outsider" rule
institutionalized racism
insurgents
intelligence

"intelligent design"
intentional communities (ICs)
intercourse
interfaith
internal nutrition
Internet
internment
interracial
intersexual
intifada
Inuit
invasion
Iranian
Iraqi sects
Irian Jaya
Irishman
Iron John
iron maiden
iron man
Ironman, The
Iroquois
irrational
Islam
Islamofascism
Islamophobia
Israeli
Israeli-Palestinian conflict
Issei
it's a man's world

j

jack/jack-/-jack
jackass
jack of all trades, master of none
jailbait
Jane Crow
Jane Doe
Jane Q. Citizen/Jane Q. Public
Japanese
Japanese American
jazzman
Jehovah
jerk
Jesus/Jesus Christ
Jew
Jew boy
"jew down"
Jewess
Jewish American Princess
Jewish mother
Jewish question
Jezebel/jezebel
jihadist
Jim Crow
jock (athlete)
jockette
joe/Joe Blow/Joe Schmo/Joe six-pack
john

John Doe
John Hancock
John Q. Citizen/John Q. Public
journalism
journeyman
judas
Judeo-Christian
jungle
junior/Jr.
junior executive
junior miss
junk
junk science
jury foreman
juryman
"just war"
juvenile

kaffeeklatsch/coffee klatsch
Kaffir/Kaafir
Kanakas
Kazakhstan
Kelly Girl
kept woman
kibei
kid
kike
Kinder, Küche, Kirche
king (noun)
kingdom
kingdom come
kingly
kingmaker
king of the hill/king of the mountain
king of the jungle
kingpin
kingpin (bowling)
king salmon
King's Counsel
king's English
kingship
king-size
king's ransom
kinsman/kinswoman
knave
knavery
knight
knight errant
knighthood
knight in shining armor
knockout
knock someone up/knock up someone
Koran
Korean American
krump dancing/crump dancing
Kurds
Kwanzaa

labor trafficking
lackey
lad
ladies and gentleman
ladies' auxiliary
ladies' room
ladies' man
ladino
lady (noun)
lady (adjective)
lady beetle/lady bird/ladybug
ladyfinger
lady friend/lady love
lady-in-waiting
lady-killer
ladylike
lady luck
lady of easy virtue/of pleasure/of the evening/
  of the night
lady of the house
ladyship
lady's maid
lady's slipper/lady's smock/lady's thumb
lame
landlady/landlord
Lapps/Lapland
La Raza
lass
last name
Latin America
Latina/Latino/Latin@
laundress
laundryman/laundrywoman
lawman
lawyer
"lay"/"easy lay"/"good lay"
layman
layman's terms
lazy
lazy Susan
leader
leading lady/leading man
leadman
learning disability
leatherneck (Marine)
lecher/lecherous/lech
left/left-winger/the left/leftist/far left
Legion of Honor/Legion of Merit
legionnaire
leper/leprosy
lesbian
lesbian separatism
lesbie/lesbo/lezzie
letterman
Lewis and Clark expedition

LGBT
LGBTQIA/GLBTQI
lib/libber
liberal
lifestyle
"like a girl"
like father, like son
Lilly Ledbetter Fair Pay Act, The
lilywhite/lily-white
limey
limousine liberal
limp-wristed
line foreman
lineman (job title)
line man (sports)
linesman
lioness
lip reading
little-boys'/little girls' room
little lady/little man
Little League
little woman, the
liveryman
living apart together (LAT)
living doll
living wage
lobbyists
lobsterman
locavore
Log Cabin Republicans
Lolita
lone wolf
long johns
longshoreman
looksism
loose woman
lord and master
lord it over someone
lordliness
lordly
lord mayor
lord of the manor, play
Lord's Day
lordship
Lothario
lounge lizard
love, honor, and obey
lover
lowerclassman
low-income
low man on the totem pole
lumberjack/lumberman
lust

ma'am/madam
macho/machismo

mademoiselle

madman/madwoman

Madras

maestro

Mafia

Magi

maharaja/maharani

maid/maidservant

maid/matron of honor

maiden (adjective)

maiden (noun)

maiden aunt

maidenhead

maidenhood

maiden name

maiden voyage

mailman

mail-order bride

main man (slang)

mainstream

maître d'hôtel

majordomo

makeup girl/makeup man

male

male bonding

male chauvinist/male chauvinist pig

male ego

male gaze

male impersonator

male privilege

mama's boy

"mammy"

man

Man/man (pseudogeneric)

man-

-man/-men

man/manned

man about town

man, act like a/be a/take it like a

man among men

man and wife

man, as one

man-at-arms

man, be his own

man-child

man Friday

manfully

manhandle

man-hater/woman-hater

manhole/manhole cover

manhood

man-hours

manhunt

man in office

man in the street

manipulative self-harm incidents

mankind

manlike/manly

man, like a

man-machine interface

manmade

manned space flight

mannequin

mannish

man of action

man of affairs

man of distinction

man of few words

man of God/man of the cloth

man of his word/man of honor

man of letters

man of means

man of the hour

man of the house

man of the world

man of the year

man-of-war

man on the street

manor

manpower (noun)

manpower (adjective)

manpowered

man's best friend

manservant

-manship

man's home is his castle

man's inhumanity to man

man-size(d)

manslaughter

man's man, a

man's work

man the barricades

man to man

mantrap

manup

man without a country

marchioness or marquise/marquis (or marquess)

mare's nest

marimacha

marine

marketing man

marksman

marksmanship

marriage

marriage penalty

married name

martinet

mascots

masculine

masculinity

masculism/masculist/masculinist

masher

Mason

massacre

masseur/masseuse

mass evictions

master (noun)
master (adjective)
master (verb)
Master (Christ)
master/master mariner
master bedroom/suite
master builder
master class
master copy
masterful
master hand
master key
master list
masterly
mastermind (noun)
mastermind (verb)
master of ceremonies/mistress of ceremonies
master of one's fate
master of the situation
masterpiece
master plan
master print
"master race"
master's degree
master sergeant
masterstroke
master switch
master tape
master teacher
masterwork
mastery
masturbation
matador
mate
mater/materfamilias
maternal
maternal death rate/maternal mortality rate
maternal instinct
maternal profiling
maternity leave
matriarch/matriarchy
matricide
matrilineal
matrimony
matron
matronly
matronym/matronymic
matron of honor
mature
maverick
may the best man win
meathead
Mecca
media
medical man
medicine man
mélange
memsahib
men (pseudogeneric)

men-
menfolk
men of goodwill
menopause/menopausal
mensch
menses/menstrual/menstruation
men's liberation/movement
men's studies
mental illness
mental retardation
mentor
men working
mercenary
mermaid/merman
mestiza/mestizo
metalhead
meter maid
meter man
métis, métisse, Métis, Métisse
metrosexual
Mexican
Mexican American
Mexican standoff
Mickey Finn
Mickey Mouse
Midas Touch
Middle America
Middle East
middleman
midget
mid-life crisis
midshipman
midwife (noun)
midwife (verb)
migrant
milady/milord
militant
militarism
"military bunker" or "civilian shelter"
Military Commissions Act
military draft
military-industrial complex
military language
military man
military wife
militiaman
milkmaid
milkman
milliner
milquetoast/milksop
miner
minister
minority
minstrel
minuteman
misanthrope/misogynist
miscegenation
misogynist
Miss

Miss America
missus/the missus
mistress
mistress of ceremonies
mixed blood
model
moderate
modern man
modiste
Mohammed
Mohammedan
Mohawk
mollycoddle
mommy track
mommy wars
monastery
moneyman
Mongolian
mongolism/mongoloid
monk
monogamist
monsignor
Montezuma's revenge
moonbats and wingnuts
Moonie
moonlighter
moral injury
more bang for the buck
Mormon
Moslem
mother (noun)
mother (verb)
mother and father
motherboard
mother cell
mother country
Mother Earth
mother hen
motherhood
motherhouse
mother-in-law
motherland
mother lode
motherly
Mother Nature
mother of all…
mother of pearl
mother of vinegar
Mother's Day
mother's helper
mother ship
mother superior
mother tongue
mother wit
motorman
mountain man/mountain woman
Mountie
movies for children
Mr. and Mrs.

Mrs.
Ms.
MTF/MTF transsexual
muezzin
Muhammad
Muhammadan
mulatto
mullah
multicultural
multiculturalism
multiracial
mumbo jumbo
mum's the word
murderess
muscleman
Muslim
Muslima/Muslimah
mute
My fellow Americans

nabob
nag (noun)
nag (verb)
name-calling
naming
nanny
natalism
nation/she
National Guardsman
national health insurance
National Organization for Women (NOW)
National Rifle Association (NRA)
nation building
native (noun)
native (adjective)
native American
Native American
Native People
nativism
nativist
"natural" father/mother/child
natural
nature/she
Navaho
Nazi/nazi
Neanderthal man
necessity is the mother of invention
née
needlewoman
negative economic growth
negative employment growth
Negress/Negro
neoconservative
Neopagan
nerd
nervous Nellie
New Age

newsboy
newsman/newspaperman
New World
Nez Perce
niggardly
nigger/nigga
niggling
night watchman
Nip
Nisei
no better than she should be
nobleman
No Child Left Behind
no man is a prophet in his own country
no-man's-land
nomenclature
non-alien
noncustodial parent
nondisabled
nonracist
nonsexist language
nontraditional career/employment
nonwhite
normal
Norseman
nosy
nosy parker
nubile
nuclear event
nuclear option
nude beach
nudist camp/colony
nukespeak
nullification
number-one man/number-two man
nun
nuncio
nuptial/nuptials
nurse
nursemaid/nurserymaid
nurseryman
nurture (verb)
Nuyorican
nymph
nymphet
nymphomaniac

oarsman
Oaxaquita/Indito
ObamaCare/Obamacare
obese/obesity
occupied territories
Occupy movement
odd-job(s)-man
odd man out
Oedipus complex

ofay
office boy/office girl
office spouse
offshoring/outsourcing
-oid
oil
oilman
Ojibwa/Ojibway
old
old as Methuselah
old-boys' network
old-girls' network
old lady/old man
old maid
old-maidish
Old Man Winter
old masters
oldster
Old Testament
old-timer
old wives' tale
old woman
oligarchy
ombudsman
one man, one vote
one-man/two-man/three-man, etc. (adjective)
one of the boys
one small step for man, one giant step for mankind
one-upmanship
openly lesbian/gay
Operation Iraqi Freedom
opportunity scholarship
opposite sex
opting out
orderly
organization man
Oriental
outcall service
outdoorsman
outing
outsourcing
overdevelopment
overlord
overmaster
overmastering
overmature trees
overseas
oversensitive
overweight
owner
"ownership society"

Pacific Islander
paddy wagon
Pagan/Neopagan
pal

paladin
palimony
pallbearer
Pandora's Box
pansy
Papago Tribe
paperboy
Papist
papoose
paramour
paraplegic
parent (noun)
parent (verb)
parlormaid
parson
"partial-birth abortion"
partner
pasha
pastor
pater/paterfamilias
paternal
paternalism
patient
patient as Job
patient bias
patient dumping
patriarchy
patrician
patricide
patrilineal
patrimony
patriot/patriotic/patriotism
Patriot Act
Patriot Movement
patrolman
patron
patronage
patroness
patronize
patronizing
patron saint
patronym/patronymic
patsy
pay equity
paymaster
Peacekeeper/peacekeeper
peace movement
peace on earth, good will to men
peach
peacock/peafowl/peahen
Peck's bad boy
pederast
pedestal
pedophile
peeping Tom
peeress
Peking man
penman

penwoman
penmanship
"people first" rule
people of faith
people of color/person of color
perky/pert
perpetrator
person/person-/-person
persona grata/persona non grata
personal accounts
personal injury lawyer
personal is political, the
"person first" rule
person of color
persons
pervert
pet
Peter principle/Paula principle
petite
pharaoh
pharmaceutical industry
philanderer
philanthropic/philanthropist/philanthropy
Philippines
physically challenged/different
pickup (woman)
pied piper
pig
Pilgrim Fathers
pillar of society/of the community
pimp
pink
pink-collar job/worker
pinko
pin money
Pinay/Pinoy
pinup girl
pioneer
Piraha Indians
pirate
pitchman
pitman (industry)
pivotman (basketball)
placeman
plainclothesman
Plain Language
plainsman
Plan B (contraceptive)
playboy
playgirl/playmate
"playing the race card"
pleased as Punch
pledge of allegiance
plowboy/plowman
plutocracy
PMS
poetess
poilu

point man
policeman
policeman of the world
political language
"politically correct"
political prisoners
political spectrum
politician
politics makes strange bedfellows
pollution rights
Pollyanna
polyamorist
polyandrist/polygynist
polyfidelity
polygamist
polysexual
pontiff
pontificate
pooh-bah
poor
popular culture
population control
populist
pork barrel
pornography
poseur
postfeminism
postman
postmaster/postmistress
postmaster general
postmodern churches
postmodernism
postracial
potentate
"pound of flesh"
poverty
powder room
pow-wow
prattle
prayer language
preacher
precision bombing
pre-emptive strike
"preferential treatment"
pregnancy
prehistoric man
prehominid
prejudice
pre-industrial
prelate
pre-literate society
premenstrual syndrome/PMS
premier danseur
prenuptial agreement
preparedness
pre-pregnant
presidentress
pressman

preventive detention
prick (man)
priest
priestess
prima ballerina
prima donna
primitive
primitive man
primogenitor
primogeniture
prince
princely
princess
princess dress
prioress
prisoner
privilege
PR man
problem
processing (of animals)
pro-choice
proconsul
procreate
procuress
prodigal son
professional/pro
Professional Secretaries Day/Week
progressive
progressive taxes
project
pro-life
promiscuous
Promise Keepers
pro-natalist
pronouns
propertyman/prop man
prophet in his own country, no man is a
prophetess
proprietress
prostitute
Protect America Act, The
protectress
protégé/protégée
provider
provocative
provoke
prudent man (legal)
pseudogeneric
pseudoscience
puberty
public diplomacy
public relations man
puerile
Puerto Rican
Pullman car/Pullman porter
pundit
purdah
purple state

purse strings
pushy
pussy
pussy-whipped
PWA/PLWA/PLA
pygmy

q

quadriplegic
Quakeress
qualified
quarryman
quartermaster
queen (noun)
queen (verb)
queen bee
queen consort
queenlike/queenly
queen-size
queer
questioning
quotas
quotation marks
Qur'an

r

rabbi
race
racialization
racial preference
racism
racketeer
raconteur
radical
radioman
raghead
ragman
raiders
raise Cain
rajah
rake
Ramadan
randy
rape
rape culture
rape victim
rapist
Rastafarian
reactionary
"real" father/mother/parent
real McCoy, the
reasonable and prudent man (law)
reasonable woman (law)
rebel
recruit
rector

redhead
red light district
red man
redneck
redskin
red state
referee
reform
reformed alcoholic
refugee
regal/regalia/regent
regime
regime change
regulation/deregulation/voluntary regulation
religious right
relocation
Renaissance man
renegades
reorientation therapy
repairman
reparative therapy
repo man
representative
reproductive justice
reproductive rights
resettlement
restaurateur
retard
revenge porn
revenue enhancement
reverend (adjective)
reverse discrimination
rewrite man
rhyme, feminine/masculine
rich as Croesus
ridiculisms
rifleman
right/right-winger/the right/far right
right-hand man
rights
right to die
right to life
right-to-work laws
ringmaster
riot grrrls
risk
riverman
road sister
roaming
riot
Robin Hood tax
rob the cradle
rock art
roger
rogue nation/rogue state
Roman Catholic
Romani/Romanies
Romani Holocaust

Romeo
rookie
roommate
roughhouse/roughneck
roundsman
roustabout
rowdy
royal/royalty
rubbing noses
rube
rugged individualism
rule of thumb
rule the roost
Rwanda/Rwandan genocide

S

saboteur
sacristan
safe-haven laws
safe sex
safety net/social safety net
sahib
salesgirl/saleslady/salesman/saleswoman
salesmanship
salutations (letters)
salvage man
Samaritan, good
Sambo
same-sex
same-sex marriage
samurai
sanctions
Sandman, the
sand nigger
sanitation man
sanitized
Sansei
Santa Claus
Sapphic
sassy/saucy
Satan/he
satyr
savage
savant
scalper
scarlet woman
scatterbrained
schizophrenic
schlemiel
schmoozer
schmuck
scold (noun)
scold (verb)
schoolboy/schoolfellow/schoolgirl
schoolmarm/schoolmaster/schoolmistress
score
Scotch
Scotsman

Scottish
scout
scoutmaster
scrapman
script girl/script man
Scrooge
sculptress
seamstress
seaman
seaman apprentice
seamanlike/seamanly
seamanship
second shift, the
second-story man
second-wave feminism
secretary
Secret Service man
secular humanist
secularist
Secure Flight
seductive
seductress
see a man about a dog/horse
seigneur/seigneury
selectman
self-determination
self-made man
self-mastery
self-regulation
seminal
seminar
seminary
senator
senility
senior airman
senior/senior citizen
separate the men from the boys
separation of church and state
serf
seropositive
serve two masters
serviceman (armed forces)
serviceman (repair)
service wife
session man
set-asides
settler
sex
sex change operation
sex differences
sex discrimination
sex industry
sex industry worker
sexism
sexist
sexist language
sexist quotations
sex-linked expressions
sex object

sexploitation
sexpot
sex reassignment surgery (SRS)
sex roles
sex slavery
sexting
sexton
sex tourist
sexual assault
sexual conquest
sexual freedom
sexual harassment
sexual intercourse
sexual orientation
sexpert
sexsomnia
sexual conversion therapy
sexual preference
sexual reorientation
sexual revolution
sex worker
Shaker
shaman
shamus
shanghai
"She asked for it"
sheikh/sheik
shelters
sheroe
shiftless
Shiites, Sunnis, Kurds
shiksa
ship/she ship/it
shock and awe
shock jock
shoeshine boy
shogun
shoot the bull
shop girl
shoreman
short
shortened forms of words
showgirl
showman
showmanship
shrew
shrill
shylock
shyster
Siamese twins
Siberia
sibyl
sideman
signalman
significant other
"silent majority"
silk stocking district
silk stocking liberal
Simon Legree

simon-pure
single
single mother/single father
single-payer health insurance/single-payer system
single-sex colleges
singular "they"
sins of the fathers are visited on the children, the
Sioux
sir
siren
sissy
sister (adjective)
sisterhood
sisterly
sizeism/sizism
skank
skinhead
skirt/a bit of skirt (woman)
slattern
slave/slavery
slave girl
slaveholders
sleepsex/sexsomnia
slum
slur
slut
smart aleck
snowman
sob sister
soccer mom
social butterfly
socialite
socialized medicine
social justice
social safety net
social titles
social welfare
sodomite
sodomy laws
"soft on crime"
soft targets
soldier
soldier of fortune
soldier-statesman
solicitor
solitary confinement
solon
"some of my best friends are…"
sommelier
songbird
songstress
sonny
son of a bitch
son of a gun
Son of God
Son of Man
sons (pseudogeneric)
sons of God
sons of man

sorceress
sororal
sorority
soubrette
sound-effects man
sound man
soul brother/soul sister
"sound science"
Southeast Asian American
sousveillance/souveillance
sovereign citizens
Soviet
sow wild oats
spaceman
Spanish
spastic
special
special-effects man
special interests
"special rights"
"special treatment"
speciesism
spend money like a drunken sailor
spin/spin control
spinning jenny
spinmeister
spinster
spinsterhood
spirits
spirituality
spokesman
spoonerism
sport of kings
sportsman
sportsmanlike/sportsmanly
sportsmanship
sport teams' names and mascots
spouse
spry
spunky
squaw
squire (noun)
squire (verb)
stableboy/stableman
stag line
stag movie
stag party
stained-glass ceiling
stand pat
starlet
star wars
state rape
"state secrets" defense
statesman
statesmanlike/statesmanly
statesmanship
stationmaster
stem cell research
stepfather/stepmother

stepmother, wicked
stereotype
sterile
stevedore
steward (manager)
steward/stewardess
stock boy/stock girl/stock man
stockman
Stone Age
storms
straight (adjective)
straw man
street people
stress positions
strict constructionists
strident
strongarm man
strongman
stud (man)
stuffed shirt
strumpet
stuntman
suave
subjects
subkingdom
submissive
subsidy
substandard English
substandard housing
success object (man)
suffers from (a condition)
suffragette
suffragist
sugar daddy
suicide
suicide bomber
suit
suitor
sultan/sultana
Sunni
superhero/superheroine
superman/superwoman
superpatriot
superstition
"support our troops"
surgical strike
surnames
surrogate mother
survivor
suttee
swain
swami
swamp
swarthy
swashbuckler
swear like a trooper
sweater girl
sweet sixteen (and never been kissed)
sweet william

swingman
switchman
swordsman

t

tailor
take off one's hat to
Taliban
talisman
tar baby
tart
taskmaster/taskmistress
tax-and-spend
taxes
taximan
tax loopholes
taxman
tax relief
teacher
Tea Party movement
tease (woman)
teen/teenager
teen moms
Tejana/Tejano
telephone man
telephone operator
television
tell it to the marines
temp
temptress
termagant
terminate with extreme prejudice
terrorist
terror, war on
testimony
testosterone
testy
that's so gay
"the" (before people)
"the" (before countries)
theaology
their/them/they
the n-word
theocracy
theodicy
therapy
thinking man
think tank
third-wave feminism
Third World
"those people"
three-man (adjective)
three sisters
three wise men, the
thug
tigress
tillerman
timberman

time-study man
time waits for no man
tin lizzie
tinman
Title IX
T-man
to a man
toastmaster/toastmistress
to boldly go where no man has gone before
to each his own
toff
token
tomato
tomboy
tomcat
tomfool/tomfoolery/tommyrot
Tommy
tommy gun
Tom Thumb
tom-tom
tonto
too big for one's britches
top banana/top brass/top dog
Torah, the
torch singer
tort reform
torture
totem pole, high man on the
totem pole, low man on the
tough cookie/tough guy
tough titty
towerman
townsman
toyboy
tradesman
"traditional family"
trafficking, labor
trafficking, sex
tragedienne
trailer
trailer park
trailing spouse
tramp (hobo)
tramp (woman)
transgender
transphobia
transsexual
transvestite
trash
trashman
travel
traveling salesman
treatment
tribal warfare
tribe
tribesman
trick
triggerman
Trinity, the

troglodyte
trooper/trouper
troops
troop sergeant
trophy wife
troubadour
truck driver
truthiness
Tuareg
turfman
tweens
twinkie
twit
two-man
two-person single career
two-spirit people
tycoon
typical
typist
tsarina

u

umpire/ump
un-American
unborn child/unborn children
uncivilized
uncle, I'll be a monkey's
Uncle Sam
uncle, say
Uncle Tom
unconventional spellings
underclass
underclassman
undercover man
underdeveloped/undeveloped countries
undermanned
underprivileged
underutilized
undocumented immigrant/worker
undomestic
uneconomical
uneducated
unemployed
unfeminine
ungentlemanly
Union Jack
union man
United Kingdom
"United we stand"
universal health care coverage
Unknown Soldier, the
unladylike
unlawful enemy combatants/unlawful
  combatants
unman
unmanliness/unmanly
unmanned

unmanned space flight
unmarried woman/unmarried man
unmarried mother
unmasculine
unsalaried
unsportsmanlike
unstatesmanlike
"Untouchables"
unwaged/unsalaried
"unwanted child"
unwed mother
unwomanly
unworkmanlike
upperclassman
urban
urban unrest
uxoricide

v

vagina
Valentino
valet/valet de chambre
valet parking
valley girl
vamp (woman)
vampire
varlet
vassal
vegetarian
verger
vestryman
veteran
vicar
vice-chairman
vicereine/viceroy
victim
"victimization, culture of"
victory for mankind
Vietnam War
vigilante
villainess
violence
violent language
violently
virago
virgin/virginity
virgin forest/virgin soil
virile
virtue/virtuous
visitation (child custody)
visual-effects man
visual impairment
vital interests
vivacious
vizier
voluntary regulation
volunteer

voodoo
voyageur
voyeur

wage earner
waiter
waitress
wallflower
Walter Mitty
wandering
wanton
war
"war"/"war on"
war bride
war diamonds
"war of liberation"
war on drugs
war on poverty
war on terror
wardrobe mistress
warehouseman
war hawk/warmaker/warmonger
warlock
warlord
"war of/between the sexes"
warpaint
warpath
warrior
warrior (Indian)
washerman/washerwoman/washwoman
WASP
watchman
waterboarding
water boy
watermanship
water witch
wave (feminism)
way to a man's heart is through his stomach, the
weaker sex, the
weapons of mass destruction (WMD)
weathergirl/weatherman
webmaster
wedding
wedlock
weekend warrior
welder
welfare
welfare mother
welsh (verb)
Welshman
wench
werewolf
West, the
Western civilization
West Indian
wetback

wet nurse
whaleman/whalerman
wharfman
wharfmaster
what evil lurks in the hearts of men?
whatsoever a man sows, that he shall also reap
wheel-chair bound
wheelsman
whine
whipping boy
whirling dervish
white (noun, referring to people)
white (adjective)
white-collar worker
white knight
white man's burden
whiteness studies
white privilege
white slavery
white supremacy
white trash/poor white trash
whore
whorehouse
whoremonger
Wicca
wicked stepmother
widow/widower
widow burning
widowhood
widow lady
widow's mite
widow's peak
widow's walk
wife
wife-beater tank top
wifehood/wifelike/wifeliness/wifely
wife-swapping
wildcrafter
wilderness
wild Indians
willy-nilly
wimmin/wimyn/womon/womyn
wingman
wingnuts
Winnebago
wireman
wise as Balaam's ass/Solomon
wise man
wise-use movement
witch
wizard
wolf
woman (noun)
woman (adjective)
woman-hater
womanhood
womanish
womanist

womanize/womanizer
womankind
womanlike/womanliness/womanly
woman's place is in the home, a
woman suffrage movement
woman's work
women and children/women and children first
"women and other minorities"
womenfolk
women-only spaces
women's intuition
women's issues
women's lib/women's libber
women's movement/women's liberation
  movement/women's rights movement
women's studies
womyn
Wonder Woman
woodsman
work ethic
workfare
working father
working girl
working man
working poor
working mother/working wife/
  working woman
workman
workmanlike/workmanly
workmanship
workmen's compensation
workplace
writing guidelines
wuss/wussy

xenophobia
Xmas

yachtsman
yachtsmanship
Yahweh
yammer
Yankee/Yank/Yanqui
yardman
yellow
yellow/yellow-bellied/yellow-bellied coward/
  yellow belly/yellow streak down one's back
"Yellow Peril"
yente/yenta
yeoman/Yeoman of the Guard/yeomanry/
  yeoman's service
yeomanly
yeoman's job
yes man

Yid
yogi
yokel
Yonsei
Yorkshireman
you guys
young lady
youngster
"you people"
youth
"You've come a long way, baby!"
yuppie/Yuppie

zamba/zambo
zines
Zionism
zoo
Zulu

Acknowledgments

Unspinning the Spin—The Women's Media Center Guide to Fair & Accurate Language is the first publication of WMC Press.

The Women's Media Center extends special thanks to the Artemis Rising Foundation and Regina K. Scully for groundbreaking support as the founding sponsor of WMC Press.

Our gratitude also goes to the Fonda Family Foundation, Ford Foundation, Libra Foundation, NoVo Foundation, Overbrook Foundation, Roland & Sylvia Schaefer Foundation, and Ruth Turner Fund, for their generous assistance in making possible this guide to bias-free language.

This book would not have been possible without all those on the Women's Media Center staff, former and current, who have contributed to its development, and to our Founding President Carol Jenkins and the WMC Board Chairs—Lauren Embrey, Jodie Evans, Pat Mitchell, and Helen Zia—who nurtured the project over the years.

The author of *Unspinning the Spin*, Rosalie Maggio, has been an acknowledged expert and widely read authority on bias-free language for more than twenty-five years. It was an honor to have collaborated with her and we're grateful for her scholarship, and her passion for fairness, accuracy, and the power of words.

Mary Thom was the editor of *Unspinning the Spin*, and we dedicate the book to her memory. This was her final act of editing in an impressive career: she was an early and long-time editor of Ms. Magazine; her books included *Inside Ms.: 25 Years of the Magazine and the Feminist Movement and Letters to Ms.: 1972-1987*. She and Suzanne Braun Levine co-edited the oral history, *Bella Abzug: How One Tough Broad from the Bronx Fought Jim Crow and Joe McCarthy, Pissed Off Jimmy Carter, Battled for the Rights of Women and Workers, Rallied Against War and for the Planet, and Shook Up Politics Along the Way*. Thom joined the Women's Media Center in 2006, assigning and editing three *WMC Features* a week of original writing by women journalists for the WMC website. In April, 2013, she died in an accident on her much-loved motorcycle.

Rosemary Ahern, line-editor of *Unspinning the Spin*, has worked with more than 200 authors as both an in-house and an independent editor, and is herself the author of *The Art of the Epigraph—How Great Books Begin*. The Women's Media Center was fortunate in having Rosemary's skill, experience, and grace in the final editing stages of *Unspinning*.

Shazdeh Omari, copy editor of *Unspinning the Spin*, is Associate Editor of the Women's Media Center, and we are grateful for her thoughtful, precise work.

Diahann Hill, designer for *Unspinning the Spin*, is an artist of perception and wit, and we thank her for her elegant, powerful imagery.

Jane Fonda, Robin Morgan, and Gloria Steinem, co-founders of the Women's Media Center, are the visionaries behind WMC Press's *Unspinning the Spin*. As word-artists and activists, they use their voices to move, enlighten, and inspire us. Their love of language is evident in the way they employ it toward the goal of making women and girls visible and powerful in media.

Julie Burton
President, Women's Media Center
October 2014